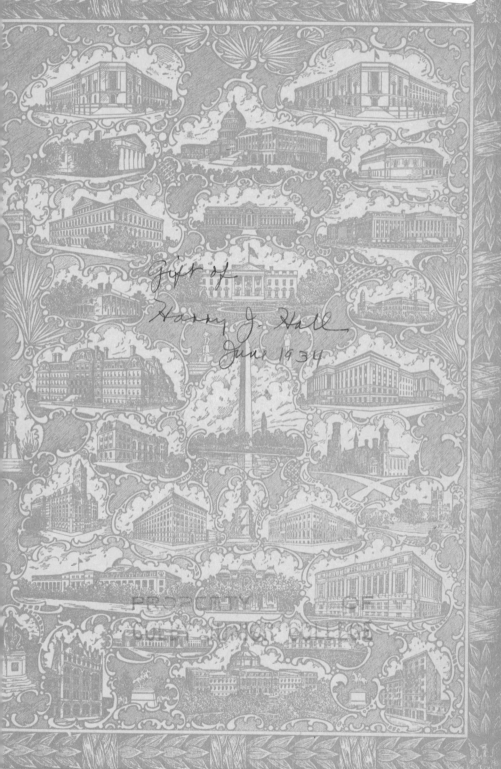

Gift of
Harry J. Hall
June 1934

State, War and Navy Departments

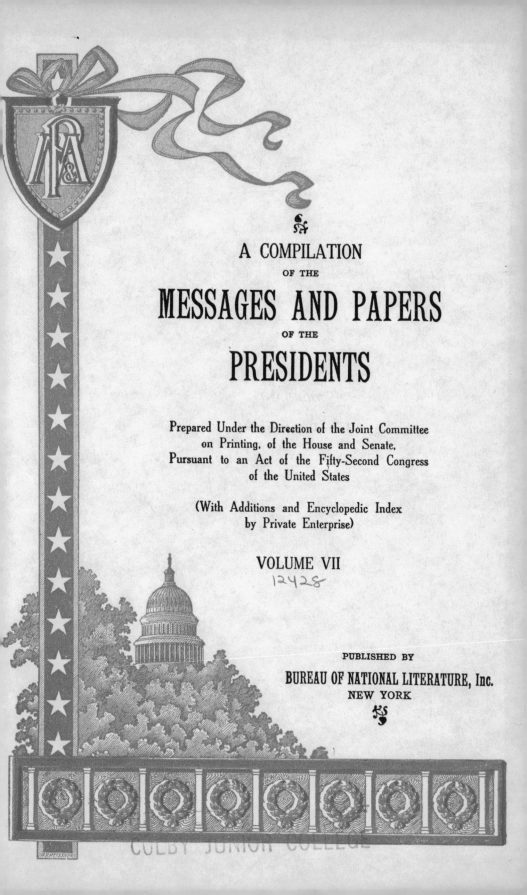

A COMPILATION

OF THE

MESSAGES AND PAPERS

OF THE

PRESIDENTS

Prepared Under the Direction of the Joint Committee
on Printing, of the House and Senate,
Pursuant to an Act of the Fifty-Second Congress
of the United States

(With Additions and Encyclopedic Index
by Private Enterprise)

VOLUME VII

12428

PUBLISHED BY

BUREAU OF NATIONAL LITERATURE, Inc.
NEW YORK

Copyright, 1897

BY

James D. Richardson

ILLUSTRATIONS IN VOLUME SEVEN

of civil war in Kansas and had produced dangerous sectional parties throughout the Confederacy. It was of a character so paramount in respect to the condition of Kansas as to rivet the anxious attention of the people of the whole country upon it, and it alone. No person thought of any other question. For my own part, when I instructed Governor Walker in general terms in favor of submitting the constitution to the people, I had no object in view except the all-absorbing question of slavery. In what manner the people of Kansas might regulate their other concerns was not a subject which attracted any attention. In fact, the general provisions of our recent State constitutions, after an experience of eight years, are so similar and so excellent that it would be difficult to go far wrong at the present day in framing a new constitution.

I then believed and still believe that under the organic act the Kansas convention were bound to submit this all-important question of slavery to the people. It was never, however, my opinion that, independently of this act, they would have been bound to submit any portion of the constitution to a popular vote in order to give it validity. Had I entertained such an opinion, this would have been in opposition to many precedents in our history, commencing in the very best age of the Republic. It would have been in opposition to the principle which pervades our institutions, and which is every day carried out into practice, that the people have the right to delegate to representatives chosen by themselves their sovereign power to frame constitutions, enact laws, and perform many other important acts without requiring that these should be subjected to their subsequent approbation. It would be a most inconvenient limitation of their own power, imposed by the people upon themselves, to exclude them from exercising their sovereignty in any lawful manner they think proper. It is true that the people of Kansas might, if they had pleased, have required the convention to submit the constitution to a popular vote; but this they have not done. The only remedy, therefore, in this case is that which exists in all other similar cases. If the delegates who framed the Kansas constitution have in any manner violated the will of their constituents, the people always possess the power to change their constitution or their laws according to their own pleasure.

The question of slavery was submitted to an election of the people of Kansas on the 21st December last, in obedience to the mandate of the constitution. Here again a fair opportunity was presented to the adherents of the Topeka constitution, if they were the majority, to decide this exciting question "in their own way" and thus restore peace to the distracted Territory; but they again refused to exercise their right of popular sovereignty, and again suffered the election to pass by default.

I heartily rejoice that a wiser and better spirit prevailed among a large majority of these people on the first Monday of January, and that they did on that day vote under the Lecompton constitution for a governor

97

and other State officers, a Member of Congress, and for members of the legislature. This election was warmly contested by the parties, and a larger vote was polled than at any previous election in the Territory. We may now reasonably hope that the revolutionary Topeka organization will be speedily and finally abandoned, and this will go far toward the final settlement of the unhappy differences in Kansas. If frauds have been committed at this election, either by one or both parties, the legislature and the people of Kansas, under their constitution, will know how to redress themselves and punish these detestable but too common crimes without any outside interference.

The people of Kansas have, then, "in their own way" and in strict accordance with the organic act, framed a constitution and State government, have submitted the all-important question of slavery to the people, and have elected a governor, a Member to represent them in Congress, members of the State legislature, and other State officers. They now ask admission into the Union under this constitution, which is republican in its form. It is for Congress to decide whether they will admit or reject the State which has thus been created. For my own part, I am decidedly in favor of its admission, and thus terminating the Kansas question. This will carry out the great principle of nonintervention recognized and sanctioned by the organic act, which declares in express language in favor of "nonintervention by Congress with slavery in the States or Territories," leaving "the people thereof perfectly free to form and regulate their domestic institutions in their own way, subject only to the Constitution of the United States." In this manner, by localizing the question of slavery and confining it to the people whom it immediately concerned, every patriot anxiously expected that this question would be banished from the halls of Congress, where it has always exerted a baneful influence throughout the whole country.

It is proper that I should briefly refer to the election held under an act of the Territorial legislature on the first Monday of January last on the Lecompton constitution. This election was held after the Territory had been prepared for admission into the Union as a sovereign State, and when no authority existed in the Territorial legislature which could possibly destroy its existence or change its character. The election, which was peaceably conducted under my instructions, involved a strange inconsistency. A large majority of the persons who voted against the Lecompton constitution were at the very same time and place recognizing its valid existence in the most solemn and authentic manner by voting under its provisions. I have yet received no official information of the result of this election.

As a question of expediency, after the right has been maintained, it may be wise to reflect upon the benefits to Kansas and to the whole country which would result from its immediate admission into the Union, as well as the disasters which may follow its rejection. Domestic peace will be the happy consequence of its admission, and that fine Territory, which has hitherto been torn by dissensions, will rapidly increase in population and wealth and speedily realize the blessings and the comforts which follow in the train of agricultural and mechanical industry. The people will then be sovereign and can regulate their own affairs in their own way. If a majority of them desire to abolish domestic slavery within the State, there is no other possible mode by which this can be effected so speedily as by prompt admission. The will of the majority is supreme and irresistible when expressed in an orderly and lawful manner. They can make and unmake constitutions at pleasure. It would be absurd to say that they can impose fetters upon their own power which they can not afterwards remove. If they could do this, they might tie their own hands for a hundred as well as for ten years. These are fundamental principles of American freedom, and are recognized, I believe, in some form or other by every State constitution; and if Congress, in the act of admission, should think proper to recognize them I can perceive no objection to such a course. This has been done emphatically in the constitution of Kansas. It declares in the bill of rights that "all political power is inherent in the people and all free governments are founded on their authority and instituted for their benefit, and therefore they have at all times an inalienable and indefeasible right to alter, reform, or abolish their form of government in such manner as they may think proper." The great State of New York is at this moment governed under a constitution framed and established in direct opposition to the mode prescribed by the previous constitution. If, therefore, the provision changing the Kansas constitution after the year 1864 could by possibility be construed into a prohibition to make such a change previous to that period, this prohibition would be wholly unavailing. The legislature already elected may at its very first session submit the question to a vote of the people whether they will or will not have a convention to amend their constitution and adopt all necessary means for giving effect to the popular will.

It has been solemnly adjudged by the highest judicial tribunal known to our laws that slavery exists in Kansas by virtue of the Constitution of the United States. Kansas is therefore at this moment as much a slave State as Georgia or South Carolina. Without this the equality of the sovereign States composing the Union would be violated and the use and enjoyment of a territory acquired by the common treasure of all the States would be closed against the people and the property of nearly half the members of the Confederacy. Slavery can therefore never be prohibited in Kansas except by means of a constitutional provision, and in no other manner can this be obtained so promptly, if a majority of the people desire it, as by admitting it into the Union under its present constitution.

On the other hand, should Congress reject the constitution under the idea of affording the disaffected in Kansas a third opportunity of prohibiting slavery in the State, which they might have done twice before if in the majority, no man can foretell the consequences.

If Congress, for the sake of those men who refused to vote for delegates to the convention when they might have excluded slavery from the constitution, and who afterwards refused to vote on the 21st December last, when they might, as they claim, have stricken slavery from the constitution, should now reject the State because slavery remains in the constitution, it is manifest that the agitation upon this dangerous subject will be renewed in a more alarming form than it has ever yet assumed.

Every patriot in the country had indulged the hope that the Kansas and Nebraska act would put a final end to the slavery agitation, at least in Congress, which had for more than twenty years convulsed the country and endangered the Union. This act involved great and fundamental principles, and if fairly carried into effect will settle the question. Should the agitation be again revived, should the people of the sister States be again estranged from each other with more than their former bitterness, this will arise from a cause, so far as the interests of Kansas are concerned, more trifling and insignificant than has ever stirred the elements of a great people into commotion. To the people of Kansas the only practical difference between admission or rejection depends simply upon the fact whether they can themselves more speedily change the present constitution if it does not accord with the will of the majority, or frame a second constitution to be submitted to Congress hereafter. Even if this were a question of mere expediency, and not of right, the small difference of time one way or the other is of not the least importance when contrasted with the evils which must necessarily result to the whole country from a revival of the slavery agitation.

In considering this question it should never be forgotten that in proportion to its insignificance, let the decision be what it may so far as it may affect the few thousand inhabitants of Kansas who have from the beginning resisted the constitution and the laws, for this very reason the rejection of the constitution will be so much the more keenly felt by the people of fourteen of the States of this Union, where slavery is recognized under the Constitution of the United States.

Again, the speedy admission of Kansas into the Union would restore peace and quiet to the whole country. Already the affairs of this Territory have engrossed an undue proportion of public attention. They have sadly affected the friendly relations of the people of the States with each other and alarmed the fears of patriots for the safety of the Union. Kansas once admitted into the Union, the excitement becomes localized and will soon die away for want of outside aliment. Then every difficulty will be settled at the ballot box.

Besides—and this is no trifling consideration—I shall then be enabled to withdraw the troops of the United States from Kansas and employ them on branches of service where they are much needed. They have been kept there, on the earnest importunity of Governor Walker, to maintain the existence of the Territorial government and secure the execution of the laws. He considered that at least 2,000 regular troops, under the command of General Harney, were necessary for this purpose. Acting upon his reliable information, I have been obliged in some degree to interfere with the expedition to Utah in order to keep down rebellion in Kansas. This has involved a very heavy expense to the Government. Kansas once admitted, it is believed there will no longer be any occasion there for troops of the United States.

I have thus performed my duty on this important question, under a deep sense of responsibility to God and my country. My public life will terminate within a brief period, and I have no other object of earthly ambition than to leave my country in a peaceful and prosperous condition and to live in the affections and respect of my countrymen. The dark and ominous clouds which now appear to be impending over the Union I conscientiously believe may be dissipated with honor to every portion of it by the admission of Kansas during the present session of Congress, whereas if she should be rejected I greatly fear these clouds will become darker and more ominous than any which have ever yet threatened the Consitution and the Union.

JAMES BUCHANAN.

To the Senate of the United States:

I transmit to the Senate for its consideration with a view to ratification, a convention for the purpose of further regulating the intercourse of American citizens within the Empire of Japan, signed at Simoda on the 17th day of June last by Townsend Harris, consul-general of the United States, and by the governors of Simoda, empowered for that purpose by their respective Governments.

FEBRUARY 10, 1858.

JAMES BUCHANAN.

WASHINGTON, *February 11, 1858.*

To the Senate of the United States:

I transmit to the Senate, for its consideration with a view to ratification, an additional article to the extradition convention between the United States and France of the 9th of November, 1843, and the additional article thereto of the 24th February, 1845, signed in this city yesterday by the Secretary of State and the minister of His Imperial Majesty the Emperor of the French.

JAMES BUCHANAN.

WASHINGTON, *February 12, 1858.*

To the House of Representatives:

I herewith transmit a report from the Secretary of State, with the accompanying documents, in reply to the resolution of the House of

Representatives of the 18th ultimo, requesting to be furnished with official information and correspondence in relation to the execution of Colonel Crabb and his associates within or near the limits of the Republic of Mexico.

JAMES BUCHANAN.

WASHINGTON CITY, *February 26, 1858.*

To the House of Representatives:

I herewith transmit to the House of Representatives the reports of the Secretaries of State, of War, of the Interior, and of the Attorney-General, containing the information called for by a resolution of the House of the 27th ultimo, requesting "the President, if not incompatible with the public interest, to communicate to the House of Representatives the information which gave rise to the military expeditions ordered to Utah Territory, the instructions to the army officers in connection with the same, and all correspondence which has taken place with said army officers, with Brigham Young and his followers, or with others throwing light upon the question as to how far said Brigham Young and his followers are in a state of rebellion or resistance to the Government of the United States."

JAMES BUCHANAN.

WASHINGTON, *March 2, 1858.*

To the Senate of the United States:

I herewith transmit to the Senate a report from the Secretary of the Navy, dated on the 24th instant [ultimo], furnishing the information called for by a resolution of the Senate adopted on the 16th instant [ultimo], requesting me "to inform the Senate in executive session on what evidence the nominees for the Marine Corps are stated to be taken from the States as designated in his message communicating the nominations of January 13."

JAMES BUCHANAN.

WASHINGTON CITY, *March 4, 1858.*

To the House of Representatives:

I herewith transmit to the House of Representatives communications from the Secretary of War and Secretary of the Interior, in answer to the resolution adopted by the House on the 5th ultimo, requesting the President to furnish certain information in relation to the number of troops, whether regulars, volunteers, drafted men, or militia, who were engaged in the service of the United States in the last war with Great Britain, etc.

JAMES BUCHANAN.

WASHINGTON, *March 9, 1858.*

To the Senate and House of Representatives:

I transmit herewith a report of the Attorney-General, with accompanying papers, dated March 1, 1858, detailing proceedings under the act approved March 3, 1855, entitled "An act to improve the laws of the District of Columbia and to codify the same."

JAMES BUCHANAN.

WASHINGTON, *March 23, 1858.*

To the House of Representatives:

In compliance with a resolution of the House of Representatives of the 26th of January, requesting the President to communicate to the House "so much of the correspondence between the late Secretary of War and Major-General John E. Wool, late commander of the Pacific Department, relative to the affairs of such department, as has not heretofore been published under a call of this House," I herewith transmit all the correspondence called for so far as is afforded by the files of the War Department.

JAMES BUCHANAN.

WASHINGTON, *April 7, 1858.*

To the Senate of the United States:

I submit to the Senate, for its consideration and constitutional action, a treaty made with the Tonawanda Indians, of New York, on the 5th of November, 1857, with the accompanying papers from the Department of the Interior.

JAMES BUCHANAN.

WASHINGTON, *April 9, 1858.*

To the House of Representatives:

I transmit to the House of Representatives a memorial addressed to myself by a committee appointed by the citizens of that portion of the Territory of Utah which is situated west of the Goose Creek range of mountains, commonly known as "Carsons Valley," in favor of the establishment of a Territorial government over them, and containing the request that I should communicate it to Congress. I have received but one copy of this memorial, which I transmit to the House upon the suggestion of James M. Crane, esq., the Delegate elect of the people of the proposed new Territory, for the reason, as he alleges, that the subject is now under consideration before the Committee on the Territories of that body.

JAMES BUCHANAN.

WASHINGTON, *April 20, 1858.*

To the Senate of the United States:

I transmit a report from the Secretary of State, with accompanying papers,* in answer to the resolution of the Senate of the 5th instant.

JAMES BUCHANAN.

WASHINGTON, *April 21, 1858.*

To the Senate of the United States:

I herewith transmit the reports of the Secretary of State and the Secretary of the Navy, with accompanying papers,† in answer to the resolution of the Senate of the 19th of January last.

JAMES BUCHANAN.

WASHINGTON, *April 28, 1858.*

To the Senate of the United States:

I transmit a report from the Secretary of State, in answer to the resolution of the Senate of the 24th ultimo, requesting information relative to the seizure in the Valley of Sitana, in Peru, by authorities of Chile of a sum of money belonging to citizens of the United States.

JAMES BUCHANAN.

WASHINGTON, *May 1, 1858.*

To the Senate of the United States:

In compliance with the resolution of the Senate of the 24th ultimo, I herewith transmit a report of the Secretary of State, with accompanying documents.‡

JAMES BUCHANAN.

WASHINGTON, *May, 1858.*

To the Senate of the United States:

1 transmit herewith, for the constitutional action of the Senate, a treaty negotiated with the Ponca tribe of Indians on the 12th of March, 1858, with the accompanying documents from the Department of the Interior.

JAMES BUCHANAN.

WASHINGTON, *May 3, 1858.*

To the House of Representatives:

In compliance with the resolutions of the House of Representatives of the 19th January, 1857, and 3d February, 1858, I herewith transmit the report of the Secretary of the Interior, with accompanying documents.§

JAMES BUCHANAN.

---

*Instructions to William B. Reed, United States commissioner to China.

†Relating to the African slave trade and to movements of the French Government to establish a colony in the possessions of that Government from the coast of Africa.

‡Relating to outrages committed against the family of Walter Dickson, an American citizen residing at Jaffa, Palestine.

§ Relating to Indian affairs in Oregon and Washington Territories and to the official conduct of Anson Dart, superintendent of Indian affairs in Oregon Territory.

WASHINGTON, *May 6, 1858.*

To the House of Representatives:

In compliance with the resolution of the House of Representatives of the 3d of February, 1858, I transmit herewith a report from the Secretary of War, with all papers and correspondence* so far as the same is afforded by the files of the Department. JAMES BUCHANAN.

WASHINGTON CITY, *May 13, 1858.*

Hon. JAMES L. ORR,
 Speaker of the House of Representatives:

SIR: I herewith transmit, to be laid before the House of Representatives, the letter of the Secretary of the Interior, dated the 12th instant, covering the report, maps, etc., of the geological survey of Oregon and Washington Territories, which has been made by John Evans, esq., United States geologist, under appropriations made by Congress for that purpose.

  Respectfully, JAMES BUCHANAN.

WASHINGTON, *May 13, 1858.*

To the Senate of the United States:

I transmit herewith, for the constitutional action of the Senate, a treaty negotiated on the 19th of April, 1858, with the Yancton tribe of Sioux or Dacotah Indians, with accompanying papers from the Department of the Interior. JAMES BUCHANAN.

WASHINGTON, *May, 1858.*

To the Senate of the United States:

I transmit to the Senate a report, dated 13th instant, with the accompanying papers, received from the Secretary of State in answer to the resolution of the Senate of the 5th instant, requesting information in regard to measures which may have been adopted for the protection of American commerce in the ports of Mexico.

  JAMES BUCHANAN.

WASHINGTON CITY, *May 18, 1858.*

Hon. J. C. BRECKINRIDGE,
 Vice-President of the United States:

SIR: In reply to the resolutions of the Senate of the United States of the 20th February and 14th March, 1857, I herewith transmit, to be laid before that body, copies of all correspondence, vouchers, and other papers having reference to the accounts of Edward F. Beale, esq., late superintendent of Indian affairs in California, which are of file or record in the Departments of the Treasury and Interior.

  JAMES BUCHANAN.

* Relating to Indian affairs in Oregon and Washington Territories and to the official conduct of Anson Dart, superintendent of Indian affairs in Oregon Territory.

WASHINGTON, *May 19, 1858.*

To the Senate of the United States:

In answer to the resolution of the Senate of the 14th instant, request-ing information concerning the recent search or seizure of American ves-sels by foreign armed cruisers in the Gulf of Mexico, I transmit reports from the Secretaries of State and of the Navy.

JAMES BUCHANAN.

WASHINGTON, *May 27, 1858.*

To the Senate of the United States:

I transmit herewith, in compliance with the resolution of the Senate of the 19th of May, a communication from the Secretary of the Navy with copies of the correspondence, etc.,* as afforded by the files of the Department.   JAMES BUCHANAN.

WASHINGTON, *May 29, 1858.*

To the Senate of the United States:

I transmit a report from the Secretary of State, with accompanying papers, in answer to the resolution of the Senate of the 22d instant, requesting information in regard to the seizure of the American vessel *Panchita* on the coast of Africa.   JAMES BUCHANAN.

WASHINGTON, *May 31, 1858.*

To the House of Representatives:

In answer to the resolution of the House of Representatives of the 17th instant, requesting information relative to attacks upon United States vessels in the Gulf of Mexico and on the coast of Cuba, I transmit a report from the Secretary of State, with the papers by which it was accompanied.   JAMES BUCHANAN.

WASHINGTON, *June 1, 1858.*

To the Senate of the United States:

I transmit herewith a report from the Secretaries of State and Navy, with the accompanying papers, in compliance with the resolution of the Senate of the 11th of March, 1858, requesting the President "to commu-nicate to the Senate any information in possession of any of the Execu-tive Departments in relation to alleged discoveries of guano in the year 1855 and the measures taken to ascertain the correctness of the same, and also any report made to the Navy Department in relation to the dis-covery of guano in Jarvis and Bakers islands, with the charts, soundings, and sailing directions for those islands.

JAMES BUCHANAN.

* Relating to the arrest of William Walker and associates within the territory of Nicaragua by the naval forces under Commodore Paulding.

WASHINGTON, *June 4, 1858.*

To the Senate of the United States:

I transmit herewith a report from the Secretary of State, together with the documents by which it is accompanied, as embracing all the information which it is practicable or expedient to communicate in reply to the resolution of the Senate of the 31st ultimo, on the subject of guano.

JAMES BUCHANAN.

WASHINGTON, *June 10, 1858.*

To the Senate and House of Representatives:

I transmit a copy of a dispatch from Governor Cumming to the Secretary of State, dated at Great Salt Lake City on the 2d of May and received at the Department of State on yesterday. From this there is reason to believe that our difficulties with the Territory of Utah have terminated and the reign of the Constitution and the laws has been restored. I congratulate you on this auspicious event.

I lose no time in communicating this information and in expressing the opinion that there will now be no occasion to make any appropriation for the purpose of calling into service the two regiments of volunteers authorized by the act of Congress approved on the 7th of April last for the purpose of quelling disturbances in the Territory of Utah, for the protection of supply and emigrant trains, and the suppression of Indian hostilities on the frontier.

I am the more gratified at this satisfactory intelligence from Utah because it will afford some relief to the Treasury at a time demanding from us the strictest economy, and when the question which now arises upon every new appropriation is whether it be of a character so important and urgent as to brook no delay and to justify and require a loan and most probably a tax upon the people to raise the money necessary for its payment.

In regard to the regiment of volunteers authorized by the same act of Congress to be called into service for the defense of the frontiers of Texas against Indian hostilities, I desire to leave this question to Congress, observing at the same time that in my opinion the State can be defended for the present by the regular troops which have not yet been withdrawn from its limits.

JAMES BUCHANAN.

WASHINGTON, *June 11, 1858.*

To the Senate of the United States:

In answer to the resolution of the Senate of the 19th ultimo, respecting the Isthmus of Tehuantepec, I transmit herewith a report from the Secretary of State, with the documents by which it is accompanied, together with the copy of a letter from the Postmaster-General of the 21st ultimo to the Department of State.

JAMES BUCHANAN.

WASHINGTON CITY, *June 11, 1858.*

To the House of Representatives:

I transmit herewith a report from the Secretary of War, with the accompanying papers,* in obedience to the resolution of the House of Representatives of the 2d of June, 1858.

JAMES BUCHANAN.

WASHINGTON CITY, *June 12, 1858.*

To the Senate and House of Representatives:

I feel it to be an indispensable duty to call your attention to the condition of the Treasury. On the 19th day of May last the Secretary of the Treasury submitted a report to Congress "on the present condition of the finances of the Government." In this report he states that after a call upon the heads of Departments he had received official information that the sum of $37,000,000 would probably be required during the first two quarters of the next fiscal year, from the 1st of July until the 1st of January. "This sum," the Secretary says, "does not include such amounts as may be appropriated by Congress over and above the estimates submitted to them by the Departments, and I have no data on which to estimate for such expenditures. Upon this point Congress is better able to form a correct opinion than I am."

The Secretary then estimates that the receipts into the Treasury from all sources between the 1st of July and the 1st of January would amount to $25,000,000, leaving a deficit of $15,000,000, inclusive of the sum of about $3,000,000, the least amount required to be in the Treasury at all times to secure its successful operation. For this amount he recommends a loan. This loan, it will be observed, was required, after a close calculation, to meet the estimates from the different Departments, and not such appropriations as might be made by Congress over and above these estimates.

There was embraced in this sum of $15,000,000 estimates to the amount of about $1,750,000 for the three volunteer regiments authorized by the act of Congress approved April 7, 1858, for two of which, if not for the third, no appropriation will now be required. To this extent a portion of the loan of $15,000,000 may be applied to pay the appropriations made by Congress beyond the estimates from the different Departments, referred to in the report of the Secretary of the Treasury.

To what extent a probable deficiency may exist in the Treasury between the 1st July and the 1st January next can not be ascertained until the appropriation bills, as well as the private bills containing appropriations, shall have finally passed.

Adversity teaches useful lessons to nations as well as individuals. The habit of extravagant expenditures, fostered by a large surplus in

* Copies of contracts for deepening the channels of the Southwest Pass and Pass à l'Outre, at the mouth of the Mississippi River, etc.

the Treasury, must now be corrected or the country will be involved in serious financial difficulties.

Under any form of government extravagance in expenditure must be the natural consequence when those who authorize the expenditure feel no responsibility in providing the means of payment. Such had been for a number of years our condition previously to the late monetary revulsion in the country. Fortunately, at least for the cause of public economy, the case is now reversed, and to the extent of the appropriations, whatever these may be, ingrafted on the different appropriation bills, as well as those made by private bills, over and above the estimates of the different Departments, it will be necessary for Congress to provide the means of payment before their adjournment. Without this the Treasury will be exhausted before the 1st of January and the public credit will be seriously impaired. This disgrace must not fall upon the country.

It is impossible for me, however, now to ascertain this amount, nor does there at present seem to be the least probability that this can be done and the necessary means provided by Congress to meet any deficiency which may exist in the Treasury before Monday next at 12 o'clock, the hour fixed for adjournment, it being now Saturday morning at half-past 11 o'clock. To accomplish this object the appropriation bills, as they shall have finally passed Congress, must be before me, and time must be allowed to ascertain the amount of the moneys appropriated and to enable Congress to provide the necessary means. At this writing it is understood that several of these bills are yet before the committee of conference and the amendments to some of them have not even been printed.

Foreseeing that such a state of things might exist at the close of the session, I stated in the annual message to Congress of December last that—

From the practice of Congress such an examination of each bill as the Constitution requires has been rendered impossible. The most important business of each session is generally crowded into its last hours, and the alternative presented to the President is either to violate the constitutional duty which he owes to the people and approve bills which for want of time it is impossible he should have examined, or by his refusal to do this subject the country and individuals to great loss and inconvenience.

*   *   *   *   *   *   *

For my own part, I have deliberately determined that I shall approve no bills which I have not examined, and it will be a case of extreme and most urgent necessity which shall ever induce me to depart from this rule.

The present condition of the Treasury absolutely requires that I should adhere to this resolution on the present occasion, for the reasons which I have heretofore presented.

In former times it was believed to be the true character of an appropriation bill simply to carry into effect existing laws and the established policy of the country. A practice has, however, grown up of late years to ingraft on such bills at the last hours of the session large appropriations for new and important objects not provided for by preexisting laws and when no time is left to the Executive for their examination and investigation. No alternative is thus left to the President but either to approve measures without examination or by vetoing an appropriation bill seriously to embarrass the operations of the Government. This practice could never have prevailed without a surplus in the Treasury sufficiently large to cover an indefinite amount of appropriations. Necessity now compels us to arrest it, at least so far as to afford time to ascertain the amount appropriated and to provide the means of its payment.

For all these reasons I recommend to Congress to postpone the day of adjournment for a brief period. I promise that not an hour shall be lost in ascertaining the amount of appropriations made by them for which it will be necessary to provide. I know it will be inconvenient for the members to attend a called session, and this above all things I desire to avoid.

JAMES BUCHANAN.

PROCLAMATIONS.

[From Statutes at Large (Little, Brown & Co.), Vol. XI, p. 794.]

BY THE PRESIDENT OF THE UNITED STATES OF AMERICA.

A PROCLAMATION.

Whereas by an act of Congress approved March 3, 1855, entitled "An act to improve the laws of the District of Columbia and to codify the same," the President of the United States was directed to appoint a time and place for taking the sense of the citizens of the District of Columbia for or against the adoption of the code prepared in pursuance of said act, and, further, to provide and proclaim the mode and rules of conducting such election:

Now, therefore, be it known that I do hereby appoint Monday, the 15th day of February, 1858, as the day for taking the sense of the citizens of the District of Columbia as aforesaid.

The polls will be opened at 9 o'clock a. m. and closed at 5 o'clock p. m. Every free white male citizen of the United States above the age of 21 years who shall have resided in the District of Columbia for one year next preceding the said 15th day of February, 1858, shall be allowed to vote at said election.

The voting shall be by ballot. Those in favor of the adoption of the revised code will vote a ballot with the words "for the revised code" written or printed upon the same, and those opposed to the adoption of the said code will vote a ballot with the words "against the revised code" written or printed upon the same.

The places where the said election shall be held and the judges who shall conduct and preside over the same will be as follows:

For the First Ward, in the city of Washington, at Samuel Drury's office, on Pennsylvania avenue. Judges: Southey S. Parker, Terence Drury, and Alexander H. Mechlin.

For the Second Ward, on Twelfth street, one door above Pennsylvania avenue. Judges: Charles L. Coltman, Charles J. Canfield, and Edward C. Dyer.

For the Third Ward, near the corner of Ninth street, between F and G, west of the Patent Office. Judges: Valentine Harbaugh, Joseph Bryan, and Harvey Cruttenden.

For the Fourth Ward, at the west end of City Hall. Judges: William A. Kennedy, John T. Clements, and Francis Mohun.

For the Fifth Ward, at the Columbia engine house. Judges: Henry C. Purdy, Thomas Hutchinson, and James A. Brown.

For the Sixth Ward, at the Anacostia engine house. Judges: John D. Brandt, George A. Bohrer, and George R. Ruff.

For the Seventh Ward, at Island Hall. Judges: Samuel Pumphrey, James Espey, and John L. Smith.

For Georgetown, at the mayor's office. Judges: Edward Chapman, John L. Kidwell, and William H. Edes.

For that portion of the county of Washington which lies west of Rock Creek, at Conrad's Tavern, in Tenallytown. Judges: Joshua Peirce, Charles R. Belt, and William D. C. Murdock.

For that portion of said county which lies between Rock Creek and the Eastern Branch of the Potomac, at Seventh street tollgate. Judges: Thomas Blagden, Dr. Henry Haw, and Abner Shoemaker.

And for that portion of said county which lies east of the Eastern Branch of the Potomac, at Goodhope Tavern. Judges: Selby B. Scaggs, Fenwick Young, and Dr. Wellford Manning.

The judges presiding at the respective places of holding the elections shall be sworn to perform their duties faithfully; and immediately after the close of the polls they shall count up the votes and certify what number were given "for the revised code" and what number "against the revised code," which certificates shall be transmitted within twenty-four hours to the Attorney-General of the United States, who will report the same to me.

Given under my hand this 24th day of December, A. D. 1857, and of Independence the eighty-second.

[SEAL.]   JAMES BUCHANAN.

BY THE PRESIDENT OF THE UNITED STATES OF AMERICA.

A PROCLAMATION.

Whereas by an act of Congress of the United States of the 24th of May, 1828, entitled "An act in addition to an act entitled 'An act concerning discriminating duties of tonnage and impost,' and to equalize the duties on Prussian vessels and their cargoes,'' it is provided that upon satisfactory evidence being given to the President of the United States by the government of any foreign nation that no discriminating duties of tonnage or impost are imposed or levied in the ports of the said nation upon vessels wholly belonging to citizens of the United States, or upon the produce, manufactures, or merchandise imported in the same from the United States or from any foreign country, the President is thereby authorized to issue his proclamation declaring that the foreign discriminating duties of tonnage and impost within the United States are and shall be suspended and discontinued so far as respects the vessels of the said foreign nation and the produce, manufactures, or merchandise imported into the United States in the same from the said foreign nation or from any other foreign country, the said suspension to take effect from the time of such notification being given to the President of the United States and to continue so long as the reciprocal exemption of vessels belonging to citizens of the United States and their cargoes, as aforesaid, shall be continued, and no longer; and

Whereas satisfactory evidence has lately been received from the Government of His Holiness the Pope, through an official communication addressed by Cardinal Antonelli, his secretary of state, to the minister resident of the United States at Rome, under date of the 7th day of December, 1857, that no discriminating duties of tonnage or impost are imposed or levied in the ports of the Pontifical States upon vessels wholly belonging to citizens of the United States, or upon the produce, manufactures, or merchandise imported in the same from the United States or from any foreign country:

Now, therefore, I, James Buchanan, President of the United States of America, do hereby declare and proclaim that the foreign discriminating duties of tonnage and impost within the United States are and shall be suspended and discontinued so far as respects the vessels of the subjects of His Holiness the Pope and the produce, manufactures, or merchandise imported into the United States in the same from the Pontifical States or from any other foreign country, the said suspension to take effect from the 7th day of December, 1857, above mentioned, and to continue so long as the reciprocal exemption of vessels belonging to citizens of the United States and their cargoes, as aforesaid, shall be continued, and no longer.

Given under my hand, at the city of Washington, the 25th day of February, A. D. 1858, and of the Independence of the United States the eighty-second.

[SEAL.]

JAMES BUCHANAN.

By the President:

LEWIS CASS,
    Secretary of State.

BY JAMES BUCHANAN, PRESIDENT OF THE UNITED STATES OF
AMERICA.

A PROCLAMATION.

Whereas the Territory of Utah was settled by certain emigrants from
the States and from foreign countries who have for several years past
manifested a spirit of insubordination to the Constitution and laws of the
United States. The great mass of those settlers, acting under the influence of leaders to whom they seem to have surrendered their judgment,
refuse to be controlled by any other authority. They have been often
advised to obedience, and these friendly counsels have been answered
with defiance. The officers of the Federal Government have been driven
from the Territory for no offense but an effort to do their sworn duty;
others have been prevented from going there by threats of assassination;
judges have been violently interrupted in the performance of their functions, and the records of the courts have been seized and destroyed or
concealed. Many other acts of unlawful violence have been perpetrated, and the right to repeat them has been openly claimed by the
leading inhabitants, with at least the silent acquiescence of nearly all
the others. Their hostility to the lawful government of the country has
at length become so violent that no officer bearing a commission from
the Chief Magistrate of the Union can enter the Territory or remain
there with safety, and all those officers recently appointed have been
unable to go to Salt Lake or anywhere else in Utah beyond the immediate power of the Army. Indeed, such is believed to be the condition to
which a strange system of terrorism has brought the inhabitants of that
region that no one among them could express an opinion favorable to
this Government, or even propose to obey its laws, without exposing his
life and property to peril.

After carefully considering this state of affairs and maturely weighing
the obligation I was under to see the laws faithfully executed, it seemed
to me right and proper that I should make such use of the military force
at my disposal as might be necessary to protect the Federal officers in
going into the Territory of Utah and in performing their duties after
arriving there. I accordingly ordered a detachment of the Army to
march for the city of Salt Lake, or within reach of that place, and to act
in case of need as a posse for the enforcement of the laws. But in the
meantime the hatred of that misguided people for the just and legal
authority of the Government had become so intense that they resolved
to measure their military strength with that of the Union. They have
organized an armed force far from contemptible in point of numbers and
trained it, if not with skill, at least with great assiduity and perseverance.
While the troops of the United States were on their march a train of
baggage wagons, which happened to be unprotected, was attacked and
destroyed by a portion of the Mormon forces and the provisions and

stores with which the train was laden were wantonly burnt. In short, their present attitude is one of decided and unreserved enmity to the United States and to all their loyal citizens. Their determination to oppose the authority of the Government by military force has not only been expressed in words, but manifested in overt acts of the most unequivocal character.

Fellow-citizens of Utah, this is rebellion against the Government to which you owe allegiance; it is levying war against the United States, and involves you in the guilt of treason. Persistence in it will bring you to condign punishment, to ruin, and to shame; for it is mere madness to suppose that with your limited resources you can successfully resist the force of this great and powerful nation.

If you have calculated upon the forbearance of the United States, if you have permitted yourselves to suppose that this Government will fail to put forth its strength and bring you to submission, you have fallen into a grave mistake. You have settled upon territory which lies, geographically, in the heart of the Union. The land you live upon was purchased by the United States and paid for out of their Treasury; the proprietary right and title to it is in them, and not in you. Utah is bounded on every side by States and Territories whose people are true to the Union. It is absurd to believe that they will or can permit you to erect in their very midst a government of your own, not only independent of the authority which they all acknowledge, but hostile to them and their interests.

Do not deceive yourselves nor try to mislead others by propagating the idea that this is a crusade against your religion. The Constitution and laws of this country can take no notice of your creed, whether it be true or false. That is a question between your God and yourselves, in which I disclaim all right to interfere. If you obey the laws, keep the peace, and respect the just rights of others, you will be perfectly secure, and may live on in your present faith or change it for another at your pleasure. Every intelligent man among you knows very well that this Government has never, directly or indirectly, sought to molest you in your worship, to control you in your ecclesiastical affairs, or even to influence you in your religious opinions.

This rebellion is not merely a violation of your legal duty; it is without just cause, without reason, without excuse. You never made a complaint that was not listened to with patience; you never exhibited a real grievance that was not redressed as promptly as it could be. The laws and regulations enacted for your government by Congress have been equal and just, and their enforcement was manifestly necessary for your own welfare and happiness. You have never asked their repeal. They are similar in every material respect to the laws which have been passed for the other Territories of the Union, and which everywhere else (with one partial exception) have been cheerfully obeyed. No people ever lived who were freer from unnecessary legal restraints than you. Human wisdom never devised a political system which bestowed more blessings or imposed lighter burdens than the Government of the United States in its operation upon the Territories.

But being anxious to save the effusion of blood and to avoid the indiscriminate punishment of a whole people for crimes of which it is not probable that all are equally guilty, I offer now a free and full pardon to all who will submit themselves to the just authority of the Federal Government. If you refuse to accept it, let the consequences fall upon your own heads. But I conjure you to pause deliberately and reflect well before you reject this tender of peace and good will.

Now, therefore, I, James Buchanan, President of the United States, have thought proper to issue this my proclamation, enjoining upon all public officers in the Territory of Utah to be diligent and faithful, to the full extent of their power, in the execution of the laws; commanding all citizens of the United States in said Territory to aid and assist the officers in the performance of their duties; offering to the inhabitants of Utah who shall submit to the laws a free pardon for the seditions and treasons heretofore by them committed; warning those who shall persist, after notice of this proclamation, in the present rebellion against the United States that they must expect no further lenity, but look to be rigorously dealt with according to their deserts; and declaring that the military forces now in Utah and hereafter to be sent there will not be withdrawn until the inhabitants of that Territory shall manifest a proper sense of the duty which they owe to this Government.

In testimony whereof I have hereunto set my hand and caused the seal of the United States to be affixed to these presents.

[SEAL.]   Done at the city of Washington the 6th day of April, 1858, and of the Independence of the United States the eighty-second.

JAMES BUCHANAN.

By the President:

LEWIS CASS, *Secretary of State.*

BY THE PRESIDENT OF THE UNITED STATES OF AMERICA.

A PROCLAMATION.

Whereas an extraordinary occasion has occurred rendering it necessary and proper that the Senate of the United States shall be convened to receive and act upon such communications as have been or may be made to it on the part of the Executive:

Now, therefore, I, James Buchanan, President of the United States, do issue this my proclamation, declaring that an extraordinary occasion requires the Senate of the United States to convene for the transaction of business at the Capitol, in the city of Washington, on the 15th day of this month, at 12 o'clock at noon of that day, of which all who shall at that time be entitled to act as members of that body are hereby required to take notice.

Given under my hand and the seal of the United States, at Washington, this 14th day of June, A. D. 1858, and of the Independence of the United States the eighty-second.

[SEAL.]

JAMES BUCHANAN.

By the President:

LEWIS CASS,
Secretary of State.

BY JAMES BUCHANAN, PRESIDENT OF THE UNITED STATES OF AMERICA.

A PROCLAMATION.

Whereas information has reached me from sources which I can not disregard that certain persons, in violation of the neutrality laws of the United States, are making a third attempt to set on foot a military expedition within their territory against Nicaragua, a foreign State with which they are at peace. In order to raise money for equipping and maintaining this expedition, persons connected therewith, as I have reason to believe, have issued and sold bonds and other contracts pledging the public lands of Nicaragua and the transit route through its territory as a security for their redemption and fulfillment.

The hostile design of this expedition is rendered manifest by the fact that these bonds and contracts can be of no possible value to their holders unless the present Government of Nicaragua shall be overthrown by force. Besides, the envoy extraordinary and minister plenipotentiary of that Government in the United States has issued a notice, in pursuance of his instructions, dated on the 27th instant, forbidding the citizens or subjects of any nation, except passengers intending to proceed through Nicaragua over the transit route from ocean to ocean, to enter its territory without a regular passport, signed by the proper minister or consul-general of the Republic resident in the country from whence they shall have departed. Such persons, with this exception, "will be stopped and compelled to return by the same conveyance that took them to the country." From these circumstances the inference is irresistible that persons engaged in this expedition will leave the United States with hostile purposes against Nicaragua. They can not, under the guise which they have assumed that they are peaceful emigrants, conceal their real intentions, and especially when they know in advance that their landing will be resisted and can only be accomplished by an overpowering force. This expedient was successfully resorted to previous to the last expedition, and the vessel in which those composing it were conveyed to Nicaragua obtained a clearance from the collector of the port of Mobile. Although, after a careful examination, no arms or munitions of war were discovered on board, yet when they arrived in Nicaragua they were found to be armed and equipped and immediately commenced hostilities.

The leaders of former illegal expeditions of the same character have openly expressed their intention to renew hostilities against Nicaragua. One of them, who has already been twice expelled from Nicaragua, has invited through the public newspapers American citizens to emigrate to that Republic, and has designated Mobile as the place of rendezvous and departure and San Juan del Norte as the port to which they are bound. This person, who has renounced his allegiance to the United States and claims to be President of Nicaragua, has given notice to the collector of the port of Mobile that two or three hundred of these emigrants will be prepared to embark from that port about the middle of November.

For these and other good reasons, and for the purpose of saving American citizens who may have been honestly deluded into the belief that they are about to proceed to Nicaragua as peaceful emigrants, if any such there be, from the disastrous consequences to which they will be exposed, I, James Buchanan, President of the United States, have thought it fit to issue this my proclamation, enjoining upon all officers of the Government, civil and military, in their respective spheres, to be vigilant, active, and faithful in suppressing these illegal enterprises and in carrying out their standing instructions to that effect; exhorting all good citizens, by their respect for the laws and their regard for the peace and welfare of the country, to aid the efforts of the public authorities in the discharge of their duties.

In testimony whereof I have hereunto set my hand and caused the seal of the United States to be affixed to these presents.

[SEAL.]   Done at the city of Washington the 30th day of October, 1858, and of the Independence of the United States the eighty-third.

JAMES BUCHANAN.

By the President:

LEWIS CASS, *Secretary of State.*

SECOND ANNUAL MESSAGE.

WASHINGTON CITY, *December 6, 1858.*

Fellow-Citizens of the Senate and House of Representatives:

When we compare the condition of the country at the present day with what it was one year ago at the meeting of Congress, we have much reason for gratitude to that Almighty Providence which has never failed to interpose for our relief at the most critical periods of our history. One year ago the sectional strife between the North and the

South on the dangerous subject of slavery had again become so intense as to threaten the peace and perpetuity of the Confederacy. The application for the admission of Kansas as a State into the Union fostered this unhappy agitation and brought the whole subject once more before Congress. It was the desire of every patriot that such measures of legislation might be adopted as would remove the excitement from the States and confine it to the Territory where it legitimately belonged. Much has been done, I am happy to say, toward the accomplishment of this object during the last session of Congress.

The Supreme Court of the United States had previously decided that all American citizens have an equal right to take into the Territories whatever is held as property under the laws of any of the States, and to hold such property there under the guardianship of the Federal Constitution so long as the Territorial condition shall remain.

This is now a well-established position, and the proceedings of the last session were alone wanting to give it practical effect. The principle has been recognized in some form or other by an almost unanimous vote of both Houses of Congress that a Territory has a right to come into the Union either as a free or a slave State, according to the will of a majority of its people. The just equality of all the States has thus been vindicated and a fruitful source of dangerous dissension among them has been removed.

Whilst such has been the beneficial tendency of your legislative proceedings outside of Kansas, their influence has nowhere been so happy as within that Territory itself. Left to manage and control its own affairs in its own way, without the pressure of external influence, the revolutionary Topeka organization and all resistance to the Territorial government established by Congress have been finally abandoned. As a natural consequence that fine Territory now appears to be tranquil and prosperous and is attracting increasing thousands of immigrants to make it their happy home.

The past unfortunate experience of Kansas has enforced the lesson, so often already taught, that resistance to lawful authority under our form of government can not fail in the end to prove disastrous to its authors. Had the people of the Territory yielded obedience to the laws enacted by their legislature, it would at the present moment have contained a large additional population of industrious and enterprising citizens, who have been deterred from entering its borders by the existence of civil strife and organized rebellion.

It was the resistance to rightful authority and the persevering attempts to establish a revolutionary government under the Topeka constitution which caused the people of Kansas to commit the grave error of refusing to vote for delegates to the convention to frame a constitution under a law not denied to be fair and just in its provisions. This refusal to vote has been the prolific source of all the evils which have followed. In their hostility to the Territorial government they disregarded the principle, absolutely essential to the working of our form of government, that a majority of those who vote, not the majority who may remain at home, from whatever cause, must decide the result of an election. For this reason, seeking to take advantage of their own error, they denied the authority of the convention thus elected to frame a constitution.

The convention, notwithstanding, proceeded to adopt a constitution unexceptionable in its general features, and providing for the submission of the slavery question to a vote of the people, which, in my opinion, they were bound to do under the Kansas and Nebraska act. This was the all-important question which had alone convulsed the Territory; and yet the opponents of the lawful government, persisting in their first error, refrained from exercising their right to vote, and preferred that slavery should continue rather than surrender their revolutionary Topeka organization.

A wiser and better spirit seemed to prevail before the first Monday of January last, when an election was held under the constitution. A majority of the people then voted for a governor and other State officers, for a Member of Congress and members of the State legislature. This election was warmly contested by the two political parties in Kansas, and a greater vote was polled than at any previous election. A large majority of the members of the legislature elect belonged to that party which had previously refused to vote. The antislavery party were thus placed in the ascendant, and the political power of the State was in their own hands. Had Congress admitted Kansas into the Union under the Lecompton constitution, the legislature might at its very first session have submitted the question to a vote of the people whether they would or would not have a convention to amend their constitution, either on the slavery or any other question, and have adopted all necessary means for giving speedy effect to the will of the majority. Thus the Kansas question would have been immediately and finally settled.

Under these circumstances I submitted to Congress the constitution thus framed, with all the officers already elected necessary to put the State government into operation, accompanied by a strong recommendation in favor of the admission of Kansas as a State. In the course of my long public life I have never performed any official act which in the retrospect has afforded me more heartfelt satisfaction. Its admission could have inflicted no possible injury on any human being, whilst it would within a brief period have restored peace to Kansas and harmony to the Union. In that event the slavery question would ere this have been finally settled according to the legally expressed will of a majority of the voters, and popular sovereignty would thus have been vindicated in a constitutional manner.

With my deep convictions of duty I could have pursued no other course. It is true that as an individual I had expressed an opinion, both before and during the session of the convention, in favor of submitting the remaining clauses of the constitution, as well as that concerning slavery, to the people. But, acting in an official character, neither myself nor any human authority had the power to rejudge the proceedings of the convention and declare the constitution which it had framed to be a nullity. To have done this would have been a violation of the Kansas and Nebraska act, which left the people of the Territory "perfectly free to form and regulate their domestic institutions in their own way, subject only to the Constitution of the United States." It would equally have violated the great principle of popular sovereignty, at the foundation of our institutions, to deprive the people of the power, if they thought proper to exercise it, of confiding to delegates elected by themselves the trust of framing a constitution without requiring them to subject their constituents to the trouble, expense, and delay of a second election. It would have been in opposition to many precedents in our history, commencing in the very best age of the Republic, of the admission of Territories as States into the Union without a previous vote of the people approving their constitution.

It is to be lamented that a question so insignificant when viewed in its practical effects on the people of Kansas, whether decided one way or the other, should have kindled such a flame of excitement throughout the country. This reflection may prove to be a lesson of wisdom and of warning for our future guidance. Practically considered, the question is simply whether the people of that Territory should first come into the Union and then change any provision in their constitution not agreeable to themselves, or accomplish the very same object by remaining out of the Union and framing another constitution in accordance with their will. In either case the result would be precisely the same. The only difference, in point of fact, is that the object would have been much sooner attained and the pacification of Kansas more speedily effected had it been admitted as a State during the last session of Congress.

My recommendation, however, for the immediate admission of Kansas failed to meet the approbation of Congress. They deemed it wiser to adopt a different measure for the settlement of the question. For my own part, I should have been willing to yield my assent to almost any constitutional measure to accomplish this object. I therefore cordially acquiesced in what has been called the English compromise and approved the "act for the admission of the State of Kansas into the Union" upon the terms therein prescribed.

Under the ordinance which accompanied the Lecompton constitution the people of Kansas had claimed double the quantity of public lands for the support of common schools which had ever been previously granted to any State upon entering the Union, and also the alternate sections of land for 12 miles on each side of two railroads proposed to be constructed from the northern to the southern boundary and from the eastern to the western boundary of the State. Congress, deeming these claims unreasonable, provided by the act of May 4, 1858, to which I have just referred, for the admission of the State on an equal footing with the original States, but "upon the fundamental condition precedent" that a majority of the people thereof, at an election to be held for that purpose, should, in place of the very large grants of public lands which they had demanded under the ordinance, accept such grants as had been made to Minnesota and other new States. Under this act, should a majority reject the proposition offered them, "it shall be deemed and held that the people of Kansas do not desire admission into the Union with said constitution under the conditions set forth in said proposition." In that event the act authorizes the people of the Territory to elect delegates to form a constitution and State government for themselves "whenever, and not before, it is ascertained by a census, duly and legally taken, that the population of said Territory equals or exceeds the ratio of representation required for a member of the House of Representatives of the Congress of the United States." The delegates thus assembled "shall first determine by a vote whether it is the wish of the people of the proposed State to be admitted into the Union at that time, and, if so, shall proceed to form a constitution and take all necessary steps for the establishment of a State government in conformity with the Federal Constitution." After this constitution shall have been formed, Congress, carrying out the principles of popular sovereignty and nonintervention, have left "the mode and manner of its approval or ratification by the people of the proposed State" to be "prescribed by law," and they "shall then be admitted into the Union as a State under such constitution, thus fairly and legally made, with or without slavery, as said constitution may prescribe."

An election was held throughout Kansas, in pursuance of the provisions of this act, on the 2d day of August last, and it resulted in the rejection by a large majority of the proposition submitted to the people by Congress. This being the case, they are now authorized to form another constitution, preparatory to admission into the Union, but not until their number, as ascertained by a census, shall equal or exceed the ratio required to elect a member to the House of Representatives.

It is not probable, in the present state of the case, that a third constitution can be lawfully framed and presented to Congress by Kansas before its population shall have reached the designated number. Nor is it to be presumed that after their sad experience in resisting the Territorial laws they will attempt to adopt a constitution in express violation of the provisions of an act of Congress. During the session of 1856 much of the time of Congress was occupied on the question of admitting Kansas under the Topeka constitution. Again, nearly the whole of the last session was devoted to the question of its admission under the Lecompton constitution. Surely it is not unreasonable to require the people of Kansas to wait before making a third attempt until the number of their inhabitants shall amount to 93,420. During this brief period the harmony of the States as well as the great business interests of the country demand that the people of the Union shall not for a third time be convulsed by another agitation on the Kansas question. By waiting for a short time and acting in obedience to law Kansas will glide into the Union without the slightest impediment.

This excellent provision, which Congress have applied to Kansas, ought to be extended and rendered applicable to all Territories which may hereafter seek admission into the Union.

Whilst Congress possess the undoubted power of admitting a new State into the Union, however small may be the number of its inhabitants, yet this power ought not, in my opinion, to be exercised before the population shall amount to the ratio required by the act for the admission of Kansas. Had this been previously the rule, the country would have escaped all the evils and misfortunes to which it has been exposed by the Kansas question.

Of course it would be unjust to give this rule a retrospective application, and exclude a State which, acting upon the past practice of the Government, has already formed its constitution, elected its legislature and other officers, and is now prepared to enter the Union.

The rule ought to be adopted, whether we consider its bearing on the people of the Territories or upon the people of the existing States. Many of the serious dissensions which have prevailed in Congress and throughout the country would have been avoided had this rule been established at an earlier period of the Government.

Immediately upon the formation of a new Territory people from different States and from foreign countries rush into it for the laudable purpose of improving their condition. Their first duty to themselves is to open and cultivate farms, to construct roads, to establish schools, to erect places of religious worship, and to devote their energies generally to reclaim the wilderness and to lay the foundations of a flourishing and prosperous commonwealth. If in this incipient condition, with a population of a few thousand, they should prematurely enter the Union, they are oppressed by the burden of State taxation, and the means necessary for the improvement of the Territory and the advancement of their own interests are thus diverted to very different purposes.

The Federal Government has ever been a liberal parent to the Territories and a generous contributor to the useful enterprises of the early settlers. It has paid the expenses of their governments and legislative assemblies out of the common Treasury, and thus relieved them from a heavy charge. Under these circumstances nothing can be better calculated to retard their material progress than to divert them from their useful employments by prematurely exciting angry political contests among themselves for the benefit of aspiring leaders. It is surely no hardship for embryo governors, Senators, and Members of Congress to wait until the number of inhabitants shall equal those of a single Congressional district. They surely ought not to be permitted to rush into the Union with a population less than one-half of several of the large counties in the interior of some of the States. This was the condition of Kansas when it made application to be admitted under the Topeka constitution. Besides, it requires some time to render the mass of a population collected in a new Territory at all homogeneous and to unite them on anything like a fixed policy. Establish the rule, and all will look forward to it and govern themselves accordingly.

But justice to the people of the several States requires that this rule should be established by Congress. Each State is entitled to two Senators and at least one Representative in Congress. Should the people of the States fail to elect a Vice-President, the power devolves upon the Senate to select this officer from the two highest candidates on the list. In case of the death of the President, the Vice-President thus elected by the Senate becomes President of the United States. On all questions of legislation the Senators from the smallest States of the Union have an equal vote with those from the largest. The same may be said in regard to the ratification of treaties and of Executive appointments. All this has worked admirably in practice, whilst it conforms in principle with the character of a Government instituted by sovereign States. I presume no American citizen would desire the slightest change in the arrangement. Still, is it not unjust and unequal to the existing States to invest some 40,000 or 50,000 people collected in a Territory with the attributes of sovereignty and place them on an equal footing with Virginia and New York in the Senate of the United States?

For these reasons I earnestly recommend the passage of a general act which shall provide that, upon the application of a Territorial legislature declaring their belief that the Territory contains a number of inhabitants which, if in a State, would entitle them to elect a Member of Congress, it shall be the duty of the President to cause a census of the inhabitants to be taken, and if found sufficient then by the terms of this act to authorize them to proceed "in their own way" to frame a State constitution preparatory to admission into the Union. I also recommend that an appropriation may be made to enable the President to take a census of the people of Kansas.

The present condition of the Territory of Utah, when contrasted with what it was one year ago, is a subject for congratulation. It was then in a state of open rebellion, and, cost what it might, the character of the Government required that this rebellion should be suppressed and the Mormons compelled to yield obedience to the Constitution and the laws. In order to accomplish this object, as I informed you in my last annual message, I appointed a new governor instead of Brigham Young, and other Federal officers to take the place of those who, consulting their personal safety, had found it necessary to withdraw from the Territory.

To protect these civil officers, and to aid them, as a *posse comitatus*, in the execution of the laws in case of need, I ordered a detachment of the Army to accompany them to Utah. The necessity for adopting these measures is now demonstrated.

On the 15th of September, 1857, Governor Young issued his proclamation, in the style of an independent sovereign, announcing his purpose to resist by force of arms the entry of the United States troops into our own Territory of Utah. By this he required all the forces in the Territory to "hold themselves in readiness to march at a moment's notice to repel any and all such invasion," and established martial law from its date throughout the Territory. These proved to be no idle threats. Forts Bridger and Supply were vacated and burnt down by the Mormons to deprive our troops of a shelter after their long and fatiguing march. Orders were issued by Daniel H. Wells, styling himself "Lieutenant-General, Nauvoo Legion," to stampede the animals of the United States troops on their march, to set fire to their trains, to burn the grass and the whole country before them and on their flanks, to keep them from sleeping by night surprises, and to blockade the road by felling trees and destroying the fords of rivers, etc.

These orders were promptly and effectually obeyed. On the 4th of October, 1857, the Mormons captured and burned, on Green River, three of our supply trains, consisting of seventy-five wagons loaded with provisions and tents for the army, and carried away several hundred animals. This diminished the supply of provisions so materially that General Johnston was obliged to reduce the ration, and even with this precaution there was only sufficient left to subsist the troops until the 1st of June.

Our little army behaved admirably in their encampment at Fort Bridger under these trying privations. In the midst of the mountains, in a dreary, unsettled, and inhospitable region, more than a thousand miles from home, they passed the severe and inclement winter without a murmur. They looked forward with confidence for relief from their country in due season, and in this they were not disappointed.

The Secretary of War employed all his energies to forward them the necessary supplies and to muster and send such a military force to Utah as would render resistance on the part of the Mormons hopeless, and thus terminate the war without the effusion of blood. In his efforts he was efficiently sustained by Congress. They granted appropriations sufficient to cover the deficiency thus necessarily created, and also provided for raising two regiments of volunteers "for the purpose of quelling disturbances in the Territory of Utah, for the protection of supply and emigrant trains, and the suppression of Indian hostilities on the frontiers." Happily, there was no occasion to call these regiments into service. If there had been, I should have felt serious embarrassment in selecting them, so great was the number of our brave and patriotic citizens anxious to serve their country in this distant and apparently dangerous expedition. Thus it has ever been, and thus may it ever be.

The wisdom and economy of sending sufficient reenforcements to Utah are established, not only by the event, but in the opinion of those who from their position and opportunities are the most capable of forming a correct judgment. General Johnston, the commander of the forces, in addressing the Secretary of War from Fort Bridger under date of October 18, 1857, expresses the opinion that "unless a large force is sent here, from the nature of the country a protracted war on their [the Mormons's] part is inevitable." This he considered necessary to terminate the war "speedily and more economically than if attempted by insufficient means."

In the meantime it was my anxious desire that the Mormons should yield obedience to the Constitution and the laws without rendering it necessary to resort to military force. To aid in accomplishing this object, I deemed it advisable in April last to dispatch two distinguished citizens of the United States, Messrs. Powell and McCulloch, to Utah. They bore with them a proclamation addressed by myself to the inhabitants of Utah, dated on the 6th day of that month, warning them of their true condition and how hopeless it was on their part to persist in rebellion against the United States, and offering all those who should submit to the laws a full pardon for their past seditions and treasons. At the same time I assured those who should persist in rebellion against the United States that they must expect no further lenity, but look to be rigorously dealt with according to their deserts. The instructions to these agents, as well as a copy of the proclamation and their reports, are herewith submitted. It will be seen by their report of the 3d of July last that they have fully confirmed the opinion expressed by General Johnston in the previous October as to the necessity of sending reenforcements to Utah. In this they state that they "are firmly impressed with the belief that the presence of the Army here and the large additional force that had been ordered to this Territory were the chief inducements that caused the Mormons to abandon the idea of resisting the authority of the United States. A less decisive policy would probably have resulted in a long, bloody, and expensive war."

These gentlemen conducted themselves to my entire satisfaction and rendered useful services in executing the humane intentions of the Government.

It also affords me great satisfaction to state that Governor Cumming has performed his duty in an able and conciliatory manner and with the happiest effect. I can not in this connection refrain from mentioning the valuable services of Colonel Thomas L. Kane, who, from motives of pure benevolence and without any official character or pecuniary compensation, visited Utah during the last inclement winter for the purpose of contributing to the pacification of the Territory.

I am happy to inform you that the governor and other civil officers of

Utah are now performing their appropriate functions without resistance. The authority of the Constitution and the laws has been fully restored and peace prevails throughout the Territory.

A portion of the troops sent to Utah are now encamped in Cedar Valley, 44 miles southwest of Salt Lake City, and the remainder have been ordered to Oregon to suppress Indian hostilities.

The march of the army to Salt Lake City through the Indian Territory has had a powerful effect in restraining the hostile feelings against the United States which existed among the Indians in that region and in securing emigrants to the far West against their depredations. This will also be the means of establishing military posts and promoting settlements along the route.

I recommend that the benefits of our land laws and preemption system be extended to the people of Utah by the establishment of a land office in that Territory.

I have occasion also to congratulate you on the result of our negotiations with China.

You were informed by my last annual message that our minister had been instructed to occupy a neutral position in the hostilities conducted by Great Britain and France against Canton. He was, however, at the same time directed to cooperate cordially with the British and French ministers in all peaceful measures to secure by treaty those just concessions to foreign commerce which the nations of the world had a right to demand. It was impossible for me to proceed further than this on my own authority without usurping the war-making power, which under the Constitution belongs exclusively to Congress.

Besides, after a careful examination of the nature and extent of our grievances, I did not believe they were of such a pressing and aggravated character as would have justified Congress in declaring war against the Chinese Empire without first making another earnest attempt to adjust them by peaceful negotiation. I was the more inclined to this opinion because of the severe chastisement which had then but recently been inflicted upon the Chinese by our squadron in the capture and destruction of the Barrier forts to avenge an alleged insult to our flag.

The event has proved the wisdom of our neutrality. Our minister has executed his instructions with eminent skill and ability. In conjunction with the Russian plenipotentiary, he has peacefully, but effectually, cooperated with the English and French plenipotentiaries, and each of the four powers has concluded a separate treaty with China of a highly satisfactory character. The treaty concluded by our own plenipotentiary will immediately be submitted to the Senate.

I am happy to announce that through the energetic yet conciliatory efforts of our consul-general in Japan a new treaty has been concluded with that Empire, which may be expected materially to augment our trade and intercourse in that quarter and remove from our countrymen the disabilities which have heretofore been imposed upon the exercise of their religion. The treaty shall be submitted to the Senate for approval without delay.

It is my earnest desire that every misunderstanding with the Government of Great Britain should be amicably and speedily adjusted. It has been the misfortune of both countries, almost ever since the period of the Revolution, to have been annoyed by a succession of irritating and dangerous questions, threatening their friendly relations. This has partially prevented the full development of those feelings of mutual friendship between the people of the two countries so natural in themselves and so conducive to their common interest. Any serious interruption of the commerce between the United States and Great Britain would be equally injurious to both. In fact, no two nations have ever existed on the face of the earth which could do each other so much good or so much harm.

Entertaining these sentiments, I am gratified to inform you that the long-pending controversy between the two Governments in relation to the question of visitation and search has been amicably adjusted. The claim on the part of Great Britain forcibly to visit American vessels on the high seas in time of peace could not be sustained under the law of nations, and it had been overruled by her own most eminent jurists. This question was recently brought to an issue by the repeated acts of British cruisers in boarding and searching our merchant vessels in the Gulf of Mexico and the adjacent seas. These acts were the more injurious and annoying, as these waters are traversed by a large portion of the commerce and navigation of the United States and their free and unrestricted use is essential to the security of the coastwise trade between the different States of the Union. Such vexatious interruptions could not fail to excite the feelings of the country and to require the interposition of the Government. Remonstrances were addressed to the British Government against these violations of our rights of sovereignty, and a naval force was at the same time ordered to the Cuban waters with directions "to protect all vessels of the United States on the high seas from search or detention by the vessels of war of any other nation." These measures received the unqualified and even enthusiastic approbation of the American people. Most fortunately, however, no collision took place, and the British Government promptly avowed its recognition of the principles of international law upon this subject as laid down by the Government of the United States in the note of the Secretary of State to the British minister at Washington of April 10, 1858, which secure the vessels of the United States upon the high seas from visitation or search in time of peace under any circumstances whatever. The claim has been abandoned in a manner reflecting honor on the British Government and evincing a just regard for the law of nations, and can not fail to strengthen the amicable relations between the two countries.

The British Government at the same time proposed to the United States that some mode should be adopted, by mutual arrangement between the two countries, of a character which may be found effective without being offensive, for verifying the nationality of vessels suspected on good grounds of carrying false colors. They have also invited the United States to take the initiative and propose measures for this purpose. Whilst declining to assume so grave a responsibility, the Secretary of State has informed the British Government that we are ready to receive any proposals which they may feel disposed to offer having this object in view, and to consider them in an amicable spirit. A strong opinion is, however, expressed that the occasional abuse of the flag of any nation is an evil far less to be deprecated than would be the establishment of any regulations which might be incompatible with the freedom of the seas. This Government has yet received no communication specifying the manner in which the British Government would propose to carry out their suggestion, and I am inclined to believe that no plan which can be devised will be free from grave embarrassments. Still, I shall form no decided opinion on the subject until I shall have carefully and in the best spirit examined any proposals which they may think proper to make.

I am truly sorry I can not also inform you that the complication between Great Britain and the United States arising out of the Clayton and Bulwer treaty of April, 1850, have been finally adjusted.

At the commencement of your last session I had reason to hope that, emancipating themselves from further unavailing discussions, the two Governments would proceed to settle the Central American questions in a practical manner, alike honorable and satisfactory to both; and this hope I have not yet abandoned. In my last annual message I stated that overtures had been made by the British Government for this purpose in a friendly spirit, which I cordially reciprocated. Their proposal was to withdraw these questions from direct negotiation between the two Governments, but to accomplish the same object by a negotiation between the British Government and each of the Central American Republics whose territorial interests are immediately involved. The settlement was to be made in accordance with the general tenor of the interpretation placed upon the Clayton and Bulwer treaty by the United States, with certain modifications. As negotiations are still pending upon this basis, it would not be proper for me now to communicate their present condition. A final settlement of these questions is greatly to be desired, as this would wipe out the last remaining subject of dispute between the two countries.

Our relations with the great Empires of France and Russia, as well as with all other Governments on the continent of Europe, except that of Spain, continue to be of the most friendly character.

With Spain our relations remain in an unsatisfactory condition. In my message of December last I informed you that our envoy extraordi-

THE TRIAL OF JOHN BROWN

JOHN BROWN'S RAID ON HARPER'S FERRY

The full account of this occurrence is given in the article entitled "Brown's Insurrection," in the Encyclopedic Index.

The eyes, not only of the United States, but also of the entire civilized world, were upon the court-room where the trial of John Brown took place. The upper panel on the preceding page reproduces a careful drawing made by an eye-witness of the scene. All the world knows the fate which was meted out to Brown; and it is his appearance as he went to meet that fate which is reproduced in the lower panel.

President Buchanan discusses the event on page 2084.

nary and minister plenipotentiary to Madrid had asked for his recall, and it was my purpose to send out a new minister to that Court with special instructions on all questions pending between the two Governments, and with a determination to have them speedily and amicably adjusted if that were possible. This purpose has been hitherto defeated by causes which I need not enumerate.

The mission to Spain has been intrusted to a distinguished citizen of Kentucky, who will proceed to Madrid without delay and make another and a final attempt to obtain justice from that Government.

Spanish officials under the direct control of the Captain-General of Cuba have insulted our national flag and in repeated instances have from time to time inflicted injuries on the persons and property of our citizens. These have given birth to numerous claims against the Spanish Government, the merits of which have been ably discussed for a series of years by our successive diplomatic representatives. Notwithstanding this, we have not arrived at a practical result in any single instance, unless we may except the case of the *Black Warrior*, under the late Administration, and that presented an outrage of such a character as would have justified an immediate resort to war. All our attempts to obtain redress have been baffled and defeated. The frequent and oft-recurring changes in the Spanish ministry have been employed as reasons for delay. We have been compelled to wait again and again until the new minister shall have had time to investigate the justice of our demands.

Even what have been denominated "the Cuban claims," in which more than 100 of our citizens are directly interested, have furnished no exception. These claims were for the refunding of duties unjustly exacted from American vessels at different custom-houses in Cuba so long ago as the year 1844. The principles upon which they rest are so manifestly equitable and just that, after a period of nearly ten years, in 1854 they were recognized by the Spanish Government. Proceedings were afterwards instituted to ascertain their amount, and this was finally fixed, according to their own statement (with which we were satisfied), at the sum of $128,635.54. Just at the moment, after a delay of fourteen years, when we had reason to expect that this sum would be repaid with interest, we have received a proposal offering to refund one-third of that amount ($42,878.41), but without interest, if we would accept this in full satisfaction. The offer is also accompanied by a declaration that this indemnification is not founded on any reason of strict justice, but is made as a special favor.

One alleged cause for procrastination in the examination and adjustment of our claims arises from an obstacle which it is the duty of the Spanish Government to remove. Whilst the Captain-General of Cuba is invested with general despotic authority in the government of that island, the power is withheld from him to examine and redress wrongs committed by officials under his control on citizens of the United States.

Instead of making our complaints directly to him at Havana, we are obliged to present them through our minister at Madrid. These are then referred back to the Captain-General for information, and much time is thus consumed in preliminary investigations and correspondence between Madrid and Cuba before the Spanish Government will consent to proceed to negotiation. Many of the difficulties between the two Governments would be obviated and a long train of negotiation avoided if the Captain-General were invested with authority to settle questions of easy solution on the spot, where all the facts are fresh and could be promptly and satisfactorily ascertained. We have hitherto in vain urged upon the Spanish Government to confer this power upon the Captain-General, and our minister to Spain will again be instructed to urge this subject on their notice. In this respect we occupy a different position from the powers of Europe. Cuba is almost within sight of our shores; our commerce with it is far greater than that of any other nation, including Spain itself, and our citizens are in habits of daily and extended personal intercourse with every part of the island. It is therefore a great grievance that when any difficulty occurs, no matter how unimportant, which might be readily settled at the moment, we should be obliged to resort to Madrid, especially when the very first step to be taken there is to refer it back to Cuba.

The truth is that Cuba, in its existing colonial condition, is a constant source of injury and annoyance to the American people. It is the only spot in the civilized world where the African slave trade is tolerated, and we are bound by treaty with Great Britain to maintain a naval force on the coast of Africa, at much expense both of life and treasure, solely for the purpose of arresting slavers bound to that island. The late serious difficulties between the United States and Great Britain respecting the right of search, now so happily terminated, could never have arisen if Cuba had not afforded a market for slaves. As long as this market shall remain open there can be no hope for the civilization of benighted Africa. Whilst the demand for slaves continues in Cuba wars will be waged among the petty and barbarous chiefs in Africa for the purpose of seizing subjects to supply this trade. In such a condition of affairs it is impossible that the light of civilization and religion can ever penetrate these dark abodes.

It has been made known to the world by my predecessors that the United States have on several occasions endeavored to acquire Cuba from Spain by honorable negotiation. If this were accomplished, the last relic of the African slave trade would instantly disappear. We would not, if we could, acquire Cuba in any other manner. This is due to our national character. All the territory which we have acquired since the origin of the Government has been by fair purchase from France, Spain, and Mexico or by the free and voluntary act of the independent State of Texas in blending her destinies with our own. This course we shall ever pursue, unless circumstances should occur which we do not now anticipate, rendering a departure from it clearly justifiable under the imperative and overruling law of self-preservation.

The island of Cuba, from its geographical position, commands the mouth of the Mississippi and the immense and annually increasing trade, foreign and coastwise, from the valley of that noble river, now embracing half the sovereign States of the Union. With that island under the dominion of a distant foreign power this trade, of vital importance to these States, is exposed to the danger of being destroyed in time of war, and it has hitherto been subjected to perpetual injury and annoyance in time of peace. Our relations with Spain, which ought to be of the most friendly character, must always be placed in jeopardy whilst the existing colonial government over the island shall remain in its present condition.

Whilst the possession of the island would be of vast importance to the United States, its value to Spain is comparatively unimportant. Such was the relative situation of the parties when the great Napoleon transferred Louisiana to the United States. Jealous as he ever was of the national honor and interests of France, no person throughout the world has imputed blame to him for accepting a pecuniary equivalent for this cession.

The publicity which has been given to our former negotiations upon this subject and the large appropriation which may be required to effect the purpose render it expedient before making another attempt to renew the negotiation that I should lay the whole subject before Congress. This is especially necessary, as it may become indispensable to success that I should be intrusted with the means of making an advance to the Spanish Government immediately after the signing of the treaty, without awaiting the ratification of it by the Senate. I am encouraged to make this suggestion by the example of Mr. Jefferson previous to the purchase of Louisiana from France and by that of Mr. Polk in view of the acquisition of territory from Mexico. I refer the whole subject to Congress and commend it to their careful consideration.

I repeat the recommendation made in my message of December last in favor of an appropriation "to be paid to the Spanish Government for the purpose of distribution among the claimants in the *Amistad* case." President Polk first made a similar recommendation in December, 1847, and it was repeated by my immediate predecessor in December, 1853. I entertain no doubt that indemnity is fairly due to these claimants under our treaty with Spain of October 27, 1795; and whilst demanding justice we ought to do justice. An appropriation promptly made for this purpose could not fail to exert a favorable influence on our negotiations with Spain.

Our position in relation to the independent States south of us on this continent, and especially those within the limits of North America, is of a peculiar character. The northern boundary of Mexico is coincident with our own southern boundary from ocean to ocean, and we must necessarily feel a deep interest in all that concerns the well-being and the fate of so near a neighbor. We have always cherished the kindest wishes for the success of that Republic, and have indulged the hope that it might at last, after all its trials, enjoy peace and prosperity under a free and stable government. We have never hitherto interfered, directly or indirectly, with its internal affairs, and it is a duty which we owe to ourselves to protect the integrity of its territory against the hostile interference of any other power. Our geographical position, our direct interest in all that concerns Mexico, and our well-settled policy in regard to the North American continent render this an indispensable duty.

Mexico has been in a state of constant revolution almost ever since it achieved its independence. One military leader after another has usurped the Government in rapid succession, and the various constitutions from time to time adopted have been set at naught almost as soon as they were proclaimed. The successive Governments have afforded no adequate protection, either to Mexican citizens or foreign residents, against lawless violence. Heretofore a seizure of the capital by a military chieftain has been generally followed by at least the nominal submission of the country to his rule for a brief period, but not so at the present crisis of Mexican affairs. A civil war has been raging for some time throughout the Republic between the central Government at the City of Mexico, which has endeavored to subvert the constitution last framed by military power, and those who maintain the authority of that constitution. The antagonist parties each hold possession of different States of the Republic, and the fortunes of the war are constantly changing. Meanwhile the most reprehensible means have been employed by both parties to extort money from foreigners, as well as natives, to carry on this ruinous contest. The truth is that this fine country, blessed with a productive soil and a benign climate, has been reduced by civil dissension to a condition of almost hopeless anarchy and imbecility. It would be vain for this Government to attempt to enforce payment in money of the claims of American citizens, now amounting to more than $10,000,000, against Mexico, because she is destitute of all pecuniary means to satisfy these demands.

Our late minister was furnished with ample powers and instructions for the adjustment of all pending questions with the central Government of Mexico, and he performed his duty with zeal and ability. The claims of our citizens, some of them arising out of the violation of an express provision of the treaty of Guadalupe Hidalgo, and others from gross injuries to persons as well as property, have remained unredressed and even unnoticed. Remonstrances against these grievances have been addressed without effect to that Government. Meantime in various parts of the Republic instances have been numerous of the murder, imprisonment, and plunder of our citizens by different parties claiming and exercising a local jurisdiction; but the central Government, although repeatedly urged thereto, have made no effort either to punish the authors of these outrages or to prevent their recurrence. No American citizen can now visit Mexico on lawful business without imminent danger to his person and property. There is no adequate protection to either, and in this respect our treaty with that Republic is almost a dead letter.

This state of affairs was brought to a crisis in May last by the promulgation of a decree levying a contribution *pro rata* upon all the capital in the Republic between certain specified amounts, whether held by Mexicans or foreigners. Mr. Forsyth, regarding this decree in the light of a "forced loan," formally protested against its application to his countrymen and advised them not to pay the contribution, but to suffer it to be forcibly exacted. Acting upon this advice, an American citizen refused to pay the contribution, and his property was seized by armed men to satisfy the amount. Not content with this, the Government proceeded still further and issued a decree banishing him from the country. Our minister immediately notified them that if this decree should be carried into execution he would feel it to be his duty to adopt "the most decided measures that belong to the powers and obligations of the representative office." Notwithstanding this warning, the banishment was enforced, and Mr. Forsyth promptly announced to the Government the suspension of the political relations of his legation with them until the pleasure of his own Government should be ascertained.

This Government did not regard the contribution imposed by the decree of the 15th May last to be in strictness a "forced loan," and as such prohibited by the tenth article of the treaty of 1826 between Great Britain and Mexico, to the benefits of which American citizens are entitled by treaty; yet the imposition of the contribution upon foreigners was considered an unjust and oppressive measure. Besides, internal factions in other parts of the Republic were at the same time levying similar exactions upon the property of our citizens and interrupting their commerce. There had been an entire failure on the part of our minister to secure redress for the wrongs which our citizens had endured, notwithstanding his persevering efforts. And from the temper manifested by the Mexican Government he had repeatedly assured us that no favorable change could be expected until the United States should "give striking evidence of their will and power to protect their citizens," and that "severe chastening is the only earthly remedy for our grievances." From this statement of facts it would have been worse than idle to direct Mr. Forsyth to retrace his steps and resume diplomatic relations with that Government, and it was therefore deemed proper to sanction his withdrawal of the legation from the City of Mexico.

Abundant cause now undoubtedly exists for a resort to hostilities against the Government still holding possession of the capital. Should they succeed in subduing the constitutional forces, all reasonable hope will then have expired of a peaceful settlement of our difficulties.

On the other hand, should the constitutional party prevail and their authority be established over the Republic, there is reason to hope that they will be animated by a less unfriendly spirit and may grant that redress to American citizens which justice requires so far as they may possess the means. But for this expectation I should at once have recommended to Congress to grant the necessary power to the President to take possession of a sufficient portion of the remote and unsettled territory of Mexico, to be held in pledge until our injuries shall be redressed and our just demands be satisfied. We have already exhausted every milder means of obtaining justice. In such a case this remedy of reprisals is recognized by the law of nations, not only as just in itself, but as a means of preventing actual war.

But there is another view of our relations with Mexico, arising from the unhappy condition of affairs along our southwestern frontier, which demands immediate action. In that remote region, where there are but few white inhabitants, large bands of hostile and predatory Indians roam promiscuously over the Mexican States of Chihuahua and Sonora and our adjoining Territories. The local governments of these States are perfectly helpless and are kept in a state of constant alarm by the Indians. They have not the power, if they possessed the will, even to restrain lawless Mexicans from passing the border and committing depredations on our remote settlers. A state of anarchy and violence prevails throughout that distant frontier. The laws are a dead letter and life and property wholly insecure. For this reason the settlement of Arizona is arrested, whilst it is of great importance that a chain of inhabitants should extend all along its southern border sufficient for their own protection and that of the United States mail passing to and from California. Well-founded apprehensions are now entertained that the Indians and wandering Mexicans, equally lawless, may break up the important stage and postal communication recently established between our Atlantic and Pacific possessions. This passes very near to the Mexican boundary throughout the whole length of Arizona. I can imagine no possible remedy for these evils and no mode of restoring law and order on that remote and unsettled frontier but for the Government of the United States to assume a temporary protectorate over the northern portions of Chihuahua and Sonora and to establish military posts within the same; and this I earnestly recommend to Congress. This protection may be withdrawn as soon as local governments shall be established in these Mexican States capable of performing their duties to the United States, restraining the lawless, and preserving peace along the border.

I do not doubt that this measure will be viewed in a friendly spirit by the governments and people of Chihuahua and Sonora, as it will prove equally effectual for the protection of their citizens on that remote and lawless frontier as for citizens of the United States.

And in this connection permit me to recall your attention to the condition of Arizona. The population of that Territory, numbering, as is alleged, more than 10,000 souls, are practically without a government, without laws, and without any regular administration of justice. Murder and other crimes are committed with impunity. This state of things calls loudly for redress, and I therefore repeat my recommendation for the establishment of a Territorial government over Arizona.

The political condition of the narrow isthmus of Central America, through which transit routes pass between the Atlantic and Pacific oceans, presents a subject of deep interest to all commercial nations. It is over these transits that a large proportion of the trade and travel between the European and Asiatic continents is destined to pass. To the United States these routes are of incalculable importance as a means of communication between their Atlantic and Pacific possessions. The latter now extend throughout seventeen degrees of latitude on the Pacific coast, embracing the important State of California and the flourishing Territories of Oregon and Washington. All commercial nations therefore have a deep and direct interest that these communications shall be rendered secure from interruption. If an arm of the sea connecting the two oceans penetrated through Nicaragua and Costa Rica, it could not be pretended that these States would have the right to arrest or retard its navigation to the injury of other nations. The transit by land over this narrow isthmus occupies nearly the same position. It is a highway in which they themselves have little interest when compared with the vast interests of the rest of the world. Whilst their rights of sovereignty ought to be respected, it is the duty of other nations to require that this important passage shall not be interrupted by the civil wars and revolutionary outbreaks which have so frequently occurred in that region. The stake is too important to be left at the mercy of rival companies claiming to hold conflicting contracts with Nicaragua. The commerce of other nations is not to stand still and await the adjustment of such petty controversies. The Government of the United States expect no more than this, and they will not be satisfied with less. They would not, if they could, derive any advantage from the Nicaragua transit not common to the rest of the world. Its neutrality and protection for the common use of all nations is their only object. They have no objection that Nicaragua shall demand and receive a fair compensation from the companies and individuals who may traverse the route, but they insist that it shall never hereafter be closed by an arbitrary decree of that Government. If disputes arise between it and those with whom they may have entered into contracts, these must be adjusted by some fair tribunal provided for the purpose, and the route must not be closed pending the controversy. This is our whole policy, and it can not fail to be acceptable to other nations.

All these difficulties might be avoided if, consistently with the good faith of Nicaragua, the use of this transit could be thrown open to general competition, providing at the same time for the payment of a reasonable rate to the Nicaraguan Government on passengers and freight.

In August, 1852, the Accessory Transit Company made its first interoceanic trip over the Nicaraguan route, and continued in successful operation, with great advantage to the public, until the 18th February, 1856,
when it was closed and the grant to this company as well as its charter
were summarily and arbitrarily revoked by the Government of President
Rivàs. Previous to this date, however, in 1854, serious disputes concern‐
ing the settlement of their accounts had arisen between the company
and the Government, threatening the interruption of the route at any
moment. These the United States in vain endeavored to compose. It
would be useless to narrate the various proceedings which took place
between the parties up till the time when the transit was discontinued.
Suffice it to say that since February, 1856, it has remained closed, greatly
to the prejudice of citizens of the United States. Since that time the
competition has ceased between the rival routes of Panama and Nicaragua, and in consequence thereof an unjust and unreasonable amount has
been exacted from our citizens for their passage to and from California.

A treaty was signed on the 16th day of November, 1857, by the Secretary of State and minister of Nicaragua, under the stipulations of which
the use and protection of the transit route would have been secured, not
only to the United States, but equally to all other nations. How and on
what pretext this treaty has failed to receive the ratification of the Nicaraguan Government will appear by the papers herewith communicated
from the State Department. The principal objection seems to have been
to the provision authorizing the United States to employ force to keep
the route open in case Nicaragua should fail to perform her duty in this
respect. From the feebleness of that Republic, its frequent changes of
government, and its constant internal dissensions, this had become a
most important stipulation, and one essentially necessary, not only for the
security of the route, but for the safety of American citizens passing and
repassing to and from our Pacific possessions. Were such a stipulation
embraced in a treaty between the United States and Nicaragua, the
knowledge of this fact would of itself most probably prevent hostile
parties from committing aggressions on the route, and render our actual
interference for its protection unnecessary.

The executive government of this country in its intercourse with foreign nations is limited to the employment of diplomacy alone. When
this fails it can proceed no further. It can not legitimately resort to force
without the direct authority of Congress, except in resisting and repelling
hostile attacks. It would have no authority to enter the territories of
Nicaragua even to prevent the destruction of the transit and protect the
lives and property of our own citizens on their passage. It is true that
on a sudden emergency of this character the President would direct any
armed force in the vicinity to march to their relief, but in doing this he
would act upon his own responsibility.

Under these circumstances I earnestly recommend to Congress the passage of an act authorizing the President, under such restrictions as they may deem proper, to employ the land and naval forces of the United States in preventing the transit from being obstructed or closed by lawless violence, and in protecting the lives and property of American citizens traveling thereupon, requiring at the same time that these forces shall be withdrawn the moment the danger shall have passed away. Without such a provision our citizens will be constantly exposed to interruption in their progress and to lawless violence.

A similar necessity exists for the passage of such an act for the protection of the Panama and Tehuantepec routes.

In reference to the Panama route, the United States, by their existing treaty with New Granada, expressly guarantee the neutrality of the Isthmus, ''with the view that the free transit from the one to the other sea may not be interrupted or embarrassed in any future time while this treaty exists.''

In regard to the Tehuantepec route, which has been recently opened under the most favorable auspices, our treaty with Mexico of the 30th December, 1853, secures to the citizens of the United States a right of transit over it for their persons and merchandise and stipulates that neither Government shall ''interpose any obstacle'' thereto. It also concedes to the United States the ''right to transport across the Isthmus, in closed bags, the mails of the United States not intended for distribution along the line of the communication; also the effects of the United States Government and its citizens which may be intended for transit and not for distribution on the Isthmus, free of custom-house or other charges by the Mexican Government.''

These treaty stipulations with New Granada and Mexico, in addition to the considerations applicable to the Nicaragua route, seem to require legislation for the purpose of carrying them into effect.

The injuries which have been inflicted upon our citizens in Costa Rica and Nicaragua during the last two or three years have received the prompt attention of this Government. Some of these injuries were of the most aggravated character. The transaction at Virgin Bay in April, 1856, when a company of unarmed Americans, who were in no way connected with any belligerent conduct or party, were fired upon by the troops of Costa Rica and numbers of them killed and wounded, was brought to the knowledge of Congress by my predecessor soon after its occurrence, and was also presented to the Government of Costa Rica for that immediate investigation and redress which the nature of the case demanded. A similar course was pursued with reference to other outrages in these countries, some of which were hardly less aggravated in their character than the transaction at Virgin Bay. At the time, however, when our present minister to Nicaragua was appointed, in December, 1857, no redress had been obtained for any of these wrongs and no reply even had been received to the demands which had been made by this

Government upon that of Costa Rica more than a year before. Our minister was instructed, therefore, to lose no time in expressing to those Governments the deep regret with which the President had witnessed this inattention to the just claims of the United States and in demanding their prompt and satisfactory adjustment. Unless this demand shall be complied with at an early day it will only remain for this Government to adopt such other measures as may be necessary in order to obtain for itself that justice which it has in vain attempted to secure by peaceful means from the Governments of Nicaragua and Costa Rica. While it has shown, and will continue to show, the most sincere regard for the rights and honor of these Republics, it can not permit this regard to be met by an utter neglect on their part of what is due to the Government and citizens of the United States.

Against New Granada we have long-standing causes of complaint, arising out of the unsatisfied claims of our citizens upon that Republic, and to these have been more recently added the outrages committed upon our citizens at Panama in April, 1856. A treaty for the adjustment of these difficulties was concluded by the Secretary of State and the minister of New Granada in September, 1857, which contained just and acceptable provisions for that purpose. This treaty was transmitted to Bogota and was ratified by the Government of New Granada, but with certain amendments. It was not, however, returned to this city until after the close of the last session of the Senate. It will be immediately transmitted to that body for their advice and consent, and should this be obtained it will remove all our existing causes of complaint against New Granada on the subject of claims.

Questions have arisen between the two Governments as to the right of New Granada to levy a tonnage duty upon the vessels of the United States in its ports of the Isthmus and to levy a passenger tax upon our citizens arriving in that country, whether with a design to remain there or to pass from ocean to ocean by the transit route; and also a tax upon the mail of the United States transported over the Panama Railroad. The Government of New Granada has been informed that the United States would consider the collection of either of these taxes as an act in violation of the treaty between the two countries, and as such would be resisted by the United States. At the same time, we are prepared to discuss these questions in a spirit of amity and justice and with a sincere desire to adjust them in a satisfactory manner. A negotiation for that purpose has already been commenced. No effort has recently been made to collect these taxes nor is any anticipated under present circumstances.

With the Empire of Brazil our relations are of the most friendly character. The productions of the two countries, and especially those of an agricultural nature, are such as to invite extensive mutual exchanges. A large quantity of American flour is consumed in Brazil, whilst more than treble the amount in value of Brazilian coffee is consumed in the United States. Whilst this is the case, a heavy duty has been levied until very recently upon the importation of American flour into Brazil. I am gratified, however, to be able to inform you that in September last this has been reduced from $1.32 to about 49 cents per barrel, and the duties on other articles of our production have been diminished in nearly the same proportion.

I regret to state that the Government of Brazil still continues to levy an export duty of about 11 per cent on coffee, notwithstanding this article is admitted free from duty in the United States. This is a heavy charge upon the consumers of coffee in our country, as we purchase half of the entire surplus crop of that article raised in Brazil. Our minister, under instructions, will reiterate his efforts to have this export duty removed, and it is hoped that the enlightened Government of the Emperor will adopt this wise, just, and equal policy. In that event, there is good reason to believe that the commerce between the two countries will greatly increase, much to the advantage of both.

The claims of our citizens against the Government of Brazil are not in the aggregate of very large amount; but some of these rest upon plain principles of justice and their settlement ought not to be longer delayed. A renewed and earnest, and I trust a successful, effort will be made by our minister to procure their final adjustment.

On the 2d of June last Congress passed a joint resolution authorizing the President "to adopt such measures and use such force as in his judgment may be necessary and advisable" "for the purpose of adjusting the differences between the United States and the Republic of Paraguay in connection with the attack on the United States steamer *Water Witch* and with other measures referred to" in his annual message, and on the 12th of July following they made an appropriation to defray the expenses and compensation of a commissioner to that Republic should the President deem it proper to make such an appointment.

In compliance with these enactments, I have appointed a commissioner, who has proceeded to Paraguay with full powers and instructions to settle these differences in an amicable and peaceful manner if this be practicable. His experience and discretion justify the hope that he may prove successful in convincing the Paraguayan Government that it is due both to honor and justice that they should voluntarily and promptly make atonement for the wrongs which they have committed against the United States and indemnify our injured citizens whom they have forcibly despoiled of their property.

Should our commissioner prove unsuccessful after a sincere and earnest effort to accomplish the object of his mission, then no alternative will remain but the employment of force to obtain "just satisfaction" from Paraguay. In view of this contingency, the Secretary of the Navy, under my direction, has fitted out and dispatched a naval force to rendezvous near Buenos Ayres, which, it is believed, will prove sufficient for the occasion. It is my earnest desire, however, that it may not be found necessary to resort to this last alternative.

When Congress met in December last the business of the country had just been crushed by one of those periodical revulsions which are the inevitable consequence of our unsound and extravagant system of bank credits and inflated currency. With all the elements of national wealth in abundance, our manufactures were suspended, our useful public and private enterprises were arrested, and thousands of laborers were deprived of employment and reduced to want. Universal distress prevailed among the commercial, manufacturing, and mechanical classes. This revulsion was felt the more severely in the United States because similar causes had produced the like deplorable effects throughout the commercial nations of Europe. All were experiencing sad reverses at the same moment. Our manufacturers everywhere suffered severely, not because of the recent reduction in the tariff of duties on imports, but because there was no demand at any price for their productions. The people were obliged to restrict themselves in their purchases to articles of prime necessity. In the general prostration of business the iron manufacturers in different States probably suffered more than any other class, and much destitution was the inevitable consequence among the great number of workmen who had been employed in this useful branch of industry. There could be no supply where there was no demand. To present an example, there could be no demand for railroad iron after our magnificent system of railroads, extending its benefits to every portion of the Union, had been brought to a dead pause. The same consequences have resulted from similar causes to many other branches of useful manufactures. It is self-evident that where there is no ability to purchase manufactured articles these can not be sold, and consequently must cease to be produced.

No government, and especially a government of such limited powers as that of the United States, could have prevented the late revulsion. The whole commercial world seemed for years to have been rushing to this catastrophe. The same ruinous consequences would have followed in the United States whether the duties upon foreign imports had remained as they were under the tariff of 1846 or had been raised to a much higher standard. The tariff of 1857 had no agency in the result. The general causes existing throughout the world could not have been controlled by the legislation of any particular country.

The periodical revulsions which have existed in our past history must continue to return at intervals so long as our present unbounded system of bank credits shall prevail. They will, however, probably be the less severe in future, because it is not to be expected, at least for many years to come, that the commercial nations of Europe, with whose interests our own are so materially involved, will expose themselves to similar calamities. But this subject was treated so much at large in my last annual message that I shall not now pursue it further. Still, I respect-fully renew the recommendation in favor of the passage of a uniform bankrupt law applicable to banking institutions. This is all the direct power over the subject which I believe the Federal Government pos-sesses. Such a law would mitigate, though it might not prevent, the evil. The instinct of self-preservation might produce a wholesome re-straint upon their banking business if they knew in advance that a sus-pension of specie payments would inevitably produce their civil death.

But the effects of the revulsion are now slowly but surely passing away. The energy and enterprise of our citizens, with our unbounded resources, will within the period of another year restore a state of whole-some industry and trade. Capital has again accumulated in our large cities. The rate of interest is there very low. Confidence is gradually reviving, and so soon as it is discovered that this capital can be profit-ably employed in commercial and manufacturing enterprises and in the construction of railroads and other works of public and private improve-ment prosperity will again smile throughout the land. It is vain, how-ever, to disguise the fact from ourselves that a speculative inflation of our currency without a corresponding inflation in other countries whose manufactures come into competition with our own must ever produce disastrous results to our domestic manufactures. No tariff short of absolute prohibition can prevent these evil consequences.

In connection with this subject it is proper to refer to our financial condition. The same causes which have produced pecuniary distress throughout the country have so reduced the amount of imports from foreign countries that the revenue has proved inadequate to meet the necessary expenses of the Government. To supply the deficiency, Con-gress, by the act of December 23, 1857, authorized the issue of $20,000,000 of Treasury notes; and this proving inadequate, they authorized, by the act of June 14, 1858, a loan of $20,000,000, "to be applied to the payment of appropriations made by law."

No statesman would advise that we should go on increasing the national debt to meet the ordinary expenses of the Government. This would be a most ruinous policy. In case of war our credit must be our chief resource, at least for the first year, and this would be greatly impaired by having contracted a large debt in time of peace. It is our true policy to increase our revenue so as to equal our expenditures. It would be ruinous to continue to borrow. Besides, it may be proper to observe that the incidental protection thus afforded by a revenue tariff would at the present moment to some extent increase the confidence of the manu-facturing interests and give a fresh impulse to our reviving business. To this surely no person will object.

In regard to the mode of assessing and collecting duties under a strictly revenue tariff, I have long entertained and often expressed the opinion that sound policy requires this should be done by specific duties in cases to which these can be properly applied. They are well adapted to commodities which are usually sold by weight or by measure, and which from their nature are of equal or of nearly equal value. Such, for example, are the articles of iron of different classes, raw sugar, and foreign wines and spirits.

In my deliberate judgment specific duties are the best, if not the only, means of securing the revenue against false and fraudulent invoices, and such has been the practice adopted for this purpose by other commercial nations. Besides, specific duties would afford to the American manufacturer the incidental advantages to which he is fairly entitled under a revenue tariff. The present system is a sliding scale to his disadvantage. Under it, when prices are high and business prosperous, the duties rise in amount when he least requires their aid. On the contrary, when prices fall and he is struggling against adversity, the duties are diminished in the same proportion, greatly to his injury.

Neither would there be danger that a higher rate of duty than that intended by Congress could be levied in the form of specific duties. It would be easy to ascertain the average value of any imported article for a series of years, and, instead of subjecting it to an *ad valorem* duty at a certain rate *per centum*, to substitute in its place an equivalent specific duty.

By such an arrangement the consumer would not be injured. It is true he might have to pay a little more duty on a given article in one year, but, if so, he would pay a little less in another, and in a series of years these would counterbalance each other and amount to the same thing so far as his interest is concerned. This inconvenience would be trifling when contrasted with the additional security thus afforded against frauds upon the revenue, in which every consumer is directly interested.

I have thrown out these suggestions as the fruit of my own observation, to which Congress, in their better judgment, will give such weight as they may justly deserve.

The report of the Secretary of the Treasury will explain in detail the operations of that Department of the Government. The receipts into the Treasury from all sources during the fiscal year ending June 30, 1858, including the Treasury notes authorized by the act of December 23, 1857, were $70,273,869.59, which amount, with the balance of $17,710,114.27 remaining in the Treasury at the commencement of the year, made an aggregate for the service of the year of $87,983,983.86.

The public expenditures during the fiscal year ending June 30, 1858, amounted to $81,585,667.76, of which $9,684,537.99 were applied to the payment of the public debt and the redemption of Treasury notes with the interest thereon, leaving in the Treasury on July 1, 1858, being the commencement of the present fiscal year, $6,398,316.10.

The receipts into the Treasury during the first quarter of the present fiscal year, commencing the 1st of July, 1858, including one-half of the loan of $20,000,000, with the premium upon it, authorized by the act of June 14, 1858, were $25,230,879.46, and the estimated receipts for the remaining three quarters to the 30th of June, 1859, from ordinary sources are $38,500,000, making, with the balance before stated, an aggregate of $70,129,195.56.

The expenditures during the first quarter of the present fiscal year were $21,708,198.51, of which $1,010,142.37 were applied to the payment of the public debt and the redemption of Treasury notes and the interest thereon. The estimated expenditures during the remaining three quarters to June 30, 1859, are $52,357,698.48, making an aggregate of $74,065,896.99, being an excess of expenditure beyond the estimated receipts into the Treasury from ordinary sources during the fiscal year to the 30th of June, 1859, of $3,936,701.43. Extraordinary means are placed by law within the command of the Secretary of the Treasury, by the reissue of Treasury notes redeemed and by negotiating the balance of the loan authorized by the act of June 14, 1858, to the extent of $11,000,000, which, if realized during the present fiscal year, will leave a balance in the Treasury on the 1st day of July, 1859, of $7,063,298.57.

The estimated receipts during the next fiscal year, ending June 30, 1860, are $62,000,000, which, with the above-estimated balance of $7,063,298.57 make an aggregate for the service of the next fiscal year of $69,063,298.57. The estimated expenditures during the next fiscal year, ending June 30, 1860, are $73,139,147.46, which leaves a deficit of estimated means, compared with the estimated expenditures, for that year, commencing on July 1, 1859, of $4,075,848.89.

In addition to this sum the Postmaster-General will require from the Treasury for the service of the Post-Office Department $3,838,728, as explained in the report of the Secretary of the Treasury, which will increase the estimated deficit on June 30, 1860, to $7,914,576.89. To provide for the payment of this estimated deficiency, which will be increased by such appropriations as may be made by Congress not estimated for in the report of the Treasury Department, as well as to provide for the gradual redemption from year to year of the outstanding Treasury notes, the Secretary of the Treasury recommends such a revision of the present tariff as will raise the required amount. After what I have already said I need scarcely add that I concur in the opinion expressed in his report—that the public debt should not be increased by an additional loan—and would therefore strongly urge upon Congress the duty of making at their present session the necessary provision for meeting these liabilities.

The public debt on July 1, 1858, the commencement of the present fiscal year, was $25,155,977.66.

During the first quarter of the present year the sum of $10,000,000 has been negotiated of the loan authorized by the act of June 14, 1858, making the present outstanding public debt, exclusive of Treasury notes,

$35,155,977.66. There was on the 1st of July, 1858, of Treasury notes issued by authority of the act of December 23, 1857, unredeemed, the sum of $19,754,800, making the amount of actual indebtedness at that date $54,910,777.66. To this will be added $10,000,000 during the present fiscal year, this being the remaining half of the loan of $20,000,000 not yet negotiated.

The rapid increase of the public debt and the necessity which exists for a modification of the tariff to meet even the ordinary expenses of the Government ought to admonish us all, in our respective spheres of duty, to the practice of rigid economy. The objects of expenditure should be limited in number, as far as this may be practicable, and the appropriations necessary to carry them into effect ought to be disbursed under the strictest accountability. Enlightened economy does not consist in the refusal to appropriate money for constitutional purposes essential to the defense, progress, and prosperity of the Republic, but in taking care that none of this money shall be wasted by mismanagement in its application to the objects designated by law.

Comparisons between the annual expenditure at the present time and what it was ten or twenty years ago are altogether fallacious. The rapid increase of our country in extent and population renders a corresponding increase of expenditure to some extent unavoidable. This is constantly creating new objects of expenditure and augmenting the amount required for the old. The true questions, then, are, Have these objects been unnecessarily multiplied, or has the amount expended upon any or all of them been larger than comports with due economy? In accordance with these principles, the heads of the different Executive Departments of the Government have been instructed to reduce their estimates for the next fiscal year to the lowest standard consistent with the efficiency of the service, and this duty they have performed in a spirit of just economy. The estimates of the Treasury, War, Navy, and Interior Departments have each been in some degree reduced, and unless a sudden and unforeseen emergency should arise it is not anticipated that a deficiency will exist in either within the present or the next fiscal year. The Post-Office Department is placed in a peculiar position, different from the other Departments, and to this I shall hereafter refer.

I invite Congress to institute a rigid scrutiny to ascertain whether the expenses in all the Departments can not be still further reduced, and I promise them all the aid in my power in pursuing the investigation.

I transmit herewith the reports made to me by the Secretaries of War, of the Navy, of the Interior, and of the Postmaster-General. They each contain valuable information and important recommendations, to which I invite the attention of Congress.

In my last annual message I took occasion to recommend the immediate construction of ten small steamers of light draft, for the purpose of increasing the efficiency of the Navy. Congress responded to the recommendation by authorizing the construction of eight of them. The progress which has been made in executing this authority is stated in the report of the Secretary of the Navy. I concur with him in the opinion that a greater number of this class of vessels is necessary for the purpose of protecting in a more efficient manner the persons and property of American citizens on the high seas and in foreign countries, as well as in guarding more effectually our own coasts. I accordingly recommend the passage of an act for this purpose.

The suggestions contained in the report of the Secretary of the Interior, especially those in regard to the disposition of the public domain, the pension and bounty-land system, the policy toward the Indians, and the amendment of our patent laws, are worthy of the serious consideration of Congress.

The Post-Office Department occupies a position very different from that of the other Departments. For many years it was the policy of the Government to render this a self-sustaining Department; and if this can not now be accomplished, in the present condition of the country, we ought to make as near an approach to it as may be practicable.

The Postmaster-General is placed in a most embarrassing position by the existing laws. He is obliged to carry these into effect. He has no other alternative. He finds, however, that this can not be done without heavy demands upon the Treasury over and above what is received for postage, and these have been progressively increasing from year to year until they amounted for the last fiscal year, ending on the 30th of June, 1858, to more than $4,500,000, whilst it is estimated that for the present fiscal year they will amount to $6,290,000. These sums are exclusive of the annual appropriation of $700,000 for "compensation for the mail service performed for the two Houses of Congress and the other Departments and officers of the Government in the transmission of free matter."

The cause of these large deficits is mainly attributable to the increased expense of transporting the mails. In 1852 the sum paid for this service was but a fraction above four millions and a quarter. Since that year it has annually increased, until in 1858 it has reached more than eight millions and a quarter, and for the service of 1859 it is estimated that it will amount to more than $10,000,000.

The receipts of the Post-Office Department can be made to approach or to equal its expenditure only by means of the legislation of Congress. In applying any remedy care should be taken that the people shall not be deprived of the advantages which they are fairly entitled to enjoy from the Post-Office Department. The principal remedies recommended to the consideration of Congress by the Postmaster-General are to restore the former rate of postage upon single letters to 5 cents; to substitute for the franking privilege the delivery to those now entitled to enjoy it of post-office stamps for their correspondence, and to direct the Department in making contracts for the transportation of the mail to confine itself to the payment of the sum necessary for this single purpose, without requiring it to be transported in post coaches or carriages of any particular description. Under the present system the expense to the Government is greatly increased by requiring that the mail shall be carried in such vehicles as will accommodate passengers. This will be done, without pay from the Department, over all roads where the travel will remunerate the contractors.

These recommendations deserve the grave consideration of Congress.

I would again call your attention to the construction of a Pacific railroad. Time and reflection have but served to confirm me in the truth and justice of the observations which I made on this subject in my last annual message, to which I beg leave respectfully to refer.

It is freely admitted that it would be inexpedient for this Government to exercise the power of constructing the Pacific railroad by its own immediate agents. Such a policy would increase the patronage of the Executive to a dangerous extent, and introduce a system of jobbing and corruption which no vigilance on the part of Federal officials could either prevent or detect. This can only be done by the keen eye and active and careful supervision of individual and private interest. The construction of this road ought therefore to be committed to companies incorporated by the States or other agencies whose pecuniary interests would be directly involved. Congress might then assist them in the work by grants of land or of money, or both, under such conditions and restrictions as would secure the transportation of troops and munitions of war free from any charge and that of the United States mail at a fair and reasonable price.

The progress of events since the commencement of your last session has shown how soon difficulties disappear before a firm and determined resolution. At that time such a road was deemed by wise and patriotic men to be a visionary project. The great distance to be overcome and the intervening mountains and deserts in the way were obstacles which, in the opinion of many, could not be surmounted. Now, after the lapse of but a single year, these obstacles, it has been discovered, are far less formidable than they were supposed to be, and mail stages with passengers now pass and repass regularly twice in each week, by a common wagon road, between San Francisco and St. Louis and Memphis in less than twenty-five days. The service has been as regularly performed as it was in former years between New York and this city.

Whilst disclaiming all authority to appropriate money for the construction of this road, except that derived from the war-making power of the Constitution, there are important collateral considerations urging us to undertake the work as speedily as possible.

The first and most momentous of these is that such a road would be a powerful bond of union between the States east and west of the Rocky Mountains. This is so self-evident as to require no illustration.

But again, in a commercial point of view, I consider this the great question of the day. With the eastern front of our Republic stretching along the Atlantic and its western front along the Pacific, if all the parts should be united by a safe, easy, and rapid intercommunication we must necessarily command a very large proportion of the trade both of Europe and Asia. Our recent treaties with China and Japan will open these rich and populous Empires to our commerce; and the history of the world proves that the nation which has gained possession of the trade with eastern Asia has always become wealthy and powerful. The peculiar geographical position of California and our Pacific possessions invites American capital and enterprise into this fruitful field. To reap the rich harvest, however, it is an indispensable prerequisite that we shall first have a railroad to convey and circulate its products throughout every portion of the Union. Besides, such a railroad through our temperate latitude, which would not be impeded by the frosts and snows of winter nor by the tropical heats of summer, would attract to itself much of the travel and the trade of all nations passing between Europe and Asia.

On the 21st of August last Lieutenant J. N. Maffit, of the United States brig *Dolphin*, captured the slaver *Echo* (formerly the *Putnam*, of New Orleans) near Kay Verde, on the coast of Cuba, with more than 300 African negroes on board. The prize, under the command of Lieutenant Bradford, of the United States Navy, arrived at Charleston on the 27th August, when the negroes, 306 in number, were delivered into the custody of the United States marshal for the district of South Carolina. They were first placed in Castle Pinckney, and afterwards in Fort Sumter, for safe-keeping, and were detained there until the 19th September, when the survivors, 271 in number, were delivered on board the United States steamer *Niagara* to be transported to the coast of Africa under the charge of the agent of the United States, pursuant to the provisions of the act of the 3d March, 1819, ''in addition to the acts prohibiting the slave trade.'' Under the second section of this act the President is ''authorized to make such regulations and arrangements as he may deem expedient for the safe-keeping, support, and removal beyond the limits of the United States of all such negroes, mulattoes, or persons of color'' captured by vessels of the United States as may be delivered to the marshal of the district into which they are brought, ''and to appoint a proper person or persons residing upon the coast of Africa as agent or agents for receiving the negroes, mulattoes, or persons of color delivered from on board vessels seized in the prosecution of the slave trade by commanders of United States armed vessels.''

A doubt immediately arose as to the true construction of this act. It is quite clear from its terms that the President was authorized to provide ''for the safe-keeping, support, and removal'' of these negroes up till the time of their delivery to the agent on the coast of Africa, but no express provision was made for their protection and support after they had reached the place of their destination. Still, an agent was to be appointed to receive them in Africa, and it could not have been supposed that Congress intended he should desert them at the moment they were received and turn them loose on that inhospitable coast to perish for want of food or to become again the victims of the slave trade. Had this been the intention of Congress, the employment of an agent to receive them, who is required to reside on the coast, was unnecessary, and they might have been landed by our vessels anywhere in Africa and left exposed to the sufferings and the fate which would certainly await them.

Mr. Monroe, in his special message of December 17, 1819, at the first session after the act was passed, announced to Congress what in his opinion was its true construction. He believed it to be his duty under it to follow these unfortunates into Africa and make provision for them there until they should be able to provide for themselves. In communicating this interpretation of the act to Congress he stated that some doubt had been entertained as to its true intent and meaning, and he submitted the question to them so that they might, "should it be deemed advisable, amend the same before further proceedings are had under it." Nothing was done by Congress to explain the act, and Mr. Monroe proceeded to carry it into execution according to his own interpretation. This, then, became the practical construction. When the Africans from on board the *Echo* were delivered to the marshal at Charleston, it became my duty to consider what disposition ought to be made of them under the law. For many reasons it was expedient to remove them from that locality as speedily as possible. Although the conduct of the authorities and citizens of Charleston in giving countenance to the execution of the law was just what might have been expected from their high character, yet a prolonged continuance of 300 Africans in the immediate vicinity of that city could not have failed to become a source of inconvenience and anxiety to its inhabitants. Where to send them was the question. There was no portion of the coast of Africa to which they could be removed with any regard to humanity except to Liberia. Under these circumstances an agreement was entered into with the Colonization Society on the 7th of September last, a copy of which is herewith transmitted, under which the society engaged, for the consideration of $45,000, to receive these Africans in Liberia from the agent of the United States and furnish them during the period of one year thereafter with comfortable shelter, clothing, provisions, and medical attendance, causing the children to receive schooling, and all, whether children or adults, to be instructed in the arts of civilized life suitable to their condition. This aggregate of $45,000 was based upon an allowance of $150 for each individual; and as there has been considerable mortality among them and may be more before they reach Africa, the society have agreed, in an equitable spirit, to make such a deduction from the amount as under the circumstances may appear just and reasonable. This can not be fixed until we shall ascertain the actual number which may become a charge to the society.

It was also distinctly agreed that under no circumstances shall this Government be called upon for any additional expenses.

The agents of the society manifested a laudable desire to conform to the wishes of the Government throughout the transaction. They assured me that after a careful calculation they would be required to expend the sum of $150 on each individual in complying with the agreement, and they would have nothing left to remunerate them for their care, trouble, and responsibility. At all events, I could make no better arrangement, and there was no other alternative. During the period when the Government itself, through its own agents, undertook the task of providing for captured negroes in Africa the cost per head was very much greater.

There having been no outstanding appropriation applicable to this purpose, I could not advance any money on the agreement. I therefore recommend that an appropriation may be made of the amount necessary to carry it into effect.

Other captures of a similar character may, and probably will, be made by our naval forces, and I earnestly recommend that Congress may amend the second section of the act of March 3, 1819, so as to free its construction from the ambiguity which has so long existed and render the duty of the President plain in executing its provisions.

I recommend to your favorable regard the local interests of the District of Columbia. As the residence of Congress and the Executive Departments of the Government, we can not fail to feel a deep concern in its welfare. This is heightened by the high character and the peaceful and orderly conduct of its resident inhabitants.

I can not conclude without performing the agreeable duty of expressing my gratification that Congress so kindly responded to the recommendation of my last annual message by affording me sufficient time before the close of their late session for the examination of all the bills presented to me for approval. This change in the practice of Congress has proved to be a wholesome reform. It exerted a beneficial influence on the transaction of legislative business and elicited the general approbation of the country. It enabled Congress to adjourn with that dignity and deliberation so becoming to the representatives of this great Republic, without having crowded into general appropriation bills provisions foreign to their nature and of doubtful constitutionality and expediency. Let me warmly and strongly commend this precedent established by themselves as a guide to their proceedings during the present session.

JAMES BUCHANAN.

SPECIAL MESSAGES.

WASHINGTON, *December 7, 1858*.

To the Senate of the United States:

I transmit to the Senate, for its consideration with a view to ratification, a treaty of amity and commerce between the United States, and Japan, concluded at the city of Yeddo on the 29th of July last.

JAMES BUCHANAN.

WASHINGTON, *December 7, 1858*.

To the Senate of the United States:

I transmit to the Senate, for its consideration with a view to ratification, a treaty between the United States and China, signed at Tien-tsin by the plenipotentiaries of the parties on the 18th day of June last.

JAMES BUCHANAN.

EXECUTIVE MANSION, *December 10, 1858*.

The PRESIDENT OF THE SENATE.

SIR: In compliance with the resolution of the Senate of June 12, 1858, I herewith communicate a report from the Secretary of the Interior, showing "the amount of money paid for pensions in each of the States and Territories since the commencement of the present Government."

JAMES BUCHANAN.

WASHINGTON, *December 10, 1858*.

To the Senate and House of Representatives:

I transmit to Congress a copy of the treaty between the United States and the Kingdom of Siam, concluded on the 29th of May, 1856, and proclaimed on the 16th of August last, and call the attention of that body to the necessity of an act for carrying into effect the provisions of Article II of the said treaty, conferring certain judicial powers upon the consul of the United States who may be appointed to reside at Bangkok. I would also suggest that the extension to the Kingdom of Siam of the provisions of the act approved August 11, 1848, entitled "An act to carry into effect certain provisions in the treaties between the United States and China and the Ottoman Porte, giving certain judicial powers to ministers and consuls of the United States in those countries," might obviate the necessity of any other legislation upon the subject.

JAMES BUCHANAN.

EXECUTIVE OFFICE,
Washington, December 15, 1858.

Hon. JAMES L. ORR,
  Speaker of the House of Representatives.

SIR: In compliance with a resolution of the House of Representatives of the 13th instant, requesting the President of the United States, if not inconsistent with the public interest, "to communicate all information in his possession, or which may shortly come into his possession, respecting the reported recent acts of visitation by officers of the British navy of American vessels in the waters of the Gulf of Mexico," I transmit the accompanying reports from the Secretaries of State and the Navy. The report from the Secretary of State is not in strictness embraced by the terms of the resolution, but I deem it advisable to communicate to the House the information therein contained.

JAMES BUCHANAN.

WASHINGTON, *December 20, 1858.*

To the Senate of the United States:

I transmit a report from the Secretary of State, with accompanying documents, in answer to the resolution of the Senate of the 7th of January last, calling for all the official dispatches and correspondence of the Hon. Robert M. McLane and of the Hon. Peter Parker, late commissioners of the United States in China, with the Department of State.

JAMES BUCHANAN.

WASHINGTON, *December 20, 1858.*

To the Senate of the United States:

The Senate will learn from the thirty-five naval nominations herewith submitted the result of my investigations under the resolutions of Congress of March 10 and May 11, 1858. In compliance with these resolutions, I have carefully examined the records of the courts of inquiry in fifty-eight cases, and have arrived at the conclusion that twenty-three of the officers ought to remain in the positions where they have been fixed by the courts of inquiry.

The records are very voluminous and the labor of examination, in which I have been materially assisted by the Secretary of the Navy, the Attorney-General, and the Commissioner of Patents, has consumed much time.

Under the act of January 17, 1857, the courts of inquiry were directed to investigate "the physical, mental, professional, and moral fitness" of each officer who applied to them for relief. These investigations it was my duty to review. They have been very extensive and searching, as the Senate will perceive from an examination of the records, embracing in many instances almost the entire professional life of the individual from his first entrance into the service.

In the performance of my duty I found the greatest difficulty in deciding what should be considered as "moral fitness" for the Navy. Physical, mental, and professional fitness may be decided with a considerable degree of accuracy by a naval court of inquiry, but the question of moral fitness is of a very different character. There has been but one perfect standard of morality on earth, and how far a departure from His precepts and example must proceed in order to disqualify an officer for the naval service is a question on which a great difference of honest opinion must always exist. On this question I have differed in several instances from the courts of inquiry.

There is one nomination which I regret that I have not the power to present to the Senate, and this is in the case of Commodore Stewart. His name stood on the Register at the head of the list of captains in the Navy until it was removed from this well-earned position by the retiring board and placed on the list of retired officers. The deeply wounded feelings of this veteran officer, who had contributed so much to the efficiency and glory of the Navy from its infancy, prevented him from applying for restoration to his rank and submitting to a court of inquiry composed of his junior officers the question of his "physical, mental, professional, and moral fitness" for the naval service. I would ere this have recommended to Congress the passage of a joint resolution to restore him to his former rank had I not believed this would more appropriately emanate from the legislative branch of Government.

I transmit herewith to the Senate the original records in the fifty-eight cases to which I have referred. After they shall have been examined by the Senate I would respectfully request that they might be returned to the Navy Department.   JAMES BUCHANAN.

WASHINGTON, *December 22, 1858.*
To the Senate of the United States:

I transmit to the Senate, for its consideration with a view to ratification, a convention between the United States and Belgium for regulating the commerce and navigation between the two countries, signed in this city on the 17th of July last.   JAMES BUCHANAN.

WASHINGTON, *December 23, 1858.*
To the Senate of the United States:

I transmit for the consideration of the Senate a convention with New Granada, signed on the 10th day of September, 1857, and a translation of the decree of the President of that Republic ratifying and confirming the same with certain modifications and explanations.

             JAMES BUCHANAN.

WASHINGTON, *December 27, 1858.*

To the Senate and House of Representatives:

I transmit a copy of a letter of the 8th of April last from the minister of the United States in China, and of the decree and regulation which accompanied it, for such revision thereof as Congress may deem expedient, pursuant to the sixth section of the act approved 11th August, 1848.

JAMES BUCHANAN.

WASHINGTON, *January 4, 1859.*

To the House of Representatives:

I herewith transmit to the House of Representatives the report of the Secretary of the Treasury, with the accompanying documents, containing the information called for by the resolution of the House of the 23d December, 1858, concerning the correspondence in reference to the clearance of vessels at the port of Mobile.

JAMES BUCHANAN.

WASHINGTON, *January 5, 1859.*

To the Senate of the United States: .

I transmit herewith, for the constitutional action of the Senate, the articles of agreement and convention made and concluded on the 19th day of June last with the Mendawakanton and Wahpakoota bands of the Dakota or Sioux Indians.

JAMES BUCHANAN.

WASHINGTON, *January 5, 1859.*

To the Senate of the United States:

I transmit herewith, for the constitutional action of the Senate, the articles of agreement and convention made and concluded on the 19th day of June last (1858) with the Sisseeton and Wahpaton bands of the Dakota or Sioux Indians, with accompanying papers from the Department of the Interior.

JAMES BUCHANAN.

WASHINGTON, *January 5, 1859.*

To the Senate of the United States:

I transmit herewith to the Senate, for its consideration with a view to ratification, a convention between the United States and the Republic of Chili, signed by the plenipotentiaries of the parties on the 10th day of November last, providing for the reference to an arbiter of the questions which have long been in controversy between the two Governments relative to a sum of money, the proceeds of the cargo of the brig *Macedonia*, alleged to have belonged to citizens of the United States, which was seized in the Valley of Sitana, in Peru, by orders of an officer in the service of the Republic of Chili.

JAMES BUCHANAN.

WASHINGTON CITY, *January 6, 1859.*

To the House of Representatives:

I herewith transmit to the House of Representatives a report from the Secretary of the Navy, with accompanying papers, in compliance with a resolution adopted December 23, 1858, requesting the President of the United States "to communicate to the House, if not deemed by him incompatible with the public interest, the instructions which have been given to our naval commanders in the Gulf of Mexico."

JAMES BUCHANAN.

WASHINGTON, *January 7, 1859.*

To the House of Representatives:

I herewith transmit reports from the Secretary of the Treasury and Postmaster-General, with the accompanying papers, in compliance with the resolution of the House adopted December 23, 1858, requesting the President of the United States to report "what action, if any, has been taken under the sixth section of the Post-Office appropriation act approved August 18, 1856, for the adjustment of the damages due Carmick & Ramsey, and if the said section of said law yet remains unexecuted that the President report the reasons therefor."

JAMES BUCHANAN.

WASHINGTON, *January 11, 1859.*

To the Senate of the United States:

In reply to the resolution of the Senate passed on the 16th ultimo, requesting me to communicate, if in my opinion not incompatible with the public interest, any information in my possession in relation to the landing of the bark *Wanderer* on the coast of Georgia with a cargo of slaves, I herewith communicate the report made to me by the Attorney-General, to whom the resolution was referred. From that report it will appear that the offense referred to in the resolution has been committed and that effective measures have been taken to see the laws faithfully executed. I concur with the Attorney-General in the opinion that it would be incompatible with the public interest at this time to communicate the correspondence with the officers of the Government at Savannah or the instructions which they have received. In the meantime every practicable effort has been made, and will be continued, to discover all the guilty parties and to bring them to justice.

JAMES BUCHANAN.

WASHINGTON CITY, *January 13, 1859.*

To the House of Representatives:

I herewith transmit a report from the Comptroller, with a copy of the letter of Messrs. Johnson and Williams, in relation to the decision upon the Carmick & Ramsey claim.

This should have accompanied the papers which have already been transmitted to the House, but was omitted by mistake.

JAMES BUCHANAN.

WASHINGTON, *January 15, 1859.*

To the House of Representatives:

I transmit a report from the Secretary of State, in answer to the resolution of the House of Representatives of the 10th instant, requesting a communication of the correspondence between this Government and France and England respecting the acquisition of Cuba by the United States.

JAMES BUCHANAN.

WASHINGTON, *January 19, 1859.*

To the Senate of the United States:

In compliance with the resolution of the Senate of the 14th of June last, requesting a list of claims of citizens of the United States on foreign governments, I transmit a report from the Secretary of State, with the documents which accompanied it.

JAMES BUCHANAN.

WASHINGTON CITY, *January 21, 1859.*

To the House of Representatives:

I have this day transmitted to the Senate a digest of the statistics of manufactures, according to the returns of the Seventh Census, prepared under the direction of the Secretary of the Interior in accordance with a provision contained in the first section of an act of Congress approved June 12, 1858, entitled "An act making appropriations for sundry civil expenses of the Government for the year ending the 30th of June, 1859." The magnitude of the work has prevented the preparation of another copy.

JAMES BUCHANAN.

WASHINGTON CITY, *January 21, 1859.*

To the Senate of the United States:

I transmit herewith a report from the Secretary of State, in answer to the resolution of the Senate of the 18th instant, requesting the President, if not incompatible with the public interest, "to communicate to the Senate any and all correspondence between the Government of the United States and the Government of Her Catholic Majesty relating to any proposition for the purchase of the island of Cuba, which correspondence has not been furnished to either House of Congress." From this it appears that no such correspondence has taken place which has not already been communicated to Congress. In my late annual message I stated in reference to the purchase of Cuba that "the publicity which has been given to our former negotiations on this subject and the large appropriation which may be required to effect the purpose render it expedient befo e making another attempt to renew the negotiation that I should lay the whole subject before Congress." I still entertain the same opinion, deeming it highly important, if not indispensable to the success of any negotiation which I might institute for this purpose, that the measure should receive the previous sanction of Congress.

JAMES BUCHANAN.

WASHINGTON, *January 21, 1859.*

To the Senate of the United States:

I herewith transmit to the Senate a digest of the statistics of manufactures according to the returns of the Seventh Census, prepared under the direction of the Secretary of the Interior in accordance with a provision in the first section of an act of Congress approved June 12, 1858, entitled "An act making appropriations for sundry civil expenses of the Government for the year ending the 30th of June, 1859."

JAMES BUCHANAN.

WASHINGTON, *January 26, 1859.*

To the Senate of the United States:

I transmit another report from the Secretary of State, in answer to the resolution of the Senate of the 14th of June last, requesting information on the subject of claims of citizens of the United States against foreign governments.

JAMES BUCHANAN.

WASHINGTON, *January 26, 1859.*

To the Senate and House of Representatives:

I transmit to Congress a report, dated the 25th instant, with the accompanying papers, received from the Secretary of State, in compliance with the requirement of the eighteenth section of the act entitled "An act to regulate the diplomatic and consular systems of the United States," approved August 18, 1856.

JAMES BUCHANAN.

WASHINGTON, *January 29, 1859.*

To the Senate and House of Representatives:

I transmit a report from the Secretary of War, with the accompanying documents, recommending the repayment to Governor Douglas, of Vancouvers Island, of the sum of $7,000, advanced by him to Governor Stevens, of Washington Territory, which was applied to the purchase of ammunition and subsistence stores for the forces of the United States in time of need and at a critical period of the late Indian war in that Territory.

As this advance was made by Governor Douglas out of his own private means and from friendly motives toward the United States, I recommend that an appropriation may be made for its immediate payment, with interest.

JAMES BUCHANAN.

WASHINGTON, *January 29, 1859.*

To the Senate of the United States:

In compliance with the resolution of the Senate of the 25th instant, I transmit a copy of the report of the special agent of the United States recently sent to Vancouvers Island and British Columbia.

JAMES BUCHANAN.

WASHINGTON, *February 5, 1859.*

To the Senate of the United States:

In reply to the resolution of the Senate of the 4th ultimo, I transmit a report from the Secretary of State, together with the papers* therein referred to.

JAMES BUCHANAN.

WASHINGTON CITY, *February 8, 1859.*

To the House of Representatives:

I transmit herewith a report from the Secretary of the Navy, in compliance with the resolution of the House of Representatives adopted on the 24th of January, requesting the President of the United States to communicate to the House "the aggregate expenditure, of whatsoever nature, including all salaries, whether special or by virtue of official position in the Army or Navy or otherwise, on account of the preparation and publication of the work known as Wilkes's Exploring Expedition;" also, what number of copies of the said work have been ordered, how they have been distributed, what number of persons are now employed thereon, how long they have been employed, respectively, and the amount of the appropriation now remaining undrawn.

JAMES BUCHANAN.

WASHINGTON, *February 12, 1859.*

To the House of Representatives:

I transmit herewith a report from the Secretary of State, with accompanying papers, in answer to the resolution of the House of Representatives

* Correspondence with the United States minister to Peru and others relative to the guano trade.

of the 14th of June last, requesting the communication of all information and correspondence which may have been received in regard to any consular officer engaged in business in violation of law.

JAMES BUCHANAN.

WASHINGTON CITY, *February 15, 1859.*

To the House of Representatives:

I transmit herewith a report from the Attorney-General, in reply to the resolution of the House of Representatives adopted on the 22d ultimo, requesting the President of the United States to ''report what information has been received by him, if any, in regard to the recent importation of Africans into the State of Georgia or any other State of this Union, and what steps have been taken to bring to trial and punishment the' persons engaged in this inhuman violation of the laws of the United States and to prevent similar violations hereafter.''

JAMES BUCHANAN.

WASHINGTON, *February 18, 1859.*

To the Senate and House of Representatives:

The brief period which remains of your present session and the great urgency and importance of legislative action before its termination for the protection of American citizens and their property whilst in transit across the Isthmus routes between our Atlantic and Pacific possessions render it my duty again to recall this subject to your notice. I have heretofore presented it in my annual messages, both in December, 1857 and 1858, to which I beg leave to refer. In the latter I state that—

The executive government of this country in its intercourse with foreign nations is limited to the employment of diplomacy alone. When this fails it can proceed no further. It can not legitimately resort to force without the direct authority of Congress, except in resisting and repelling hostile attacks. It would have no authority to enter the territories of Nicaragua even to prevent the destruction of the transit and protect the lives and property of our own citizens on their passage. It is true that on a sudden emergency of this character the President would direct any armed force in the vicinity to march to their relief, but in doing this he would act upon his own responsibility.

Under these circumstances I earnestly recommend to Congress the passage of an act authorizing the President, under such restrictions as they may deem proper, to employ the land and naval forces of the United States in preventing the transit from being obstructed or closed by lawless violence and in protecting the lives and property of American citizens traveling thereupon, requiring at the same time that these forces shall be withdrawn the moment the danger shall have passed away. Without such a provision our citizens will be constantly exposed to interruption in their progress and to lawless violence.

A similar necessity exists for the passage of such an act for the protection of the Panama and Tehuantepec routes.

Another subject, equally important, commanded the attention of the Senate at the last session of Congress.

The Republics south of the United States on this continent have, unfortunately, been frequently in a state of revolution and civil war ever since they achieved their independence. As one or the other party has prevailed and obtained possession of the ports open to foreign commerce, they have seized and confiscated American vessels and their cargoes in an arbitrary and lawless manner and exacted money from American citizens by forced loans and other violent proceedings to enable them to carry on hostilities. The executive governments of Great Britain, France, and other countries, possessing the war-making power, can promptly employ the necessary means to enforce immediate redress for similar outrages upon their subjects. Not so the executive government of the United States.

If the President orders a vessel of war to any of these ports to demand prompt redress for outrages committed, the offending parties are well aware that in case of refusal the commander can do no more than remonstrate. He can resort to no hostile act. The question must then be referred to diplomacy, and in many cases adequate redress can never be obtained. Thus American citizens are deprived of the same protection under the flag of their country which the subjects of other nations enjoy. The remedy for this state of things can only be supplied by Congress, since the Constitution has confided to that body alone the power to make war. Without the authority of Congress the Executive can not lawfully direct any force, however near it may be to the scene of difficulty, to enter the territory of Mexico, Nicaragua, or New Granada for the purpose of defending the persons and property of American citizens, even though they may be violently assailed whilst passing in peaceful transit over the Tehuantepec, Nicaragua, or Panama routes. He can not, without transcending his constitutional power, direct a gun to be fired into a port or land a seaman or marine to protect the lives of our countrymen on shore or to obtain redress for a recent outrage on their property. The banditti which infest our neighboring Republic of Mexico, always claiming to belong to one or other of the hostile parties, might make a sudden descent on Vera Cruz or on the Tehuantepec route, and he would have no power to employ the force on shipboard in the vicinity for their relief, either to prevent the plunder of our merchants or the destruction of the transit.

In reference to countries where the local authorities are strong enough to enforce the laws, the difficulty here indicated can seldom happen; but where this is not the case and the local authorities do not possess the physical power, even if they possess the will, to protect our citizens within their limits recent experience has shown that the American Executive should itself be authorized to render this protection. Such a grant of **authority, thus limited in its extent,** could in no just sense be regarded as a transfer of the war-making power to the Executive, but only as an appropriate exercise of that power by the body to whom it exclusively belongs. The riot at Panama in 1856, in which a great number of our citizens lost their lives, furnishes a pointed illustration of the necessity which may arise for the exertion of this authority.

I therefore earnestly recommend to Congress, on whom the responsibility exclusively rests, to pass a law before their adjournment conferring on the President the power to protect the lives and property of American citizens in the cases which I have indicated, under such restrictions and conditions as they may deem advisable. The knowledge that such a law exists would of itself go far to prevent the outrages which it is intended to redress and to render the employment of force unnecessary.

Without this the President may be placed in a painful position before the meeting of the next Congress. In the present disturbed condition of Mexico and one or more of the other Republics south of us, no person can foresee what occurrences may take place before that period. In case of emergency, our citizens, seeing that they do not enjoy the same protection with subjects of European Governments, will have just cause to complain. On the other hand, should the Executive interpose, and especially should the result prove disastrous and valuable lives be lost, he might subject himself to severe censure for having assumed a power not confided to him by the Constitution. It is to guard against this contingency that I now appeal to Congress.

Having thus recommended to Congress a measure which I deem necessary and expedient for the interest and honor of the country, I leave the whole subject to their wisdom and discretion.

JAMES BUCHANAN.

WASHINGTON, *February 18, 1859.*

To the Senate of the United States:

I transmit to the Senate, for its consideration with a view to ratification, two conventions between the United States and China, one providing for the adjustment of claims of citizens of the United States on the Government of that Empire, the other for the regulation of trade, both signed at Shanghai on the 8th of November last. A copy of the dispatches of Mr. Reed to the Department of State on the subject is also herewith transmitted.

JAMES BUCHANAN.

WASHINGTON CITY, *February 25, 1859.*

To the House of Representatives:

I transmit herewith a report from the Secretary of the Navy, with the accompanying documents, in obedience to the resolution of the House of Representatives adopted on the 28th of January, requesting the Presi-

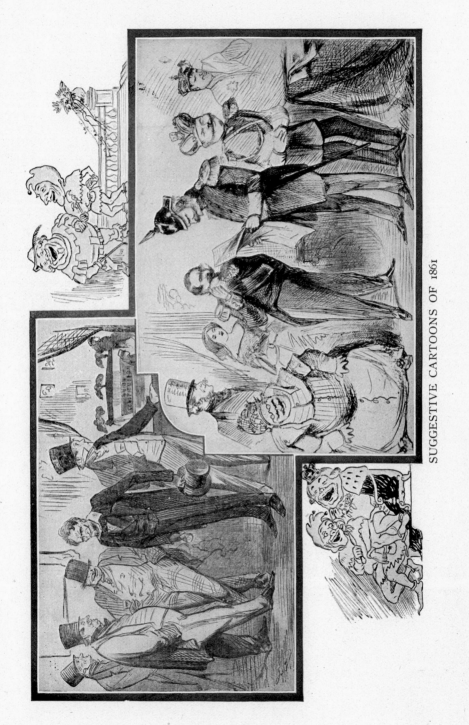

SUGGESTIVE CARTOONS OF 1861.

The lower one, showing foreign potentates receiving with pleasure the news of disunion, is a true presentation of conditions. England hastened to accord belligerent rights to the South, which raised the Confederate commerce-destroyers, in the eyes of nations, from pirate vessels whose crews should be executed when caught, to privateers legitimately warring on the enemy's trade. Napoleon III, Emperor of France, was constantly in negotiation with the Confederates, trying to find an opportunity to do the Federal Government harm. Following the lead of England and France, the other nations, deprived of cotton by our blockade, were equally unfriendly. Aristocracy in Europe sympathized with oligarchy in America.

The upper cartoon, from the most influential publication of the time, Harper's Weekly, reveals a phase of Lincoln's troubles that is little recognized. His place in the memories of his countrymen is now wreathed with the rarest garlands they can bestow. When his administration began, however, he was misunderstood and underrated. He was represented as telling questionable yarns when he should be attending to vital business. One of the keenest newspaper men of the time considered him a "simple Susan." His secret trip through Baltimore, where assassins awaited him, branded him with cowardice. And his habitual optimism earned for him the reputation of caring little whether the Union lived or died. The cartoon represents him as maudlin drunk while the funeral of the Union passes by.

dent of the United States "to communicate to this House a copy of all instructions given to the commanders of our African squadron since the ratification of the treaty of 1842, called the Washington treaty, with a copy or statement of whatever regulations were entered into by the commanders of the two squadrons for more fully accomplishing the object of the eighth article of said treaty," etc.

JAMES BUCHANAN.

WASHINGTON, *February 26, 1859.*

To the Senate of the United States:

In answer to the resolution of the Senate of the 23d instant, requesting a copy of certain letters of Horatio J. Perry, late secretary to the legation of the United States at Madrid, I transmit a report from the Secretary of State, with the documents which accompanied it.

JAMES BUCHANAN.

WASHINGTON CITY, *March 1, 1859.*

To the Senate of the United States:

I transmit herewith a report from the Secretary of War, with accompanying paper, in obedience to the resolution of the Senate adopted 23d February, requesting the President of the United States "to communicate to the Senate a copy of the opinion of Judge Brewer in the Great Falls land condemnation case, involving a claim for damages to be paid by the United States."

JAMES BUCHANAN.

WASHINGTON, *March 2, 1859.*

To the Senate of the United States:

I transmit to the Senate, in executive session, the report of the Secretary of State, with the accompanying documents, in reply to the resolution of the Senate adopted in open session on the 11th January last, relating to outrages committed on citizens of the United States on the Isthmus of Panama.

JAMES BUCHANAN.

To the House of Representatives:

In compliance with the resolution of the House of Representatives of the 25th ultimo, I transmit a copy of the report of the special agent of the United States recently sent to Vancouvers Island and British Columbia.

JAMES BUCHANAN.

MARCH 3, 1859.

WASHINGTON, *March 3, 1859.*

To the Senate and House of Representatives:

An imperative sense of duty compels me to make an appeal to Congress to preserve the credit of the country. This is the last day of the present Congress, and no provision has yet been made for the payment of appropriations and to meet the outstanding Treasury notes issued under the authority of law. From the information which has already been communicated to Congress by the Secretary of the Treasury it is manifest that the ordinary receipts into the Treasury, even under the most favorable circumstances, will scarcely meet the ordinary expenses of the Government during the remainder of the present fiscal year, ending on the 30th of June. At that time nearly eighteen millions of Treasury notes will have become due, and many of those not yet due are daily paid for duties at the different ports, and there will be no means in the Treasury to meet them. Thus the country, which is full of resources, will be dishonored before the world, and the American people, who are a debt-paying people, will be disgraced by the omission on our part to do our duty. It is impossible to avoid this catastrophe unless we make provision this very day to meet the lawful demands on the public Treasury. If this were the first instead of the last session of a Congress, the case would be different. You might then be convened by proclamation for to-morrow morning. But there are now thirteen States of the Union, entitled to seventy-eight Representatives, in which none have been elected. It will therefore be impracticable for a large majority of these States to elect their Members before the Treasury shall be compelled to stop payment.

Under these circumstances I earnestly recommend to Congress to make provision within the few remaining hours of the session for the preservation of the public credit. The urgency of the case not only justifies but demands that, if necessary, this shall be done by a separate bill. We ought to incur no risk when the good faith of the country is at stake.

JAMES BUCHANAN.

VETO MESSAGES.*

WASHINGTON, *January 7, 1859.*

To the House of Representatives:

On the last day of the last session of Congress, as appears by the Journal of the House of Representatives, "a joint resolution in regard to the carrying the United States mails from Saint Josephs, Missouri, to Placerville, California," was presented to me for my approval. This resolution

* The first is a pocket veto.

authorized and directed the Postmaster-General "to order an increase of speed upon said route, requiring the mails to be carried through in thirty days, instead of thirty-eight days, according to the existing contract: *Provided*, The same can be done upon a *pro rata* increase of compensation to the contractors."

I did not approve this joint resolution: First, because it was presented to me at so late a period that I had not the time necessary on the day of the adjournment of the last session for an investigation of the subject. Besides, no injury could result to the public, as the Postmaster-General already possessed the discretionary power under existing laws to increase the speed upon this as well as all other mail routes.

Second. Because the Postmaster-General, at the moment in the Capitol, informed me that the contractors themselves had offered to increase the speed on this route to thirty instead of thirty-eight days at a less cost than that authorized by the joint resolution. Upon subsequent examination it has been ascertained at the Post-Office Department that their bid, which is still depending, proposes to perform this service for a sum less by $49,000 than that authorized by the resolution.

JAMES BUCHANAN.

WASHINGTON CITY, *February 24, 1859.*

To the House of Representatives of the United States:

I return with my objections to the House of Representatives, in which it originated, the bill entitled "An act donating public lands to the several States and Territories which may provide colleges for the benefit of agriculture and the mechanic arts," presented to me on the 18th instant.

This bill makes a donation to the several States of 20,000 acres of the public lands for each Senator and Representative in the present Congress, and also an additional donation of 20,000 acres for each additional Representative to which any State may be entitled under the census of 1860.

According to a report from the Interior Department, based upon the present number of Senators and Representatives, the lands given to the States amount to 6,060,000 acres, and their value, at the minimum Government price of $1.25 per acre, to $7,575,000.

The object of this gift, as stated by the bill, is "the endowment, support, and maintenance of at least one college [in each State] where the leading object shall be, without excluding other scientific or classical studies, to teach such branches of learning as are related to agriculture and the mechanic arts, as the legislatures of the States may respectively prescribe, in order to promote the liberal and practical education of the industrial classes in the several pursuits and professions in life "

As there does not appear from the bill to be any beneficiaries in existence to which this endowment can be applied, each State is required

Messages and Papers of the Presidents

"to provide, within five years at least, not less than one college, or the grant to said State shall cease." In that event the "said State shall be bound to pay the United States the amount received of any lands previously sold, and that the title to purchasers under the State shall be valid."

The grant in land itself is confined to such States as have public lands within their limits worth $1.25 per acre in the opinion of the governor. For the remaining States the Secretary of the Interior is directed to issue "land scrip to the amount of their distributive shares in acres under the provisions of this act, said scrip to be sold by said States, and the proceeds thereof applied to the uses and purposes prescribed in this act, and for no other use or purpose whatsoever." The lands are granted and the scrip is to be issued "in sections or subdivisions of sections of not less than one-quarter of a section."

According to an estimate from the Interior Department, the number of acres which will probably be accepted by States having public lands within their own limits will not exceed 580,000 acres (and it may be much less), leaving a balance of 5,480,000 acres to be provided for by scrip. These grants of land and land scrip to each of the thirty-three States are made upon certain conditions, the principal of which is that if the fund shall be lost or diminished on account of unfortunate investments or otherwise the deficiency shall be replaced and made good by the respective States.

I shall now proceed to state my objections to this bill. I deem it to be both inexpedient and unconstitutional.

1. This bill has been passed at a period when we can with great difficulty raise sufficient revenue to sustain the expenses of the Government. Should it become a law the Treasury will be deprived of the whole, or nearly the whole, of our income from the sale of public lands, which for the next fiscal year has been estimated at $5,000,000.

A bare statement of the case will make this evident. The minimum price at which we dispose of our lands is $1.25 per acre. At the present moment, however, the price has been reduced to those who purchase the bounty-land warrants of the old soldiers to 85 cents per acre, and of these warrants there are still outstanding and unlocated, as appears by a report (February 12, 1859) from the General Land Office, the amount of 11,990,391 acres. This has already greatly reduced the current sales by the Government and diminished the revenue from this source. If in addition thirty-three States shall enter the market with their land scrip, the price must be greatly reduced below even 85 cents per acre, as much to the prejudice of the old soldiers who have not already parted with their land warrants as to Government. It is easy to perceive that with this glut of the market Government can sell little or no lands at $1.25 per acre, when the price of bounty-land warrants and scrip shall be reduced to half this sum. This source of revenue will be almost entirely dried up. Under the bill the States may sell their land scrip at any price it may bring. . There is no limitation whatever in this respect. Indeed, they must sell for what the scrip will bring, for without this fund they can not proceed to establish their colleges within the five years to which they are limited. It is manifest, therefore, that to the extent to which this bill will prevent the sale of public lands at $1.25 per acre, to that amount it will have precisely the same effect upon the Treasury as if we should impose a tax to create a loan to endow these State colleges.

Surely the present is the most unpropitious moment which could have been selected for the passage of this bill.

2. Waiving for the present the question of constitutional power, what effect will this bill have on the relations established between the Federal and State Governments? The Constitution is a grant to Congress of a few enumerated but most important powers, relating chiefly to war, peace, foreign and domestic commerce, negotiation, and other subjects which can be best or alone exercised beneficially by the common Government. All other powers are reserved to the States and to the people. For the efficient and harmonious working of both, it is necessary that their several spheres of action should be kept distinct from each other. This alone can prevent conflict and mutual injury. Should the time ever arrive when the State governments shall look to the Federal Treasury for the means of supporting themselves and maintaining their systems of education and internal policy, the character of both Governments will be greatly deteriorated. The representatives of the States and of the people, feeling a more immediate interest in obtaining money to lighten the burdens of their constituents than for the promotion of the more distant objects intrusted to the Federal Government, will naturally incline to obtain means from the Federal Government for State purposes. If a question shall arise between an appropriation of land or money to carry into effect the objects of the Federal Government and those of the States, their feelings will be enlisted in favor of the latter. This is human nature; and hence the necessity of keeping the two Governments entirely distinct. The preponderance of this home feeling has been manifested by the passage of the present bill. The establishment of these colleges has prevailed over the pressing wants of the common Treasury. No nation ever had such an inheritance as we possess in the public lands. These ought to be managed with the utmost care, but at the same time with a liberal spirit toward actual settlers.

In the first year of a war with a powerful naval nation the revenue from customs must in a great degree cease. A resort to loans will then become necessary, and these can always be obtained, as our fathers obtained them, on advantageous terms by pledging the public lands as security. In this view of the subject it would be wiser to grant money to the States for domestic purposes than to squander away the public lands and transfer them in large bodies into the hands of speculators.

A successful struggle on the part of the State governments with the

General Government for the public lands would deprive the latter of the means of performing its high duties, especially at critical and dangerous periods. Besides, it would operate with equal detriment to the best interests of the States. It would remove the most wholesome of all restraints on legislative bodies—that of being obliged to raise money by taxation from their constituents—and would lead to extravagance, if not to corruption. What is obtained easily and without responsibility will be lavishly expended.

3. This bill, should it become a law, will operate greatly to the injury of the new States. The progress of settlements and the increase of an industrious population owning an interest in the soil they cultivate are the causes which will build them up into great and flourishing commonwealths. Nothing could be more prejudicial to their interests than for wealthy individuals to acquire large tracts of the public land and hold them for speculative purposes. The low price to which this land scrip will probably be reduced will tempt speculators to buy it in large amounts and locate it on the best lands belonging to the Government. The eventual consequence must be that the men who desire to cultivate the soil will be compelled to purchase these very lands at rates much higher than the price at which they could be obtained from the Government.

4. It is extremely doubtful, to say the least, whether this bill would contribute to the advancement of agriculture and the mechanic arts—objects the dignity and value of which can not be too highly appreciated. The Federal Government, which makes the donation, has confessedly no constitutional power to follow it into the States and enforce the application of the fund to the intended objects. As donors we shall possess no control over our own gift after it shall have passed from our hands. It is true that the State legislatures are required to stipulate that they will faithfully execute the trust in the manner prescribed by the bill. But should they fail to do this, what would be the consequence? The Federal Government has no power, and ought to have no power, to compel the execution of the trust. It would be in as helpless a condition as if, even in this, the time of great need, we were to demand any portion of the many millions of surplus revenue deposited with the States for safe-keeping under the act of 1836.

5. This bill will injuriously interfere with existing colleges in the different States, in many of which agriculture is taught as a science and in all of which it ought to be so taught. These institutions of learning have grown up with the growth of the country, under the fostering care of the States and the munificence of individuals, to meet the advancing demands for education. They have proved great blessings to the people. Many, indeed most, of them are poor and sustain themselves with difficulty. What the effect will be on these institutions of creating an indefinite number of rival colleges sustained by the endowment of the Federal Government it is not difficult to determine.

Under this bill it is provided that scientific and classical studies shall not be excluded from them. Indeed, it would be almost impossible to sustain them without such a provision, for no father would incur the expense of sending a son to one of these institutions for the sole purpose of making him a scientific farmer or mechanic. The bill itself negatives this idea, and declares that their object is "to promote the liberal and practical education of the industrial classes in the several pursuits and professions of life." This certainly ought to be the case. In this view of the subject it would be far better, if such an appropriation of land must be made to institutions of learning in the several States, to apply it directly to the establishment of professorships of agriculture and the mechanic arts in existing colleges, without the intervention of the State legislatures. It would be difficult to foresee how these legislatures will manage this fund. Each Representative in Congress for whose district the proportion of 20,000 acres has been granted will probably insist that the proceeds shall be expended within its limits. There will undoubtedly be a struggle between different localities in each State concerning the division of the gift, which may end in disappointing the hopes of the true friends of agriculture. For this state of things we are without remedy. Not so in regard to State colleges. We might grant land to these corporations to establish agricultural and mechanical professorships, and should they fail to comply with the conditions on which they accepted the grant we might enforce specific performance of these before the ordinary courts of justice.

6. But does Congress possess the power under the Constitution to make a donation of public lands to the different States of the Union to provide colleges for the purpose of educating their own people?

I presume the general proposition is undeniable that Congress does not possess the power to appropriate money in the Treasury, raised by taxes on the people of the United States, for the purpose of educating the people of the respective States. It will not be pretended that any such power is to be found among the specific powers granted to Congress nor that "it is necessary and proper for carrying into execution" any one of these powers. Should Congress exercise such a power, this would be to break down the barriers which have been so carefully constructed in the Constitution to separate Federal from State authority. We should then not only "lay and collect taxes, duties, imposts, and excises" for Federal purposes, but for every State purpose which Congress might deem expedient or useful. This would be an actual consolidation of the Federal and State Governments so far as the great taxing and money power is concerned, and constitute a sort of partnership between the two in the Treasury of the United States, equally ruinous to both.

But it is contended that the public lands are placed upon a different footing from money raised by taxation and that the proceeds arising from their sale are not subject to the limitations of the Constitution, but may be appropriated or given away by Congress, at its own discretion, to States, corporations, or individuals for any purpose they may deem expedient.

The advocates of this bill attempt to sustain their position upon the language of the second clause of the third section of the fourth article of the Constitution, which declares that "the Congress shall have power to dispose of and make all needful rules and regulations respecting the territory or other property belonging to the United States." They contend that by a fair interpretation of the words "dispose of" in this clause Congress possesses the power to make this gift of public lands to the States for purposes of education.

It would require clear and strong evidence to induce the belief that the framers of the Constitution, after having limited the powers of Congress to certain precise and specific objects, intended by employing the words "dispose of" to give that body unlimited power over the vast public domain. It would be a strange anomaly, indeed, to have created two funds—the one by taxation, confined to the execution of the enumerated powers delegated to Congress, and the other from the public lands, applicable to all subjects, foreign and domestic, which Congress might designate; that this fund should be "disposed of," not to pay the debts of the United States, nor "to raise and support armies," nor "to provide and maintain a navy," nor to accomplish any one of the other great objects enumerated in the Constitution, but be diverted from them to pay the debts of the States, to educate their people, and to carry into effect any other measure of their domestic policy. This would be to confer upon Congress a vast and irresponsible authority, utterly at war with the well-known jealousy of Federal power which prevailed at the formation of the Constitution. The natural intendment would be that as the Constitution confined Congress to well-defined specific powers, the funds placed at their command, whether in land or money, should be appropriated to the performance of the duties corresponding with these powers. If not, a Government has been created with all its other powers carefully limited, but without any limitation in respect to the public lands.

But I can not so read the words "dispose of" as to make them embrace the idea of "giving away." The true meaning of words is always to be ascertained by the subject to which they are applied and the known general intent of the lawgiver. Congress is a trustee under the Constitution for the people of the United States to "dispose of" their public lands, and I think I may venture to assert with confidence that no case can be found in which a trustee in the position of Congress has been authorized to "*dispose of*" property by its owner where it has been held that these words authorized such trustee to give away the fund intrusted to his care. No trustee, when called upon to account for the disposition of the property placed under his management before any judicial tribunal, would venture to present such a plea in his defense. The true meaning of these words is clearly stated by Chief Justice Taney in delivering the opinion of the court (19 Howard, p. 436). He says in reference to this clause of the Constitution:

It begins its enumeration of powers by that of disposing; in other words, making sale of the lands or raising money from them, which, as we have already said, was the main object of the cession (from the States), and which is the first thing provided for in the article.

It is unnecessary to refer to the history of the times to establish the known fact that this statement of the Chief Justice is perfectly well founded. That it never was intended by the framers of the Constitution that these lands should be given away by Congress is manifest from the concluding portion of the same clause. By it Congress has power not only "to dispose of" the territory, but of the "other property of the United States." In the language of the Chief Justice (p. 437):

And the same power of making needful rules respecting the territory is in precisely the same language applied to the other property of the United States, associating the power over the territory in this respect with the power over movable or personal property; that is, the ships, arms, or munitions of war which then belonged in common to the State sovereignties.

The question is still clearer in regard to the public lands in the States and Territories within the Louisiana and Florida purchases. These lands were paid for out of the public Treasury from money raised by taxation. Now if Congress had no power to appropriate the money with which these lands were purchased, is it not clear that the power over the lands is equally limited? The mere conversion of this money into land could not confer upon Congress new power over the disposition of land which they had not possessed over money. If it could, then a trustee, by changing the character of the fund intrusted to his care for special objects from money into land, might give the land away or devote it to any purpose he thought proper, however foreign from the trust. The inference is irresistible that this land partakes of the very same character with the money paid for it, and can be devoted to no objects different from those to which the money could have been devoted. If this were not the case, then by the purchase of a new territory from a foreign government out of the public Treasury Congress could enlarge their own powers and appropriate the proceeds of the sales of the land thus purchased, at their own discretion, to other and far different objects from what they could have applied the purchase money which had been raised by taxation.

It has been asserted truly that Congress in numerous instances have granted lands for the purposes of education. These grants have been chiefly, if not exclusively, made to the new States as they successively entered the Union, and consisted at the first of one section and afterwards of two sections of the public land in each township for the use of schools, as well as of additional sections for a State university. Such grants are not, in my opinion, a violation of the Constitution. The United States is a great landed proprietor, and from the very nature of this relation it is both the right and the duty of Congress as their trustee to manage these lands as any other prudent proprietor would manage them for his own best advantage. Now no consideration could be presented of a stronger character to induce the American people to brave the difficulties and hardships of frontier life and to settle upon these lands and to purchase them at a fair price than to give to them and to their children an assurance of the means of education. If any prudent individual had held these lands, he could not have adopted a wiser course to bring them into market and enhance their value than to give a portion of them for purposes of education. As a mere speculation he would pursue this course. No person will contend that donations of land to all the States of the Union for the erection of colleges within the limits of each can be embraced by this principle. It can not be pretended that an agricultural college in New York or Virginia would aid the settlement or facilitate the sale of public lands in Minnesota or California. This can not possibly be embraced within the authority which a prudent proprietor of land would exercise over his own possessions. I purposely avoid any attempt to define what portions of land may be granted, and for what purposes, to improve the value and promote the settlement and sale of the remainder without violating the Constitution. In this case I adopt the rule that "sufficient unto the day is the evil thereof."

JAMES BUCHANAN.

PROCLAMATION.

BY THE PRESIDENT OF THE UNITED STATES OF AMERICA.

A PROCLAMATION.

Whereas an extraordinary occasion has occurred rendering it necessary and proper that the Senate of the United States shall be convened to receive and act upon such communications as have been or may be made to it on the part of the Executive:

Now, therefore, I, James Buchanan, President of the United States, do issue this my proclamation, declaring that an extraordinary occasion requires the Senate of the United States to convene for the transaction of business at the Capitol, in the city of Washington, on the 4th day of next month, at 12 o'clock at noon of that day, of which all who shall then be entitled to act as members of that body are hereby required to take notice.

Given under my hand and the seal of the United States, at Washing-
[SEAL.] ton, this 26th day of February, A. D. 1859, and of the Independence of the United States the eighty-third.

JAMES BUCHANAN.

By the President:
LEWIS CASS, *Secretary of State.*

SPECIAL MESSAGE.

WASHINGTON, *March 9, 1859.*

To the Senate of the United States:

It has become my sad duty to announce to the Senate the death of
Aaron V. Brown, late Postmaster-General, at his residence in this city on
yesterday morning at twenty minutes past 9 o'clock.

The death of this distinguished public officer, especially at the present
moment, when his eminent services are so much needed, is a great loss to
his country. He was able, honest, and indefatigable in the discharge
of his high and responsible duties, whilst his benevolent heart and his
kind deportment endeared him to all who approached him.

Submitting, as I do, with humble resignation to the will of Divine
Providence in this calamitous dispensation, I shall ever cherish his memory with affectionate regard.

JAMES BUCHANAN.

EXECUTIVE ORDERS.

[From the Evening Star, March 10, 1859.]

GENERAL ORDER.

WAR DEPARTMENT,
Washington, March 8, 1859.

Under instructions from the President of the United States, the Secretary of War with unfeigned sorrow announces to the Army the decease
of the Hon. A. V. Brown, Postmaster-General, which occurred in this city
at an early hour this morning.

An enlightened statesman and a distinguished and able member of
the General Government has thus been stricken down at his post. The
nation will mourn the afflicting dispensation which has left so great a
void in its councils. A worthy and estimable citizen has been removed
from the circle of his numerous friends. Society will mingle its grief
with the patriotic regrets which the loss of a statesman will not fail to
call forth.

While the President, with the surviving members of the Cabinet, the legislative and judicial departments of the Government, will unite in every testimonial the sad occasion demands, it is fitting a similar respect should be shown to the memory of the distinguished deceased by the national arms of defense. Accordingly, half-hour guns will be fired from sunrise to sunset at every garrisoned military post the day succeeding the receipt of this order, the national flag will be displayed at half-staff during the same time, and officers of the Army will wear for three months the proper badge of military mourning.

The War Department and its bureaus will be closed until the day succeeding the funeral obsequies.

JOHN B. FLOYD,
Secretary of War.

[From the Daily National Intelligencer, March 10, 1859.]

GENERAL ORDER.

NAVY DEPARTMENT, *March 9, 1859.*

The Secretary of the Navy, by the direction of the President, announces to the Navy and to the Marine Corps the lamented death of the Hon. Aaron V. Brown, Postmaster-General of the United States. He died at his residence in the city of Washington on the 8th of the present month.

As a mark of respect to his high character, his eminent position, and great public services, it is directed that on the day after the receipt of this order by the different navy-yards and stations and vessels of war of the United States in commission the flags be hoisted at half-mast from sunrise to sunset and that seventeen minute guns be fired at noon.

Officers of the Navy and Marine Corps will wear crape on the left arm for thirty days.

The Navy Department will be draped in mourning and will be closed until after the funeral.

ISAAC TOUCEY,
Secretary of the Navy.

THIRD ANNUAL MESSAGE.

WASHINGTON CITY, *December 19, 1859.*
Fellow-Citizens of the Senate and House of Representatives:

Our deep and heartfelt gratitude is due to that Almighty Power which has bestowed upon us such varied and numerous blessings throughout the past year. The general health of the country has been excellent, our harvests have been unusually plentiful, and prosperity smiles throughout the land. Indeed, notwithstanding our demerits, we have much reason to believe from the past events in our history that we have enjoyed the special protection of Divine Providence ever since our origin as a nation. We have been exposed to many threatening and alarming difficulties in our progress, but on each successive occasion the impending cloud has been dissipated at the moment it appeared ready to burst upon our head, and the danger to our institutions has passed away. May we ever be under the divine guidance and protection.

Whilst it is the duty of the President "from time to time to give to Congress information of the state of the Union," I shall not refer in detail to the recent sad and bloody occurrences at Harpers Ferry. Still, it is proper to observe that these events, however bad and cruel in themselves, derive their chief importance from the apprehension that they are but symptoms of an incurable disease in the public mind, which may break out in still more dangerous outrages and terminate at last in an open war by the North to abolish slavery in the South.

Whilst for myself I entertain no such apprehension, they ought to afford a solemn warning to us all to beware of the approach of danger. Our Union is a stake of such inestimable value as to demand our constant and watchful vigilance for its preservation. In this view, let me implore my countrymen, North and South, to cultivate the ancient feelings of mutual forbearance and good will toward each other and strive to allay the demon spirit of sectional hatred and strife now alive in the land. This advice proceeds from the heart of an old public functionary whose service commenced in the last generation, among the wise and conservative statesmen of that day, now nearly all passed away, and whose first and dearest earthly wish is to leave his country tranquil, prosperous, united, and powerful.

We ought to reflect that in this age, and especially in this country, there is an incessant flux and reflux of public opinion. Questions which in their day assumed a most threatening aspect have now nearly gone from the memory of men. They are "volcanoes burnt out, and on the lava and ashes and squalid scoria of old eruptions grow the peaceful olive, the cheering vine, and the sustaining corn." Such, in my opinion, will prove to be the fate of the present sectional excitement should those who wisely seek to apply the remedy continue always to confine their efforts within the pale of the Constitution. If this course be pursued, the existing agitation on the subject of domestic slavery, like everything human, will have its day and give place to other and less threatening controversies. Public opinion in this country is all-powerful, and when it reaches a dangerous excess upon any question the good sense of the people will furnish the corrective and bring it back within safe limits. Still, to hasten this auspicious result at the present crisis we ought to remember that every rational creature must be presumed to intend the natural consequences of his own teachings. Those who announce abstract doctrines subversive of the Constitution and the Union must not be surprised should their heated partisans advance one step further and attempt by violence to carry these doctrines into practical effect. In this view of the subject, it ought never to be forgotten that however great may have been the political advantages resulting from the Union to every portion of our common country, these would all prove to be as nothing should the time ever arrive when they can not be enjoyed without serious danger to the personal safety of the people of fifteen members of the Confederacy. If the peace of the domestic fireside throughout these States should ever be invaded, if the mothers of families within this extensive region should not be able to retire to rest at night without suffering dreadful apprehensions of what may be their own fate and that of their children before the morning, it would be vain to recount to such a people the political benefits which result to them from the Union. Self-preservation is the first instinct of nature, and therefore any state of society in which the sword is all the time suspended over the heads of the people must at last become intolerable. But I indulge in no such gloomy forebodings. On the contrary, I firmly believe that the events at Harpers Ferry, by causing the people to pause and reflect upon the possible peril to their cherished institutions, will be the means under Providence of allaying the existing excitement and preventing further outbreaks of a similar character. They will resolve that the Constitution and the Union shall not be endangered by rash counsels, knowing that should "the silver cord be loosed or the golden bowl be broken * * * at the fountain" human power could never reunite the scattered and hostile fragments.

I cordially congratulate you upon the final settlement by the Supreme Court of the United States of the question of slavery in the Territories, which had presented an aspect so truly formidable at the commencement of my Administration. The right has been established of every citizen to take his property of any kind, including slaves, into the common Territories belonging equally to all the States of the Confederacy, and to have it protected there under the Federal Constitution. Neither Congress nor a Territorial legislature nor any human power has any authority to annul or impair this vested right. The supreme judicial tribunal of the country, which is a coordinate branch of the Government, has sanctioned and affirmed these principles of constitutional law, so manifestly just in themselves and so well calculated to promote peace and harmony among the States. It is a striking proof of the sense of justice which is inherent in our people that the property in slaves has never been disturbed, to my knowledge, in any of the Territories. Even throughout the late troubles in Kansas there has not been any attempt, as I am credibly informed, to interfere in a single instance with the right of the master. Had any such attempt been made, the judiciary would doubtless have afforded an adequate remedy. Should they fail to do this hereafter, it will then be time enough to strengthen their hands by further legislation. Had it been decided that either Congress or the Territorial legislature possess the power to annul or impair the right to property in slaves, the evil would be intolerable. In the latter event there would be a struggle for a majority of the members of the legislature at each successive election, and the sacred rights of property held under the Federal Constitution would depend for the time being on the result. The agitation would thus be rendered incessant whilst the Territorial condition remained, and its baneful influence would keep alive a dangerous excitement among the people of the several States.

Thus has the status of a Territory during the intermediate period from its first settlement until it shall become a State been irrevocably fixed by the final decision of the Supreme Court. Fortunate has this been for the prosperity of the Territories, as well as the tranquillity of the States. Now emigrants from the North and the South, the East and the West, will meet in the Territories on a common platform, having brought with them that species of property best adapted, in their own opinion, to promote their welfare. From natural causes the slavery question will in each case soon virtually settle itself, and before the Territory is prepared for admission as a State into the Union this decision, one way or the other, will have been a foregone conclusion. Meanwhile the settlement of the new Territory will proceed without serious interruption, and its progress and prosperity will not be endangered or retarded by violent political struggles.

When in the progress of events the inhabitants of any Territory shall have reached the number required to form a State, they will then proceed in a regular manner and in the exercise of the rights of popular sovereignty to form a constitution preparatory to admission into the Union. After this has been done, to employ the language of the Kansas and Nebraska act, they "shall be received into the Union with or without slavery, as their constitution may prescribe at the time of their admission." This sound principle has happily been recognized in some form or other by an almost unanimous vote of both Houses of the last Congress.

All lawful means at my command have been employed, and shall continue to be employed, to execute the laws against the African slave trade. After a most careful and rigorous examination of our coasts and a thorough investigation of the subject, we have not been able to discover that any slaves have been imported into the United States except the cargo by the *Wanderer*, numbering between three and four hundred. Those engaged in this unlawful enterprise have been rigorously prosecuted, but not with as much success as their crimes have deserved. A number of them are still under prosecution.

Our history proves that the fathers of the Republic, in advance of all other nations, condemned the African slave trade. It was, notwithstanding, deemed expedient by the framers of the Constitution to deprive Congress of the power to prohibit "the migration or importation of such persons as any of the States now existing shall think proper to admit " "prior to the year 1808." It will be seen that this restriction on the power of Congress was confined to such States only as might think proper to admit the importation of slaves. It did not extend to other States or to the trade carried on abroad. Accordingly, we find that so early as the 22d March, 1794, Congress passed an act imposing severe penalties and punishments upon citizens and residents of the United States who should engage in this trade between foreign nations. The provisions of this act were extended and enforced by the act of 10th May, 1800.

Again, the States themselves had a clear right to waive the constitutional privilege intended for their benefit, and to prohibit by their own laws this trade at any time they thought proper previous to 1808. Several of them exercised this right before that period, and among them some containing the greatest number of slaves. This gave to Congress the immediate power to act in regard to all such States, because they themselves had removed the constitutional barrier. Congress accordingly passed an act on 28th February, 1803, "to prevent the importation of certain persons into certain States where by the laws thereof their admission is prohibited." In this manner the importation of African slaves into the United States was to a great extent prohibited some years in advance of 1808.

As the year 1808 approached Congress determined not to suffer this trade to exist even for a single day after they had the power to abolish it. On the 2d of March, 1807, they passed an act, to take effect "from and after the 1st day of January, 1808," prohibiting the importation of African slaves into the United States. This was followed by subsequent acts of a similar character, to which I need not specially refer. Such were the principles and such the practice of our ancestors more than fifty years ago in regard to the African slave trade. It did not occur to the revered patriots who had been delegates to the Convention, and afterwards became members of Congress, that in passing these laws they had violated the Constitution which they had framed with so much care and deliberation. They supposed that to prohibit Congress in express terms from exercising a specified power before an appointed day necessarily involved the right to exercise this power after that day had arrived.

If this were not the case, the framers of the Constitution had expended much labor in vain. Had they imagined that Congress would possess no power to prohibit the trade either before or after 1808, they would not have taken so much care to protect the States against the exercise of this power before that period. Nay, more, they would not have attached such vast importance to this provision as to have excluded it from the possibility of future repeal or amendment, to which other portions of the Constitution were exposed. It would, then, have been wholly unnecessary to ingraft on the fifth article of the Constitution, prescribing the mode of its own future amendment, the proviso "that no amendment which may be made prior to the year 1808 shall in any manner affect" the provision in the Constitution securing to the States the right to admit the importation of African slaves previous to that period. According to the adverse construction, the clause itself, on which so much care and discussion had been employed by the members of the Convention, was an absolute nullity from the beginning, and all that has since been done under it a mere usurpation.

It was well and wise to confer this power on Congress, because had it been left to the States its efficient exercise would have been impossible. In that event any one State could have effectually continued the trade, not only for itself, but for all the other slave States, though never so much against their will. And why? Because African slaves, when once brought within the limits of any one State in accordance with its laws, can not practically be excluded from any State where slavery exists. And even if all the States had separately passed laws prohibiting the importation of slaves, these laws would have failed of effect for want of a naval force to capture the slavers and to guard the coast. Such a force no State can employ in time of peace without the consent of Congress.

These acts of Congress, it is believed, have, with very rare and insignificant exceptions, accomplished their purpose. For a period of more than half a century there has been no perceptible addition to the number of our domestic slaves. During this period their advancement in civilization has far surpassed that of any other portion of the African race. The light and the blessings of Christianity have been extended to them, and both their moral and physical condition has been greatly improved.

Reopen the trade and it would be difficult to determine whether the effect would be more deleterious on the interests of the master or on those of the native-born slave. Of the evils to the master, the one most to be dreaded would be the introduction of wild, heathen, and ignorant barbarians among the sober, orderly, and quiet slaves whose ancestors have been on the soil for several generations. This might tend to barbarize, demoralize, and exasperate the whole mass and produce most deplorable consequences.

The effect upon the existing slave would, if possible, be still more deplorable. At present he is treated with kindness and humanity. He is well fed, well clothed, and not overworked. His condition is incomparably better than that of the coolies which modern nations of high civilization have employed as a substitute for African slaves. Both the philanthropy and the self-interest of the master have combined to produce this humane result. But let this trade be reopened and what will be the effect? The same to a considerable extent as on a neighboring island, the only spot now on earth where the African slave trade is openly tolerated, and this in defiance of solemn treaties with a power abundantly able at any moment to enforce their execution. There the master, intent upon present gain, extorts from the slave as much labor as his physical powers are capable of enduring, knowing that when death comes to his relief his place can be supplied at a price reduced to the lowest point by the competition of rival African slave traders. Should this ever be the case in our country, which I do not deem possible, the present useful character of the domestic institution, wherein those too old and too young to work are provided for with care and humanity and those capable of labor are not overtasked, would undergo an unfortunate change. The feeling of reciprocal dependence and attachment which now exists between master and slave would be converted into mutual distrust and hostility.

But we are obliged as a Christian and moral nation to consider what would be the effect upon unhappy Africa itself if we should reopen the slave trade. This would give the trade an impulse and extension which it has never had, even in its palmiest days. The numerous victims required to supply it would convert the whole slave coast into a perfect pandemonium, for which this country would be held responsible in the eyes both of God and man. Its petty tribes would then be constantly engaged in predatory wars against each other for the purpose of seizing slaves to supply the American market. All hopes of African civilization would thus be ended.

On the other hand, when a market for African slaves shall no longer be furnished in Cuba, and thus all the world be closed against this trade, we may then indulge a reasonable hope for the gradual improvement of Africa. The chief motive of war among the tribes will cease whenever there is no longer any demand for slaves. The resources of that fertile but miserable country might then be developed by the hand of industry and afford subjects for legitimate foreign and domestic commerce. In this manner Christianity and civilization may gradually penetrate the existing gloom.

The wisdom of the course pursued by this Government toward China has been vindicated by the event. Whilst we sustained a neutral position in the war waged by Great Britain and France against the Chinese Empire, our late minister, in obedience to his instructions, judiciously cooperated with the ministers of these powers in all peaceful measures to secure by treaty the just concessions demanded by the interests of foreign commerce. The result is that satisfactory treaties have been concluded with China by the respective ministers of the United States, Great Britain, France, and Russia. Our "treaty, or general convention, of peace, amity, and commerce" with that Empire was concluded at Tien-tsin on the 18th June, 1858, and was ratified by the President, by and with the advice and consent of the Senate, on the 21st December following. On the 15th December, 1858, John E. Ward, a distinguished citizen of Georgia, was duly commissioned as envoy extraordinary and minister plenipotentiary to China.

He left the United States for the place of his destination on the 5th of February, 1859, bearing with him the ratified copy of this treaty, and arrived at Shanghai on the 28th May. From thence he proceeded to Peking on the 16th June, but did not arrive in that city until the 27th July. According to the terms of the treaty, the ratifications were to be exchanged on or before the 18th June, 1859. This was rendered impossible by reasons and events beyond his control, not necessary to detail; but still it is due to the Chinese authorities at Shanghai to state that they always assured him no advantage should be taken of the delay, and this pledge has been faithfully redeemed.

On the arrival of Mr. Ward at Peking he requested an audience of the Emperor to present his letter of credence. This he did not obtain, in consequence of his very proper refusal to submit to the humiliating ceremonies required by the etiquette of this strange people in approaching their sovereign. Nevertheless, the interviews on this question were conducted in the most friendly spirit and with all due regard to his personal feelings and the honor of his country. When a presentation to His Majesty was found to be impossible, the letter of credence from the President was received with peculiar honors by Kweiliang, "the Emperor's prime minister and the second man in the Empire to the Emperor himself." The ratifications of the treaty were afterwards, on the 16th of August, exchanged in proper form at Pei-tsang. As the exchange did not take place until after the day prescribed by the treaty, it is deemed proper before its publication again to submit it to the Senate. It is but simple justice to the Chinese authorities to observe that throughout the whole transaction they appear to have acted in good faith and in a friendly spirit toward the United States. It is true this has been done after their own peculiar fashion; but we ought to regard with a lenient eye the ancient customs of an empire dating back for thousands of years, so far as this may be consistent with our own national honor. The conduct of our minister on the occasion has received my entire approbation.

In order to carry out the spirit of this treaty and to give it full effect it became necessary to conclude two supplemental conventions, the one for the adjustment and satisfaction of the claims of our citizens and the other to fix the tariff on imports and exports and to regulate the transit duties and trade of our merchants with China. This duty was satisfactorily performed by our late minister. These conventions bear date at Shanghai on the 8th November, 1858. Having been considered in the light of binding agreements subsidiary to the principal treaty, and to be carried into execution without delay, they do not provide for any formal ratification or exchange of ratifications by the contracting parties. This was not deemed necessary by the Chinese, who are already proceeding in good faith to satisfy the claims of our citizens and, it is hoped, to carry out the other provisions of the conventions. Still, I thought it was proper to submit them to the Senate, by which they were ratified on the

3d of March, 1859. The ratified copies, however, did not reach Shanghai until after the departure of our minister to Peking, and these conventions could not, therefore, be exchanged at the same time with the principal treaty. No doubt is entertained that they will be ratified and exchanged by the Chinese Government should this be thought advisable; but under the circumstances presented I shall consider them binding engagements from their date on both parties, and cause them to be published as such for the information and guidance of our merchants trading with the Chinese Empire.

It affords me much satisfaction to inform you that all our difficulties with the Republic of Paraguay have been satisfactorily adjusted. It happily did not become necessary to employ the force for this purpose which Congress had placed at my command under the joint resolution of 2d June, 1858. On the contrary, the President of that Republic, in a friendly spirit, acceded promptly to the just and reasonable demands of the Government of the United States. Our commissioner arrived at Assumption, the capital of the Republic, on the 25th of January, 1859, and left it on the 17th of February, having in three weeks ably and successfully accomplished all the objects of his mission. The treaties which he has concluded will be immediately submitted to the Senate.

In the view that the employment of other than peaceful means might become necessary to obtain "just satisfaction" from Paraguay, a strong naval force was concentrated in the waters of the La Plata to await contingencies whilst our commissioner ascended the rivers to Assumption. The Navy Department is entitled to great credit for the promptness, efficiency, and economy with which this expedition was fitted out and conducted. It consisted of 19 armed vessels, great and small, carrying 200 guns and 2,500 men, all under the command of the veteran and gallant Shubrick. The entire expenses of the expedition have been defrayed out of the ordinary appropriations for the naval service, except the sum of $289,000, applied to the purchase of seven of the steamers constituting a part of it, under the authority of the naval appropriation act of the 3d March last. It is believed that these steamers are worth more than their cost, and they are all now usefully and actively employed in the naval service.

The appearance of so large a force, fitted out in such a prompt manner, in the far-distant waters of the La Plata, and the admirable conduct of the officers and men employed in it, have had a happy effect in favor of our country throughout all that remote portion of the world.

Our relations with the great Empires of France and Russia, as well as with all other governments on the continent of Europe, unless we may except that of Spain, happily continue to be of the most friendly character.

In my last annual message I presented a statement of the unsatisfactory condition of our relations with Spain, and I regret to say that this has not materially improved.

Without special reference to other claims, even the "Cuban claims," the payment of which has been ably urged by our ministers, and in which more than a hundred of our citizens are directly interested, remain unsatisfied, notwithstanding both their justice and their amount ($128,635.54) had been recognized and ascertained by the Spanish Government itself.

I again recommend that an appropriation be made "to be paid to the Spanish Government for the purpose of distribution among the claimants in the *Amistad* case." In common with two of my predecessors, I entertain no doubt that this is required by our treaty with Spain of the 27th October, 1795. The failure to discharge this obligation has been employed by the cabinet of Madrid as a reason against the settlement of our claims.

I need not repeat the arguments which I urged in my last annual message in favor of the acquisition of Cuba by fair purchase. My opinions on that measure remain unchanged. I therefore again invite the serious attention of Congress to this important subject. Without a recognition of this policy on their part it will be almost impossible to institute negotiations with any reasonable prospect of success.

Until a recent period there was good reason to believe that I should be able to announce to you on the present occasion that our difficulties with Great Britain arising out of the Clayton and Bulwer treaty had been finally adjusted in a manner alike honorable and satisfactory to both parties. From causes, however, which the British Government had not anticipated, they have not yet completed treaty arrangements with the Republics of Honduras and Nicaragua, in pursuance of the understanding between the two Governments. It is, nevertheless, confidently expected that this good work will ere long be accomplished.

Whilst indulging the hope that no other subject remained which could disturb the good understanding between the two countries, the question arising out of the adverse claims of the parties to the island of San Juan, under the Oregon treaty of the 15th June, 1846, suddenly assumed a threatening prominence. In order to prevent unfortunate collisions on that remote frontier, the late Secretary of State, on the 17th July, 1855, addressed a note to Mr. Crampton, then British minister at Washington, communicating to him a copy of the instructions which he (Mr. Marcy) had given on the 14th July to Governor Stevens, of Washington Territory, having a special reference to an "apprehended conflict between our citizens and the British subjects on the island of San Juan." To prevent this the governor was instructed "that the officers of the Territory should abstain from all acts on the disputed grounds which are calculated to provoke any conflicts, so far as it can be done without implying the concession to the authorities of Great Britain of an exclusive right over the premises. The title ought to be settled before either party should attempt to exclude the other by force or exercise complete and exclusive sovereign rights within the fairly disputed limits."

In acknowledging the receipt on the next day of Mr. Marcy's note the British minister expressed his entire concurrence "in the propriety of the course recommended to the governor of Washington Territory by your [Mr. Marcy's] instructions to that officer," and stating that he had "lost no time in transmitting a copy of that document to the Governor-General of British North America" and had "earnestly recommended to His Excellency to take such measures as to him may appear best calculated to secure on the part of the British local authorities and the inhabitants of the neighborhood of the line in question the exercise of the same spirit of forbearance which is inculcated by you [Mr. Marcy] on the authorities and citizens of the United States."

Thus matters remained upon the faith of this arrangement until the 9th July last, when General Harney paid a visit to the island. He found upon it twenty-five American residents with their families, and also an establishment of the Hudsons Bay Company for the purpose of raising sheep. A short time before his arrival one of these residents had shot an animal belonging to the company whilst trespassing upon his premises, for which, however, he offered to pay twice its value, but that was refused. Soon after "the chief factor of the company at Victoria, Mr. Dalles, son-in-law of Governor Douglas, came to the island in the British sloop of war *Satellite* and threatened to take this American [Mr. Cutler] by force to Victoria to answer for the trespass he had committed. The American seized his rifle and told Mr. Dalles if any such attempt was made he would kill him upon the spot. The affair then ended."

Under these circumstances the American settlers presented a petition to the General "through the United States inspector of customs, Mr. Hubbs, to place a force upon the island to protect them from the Indians, as well as the oppressive interference of the authorities of the Hudsons Bay Company at Victoria with their rights as American citizens." The General immediately responded to this petition, and ordered Captain George E. Pickett, Ninth Infantry, "to establish his company on Bellevue, or San Juan Island, on some suitable position near the harbor at the southeastern extremity." This order was promptly obeyed and a military post was established at the place designated. The force was afterwards increased, so that by the last return the whole number of troops then on the island amounted in the aggregate to 691 men.

Whilst I do not deem it proper on the present occasion to go further into the subject and discuss the weight which ought to be attached to the statements of the British colonial authorities contesting the accuracy of the information on which the gallant General acted, it was due to him that I should thus present his own reasons for issuing the order to Captain Pickett. From these it is quite clear his object was to prevent the British authorities on Vancouvers Island from exercising jurisdiction over American residents on the island of San Juan, as well as to protect them against the incursions of the Indians. Much excitement prevailed for some time throughout that region, and serious danger of collision between the parties was apprehended. The British had a large naval force in the vicinity, and it is but an act of simple justice to the admiral on that station to state that he wisely and discreetly forbore to commit any hostile act, but determined to refer the whole affair to his Government and await their instructions.

This aspect of the matter, in my opinion, demanded serious attention. It would have been a great calamity for both nations had they been precipitated into acts of hostility, not on the question of title to the island, but merely concerning what should be its condition during the intervening period whilst the two Governments might be employed in settling the question to which of them it belongs. For this reason Lieutenant-General Scott was dispatched, on the 17th of September last, to Washington Territory to take immediate command of the United States forces on the Pacific Coast, should he deem this necessary. The main object of his mission was to carry out the spirit of the precautionary arrangement between the late Secretary of State and the British minister, and thus to preserve the peace and prevent collision between the British and American authorities pending the negotiations between the two Governments. Entertaining no doubt of the validity of our title, I need scarcely add that in any event American citizens were to be placed on a footing at least as favorable as that of British subjects, it being understood that Captain Pickett's company should remain on the island. It is proper to observe that, considering the distance from the scene of action and in ignorance of what might have transpired on the spot before the General's arrival, it was necessary to leave much to his discretion; and I am happy to state the event has proven that this discretion could not have been intrusted to more competent hands. General Scott has recently returned from his mission, having successfully accomplished its objects, and there is no longer any good reason to apprehend a collision between the forces of the two countries during the pendency of the existing negotiations.

I regret to inform you that there has been no improvement in the affairs of Mexico since my last annual message, and I am again obliged to ask the earnest attention of Congress to the unhappy condition of that Republic.

The constituent Congress of Mexico, which adjourned on the 17th February, 1857, adopted a constitution and provided for a popular election. This took place in the following July (1857), and General Comonfort was chosen President almost without opposition. At the same election a new Congress was chosen, whose first session commenced on the 16th of September (1857). By the constitution of 1857 the Presidential term was to begin on the 1st of December (1857) and continue for four years. On that day General Comonfort appeared before the assembled Congress in the City of Mexico, took the oath to support the new constitution, and **was duly inaugurated as President.** Within a month afterwards he had been driven from the capital and a military rebellion had assigned the supreme power of the Republic to General Zuloaga. The constitution provided that in the absence of the President his office should devolve upon the chief justice of the supreme court; and General Comonfort having left the country, this functionary, General Juarez, proceeded to form at Guanajuato a constitutional Government. Before this was officially known, however, at the capital the Government of Zuloaga had been recognized by the entire diplomatic corps, including the minister of the United States, as the *de facto* Government of Mexico. The constitutional President, nevertheless, maintained his position with firmness, and was soon established, with his cabinet, at Vera Cruz. Meanwhile the Government of Zuloaga was earnestly resisted in many parts of the Republic, and even in the capital, a portion of the army having pronounced against it, its functions were declared terminated, and an assembly of citizens was invited for the choice of a new President. This assembly elected General Miramon, but that officer repudiated the plan under which he was chosen, and Zuloaga was thus restored to his previous position. He assumed it, however, only to withdraw from it; and Miramon, having become by his appointment "President substitute," continues with that title at the head of the insurgent party.

In my last annual message I communicated to Congress the circumstances under which the late minister of the United States suspended his official relations with the central Government and withdrew from the country. It was impossible to maintain friendly intercourse with a government like that at the capital, under whose usurped authority wrongs were constantly committed, but never redressed. Had this been an established government, with its power extending by the consent of the people over the whole of Mexico, a resort to hostilities against it would have been quite justifiable, and, indeed, necessary. But the country was a prey to civil war, and it was hoped that the success of the constitutional President might lead to a condition of things less injurious to the United States. This success became so probable that in January last I employed a reliable agent to visit Mexico and report to me the actual condition and prospects of the contending parties. In consequence of his report and from information which reached me from other sources favorable to the prospects of the constitutional cause, I felt justified in appointing a new minister to Mexico, who might embrace the earliest suitable opportunity of restoring our diplomatic relations with that Republic. For this purpose a distinguished citizen of Maryland was selected, who proceeded on his mission on the 8th of March last, with discretionary authority to recognize the Government of President Juarez if on his arrival in Mexico he should find it entitled to such recognition according to the established practice of the United States.

On the 7th of April following Mr. McLane presented his credentials to President Juarez, having no hesitation "in pronouncing the Government of Juarez to be the only existing government of the Republic.'' He was cordially received by the authorities at Vera Cruz, and they have ever since manifested the most friendly disposition toward the United States.

Unhappily, however, the constitutional Government has not been able to establish its power over the whole Republic.

It is supported by a large majority of the people and the States, but there are important parts of the country where it can enforce no obedience.

General Miramon maintains himself at the capital, and in some of the distant Provinces there are military governors who pay little respect to the decrees of either Government. In the meantime the excesses which always attend upon civil war, especially in Mexico, are constantly recurring. Outrages of the worst description are committed both upon persons and property. There is scarcely any form of injury which has not been suffered by our citizens in Mexico during the last few years. We have been nominally at peace with that Republic, but ''so far as the interests of our commerce, or of our citizens who have visited the country as merchants, shipmasters, or in other capacities, are concerned, we might as well have been at war.'' Life has been insecure, property unprotected, and trade impossible except at a risk of loss which prudent men can not be expected to incur. Important contracts, involving large expenditures, entered into by the central Government, have been set at defiance by the local governments. Peaceful American residents, occupying their rightful possessions, have been suddenly expelled the country, in defiance of treaties and by the mere force of arbitrary power. Even the course of justice has not been safe from control, and a recent decree of Miramon permits the intervention of Government in all suits where either party is a foreigner. Vessels of the United States have been seized without law, and a consular officer who protested against such seizure has been fined and imprisoned for disrespect to the authorities. Military contributions have been levied in violation of every principle of right, and the American who resisted the lawless demand has had his property forcibly taken away and has been himself banished. From a conflict of authority in different parts of the country tariff duties which have been paid in one place have been exacted over again in another place. Large numbers of our citizens have been arrested and imprisoned without any form of examination or any opportunity for a hearing, and even when released have only obtained their liberty after much suffering and injury, and without any hope of redress. The wholesale massacre of Crabbe and his associates without trial in Sonora, as well as the seizure and murder of four sick Americans who had taken shelter in the house of an American upon the soil of the United States, was communicated to Congress at its last session. Murders of a still more atrocious character have been committed in the very heart of Mexico, under the authority of Miramon's Government, during the present year. Some of these were only worthy of a barbarous age, and if they had not been clearly proven would have seemed impossible in a country which claims to be civilized. Of this description was the brutal massacre in April last, by order of General Marquez, of three American physicians who were seized in the hospital at Tacubaya while attending upon the sick and the dying of both parties, and without trial, as without crime, were hurried away to speedy execution. Little less shocking was the recent fate of Ormond Chase, who was shot in Tepic on the 7th of August by order of the same Mexican general, not only without a trial, but without any conjecture by his friends of the cause of his arrest. He is represented as a young man of good character and intelligence, who had made numerous friends in Tepic by the courage and humanity which he had displayed on several trying occasions; and his death was as unexpected as it was shocking to the whole community. Other outrages might be enumerated, but these are sufficient to illustrate the wretched state of the country and the unprotected condition of the persons and property of our citizens in Mexico.

In all these cases our ministers have been constant and faithful in their demands for redress, but both they and this Government, which they have successively represented, have been wholly powerless to make their demands effective. Their testimony in this respect and in reference to the only remedy which in their judgments would meet the exigency has been both uniform and emphatic. "Nothing but a manifestation of the power of the Government of the United States," wrote our late minister in 1856, "and of its purpose to punish these wrongs will avail. I assure you that the universal belief here is that there is nothing to be apprehended from the Government of the United States, and that local Mexican officials can commit these outrages upon American citizens with absolute impunity." "I hope the President," wrote our present minister in August last, "will feel authorized to ask from Congress the power to enter Mexico with the military forces of the United States at the call of the constitutional authorities, in order to protect the citizens and the treaty rights of the United States. Unless such a power is conferred upon him, neither the one nor the other will be respected in the existing state of anarchy and disorder, and the outrages already perpetrated will never be chastised; and, as I assured you in my No. 23, all these evils must increase until every vestige of order and government disappears from the country." I have been reluctantly led to the same opinion, and in justice to my countrymen who have suffered wrongs from Mexico and who may still suffer them I feel bound to announce this conclusion to Congress.

The case presented, however, is not merely a case of individual claims, although our just claims against Mexico have reached a very large amount; nor is it merely the case of protection to the lives and property of the few Americans who may still remain in Mexico, although the life and property of every American citizen ought to be sacredly protected in every quarter of the world; but it is a question which relates to the future as well as to the present and the past, and which involves, indirectly at least, the whole subject of our duty to Mexico as a neighboring State. The exercise of the power of the United States in that country to redress the wrongs and protect the rights of our own citizens is none the less to be desired because efficient and necessary aid may thus be rendered at the same time to restore peace and order to Mexico itself. In the accomplishment of this result the people of the United States must necessarily feel a deep and earnest interest. Mexico ought to be a rich and prosperous and powerful Republic. She possesses an extensive territory, a fertile soil, and an incalculable store of mineral wealth. She occupies an important position between the Gulf and the ocean for transit routes and for commerce. Is it possible that such a country as this can be given up to anarchy and ruin without an effort from any quarter for its rescue and its safety? Will the commercial nations of the world, which have so many interests connected with it, remain wholly indifferent to such a result? Can the United States especially, which ought to share most largely in its commercial intercourse, allow their immediate neighbor thus to destroy itself and injure them? Yet without support from some quarter it is impossible to perceive how Mexico can resume her position among nations and enter upon a career which promises any good results. The aid which she requires, and which the interests of all commercial countries require that she should have, it belongs to this Government to render, not only by virtue of our neighborhood to Mexico, along whose territory we have a continuous frontier of nearly a thousand miles, but by virtue also of our established policy, which is inconsistent with the intervention of any European power in the domestic concerns of that Republic.

The wrongs which we have suffered from Mexico are before the world and must deeply impress every American citizen. A government which is either unable or unwilling to redress such wrongs is derelict to its highest duties. The difficulty consists in selecting and enforcing the remedy. We may in vain apply to the constitutional Government at Vera Cruz, although it is well disposed to do us justice, for adequate redress. Whilst its authority is acknowledged in all the important ports and throughout the seacoasts of the Republic, its power does not extend to the City of Mexico and the States in its vicinity, where nearly all the recent outrages have been committed on American citizens. We must penetrate into the interior before we can reach the offenders, and this can only be done by passing through the territory in the occupation of the constitutional Government. The most acceptable and least difficult mode of accomplishing the object will be to act in concert with that Government. Their consent and their aid might, I believe, be obtained; but if not, our obligation to protect our own citizens in their just rights secured by treaty would not be the less imperative. For these reasons I recommend to Congress to pass a law authorizing the President, under such conditions as they may deem expedient, to employ a sufficient military force to enter Mexico for the purpose of obtaining indemnity for the past and security for the future. I purposely refrain from any suggestion as to whether this force shall consist of regular troops or volunteers, or both. This question may be most appropriately left to the decision of Congress. I would merely observe that should volunteers be selected such a force could be easily raised in this country among those who sympathize with the sufferings of our unfortunate fellow-citizens in Mexico and with the unhappy condition of that Republic. Such an accession to the forces of the constitutional Government would enable it soon to reach the City of Mexico and extend its power over the whole Republic. In that event there is no reason to doubt that the just claims of our citizens would be satisfied and adequate redress obtained for the injuries inflicted upon them. The constitutional Government have ever evinced a strong desire to do justice, and this might be secured in advance by a preliminary treaty.

It may be said that these measures will, at least indirectly, be inconsistent with our wise and settled policy not to interfere in the domestic concerns of foreign nations. But does not the present case fairly constitute an exception? An adjoining Republic is in a state of anarchy and confusion from which she has proved wholly unable to extricate herself. She is entirely destitute of the power to maintain peace upon her borders or to prevent the incursions of banditti into our territory. In her fate and in her fortune, in her power to establish and maintain a settled government, we have a far deeper interest, socially, commercially, and politically, than any other nation. She is now a wreck upon the ocean, drifting about as she is impelled by different factions. As a good neighbor, shall we not extend to her a helping hand to save her? If we do not, it would not be surprising should some other nation undertake the task, and thus force us to interfere at last, under circumstances of increased difficulty, for the maintenance of our established policy.

I repeat the recommendation contained in my last annual message that authority may be given to the President to establish one or more temporary military posts across the Mexican line in Sonora and Chihuahua, where these may be necessary to protect the lives and property of American and Mexican citizens against the incursions and depredations of the Indians, as well as of lawless rovers, on that remote region. The establishment of one such post at a point called Arispe, in Sonora, in a country now almost depopulated by the hostile inroads of the Indians from our side of the line, would, it is believed, have prevented much injury and many cruelties during the past season. A state of lawlessness and violence prevails on that distant frontier. Life and property are there wholly insecure. The population of Arizona, now numbering more than 10,000 souls, are practically destitute of government, of laws, or of any regular administration of justice. Murder, rapine, and other crimes are committed with impunity. I therefore again call the attention of Congress to the necessity for establishing a Territorial government over Arizona.

The treaty with Nicaragua of the 16th of February, 1857, to which I referred in my last annual message, failed to receive the ratification of the Government of that Republic, for reasons which I need not enumerate. A similar treaty has been since concluded between the parties, bearing date on the 16th March, 1859, which has already been ratified by the Nicaraguan Congress. This will be immediately submitted to the Senate for their ratification. . Its provisions can not, I think, fail to be acceptable to the people of both countries.

Our claims against the Governments of Costa Rica and Nicaragua remain unredressed, though they are pressed in an earnest manner and not without hope of success.

I deem it to be my duty once more earnestly to recommend to Congress the passage of a law authorizing the President to employ the naval force at his command for the purpose of protecting the lives and property of American citizens passing in transit across the Panama, Nicaragua, and Tehuantepec routes against sudden and lawless outbreaks and depredations. I shall not repeat the arguments employed in former messages in support of this measure. Suffice it to say that the lives of many of our people and the security of vast amounts of treasure passing and repassing over one or more of these routes between the Atlantic and Pacific may be deeply involved in the action of Congress on this subject.

I would also again recommend to Congress that authority be given to the President to employ the naval force to protect American merchant vessels, their crews and cargoes, against violent and lawless seizure and confiscation in the ports of Mexico and the Spanish American States when these countries may be in a disturbed and revolutionary condition. The mere knowledge that such an authority had been conferred, as I have already stated, would of itself in a great degree prevent the evil. Neither would this require any additional appropriation for the naval service.

The chief objection urged against the grant of this authority is that Congress by conferring it would violate the Constitution; that it would be a transfer of the war-making, or, strictly speaking, the war-declaring, power to the Executive. If this were well founded, it would, of course, be conclusive. A very brief examination, however, will place this objection at rest.

Congress possess the sole and exclusive power under the Constitution "to declare war." They alone can "raise and support armies" and "provide and maintain a navy." But after Congress shall have declared war and provided the force necessary to carry it on the President, as Commander in Chief of the Army and Navy, can alone employ this force in making war against the enemy. This is the plain language, and history proves that it was the well-known intention of the framers, of the Constitution.

It will not be denied that the general "power to declare war" is without limitation and embraces within itself not only what writers on the law of nations term a public or perfect war, but also an imperfect war, and, in short, every species of hostility, however confined or limited. Without the authority of Congress the President can not fire a hostile gun in any case except to repel the attacks of an enemy. It will not be doubted that under this power Congress could, if they thought proper, authorize the President to employ the force at his command to seize a vessel belonging to an American citizen which had been illegally and unjustly captured in a foreign port and restore it to its owner. But can Congress only act after the fact, after the mischief has been done? Have they no power to confer upon the President the authority in advance to furnish instant redress should such a case afterwards occur? Must they wait until the mischief has been done, and can they apply the remedy only when it is too late? To confer this authority to meet future cases under circumstances strictly specified is as clearly within the war-declaring power as such an authority conferred upon the President by act of Congress after the deed had been done. In the progress of a great nation many exigencies must arise imperatively requiring that Congress should authorize the President to act promptly on certain conditions which may or may not afterwards arise. Our history has already presented a number of such cases. I shall refer only to the latest.

Under the resolution of June 2, 1858, "for the adjustment of difficulties with the Republic of Paraguay," the President is "authorized to adopt such measures and use such force as in his judgment may be necessary and advisable in the event of a refusal of just satisfaction by the Government of Paraguay." "Just satisfaction" for what? For "the attack on the United States steamer *Water Witch*" and "other matters referred to in the annual message of the President." Here the power is expressly granted upon the condition that the Government of Paraguay shall refuse to render this "just satisfaction." In this and other similar cases Congress have conferred upon the President power in advance to employ the Army and Navy upon the happening of contingent future events; and this most certainly is embraced within the power to declare war.

Now, if this conditional and contingent power could be constitutionally conferred upon the President in the case of Paraguay, why may it not be conferred for the purpose of protecting the lives and property of American citizens in the event that they may be violently and unlawfully attacked in passing over the transit routes to and from California or assailed by the seizure of their vessels in a foreign port? To deny this power is to render the Navy in a great degree useless for the protection of the lives and property of American citizens in countries where neither protection nor redress can be otherwise obtained.

The Thirty-fifth Congress terminated on the 3d of March, 1859, without having passed the " act making appropriations for the service of the

Post-Office Department during the fiscal year ending the 30th of June, 1860." This act also contained an appropriation "to supply deficiencies in the revenue of the Post-Office Department for the year ending 30th June, 1859." I believe this is the first instance since the origin of the Federal Government, now more than seventy years ago, when any Congress went out of existence without having passed all the general appropriation bills necessary to carry on the Government until the regular period for the meeting of a new Congress. This event imposed on the Executive a grave responsibility. It presented a choice of evils.

Had this omission of duty occurred at the first session of the last Congress, the remedy would have been plain. I might then have instantly recalled them to complete their work, and this without expense to the Government. But on the 4th of March last there were fifteen of the thirty-three States which had not elected any Representatives to the present Congress. Had Congress been called together immediately, these States would have been virtually disfranchised. If an intermediate period had been selected, several of the States would have been compelled to hold extra sessions of their legislatures, at great inconvenience and expense, to provide for elections at an earlier day than that previously fixed by law. In the regular course ten of these States would not elect until after the beginning of August, and five of these ten not until October and November.

On the other hand, when I came to examine carefully the condition of the Post-Office Department, I did not meet as many or as great difficulties as I had apprehended. Had the bill which failed been confined to appropriations for the fiscal year ending on the 30th June next, there would have been no reason of pressing importance for the call of an extra session. Nothing would become due on contracts (those with railroad companies only excepted) for carrying the mail for the first quarter of the present fiscal year, commencing on the 1st of July, until the 1st of December—less than one week before the meeting of the present Congress. The reason is that the mail contractors for this and the current year did not complete their first quarter's service until the 30th September last, and by the terms of their contracts sixty days more are allowed for the settlement of their accounts before the Department could be called upon for payment.

The great difficulty and the great hardship consisted in the failure to provide for the payment of the deficiency in the fiscal year ending the 30th June, 1859. The Department had entered into contracts, in obedience to existing laws, for the service of that fiscal year, and the contractors were fairly entitled to their compensation as it became due. The deficiency as stated in the bill amounted to $3,838,728, but after a careful settlement of all these accounts it has been ascertained that it amounts to $4,296,009. With the scanty means at his command the Postmaster-General has managed to pay that portion of this deficiency which occurred in the first two quarters of the past fiscal year, ending on the 31st

December last. In the meantime the contractors themselves, under these trying circumstances, have behaved in a manner worthy of all commendation. They had one resource in the midst of their embarrassments. After the amount due to each of them had been ascertained and finally settled according to law, this became a specific debt of record against the United States, which enabled them to borrow money on this unquestionable security. Still, they were obliged to pay interest in consequence of the default of Congress, and on every principle of justice ought to receive interest from the Government. This interest should commence from the date when a warrant would have issued for the payment of the principal had an appropriation been made for this purpose. Calculated up to the 1st December, it will not exceed $96,660—a sum not to be taken into account when contrasted with the great difficulties and embarrassments of a public and private character, both to the people and the States, which would have resulted from convening and holding a special session of Congress.

For these reasons I recommend the passage of a bill at as early a day as may be practicable to provide for the payment of the amount, with interest, due to these last-mentioned contractors, as well as to make the necessary appropriations for the service of the Post-Office Department for the current fiscal year.

The failure to pass the Post-Office bill necessarily gives birth to serious reflections. Congress, by refusing to pass the general appropriation bills necessary to carry on the Government, may not only arrest its action, but might even destroy its existence. The Army, the Navy, the judiciary, in short, every department of the Government, can no longer perform their functions if Congress refuse the money necessary for their support. If this failure should teach the country the necessity of electing a full Congress in sufficient time to enable the President to convene them in any emergency, even immediately after the old Congress has expired, it will have been productive of great good. In a time of sudden and alarming danger, foreign or domestic, which all nations must expect to encounter in their progress, the very salvation of our institutions may be staked upon the assembling of Congress without delay. If under such circumstances the President should find himself in the condition in which he was placed at the close of the last Congress, with nearly half the States of the Union destitute of representatives, the consequences might be disastrous. I therefore recommend to Congress to carry into effect the provisions of the Constitution on this subject, and to pass a law appointing some day previous to the 4th March in each year of odd number for the election of Representatives throughout all the States. They have already appointed a day for the election of electors for President and Vice-President, and this measure has been approved by the country.

I would again express a most decided opinion in favor of the construction of a Pacific railroad, for the reasons stated in my two last annual messages. When I reflect upon what would be the defenseless condition of our States and Territories west of the Rocky Mountains in case of a

PRESIDENT BUCHANAN'S NOTE TO SENATE RELATING TO
UTAH MASSACRES.

war with a naval power sufficiently strong to interrupt all intercourse with them by the routes across the Isthmus, I am still more convinced than ever of the vast importance of this railroad. I have never doubted the constitutional competency of Congress to provide for its construction, but this exclusively under the war-making power. Besides, the Constitution expressly requires as an imperative duty that "the United States shall protect each of them [the States] against invasion." I am at a loss to conceive how this protection can be afforded to California and Oregon against such a naval power by any other means. I repeat the opinion contained in my last annual message that it would be inexpedient for the Government to undertake this great work by agents of its own appointment and under its direct and exclusive control. This would increase the patronage of the Executive to a dangerous extent and would foster a system of jobbing and corruption which no vigilance on the part of Federal officials could prevent. The construction of this road ought, therefore, to be intrusted to incorporated companies or other agencies who would exercise that active and vigilant supervision over it which can be inspired alone by a sense of corporate and individual interest. I venture to assert that the additional cost of transporting troops, munitions of war, and necessary supplies for the Army across the vast intervening plains to our possessions on the Pacific Coast would be greater in such a war than the whole amount required to construct the road. And yet this resort would after all be inadequate for their defense and protection.

We have yet scarcely recovered from the habits of extravagant expenditure produced by our overflowing Treasury during several years prior to the commencement of my Administration. The financial reverses which we have since experienced ought to teach us all to scrutinize our expenditures with the greatest vigilance and to reduce them to the lowest possible point. The Executive Departments of the Government have devoted themselves to the accomplishment of this object with considerable success, as will appear from their different reports and estimates. To these I invite the scrutiny of Congress, for the purpose of reducing them still lower, if this be practicable consistent with the great public interests of the country. In aid of the policy of retrenchment, I pledge myself to examine closely the bills appropriating lands or money, so that if any of these should inadvertently pass both Houses, as must sometimes be the case, I may afford them an opportunity for reconsideration. At the same time, we ought never to forget that true public economy consists not in withholding the means necessary to accomplish important national objects confided to us by the Constitution, but in taking care that the money appropriated for these purposes shall be faithfully and frugally expended.

It will appear from the report of the Secretary of the Treasury that it is extremely doubtful, to say the least, whether we shall be able to pass through the present and the next fiscal year without providing additional revenue. This can only be accomplished by strictly confining the appropriations within the estimates of the different Departments, without making an allowance for any additional expenditures which Congress may think proper, in their discretion, to authorize, and without providing for the redemption of any portion of the $20,000,000 of Treasury notes which have been already issued. In the event of a deficiency, which I consider probable, this ought never to be supplied by a resort to additional loans. It would be a ruinous practice in the days of peace and prosperity to go on increasing the national debt to meet the ordinary expenses of the Government. This policy would cripple our resources and impair our credit in case the existence of war should render it necessary to borrow money. Should such a deficiency occur as I apprehend, I would recommend that the necessary revenue be raised by an increase of our present duties on imports. I need not repeat the opinions expressed in my last annual message as to the best mode and manner of accomplishing this object, and shall now merely observe that these have since undergone no change.

The report of the Secretary of the Treasury will explain in detail the operations of that Department of the Government.

The receipts into the Treasury from all sources during the fiscal year ending June 30, 1859, including the loan authorized by the act of June 14, 1858, and the issues of Treasury notes authorized by existing laws, were $81,692,471.01, which sum, with the balance of $6,398,316.10 remaining in the Treasury at the commencement of that fiscal year, made an aggregate for the service of the year of $88,090,787.11.

The public expenditures during the fiscal year ending June 30, 1859, amounted to $83,751,511.57. Of this sum $17,405,285.44 were applied to the payment of interest on the public debt and the redemption of the issues of Treasury notes. The expenditures for all other branches of the public service during that fiscal year were therefore $66,346,226.13.

The balance remaining in the Treasury on the 1st July, 1859, being the commencement of the present fiscal year, was $4,339,275.54.

The receipts into the Treasury during the first quarter of the present fiscal year, commencing July 1, 1859, were $20,618,865.85. Of this amount $3,821,300 was received on account of the loan and the issue of Treasury notes, the amount of $16,797,565.85 having been received during the quarter from the ordinary sources of public revenue. The estimated receipts for the remaining three quarters of the present fiscal year, to June 30, 1860, are $50,426,400. Of this amount it is estimated that $5,756,400 will be received for Treasury notes which may be reissued under the fifth section of the act of 3d March last, and $1,170,000 on account of the loan authorized by the act of June 14, 1858, making $6,926,400 from these extraordinary sources, and $43,500,000 from the ordinary sources of the public revenue, making an aggregate, with the balance in the Treasury on the 1st July, 1859, of $75,384,541.89 for the estimated means of the present fiscal year, ending June 30, 1860.

The expenditures during the first quarter of the present fiscal year were $20,007,174.76. Four million six hundred and sixty-four thousand three hundred and sixty-six dollars and seventy-six cents of this sum were applied to the payment of interest on the public debt and the redemption of the issues of Treasury notes, and the remainder, being $15,342,808, were applied to ordinary expenditures during the quarter. The estimated expenditures during the remaining three quarters, to June 30, 1860, are $40,995,558.23, of which sum $2,886,621.34 are estimated for the interest on the public debt. The ascertained and estimated expenditures for the fiscal year ending June 30, 1860, on account of the public debt are accordingly $7,550,988.10, and for the ordinary expenditures of the Government $53,451,744.89, making an aggregate of $61,002,732.99, leaving an estimated balance in the Treasury on June 30, 1860, of $14,381,808.40.

The estimated receipts during the next fiscal year, ending June 30, 1861, are $66,225,000, which, with the balance estimated, as before stated, as remaining in the Treasury on the 30th June, 1860, will make an aggregate for the service of the next fiscal year of $80,606,808.40.

The estimated expenditures during the next fiscal year, ending 30th June, 1861, are $66,714,928.79. Of this amount $3,386,621.34 will be required to pay the interest on the public debt, leaving the sum of $63,328,307.45 for the estimated ordinary expenditures during the fiscal year ending 30th June, 1861. Upon these estimates a balance will be left in the Treasury on the 30th June, 1861, of $13,891,879.61.

But this balance, as well as that estimated to remain in the Treasury on the 1st July, 1860, will be reduced by such appropriations as shall be made by law to carry into effect certain Indian treaties during the present fiscal year, asked for by the Secretary of the Interior, to the amount of $539,350; and upon the estimates of the Postmaster-General for the service of his Department the last fiscal year, ending 30th June, 1859, amounting to $4,296,009, together with the further estimate of that officer for the service of the present fiscal year, ending 30th June, 1860, being $5,526,324, making an aggregate of $10,361,683.

Should these appropriations be made as requested by the proper Departments, the balance in the Treasury on the 30th June, 1861, will not, it is estimated, exceed $3,530,196.61.

I transmit herewith the reports of the Secretaries of War, of the Navy, of the Interior, and of the Postmaster-General. They each contain valuable information and important recommendations well worthy of the serious consideration of Congress.

It will appear from the report of the Secretary of War that the Army expenditures have been materially reduced by a system of rigid economy, which in his opinion offers every guaranty that the reduction will be permanent. The estimates of the Department for the next have been reduced nearly $2,000,000 below the estimates for the present fiscal year and $500,000 below the amount granted for this year at the last session of Congress.

The expenditures of the Post-Office Department during the past fiscal year, ending on the 30th June, 1859, exclusive of payments for mail service specially provided for by Congress out of the general Treasury, amounted to $14,964,493.33 and its receipts to $7,968,484.07, showing a deficiency to be supplied from the Treasury of $6,996,009.26, against $5,235,677.15 for the year ending 30th June, 1858. The increased cost of transportation, growing out of the expansion of the service required by Congress, explains this rapid augmentation of the expenditures. It is gratifying, however, to observe an increase of receipts for the year ending on the 30th of June, 1859, equal to $481,691.21 compared with those in the year ending on the 30th June, 1858.

It is estimated that the deficiency for the current fiscal year will be $5,988,424.04, but that for the year ending 30th June, 1861, it will not exceed $1,342,473.90 should Congress adopt the measures of reform proposed and urged by the Postmaster-General. Since the month of March retrenchments have been made in the expenditures amounting to $1,826,471 annually, which, however, did not take effect until after the commencement of the present fiscal year. The period seems to have arrived for determining the question whether this Department shall become a permanent and ever-increasing charge upon the Treasury, or shall be permitted to resume the self-sustaining policy which had so long controlled its administration. The course of legislation recommended by the Postmaster-General for the relief of the Department from its present embarrassments and for restoring it to its original independence is deserving of your early and earnest consideration.

In conclusion I would again commend to the just liberality of Congress the local interests of the District of Columbia. Surely the city bearing the name of Washington, and destined, I trust, for ages to be the capital of our united, free, and prosperous Confederacy, has strong claims on our favorable regard.

JAMES BUCHANAN.

SPECIAL MESSAGES.

WASHINGTON, *December 7, 1859.*

To the Senate of the United States:

I transmit to the Senate a report from the Secretary of State and the papers referred to therein, in answer to the resolution of the Senate of the 21st of December last, in relation to the suspension of diplomatic relations with Mexico by the United States legation in that country.

JAMES BUCHANAN.

WASHINGTON, *December 16, 1859.*

To the Senate of the United States:

Having ratified the treaty between the United States and the Empire of China, pursuant to the advice and consent of the Senate as expressed in their resolution of the 15th of December last, I lost no time in forwarding my ratification thither, in the hope that it might reach that country in season to be exchanged for the ratification of the Emperor within the time limited for that purpose. Unforeseen circumstances, however, retarded the exchange until the 16th of August last. I consequently submit the instrument anew to the Senate, in order that they may declare their assent to the postponement of the exchange of the ratifications in such way as they may deem most expedient.

JAMES BUCHANAN.

WASHINGTON, *December 19, 1859.*

To the Senate of the United States:

I transmit to the Senate, with a view to ratification, a treaty of friendship, commerce, and navigation concluded at Asuncion on the 4th of February last between the plenipotentiaries of the United States and Paraguay.

JAMES BUCHANAN.

WASHINGTON, *December 19, 1859.*

To the Senate of the United States:

I transmit to the Senate, for consideration with a view to ratification, a treaty of friendship and commerce between the United States and Nicaragua, signed by their respective plenipotentiaries at Managua on the 16th March last, together with papers explanatory of the same, of which a list is herewith furnished.

I invite attention especially to the last document accompanying the treaty, being a translation of a note of 26th September ultimo from Mr. Molina, chargé d'affaires *ad interim* of Nicaragua, to the Secretary of State, together with the translation of the ratification of the treaty by the Nicaraguan Government, thereto annexed.

The amendment stipulated in the second article of the decree of ratification by Nicaragua is in conformity with the views of this Government, to which the omitted clause was obnoxious, as will be seen by reference to the note of the Secretary of State to Mr. Trisarri of 26th May, 1859, a copy of which is among the documents referred to.

JAMES BUCHANAN.

WASHINGTON, *December 19, 1859.*

To the Senate of the United States:

I transmit to the Senate, with a view to ratification, the special convention concluded at Asuncion on the 4th of February last between the plenipotentiaries of the United States and Paraguay, providing for the settlement of the claims of the United States and Paraguay Navigation Company.

JAMES BUCHANAN.

WASHINGTON, *January 4, 1860.*

To the Senate of the United States:

I transmit to the Senate, for consideration with a view to ratification, a "treaty of transits and commerce between the United States of America and the Mexican Republic," and also a "convention to enforce treaty stipulations" between the same parties, both of which were signed by the plenipotentiaries of the respective Governments at Vera Cruz on the 14th December ultimo.

I also transmit a copy of a dispatch of the minister of the United States accredited to the Mexican Government to the Secretary of State, relative to these instruments.

JAMES BUCHANAN.

WASHINGTON, *January 10, 1860.*

To the Senate of the United States:

I transmit herewith, for your constitutional action thereon, articles of agreement and convention made and concluded on the 5th day of October, 1859, with the Kansas, and recommend that the same be ratified.

JAMES BUCHANAN.

WASHINGTON, *January 10, 1860.*

To the Senate of the United States:

I transmit herewith, for your constitutional action thereon, articles of agreement and convention made and concluded on the 1st day of October, 1859, with the Sacs and Foxes of the Mississippi, and recommend that the same be ratified.

JAMES BUCHANAN.

WASHINGTON, *January 10, 1860.*

To the Senate of the United States:

I transmit herewith, for your constitutional action thereon, articles of agreement and convention made and concluded on the 15th day of April, 1859, with the Winnebagoes, and recommend that the same be ratified.

JAMES BUCHANAN.

WASHINGTON, *January 12, 1860.*

To the Senate of the United States:

In compliance with the resolution of the Senate in executive session of the 10th instant, I transmit herewith the report of the Secretary of State and the papers accompanying it, relating to the treaties lately negotiated by Mr. McLane and to the condition of the existing Government of Mexico.

It will be observed from the report that these papers are originals, and that it is indispensable they should be restored to the files of the Department when the subject to which they relate shall have been disposed of.

JAMES BUCHANAN.

WASHINGTON, *January 20, 1860.*

To the Senate of the United States:

I transmit herewith, for your constitutional action, articles of agreement and convention made and concluded on the 16th day of July, 1859, with the Chippewas of Swan Creek and Black River and the Christian Indians, and recommend that the same be ratified.

JAMES BUCHANAN.

WASHINGTON, *January 23, 1860.*

To the Senate of the United States:

In answer to the resolution of the Senate of the 12th instant, requesting information respecting an alleged outrage upon an American family at Perugia, in the Pontifical States, I transmit a report from the Secretary of State and the documents by which it is accompanied.

JAMES BUCHANAN.

WASHINGTON, *January 25, 1860.*

To the Senate of the United States:

In compliance with the resolution of the Senate of the 11th June, 1858, requesting the President of the United States, if in his judgment compatible with the public interests, to communicate to that body "such information as the Executive Departments may afford of the contracts, agreements, and arrangements which have been made and of proposals which have been received for heating and ventilating the Capitol extension, the Post-Office, and other public buildings in course of construction under the management of Captain Meigs, and of the action of the Secretary of War and Captain Meigs thereon," I transmit herewith all the papers called for by the resolution.

JAMES BUCHANAN.

WASHINGTON, *January 30, 1860.*

To the Senate of the United States:

I transmit herewith a report of the Secretary of War, with accompanying papers, in answer to the resolution of the 9th instant, requesting the President "to communicate to the Senate the official correspondence of Lieutenant-General Winfield Scott in reference to the island of San Juan, and of Brigadier-General William S. Harney, in command of the Department of Oregon."

JAMES BUCHANAN.

WASHINGTON, *February 6, 1860.*

To the Senate and House of Representatives:

I transmit a copy of a letter of the 22d of April last from the chargé a affaires *ad interim* of the United States in China, and of the regulations for consular courts which accompanied it, for such revision thereof as Congress may deem expedient, pursuant to the sixth section of the act approved the 11th of August, 1848.   JAMES BUCHANAN.

WASHINGTON, *February 9, 1860.*

To the Senate of the United States:

I transmit for the approval of the Senate an informal convention with the Republic of Venezuela for the adjustment of claims of citizens of the United States on the Government of that Republic growing out of their forcible expulsion by Venezuelan authorities from the guano island of Aves, in the Caribbean Sea.   Usually it is not deemed necessary to consult the Senate in regard to similar instruments relating to private claims of small amount when the aggrieved parties are satisfied with their terms. In this instance, however, although the convention was negotiated under the authority of the Venezuelan Executive and has been approved by the National Convention of that Republic, there is some reason to apprehend that, owing to the frequent changes in that Government, the payments for which it provides may be refused or delayed upon the pretext that the instrument has not received the constitutional sanction of this Government.   It is understood that if the payments adverted to shall be made as stipulated the convention will be acceptable to the claimants.

JAMES BUCHANAN.

WASHINGTON, *February 9, 1860.*

To the Senate of the United States:

I transmit to the Senate, for its consideration with a view to ratification, a treaty of peace, friendship, commerce, and navigation between the United States and the Republic of Bolivia, signed by their respective plenipotentiaries at La Paz on the 13th of May, 1858.

JAMES BUCHANAN.

WASHINGTON, *February 20, 1860.*

To the Senate and House of Representatives of the United States:

Eight memorials numerously signed by our fellow-citizens, "residents for the most part within the territorial limits of Kansas and Nebraska at and near the eastern slope of the Rocky Mountains," have been presented to me, containing the request that I would submit the condition of the memorialists to the two Houses of Congress in a special message. Accordingly, I transmit four of these memorials to the Senate and four to the House of Representatives.

These memorialists invoke the interposition of Congress and of the Executive "for the early extinguishment of the Indian title, a consequent survey and sale of the public land, and the establishment of an assay office in the immediate and daily reach of the citizens of that region." They also urge "the erection of a new Territory from contiguous portions of New Mexico, Utah, Kansas, and Nebraska," with the boundaries set forth in their memorial. They further state, if this request should not be granted, "that (inasmuch as during this year a census is to be taken) an enabling act be passed with provision upon condition that if on the 1st day of July, 1860, 30,000 resident inhabitants be found within the limits of the mineral region, then a Territorial government is constituted by Executive proclamation; or if on the 1st day of September, 1860, 150,000 shall be returned, then a State organization to occur."

In transmitting these memorials to Congress I recommend that such provision may be made for the protection and prosperity of our fellow-citizens at and near the eastern slope of the Rocky Mountains as their distance and the exigencies of their condition may require for their government.

JAMES BUCHANAN.

WASHINGTON, *February 25, 1860.*

To the House of Representatives:

In compliance with the resolution of the House of Representatives of the 16th instant, requesting a copy of a letter of the Emperor of France upon the subject of commerce and free trade, I transmit a report from the Secretary of State, to whom the resolution was referred.

JAMES BUCHANAN.

WASHINGTON, *February 29, 1860.*

To the Senate of the United States:

In answer to the resolution of the Senate of yesterday, requesting information with regard to the present condition of the work of marking the boundary pursuant to the first article of the treaty between the United States and Great Britain of the 15th of June, 1846, I transmit a report from the Secretary of State and the papers by which it was accompanied.

JAMES BUCHANAN.

WASHINGTON, *March 1, 1860.*

To the Senate of the United States:

I transmit herewith, in compliance with the resolution of the Senate of the 1st of February, 1860, a report from the Secretary of War, communicating the information desired relative to the payments, agreements, arrangements, etc., in connection with the heating and ventilating of the Capitol and Post-Office extensions.

JAMES BUCHANAN.

WASHINGTON, *March 5, 1860.*

To the Senate of the United States:

In compliance with the resolution of the Senate of the 23d of February, 1860, I transmit to that body a communication* of the Secretary of War, furnishing all the information requested in said resolution.

JAMES BUCHANAN.

WASHINGTON, *March 8, 1860.*

To the Senate of the United States:

I transmit herewith a report from the Secretary of State, together with the papers accompanying it, in answer to the resolution of the Senate in executive session of the 28th ultimo, calling for the instructions to our minister or ministers in Mexico which resulted in the negotiation of the treaty with that country now before the Senate.

JAMES BUCHANAN.

WASHINGTON, *March 12, 1860.*

To the Senate of the United States:

In answer to the resolution of the Senate of the 6th ultimo, requesting copies of the instructions to and dispatches from the late and from the present minister of the United States in China down to the period of the exchange of ratifications of the treaty of Tien-tsin, and also a copy of the instructions from the Department of State of February, 1857, to Mr. Parker, former commissioner in China, I transmit a report from the Secretary of State and the papers by which it was accompanied.

JAMES BUCHANAN.

WASHINGTON, *March 15, 1860.*

To the Senate of the United States:

Referring to my communication of the 5th instant to the Senate, in answer to its resolution of the 23d February, calling for any ''communication which may have been received from the governor of Texas, and the documents accompanying it, concerning alleged hostilities now existing on the Rio Grande,'' I have the honor herewith to submit for the consideration of that body the following papers:

Dispatch from the Secretary of War to the governor of Texas, dated 28th February, 1860.

Dispatch from the governor of Texas to the Secretary of War, dated 8th March, 1860.

Dispatch from Acting Secretary of War to the governor of Texas, dated 14th March, 1860.

JAMES BUCHANAN.

* Relating to disturbances on the Rio Grande between citizens and military authorities of Mexico and Texas.

WASHINGTON, *March 15, 1860.*

To the Senate of the United States:

In compliance with the resolution* of the Senate in executive session on the 12th instant, I transmit a report from the Secretary of State, with the accompanying copies of Mr. Churchwell's correspondence.

JAMES BUCHANAN.

WASHINGTON, *March 16, 1860.*

To the Senate of the United States:

I transmit herewith a report from the Acting Secretary of War, with its accompanying papers, communicating the information called for by the resolution of the Senate of the 9th instant, respecting the marble columns for the Capitol extension.

JAMES BUCHANAN.

WASHINGTON, *March 16, 1860.*

To the Senate and House of Representatives:

I transmit a copy of the convention between the United States and the Republic of Paraguay, concluded on the 4th February, 1859, and proclaimed on the 12th instant, and invite the attention of Congress to the expediency of such legislation as may be deemed necessary to carry into effect the stipulations of the convention relative to the organization of the commission provided for therein.

The commissioner on the part of Paraguay is now in this city, and is prepared to enter upon the duties devolved upon the joint commission.

JAMES BUCHANAN.

WASHINGTON, *March 21, 1860.*

To the Senate of the United States:

In compliance with the request of the Senate contained in their resolution of yesterday, the 20th instant, I return to them the resolution of the 16th instant, "that the Senate do not advise and consent to the ratification of the treaty of friendship and commerce between the United States and Nicaragua, signed at Managua on the 16th day of March, 1859." I also return the treaty itself, presuming that the Senate so intended.

JAMES BUCHANAN.

WASHINGTON, *March 22, 1860.*

To the Senate of the United States:

I transmit to the Senate, for its consideration with a view to ratification, a convention concluded on the 21st instant between the United States and His Majesty the King of Sweden and Norway for the mutual surrender of fugitive criminals.

JAMES BUCHANAN.

* Calling for the report of the agent sent to Mexico to ascertain the condition of that country.

WASHINGTON, *March 29, 1860.*

To the Senate of the United States:

In compliance with the resolution of the Senate of the 21st of March, 1860, requesting the President of the United States "to inform the Senate, if in his opinion it be not incompatible with the public interest, if any instructions have been given to any of the officers of the Navy of the United States by which, in any event, the naval force of the United States or any part thereof were to take part in the civil war now existing in Mexico, and if the recent capture of two war steamers of Mexico by the naval force of the United States was done in pursuance of orders issued by this Government, and also by what authority those steamers have been taken in possession by the naval force of the United States and the men on board made prisoners," I transmit the inclosed report, with accompanying papers, from the Secretary of the Navy.

JAMES BUCHANAN.

WASHINGTON, *March 29, 1860.*

To the House of Representatives:

I transmit herewith a report of the Secretary of War, with its accompaniments, communicating the information called for by the resolution of the House of Representatives of the 1st instant, concerning the difficulties on the southwestern frontier.

JAMES BUCHANAN.

WASHINGTON, *March 30, 1860.*

To the House of Representatives:

In answer to the resolution of the 26th instant, requesting information touching the imprisonment of an American citizen in the island of Cuba, I transmit a report from the Secretary of State and the documents by which it was accompanied.

JAMES BUCHANAN.

WASHINGTON, *April 2, 1860.*

To the Senate of the United States:

In compliance with the resolution of the Senate of the 28th of February last, relative to the uniform or costume of persons in the diplomatic or consular service, I transmit a report from the Secretary of State and the papers by which it was accompanied.

JAMES BUCHANAN.

WASHINGTON CITY, *April 3, 1860.*

To the Senate of the United States:

I herewith transmit to the Senate a report of the Attorney-General, in answer to a resolution of the Senate of the 21st of March, "that the

President be respectfully requested to communicate to the Senate the correspondence between the judges of Utah and the Attorney-General or the President with reference to the legal proceedings and condition of affairs in the Territory of Utah.''

JAMES BUCHANAN.

WASHINGTON, *April 5, 1860.*

To the Senate of the United States:

I transmit, for the consideration of the Senate with a view to ratification, a treaty of friendship, commerce, and navigation between the United States and the Republic of Honduras, signed by the plenipotentiaries of the parties in this city on the 28th day of last month.

The fourteenth article of this treaty is an exact copy of the supplemental article of the "treaty of friendship, commerce, and navigation between Great Britain and the Republic of Honduras," dated 26th day of August, 1856, with the necessary changes in names and dates. Under this article the Government and people of the United States will enjoy in the fullest and most satisfactory manner the use of the "Honduras Interoceanic Railway," in consideration of which the United States recognizes the rights of sovereignty and property of Honduras over the line of the road and guarantees its neutrality, and, when "the road shall have been completed, equally engages, in conjunction with Honduras, to protect the same from interruption, seizure, or unjust confiscation, from whatever quarter the attempt may proceed.''

This treaty is in accordance with the policy inaugurated by the Government of the United States, and in an especial manner by the Senate, in the year 1846, and several treaties have been concluded to carry it into effect. It is simple, and may be embraced in a few words. On the one side a grant of free and uninterrupted transit for the Government and people of the United States over the transit routes across the Isthmus, and on the other a guaranty of the neutrality and protection of these routes, not only for the benefit of the Republics through which they pass, but, in the language of our treaty with New Granada, in order to secure to themselves the tranquil and constant enjoyment of these interoceanic communications.

The first in the series of these treaties is that with New Granada of the 12th December, 1846. This treaty was concluded before our acquisition of California and when our interests on the Pacific Coast were of far less magnitude than at the present day. For years before this period, however, the routes across the Isthmus had attracted the serious attention of this Government.

This treaty, after granting us the right of transit across the Isthmus of Panama in the most ample terms, binds this Government to guarantee to New Granada "the perfect neutrality of the before-mentioned Isthmus, with the view that the free transit from the one to the other sea may not be interrupted or embarrassed in any future time while this treaty exists."

In one respect it goes further than any of its successors, because it not only guarantees the neutrality of the route itself, but "the rights of sovereignty and property" of New Granada over the entire Province of Panama. It is worthy of remark that when it was sent to the Senate it was accompanied by a message of President Polk, dated February 10, 1847, in which the attention of that body was especially called to these important stipulations of the thirty-fifth article, and in which it was stated, moreover, that our chargé d'affaires who negotiated the treaty "acted in this particular upon his own responsibility and without instructions." Under these circumstances the treaty was approved by the Senate and the transit policy to which I have referred was deliberately adopted. A copy of the executive document (confidential), Twenty-ninth Congress, second session, containing this message of President Polk and the papers which accompanied it is hereto annexed.

The next in order of time of these treaties of transit and guaranty is that of the 19th April, 1850, with Great Britain, commonly called the Clayton and Bulwer treaty. This treaty, in affirmance of the policy of the New Granada treaty, established a general principle which has ever since, I believe, guided the proceedings of both Governments. The eighth article of that treaty contains the following stipulations:

The Government of the United States having not only desired in entering into this convention to accomplish a particular object, but also to establish a general principle, they hereby agree to extend their protection by treaty stipulations to any other practicable communications, whether by canal or railway, across the isthmus which connects North and South America, and especially to the interoceanic communications, should the same prove to be practicable, whether by canal or railway, which are now proposed to be established by the way of Tehuantepec or Panama.

And that the said—

Canals or railways shall also be open on like terms to the citizens and subjects of every other state which is willing to grant thereto such protection as the United States and Great Britain propose to afford.

The United States, in a short time after the Clayton and Bulwer treaty was concluded, carried this stipulation in regard to the Tehuantepec route into effect by their treaty with Mexico of the 30th December, 1853. The eighth article of this treaty, after granting to us the transit privileges therein mentioned, stipulates that "the Mexican Government having agreed to protect with its whole power the prosecution, preservation, and security of the work, the United States may extend its protection as it shall judge wise, to use it when it may feel sanctioned and warranted by the public or international law."

This is a sweeping grant of power to the United States, which no nation ought to have conceded, but which, it is believed, has been confined within safe limits by our treaty with Mexico now before the Senate.

Such was believed to be the established policy of the Government at the commencement of this Administration, viz, the grant of transits in our favor and the guaranty of our protection as an equivalent. This guaranty can never be dangerous under our form of government, because it can never be carried into execution without the express authority of Congress. Still, standing on the face of treaties, as it does, it deters all evil-disposed parties from interfering with these routes.

Under such circumstances the attention of the Executive was early turned to the Nicaragua route as in many respects the most important and valuable to the citizens of our country. In concluding a treaty to secure our rights of transit over this route I experienced many difficulties, which I need not now enumerate, because they are detailed in different messages to Congress. Finally a treaty was negotiated exactly in accordance with the established policy of the Government and the views of the Executive, and clear from the embarrassments which might arise under the phraseology of previous treaties. The fourteenth article of the treaty contains a full, clear, and specific grant of the right of transit to the United States and their citizens, and is believed to be perfectly unexceptionable. The fifteenth article, instead of leaving one equivalent duty of protection, general and unlimited, as in our treaty with New Granada and in the Clayton and Bulwer treaty, or instead of that general right assured to the Government in the Mexican treaty of extending its protection as it shall itself judge wise, when it may feel sanctioned and warranted by the public or international law, confines the interference conceded within just and specific limits.

Under the sixteenth article of this treaty the Government of the United States has no right to interpose for the protection of the Nicaragua route except with the consent or at the request of the Government of Nicaragua, or of the minister thereof at Washington, or of the competent, legally appointed local authorities, civil or military; and when in the opinion of the Government of Nicaragua the necessity ceases such force shall be immediately withdrawn. Nothing can be more carefully guarded than this provision. No force can be employed unless upon the request of the Government of Nicaragua, and it must be immediately withdrawn whenever in the opinion of that Government the necessity ceases.

When Congress shall come to adopt the measures necessary to carry this provision of the treaty into effect they can guard it from any abuses which may possibly arise.

The general policy contained in these articles, although inaugurated by the United States, has been fully adopted by the Governments of Great Britain and France. The plenipotentiaries of both these Governments have recently negotiated treaties with Nicaragua, which are but transcripts of the treaty between the United States and Nicaragua now before the Senate. The treaty with France has been ratified, it is understood, by both the French and Nicaraguan Governments, and is now in operation. That with Great Britain has been delayed by other negotiations in Nicaragua, but it is believed that these are now concluded and that the ratifications of the British treaty will soon, therefore, be exchanged.

It is presumed that no objection will be made to "the exceptional case" of the sixteenth article, which is only intended to provide for the landing of sailors or marines from our vessels which may happen to be within reach of the point of difficulty, in order to protect the lives and property of citizens of the United States from unforeseen and imminent danger.

The same considerations may be suggested with respect to the fifth article of the treaty with Mexico, which is also pending before the Senate. This article is an exact copy of the sixteenth article, just referred to, of the treaty with Nicaragua.

The treaty with Honduras, which is now submitted to the Senate, follows on this subject the language of the British treaty with that Republic, and is not, therefore, identical in its terms with the Nicaraguan and Mexican treaties. The same policy, however, has been adopted in all of them, and it will not fail, I am persuaded, to receive from the Senate all that consideration which it so eminently deserves. The importance to the United States of securing free and safe transit routes across the American Isthmus can not well be overestimated. These routes are of great interest, of course, to all commercial nations, but they are especially so to us from our geographical and political position as an American State and because they furnish a necessary communication between our Atlantic and Pacific States and Territories.

The Government of the United States can never permit these routes to be permanently interrupted, nor can it safely allow them to pass under the control of other rival nations. While it seeks no exclusive privileges upon them for itself, it can never consent to be made tributary to their use to any European power. It is worthy of consideration, however, whether to some extent it would not necessarily become so if after Great Britain and France have adopted our policy and made treaties with the Isthmian Governments in pursuance of it we should ourselves reconsider it and refuse to pursue it in the treaties of the United States. I might add that the opening of these transit routes can not fail to extend the trade and commerce of the United States with the countries through which they pass; to afford an outlet and a market for our manufactures within their territories; to encourage American citizens to develop their vast stores of mining and mineral wealth for our benefit, and to introduce among them a wholesome American influence calculated to prevent revolutions and to render their governments stable.

JAMES BUCHANAN.

WASHINGTON, *April 10, 1860.*

To the House of Representatives:

I communicate herewith a report from the Secretary of State, in reply to the resolution of the House of Representatives of the 6th instant, respecting the expulsion of American citizens from Mexico and the confiscation of their property by General Miramon.

JAMES BUCHANAN.

WASHINGTON, *April 10, 1860.*

To the House of Representatives:

In compliance with the resolution of the House of Representatives of the 23d of December, 1858, requesting information in regard to the duties on tobacco in foreign countries, I transmit a report from the Secretary of State and the documents by which it was accompanied.

JAMES BUCHANAN.

WASHINGTON, D. C., *April 11, 1860.*

To the House of Representatives of the United States:

In compliance with the resolution of the House of Representatives of March 26, 1860, requesting me "to transmit to the House all information in the possession of the officer in charge of the Coast Survey showing the practicability of making Harlem River navigable for commercial purposes, and the expenses thereof," I herewith transmit a report from the Secretary of the Treasury containing the desired information.

JAMES BUCHANAN.

WASHINGTON, *April 11, 1860.*

To the Senate of the United States:

In compliance with the resolution of the Senate of the 2d February, 1859, requesting information in regard to the compulsory enlistment of citizens of the United States in the army of Prussia, I transmit a report from the Secretary of State and the documents by which it was accompanied.

JAMES BUCHANAN.

WASHINGTON, *April 12, 1860.*

To the Senate of the United States:

In compliance with the resolution of the Senate of the 23d of February last, requesting information in regard to the occupation by American citizens of the island of Navassa, in the West Indies, I transmit a report from the Secretary of State and the documents by which it was accompanied.

JAMES BUCHANAN.

WASHINGTON, *April 12, 1860.*

To the House of Representatives:

I transmit herewith a report of the Secretary of War, with its accompaniments, communicating the information called for by the resolution of the House of Representatives of the 20th ultimo, respecting Indian hostilities in New Mexico.   JAMES BUCHANAN.

WASHINGTON, *April 16. 1860.*

To the Senate of the United States:

In compliance with the resolution of the Senate of the 4th instant, requesting information not heretofore called for relating to the claim of any foreign governments to the military services of naturalized American citizens, I transmit a report from the Secretary of State and the documents by which it was accompanied.   JAMES BUCHANAN.

WASHINGTON, D. C., *April 17, 1860.*

To the Senate of the United States:

I transmit herewith, for the information of the Senate, the Paris Moniteur of the 4th February last, the official journal of the French Government, containing an imperial decree promulgating a treaty of friendship, commerce, and navigation, concluded on the 11th April, 1859, between France and the Republic of Nicaragua. It will be found in all respects similar to the treaty between the United States and Nicaragua now pending in the Senate.   JAMES BUCHANAN.

WASHINGTON, *April 20, 1860.*

To the House of Representatives:

I transmit herewith a report of the Secretary of the Navy, to whom was referred the resolution of the House of Representatives of April 10, 1860, requesting the President to communicate to the House, in addition to the information asked in the resolution adopted in reference to the African slave trade, "the number of officers and men in the service of the United States belonging to the African Squadron who have died in that service since the date of the Ashburton treaty up to the present time."   JAMES BUCHANAN.

WASHINGTON, *April 20, 1860.*

To the House of Representatives:

In answer to the resolution of the House of Representatives "that the President be requested to communicate to the House, if not incompatible with the public service, all such information as he may possess in relation to the existence " of the Territory of Minnesota, he has to state that he possesses no information upon the subject except what has been derived from the acts of Congress and the proceedings of the House itself. Since the date of the act of the 11th of May, 1858, admitting a portion of the Territory of Minnesota as a State into the Union, no act has been performed by the Executive either affirming or denying the existence of such Territory. The question in regard to that portion of the Territory without the limits of the existing State remains for the decision of Congress, and is in the same condition it was when the State was admitted into the Union. JAMES BUCHANAN.

WASHINGTON, *April 22, 1860.*

To the Senate of the United States:

I return to the Senate the original convention between the United States and the Republic of New Granada, signed on the 10th September, 1857, and ratified by me as amended by the Senate on the 12th March, 1859.

The amendments of the Senate were immediately transmitted to New Granada for acceptance, but they arrived at Bogota three days after the adjournment of the Congress of that Republic, notwithstanding the session had been protracted for twenty days solely with a view to the consideration of the convention after it should have received the sanction of this Government.

At the earliest moment after the assembling of the New Granadian Congress, on the 1st of February last, the convention as amended and ratified was laid before that body, and on the 25th of the same month it was approved with the amendments. Inasmuch, however, as the period had expired within which by the third amendment of the Senate the ratifications should have been exchanged, the Congress of New Granada provided that "the convention should be ratified and the ratification should be exchanged at whatever time the Governments of the two Republics may deem convenient for the purpose, and therefore the period has been extended which the Senate of the United States had fixed."

The expediency of authorizing the exchange of ratifications at such time as may be convenient to the two Governments is consequently submitted to the consideration of the Senate. JAMES BUCHANAN.

WASHINGTON, *April 23, 1860.*

To the Senate of the United States:

In answer to the resolution of the Senate of the 18th instant, requesting a copy of the instructions from the Department of State to Mr. McLane when appointed minister to China, I transmit a report from the Secretary of State, with the instructions which accompanied it. JAMES BUCHANAN.

WASHINGTON, *April 24, 1860.*

To the House of Representatives:

In compliance with the resolutions of the House of Representatives of the 2d March, 1859, and of the 26th ultimo, requesting information relative to discriminations in Switzerland against citizens of the United States of the Hebrew persuasion, I transmit a report of the Secretary of State, with the documents by which it was accompanied.

JAMES BUCHANAN.

WASHINGTON, *April 25, 1860.*

To the Senate of the United States:

In compliance with a resolution of the Senate of the 22d ultimo, calling for information concerning the expulsion from Prussia of Eugene Dullye, a naturalized citizen of the United States, I transmit a report from the Secretary of State, dated the 24th instant.

JAMES BUCHANAN.

WASHINGTON, *April 27, 1860.*

To the House of Representatives:

In compliance with the resolution of the House of Representatives of March 26, 1860, requesting "copies of all official correspondence between the civil and military officers stationed in Utah Territory with the heads or bureaus of their respective Departments, or between any of said officers, illustrating or tending to show the condition of affairs in said Territory since the 1st day of October, 1857, and which may not have been heretofore officially published," I transmit reports from the Secretaries of State and War and the documents by which they were accompanied.

JAMES BUCHANAN.

WASHINGTON, *April 30, 1860.*

To the Senate of the United States:

In compliance with the resolution of the Senate of the 2d of February, 1859, requesting information in regard to the compulsory service of citizens of the United States in the army of Prussia, I transmit an additional report from the Secretary of State and the document by which it is accompanied.

JAMES BUCHANAN.

EXECUTIVE MANSION, *May 1, 1860.*

To the Senate:

In compliance with the resolution of the Senate adopted March 19, 1860, calling for the correspondence, etc., in relation to the Mountain Meadow and other massacres in Utah Territory, I have the honor to transmit the report, with the accompanying documents, of the Secretary of the Interior, who was instructed to collect the information.

JAMES BUCHANAN.

WASHINGTON, *May 3, 1860.*

To the Senate of the United States:

I transmit to the Senate, for its consideration with a view to ratification, a convention between the United States and Spain for the settlement of claims, signed at Madrid on the 5th of March last.

JAMES BUCHANAN.

WASHINGTON, *May 19, 1860.*

To the Senate and House of Representatives:

On the 26th day of April last Lieutenant Craven, of the United States steamer *Mohawk*, captured the slaver *Wildfire* on the coast of Cuba, with 507 African negroes on board. The prize was brought into Key West on the 31st April and the negroes were delivered into the custody of Fernando J. Moreno, marshal of the southern district of Florida.

The question which now demands immediate decision is, What disposition shall be made of these Africans? In the annual message to Congress of December 6, 1858, I expressed my opinion in regard to the construction of the act of the 3d March, 1819, "in addition to the acts prohibiting the slave trade," so far as the same is applicable to the present case. From this I make the following extract:

Under the second section of this act the President is "authorized to make such regulations and arrangements as he may deem expedient for the safe-keeping, support, and removal beyond the limits of the United States of all such negroes, mulattoes, or persons of color" captured by vessels of the United States as may be delivered to the marshal of the district into which they are brought, "and to appoint a proper person or persons residing upon the coast of Africa as agent or agents for receiving the negroes, mulattoes, or persons of color delivered from on board vessels seized in the prosecution of the slave trade by commanders of United States armed vessels."

A doubt immediately arose as to the true construction of this act. It is quite clear from its terms that the President was authorized to provide "for the safe-keeping, support, and removal" of these negroes up till the time of their delivery to the agent on the coast of Africa, but no express provision was made for their protection and support after they had reached the place of their destination. Still, an agent was to be appointed to receive them in Africa, and it could not have been supposed that Congress intended he should desert them at the moment they were received and turn them loose on that inhospitable coast to perish for want of food or to become again the victims of the slave trade. Had this been the intention of Congress, the employment of an agent to receive them, who is required to reside on the coast, was unnecessary, and they might have been landed by our vessels anywhere in Africa and left exposed to the sufferings and the fate which would certainly await them.

Mr. Monroe, in his special message of December 17, 1819, at the first session after the act was passed, announced to Congress what in his opinion was its true construction. He believed it to be his duty under it to follow these unfortunates into Africa and make provision for them there until they should be able to provide for themselves. In communicating this interpretation of the act to Congress he stated that some doubt had been entertained as to its true intent and meaning, and he submitted the question to them so that they might, "should it be deemed advisable, amend the same before further proceedings are had under it." Nothing was done by Congress to explain the act, and Mr. Monroe proceeded to carry it into execution according to his own interpretation. This, then, became the practical construction.

Adopting this construction of President Monroe, I entered into an agreement with the Colonization Society, dated 7th September, 1858, to receive the Africans which had been captured on the slaver *Echo* from the agent of the United States in Liberia, to furnish them during the period of one year thereafter with comfortable shelter, clothing, and provisions, and to cause them to be instructed in the arts of civilized life suitable to their condition, at the rate of $150 for each individual. It was believed that within that period they would be prepared to become citizens of Liberia and to take care of themselves.

As Congress was not then in session and as there was no outstanding appropriation applicable to this purpose, the society were obliged to depend for payment on the future action of that body. I recommended this appropriation, and $75,000 were granted by the act of 3d March, 1859 (the consular and diplomatic bill), "to enable the President of the United States to carry into effect the act of Congress of 3d March, 1819, and any subsequent acts now in force for the suppression of the slave trade." Of this appropriation there remains unexpended the sum of $24,350.90, after deducting from it an advance made by the Secretary of the Interior out of the judiciary fund of $11,348.10.

I regret to say that under the mode adopted in regard to the Africans captured on board the *Echo* the expense will be large, but this seems to a great extent to be inevitable without a violation of the laws of humanity. The expenditure upon this scale for those captured on board the *Wildfire* will not be less than $100,000, and may considerably exceed that sum. Still, it ought to be observed that during the period when the Government itself, through its own agents, undertook the task of providing for captured negroes in Africa the cost per head was much greater than that which I agreed to pay the Colonization Society.

But it will not be sufficient for Congress to limit the amount appropriated to the case of the *Wildfire*. It is probable, judging from the increased activity of the slave trade and the vigilance of our cruisers, that several similar captures may be made before the end of the year. An appropriation ought therefore to be granted large enough to cover such contingencies.

The period has arrived when it is indispensable to provide some specific legislation for the guidance of the Executive on this subject. With this view I would suggest that Congress might authorize the President to enter into a general agreement with the Colonization Society binding them to receive on the coast of Africa, from an agent there, all the captured Africans which may be delivered to him, and to maintain them for a limited period, upon such terms and conditions as may combine humanity toward these unfortunates with a just economy. This would obviate the necessity of making a new bargain with every new capture and would prevent delay and avoid expense in the disposition of the captured. The law might then provide that in all cases where this may be practicable the captor should carry the negroes directly to Africa and deliver them to the American agent there, afterwards bringing the captured vessel to the United States for adjudication.

The capturing officer, in case he should bring his prize directly to the United States, ought to be required to land the negroes in some one or more ports, to be designated by Congress, where the prevailing health throughout the year is good. At these ports cheap but permanent accommodations might be provided for the negroes until they could be sent away, without incurring the expense of erecting such accommodations at every port where the capturing officer may think proper to enter. On the present occasion these negroes have been brought to Key West, and, according to the estimate presented by the marshal of the southern district of Florida to the Secretary of the Interior, the cost of providing temporary quarters for them will be $2,500 and the aggregate expenses for the single month of May will amount to $12,000. But this is far from being the worst evil. Within a few weeks the yellow fever will most probably prevail at Key West, and hence the marshal urges their removal from their present quarters at an early day, which must be done, in any event, as soon as practicable. For these reasons I earnestly commend this subject to the immediate attention of Congress. I transmit herewith a copy of the letter and estimate of Fernando J. Moreno, marshal of the southern district of Florida, to the Secretary of the Interior, dated 10th May, 1860, together with a copy of the letter of the Secretary of the Interior to myself, dated 16th May.

It is truly lamentable that Great Britain and the United States should be obliged to expend such a vast amount of blood and treasure for the suppression of the African slave trade, and this when the only portions of the civilized world where it is tolerated and encouraged are the Spanish islands of Cuba and Porto Rico.

JAMES BUCHANAN.

WASHINGTON, *May 22, 1860.*

To the Senate and House of Representatives:

I transmit herewith the copy of a letter, dated yesterday, from the Secretary of the Interior, communicating the copy of a letter addressed to him on the 13th instant by Fernando J. Moreno, marshal of the southern district of Florida. From this it appears that Lieutenant Stanly, of the United States steamer *Wyandotte*, captured the bark *William*, with about 550 African negroes on board, on the south side of Cuba, near the Isle of Pines, and brought her into Key West on the 12th instant. These negroes have doubtless been delivered to the marshal, and with those captured on board the *Wildfire* will make the number in his custody about 1,000.   More may be daily expected at Key West, which, both on account of a deficiency of water and provisions and its exposure to yellow fever, is one of the worst spots for an African negro depot which could be found on the coast of the United States.

JAMES BUCHANAN.

WASHINGTON, May 22, 1860.

To the House of Representatives:

In answer to the resolution passed on the 26th of March last, calling for a detailed statement of the expenditures from the "appropriations made during the first session of the Thirty-fourth Congress and the first and second sessions of the Thirty-fifth Congress for legal assistance and other necessary expenditures in the disposal of private land claims in California and for the service of special counsel and other extraordinary expenses of such land claims, amounting in all to $114,000," I have the honor to transmit to the House of Representatives a report of the Attorney-General, which, with the accompanying documents, contains the information required.

JAMES BUCHANAN.

WASHINGTON, May 26, 1860.

To the House of Representatives:

In compliance with the resolution of the House of Representatives of the 21st instant, requesting any information recently received respecting the Chinese cooly trade which has not been heretofore communicated to Congress, I transmit a report from the Secretary of State, with the documents which accompanied it.

JAMES BUCHANAN.

WASHINGTON, June 14, 1860.

To the Senate of the United States:

I submit, for the consideration of the Senate, articles of agreement and convention with the Delaware Indians, concluded May 13, 1860.   I concur in the recommendation of the Secretary of the Interior that the treaty should be ratified, with the amendments suggested by the Commissioner of Indian Affairs.

JAMES BUCHANAN.

JUNE 23, 1860.

To the Senate and House of Representatives.

GENTLEMEN: I feel it my duty to communicate to you that it has been found impracticable to conclude a contract for the transportation of the mails between our Atlantic and Pacific ports on the terms authorized by the fourth section of an act entitled "An act making appropriations for the service of the Post-Office Department during the fiscal year ending

30th June, 1861," approved 15th June, 1860. The Postmaster-General has offered the California mails to the several companies and shipowners engaged in the trade with the Pacific via the Isthmus, but they have all declined carrying them for the postages. They demand a higher rate of compensation, and unless power is given to the Postmaster-General to accede to this demand I am well satisfied that these mails can not be forwarded. It should not be forgotten that, in consequence of the diversion of a large part of the letter mail to the overland route, the postages derived from the California service have been greatly reduced and afford a wholly inadequate remuneration for the ocean transportation. The weight of these mails, averaging from 12 to 15 tons semimonthly, renders it, in view of the climate and character of the road, manifestly impossible to forward them overland without involving an expenditure which no wise administration of the Government would impose upon the Treasury. I therefore earnestly recommend that the act referred to be so modified as to empower the Postmaster-General to provide for carrying the California mails at a rate of compensation which may be deemed reasonable and just.

JAMES BUCHANAN.

WASHINGTON, *June 25, 1860.*

To the House of Representatives:

I have approved and signed the bill entitled "An act making appropriation for sundry civil expenses of the Government for the year ending the 30th of June, 1861."

In notifying the House of my approval of this bill I deem it proper, under the peculiar circumstances of the case, to make a few explanatory observations, so that my course may not hereafter be misunderstood.

Amid a great variety of important appropriations, this bill contains an appropriation "for the completion of the Washington Aqueduct, $500,000, to be expended according to the plans and estimates of Captain Meigs and under his superintendence: *Provided*, That the office of engineer of the Potomac Waterworks is hereby abolished and its duties shall hereafter be discharged by the chief engineer of the Washington Aqueduct." To this appropriation, for a wise and beneficial object, I have not the least objection. It is true I had reason to believe when the last appropriation was made of $800,000 on the 12th of June, 1858, "*for the completion of the Washington Aqueduct,*" this would have been sufficient for the purpose. It is now discovered, however, that it will require half a million more "*for the completion of the Washington Aqueduct,*" and this ought to be granted.

The Captain Meigs to whom the bill refers is Montgomery C. Meigs, a captain in the Corps of Engineers of the Army of the United States, who has superintended this work from its commencement under the authority of the late and present Secretary of War.

Had this appropriation been made in the usual form, no difficulty could have arisen upon it. This bill, however, annexes a declaration to the appropriation that the money is to be expended under the superintendence of Captain Meigs.

The first aspect in which this clause presented itself to my mind was that it interfered with the right of the President to be "Commander in Chief of the Army and Navy of the United States." If this had really been the case, there would have been an end to the question. Upon further examination I deemed it impossible that Congress could have intended to interfere with the clear right of the President to command the Army and to order its officers to any duty he might deem most expedient for the public interest. If they could withdraw an officer from the command of the President and select him for the performance of an executive duty, they might upon the same principle annex to an appropriation to carry on a war a condition requiring it not to be used for the defense of the country unless a particular person of its own selection should command the Army. It was impossible that Congress could have had such an intention, and therefore, according to my construction of the clause in question, it merely designated Captain Meigs as its preference for the work, without intending to deprive the President of the power to order him to any other army duty for the performance of which he might consider him better adapted. Still, whilst this clause may not be, and I believe is not, a violation of the Constitution, yet how destructive it would be to all proper subordination and how demoralizing its effect upon the morale of the Army if it should become a precedent for future legislation! Officers might then be found, instead of performing their appropriate duties, besieging the halls of Congress for the purpose of obtaining special favors and choice places by legislative enactment. Under these circumstances I have deemed it but fair to inform Congress that whilst I do not consider the bill unconstitutional, this is only because, in my opinion, Congress did not intend by the language which they have employed to interfere with my absolute authority to order Captain Meigs to any other service I might deem expedient. My perfect right still remains, notwithstanding the clause, to send him away from Washington to any part of the Union to superintend the erection of a fortification or on any other appropriate duty.

It has been alleged, I think without sufficient cause, that this clause is unconstitutional because it has created a new office and has appointed Captain Meigs to perform its duties. If it had done this, it would have been a clear question, because Congress have no right to appoint to any office, this being specially conferred upon the President and Senate. It is evident that Congress intended nothing more by this clause than to express a decided opinion that Captain Meigs should be continued in the employment to which he had been previously assigned by competent authority.

It is not improbable that another question of grave importance may arise out of this clause. Is the appropriation conditional and will it fall provided I do not deem it proper that it shall be expended under the superintendence of Captain Meigs? This is a question which shall receive serious consideration, because upon its decision may depend whether the completion of the waterworks shall be arrested for another season. It is not probable that Congress could have intended that this great and important work should depend upon the various casualties and vicissitudes incident to the natural or official life of a single officer of the Army. This would be to make the work subordinate to the man, and not the man to the work, and to reverse our great axiomatic rule of "principles, not men." I desire to express no opinion upon the subject. Should the question ever arise, it shall have my serious consideration.

JAMES BUCHANAN.

VETO MESSAGES.*

WASHINGTON CITY, *February 1, 1860.*

To the Senate of the United States:

On the last day of the last Congress a bill, which had passed both Houses, entitled "An act making an appropriation for deepening the channel over the St. Clair flats, in the State of Michigan," was presented to me for approval.

It is scarcely necessary to observe that during the closing hours of a session it is impossible for the President on the instant to examine into the merits or demerits of an important bill, involving, as this does, grave questions both of expediency and of constitutional power, with that care and deliberation demanded by his public duty as well as by the best interests of the country. For this reason the Constitution has in all cases allowed him ten days for deliberation, because if a bill be presented to him within the last ten days of the session he is not required to return it, either with an approval or a veto, but may retain it, "in which case it shall not be a law." Whilst an occasion can rarely occur when so long a period as ten days would be required to enable the President to decide whether he should approve or veto a bill, yet to deny him even two days on important questions before the adjournment of each session for this purpose, as recommended by a former annual message, would not only be unjust to him, but a violation of the spirit of the Constitution. To require him to approve a bill when it is impossible he could examine into its merits would be to deprive him of the exercise of his constitutional discretion and convert him into a mere register of

* The messages of February 1 and February 6, 1860, are pocket vetoes.

the decrees of Congress. I therefore deem it a sufficient reason for having retained the bill in question that it was not presented to me until the last day of the session.

Since the termination of the last Congress I have made a thorough examination of the questions involved in the bill to deepen the channel over the St. Clair flats, and now proceed to express the opinions which I have formed upon the subject; and

1. Even if this had been a mere question of expediency, it was, to say the least, extremely doubtful whether the bill ought to have been approved, because the object which Congress intended to accomplish by the appropriation which it contains of $55,000 had been already substantially accomplished. I do not mean to allege that the work had been completed in the best manner, but it was sufficient for all practical purposes.

The St. Clair flats are formed by the St. Clair River, which empties into the lake of that name by several mouths, and which forms a bar or shoal on which in its natural state there is not more than 6 or 7 feet of water. This shoal is interposed between the mouth of the river and the deep water of the lake, a distance of 6,000 feet, and in its natural condition was a serious obstruction to navigation. The obvious remedy for this was to deepen a channel through these flats by dredging, so as to enable vessels which could navigate the lake and the river to pass through this intermediate channel. This object had been already accomplished by previous appropriations, but without my knowledge, when the bill was presented to me. Captain Whipple, of the Topographical Engineers, to whom the expenditure of the last appropriation of $45,000 for this purpose in 1856 was intrusted, in his annual report of the 1st October, 1858, stated that the dredging was discontinued on the 26th August, 1858, when a channel had been cut averaging 275 feet wide, with a depth varying from 12 to 15½ feet. He says:

So long as the lake retains its present height we may assume that the depth in the channel will be at least 13½ feet.

With this result, highly creditable to Captain Whipple, he observes that if he has been correctly informed "all the lake navigators are gratified." Besides, afterwards, and during the autumn of 1858, the Canadian Government expended $20,000 in deepening and widening the inner end of the channel excavated by the United States. No complaint had been made previous to the passage of the bill of obstructions to the commerce and navigation across the St. Clair flats. What, then, was the object of the appropriation proposed by the bill?

It appears that the surface of the water in Lake St. Clair has been gradually rising, until in 1858 it had attained an elevation of 4 feet above what had been its level in 1841. It is inferred, whether correctly or not it is not for me to say, that the surface of the water may gradually sink to the level of 1841, and in that event the water, which was, when the bill passed, 13½ feet deep in the channel, might sink to 9½ feet, and thus obstruct the passage.

To provide for this contingency, Captain Whipple suggested "the propriety of placing the subject before Congress, with an estimate for excavating a cut through the center of the new channel 150 feet in width and 4½ feet deep, so as to obtain from the river to the lake a depth of 18 feet during seasons of extreme high water and 12 feet at periods of extreme low water." It was not alleged that any present necessity existed for this narrower cut in the bottom of the present channel, but it is inferred that for the reason stated it may hereafter become necessary. Captain Whipple's estimate amounted to $50,000, but Congress by the bill have granted $55,000. Now, if no other objection existed against this measure, it would not seem necessary that the appropriation should have been made for the purpose indicated. The channel was sufficiently deep for all practical purposes; but from natural causes constantly operating in the lake, which I need not explain, this channel is peculiarly liable to fill up. What is really required is that it should at intervals be dredged out, so as to preserve its present depth; and surely the comparatively trifling expense necessary for this purpose ought not to be borne by the United States. After an improvement has been once constructed by appropriations from the Treasury it is not too much to expect that it should be kept in repair by that portion of the commercial and navigating interests which enjoys its peculiar benefits.

The last report made by Captain Whipple, dated on the 13th September last, has been submitted to Congress by the Secretary of War, and to this I would refer for information, which is, upon the whole, favorable, in relation to the present condition of the channel through the St. Clair flats.

2. But the far more important question is, Does Congress possess the power under the Constitution to deepen the channels of rivers and to create and improve harbors for purposes of commerce?

The question of the constitutional power of Congress to construct internal improvements within the States has been so frequently and so elaborately discussed that it would seem useless on this occasion to repeat or to refute at length arguments which have been so often advanced. For my own opinions on this subject I might refer to President Polk's carefully considered message of the 15th December, 1847, addressed to the House of Representatives whilst I was a member of his Cabinet.

The power to pass the bill in question, if it exist at all, must be derived from the power "to regulate commerce with foreign nations and among the several States and with the Indian tribes."

The power "to regulate:" Does this ever embrace the power to create or to construct? To say that it does is to confound the meaning of words of well-known signification. The word "regulate" has several shades of meaning, according to its application to different subjects, but never does it approach the signification of creative power. The regulating power necessarily presupposes the existence of something to be regulated. As applied to commerce, it signifies, according to the lexicographers, "to subject to rules or restrictions, as to regulate trade," etc. The Constitution itself is its own best expounder of the meaning of words employed by its framers. Thus, Congress have the power "to coin money." This is the creative power. Then immediately follows the power "to regulate the value thereof"—that is, of the coined money thus brought into existence. The words "regulate," "regulation," and "regulations" occur several times in the Constitution, but always with this subordinate meaning. Thus, after the creative power "to raise and support armies" and "to provide and maintain a navy" had been conferred upon Congress, then follows the power "to make rules for the government and regulation of the land and naval forces" thus called into being. So the Constitution, acting upon the self-evident fact that "commerce with foreign nations and among the several States and with the Indian tribes" already existed, conferred upon Congress the power "to regulate" this commerce. Thus, according to Chief Justice Marshall, the power to regulate commerce "is the power to prescribe the rule by which commerce is to be governed." And Mr. Madison, in his veto message of the 3d March, 1817, declares that—

"The power to regulate commerce among the several States" can not include a power to construct roads and canals and to improve the navigation of water courses, in order to facilitate, promote, and secure such commerce, without a latitude of construction departing from the ordinary import of the terms, strengthened by the known inconveniences which doubtless led to the grant of this remedial power to Congress.

We know from the history of the Constitution what these inconveniences were. Different States admitted foreign imports at different rates of duty. Those which had prescribed a higher rate of duty for the purpose of increasing their revenue were defeated in this object by the legislation of neighboring States admitting the same foreign articles at lower rates. Hence jealousies and dangerous rivalries had sprung up between the different States. It was chiefly in the desire to provide a remedy for these evils that the Federal Convention originated. The Constitution, for this purpose, conferred upon Congress the power to regulate commerce in such a manner that duties should be uniform in all the States composing the Confederacy, and, moreover, expressly provided that "no preference shall be given by any regulation of commerce or revenue to the ports of one State over those of another." If the construction of a harbor or deepening the channel of a river be a regulation of commerce, as the advocates of this power contend, this would give the ports of the State within which these improvements were made a preference over the ports of other States, and thus be a violation of the Constitution.

It is not too much to assert that no human being in existence when the Constitution was framed entertained the idea or the apprehension that by conferring upon Congress the power to regulate commerce its framers intended to embrace the power of constructing roads and canals and of creating and improving harbors and deepening the channels of rivers throughout our extensive Confederacy. Indeed, one important branch of this very power had been denied to Congress in express terms by the Convention. A proposition was made in the Convention to confer on Congress the power "to provide for the cutting of canals when deemed necessary." This was rejected by the strong majority of eight States to three. Among the reasons given for this rejection was that "the expense in such cases will fall on the United States and the benefits accrue to the places where the canals may be cut."

To say that the simple power of regulating commerce embraces within itself that of constructing harbors, of deepening the channels of rivers— in short, of creating a system of internal improvements for the purpose of facilitating the operations of commerce—would be to adopt a latitude of construction under which all political power might be usurped by the Federal Government. Such a construction would be in conflict with the well-known jealousy against Federal power which actuated the framers of the Constitution. It is certain that the power in question is not enumerated among the express grants to Congress contained in the instrument. In construing the Constitution we must then next inquire, Is its exercise "necessary and proper"?—not whether it may be convenient or useful "for carrying into execution" the power to regulate commerce among the States. But the jealous patriots of that day were not content even with this strict rule of construction. Apprehending that a dangerous latitude of interpretation might be applied in future times to the enumerated grants of power, they procured an amendment to be made to the original instrument, which declares that "the powers not delegated to the United States by the Constitution nor prohibited by it to the States are reserved to the States respectively or to the people."

The distinctive spirit and character which pervades the Constitution is that the powers of the General Government are confined chiefly to our intercourse with foreign nations, to questions of peace and war, and to subjects of common interest to all the States, carefully leaving the internal and domestic concerns of each individual State to be controlled by its own people and legislature. Without specifically enumerating these powers, it must be admitted that this well-marked distinction runs through the whole instrument. In nothing does the wisdom of its framers appear more conspicuously than in the care with which they sought to avoid the danger to our institutions which must necessarily result from the interference of the Federal Government with the local concerns of the States. The jarring and collision which would occur from the exercise by two separate governments of jurisdiction over the same subjects could not fail to produce disastrous consequences. Besides, the corrupting and seducing money influence exerted by the General Government in carrying into effect a system of internal improvements might be perverted to increase and consolidate its own power to the detriment of the rights of the States.

If the power existed in Congress to pass the present bill, then taxes must be imposed and money borrowed to an unlimited extent to carry such a system into execution. Equality among the States is equity. This equality is the very essence of the Constitution. No preference can justly be given to one of the sovereign States over another. According to the best estimate, our immense coast on the Atlantic, the Gulf of Mexico, the Pacific, and the Lakes embraces more than 9,500 miles, and, measuring by its indentations and to the head of tide water on the rivers, the distance is believed to be more than 33,000 miles. This everywhere throughout its vast extent contains numerous rivers and harbors, all of which may become the objects of Congressional appropriation. You can not deny to one State what you have granted to another. Such injustice would produce strife, jealousy, and alarming dissensions among them. Even within the same State improvements may be made in one river or harbor which would essentially injure the commerce and industry of another river or harbor. The truth is that most of these improvements are in a great degree local in their character and for the especial benefit of corporations or individuals in their vicinity, though they may have an odor of nationality on the principle that whatever benefits any part indirectly benefits the whole.

From our past history we may have a small foretaste of the cost of reviving the system of internal improvements.

For more than thirty years after the adoption of the Federal Constitution the power to appropriate money for the construction of internal improvements was neither claimed nor exercised by Congress. After its commencement, in 1820 and 1821, by very small and modest appropriations for surveys, it advanced with such rapid strides that within the brief period of ten years, according to President Polk, "the sum asked for from the Treasury for various projects amounted to more than $200,000,000." The vetoes of General Jackson and several of his successors have impeded the progress of the system and limited its extent, but have not altogether destroyed it. The time has now arrived for a final decision of the question. If the power exists, a general system should be adopted which would make some approach to justice among all the States, if this be possible.

What a vast field would the exercise of this power open for jobbing and corruption! Members of Congress, from an honest desire to promote the interest of their constituents, would struggle for improvements within their own districts, and the body itself must necessarily be converted into an arena where each would endeavor to obtain from the

SOUTH CAROLINA'S ORDINANCE OF SECESSION.

Treasury as much money as possible for his own locality. The temptation would prove irresistible. A system of "*logrolling*" (I know no word so expressive) would be inaugurated, under which the Treasury would be exhausted and the Federal Government be deprived of the means necessary to execute those great powers clearly confided to it by the Constitution for the purpose of promoting the interests and vindicating the honor of the country.

Whilst the power over internal improvements, it is believed, was "reserved to the States respectively," the framers of the Constitution were not unmindful that it might be proper for the State legislatures to possess the power to impose tonnage duties for the improvement of rivers and harbors within their limits. The self-interest of the different localities would prevent this from being done to such an extent as to injure their trade. The Constitution, therefore, which had in a previous clause provided that all duties should be uniform throughout the United States, subsequently modified the general rule so far as to declare that "no State shall without the consent of Congress levy any duty of tonnage." The inference is therefore irresistible that with the consent of Congress such a duty may be imposed by the States. Thus those directly interested in the improvement may lay a tonnage duty for its construction without imposing a tax for this purpose upon all the people of the United States.

To this provision several of the States resorted until the period when they began to look to the Federal Treasury instead of depending upon their own exertions. Massachusetts, Rhode Island, Pennsylvania, Maryland, Virginia, North Carolina, South Carolina, and Georgia, with the consent of Congress, imposed small tonnage duties on vessels at different periods for clearing and deepening the channels of rivers and improving harbors where such vessels entered. The last of these legislative acts believed to exist is that of Virginia, passed on the 22d February, 1826, levying a tonnage duty on vessels for "improving the navigation of James River from Warwick to Rocketts Landing." The latest act of Congress on this subject was passed on the 24th of February, 1843, giving its consent to the law of the legislature of Maryland laying a tonnage duty on vessels for the improvement of the harbor of Baltimore, and continuing it in force until 1st June, 1850.

Thus a clear constitutional mode exists by which the legislature of Michigan may, in its discretion, raise money to preserve the channel of the St. Clair River at its present depth or to render it deeper. A very insignificant tonnage duty on American vessels using this channel would be sufficient for the purpose; and as the St. Clair River is the boundary line between the United States and the Province of Upper Canada, the provincial British authorities would doubtless be willing to impose a similar tonnage duty on British vessels to aid in the accomplishment of this object. Indeed, the legislature of that Province have already evinced their interest on this subject by having but recently expended $20,000 on the improvement of the St. Clair flats. Even if the Constitution of the United States had conferred upon Congress the power of deepening the channel of the St. Clair River, it would be unjust to impose upon the people of the United States the entire burden, which ought to be borne jointly by the two parties having an equal interest in the work. Whenever the State of Michigan shall cease to depend on the Treasury of the United States, I doubt not that she, in conjunction with Upper Canada, will provide the necessary means for keeping this work in repair in the least expensive and most effective manner and without being burdensome to any interest.

It has been contended in favor of the existence of the power to construct internal improvements that Congress have from the beginning made appropriations for light-houses, and that upon the same principle of construction they possess the power of improving harbors and deepening the channels of rivers. As an original question the authority to erect light-houses under the commercial power might be considered doubtful; but even were it more doubtful than it is I should regard it as settled after an uninterrupted exercise of the power for seventy years. Such a long and uniform practical construction of the Constitution is entitled to the highest respect, and has finally determined the question.

Among the first acts which passed Congress after the Federal Government went into effect was that of August 7, 1789, providing "for the establishment and support of light-houses, beacons, buoys, and public piers." Under this act the expenses for the maintenance of all such erections then in existence were to be paid by the Federal Government and provision was made for the cession of jurisdiction over them by the respective States to the United States. In every case since before a light-house could be built a previous cession of jurisdiction has been required. This practice doubtless originated from that clause of the Constitution authorizing Congress "to exercise exclusive legislation * * * over all places purchased by the consent of the legislature of the State in which the same shall be, for the erection of forts, magazines, arsenals, dockyards, and other *needful buildings.*" Among these "*needful buildings*" light-houses must in fact have been included.

The bare statement of these facts is sufficient to prove that no analogy exists between the power to erect a light-house as a "needful building" and that to deepen the channel of a river.

In what I have said I do not mean to intimate a doubt of the power of Congress to construct such internal improvements as may be essentially necessary for defense and protection against the invasion of a foreign enemy. The power to declare war and the obligation to protect each State against invasion clearly cover such cases. It will scarcely be claimed, however, that the improvement of the St. Clair River is within this category. This river is the boundary line between the United States and the British Province of Upper Canada. **Any improvement** of its **navigation, therefore, which we could make for purposes of war would equally inure to the benefit of Great Britain, the only enemy which could possibly confront us in that quarter.** War would be a sad calamity for both nations, but should it ever, unhappily, exist, the battles will not be fought on the St. Clair River or on the lakes with which it communicates.

JAMES BUCHANAN.

WASHINGTON, *February 6, 1860.*

To the Senate of the United States:

On the last day of the last session of Congress a resolution, which had passed both Houses, "in relation to removal of obstructions to navigation in the mouth of the Mississippi River" was presented to me for approval. I have retained this resolution because it was presented to me at a period when it was impossible to give the subject that examination to which it appeared to be entitled. I need not repeat the views on this point presented in the introductory portion of my message to the Senate of the 2d [1st] instant.

In addition I would merely observe that although at different periods sums, amounting in the aggregate to $690,000, have been appropriated by Congress for the purpose of removing the bar and obstructions at the mouth of the Mississippi, yet it is now acknowledged that this money has been expended with but little, if any, practical benefit to its navigation.

JAMES BUCHANAN.

WASHINGTON, *April 17, 1860.*

To the Senate of the United States:

I return with my objections to the Senate, for their reconsideration, the bill entitled "An act for the relief of Arthur Edwards and his associates," presented to me on the 10th instant.

This bill directs the Postmaster-General "to audit and settle the accounts of Arthur Edwards and his associates for transporting the United States through mail on their steamers during the years 1849 and 1853 and intervening years" between Cleveland and Detroit, between Sandusky and Detroit, and between Toledo and Detroit, and "to allow and pay them not less than $28.60 for each and every passage of said steamers between said places during the aforementioned time when the mails were on board."

I have caused a statement to be made at the Post-Office Department of the least sum which can be paid to Mr. Edwards and his associates under the bill should it become a law, and from this it appears the amount will be $80,405.23.

Mr. Edwards and his associates, in 1854, a short time after the alleged services had been rendered, presented a claim to the Postmaster-General for $25,180 as compensation for these services. This claim consisted of nine items, setting forth specifically all the services embraced by the present bill. It is fair to presume that the parties best knew the value of their own services and that they would not by an underestimate do themselves injustice. The whole claim of $25,180 was rejected by the Postmaster-General for reasons which it is no part of my present purpose to discuss.

The claimants next presented a petition to the Court of Claims in June, 1855, "for a reasonable compensation" for these services, and "pray the judgment of your honorable court for the actual value of the service rendered by them and received by the United States, which amounts to the sum of $50,000." Thus the estimate which they placed upon their services had nearly doubled between 1854 and 1855—had risen from $25,180 to $50,000. On the ———, after a full hearing, the court decided against the claim, and delivered an opinion in support of this decision which can not, I think, be contested on legal principles. But they state in the conclusion of the opinion that "for any compensation for their services beyond what they have received they must depend upon the discretion of Congress."

This decision of the Court of Claims was reported to Congress on the 1st of April, 1858, and from it the present bill has originated. The amount granted by it is more by upward of $55,000 than the parties themselves demanded from the Postmaster-General in 1854, and is more by upward of $30,000 than they demanded when before the Court of Claims. The enormous difference in their favor between their own original demand and the amount granted by the present bill constitutes my chief objection to it. In presenting this objection I do not propose to enter into the question whether the claimants are entitled in equity to any compensation for their services beyond that which it is alleged they have already received, or, if so, what would be "a reasonable and fair compensation." My sole purpose is to afford Congress an opportunity of reconsidering this case on account of its peculiar circumstances. I transmit to the Senate the reports of Horatio King, Acting Postmaster-General, and of A. N. Zevely, Third Assistant Postmaster-General, both dated on the 14th of April, 1860, on the subject of this claim.

JAMES BUCHANAN.

WASHINGTON, *June 22, 1860.*

To the Senate of the United States:

I return with my objections to the Senate, in which it originated, the bill entitled "An act to secure homesteads to actual settlers on the public domain, and for other purposes," presented to me on the 20th instant.

This bill gives to every citizen of the United States "who is the head of a family," and to every person of foreign birth residing in the country who has declared his intention to become a citizen, though he may not be the head of a family, the privilege of appropriating to himself 160 acres of Government land, of settling and residing upon it for five years; and should his residence continue until the end of this period, he shall then receive a patent on the payment of 25 cents per acre, or one-fifth of the present Government price. During this period the land is protected from all the debts of the settler.

This bill also contains a cession to the States of all the public lands within their respective limits "which have been subject to sale at private entry, and which remain unsold after the lapse of thirty years." This provision embraces a present donation to the States of 12,229,731 acres, and will from time to time transfer to them large bodies of such lands which from peculiar circumstances may not be absorbed by private purchase and settlement.

To the actual settler this bill does not make an absolute donation, but the price is so small that it can scarcely be called a sale. It is nominally 25 cents per acre, but considering this is not to be paid until the end of five years, it is in fact reduced to about 18 cents per acre, or one-seventh of the present minimum price of the public lands. In regard to the States, it is an absolute and unqualified gift.

1. This state of the facts raises the question whether Congress, under the Constitution, has the power to give away the public lands either to States or individuals. On this question I expressed a decided opinion in my message to the House of Representatives of the 24th February, 1859, returning the agricultural-college bill. This opinion remains unchanged. The argument then used applies as a constitutional objection with greater force to the present bill. *There* it had the plea of consideration, growing out of a specific beneficial purpose; *here* it is an absolute gratuity to the States, without the pretext of consideration. I am compelled for want of time in these the last hours of the session to quote largely from this message.

I presume the general proposition will be admitted that Congress does not possess the power to make donations of money already in the Treasury, raised by taxes on the people, either to States or individuals.

But it is contended that the public lands are placed upon a different footing from money raised by taxation and that the proceeds arising from their sale are not subject to the limitations of the Constitution, but may be appropriated or given away by Congress, at its own discretion, to States, corporations, or individuals for any purpose they may deem expedient.

The advocates of this bill attempt to sustain their position upon the language of the second clause of the third section of the fourth article of the Constitution, which declares that "the Congress shall have power to dispose of and make all needful rules and regulations respecting the territory or other property belonging to the United States." They contend that by a fair interpretation of the words "dispose of" in this clause Congress possesses the power to make this gift of public lands to the States for purposes of education.

It would require clear and strong evidence to induce the belief that the framers of the Constitution, after having limited the powers of Congress to certain precise and specific objects, intended by employing the words "dispose of" to give that body unlimited power over the vast public domain. It would be a strange anomaly indeed to have created two funds—the one by taxation, confined to the execution of the enumerated powers delegated to Congress, and the other from the public lands, applicable to all subjects, foreign and domestic, which Congress might designate; that this fund should be "disposed of," not to pay the debts of the United States, nor "to raise and support armies," nor "to provide and maintain a navy," nor to accomplish any one of the other great objects enumerated in the Constitution, but be diverted from them to pay the debts of the States, to educate their people, and to carry into effect any other measure of their domestic policy. This would be to confer upon Congress a vast and irresponsible authority utterly at war with the well-known jealousy of Federal power which prevailed at the formation of the Constitution. The natural intendment would be that as the Constitution confined Congress to well-defined specific powers, the funds placed at their command, whether in land or money, should be appropriated to the performance of the duties corresponding with these powers. If not, a Government has been created with all its other powers carefully limited, but without any limitation in respect to the public lands.

But I can not so read the words "dispose of" as to make them embrace the idea of "giving away." The true meaning of words is always to be ascertained by the subject to which they are applied and the known general intent of the lawgiver. Congress is a trustee under the Constitution for the people of the United States to "dispose of" their public lands, and I think I may venture to assert with confidence that no case can be found in which a trustee in the position of Congress has been authorized to *"dispose of"* property by its owner where it has been held that these words authorized such trustee to give away the fund intrusted to his care. No trustee, when called upon to account for the disposition of the property placed under his management before any judicial tribunal, would venture to present such a plea in his defense. The true meaning of these words is clearly stated by Chief Justice Taney in delivering the opinion of the court (19 Howard, p. 436). He says in reference to this clause of the Constitution: "It begins its enumeration of powers by that of disposing; in other words, making sale of the lands or raising money from them, which, as we have already said, was the main object of the cession (from the States), and which is the first thing provided for in the article." It is unnecessary to refer to the history of the times to establish the known fact that this statement of the Chief Justice is perfectly well founded. That it never was intended by the framers of the Constitution that these lands should be given away by Congress is manifest from the concluding portion of the same clause. By it Congress has power not only "to dispose of" the territory, but of the "other property of the United States." In the language of the Chief Justice (p. 437): "And the same power of making needful rules respecting the territory is in precisely the same language applied to the other property of the United States, associating the power over the territory in this respect with the power over movable or personal property; that is, the ships, arms, or munitions of war, which then belonged in common to the State sovereignties."

The question is still clearer in regard to the public lands in the States and Territories within the Louisiana and Florida purchases. These lands were paid for out of the public Treasury from money raised by taxation. Now if Congress had no power to appropriate the money with which these lands were purchased, is it not clear that the power over the lands is equally limited? The mere conversion of this money into land could not confer upon Congress new power over the disposition of land which they had not possessed over money. If it could, then a trustee, by changing the character of the fund intrusted to his care for special objects from money into land, might give the land away or devote it to any purpose he thought proper, however foreign from the trust. The inference is irresistible that this land partakes of the very same character with the money paid for it, and can be devoted to no objects different from those to which the money could have been devoted. If this were not the case, then by the purchase of a new territory from a foreign government out of the public Treasury Congress could enlarge their own powers and appropriate the proceeds of the sales of the land thus purchased, at their own discretion, to other and far different objects from what they could have applied the purchase money which had been raised by taxation.

2. It will prove unequal and unjust in its operation among the actual settlers themselves.

The first settlers of a new country are a most meritorious class. They brave the dangers of savage warfare, suffer the privations of a frontier life, and with the hand of toil bring the wilderness into cultivation. The "old settlers," as they are everywhere called, are public benefactors. This class have all paid for their lands the Government price, or $1.25 per acre. They have constructed roads, established schools, and laid the foundation of prosperous commonwealths. Is it just, is it equal, that after they have accomplished all this by their labor new settlers should come in among them and receive their farms at the price of 25 or 18 cents per acre? Surely the old settlers, as a class, are entitled to at least equal benefits with the new. If you give the new settlers their land for a comparatively nominal price, upon every principle of equality and justice you will be obliged to refund out of the common Treasury the difference which the old have paid above the new settlers for their land.

3. This bill will do great injustice to the old soldiers who have received land warrants for their services in fighting the battles of their country. It will greatly reduce the market value of these warrants. Already their value has sunk for 160-acre warrants to 67 cents per acre under an apprehension that such a measure as this might become a law. What price would they command when any head of a family may take possession of a quarter section of land and not pay for it until the end of five years, and then at the rate of only 25 cents per acre? The magnitude of the interest to be affected will appear in the fact that there are outstanding unsatisfied land warrants reaching back to the last war with Great Britain, and even Revolutionary times, amounting in round numbers to seven and a half millions of acres.

4. This bill will prove unequal and unjust in its operation, because from its nature it is confined to one class of our people. It is a boon exclusively conferred upon the cultivators of the soil. Whilst it is cheerfully admitted that these are the most numerous and useful class of our fellow-citizens and eminently deserve all the advantages which our laws have already extended to them, yet there should be no new legislation which would operate to the injury or embarrassment of the large body of respectable artisans and laborers. The mechanic who emigrates to the West and pursues his calling must labor long before he can purchase a quarter section of land, whilst the tiller of the soil who accompanies him obtains a farm at once by the bounty of the Government. The

numerous body of mechanics in our large cities can not, even by emi-grating to the West, take advantage of the provisions of this bill with-out entering upon a new occupation for which their habits of life have rendered them unfit.

5. This bill is unjust to the old States of the Union in many respects; and amongst these States, so far as the public lands are concerned, we may enumerate every State east of the Mississippi with the exception of Wisconsin and a portion of Minnesota.

It is a common belief within their limits that the older States of the Confederacy do not derive their proportionate benefit from the public lands. This is not a just opinion. It is doubtful whether they could be rendered more beneficial to these States under any other system than that which at present exists. Their proceeds go into the common Treas-ury to accomplish the objects of the Government, and in this manner all the States are benefited in just proportion. But to give this common inheritance away would deprive the old States of their just proportion of this revenue without holding out any the least corresponding advan-tage. Whilst it is our common glory that the new States have become so prosperous and populous, there is no good reason why the old States should offer premiums to their own citizens to emigrate from them to the West. That land of promise presents in itself sufficient allurements to our young and enterprising citizens without any adventitious aid. The offer of free farms would probably have a powerful effect in encourag-ing emigration, especially from States like Illinois, Tennessee, and Ken-tucky, to the west of the Mississippi, and could not fail to reduce the price of property within their limits. An individual in States thus sit-uated would not pay its fair value for land when by crossing the Missis-sippi he could go upon the public lands and obtain a farm almost without money and without price.

6. This bill will open one vast field for speculation. Men will not pay $1.25 for lands when they can purchase them for one-fifth of that price. Large numbers of actual settlers will be carried out by capitalists upon agreements to give them half of the land for the improvement of the other half. This can not be avoided. Secret agreements of this kind will be numerous. In the entry of graduated lands the experience of the Land Office justifies this objection.

7. We ought ever to maintain the most perfect equality between native and naturalized citizens. They are equal, and ought always to remain equal, before the laws. Our laws welcome foreigners to our shores, and their rights will ever be respected. Whilst these are the sentiments on which I have acted through life, it is not, in my opinion, expedient to proclaim to all the nations of the earth that whoever shall arrive in this country from a foreign shore and declare his intention to become a citi-zen shall receive a farm of 160 acres at a cost of 25 or 20 cents per acre if he will only reside on it and cultivate it. The invitation extends to

all, and if this bill becomes a law we may have numerous actual settlers from China and other Eastern nations enjoying its benefits on the great Pacific Slope. The bill makes a distinction in favor of such persons over native and naturalized citizens. When applied to such citizens, it is confined to such as are the heads of families, but when applicable to persons of foreign birth recently arrived on our shores there is no such restriction. Such persons need not be the heads of families provided they have filed a declaration of intention to become citizens. Perhaps this distinction was an inadvertence, but it is, nevertheless, a part of the bill.

8. The bill creates an unjust distinction between persons claiming the benefit of the preemption laws. Whilst it reduces the price of the land to existing preemptors to 62½ cents per acre and gives them a credit on this sum for two years from the present date, no matter how long they may have hitherto enjoyed the land, future preemptors will be compelled to pay double this price per acre. There is no reason or justice in this discrimination.

9. The effect of this bill on the public revenue must be apparent to all. Should it become a law, the reduction of the price of land to actual settlers to 25 cents per acre, with a credit of five years, and the reduction of its price to existing preemptors to 62½ cents per acre, with a credit of two years, will so diminish the sale of other public lands as to render the expectation of future revenue from that source, beyond the expenses of survey and management, illusory. The Secretary of the Interior estimated the revenue from the public lands for the next fiscal year at $4,000,000, on the presumption that the present land system would remain unchanged. Should this bill become a law, he does not believe that $1,000,000 will be derived from this source.

10. This bill lays the ax at the root of our present admirable land system. The public land is an inheritance of vast value to us and to our descendants. It is a resource to which we can resort in the hour of difficulty and danger. It has been managed heretofore with the greatest wisdom under existing laws. I this management the rights of actual settlers have been conciliated with the interests of the Government. The price to all has been reduced from $2 per acre to $1.25 for fresh lands, and the claims of actual settlers have been secured by our preemption laws. Any man can now acquire a title in fee simple to a homestead of 80 acres, at the minimum price of $1.25 per acre, for $100. Should the present system remain, we shall derive a revenue from the public lands of $10,000,000 per annum, when the bounty-land warrants are satisfied, without oppression to any human being. In time of war, when all other sources of revenue are seriously impaired, this will remain intact. It may become the best security for public loans hereafter, in times of difficulty and danger, as it has been heretofore. Why should we impair or destroy the system at the present moment? What necessity exists for it?

The people of the United States have advanced with steady but rapid strides to their present condition of power and prosperity. They have been guided in their progress by the fixed principle of protecting the equal rights of all, whether they be rich or poor. No agrarian sentiment has ever prevailed among them. The honest poor man, by frugality and industry, can in any part of our country acquire a competence for himself and his family, and in doing this he feels that he eats the bread of independence. He desires no charity, either from the Government or from his neighbors. This bill, which proposes to give him land at an almost nominal price out of the property of the Government, will go far to demoralize the people and repress this noble spirit of independence. It may introduce among us those pernicious social theories which have proved so disastrous in other countries.

JAMES BUCHANAN.

PROTESTS.

WASHINGTON, March 28, 1860.

To the House of Representatives:

After a delay which has afforded me ample time for reflection, and after much and careful deliberation, I find myself constrained by an imperious sense of duty, as a coordinate branch of the Federal Government, to protest against the first two clauses of the first resolution adopted by the House of Representatives on the 5th instant, and published in the Congressional Globe on the succeeding day. These clauses are in the following words:

Resolved, That a committee of five members be appointed by the Speaker for the purpose, first, of investigating whether the President of the United States or any other officer of the Government has, by money, patronage, or other improper means, sought to influence the action of Congress or any committee thereof for or against the passage of any law appertaining to the rights of any State or Territory; and, second, also to inquire into and investigate whether any officer or officers of the Government have, by combination or otherwise, prevented or defeated, or attempted to prevent or defeat, the execution of any law or laws now upon the statute book, and whether the President has failed or refused to compel the execution of any law thereof.

I confine myself exclusively to these two branches of the resolution, because the portions of it which follow relate to alleged abuses in postoffices, navy-yards, public buildings, and other public works of the United States. In such cases inquiries are highly proper in themselves and belong equally to the Senate and the House, as incident to their legislative duties and being necessary to enable them to discover and to provide the appropriate legislative remedies for any abuses which may be ascertained. Although the terms of the latter portion of the resolution are extremely vague and general, yet my sole purpose in adverting to them at present is to mark the broad line of distinction between the accusatory and the remedial clauses of this resolution. The House of Representatives possess no power under the Constitution over the first or accusatory portion of the resolution except as an impeaching body, whilst over the last, in common with the Senate, their authority as a legislative body is fully and cheerfully admitted.

It is solely in reference to the first or impeaching power that I propose to make a few observations. Except in this single case, the Constitution has invested the House of Representatives with no power, no jurisdiction, no supremacy whatever over the President. In all other respects he is quite as independent of them as they are of him. As a coordinate branch of the Government he is their equal. Indeed, he is the only direct representative on earth of the people of all and each of the sovereign States. To them, and to them alone, is he responsible whilst acting within the sphere of his constitutional duty, and not in any manner to the House of Representatives. The people have thought proper to invest him with the most honorable, responsible, and dignified office in the world, and the individual, however unworthy, now holding this exalted position, will take care, so far as in him lies, that their rights and prerogatives shall never be violated in his person, but shall pass to his successors unimpaired by the adoption of a dangerous precedent. He will defend them to the last extremity against any unconstitutional attempt, come from what quarter it may, to abridge the constitutional rights of the Executive and render him subservient to any human power except themselves.

The people have not confined the President to the exercise of executive duties. They have also conferred upon him a large measure of legislative discretion. No bill can become a law without his approval, as representing the people of the United States, unless it shall pass after his veto by a majority of two-thirds of both Houses. In his legislative capacity he might, in common with the Senate and the House, institute an inquiry to ascertain any facts which ought to influence his judgment in approving or vetoing any bill.

This participation in the performance of legislative duties between the coordinate branches of the Government ought to inspire the conduct of all of them in their relations toward each other with mutual forbearance and respect. At least each has a right to demand justice from the other. The cause of complaint is that the constitutional rights and immunities of the Executive have been violated in the person of the President.

The trial of an impeachment of the President before the Senate on charges preferred and prosecuted against him by the House of Representatives would be an imposing spectacle for the world. In the result not only his removal from the Presidential office would be involved, but, what is of infinitely greater importance to himself, his character, both in the eyes of the present and of future generations, might possibly be tarnished. The disgrace cast upon him would in some degree be reflected upon the character of the American people, who elected him. Hence the precautions adopted by the Constitution to secure a fair trial. On such a trial it declares that "the Chief Justice shall preside." This was doubtless because the framers of the Constitution believed it to be possible that the Vice-President might be biased by the fact that "in case of the removal of the President from office * * * the same shall devolve on the Vice-President."

The preliminary proceedings in the House in the case of charges which may involve impeachment have been well and wisely settled by long practice upon principles of equal justice both to the accused and to the people. The precedent established in the case of Judge Peck, of Missouri, in 1831, after a careful review of all former precedents, will, I venture to predict, stand the test of time.

In that case Luke Edward Lawless, the accuser, presented a petition to the House, in which he set forth minutely and specifically his causes of complaint. He prayed "that the conduct and proceedings in this behalf of said Judge Peck may be inquired into by your honorable body, and such decision made thereon as to your wisdom and justice shall seem proper." This petition was referred to the Judiciary Committee; such has ever been deemed the appropriate committee to make similar investigations. It is a standing committee, supposed to be appointed without reference to any special case, and at all times is presumed to be composed of the most eminent lawyers in the House from different portions of the Union, whose acquaintance with judicial proceedings and whose habits of investigation qualify them peculiarly for the task. No tribunal, from their position and character, could in the nature of things be more impartial. In the case of Judge Peck the witnesses were selected by the committee itself, with a view to ascertain the truth of the charge. They were cross-examined by him, and everything was conducted in such a manner as to afford him no reasonable cause of complaint. In view of this precedent, and, what is of far greater importance, in view of the Constitution and the principles of eternal justice, in what manner has the President of the United States been treated by the House of Representatives? Mr. John Covode, a Representative from Pennsylvania, is the accuser of the President. Instead of following the wise precedents of former times, and especially that in the case of Judge Peck, and referring the accusation to the Committee on the Judiciary, the House have made my accuser one of my judges.

To make the accuser the judge is a violation of the principles of universal justice, and is condemned by the practice of all civilized nations. Every freeman must revolt at such a spectacle. I am to appear before Mr. Covode, either personally or by a substitute, to cross-examine the witnesses which he may produce before himself to sustain his own accusations against me; and perhaps even this poor boon may be denied to the President.

And what is the nature of the investigation which his resolution proposes to institute? It is as vague and general as the English language affords words in which to make it. The committee is to inquire, not into any specific charge or charges, but whether the President has, by "money, patronage, or other improper means, sought to influence," not the action of any individual member or members of Congress, but "the action" of the entire body "of Congress" itself "or any committee thereof." The President might have had some glimmering of the nature of the offense to be investigated had his accuser pointed to the act or acts of Congress which he sought to pass or to defeat by the employment of "money, patronage, or other improper means." But the accusation is bounded by no such limits. It extends to the whole circle of legislation—to interference "for or against the passage of any law appertaining to the rights of any State or Territory." And what law does not appertain to the rights of some State or Territory? And what law or laws has the President failed to execute? These might easily have been pointed out had any such existed.

Had Mr. Lawless asked an inquiry to be made by the House whether Judge Peck, in general terms, had not violated his judicial duties, without the specification of any particular act, I do not believe there would have been a single vote in that body in favor of the inquiry.

Since the time of the star-chamber and of general warrants there has been no such proceeding in England.

The House of Representatives, the high impeaching power of the country, without consenting to hear a word of explanation, have indorsed this accusation against the President and made it their own act. They even refused to permit a Member to inquire of the President's accuser what were the specific charges against him. Thus, in this preliminary accusation of "high crimes and misdemeanors" against a coordinate branch of the Government, under the impeaching power, the House refused to hear a single suggestion, even in regard to the correct mode of proceeding, but without a moment's delay passed the accusatory resolutions under the pressure of the previous question.

In the institution of a prosecution for any offense against the most humble citizen—and I claim for myself no greater rights than he enjoys—the constitutions of the United States and of the several States require that he shall be informed in the very beginning of the nature and cause of the accusation against him, in order to enable him to prepare for his defense. There are other principles which I might enumerate, not less sacred, presenting an impenetrable shield to protect every citizen falsely charged with a criminal offense. These have been violated in the prosecution instituted by the House of Representatives against the executive branch of the Government. Shall the President alone be deprived of the protection of these great principles which prevail in every land where a ray of liberty penetrates the gloom of despotism? Shall the Executive alone be deprived of rights which all his fellow-citizens enjoy? The whole proceeding against him justifies the fears of those wise and great men who, before the Constitution was adopted by the States, apprehended that the tendency of the Government was to the aggrandizement of the legislative at the expense of the executive and judicial departments.

I again declare emphatically that I make this protest for no reason personal to myself, and I do it with perfect respect for the House of Representatives, in which I had the honor of serving as a member for five successive terms. I have lived long in this goodly land, and have enjoyed all the offices and honors which my country could bestow. Amid all the political storms through which I have passed, the present is the first attempt which has ever been made, to my knowledge, to assail my personal or official integrity; and this as the time is approaching when I shall voluntarily retire from the service of my country. I feel proudly conscious that there is no public act of my life which will not bear the strictest scrutiny. I defy all investigation. Nothing but the basest perjury can sully my good name. I do not fear even this, because I cherish an humble confidence that the gracious Being who has hitherto defended and protected me against the shafts of falsehood and malice will not desert me now when I have become "old and gray headed." I can declare before God and my country that no human being (with an exception scarcely worthy of notice) has at any period of my life dared to approach me with a corrupt or dishonorable proposition, and until recent developments it had never entered into my imagination that any person, even in the storm of exasperated political excitement, would charge me in the most remote degree with having made such a proposition to any human being. I may now, however, exclaim in the language of complaint employed by my first and greatest predecessor, that I have been abused "in such exaggerated and indecent terms as could scarcely be applied to a Nero, to a notorious defaulter, or even to a common pickpocket."

I do therefore, for the reasons stated and in the name of the people of the several States, solemnly protest against these proceedings of the House of Representatives, because they are in violation of the rights of the coordinate executive branch of the Government and subversive of its constitutional independence; because they are calculated to foster a band of interested parasites and informers, ever ready, for their own advantage, to swear before *ex parte* committees to pretended private conversations between the President and themselves, incapable from their nature of being disproved, thus furnishing material for harassing him, degrading him in the eyes of the country, and eventually, should he be a weak or a timid man, rendering him subservient to improper influences in order to avoid such persecutions and annoyances; because they tend to destroy that harmonious action for the common good which ought to be maintained, and which I sincerely desire to cherish, between coordinate branches of the Government; and, finally, because, if unresisted, they would establish a precedent dangerous and embarrassing to all my successors, to whatever political party they might be attached.

JAMES BUCHANAN.

WASHINGTON, *June 22, 1860.*

To the House of Representatives:

In my message to the House of Representatives of the 28th March last I solemnly protested against the creation of a committee, at the head of which was placed my accuser, for the purpose of investigating whether the President had, "by money, patronage, or other improper means, sought to influence the action of Congress or any committee thereof for or against the passage of any law appertaining to the rights of any State or Territory." I protested against this because it was destitute of any specification; because it referred to no particular act to enable the President to prepare for his defense; because it deprived him of the constitutional guards which, in common with every citizen of the United States, he possesses for his protection, and because it assailed his constitutional independence as a coordinate branch of the Government.

There is an enlightened justice, as well as a beautiful symmetry, in every part of the Constitution. This is conspicuously manifested in regard to impeachments. The House of Representatives possesses "the sole power of impeachment," the Senate "the sole power to try all impeachments;" and the impeachable offenses are "treason, bribery, or other high crimes or misdemeanors." The practice of the House from the earliest times had been in accordance with its own dignity, the rights of the accused, and the demands of justice. At the commencement of each judicial investigation which might lead to an impeachment specific charges were always preferred; the accused had an opportunity of cross-examining the witnesses, and he was placed in full possession of the precise nature of the offense which he had to meet. An impartial and elevated standing committee was charged with this investigation, upon which no member inspired with the ancient sense of honor and justice would have served had he ever expressed an opinion against the accused. Until the present occasion it was never deemed proper to transform the accuser into the judge and to confer upon him the selection of his own committee.

The charges made against me in vague and general terms were of such a false and atrocious character that I did not entertain a moment's apprehension for the result. They were abhorrent to every principle instilled into me from my youth and every practice of my life, and I did not believe it possible that the man existed who would so basely perjure himself as to swear to the truth of any such accusations. In this conviction I am informed I have not been mistaken.

In my former protest, therefore, I truly and emphatically declared that it was made for no reason personal to myself, but because the proceedings of the House were in violation of the rights of the coordinate executive branch of the Government, subversive of its constitutional independence, and if unresisted would establish a precedent dangerous and embarrassing to all my successors. Notwithstanding all this, if the committee had not transcended the authority conferred upon it by the resolution of the House of Representatives, broad and general as this was, I should have remained silent upon the subject. What I now charge is that they have acted as though they possessed unlimited power, and, without any warrant whatever in the resolution under which they were appointed, have pursued a course not merely at war with the constitutional rights of the Executive, but tending to degrade the Presidential office itself to such a degree as to render it unworthy of the acceptance of any man of honor or principle.

The resolution of the House, so far as it is accusatory of the President, is confined to an inquiry whether he had used corrupt or improper means to influence the action of Congress or any of its committees on legislative measures pending before them—nothing more, nothing less. I have not learned through the newspapers or in any other mode that the committee have touched the other accusatory branch of the resolution, charging the President with a violation of duty in failing to execute some law or laws. This branch of the resolution is therefore out of the question. By what authority, then, have the committee undertaken to investigate the course of the President in regard to the convention which framed the Lecompton constitution? By what authority have they undertaken to pry into our foreign relations for the purpose of assailing him on account of the instructions given by the Secretary of State to our minister in Mexico relative to the Tehuantepec route? By what authority have they inquired into the causes of removal from office, and this from the parties themselves removed, with a view to prejudice his character, notwithstanding this power of removal belongs exclusively to the President under the Constitution, was so decided by the First Congress in the year 1789, and has accordingly ever since been exercised? There is in the resolution no pretext of authority for the committee to investigate the question of the printing of the post-office blanks; nor is it to be supposed that the House, if asked, would have granted such an authority, because this question had been previously committed to two other committees—one in the Senate and the other in the House. Notwithstanding this absolute want of power, the committee rushed into this investigation in advance of all other subjects.

The committee proceeded for months, from March 22, 1860, to examine *ex parte* and without any notice to myself into every subject which could possibly affect my character. Interested and vindictive witnesses were summoned and examined before them; and the first and only information of their testimony which, in almost every instance, I received was obtained from the publication of such portions of it as could injuriously affect myself in the New York journals. It mattered not that these statements were, so far as I have learned, disproved by the most respectable witnesses who happened to be on the spot. The telegraph was silent respecting these contradictions. It was a secret committee in regard to the testimony in my defense, but it was public in regard to all the testimony which could by possibility reflect on my character. The poison was left to produce its effect upon the public mind, whilst the antidote was carefully withheld.

In their examinations the committee violated the most sacred and honorable confidences existing among men. Private correspondence, which a truly honorable man would never even entertain a distant thought of divulging, was dragged to light. Different persons in official and confidential relations with myself, and with whom it was supposed I might have held conversations the revelation of which would do me injury, were examined. Even members of the Senate and members of my own Cabinet, both my constitutional advisers, were called upon to testify, for the purpose of discovering something, if possible, to my discredit.

The distribution of the patronage of the Government is by far the most disagreeable duty of the President. Applicants are so numerous and their applications are pressed with such eagerness by their friends, both in and out of Congress, that the selection of one for any desirable office gives offense to many. Disappointed applicants, removed officers, and those who for any cause, real or imaginary, had become hostile to the Administration presented themselves or were invited by a summons to appear before the committee. These are the most dangerous witnesses. Even with the best intentions they are so influenced by prejudice and disappointment that they almost inevitably discolor truth. They swear to their own version of private conversations with the President without the possibility of contradiction. His lips are sealed, and he is left at their mercy. He can not, as a coordinate branch of the Government, appear before a committee of investigation to contradict the oaths of such witnesses. Every coward knows that he can employ insulting language against the President with impunity, and every false or prejudiced witness can attempt to swear away his character before such a committee without the fear of contradiction.

Thus for months, whilst doing my best at one end of the Avenue to perform my high and responsible duties to the country, has there been a committee of the House of Representatives in session at the other end of the Avenue spreading a drag net, without the shadow of authority from the House, over the whole Union, to catch any disappointed man willing to malign my character; and all this in secret conclave. The lion's mouth at Venice, into which secret denunciations were dropped, is an apt illustration of the Covode committee. The star-chamber, tyrannical and odious as it was, never proceeded in such a manner. For centuries there has been nothing like it in any civilized country, except the revolutionary tribunal of France in the days of Robespierre. Now I undertake to state and to prove that should the proceedings of the committee be sanctioned by the House and become a precedent for future times the balance of the Constitution will be entirely upset, and there will no longer remain the three coordinate and independent branches of the Government—legislative, executive, and judicial. The worst fears of the patriots and statesmen who framed the Constitution in regard to the usurpations of the legislative on the executive and judicial branches will then be realized. In the language of Mr. Madison, speaking on this very subject in the forty-eighth number of the Federalist:

In a representative republic, where the executive magistracy is carefully limited, both in the extent and duration of its power, and where the legislative power is exercised by an assembly which is inspired, by a supposed influence over the people, with an intrepid confidence in its own strength, which is sufficiently numerous to feel all the passions which actuate a multitude, yet not so numerous as to be incapable of pursuing the objects of its passions by means which reason prescribes, it is against the enterprising ambition of this department that the people ought to indulge all their jealousy and exhaust all their precautions.

And in the expressive and pointed language of Mr. Jefferson, when speaking of the tendency of the legislative branch of Government to usurp the rights of the weaker branches:

The concentrating these in the same hands is precisely the definition of despotic government. It will be no alleviation that these powers will be exercised by a plurality of hands, and not by a single one. One hundred and seventy-three despots would surely be as oppressive as one. Let those who doubt it turn their eyes on the Republic of Venice. As little will it avail us that they are chosen by ourselves. An elective despotism was not the government we fought for, but one which should not only be founded on free principles, but in which the powers of government should be so divided and balanced among several bodies of magistracy as that no one could transcend their legal limits without being effectually checked and controlled by the others.

Should the proceedings of the Covode committee become a precedent, both the letter and spirit of the Constitution will be violated. One of the three massive columns on which the whole superstructure rests will be broken down. Instead of the Executive being a coordinate it will become a subordinate branch of the Government. The Presidential office will be dragged into the dust. The House of Representatives will then have rendered the Executive almost necessarily subservient to its wishes, instead of being independent. How is it possible that two powers in the State can be coordinate and independent of each other if the one claims and exercises the power to reprove and to censure all the official acts and all the private conversations of the other, and this upon *ex parte* testimony before a secret inquisitorial committee; in short, to assume a general censorship over the other? The idea is as absurd in public as it would be in private life. Should the President attempt to assert and maintain his own independence, future Covode committees may dragoon him into submission by collecting the hosts of disappointed office hunters, removed officers, and those who desire to live upon the public Treasury, which must follow in the wake of every Administration, and they in secret conclave will swear away his reputation. Under such circumstances he must be a very bold man should he not surrender at discretion and consent to exercise his authority according to the will of those invested with this terrific power. The sovereign people of the several States have elected him to the highest and most honorable office in the world. He is their only direct representative in the Government. By their Constitution they have made him Commander in Chief of their Army and Navy. He represents them in their intercourse with foreign nations. Clothed with their dignity and authority, he occupies a proud position before all nations, civilized and savage. With the consent of the Senate, he appoints all the important officers of the Government. He exercises the veto power, and to that extent controls the legislation of Congress. For the performance of these high duties he is responsible to the people of the several States, and not in any degree to the House of Representatives.

Shall he surrender these high powers, conferred upon him as the representative of the American people for their benefit, to the House to be exercised under their overshadowing influence and control? Shall he alone of all the citizens of the United States be denied a fair trial? Shall he alone not be "informed of the nature and cause of the accusation" against him? Shall he alone not "be confronted with the witnesses" against him? Shall the House of Representatives, usurping the powers of the Senate, proceed to try the President through the agency of a secret committee of the body, where it is impossible he can make any defense, and then, without affording him an opportunity of being heard, pronounce a judgment of censure against him? The very same rule might be applied for the very same reason to every judge of every court of the United States. From what part of the Constitution is this terrible secret inquisitorial power derived? No such express power exists. From which of the enumerated powers can it be inferred? It is true the House can not pronounce the formal judgment against him of "removal from office," but they can by their judgment of censure asperse his reputation, and thus to the extent of their influence render the office contemptible. An example is at hand of the reckless manner in which this power of censure can be employed in high party times. The House on a recent occasion have attempted to degrade the President by adopting the resolution of Mr. John Sherman declaring that he, in conjunction with the Secretary of the Navy, " by receiving and considering the party relations of bidders for contracts and the effect of awarding contracts upon pending elections, have set an example dangerous to the public safety and deserving the reproof of this House."

It will scarcely be credited that the sole pretext for this vote of censure was the simple fact that in disposing of the numerous letters of every imaginable character which I daily receive I had in the usual course of business referred a letter from Colonel Patterson, of Philadelphia, in relation to a contract, to the attention of the Secretary of the Navy, the head of the appropriate Department, without expressing or intimating any opinion whatever on the subject; and to make the matter if possible still plainer, the Secretary had informed the committee that "*the President did not in any manner interfere in this case, nor has he in any other case of contract since I have been in the Department.*" The absence of all proof to sustain this attempt to degrade the President, whilst it manifests the venom of the shaft aimed at him, has destroyed the vigor of the bow.

To return after this digression: Should the House, by the institution of Covode committees, votes of censure, and other devices to harass the President, reduce him to subservience to their will and render him their creature, then the well-balanced Government which our fathers framed will be annihilated. This conflict has already been commenced in earnest by the House against the Executive. A bad precedent rarely, if ever, dies. It will, I fear, be pursued in the time of my successors, no matter what may be their political character. Should secret committees be appointed with unlimited authority to range over all the words and actions, and, if possible, the very thoughts, of the President with a view to discover something in his past life prejudicial to his character from parasites and informers, this would be an ordeal which scarcely any mere man since the fall could endure. It would be to subject him to a reign of terror from which the stoutest and purest heart might shrink. I have passed triumphantly through this ordeal. My vindication is complete. The committee have reported no resolution looking to an impeachment against me; no resolution of censure; not even a resolution pointing out any abuses in any of the Executive Departments of the Government to be corrected by legislation. This is the highest commendation which could be bestowed on the heads of these Departments. The sovereign people of the States will, however, I trust, save my successors, whoever they may be, from any such ordeal. They are frank, bold, and honest. They detest delators and informers. I therefore, in the name and as the representative of this great people, and standing upon the ramparts of the Constitution which they "have ordained and established," do solemnly protest against these unprecedented and unconstitutional proceedings.

There was still another committee raised by the House on the 6th March last, on motion of Mr. Hoard, to which I had not the slightest objection. The resolution creating it was confined to specific charges, which I have ever since been ready and willing to meet. I have at all times invited and defied fair investigation upon constitutional principles. I have received no notice that this committee have ever proceeded to the investigation.

Why should the House of Representatives desire to encroach on the other departments of the Government? Their rightful powers are ample for every legitimate purpose. They are the impeaching body. In their legislative capacity it is their most wise and wholesome prerogative to institute rigid examinations into the manner in which all departments of the Government are conducted, with a view to reform abuses, to promote economy, and to improve every branch of administration. Should they find reason to believe in the course of their examinations that any grave offense had been committed by the President or any officer of the Government rendering it proper, in their judgment, to resort to impeachment, their course would be plain. They would then transfer the question from their legislative to their accusatory jurisdiction, and take care that in all the preliminary judicial proceedings preparatory to the vote of articles of impeachment the accused should enjoy the benefit of cross-examining the witnesses and all the other safeguards with which the Constitution surrounds every American citizen.

If in a legislative investigation it should appear that the public interest required the removal of any officer of the Government, no President has ever existed who, after giving him a fair hearing, would hesitate to apply the remedy.

This I take to be the ancient and well-established practice. An adherence to it will best promote the harmony and the dignity of the intercourse between the coordinate branches of the Government and render us all more respectable both in the eyes of our own countrymen and of foreign nations.

JAMES BUCHANAN.

PROCLAMATION.

BY THE PRESIDENT OF THE UNITED STATES OF AMERICA.

A PROCLAMATION.

Whereas an extraordinary occasion has occurred rendering it necessary and proper that the Senate of the United States shall be convened to receive and act upon such communications as have been or may be made to it on the part of the Executive:

Now, therefore, I, James Buchanan, President of the United States, do issue this my proclamation, declaring that an extraordinary occasion requires the Senate of the United States to convene for the transaction of business at the Capitol, in the city of Washington, on the 26th day of

June instant, at 12 o'clock at noon of that day, of which all who shall then be entitled to act as members of that body are hereby required to take notice.

Given under my hand and the seal of the United States, at Washington, this 25th day of June, A. D. 1860, and of the Independence of the United States the eighty-fourth.

[SEAL.]

JAMES BUCHANAN.

By the President:
LEWIS CASS,
Secretary of State.

FOURTH ANNUAL MESSAGE.

WASHINGTON CITY, *December 3, 1860.*

Fellow-Citizens of the Senate and House of Representatives:

Throughout the year since our last meeting the country has been eminently prosperous in all its material interests. The general health has been excellent, our harvests have been abundant, and plenty smiles throughout the land. Our commerce and manufactures have been prosecuted with energy and industry, and have yielded fair and ample returns. In short, no nation in the tide of time has ever presented a spectacle of greater material prosperity than we have done until within a very recent period.

Why is it, then, that discontent now so extensively prevails, and the Union of the States, which is the source of all these blessings, is threatened with destruction?

The long-continued and intemperate interference of the Northern people with the question of slavery in the Southern States has at length produced its natural effects. The different sections of the Union are now arrayed against each other, and the time has arrived, so much dreaded by the Father of his Country, when hostile geographical parties have been formed.

I have long foreseen and often forewarned my countrymen of the now impending danger. This does not proceed solely from the claim on the part of Congress or the Territorial legislatures to exclude slavery from the Territories, nor from the efforts of different States to defeat the execution of the fugitive-slave law. All or any of these evils might have been endured by the South without danger to the Union (as others have been) in the hope that time and reflection might apply the remedy. The immediate peril arises not so much from these causes as from the fact that the incessant and violent agitation of the slavery question throughout the North for the last quarter of a century has at length produced its malign influence on the slaves and inspired them with vague notions of freedom. Hence a sense of security no longer exists around the family altar. This feeling of peace at home has given place to apprehensions of servile insurrections. Many a matron throughout the South retires at night in dread of what may befall herself and children before the morning. Should this apprehension of domestic danger, whether real or imaginary, extend and intensify itself until it shall pervade the masses of the Southern people, then disunion will become inevitable. Self-preservation is the first law of nature, and has been implanted in the heart of man by his Creator for the wisest purpose; and no political union, however fraught with blessings and benefits in all other respects, can long continue if the necessary consequence be to render the homes and the firesides of nearly half the parties to it habitually and hopelessly insecure. Sooner or later the bonds of such a union must be severed. It is my conviction that this fatal period has not yet arrived, and my prayer to God is that He would preserve the Constitution and the Union throughout all generations.

But let us take warning in time and remove the cause of danger. It can not be denied that for five and twenty years the agitation at the North against slavery has been incessant. In 1835 pictorial handbills and inflammatory appeals were circulated extensively throughout the South of a character to excite the passions of the slaves, and, in the language of General Jackson, "to stimulate them to insurrection and produce all the horrors of a servile war." This agitation has ever since been continued by the public press, by the proceedings of State and county conventions and by abolition sermons and lectures. The time of Congress has been occupied in violent speeches on this never-ending subject, and appeals, in pamphlet and other forms, indorsed by distinguished names, have been sent forth from this central point and spread broadcast over the Union.

How easy would it be for the American people to settle the slavery question forever and to restore peace and harmony to this distracted country! They, and they alone, can do it. All that is necessary to accomplish the object, and all for which the slave States have ever contended, is to be let alone and permitted to manage their domestic institutions in their own way. As sovereign States, they, and they alone, are responsible before God and the world for the slavery existing among them. For this the people of the North are not more responsible and have no more right to interfere than with similar institutions in Russia or in Brazil.

Upon their good sense and patriotic forbearance I confess I still greatly rely. Without their aid it is beyond the power of any President, no matter what may be his own political proclivities, to restore peace and harmony among the States. Wisely limited and restrained as is his power under our Constitution and laws, he alone can accomplish but little for good or for evil on such a momentous question.

And this brings me to observe that the election of any one of our fellow-citizens to the office of President does not of itself afford just cause for dissolving the Union. This is more especially true if his election has been effected by a mere plurality, and not a majority of the people, and has resulted from transient and temporary causes, which may probably never again occur. In order to justify a resort to revolutionary resistance, the Federal Government must be guilty of "a deliberate, palpable, and dangerous exercise" of powers not granted by the Constitution. The late Presidential election, however, has been held in strict conformity with its express provisions. How, then, can the result justify a revolution to destroy this very Constitution? Reason, justice, a regard for the Constitution, all require that we shall wait for some overt and dangerous act on the part of the President elect before resorting to such a remedy. It is said, however, that the antecedents of the President elect have been sufficient to justify the fears of the South that he will attempt to invade their constitutional rights. But are such apprehensions of contingent danger in the future sufficient to justify the immediate destruction of the noblest system of government ever devised by mortals? From the very nature of his office and its high responsibilities he must necessarily be conservative. The stern duty of administering the vast and complicated concerns of this Government affords in itself a guaranty that he will not attempt any violation of a clear constitutional right.

After all, he is no more than the chief executive officer of the Government. His province is not to make but to execute the laws. And it is a remarkable fact in our history that, notwithstanding the repeated efforts of the antislavery party, no single act has ever passed Congress, unless we may possibly except the Missouri compromise, impairing in the slightest degree the rights of the South to their property in slaves; and it may also be observed, judging from present indications, that no probability exists of the passage of such an act by a majority of both Houses, either in the present or the next Congress. Surely under these circumstances we ought to be restrained from present action by the precept of Him who spake as man never spoke, that "sufficient unto the day is the evil thereof." The day of evil may never come unless we shall rashly bring it upon ourselves.

It is alleged as one cause for immediate secession that the Southern States are denied equal rights with the other States in the common Territories. But by what authority are these denied? Not by Congress, which has never passed, and I believe never will pass, any act to exclude slavery from these Territories; and certainly not by the Supreme Court, which has solemnly decided that slaves are property, and, like all other property, their owners have a right to take them into the common Territories and hold them there under the protection of the Constitution.

So far then, as Congress is concerned, the objection is not to anything they have already done, but to what they may do hereafter. It will surely be admitted that this apprehension of future danger is no good reason for an immediate dissolution of the Union. It is true that the Territorial legislature of Kansas, on the 23d February, 1860, passed in great haste an act over the veto of the governor declaring that slavery "is and shall be forever prohibited in this Territory." Such an act, however, plainly violating the rights of property secured by the Constitution, will surely be declared void by the judiciary whenever it shall be presented in a legal form.

Only three days after my inauguration the Supreme Court of the United States solemnly adjudged that this power did not exist in a Territorial legislature. Yet such has been the factious temper of the times that the correctness of this decision has been extensively impugned before the people, and the question has given rise to angry political conflicts throughout the country. Those who have appealed from this judgment of our highest constitutional tribunal to popular assemblies would, if they could, invest a Territorial legislature with power to annul the sacred rights of property. This power Congress is expressly forbidden by the Federal Constitution to exercise. Every State legislature in the Union is forbidden by its own constitution to exercise it. It can not be exercised in any State except by the people in their highest sovereign capacity, when framing or amending their State constitution. In like manner it can only be exercised by the people of a Territory represented in a convention of delegates for the purpose of framing a constitution preparatory to admission as a State into the Union. Then, and not until then, are they invested with power to decide the question whether slavery shall or shall not exist within their limits. This is an act of sovereign authority, and not of subordinate Territorial legislation. Were it otherwise, then indeed would the equality of the States in the Territories be destroyed, and the rights of property in slaves would depend not upon the guaranties of the Constitution, but upon the shifting majorities of an irresponsible Territorial legislature. Such a doctrine, from its intrinsic unsoundness, can not long influence any considerable portion of our people, much less can it afford a good reason for a dissolution of the Union.

The most palpable violations of constitutional duty which have yet been committed consist in the acts of different State legislatures to defeat the execution of the fugitive-slave law. It ought to be remembered, however, that for these acts neither Congress nor any President can justly be held responsible. Having been passed in violation of the Federal Constitution, they are therefore null and void. All the courts, both State and national, before whom the question has arisen have from the beginning declared the fugitive-slave law to be constitutional. The single exception is that of a State court in Wisconsin, and this has not only been reversed by the proper appellate tribunal, but has met with such universal reprobation that there can be no danger from it as a precedent. The validity of this law has been established over and over again by the Supreme Court of the United States with perfect unanimity. It is founded upon an express provision of the Constitution, requiring that fugitive slaves who escape from service in one State to another shall be "delivered up" to their masters. Without this provision it is a well-known historical fact that the Constitution itself could never have been adopted by the Convention. In one form or other, under the acts of 1793 and 1850, both being substantially the same, the fugitive-slave law has been the law of the land from the days of Washington until the present moment. Here, then, a clear case is presented in which it will be the duty of the next President, as it has been my own, to act with vigor in executing this supreme law against the conflicting enactments of State legislatures. Should he fail in the performance of this high duty, he will then have manifested a disregard of the Constitution and laws, to the great injury of the people of nearly one-half of the States of the Union. But are we to presume in advance that he will thus violate his duty? This would be at war with every principle of justice and of Christian charity. Let us wait for the overt act. The fugitive-slave law has been carried into execution in every contested case since the commencement of the present Administration, though often, it is to be regretted, with great loss and inconvenience to the master and with considerable expense to the Government. Let us trust that the State legislatures will repeal their unconstitutional and obnoxious enactments. Unless this shall be done without unnecessary delay, it is impossible for any human power to save the Union.

The Southern States, standing on the basis of the Constitution, have a right to demand this act of justice from the States of the North. Should it be refused, then the Constitution, to which all the States are parties, will have been willfully violated by one portion of them in a provision essential to the domestic security and happiness of the remainder. In that event the injured States, after having first used all peaceful and constitutional means to obtain redress, would be justified in revolutionary resistance to the Government of the Union.

I have purposely confined my remarks to revolutionary resistance, because it has been claimed within the last few years that any State, whenever this shall be its sovereign will and pleasure, may secede from the Union in accordance with the Constitution and without any violation of the constitutional rights of the other members of the Confederacy; that as each became parties to the Union by the vote of its own people assembled in convention, so any one of them may retire from the Union in a similar manner by the vote of such a convention.

In order to justify secession as a constitutional remedy, it must be on the principle that the Federal Government is a mere voluntary association of States, to be dissolved at pleasure by any one of the contracting parties.   If this be so, the Confederacy is a rope of sand, to be penetrated and dissolved by the first adverse wave of public opinion in any of the States.   In this manner our thirty-three States may resolve themselves into as many petty, jarring, and hostile republics, each one retiring from the Union without responsibility whenever any sudden excitement might impel them to such a course.   By this process a Union might be entirely broken into fragments in a few weeks which cost our forefathers many years of toil, privation, and blood to establish.

Such a principle is wholly inconsistent with the history as well as the character of the Federal Constitution.   After it was framed with the greatest deliberation and care it was submitted to conventions of the people of the several States for ratification.   Its provisions were discussed at length in these bodies, composed of the first men of the country.   Its opponents contended that it conferred powers upon the Federal Government dangerous to the rights of the States, whilst its advocates maintained that under a fair construction of the instrument there was no foundation for such apprehensions.   In that mighty struggle between the first intellects of this or any other country it never occurred to any individual, either among its opponents or advocates, to assert or even to intimate that their efforts were all vain labor, because the moment that any State felt herself aggrieved she might secede from the Union. What a crushing argument would this have proved against those who dreaded that the rights of the States would be endangered by the Constitution!   The truth is that it was not until many years after the origin of the Federal Government that such a proposition was first advanced. It was then met and refuted by the conclusive arguments of General Jackson, who in his message of the 16th of January, 1833, transmitting the nullifying ordinance of South Carolina to Congress, employs the following language:

The right of the people of a single State to absolve themselves at will and without the consent of the other States from their most solemn obligations, and hazard the liberties and happiness of the millions composing this Union, can not be acknowledged. Such authority is believed to be utterly repugnant both to the principles upon which the General Government is constituted and to the objects which it is expressly formed to attain.

It is not pretended that any clause in the Constitution gives countenance to such a theory.   It is altogether founded upon inference; not from any language contained in the instrument itself, but from the sovereign character of the several States by which it was ratified.   But is it beyond the power of a State, like an individual, to yield a portion of its sovereign rights to secure the remainder?   In the language of Mr. Madison, who has been called the father of the Constitution—

It was formed by the States; that is, by the people in each of the States acting in their highest sovereign capacity, and formed, consequently, by the same authority which formed the State constitutions.   *   *   *   Nor is the Government of the United States, created by the Constitution, less a government, in the strict sense of the term, within the sphere of its powers than the governments created by the constitutions of the States are within their several spheres. It is, like them, organized into legislative, executive, and judiciary departments. It operates, like them directly on persons and things, and, like them, it has at command a physical force for executing the powers committed to it.

It was intended to be perpetual, and not to be annulled at the pleasure of any one of the contracting parties. The old Articles of Confederation were entitled "Articles of Confederation and Perpetual Union between the States," and by the thirteenth article it is expressly declared that "the articles of this Confederation shall be inviolably observed by every State, and the Union shall be perpetual." The preamble to the Constitution of the United States, having express reference to the Articles of Confederation, recites that it was established "in order to form a more perfect union." And yet it is contended that this "more perfect union" does not include the essential attribute of perpetuity.

But that the Union was designed to be perpetual appears conclusively from the nature and extent of the powers conferred by the Constitution on the Federal Government. These powers embrace the very highest attributes of national sovereignty. They place both the sword and the purse under its control. Congress has power to make war and to make peace, to raise and support armies and navies, and to conclude treaties with foreign governments. It is invested with the power to coin money and to regulate the value thereof, and to regulate commerce with foreign nations and among the several States. It is not necessary to enumerate the other high powers which have been conferred upon the Federal Government. In order to carry the enumerated powers into effect, Congress possesses the exclusive right to lay and collect duties on imports, and, in common with the States, to lay and collect all other taxes.

But the Constitution has not only conferred these high powers upon Congress, but it has adopted effectual means to restrain the States from interfering with their exercise. For that purpose it has in strong prohibitory language expressly declared that—

No State shall enter into any treaty, alliance, or confederation; grant letters of marque and reprisal; coin money; emit bills of credit; make anything but gold and silver coin a tender in payment of debts; pass any bill of attainder, *ex post facto* law, or law impairing the obligation of contracts.

Moreover—

No State shall without the consent of the Congress lay any imposts or duties on imports or exports, except what may be absolutely necessary for executing its inspection laws.

And if they exceed this amount the excess shall belong to the United States. And—

No State shall without the consent of Congress lay any duty of tonnage, keep troops or ships of war in time of peace, enter into any agreement or compact with another State or with a foreign power, or engage in war, unless actually invaded or in such imminent danger as will not admit of delay.

In order still further to secure the uninterrupted exercise of these high powers against State interposition, it is provided that—

This Constitution and the laws of the United States which shall be made in pursuance thereof, and all treaties made or which shall be made under the authority of the United States, shall be the supreme law of the land, and the judges in every State shall be bound thereby, anything in the constitution or laws of any State to the contrary notwithstanding.

The solemn sanction of religion has been superadded to the obligations of official duty, and all Senators and Representatives of the United States, all members of State legislatures, and all executive and judicial officers, "both of the United States and of the several States, shall be bound by oath or affirmation to support this Constitution."

In order to carry into effect these powers, the Constitution has established a perfect Government in all its forms—legislative, executive, and judicial; and this Government to the extent of its powers acts directly upon the individual citizens of every State, and executes its own decrees by the agency of its own officers. In this respect it differs entirely from the Government under the old Confederation, which was confined to making requisitions on the States in their sovereign character. This left it in the discretion of each whether to obey or to refuse, and they often declined to comply with such requisitions. It thus became necessary for the purpose of removing this barrier and "in order to form a more perfect union" to establish a Government which could act directly upon the people and execute its own laws without the intermediate agency of the States. This has been accomplished by the Constitution of the United States. In short, the Government created by the Constitution, and deriving its authority from the sovereign people of each of the several States, has precisely the same right to exercise its power over the people of all these States in the enumerated cases that each one of them possesses over subjects not delegated to the United States, but "reserved to the States respectively or to the people."

To the extent of the delegated powers the Constitution of the United States is as much a part of the constitution of each State and is as binding upon its people as though it had been textually inserted therein.

This Government, therefore, is a great and powerful Government, invested with all the attributes of sovereignty over the special subjects to which its authority extends. Its framers never intended to implant in its bosom the seeds of its own destruction, nor were they at its creation guilty of the absurdity of providing for its own dissolution. It was not intended by its framers to be the baseless fabric of a vision, which at the touch of the enchanter would vanish into thin air, but a substantial and mighty fabric, capable of resisting the slow decay of time and of defying the storms of ages. Indeed, well may the jealous patriots of that day have indulged fears that a Government of such high powers might violate the reserved rights of the States, and wisely did they adopt the rule of a strict construction of these powers to prevent the danger. But they did not fear, nor had they any reason to imagine, that the Constitution would ever be so interpreted as to enable any State by her own act, and without the consent of her sister States, to discharge her people from all or any of their federal obligations.

It may be asked, then, Are the people of the States without redress against the tyranny and oppression of the Federal Government? By no means. The right of resistance on the part of the governed against the oppression of their governments can not be denied. It exists independently of all constitutions, and has been exercised at all periods of the world's history. Under it old governments have been destroyed and new ones have taken their place. It is embodied in strong and express language in our own Declaration of Independence. But the distinction must ever be observed that this is revolution against an established government, and not a voluntary secession from it by virtue of an inherent constitutional right. In short, let us look the danger fairly in the face. Secession is neither more nor less than revolution. It may or it may not be a justifiable revolution, but still it is revolution.

What, in the meantime, is the responsibility and true position of the Executive? He is bound by solemn oath, before God and the country, "to take care that the laws be faithfully executed," and from this obligation he can not be absolved by any human power. But what if the performance of this duty, in whole or in part, has been rendered impracticable by events over which he could have exercised no control? Such at the present moment is the case throughout the State of South Carolina so far as the laws of the United States to secure the administration of justice by means of the Federal judiciary are concerned. All the Federal officers within its limits through whose agency alone these laws can be carried into execution have already resigned. We no longer have a district judge, a district attorney, or a marshal in South Carolina. In fact, the whole machinery of the Federal Government necessary for the distribution of remedial justice among the people has been demolished, and it would be difficult, if not impossible, to replace it.

The only acts of Congress on the statute book bearing upon this subject are those of February 28, 1795, and March 3, 1807. These authorize the President, after he shall have ascertained that the marshal, with his *posse comitatus*, is unable to execute civil or criminal process in any particular case, to call forth the militia and employ the Army and Navy to aid him in performing this service, having first by proclamation commanded the insurgents "to disperse and retire peaceably to their respective abodes within a limited time." This duty can not by possibility be performed in a State where no judicial authority exists to issue process, and where there is no marshal to execute it, and where, even if there were such an officer, the entire population would constitute one solid combination to resist him.

The bare enumeration of these provisions proves how inadequate they are without further legislation to overcome a united opposition in a single State, not to speak of other States who may place themselves in a similar attitude. Congress alone has power to decide whether the present laws can or can not be amended so as to carry out more effectually the objects of the Constitution.

The same insuperable obstacles do not lie in the way of executing the laws for the collection of the customs. The revenue still continues to be collected as heretofore at the custom-house in Charleston, and should the collector unfortunately resign a successor may be appointed to perform this duty.

Then, in regard to the property of the United States in South Carolina. This has been purchased for a fair equivalent, "by the consent of the legislature of the State," "for the erection of forts, magazines, arsenals," etc., and over these the authority "to exercise exclusive legislation" has been expressly granted by the Constitution to Congress. It is not believed that any attempt will be made to expel the United States from this property by force; but if in this I should prove to be mistaken, the officer in command of the forts has received orders to act strictly on the defensive. In such a contingency the responsibility for consequences would rightfully rest upon the heads of the assailants.

Apart from the execution of the laws, so far as this may be practicable, the Executive has no authority to decide what shall be the relations between the Federal Government and South Carolina. He has been invested with no such discretion. He possesses no power to change the relations heretofore existing between them, much less to acknowledge the independence of that State. This would be to invest a mere executive officer with the power of recognizing the dissolution of the confederacy among our thirty-three sovereign States. It bears no resemblance to the recognition of a foreign *de facto* government, involving no such responsibility. Any attempt to do this would, on his part, be a naked act of usurpation. It is therefore my duty to submit to Congress the whole question in all its bearings. The course of events is so rapidly hastening forward that the emergency may soon arise when you may be called upon to decide the momentous question whether you possess the power by force of arms to compel a State to remain in the Union. I should feel myself recreant to my duty were I not to express an opinion on this important subject.

The question fairly stated is, Has the Constitution delegated to Congress the power to coerce a State into submission which is attempting to withdraw or has actually withdrawn from the Confederacy? If answered in the affirmative, it must be on the principle that the power has been conferred upon Congress to declare and to make war against a State. After much serious reflection I have arrived at the conclusion that no such power has been delegated to Congress or to any other department of the Federal Government. It is manifest upon an inspection of the Constitution that this is not among the specific and enumerated powers granted to Congress, and it is equally apparent that its exercise is not "necessary and proper for carrying into execution" any one of these powers. So far from this power having been delegated to Congress, it was expressly refused by the Convention which framed the Constitution.

It appears from the proceedings of that body that on the 31st May, 1787, the clause "*authorizing an exertion of the force of the whole against a delinquent State*" came up for consideration. Mr. Madison opposed it in a brief but powerful speech, from which I shall extract but a single sentence. He observed:

The use of force against a State would look more like a declaration of war than an infliction of punishment, and would probably be considered by the party attacked as a dissolution of all previous compacts by which it might be bound.

Upon his motion the clause was unanimously postponed, and was never, I believe, again presented. Soon afterwards, on the 8th June, 1787, when incidentally adverting to the subject, he said: "Any government for the United States formed on the supposed practicability of using force against the unconstitutional proceedings of the States would prove as visionary and fallacious as the government of Congress," evidently meaning the then existing Congress of the old Confederation.

Without descending to particulars, it may be safely asserted that the power to make war against a State is at variance with the whole spirit and intent of the Constitution. Suppose such a war should result in the conquest of a State; how are we to govern it afterwards? Shall we hold it as a province and govern it by despotic power? In the nature of things, we could not by physical force control the will of the people and compel them to elect Senators and Representatives to Congress and to perform all the other duties depending upon their own volition and required from the free citizens of a free State as a constituent member of the Confederacy.

But if we possessed this power, would it be wise to exercise it under existing circumstances? The object would doubtless be to preserve the Union. War would not only present the most effectual means of destroying it, but would vanish all hope of its peaceable reconstruction. Besides, in the fraternal conflict a vast amount of blood and treasure would be expended, rendering future reconciliation between the States impossible. In the meantime, who can foretell what would be the sufferings and privations of the people during its existence?

The fact is that our Union rests upon public opinion, and can never be cemented by the blood of its citizens shed in civil war. If it can not live in the affections of the people, it must one day perish. Congress possesses many means of preserving it by conciliation, but the sword was not placed in their hand to preserve it by force.

But may I be permitted solemnly to invoke my countrymen to pause and deliberate before they determine to destroy this the grandest temple which has ever been dedicated to human freedom since the world began? It has been consecrated by the blood of our fathers, by the glories of the past, and by the hopes of the future. The Union has already made us the most prosperous, and ere long will, if preserved, render us the most powerful, nation on the face of the earth. In every foreign region of the globe the title of American citizen is held in the highest respect, and when pronounced in a foreign land it causes the hearts of our countrymen to swell with honest pride. Surely when we reach the brink of the yawning abyss we shall recoil with horror from the last fatal plunge.

By such a dread catastrophe the hopes of the friends of freedom throughout the world would be destroyed, and a long night of leaden despotism would enshroud the nations. Our example for more than eighty years would not only be lost, but it would be quoted as a conclusive proof that man is unfit for self-government.

It is not every wrong—nay, it is not every grievous wrong—which can justify a resort to such a fearful alternative. This ought to be the last desperate remedy of a despairing people, after every other constitutional means of conciliation had been exhausted. We should reflect that under this free Government there is an incessant ebb and flow in public opinion. The slavery question, like everything human, will have its day. I firmly believe that it has reached and passed the culminating point. But if in the midst of the existing excitement the Union shall perish, the evil may then become irreparable.

Congress can contribute much to avert it by proposing and recommending to the legislatures of the several States the remedy for existing evils which the Constitution has itself provided for its own preservation. This has been tried at different critical periods of our history, and always with eminent success. It is to be found in the fifth article, providing for its own amendment. Under this article amendments have been proposed by two-thirds of both Houses of Congress, and have been "ratified by the legislatures of three-fourths of the several States," and have consequently become parts of the Constitution. To this process the country is indebted for the clause prohibiting Congress from passing any law respecting an establishment of religion or abridging the freedom of speech or of the press or of the right of petition. To this we are also indebted for the bill of rights which secures the people against any abuse of power by the Federal Government. Such were the apprehensions justly entertained by the friends of State rights at that period as to have rendered it extremely doubtful whether the Constitution could have long survived without those amendments.

Again the Constitution was amended by the same process, after the election of President Jefferson by the House of Representatives, in February, 1803. This amendment was rendered necessary to prevent a recurrence of the dangers which had seriously threatened the existence of the Government during the pendency of that election. The article for its own amendment was intended to secure the amicable adjustment of conflicting constitutional questions like the present which might arise between the governments of the States and that of the United States. This appears from contemporaneous history. In this connection I shall merely call attention to a few sentences in Mr. Madison's justly celebrated report, in 1799, to the legislature of Virginia. In this he ably and conclusively defended the resolutions of the preceding legislature against the strictures of several other State legislatures. These were mainly founded upon the protest of the Virginia legislature against the "alien and sedition acts," as "palpable and alarming infractions of the Constitution." In pointing out the peaceful and constitutional remedies—and he referred to none other—to which the States were authorized to resort on such occasions, he concludes by saying that—

The legislatures of the States might have made a direct representation to Congress with a view to obtain a rescinding of the two offensive acts, or they might have represented to their respective Senators in Congress their wish that two-thirds thereof would propose an explanatory amendment to the Constitution; or two-thirds of themselves, if such had been their option, might by an application to Congress have obtained a convention for the same object.

This is the very course which I earnestly recommend in order to obtain an "explanatory amendment" of the Constitution on the subject of slavery. This might originate with Congress or the State legislatures, as may be deemed most advisable to attain the object. The explanatory amendment might be confined to the final settlement of the true construction of the Constitution on three special points:

1. An express recognition of the right of property in slaves in the States where it now exists or may hereafter exist.

2. The duty of protecting this right in all the common Territories throughout their Territorial existence, and until they shall be admitted as States into the Union, with or without slavery, as their constitutions may prescribe.

3. A like recognition of the right of the master to have his slave who has escaped from one State to another restored and "delivered up" to him, and of the validity of the fugitive-slave law enacted for this purpose, together with a declaration that all State laws impairing or defeating this right are violations of the Constitution, and are consequently null and void. It may be objected that this construction of the Constitution has already been settled by the Supreme Court of the United States, and what more ought to be required? The answer is that a very large proportion of the people of the United States still contest the correctness of this decision, and never will cease from agitation and admit its binding force until clearly established by the people of the several States in their sovereign character. Such an explanatory amendment would, it is believed, forever terminate the existing dissensions, and restore peace and harmony among the States.

It ought not to be doubted that such an appeal to the arbitrament established by the Constitution itself would be received with favor by all the States of the Confederacy. In any event, it ought to be tried in a spirit of conciliation before any of these States shall separate themselves from the Union.

When I entered upon the duties of the Presidential office, the aspect neither of our foreign nor domestic affairs was at all satisfactory. We were involved in dangerous complications with several nations, and two of our Territories were in a state of revolution against the Government. A restoration of the African slave trade had numerous and powerful advocates. Unlawful military expeditions were countenanced by many of our citizens, and were suffered, in defiance of the efforts of the Government, to escape from our shores for the purpose of making war upon the offending people of neighboring republics with whom we were at peace. In addition to these and other difficulties, we experienced a revulsion in monetary affairs soon after my advent to power of unexampled severity and of ruinous consequences to all the great interests of the country. When we take a retrospect of what was then our condition and contrast this with its material prosperity at the time of the late Presidential election, we have abundant reason to return our grateful thanks to that merciful Providence which has never forsaken us as a nation in all our past trials.

Our relations with Great Britain are of the most friendly character. Since the commencement of my Administration the two dangerous questions arising from the Clayton and Bulwer treaty and from the right of search claimed by the British Government have been amicably and honorably adjusted.

The discordant constructions of the Clayton and Bulwer treaty between the two Governments, which at different periods of the discussion bore a threatening aspect, have resulted in a final settlement entirely satisfactory to this Government. In my last annual message I informed Congress that the British Government had not then "completed treaty arrangements with the Republics of Honduras and Nicaragua in pursuance of the understanding between the two Governments. It is, nevertheless, confidently expected that this good work will ere long be accomplished." This confident expectation has since been fulfilled. Her Britannic Majesty concluded a treaty with Honduras on the 28th November, 1859, and with Nicaragua on the 28th August, 1860, relinquishing the Mosquito protectorate. Besides, by the former the Bay Islands are recognized as a part of the Republic of Honduras. It may be observed that the stipulations of these treaties conform in every important particular to the amendments adopted by the Senate of the United States to the treaty concluded at London on the 17th October, 1856, between the two Governments. It will be recollected that this treaty was rejected by the British Government because of its objection to the just and important amendment of the Senate to the article relating to Ruatan and the other islands in the Bay of Honduras.

It must be a source of sincere satisfaction to all classes of our fellow-citizens, and especially to those engaged in foreign commerce, that the claim on the part of Great Britain forcibly to visit and search American merchant vessels on the high seas in time of peace has been abandoned. This was by far the most dangerous question to the peace of the two countries which has existed since the War of 1812. Whilst it remained open they might at any moment have been precipitated into a war. This was rendered manifest by the exasperated state of public feeling throughout our entire country produced by the forcible search of American merchant vessels by British cruisers on the coast of Cuba in the spring of 1858. The American people hailed with general acclaim the orders of the Secretary of the Navy to our naval force in the Gulf of Mexico "to protect all vessels of the United States on the high seas from search or detention by the vessels of war of any other nation." These orders might have produced an immediate collision between the naval forces of the two countries. This was most fortunately prevented by an appeal to the justice of Great Britain and to the law of nations as expounded by her own most eminent jurists.

The only question of any importance which still remains open is the disputed title between the two Governments to the island of San Juan, in the vicinity of Washington Territory. As this question is still under negotiation, it is not deemed advisable at the present moment to make any other allusion to the subject.

The recent visit of the Prince of Wales, in a private character, to the people of this country has proved to be a most auspicious event. In its consequences it can not fail to increase the kindred and kindly feelings which I trust may ever actuate the Government and people of both countries in their political and social intercourse with each other.

With France, our ancient and powerful ally, our relations continue to be of the most friendly character. A decision has recently been made by a French judicial tribunal, with the approbation of the Imperial Government, which can not fail to foster the sentiments of mutual regard that have so long existed between the two countries. Under the French law no person can serve in the armies of France unless he be a French citizen. The law of France recognizing the natural right of expatriation, it follows as a necessary consequence that a Frenchman by the fact of having become a citizen of the United States has changed his allegiance and has lost his native character. He can not therefore be compelled to serve in the French armies in case he should return to his native country. These principles were announced in 1852 by the French minister of war, and in two late cases have been confirmed by the French judiciary. In these, two natives of France have been discharged from the French army because they had become American citizens. To employ the language of our present minister to France, who has rendered good service on this occasion, "I do not think our French naturalized fellow-citizens will hereafter experience much annoyance on this subject."

I venture to predict that the time is not far distant when the other continental powers will adopt the same wise and just policy which has done so much honor to the enlightened Government of the Emperor. In any event, our Government is bound to protect the rights of our naturalized citizens everywhere to the same extent as though they had drawn their first breath in this country. We can recognize no distinction between our native and naturalized citizens.

Between the great Empire of Russia and the United States the mutual friendship and regard which has so long existed still continues to prevail, and if possible to increase. Indeed, our relations with that Empire are all that we could desire. Our relations with Spain are now of a more complicated, though less dangerous, character than they have been for many years. Our citizens have long held and continue to hold numerous claims against the Spanish Government. These had been ably urged for a series of years by our successive diplomatic representatives at Madrid, but without obtaining redress. The Spanish Government finally agreed to institute a joint commission for the adjustment of these claims, and on the 5th day of March, 1860, concluded a convention for this purpose with our present minister at Madrid.

Under this convention what have been denominated the "Cuban claims," amounting to $128,635.54, in which more than 100 of our fellow-citizens are interested, were recognized, and the Spanish Government agreed to pay $100,000 of this amount "within three months following the exchange of ratifications." The payment of the remaining $28,635.54 was to await the decision of the commissioners for or against the *Amistad* claim; but in any event the balance was to be paid to the claimants either by Spain or the United States. These terms, I have every reason to know, are highly satisfactory to the holders of the Cuban claims. Indeed, they have made a formal offer authorizing the State Department to settle these claims and to deduct the amount of the *Amistad* claim from the sums which they are entitled to receive from Spain. This offer, of course, can not be accepted. All other claims of citizens of the United States against Spain, or the subjects of the Queen of Spain against the United States, including the *Amistad* claim, were by this convention referred to a board of commissioners in the usual form. Neither the validity of the *Amistad* claim nor of any other claim against either party, with the single exception of the Cuban claims, was recognized by the convention. Indeed, the Spanish Government did not insist that the validity of the *Amistad* claim should be thus recognized, notwithstanding its payment had been recommended to Congress by two of my predecessors, as well as by myself, and an appropriation for that purpose had passed the Senate of the United States.

They were content that it should be submitted to the board for examination and decision like the other claims. Both Governments were bound respectively to pay the amounts awarded to the several claimants "at such times and places as may be fixed by and according to the tenor of said awards."

I transmitted this convention to the Senate for their constitutional action on the 3d of May, 1860, and on the 27th of the succeeding June they determined that they would "not advise and consent" to its ratification.

These proceedings place our relations with Spain in an awkward and embarrassing position. It is more than probable that the final adjustment of these claims will devolve upon my successor.

I reiterate the recommendation contained in my annual message of December, 1858, and repeated in that of December, 1859, in favor of the acquisition of Cuba from Spain by fair purchase. I firmly believe that such an acquisition would contribute essentially to the well-being and prosperity of both countries in all future time, as well as prove the certain means of immediately abolishing the African slave trade throughout the world. I would not repeat this recommendation upon the present occasion if I believed that the transfer of Cuba to the United States upon conditions highly favorable to Spain could justly tarnish the national honor of the proud and ancient Spanish monarchy. Surely no person ever attributed to the first Napoleon a disregard of the national honor of France for transferring Louisiana to the United States for a fair equivalent, both in money and commercial advantages.

With the Emperor of Austria and the remaining continental powers of Europe, including that of the Sultan, our relations continue to be of the most friendly character.

The friendly and peaceful policy pursued by the Government of the United States toward the Empire of China has produced the most satisfactory results. The treaty of Tien-tsin of the 18th June, 1858, has been faithfully observed by the Chinese authorities. The convention of the 8th November, 1858, supplementary to this treaty, for the adjustment and satisfaction of the claims of our citizens on China referred to in my last annual message, has been already carried into effect so far as this was practicable. Under this convention the sum of 500,000 taels, equal to about $700,000, was stipulated to be paid in satisfaction of the claims of American citizens out of the one-fifth of the receipts for tonnage, import, and export duties on American vessels at the ports of Canton, Shanghai, and Fuchau, and it was "agreed that this amount shall be in full liquidation of all claims of American citizens at the various ports to this date." Debentures for this amount, to wit, 300,000 taels for Canton, 100,000 for Shanghai, and 100,000 for Fuchau, were delivered, according to the terms of the convention, by the respective Chinese collectors of the customs of these ports to the agent selected by our minister to receive the same. Since that time the claims of our citizens have been adjusted by the board of commissioners appointed for that purpose under the act of March 3, 1859, and their awards, which proved satisfactory to the claimants, have been approved by our minister. In the aggregate they amount to the sum of $498,694.78. The claimants have already received a large proportion of the sums awarded to them out of the fund provided, and it is confidently expected that the remainder will ere long be entirely paid. After the awards shall have been satisfied there will remain a surplus of more than $200,000 at the disposition of Congress. As this will, in equity, belong to the Chinese Government, would not justice require its appropriation to some benevolent object in which the Chinese may be specially interested?

Our minister to China, in obedience to his instructions, has remained perfectly neutral in the war between Great Britain and France and the Chinese Empire, although, in conjunction with the Russian minister, he was ever ready and willing, had the opportunity offered, to employ his good offices in restoring peace between the parties. It is but an act of simple justice, both to our present minister and his predecessor, to state that they have proved fully equal to the delicate, trying, and responsible positions in which they have on different occasions been placed.

The ratifications of the treaty with Japan concluded at Yeddo on the 29th July, 1858, were exchanged at Washington on the 22d May last, and the treaty itself was proclaimed on the succeeding day. There is good reason to expect that under its protection and influence our trade and intercourse with that distant and interesting people will rapidly increase.

The ratifications of the treaty were exchanged with unusual solemnity. For this purpose the Tycoon had accredited three of his most distinguished subjects as envoys extraordinary and ministers plenipotentiary, who were received and treated with marked distinction and kindness, both by the Government and people of the United States. There is every reason to believe that they have returned to their native land entirely satisfied with their visit and inspired by the most friendly feelings for our country. Let us ardently hope, in the language of the treaty itself, that ''there shall henceforward be perpetual peace and friendship between the United States of America and His Majesty the Tycoon of Japan and his successors.''

With the wise, conservative, and liberal Government of the Empire of Brazil our relations continue to be of the most amicable character.

The exchange of the ratifications of the convention with the Republic of New Granada signed at Washington on the 10th of September, 1857, has been long delayed from accidental causes for which neither party is censurable. These ratifications were duly exchanged in this city on the 5th of November last. Thus has a controversy been amicably terminated which had become so serious at the period of my inauguration as to require me, on the 17th of April, 1857, to direct our minister to demand his passports and return to the United States.

Under this convention the Government of New Granada has specially acknowledged itself to be responsible to our citizens "for damages which were caused by the riot at Panama on the 15th April, 1856." These claims, together with other claims of our citizens which had been long urged in vain, are referred for adjustment to a board of commissioners. I submit a copy of the convention to Congress, and recommend the legislation necessary to carry it into effect.

Persevering efforts have been made for the adjustment of the claims of American citizens against the Government of Costa Rica, and I am happy to inform you that these have finally prevailed. A convention was signed at the city of San Jose on the 2d July last, between the minister resident of the United States in Costa Rica and the plenipotentiaries of that Republic, referring these claims to a board of commissioners and providing for the payment of their awards. This convention will be submitted immediately to the Senate for their constitutional action.

The claims of our citizens upon the Republic of Nicaragua have not yet been provided for by treaty, although diligent efforts for this purpose have been made by our minister resident to that Republic. These are still continued, with a fair prospect of success.

Our relations with Mexico remain in a most unsatisfactory condition. In my last two annual messages I discussed extensively the subject of these relations, and do not now propose to repeat at length the facts and arguments then presented. They proved conclusively that our citizens residing in Mexico and our merchants trading thereto had suffered a series of wrongs and outrages such as we have never patiently borne from any other nation. For these our successive ministers, invoking the faith of treaties, had in the name of their country persistently demanded redress and indemnification, but without the slightest effect. Indeed, so confident had the Mexican authorities become of our patient endurance that they universally believed they might commit these outrages upon American citizens with absolute impunity. Thus wrote our minister in 1856, and expressed the opinion that "nothing but a manifestation of the power of the Government and of its purpose to punish these wrongs will avail."

Afterwards, in 1857, came the adoption of a new constitution for Mexico, the election of a President and Congress under its provisions, and the inauguration of the President. Within one short month, however, this President was expelled from the capital by a rebellion in the army, and the supreme power of the Republic was assigned to General Zuloaga. This usurper was in his turn soon compelled to retire and give place to General Miramon.

Under the constitution which had thus been adopted Señor Juarez, as chief justice of the supreme court, became the lawful President of the

Republic, and it was for the maintenance of the constitution and his authority derived from it that the civil war commenced and still continues to be prosecuted.

Throughout the year 1858 the constitutional party grew stronger and stronger. In the previous history of Mexico a successful military revolution at the capital had almost universally been the signal for submission throughout the Republic. Not so on the present occasion. A majority of the citizens persistently sustained the constitutional Government. When this was recognized, in April, 1859, by the Government of the United States, its authority extended over a large majority of the Mexican States and people,. including Vera Cruz and all the other important seaports of the Republic. From that period our commerce with Mexico began to revive, and the constitutional Government has afforded it all the protection in its power.

Meanwhile the Government of Miramon still held sway at the capital and over the surrounding country, and continued its outrages against the few American citizens who still had the courage to remain within its power. To cap the climax, after the battle of Tacubaya, in April, 1859, General Marquez ordered three citizens of the United States, two of them physicians, to be seized in the hospital at that place, taken out and shot, without crime and without trial. This was done, notwithstanding our unfortunate countrymen were at the moment engaged in the holy cause of affording relief to the soldiers of both parties who had been wounded in the battle, without making any distinction between them.

The time had arrived, in my opinion, when this Government was bound to exert its power to avenge and redress the wrongs of our citizens and to afford them protection in Mexico. The interposing obstacle was that the portion of the country under the sway of Miramon could not be reached without passing over territory under the jurisdiction of the constitutional Government. Under these circumstances I deemed it my duty to recommend to Congress in my last annual message the employment of a sufficient military force to penetrate into the interior, where the Government of Miramon was to be found, with or, if need be, without the consent of the Juarez Government, though it was not doubted that this consent could be obtained. Never have I had a clearer conviction on any subject than of the justice as well as wisdom of such a policy. No other alternative was left except the entire abandonment of our fellow-citizens who had gone to Mexico under the faith of treaties to the systematic injustice, cruelty, and oppression of Miramon's Government. Besides, it is almost certain that the simple authority to employ this force would of itself have accomplished all our objects without striking a single blow. The constitutional Government would then ere this have been established at the City of Mexico, and would have been ready and willing to the extent of its ability to do us justice.

In addition—and I deem this a most important consideration—European Governments would have been deprived of all pretext to interfere in the territorial and domestic concerns of Mexico. We should thus have been relieved from the obligation of resisting, even by force should this become necessary, any attempt by these Governments to deprive our neighboring Republic of portions of her territory—a duty from which we could not shrink without abandoning the traditional and established policy of the American people. I am happy to observe that, firmly relying upon the justice and good faith of these Governments, there is no present danger that such a contingency will happen.

Having discovered that my recommendations would not be sustained by Congress, the next alternative was to accomplish in some degree, if possible, the same objects by treaty stipulations with the constitutional Government. Such treaties were accordingly concluded by our late able and excellent minister to Mexico, and on the 4th of January last were submitted to the Senate for ratification. As these have not yet received the final action of that body, it would be improper for me to present a detailed statement of their provisions. Still, I may be permitted to express the opinion in advance that they are calculated to promote the agricultural, manufacturing, and commercial interests of the country and to secure our just influence with an adjoining Republic as to whose fortunes and fate we can never feel indifferent, whilst at the same time they provide for the payment of a considerable amount toward the satisfaction of the claims of our injured fellow-citizens.

At the period of my inauguration I was confronted in Kansas by a revolutionary government existing under what is called the "Topeka constitution." Its avowed object was to subdue the Territorial government by force and to inaugurate what was called the "Topeka government" in its stead. To accomplish this object an extensive military organization was formed, and its command intrusted to the most violent revolutionary leaders. Under these circumstances it became my imperative duty to exert the whole constitutional power of the Executive to prevent the flames of civil war from again raging in Kansas, which in the excited state of the public mind, both North and South, might have extended into the neighboring States. The hostile parties in Kansas had been inflamed against each other by emissaries both from the North and the South to a degree of malignity without parallel in our history. To prevent actual collision and to assist the civil magistrates in enforcing the laws, a strong detachment of the Army was stationed in the Territory, ready to aid the marshal and his deputies when lawfully called upon as a *posse comitatus* in the execution of civil and criminal process. Still, the troubles in Kansas could not have been permanently settled without an election by the people.

The ballot box is the surest arbiter of disputes among freemen. Under this conviction every proper effort was employed to induce the hostile parties to vote at the election of delegates to frame a State constitution, and afterwards at the election to decide whether Kansas should be a slave or free State.

The insurgent party refused to vote at either, lest this might be considered a recognition on their part of the Territorial government established by Congress. A better spirit, however, seemed soon after to prevail, and the two parties met face to face at the third election, held on the first Monday of January, 1858, for members of the legislature and State officers under the Lecompton constitution. The result was the triumph of the antislavery party at the polls. This decision of the ballot box proved clearly that this party were in the majority, and removed the danger of civil war. From that time we have heard little or nothing of the Topeka government, and all serious danger of revolutionary troubles in Kansas was then at an end.

The Lecompton constitution, which had been thus recognized at this State election by the votes of both political parties in Kansas, was transmitted to me with the request that I should present it to Congress. This I could not have refused to do without violating my clearest and strongest convictions of duty. The constitution and all the proceedings which preceded and followed its formation were fair and regular on their face. I then believed, and experience has proved, that the interests of the people of Kansas would have been best consulted by its admission as a State into the Union, especially as the majority within a brief period could have amended the constitution according to their will and pleasure. If fraud existed in all or any of these proceedings, it was not for the President but for Congress to investigate and determine the question of fraud and what ought to be its consequences. If at the first two elections the majority refused to vote, it can not be pretended that this refusal to exercise the elective franchise could invalidate an election fairly held under lawful authority, even if they had not subsequently voted at the third election. It is true that the whole constitution had not been submitted to the people, as I always desired; but the precedents are numerous of the admission of States into the Union without such submission. It would not comport with my present purpose to review the proceedings of Congress upon the Lecompton constitution. It is sufficient to observe that their final action has removed the last vestige of serious revolutionary troubles. The desperate band recently assembled under a notorious outlaw in the southern portion of the Territory to resist the execution of the laws and to plunder peaceful citizens will, I doubt not, be speedily subdued and brought to justice.

Had I treated the Lecompton constitution as a nullity and refused to transmit it to Congress, it is not difficult to imagine, whilst recalling the position of the country at that moment, what would have been the disastrous consequences, both in and out of the Territory, from such a dereliction of duty on the part of the Executive.

Peace has also been restored within the Territory of Utah, which at the commencement of my Administration was in a state of open rebellion. This was the more dangerous, as the people, animated by a fanatical spirit and intrenched within their distant mountain fastnesses, might have made a long and formidable resistance. Cost what it might, it was necessary to bring them into subjection to the Constitution and the laws. Sound policy, therefore, as well as humanity, required that this object should if possible be accomplished without the effusion of blood. This could only be effected by sending a military force into the Territory sufficiently strong to convince the people that resistance would be hopeless, and at the same time to offer them a pardon for past offenses on condition of immediate submission to the Government. This policy was pursued with eminent success, and the only cause for regret is the heavy expenditure required to march a large detachment of the Army to that remote region and to furnish it subsistence.

Utah is now comparatively peaceful and quiet, and the military force has been withdrawn, except that portion of it necessary to keep the Indians in check and to protect the emigrant trains on their way to our Pacific possessions.

In my first annual message I promised to employ my best exertions in cooperation with Congress to reduce the expenditures of the Government within the limits of a wise and judicious economy. An overflowing Treasury had produced habits of prodigality and extravagance which could only be gradually corrected. The work required both time and patience. I applied myself diligently to this task from the beginning and was aided by the able and energetic efforts of the heads of the different Executive Departments. The result of our labors in this good cause did not appear in the sum total of our expenditures for the first two years, mainly in consequence of the extraordinary expenditure necessarily incurred in the Utah expedition and the very large amount of the contingent expenses of Congress during this period. These greatly exceeded the pay and mileage of the members. For the year ending June 30, 1858, whilst the pay and mileage amounted to $1,490,214, the contingent expenses rose to $2,093,309.79; and for the year ending June 30, 1859, whilst the pay and mileage amounted to $859,093.66, the contingent expenses amounted to $1,431,565.78. I am happy, however, to be able to inform you that during the last fiscal year, ending June 30, 1860, the total expenditures of the Government in all its branches—legislative, executive, and judicial—exclusive of the public debt, were reduced to the sum of $55,402,-465.46. This conclusively appears from the books of the Treasury. In the year ending June 30, 1858, the total expenditure, exclusive of the public debt, amounted to $71,901,129.77, and that for the year ending June 30, 1859, to $66,346,226.13. Whilst the books of the Treasury show an actual expenditure of $59,848,474.72 for the year ending June 30, 1860, including $1,040,667.71 for the contingent expenses of Congress, there must be deducted from this amount the sum of $4,296,009.26, with the interest upon it of $150,000, appropriated by the act of February 15, 1860, "for the purpose of supplying the deficiency in the revenues and defraying the expenses of the Post-Office Department for the year ending June 30, 1859." This sum, therefore, justly chargeable to the year 1859, must be deducted from the sum of $59,848,474.72 in order to ascertain the expenditure for the year ending June 30, 1860, which leaves a balance for the expenditures of that year of $55,402,465.46. The interest on the public debt, including Treasury notes, for the same fiscal year, ending June 30, 1860, amounted to $3,177,314.62, which, added to the above sum of $55,402,465.46, makes the aggregate of $58,579,780.08.

It ought in justice to be observed that several of the estimates from the Departments for the year ending June 30, 1860, were reduced by Congress below what was and still is deemed compatible with the public interest. Allowing a liberal margin of $2,500,000 for this reduction and for other causes, it may be safely asserted that the sum of $61,000,000, or, at the most, $62,000,000, is amply sufficient to administer the Government and to pay the interest on the public debt, unless contingent events should hereafter render extraordinary expenditures necessary.

This result has been attained in a considerable degree by the care exercised by the appropriate Departments in entering into public contracts. I have myself never interfered with the award of any such contract, except in a single case, with the Colonization Society, deeming it advisable to cast the whole responsibility in each case on the proper head of the Department, with the general instruction that these contracts should always be given to the lowest and best bidder. It has ever been my opinion that public contracts are not a legitimate source of patronage to be conferred upon personal or political favorites, but that in all such cases a public officer is bound to act for the Government as a prudent individual would act for himself.

It is with great satisfaction I communicate the fact that since the date of my last annual message not a single slave has been imported into the United States in violation of the laws prohibiting the African slave trade. This statement is founded upon a thorough examination and investigation of the subject. Indeed, the spirit which prevailed some time since among a portion of our fellow-citizens in favor of this trade seems to have entirely subsided.

I also congratulate you upon the public sentiment which now exists against the crime of setting on foot military expeditions within the limits of the United States to proceed from thence and make war upon the people of unoffending States with whom we are at peace. In this respect a happy change has been effected since the commencement of my Administration. It surely ought to be the prayer of every Christian and patriot that such expeditions may never again receive countenance in our country or depart from our shores.

It would be a useless repetition to do more than refer with earnest commendation to my former recommendations in favor of the Pacific railroad; of the grant of power to the President to employ the naval force in the vicinity for the protection of the lives and property of our fellow-citizens passing in transit over the different Central American routes against sudden and lawless outbreaks and depredations, and also to protect American merchant vessels, their crews and cargoes, against violent and unlawful seizure and confiscation in the ports of Mexico and the South American Republics when these may be in a disturbed and revolutionary condition. It is my settled conviction that without such a power we do not afford that protection to those engaged in the commerce of the country which they have a right to demand.

I again recommend to Congress the passage of a law, in pursuance of the provisions of the Constitution, appointing a day certain previous to the 4th March in each year of an odd number for the election of Representatives throughout all the States. A similar power has already been exercised, with general approbation, in the appointment of the same day throughout the Union for holding the election of electors for President and Vice-President of the United States. My attention was earnestly directed to this subject from the fact that the Thirty-fifth Congress terminated on the 3d March, 1859, without making the necessary appropriation for the service of the Post-Office Department. I was then forced to consider the best remedy for this omission, and an immediate call of the present Congress was the natural resort. Upon inquiry, however, I ascertained that fifteen out of the thirty-three States composing the Confederacy were without Representatives, and that consequently these fifteen States would be disfranchised by such a call. These fifteen States will be in the same condition on the 4th March next. Ten of them can not elect Representatives, according to existing State laws, until different periods, extending from the beginning of August next until the months of October and November. In my last message I gave warning that in a time of sudden and alarming danger the salvation of our institutions might depend upon the power of the President immediately to assemble a full Congress to meet the emergency.

It is now quite evident that the financial necessities of the Government will require a modification of the tariff during your present session for the purpose of increasing the revenue. In this aspect, I desire to reiterate the recommendation contained in my last two annual messages in favor of imposing specific instead of *ad valorem* duties on all imported articles to which these can be properly applied. From long observation and experience I am convinced that specific duties are necessary, both to protect the revenue and to secure to our manufacturing interests that amount of incidental encouragement which unavoidably results from a revenue tariff.

As an abstract proposition it may be admitted that *ad valorem* duties would in theory be the most just and equal. But if the experience of this and of all other commercial nations has demonstrated that such duties can not be assessed and collected without great frauds upon the revenue, then it is the part of wisdom to resort to specific duties. Indeed, from the very nature of an *ad valorem* duty this must be the result. Under it the inevitable consequence is that foreign goods will be entered at less than their true value. The Treasury will therefore lose the duty on the difference between their real and fictitious value, and to this extent we are defrauded.

The temptations which *ad valorem* duties present to a dishonest importer are irresistible. His object is to pass his goods through the custom-house at the very lowest valuation necessary to save them from confiscation. In this he too often succeeds in spite of the vigilance of the revenue officers. Hence the resort to false invoices, one for the purchaser and another for the custom-house, and to other expedients to defraud the Government. The honest importer produces his invoice to the collector, stating the actual price at which he purchased the articles abroad. Not so the dishonest importer and the agent of the foreign manufacturer. And here it may be observed that a very large proportion of the manufactures imported from abroad are consigned for sale to commission merchants, who are mere agents employed by the manufacturers. In such cases no actual sale has been made to fix their value. The foreign manufacturer, if he be dishonest, prepares an invoice of the goods, not at their actual value, but at the very lowest rate necessary to escape detection. In this manner the dishonest importer and the foreign manufacturer enjoy a decided advantage over the honest merchant. They are thus enabled to undersell the fair trader and drive him from the market. In fact the operation of this system has already driven from the pursuits of honorable commerce many of that class of regular and conscientious merchants whose character throughout the world is the pride of our country.

The remedy for these evils is to be found in specific duties, so far as this may be practicable. They dispense with any inquiry at the custom-house into the actual cost or value of the article, and it pays the precise amount of duty previously fixed by law. They present no temptations to the appraisers of foreign goods, who receive but small salaries, and might by undervaluation in a few cases render themselves independent.

Besides, specific duties best conform to the requisition in the Constitution that "no preference shall be given by any regulation of commerce or revenue to the ports of one State over those of another." Under our *ad valorem* system such preferences are to some extent inevitable, and complaints have often been made that the spirit of this provision has been violated by a lower appraisement of the same articles at one port than at another.

An impression strangely enough prevails to some extent that specific duties are necessarily protective duties. Nothing can be more fallacious. Great Britain glories in free trade, and yet her whole revenue from imports is at the present moment collected under a system of specific duties. It is a striking fact in this connection that in the commercial treaty of January 23, 1860, between France and England one of the articles provides that the *ad valorem* duties which it imposes shall be converted into specific duties within six months from its date, and these are to be ascertained by making an average of the prices for six months previous to that time. The reverse of the propositions would be nearer to the truth, because a much larger amount of revenue would be collected by merely converting the *ad valorem* duties of a tariff into equivalent specific duties. To this extent the revenue would be increased, and in the same proportion the specific duty might be diminished.

Specific duties would secure to the American manufacturer the incidental protection to which he is fairly entitled under a revenue tariff, and to this surely no person would object. The framers of the existing tariff have gone further, and in a liberal spirit have discriminated in favor of large and useful branches of our manufactures, not by raising the rate of duty upon the importation of similar articles from abroad, but, what is the same in effect, by admitting articles free of duty which enter into the composition of their fabrics.

Under the present system it has been often truly remarked that this incidental protection decreases when the manufacturer needs it most and increases when he needs it least, and constitutes a sliding scale which always operates against him. The revenues of the country are subject to similar fluctuations. Instead of approaching a steady standard, as would be the case under a system of specific duties, they sink and rise with the sinking and rising prices of articles in foreign countries. It would not be difficult for Congress to arrange a system of specific duties which would afford additional stability both to our revenue and our manufactures and without injury or injustice to any interest of the country. This might be accomplished by ascertaining the average value of any given article for a series of years at the place of exportation and by simply converting the rate of *ad valorem* duty upon it which might be deemed necessary for revenue purposes into the form of a specific duty. Such an arrangement could not injure the consumer. If he should pay a greater amount of duty one year, this would be counterbalanced by a lesser amount the next, and in the end the aggregate would be the same.

I desire to call your immediate attention to the present condition of the Treasury, so ably and clearly presented by the Secretary in his report to

Congress, and to recommend that measures be promptly adopted to enable it to discharge its pressing obligations. The other recommendations of the report are well worthy of your favorable consideration.

I herewith transmit to Congress the reports of the Secretaries of War, of the Navy, of the Interior, and of the Postmaster-General. The recommendations and suggestions which they contain are highly valuable and deserve your careful attention.

The report of the Postmaster-General details the circumstances under which Cornelius Vanderbilt, on my request, agreed in the month of July last to carry the ocean mails between our Atlantic and Pacific coasts. Had he not thus acted this important intercommunication must have been suspended, at least for a season. The Postmaster-General had no power to make him any other compensation than the postages on the mail matter which he might carry. It was known at the time that these postages would fall far short of an adequate compensation, as well as of the sum which the same service had previously cost the Government. Mr. Vanderbilt, in a commendable spirit, was willing to rely upon the justice of Congress to make up the deficiency, and I therefore recommend that an appropriation may be granted for this purpose.

I should do great injustice to the Attorney-General were I to omit the mention of his distinguished services in the measures adopted and prosecuted by him for the defense of the Government against numerous and unfounded claims to land in California purporting to have been made by the Mexican Government previous to the treaty of cession. The successful opposition to these claims has saved the United States public property worth many millions of dollars and to individuals holding title under them to at least an equal amount.

It has been represented to me from sources which I deem reliable that the inhabitants in several portions of Kansas have been reduced nearly to a state of starvation on account of the almost total failure of their crops, whilst the harvests in every other portion of the country have been abundant. The prospect before them for the approaching winter is well calculated to enlist the sympathies of every heart. The destitution appears to be so general that it can not be relieved by private contributions, and they are in such indigent circumstances as to be unable to purchase the necessaries of life for themselves. I refer the subject to Congress. If any constitutional measure for their relief can be devised, I would recommend its adoption.

I cordially commend to your favorable regard the interests of the people of this District. They are eminently entitled to your consideration, especially since, unlike the people of the States, they can appeal to no government except that of the Union.

JAMES BUCHANAN.

SPECIAL MESSAGES.

WASHINGTON, *December 5, 1860.*
To the Senate of the United States:

I transmit, for the consideration of the Senate with a view to ratification, a convention for the adjustment of claims of citizens of the United States against the Government of the Republic of Costa Rica, signed by the plenipotentiaries of the contracting parties at San Jose on the 2d day of July last.

JAMES BUCHANAN.

WASHINGTON, *December 5, 1860.*
To the House of Representatives:

In answer to the resolution of the House of Representatives of the 9th of April last, requesting information concerning the African slave trade, I transmit a report from the Secretary of State and the documents by which it was accompanied.

JAMES BUCHANAN.

WASHINGTON, *January 2, 1861.*
To the Senate of the United States:

I transmit to the Senate, for its consideration with a view to ratification, a treaty of amity, commerce, and navigation, and for the surrender of fugitive criminals, between the United States and the Republic of Venezuela, signed at Caracas on the 27th of August last.

A similar treaty was concluded on the 10th July, 1856, was submitted to the Senate, and was by a resolution of that body approved, with an amendment, on the 10th March, 1857. Before this amendment could be laid before the Government of Venezuela for acceptance a new minister of the United States was accredited to that Government. Meantime the attention of this Government had been drawn to the disadvantage which would result to our citizens residing in Venezuela if the second article of the treaty of 1856 were permitted to go into effect, the "pecuniary equivalent" for exemption from military duty being an arbitrary and generally an excessive sum. In view of this fact it was deemed preferable to instruct our new minister to negotiate a new treaty which should omit the objectionable second article and also the few words of the twenty-eighth article which had been stricken out by the Senate.

With these changes, and with the addition of the last clause to the twenty-seventh article, the treaty is the same as that already approved by the Senate.

JAMES BUCHANAN.

WASHINGTON CITY, *January 8, 1861.*

To the Senate and House of Representatives:

At the opening of your present session I called your attention to the dangers which threatened the existence of the Union. I expressed my opinion freely concerning the original causes of those dangers, and recommended such measures as I believed would have the effect of tranquilizing the country and saving it from the peril in which it had been needlessly and most unfortunately involved. Those opinions and recommendations I do not propose now to repeat. My own convictions upon the whole subject remain unchanged.

The fact that a great calamity was impending over the nation was even at that time acknowledged by every intelligent citizen. It had already made itself felt throughout the length and breadth of the land. The necessary consequences of the alarm thus produced were most deplorable. The imports fell off with a rapidity never known before, except in time of war, in the history of our foreign commerce; the Treasury was unexpectedly left without the means which it had reasonably counted upon to meet the public engagements; trade was paralyzed; manufactures were stopped; the best public securities suddenly sunk in the market; every species of property depreciated more or less, and thousands of poor men who depended upon their daily labor for their daily bread were turned out of employment.

I deeply regret that I am not able to give you any information upon the state of the Union which is more satisfactory than what I was then obliged to communicate. On the contrary, matters are still worse at present than they then were. When Congress met, a stronge hope pervaded the whole public mind that some amicable adjustment of the subject would speedily be made by the representatives of the States and of the people which might restore peace between the conflicting sections of the country. That hope has been diminished by every hour of delay, and as the prospect of a bloodless settlement fades away the public distress becomes more and more aggravated. As evidence of this it is only necessary to say that the Treasury notes authorized by the act of 17th of December last were advertised according to the law and that no responsible bidder offered to take any considerable sum at par at a lower rate of interest than 12 per cent. From these facts it appears that in a government organized like ours domestic strife, or even a well-grounded fear of civil hostilities, is more destructive to our public and private interests than the most formidable foreign war.

In my annual message I expressed the conviction, which I have long deliberately held, and which recent reflection has only tended to deepen and confirm, that no State has a right by its own act to secede from the Union or throw off its federal obligations at pleasure. I also declared my opinion to be that even if that right existed and should be exercised by any State of the Confederacy the executive department of this Government had no authority under the Constitution to recognize its validity by acknowledging the independence of such State. This left me no alternative, as the chief executive officer under the Constitution of the United States, but to collect the public revenues and to protect the public property so far as this might be practicable under existing laws. This is still my purpose. My province is to execute and not to make the laws. It belongs to Congress exclusively to repeal, to modify, or to enlarge their provisions to meet exigencies as they may occur. I possess no dispensing power.

I certainly had no right to make aggressive war upon any State, and I am perfectly satisfied that the Constitution has wisely withheld that power even from Congress. But the right and the duty to use military force defensively against those who resist the Federal officers in the execution of their legal functions and against those who assail the property of the Federal Government is clear and undeniable.

But the dangerous and hostile attitude of the States toward each other has already far transcended and cast in the shade the ordinary executive duties already provided for by law, and has assumed such vast and alarming proportions as to place the subject entirely above and beyond Executive control. The fact can not be disguised that we are in the midst of a great revolution. In all its various bearings, therefore, I commend the question to Congress as the only human tribunal under Providence possessing the power to meet the existing emergency. To them exclusively belongs the power to declare war or to authorize the employment of military force in all cases contemplated by the Constitution, and they alone possess the power to remove grievances which might lead to war and to secure peace and union to this distracted country. On them, and on them alone, rests the responsibility.

The Union is a sacred trust left by our Revolutionary fathers to their descendants, and never did any other people inherit so rich a legacy. It has rendered us prosperous in peace and triumphant in war. The national flag has floated in glory over every sea. Under its shadow American citizens have found protection and respect in all lands beneath the sun. If we descend to considerations of purely material interest, when in the history of all time has a confederacy been bound together by such strong ties of mutual interest? Each portion of it is dependent on all and all upon each portion for prosperity and domestic security. Free trade throughout the whole supplies the wants of one portion from the productions of another and scatters wealth everywhere. The great planting and farming States require the aid of the commercial and navigating States to send their productions to domestic and foreign markets and to furnish the naval power to render their transportation secure against all hostile attacks.

Should the Union perish in the midst of the present excitement, we have already had a sad foretaste of the universal suffering which would result from its destruction. The calamity would be severe in every portion of the Union and would be quite as great, to say the least, in the Southern as in the Northern States. The greatest aggravation of the evil, and that which would place us in the most unfavorable light both before the world and posterity, is, as I am firmly convinced, that the secession movement has been chiefly based upon a misapprehension at the South of the sentiments of the majority in several of the Northern States. Let the question be transferred from political assemblies to the ballot box, and the people themselves would speedily redress the serious grievances which the South have suffered. But, in Heaven's name, let the trial be made before we plunge into armed conflict upon the mere assumption that there is no other alternative. Time is a great conservative power. Let us pause at this momentous point and afford the people, both North and South, an opportunity for reflection. Would that South Carolina had been convinced of this truth before her precipitate action! I therefore appeal through you to the people of the country to declare in their might that the Union must and shall be preserved by all constitutional means. I most earnestly recommend that you devote yourselves exclusively to the question how this can be accomplished in peace. All other questions, when compared to this, sink into insignificance. The present is no time for palliations. Action, prompt action, is required. A delay in Congress to prescribe or to recommend a distinct and practical proposition for conciliation may drive us to a point from which it will be almost impossible to recede.

A common ground on which conciliation and harmony can be produced is surely not unattainable. The proposition to compromise by letting the North have exclusive control of the territory above a certain line and to give Southern institutions protection below that line ought to receive universal approbation. In itself, indeed, it may not be entirely satisfactory, but when the alternative is between a reasonable concession on both sides and a destruction of the Union it is an imputation upon the patriotism of Congress to assert that its members will hesitate for a moment.

Even now the danger is upon us. In several of the States which have not yet seceded the forts, arsenals, and magazines of the United States have been seized. This is by far the most serious step which has been taken since the commencement of the troubles. This public property has long been left without garrisons and troops for its protection, because no person doubted its security under the flag of the country in any State of the Union. Besides, our small Army has scarcely been sufficient to guard our remote frontiers against Indian incursions. The seizure of this property, from all appearances, has been purely aggressive, and not in resistance to any attempt to coerce a State or States to remain in the Union.

At the beginning of these unhappy troubles I determined that no act of mine should increase the excitement in either section of the country. If the political conflict were to end in a civil war, it was my determined purpose not to commence it nor even to furnish an excuse for it by any act of this Government. My opinion remains unchanged that justice as well as sound policy requires us still to seek a peaceful solution of the questions at issue between the North and the South. Entertaining this conviction, I refrained even from sending reenforcements to Major Anderson, who commanded the forts in Charleston Harbor, until an absolute necessity for doing so should make itself apparent, lest it might unjustly be regarded as a menace of military coercion, and thus furnish, if not a provocation, at least a pretext for an outbreak on the part of South Carolina. No necessity for these reenforcements seemed to exist. I was assured by distinguished and upright gentlemen of South Carolina that no attack upon Major Anderson was intended, but that, on the contrary, it was the desire of the State authorities as much as it was my own to avoid the fatal consequences which must eventually follow a military collision.

And here I deem it proper to submit for your information copies of a communication, dated December 28, 1860, addressed to me by R. W. Barnwell, J. H. Adams, and James L. Orr, "commissioners" from South Carolina, with the accompanying documents, and copies of my answer thereto, dated December 31.

In further explanation of Major Anderson's removal from Fort Moultrie to Fort Sumter, it is proper to state that after my answer to the South Carolina "commissioners" the War Department received a letter from that gallant officer, dated on the 27th of December, 1860, the day after this movement, from which the following is an extract:

I will add as my opinion that many things convinced me that the authorities of the State designed to proceed to a hostile act.

Evidently referring to the orders, dated December 11, of the late Secretary of War.

Under this impression I could not hesitate that it was my solemn duty to move my command from a fort which we could not probably have held longer than forty-eight or sixty hours to this one, where my power of resistance is increased to a very great degree.

It will be recollected that the concluding part of these orders was in the following terms:

The smallness of your force will not permit you, perhaps, to occupy more than one of the three forts, but an attack on or attempt to take possession of either one of them will be regarded as an act of hostility, and you may then put your command into either of them which you may deem most proper to increase its power of resistance. You are also authorized to take similar defensive steps whenever you have tangible evidence of a design to proceed to a hostile act.

It is said that serious apprehensions are to some extent entertained (in which I do not share) that the peace of this District may be disturbed before the 4th of March next. In any event, it will be my duty to preserve it, and this duty shall be performed.

In conclusion it may be permitted to me to remark that I have often warned my countrymen of the dangers which now surround us. This may be the last time I shall refer to the subject officially. I feel that my duty has been faithfully, though it may be imperfectly, performed, and, whatever the result may be, I shall carry to my grave the consciousness that I at least meant well for my country.

JAMES BUCHANAN.

WASHINGTON, *January 15, 1861.*

To the Senate of the United States:

In compliance with the resolution of the Senate passed on the 10th instant, requesting me to inform that body, if not incompatible with the public interest, "whether John B. Floyd, whose appointment as Secretary of War was confirmed by the Senate on the 6th of March, 1857, still continues to hold said office, and, if not, when and how said office became vacant; and, further, to inform the Senate how and by whom the duties of said office are now discharged, and, if an appointment of an acting or provisional Secretary of War has been made, how, when, and by what authority it was so made, and why the fact of said appointment has not been communicated to the Senate," I have to inform the Senate that John B. Floyd, the late Secretary of the War Department, resigned that office on the 29th day of December last, and that on the 1st day of January instant Joseph Holt was authorized by me to perform the duties of the said office until a successor should be appointed or the vacancy filled. Under this authority the duties of the War Department have been performed by Mr. Holt from the day last mentioned to the present time.

The power to carry on the business of the Government by means of a provisional appointment when a vacancy occurs is expressly given by the act of February 13, 1795, which enacts—

That in case of vacancy in the office of Secretary of State, Secretary of the Treasury, or of the Secretary of the Department of War, or of any officer of either of the said Departments whose appointment is not in the head thereof, whereby they can not perform the duties of their respective offices, it shall be lawful for the President of the United States, in case he shall think it necessary, to authorize any person or persons, at his discretion, to perform the duties of the said respective offices until a successor be appointed or such vacancy be filled: *Provided*, That no one vacancy shall be supplied in manner aforesaid for a longer period than six months.

It is manifest that if the power which this law gives had been withheld the public interest would frequently suffer very serious detriment. Vacancies may occur at any time in the most important offices which can not be immediately and permanently filled in a manner satisfactory to the appointing power. It was wise to make a provision which would enable the President to avoid a total suspension of business in the interval, and equally wise so to limit the Executive discretion as to prevent any serious abuse of it. This is what the framers of the act of 1795 did, and neither the policy nor the constitutional validity of their law has been questioned for sixty-five years.

The practice of making such appointments, whether in a vacation or during the session of Congress, has been constantly followed during every Administration from the earliest period of the Government, and its perfect lawfulness has never to my knowledge been questioned or denied. Without going back further than the year 1829, and without taking into the calculation any but the chief officers of the several Departments, it will be found that provisional appointments to fill vacancies were made to the number of 179 from the commencement of General Jackson's Administration to the close of General Pierce's. This number would probably be greatly increased if all the cases which occurred in the subordinate offices and bureaus were added to the count. Some of them were made while the Senate was in session; some which were made in vacation were continued in force long after the Senate assembled. Sometimes the temporary officer was the commissioned head of another Department, sometimes a subordinate in the same Department. Sometimes the affairs of the Navy Department have been directed *ad interim* by a commodore and those of the War Department by a general. In most, if not all, of the cases which occurred previous to 1852 it is believed that the compensation provided by law for the officer regularly commissioned was paid to the person who discharged the duties *ad interim*. To give the Senate a more detailed and satisfactory view of the subject, I send the accompanying tabular statement, certified by the Secretary of State, in which the instances are all set forth in which provisional as well as permanent appointments were made to the highest executive offices from 1829 nearly to the present time, with their respective dates.

It must be allowed that these precedents, so numerous and so long continued, are entitled to great respect, since we can scarcely suppose that the wise and eminent men by whom they were made could have been mistaken on a point which was brought to their attention so often. Still less can it be supposed that any of them willfully violated the law or the Constitution.

The lawfulness of the practice rests upon the exigencies of the public service, which require that the movements of the Government shall not be arrested by an accidental vacancy in one of the Departments; upon an act of Congress expressly and plainly giving and regulating the power, and upon long and uninterrupted usage of the Executive, which has never been challenged as illegal by Congress.

This answers the inquiry of the Senate so far as it is necessary to show "how and by whom the duties of said office are now discharged." Nor is it necessary to explain further than I have done "how, when, and by what authority" the provisional appointment has been made; but the resolution makes the additional inquiry "*why* the fact of said appointment has not been communicated to the Senate."

I take it for granted that the Senate did not mean to call for the reasons upon which I acted in performing an Executive duty nor to demand an account of the motives which governed me in an act which the law and the Constitution left to my own discretion. It is sufficient, therefore, for that part of the resolution to say that a provisional or temporary appointment like that in question is not required by law to be communicated to the Senate, and that there is no instance on record where such communication ever has been made.   JAMES BUCHANAN.

WASHINGTON, *January 22, 1861.*
To the House of Representatives:

I herewith transmit to the House of Representatives a communication from the Secretary of the Navy, with accompanying reports, of the persons who were sent to the Isthmus of Chiriqui to make the examinations required by the fifth section of the act making appropriations for the naval service, approved June 22, 1860.

JAMES BUCHANAN.

WASHINGTON, *January 24, 1861.*
To the Senate of the United States:

In compliance with the resolution of the Senate of the 19th instant, requesting a copy of correspondence between the Department of State and ministers of foreign powers at Washington in regard to foreign vessels in Charleston, I transmit a report from the Secretary of State and the documents by which it was accompanied.

JAMES BUCHANAN.

WASHINGTON CITY, *January 28, 1861.*
To the Senate and House of Representatives of the United States:

I deem it my duty to submit to Congress a series of resolutions adopted by the legislature of Virginia on the 19th instant, having in view a peaceful settlement of the exciting questions which now threaten the Union. They were delivered to me on Thursday, the 24th instant, by ex-President Tyler, who has left his dignified and honored retirement in the hope that he may render service to his country in this its hour of peril. These resolutions, it will be perceived, extend an invitation "to all such States, whether slaveholding or nonslaveholding, as are willing to unite with Virginia in an earnest effort to adjust the present unhappy controversies in the spirit in which the Constitution was originally formed, and consistently with its principles, so as to afford to the people of the slaveholding States adequate guaranties for the securities of their rights, to appoint commissioners to meet, on the 4th day of February next, in the city of Washington, similar commissioners appointed by Virginia, to consider and, if practicable, agree upon some suitable adjustment.''

I confess I hail this movement on the part of Virginia with great satisfaction. From the past history of this ancient and renowned Commonwealth we have the fullest assurance that what she has undertaken she will accomplish if it can be done by able, enlightened, and persevering efforts. It is highly gratifying to know that other patriotic States have appointed and are appointing commissioners to meet those of Virginia in council. When assembled, they will constitute a body entitled in an eminent degree to the confidence of the country.

The general assembly of Virginia have also resolved—

That ex-President John Tyler is hereby appointed, by the concurrent vote of each branch of the general assembly, a commissioner to the President of the United States, and Judge John Robertson is hereby appointed, by a like vote, a commissioner to the State of South Carolina and the other States that have seceded or shall secede, with instructions respectfully to request the President of the United States and the authorities of such States to agree to abstain, pending the proceedings contemplated by the action of this general assembly, from any and all acts calculated to produce a collision of arms between the States and the Government of the United States.

However strong may be my desire to enter into such an agreement, I am convinced that I do not possess the power. Congress, and Congress alone, under the war-making power, can exercise the discretion of agreeing to abstain ''from any and all acts calculated to produce a collision of arms'' between this and any other government. It would therefore be a usurpation for the Executive to attempt to restrain their hands by an agreement in regard to matters over which he has no constitutional control. If he were thus to act, they might pass laws which he should be bound to obey, though in conflict with his agreement.

Under existing circumstances, my present actual power is confined within narrow limits. It is my duty at all times to defend and protect the public property within the seceding States so far as this may be practicable, and especially to employ all constitutional means to protect the property of the United States and to preserve the public peace at this the seat of the Federal Government. If the seceding States abstain ''from any and all acts calculated to produce a collision of arms,'' then the danger so much to be deprecated will no longer exist. Defense, and not aggression, has been the policy of the Administration from the beginning.

But whilst I can enter into no engagement such as that proposed, I cordially commend to Congress, with much confidence that it will meet their approbation, to abstain from passing any law calculated to produce a collision of arms pending the proceedings contemplated by the action of the general assembly of Virginia. I am one of those who will never despair of the Republic. I yet cherish the belief that the American people will perpetuate the Union of the States on some terms just and honorable for all sections of the country.   I trust that the mediation of Virginia may be the destined means, under Providence, of accomplishing this inestimable benefit.   Glorious as are the memories of her past history, such an achievement, both in relation to her own fame and the welfare of the whole country, would surpass them all.

JAMES BUCHANAN.

WASHINGTON, *January 30, 1861.*

To the Senate of the United States:

I have received the resolution of the Senate of the 24th instant, requesting the return to that body of the convention between the United States and the Republic of Venezuela on the subject of the Aves Island. That instrument is consequently herewith returned.   It was approved by the Senate on the 24th June last with the following amendment:

Article III: Strike out this article, in the following words:

In consideration of the above agreement and indemnification, the Government of the United States and the individuals in whose behalf they have been made agree to desist from all further reclamation respecting the island of Aves, abandoning to the Republic of Venezuela whatever rights might pertain to them.

The amendment does not seem necessary to secure any right either of the United States or of any American citizen claiming under them. Neither the Government nor the citizens in whose behalf the convention has been concluded have any further claims upon the island of Aves. Nor is it known or believed that there are any claims against the Government of Venezuela having any connection with that island other than those provided for in this convention.   I therefore recommend the reconsideration of the subject.

No steps have yet been taken toward making known to the Venezuelan Government the conditional approval of the convention by the Senate. This might have been necessary if the instrument had stipulated for a ratification in the usual form and it had been ratified accordingly.   Inasmuch, however, as the convention contains no such stipulation, and as some of the installments had been paid according to its terms, it has been deemed preferable to suspend further proceedings in regard to it, especially as it was not deemed improbable that the Senate might request it to be returned.   This anticipation has been realized.

JAMES BUCHANAN.

WASHINGTON, *February 5, 1861.*

To the Senate and House of Representatives:

I have received from the governor of Kentucky certain resolutions adopted by the general assembly of that Commonwealth, containing an application to Congress for the call of a convention for proposing amendments to the Constitution of the United States, with a request that I should immediately place the same before that body.   It affords me great satisfaction to perform this duty, and I feel quite confident that Congress will bestow upon these resolutions the careful consideration to which they are eminently entitled on account of the distinguished and patriotic source from which they proceed, as well as the great importance of the subject which they involve.

JAMES BUCHANAN.

WASHINGTON, *February 8, 1861.*

To the Senate and House of Representatives:

I deemed it a duty to transmit to Congress with my message of the 8th of January the correspondence which occurred in December last between the "commissioners" of South Carolina and myself.

Since that period, on the 14th of January, Colonel Isaac W. Hayne, the attorney-general of South Carolina, called and informed me that he was the bearer of a letter from Governor Pickens to myself which he would deliver the next day. He was, however, induced by the interposition of Hon. Jefferson Davis and nine other Senators from the seceded and seceding States not to deliver it on the day appointed, nor was it communicated to me until the 31st of January, with his letter of that date. Their letter to him urging this delay bears date January 15, and was the commencement of a correspondence, the whole of which in my possession I now submit to Congress. A reference to each letter of the series in proper order accompanies this message.

JAMES BUCHANAN.

WASHINGTON CITY, *February 12, 1861.*

To the Senate of the United States:

I herewith submit to the Senate, for their advice, the proceedings and award of the commissioners under the convention between the United States of America and the Republic of Paraguay, proclaimed by the President on the 12th of March, 1860. It is decided by the award of these commissioners that "the United States and Paraguay Navigation Company have not proved or established any right to damages upon their said claim against the Government of the Republic of Paraguay, and that upon the proofs aforesaid the said Government is not responsible to the said company in any damages or pecuniary compensation whatever in all the premises.

The question arises, Had the commissioners authority under the convention to make such an award, or were they not confined to the assessment of damages which the company had sustained from the Government of Paraguay?

Our relations with that Republic had for years been of a most unsatisfactory character. They had been investigated by the preceding and by the present Administration. The latter came to the conclusion that both the interest and honor of the country required that our rights against that Government for their attack on the *Water Witch* and for the injuries they had inflicted on this company should, if necessary, be enforced. Accordingly, the President in his annual message of December, 1857, called the attention of Congress to the subject in the following language:

A demand for these purposes will be made in a firm but conciliatory spirit. This will the more probably be granted if the Executive shall have authority to use other means in the event of a refusal. This is accordingly recommended.

After due deliberation, Congress, on the 2d of June, 1858, authorized the President "to adopt such measures and use such force as in his judgment may be necessary and advisable" in the premises. A commissioner was accordingly appointed and a force fitted out and dispatched to Paraguay for the purpose, if necessary, of enforcing atonement for these wrongs.

The expedition appeared in the waters of the La Plata and our commissioner succeeded in concluding a treaty and convention embracing both branches of our demand. The convention of indemnity was signed on the 4th of February, 1859. The preamble of this convention refers to the interruption for a time of the good understanding and harmony between the two nations which has rendered that distant armament necessary. By the first article the Government of Paraguay "binds itself for the responsibility in favor of the United States and Paraguay Navigation Company which may result from the decree of commissioners" to be appointed in the manner provided by article 2. This was in accordance with the instructions to our commissioner, who was told that an indispensable preliminary to the negotiation would, "of course, be an acknowledgment on the part of the Paraguayan Government of its liability to the company." The first paragraph of this second article clearly specifies the object of the convention. This was not to ascertain whether the claim was just, to enforce which we had sent a fleet to Paraguay, but to constitute a commission to "determine," not the existence, but "the amount, of said reclamations." The final paragraph provides that "the two commissioners named in the said manner shall meet in the city of Washington to investigate, adjust, and *determine the amount* of the claims of the above-mentioned company upon sufficient proofs of the charges and defenses of the contending parties." By the fifth article the Government of Paraguay "binds itself to pay to the Government of the United States of America, in the city of Assumption, Paraguay, thirty days after presentation to the Government of the Republic, the draft which that of the United States of America shall issue for the amount for which the two commissioners concurring, or by the umpire, shall declare it responsible to the said company."

The act of Congress of May 16, 1860, employs the same language that is used in the convention, "to investigate, adjust, and determine the amount" of the claims against Paraguay. Congress, not doubting that an award would be made in favor of the company for some certain amount of damages, in the sixth section of the act referred to provides that the money paid out of the Treasury for the expenses of the commission "shall be retained by the United States out of the money" (not any money) "that may, pursuant to the terms of said convention, be received from Paraguay."

After all this had been done, after we had fitted out a warlike expedition in part to obtain satisfaction for this very claim, after these solemn acts had been performed by the two Republics, the commissioners have felt themselves competent to decide that they could go behind the action of the legislative and executive branches of this Government and determine that there was no justice in the original claim. A commissioner of Paraguay might have been a proper person to act merely in assessing the amount of damages when an arbiter had been provided to decide between him and the commissioner on the part of the United States, but to have authorized him to decide upon the original justice of the claim against his own Government would have been a novelty. The American commissioner is as pure and honest a man as I have ever known, but I think he took a wrong view of his powers under the convention.

The principle of the liability of Paraguay having been established by the highest political acts of the United States and that Republic in their sovereign capacity, the commissioners, who would seem to have misapprehended their powers, have investigated and undertaken to decide whether the Government of the United States was right or wrong in the authority which they gave to make war if necessary to secure the indemnity. Governments may be, and doubtless often have been, wrong in going to war to enforce claims; but after this has been done, and the inquiry which led to the reclamations has been acknowledged by the Government that inflicted it, it does not appear to me to be competent for commissioners authorized to ascertain the indemnity for the injury to go behind their authority and decide upon the original merits of the claim for which the war was made. If a commissioner were appointed under a convention to ascertain the damage sustained by an American citizen in consequence of the capture of a vessel admitted by the foreign government to be illegal, and he should go behind the convention and decide that the original capture was a lawful prize, it would certainly be regarded as an extraordinary assumption of authority.

The present appears to me to be a case of this character, and for these reasons I have deemed it advisable to submit the whole subject for the consideration of the Senate.

JAMES BUCHANAN.

WASHINGTON, *February 21, 1861.*

To the Senate of the United States:

The treaty concluded between Great Britain and the United States on the 15th of June, 1846, provided in its first article that the line of boundary between the territories of Her Britannic Majesty and those of the United States from the point on the forty-ninth parallel of north latitude up to which it had already been ascertained should be continued westward along the said parallel "to the middle of the channel which separates the continent from Vancouvers Island, and thence southerly through the middle of said channel and of Fucas Straits to the Pacific Ocean." When the commissioners appointed by the two Governments to mark the boundary line came to that point of it which is required to run southerly through the channel which divides the continent from Vancouvers Island, they differed entirely in their opinions, not only concerning the true point of deflection from the forty-ninth parallel, but also as to the channel intended to be designated in the treaty. After a long-continued and very able discussion of the subject, which produced no result, they reported their disagreement to their respective Governments. Since that time the two Governments, through their ministers here and at London, have had a voluminous correspondence on the point in controversy, each sustaining the view of its own commissioner and neither yielding in any degree to the claims of the other. In the meantime the unsettled condition of this affair has produced some serious local disturbances, and on one occasion at least has threatened to destroy the harmonious relations existing between Great Britain and the United States. The island of San Juan will fall to the United States if our construction of the treaty be right, while if the British interpretation be adopted it will be on their side of the line. That island is an important possession to this country, and valuable for agricultural as well as military purposes. I am convinced that it is ours by the treaty fairly and impartially construed. But argument has been exhausted on both sides without increasing the probability of final adjustment. On the contrary, each party seems now to be more convinced than at first of the justice of its own demands. There is but one mode left of settling the dispute, and that is by submitting it to the arbitration of some friendly and impartial power. Unless this be done, the two countries are exposed to the constant danger of a collision which may end in war.

It is under these circumstances that the British Government, through its minister here, has proposed the reference of the matter in controversy to the King of Sweden and Norway, the King of the Netherlands, or to the Republic of the Swiss Confederation. Before accepting this proposition I have thought it right to take the advice of the Senate.

The precise questions which I submit are these: Will the Senate approve a treaty referring to either of the sovereign powers above named the dispute now existing between the Governments of the United States and Great Britain concerning the boundary line between Vancouvers Island and the American continent? In case the referee shall find himself unable to decide where the line is by the description of it in the treaty of 15th June, 1846, shall he be authorized to establish a line according to the treaty as nearly as possible? Which of the three powers named by Great Britain as an arbiter shall be chosen by the United States?

All important papers bearing on the questions are herewith communicated in the originals. Their return to the Department of State is requested when the Senate shall have disposed of the subject.

JAMES BUCHANAN.

WASHINGTON, *February 23, 1861.*

To the Senate of the United States:

In compliance with the resolutions of the Senate of the 17th and 18th February, 1858, requesting information upon the subject of the Aves Island, I transmit a report from the Secretary of State and the documents which accompanied it.

JAMES BUCHANAN.

WASHINGTON, *February 23, 1861.*

Hon. JOHN C. BRECKINRIDGE,
     President of the Senate.

SIR: Herewith I inclose, for constitutional action of the Senate thereon should it approve the same, supplemental articles of agreement made and concluded with the authorities of the Delaware Indians on the 21st July last, with a view to the abrogation of the sixth article of the treaty of May 30, 1860.

JAMES BUCHANAN.

WASHINGTON, *February 23, 1861.*

To the House of Representatives of the United States:

In answer to a resolution of the House of Representatives adopted on the 11th instant, respecting the seizure of the mint at New Orleans, with a large amount of money therein, by the authorities of the State of Louisiana, the refusal of the branch mint to pay drafts of the United States, etc., I have to state that all the information within my possession or power on these subjects was communicated to the House by the Secretary of the Treasury on the 21st instant, and was prepared under the resolution above referred to and a resolution of the same date addressed to himself.

JAMES BUCHANAN.

WASHINGTON, *February 26, 1861.*

To the Senate of the United States:

In answer to the resolution of the Senate of the 25th instant, requesting information relative to the extradition of one Anderson, a man of color, charged with the commission of murder in the State of Missouri,

MORMON TEMPLE AND TABERNACLE—YOUNG'S MILL—A MORMON FAMILY

BRIGHAM YOUNG MUSTERING ARMY TO OPPOSE U. S. TROOPS

THE MORMONS (LATTER DAY SAINTS).

The Mormon sect originated with Joseph Smith, who, at the age of 15, claimed to have seen divine visions while living in Ontario County, N. Y. From revelations made to him, he dictated the Book of Mormon, or Golden Bible, which consists of sixteen books, written largely in the diction of the Saint James version of the Bible, and composed of utterances claimed to have been written down at different periods by different prophets. In 1832, Brigham Young of Vermont joined the sect, and soon became its virtual leader. After trouble with the authorities in Ohio, Missouri, and Illinois, 143 families set out for the West in 1847, and after many hardships settled Salt Lake City in Utah. In 1852, the Mormons announced publicly that they were practising polygamy, according to what Young claimed was a divine revelation given him in 1843. When Utah became a United States territory, the Mormons resisted the authority of the United States, and had to be subdued by a military expedition in 1856. The government had constant trouble with the Mormons because of polygamous practises, until they agreed in 1890 to yield to a Supreme Court opinon declaring the anti-polygamy statute of the United States to be legal. In a recent year the Mormon creed in the United States possessed 624 church buildings, with a membership of 215,796. (See article Mormons in Encyclopedic Index.)

I transmit a report from the Secretary of State and the documents by which it was accompanied. The dispatch of Mr. Dallas being in the original, its return to the Department of State is requested.

JAMES BUCHANAN.

WASHINGTON, *March 1, 1861.*

To the House of Representatives:

In answer to their resolution of the 11th instant [ultimo], "that the President of the United States furnish to the House, if not incompatible with the public service, the reasons that have induced him to assemble so large a number of troops in this city, and why they are kept here; and whether he has any information of a conspiracy upon the part of any portion of the citizens of this country to seize upon the capital and prevent the inauguration of the President elect," the President submits that the number of troops assembled in this city is not large, as the resolution presupposes, its total amount being 653 men exclusive of the marines, who are, of course, at the navy-yard as their appropriate station. These troops were ordered here to act as a *posse comitatus*, in strict subordination to the civil authority, for the purpose of preserving peace and order in the city of Washington should this be necessary before or at the period of the inauguration of the President elect.

Since the date of the resolution Hon. Mr. Howard, from the select committee, has made a report to the House on this subject. It was thoroughly investigated by the committee, and although they have expressed the opinion that the evidence before them does not prove the existence of a secret organization here or elsewhere hostile to the Government that has for its object, upon its own responsibility, an attack upon the capital or any of the public property here, or an interruption of any of the functions of the Government, yet the House laid upon the table by a very large majority a resolution expressing the opinion "that the regular troops now in this city ought to be forthwith removed therefrom." This of itself was a sufficient reason for not withdrawing the troops.

But what was the duty of the President at the time the troops were ordered to this city? Ought he to have waited before this precautionary measure was adopted until he could obtain proof that a secret organization existed to seize the capital? In the language of the select committee, this was "in a time of high excitement consequent upon revolutionary events transpiring all around us, the very air filled with rumors and individuals indulging in the most extravagant expressions of fears and threats." Under these and other circumstances, which I need not detail, but which appear in the testimony before the select committee, I was convinced that I ought to act. The safety of the immense amount of public property in this city and that of the archives of the Government, in which all the States, and especially the new States in which the public lands are situated, have a deep interest; the peace and order of the city itself and the security of the inauguration of the President elect, were objects of such vast importance to the whole country that I could not hesitate to adopt precautionary defensive measures. At the present moment, when all is quiet, it is difficult to realize the state of alarm which prevailed when the troops were first ordered to this city. This almost instantly subsided after the arrival of the first company, and a feeling of comparative peace and security has since existed both in Washington and throughout the country. Had I refused to adopt this precautionary measure, and evil consequences, which many good men at the time apprehended, had followed, I should never have forgiven myself.

JAMES BUCHANAN.

WASHINGTON, *March 2, 1861.*

To the Senate of the United States:

I deem it proper to invite the attention of the Senate to the fact that with this day expires the limitation of time for the exchange of the ratifications of the treaty with Costa Rica of 2d July, 1860.

The minister of that Republic is disappointed in not having received the copy intended for exchange, and the period will lapse without the possibility of carrying out the provisions of the convention in this respect.

I submit, therefore, the expediency of the passage of a resolution authorizing the exchange of ratifications at such time as may be convenient, the limitations of the ninth article to the contrary notwithstanding.

JAMES BUCHANAN.

VETO MESSAGE.

WASHINGTON CITY, *January 25, 1861.*

To the House of Representatives of the United States:

I return with my objections to the House, in which it originated, the bill entitled "An act for the relief of Hockaday & Leggit," presented to me on the 15th instant.

This bill appropriates $59,576 "to Hockaday & Leggit, in full payment for damages sustained by them in reduction of pay for carrying the mails on route No. 8911; and that said amount be paid to William Leggit for and on account of Hockaday & Leggit, and for their benefit."

A bill containing the same language, with the single exception that the sum appropriated therein was $40,000 instead of $59,576, passed both Houses of Congress at their last session; but it was presented to me at so late a period of the session that I could not examine its merits before the time fixed for the adjournment, and it therefore, under the Constitution, failed to become a law. The increase of the sum appropriated in the present bill over that in the bill of the last session, being within a fraction of $20,000, has induced me to examine the question with some attention, and I find that the bill involves an important principle, which if established by Congress may take large sums out of the Treasury.

It appears that on the 1st day of April, 1858, John M. Hockaday entered into a contract with the Postmaster-General for transporting the mail on route No. 8911, from St. Joseph, Mo., by Fort Kearney, Nebraska Territory, and Fort Leavenworth, to Salt Lake City, for the sum of $190,000 per annum for a weekly service. The service was to commence on the 1st day of May, 1858, and to terminate on the 30th November, 1860. By this contract the Postmaster-General reserved to himself the right "to reduce the service to semimonthly whenever the necessities of the public and the condition of affairs in the Territory of Utah may not require it more frequently." And again:

That the Postmaster-General may discontinue or curtail the service, in whole or in part, in order to place on the route a greater degree of service, or whenever the public interests require such discontinuance for any other cause, he allowing one month's extra pay on the amount of service dispensed with.

On the 11th April, 1859, the Postmaster-General curtailed the service, which he had a clear right to do under the contract, to semimonthly, with an annual deduction of $65,000, leaving the compensation $125,000 for twenty-four trips per year instead of $190,000 for fifty-two trips. This curtailment was not to take effect till the 1st of July, 1859.

At the time the contract was made it was expected that the army in Utah might be engaged in active operations, and hence the necessity of frequent communications between the War Department and that Territory. The reservation of the power to curtail the service to semimonthly trips itself proves that the parties had in view the contingency of such curtailment "whenever the necessities of the public and the condition of affairs in the Territory of Utah may not require it more frequently."

Before the Postmaster-General ordered this curtailment he had an interview with the Secretary of War upon the subject, in the course of which the Secretary agreed that a weekly mail to St. Joseph and Salt Lake City was no longer needed for the purposes of the Government—this, evidently, because the trouble in Utah had ended.

Mr. Hockaday faithfully complied with his contract, and the full compensation was paid, at the rate of $190,000 per annum, up to the 1st July, 1859, and "one month's extra pay on the amount of service dispensed with," according to the contract.

Previous to that date, as has been already stated, on the 14th of April, 1859, the Postmaster-General curtailed the service to twice per month, and on the 11th May, 1859, Messrs. Hockaday & Co. assigned the contract to Jones, Russell & Co. for a bonus of $50,000. Their property connected with the route was to be appraised, which was effected, and they received on this account about $94,000, making the whole amount about $144,000.

There is no doubt that the contractors have sustained considerable loss in the whole transaction. The amount I shall not pretend to decide, whether $40,000 or $59,576, or any other sum.

It will be for Congress to consider whether the precedent established by this bill will not in effect annul all restrictions contained in the mail contracts enabling the Postmaster-General to reduce or curtail the postal service according to the public exigencies as they may arise. I have no other solicitude upon the subject. I am informed that there are many cases in the Post-Office Department depending upon the same principle.

JAMES BUCHANAN.

PROCLAMATION.

BY THE PRESIDENT OF THE UNITED STATES OF AMERICA.

A PROCLAMATION.

Whereas objects of interest to the United States require that the Senate should be convened at 12 o'clock on the 4th of March next to receive and act upon such communications as may be made to it on the part of the Executive:

Now, therefore, I, James Buchanan, President of the United States, have considered it to be my duty to issue this my proclamation, declaring that an extraordinary occasion requires the Senate of the United States to convene for the transaction of business at the Capitol, in the city of Washington, on the 4th day of March next, at 12 o'clock at noon on that day, of which all who shall at that time be entitled to act as members of that body are hereby required to take notice.

Given under my hand and the seal of the United States, at Washington, the 11th day of February, A. D. 1861, and of the Independence of the United States the eighty-fifth.

[SEAL.]

JAMES BUCHANAN.

By the President:

    J. S. BLACK,
        Secretary of State.

QUESTIONS.

1. What were the provisions of the Clayton-Bulwer Treaty? Page 3170.

2. What two directly opposite constructions were placed on the Clayton-Bulwer Treaty by its signatories? Page 2973.

3. What precautionary measure did Buchanan suggest to prevent financial panics? Page 2972.

4. When did a President recommend the passage of United States troops through a friendly neutral country, either with or without its consent, to reach an enemy beyond? Pages 3098, 3176.

5. What constitutional amendment did Buchanan propose in order to avert the Civil War? Page 3169.

6. When was the first Homestead Law passed? Page 3139.

7. What were Buchanan's reasons for vetoing the Agricultural College Land Bill? Page 3074.

8. What did Mr. Forsyth declare were the only means by which American citizens might secure justice in Mexico? Page 3044.

9. How does the Bank of England secure deposits and circulating medium? Page 2969.

SUGGESTIONS.

Buchanan's administration was embarrassed by a panic, following the inflation of currency. Page 2967. (See also Panics, Encyclopedic Index.)

The preliminary rumblings of slavery troubles reached alarming proportions. Pages 2962, 2981, 3028, 3084, 3157, 3186.

John Brown's raid took place. Opposite page 3039, and page 3072. (See Brown's Insurrection, Encyclopedic Index.)

See Dred Scott Case, Encyclopedic Index, and references.

Read Buchanan's discussion of secession. Pages 3159, 3186.

Read Buchanan's Foreign Policy. Pages 2966, 2998, 3037, 3041, 3066, 3089, 3092, 3173, 3177.

NOTE.

For further suggestions on Buchanan's administration, see Buchanan, James, Encyclopedic Index.

By reading the Foreign Policy of each President, and by scanning the messages as to the state of the nation, a thorough knowledge of the history of the United States will be acquired from the most authentic sources; because, as has been said, "Each President reviews the past, depicts the present and forecasts the future of the nation."

Abraham Lincoln

March 4, 1861, to April 15, 1865

SEE ENCYCLOPEDIC INDEX.

The Encyclopedic Index is not only an index to the other volumes, not only a key that unlocks the treasures of the entire publication, but it is in itself an alphabetically arranged brief history or story of the great controlling events constituting the History of the United States.

Under its proper alphabetical classification the story is told of every great subject referred to by any of the Presidents in their official Messages, and at the end of each article the official utterances of the Presidents themselves are cited upon the subject, so that you may readily turn to the page in the body of the work itself for this original information.

Next to the possession of knowledge is the ability to turn at will to where knowledge is to be found.

A. Lincoln

LINCOLN

Tested by the standard of many other great men, Lincoln was not great, but tested by the only true standard of his own achievements, he may justly appear in history as one of the greatest American statesmen. Indeed, in some most essential attributes of greatness I doubt whether any of our public men ever equalled him. If there are yet any intelligent Americans who believe that Lincoln was an innocent, rural, unsophisticated character, it is time that they should be undeceived. I venture the assertion, without fear of successful contradiction, that Abraham Lincoln was the most sagacious of all the public men of his day in either political party. He was, therefore, the master-politician of his time. He was not a politician as the term is now commonly applied and understood; he knew nothing about the countless methods which are employed in the details of political effort; but no man knew better, indeed, I think no man knew so well as he did, how to summon and dispose of political ability to attain great political results; and this work he performed with unfailing wisdom and discretion in every contest for himself and for the country.

Lincoln's intellectual organization has been portrayed by many writers, but so widely at variance as to greatly confuse the general reader. Indeed, he was the most difficult of all men to analyze. He sought information from every attainable source. He sought it persistently, weighed it earnestly, and in the end reached his own conclusions. When he had once reached a conclusion as to a public duty, there was no human power equal to the task of changing his purpose. He was self-reliant to an uncommon degree, and yet as entirely free from arrogance of opinion as any public man I have ever known.

Unlike all Presidents who had preceded him, he came into office without a fixed and accepted policy. Civil war plunged the Government into new and most perplexing duties. But Lincoln waited patiently—waited until in the fullness of time the judgment of the people was ripened for action, and then, and then only, did Lincoln act. Had he done otherwise, he would have involved the country in fearful peril both at home and abroad, and it was his constant study of, and obedience to, the honest judgment of the people of the Nation that saved the Republic and that enshrined him in history as the greatest of modern rulers.

While Lincoln had little appreciation of himself as candidate for President as late as 1859, the dream of reaching the Presidency evidently took possession of him in the early part of 1860, and his efforts to advance himself as a candidate were singularly awkward and infelicitous.

He had then no experience whatever as a leader of leaders, and it was not until he had made several discreditable blunders that he learned how much he must depend upon others if he would make himself President.

There were no political movements of National importance during Lincoln's Administration in which he did not actively, although often hiddenly, participate. It was Lincoln who finally, after the most conclusive efforts to get Missouri into line with the Administration, effected a reconciliation of disputing parties which brought Brown and Henderson into the Senate, and it was Lincoln who in 1863 took a leading part in attaining the declination of Curtin as a gubernatorial candidate that year.

Abraham Lincoln was not a sentimental Abolitionist. Indeed, he was not a sentimentalist on any subject. He was a man of earnest conviction and of sublime devotion to his faith. In many of his public letters and state papers he was as poetic as he was epigrammatic, and he was singularly felicitous in the pathos that was so often interwoven with his irresistible logic. But he never contemplated the abolition of slavery until the events of the war not only made it clearly possible, but made it an imperious necessity. As the sworn Executive of the Nation, it was his duty to obey the Constitution in all its provisions, and he accepted that duty without reservation. He knew that slavery was the immediate cause of the political disturbance that culminated in civil war, and I know that he believed from the beginning that if war should be persisted in, it could end only in the severance of the Union or the destruction of slavery. His supreme desire was peace, alike before the war, during the war, and in closing the war. He exhausted every means within his power to teach the Southern people that slavery could not be disturbed by his Administration as long as they themselves obeyed the Constitution and laws which protected slavery, and he never uttered a word or did an act to justify, or even excuse, the South in assuming that he meant to make any warfare upon the institution of slavery beyond protecting the free territories from its desolating tread.

It was not until the war had been in progress for nearly two years that Lincoln decided to proclaim the policy of Emancipation, and then he was careful to assume the power as warranted under the Constitution only by the supreme necessities of war. There was no time from the inauguration of Lincoln until the 1st of January, 1863, that the South could not have returned to the Union with slavery intact in every State.

A K McClure

MARY TODD LINCOLN

MARY TODD, born in Lexington, Ky., had from girlhood a supreme desire to become mistress of the White House, which, however, did not seem probable when she married Abraham Lincoln in 1842. She was short, attractive in appearance, inclined to stoutness, self possessed in manner, and would have enjoyed her high position had not the troublous events of the Rebellion prevented all festivities and converted the White House into a public institution. The death of her second son preyed sorely upon her, but when in 1865 her husband was assassinated, the shock was too great, and that, added to the blow of her youngest boy's death soon after his father's, partly unsettled her reason. Although she traveled much abroad, she never recovered, mentally or physically. She died of paralysis in her sister's home at Springfield, Ill., in 1882, and was interred in the Lincoln Monument vault with her husband and children.

Abraham Lincoln

ABRAHAM LINCOLN was born in Hardin County, Ky., February 12, 1809. His earliest ancestor in America was Samuel Lincoln, of Norwich, England, who settled in Hingham, Mass., where he died, leaving a son, Mordecai, whose son of the same name removed to Monmouth, N. J., and thence to Berks County, Pa., where he died in 1735. One of his sons, John, removed to Rockingham County, Va., and died there, leaving five sons, one of whom, named Abraham, emigrated to Kentucky about 1780. About 1784 he was killed by Indians, leaving three sons, Mordecai, Josiah, and Thomas, and two daughters. Their mother then located in Washington County, Ky., and there brought up her family. The youngest son, Thomas, learned the trade of a carpenter, and in 1806 married Nancy Hanks, a niece of the man with whom he learned his trade. They had three children, the second being Abraham, the future President of the United States. In 1816 Thomas Lincoln removed to Indiana, and settled on Little Pigeon Creek, not far distant from the Ohio River, where Abraham grew to manhood. He made the best use of his limited opportunities to acquire an education and at the same time prepare himself for business. At the age of 19 years he was intrusted with a cargo of farm products, which he took to New Orleans and sold. In 1830 his father again emigrated, and located in Macon County, Ill. Abraham by this time had attained the unusual stature of 6 feet 4 inches, and was of great muscular strength; joined with his father in building his cabin, clearing the field, and splitting the rails for fencing the farm. It was not long, however, before his father again changed his home, locating this time in Coles County, where he died in 1851 at the age of 73 years. Abraham left his father as soon as his farm was fenced and cleared and hired himself to a man named Denton Offutt, in Sangamon County, whom he assisted to build a flatboat; accompanied him to New Orleans on a trading voyage and returned with him to New Salem, Menard County, where Offutt opened a store for the sale of general merchandise. Mr. Lincoln remained with him for a time, during which he employed his leisure in constant reading and study. Learned the elements of English grammar and made a beginning in the study of surveying and the principles of law. But the next year an Indian war began, and Lincoln volunteered in a company raised in Sangamon County and was immediately elected captain. His company was organized at Richland April 21, 1832; but his service in command of it was brief, for it was mustered out on May 27. Mr. Lincoln immediately reenlisted as a private and served for several weeks, being finally mustered out on June 16, 1832, by Lieutenant Robert Anderson, who afterwards commanded Fort Sumter at the beginning of the civil war. He returned to his home and made a brief but active canvass for the legislature, but was defeated. At this time he thought seriously of learning the blacksmith's trade, but an opportunity was offered him to buy a store, which he did, giving his notes for the purchase money. He was unfortunate in his selection of a partner, and the business soon went to wreck, leaving him burdened with a heavy debt, which he finally paid in full. He then applied himself earnestly to the study of the law. Was appointed postmaster of New Salem in 1833, and filled the office for three years. At the same time was appointed deputy county surveyor. In 1834 was elected to the legislature, and was reelected in 1836, 1838, and 1840, after which he declined further election. In his last two terms he was the candidate of his party for the speakership of the house of representatives. In 1837 removed to Springfield, where he entered into partnership with John T. Stuart and began the practice of the law. November 4, 1842, married Miss Mary Todd, daughter of Robert S. Todd, of Kentucky. In 1846 was elected to Congress over Rev. Peter Cartwright. Served only one term, and was not a candidate for reelection. While a member he advocated the abolition of slavery in the District of Columbia. Was an unsuccessful applicant for Commissioner of the General Land Office under President Taylor; was tendered the office of governor of Oregon Territory, which he declined. Was an able and influential exponent of the principles of the Whig party in Illinois, and did active campaign work. Was voted for by the Whig minority in the State legislature for United States Senator in 1855. As soon as the Republican party was fully organized throughout the country he became its leader in Illinois. In 1858 he was chosen by his party to oppose Stephen A. Douglas for the Senate, and challenged him to a joint debate. The challenge was accepted, and a most exciting debate followed, which attracted national attention. The legislature chosen was favorable to Mr. Douglas, and he was elected. In May, 1860, when the Republican convention met in Chicago, Mr. Lincoln was nominated for the Presidency, on the third ballot, over William H. Seward, who was his principal competitor. Was elected on November 6, receiving 180 electoral votes to 72 for John C. Breckinridge, 39 for John Bell, and 12 for Stephen A. Douglas. Was inaugurated March 4, 1861. On June 8, 1864, was unanimously renominated for the Presidency by the Republican convention at Baltimore, and at the election in November received

212 electoral votes to 21 for General McClellan. Was inaugurated for his second term March 4, 1865. Was shot by John Wilkes Booth at Ford's Theater, in Washington, April 14, 1865, and died the next day. Was buried at Oak Ridge, near Springfield, Ill.

FIRST INAUGURAL ADDRESS.

Fellow-Citizens of the United States:

In compliance with a custom as old as the Government itself, I appear before you to address you briefly and to take in your presence the oath prescribed by the Constitution of the United States to be taken by the President "before he enters on the execution of his office."

I do not consider it necessary at present for me to discuss those matters of administration about which there is no special anxiety or excitement.

Apprehension seems to exist among the people of the Southern States that by the accession of a Republican Administration their property and their peace and personal security are to be endangered. There has never been any reasonable cause for such apprehension. Indeed, the most ample evidence to the contrary has all the while existed and been open to their inspection. It is found in nearly all the published speeches of him who now addresses you. I do but quote from one of those speeches when I declare that—

I have no purpose, directly or indirectly, to interfere with the institution of slavery in the States where it exists. I believe I have no lawful right to do so, and I have no inclination to do so.

Those who nominated and elected me did so with full knowledge that I had made this and many similar declarations and had never recanted them; and more than this, they placed in the platform for my acceptance, and as a law to themselves and to me, the clear and emphatic resolution which I now read:

Resolved, That the maintenance inviolate of the rights of the States, and especially the right of each State to order and control its own domestic institutions according to its own judgment exclusively, is essential to that balance of power on which the perfection and endurance of our political fabric depend; and we denounce the lawless invasion by armed force of the soil of any State or Territory, no matter under what pretext, as among the gravest of crimes.

I now reiterate these sentiments, and in doing so I only press upon the public attention the most conclusive evidence of which the case is susceptible that the property, peace, and security of no section are to be in any wise endangered by the now incoming Administration. I add, too, that all the protection which, consistently with the Constitution and the

3207 Messages and Papers of the Presidents

laws, can be given will be cheerfully given to all the States when lawfully demanded, for whatever cause—as cheerfully to one section as to another.

There is much controversy about the delivering up of fugitives from service or labor. The clause I now read is as plainly written in the Constitution as any other of its provisions:

> No person held to service or labor in one State, under the laws thereof, escaping into another, shall in consequence of any law or regulation therein be discharged from such service or labor, but shall be delivered up on claim of the party to whom such service or labor may be due.

It is scarcely questioned that this provision was intended by those who made it for the reclaiming of what we call fugitive slaves; and the intention of the lawgiver is the law. All members of Congress swear their support to the whole Constitution—to this provision as much as to any other. To the proposition, then, that slaves whose cases come within the terms of this clause "shall be delivered up" their oaths are unanimous. Now, if they would make the effort in good temper, could they not with nearly equal unanimity frame and pass a law by means of which to keep good that unanimous oath?

There is some difference of opinion whether this clause should be enforced by national or by State authority, but surely that difference is not a very material one. If the slave is to be surrendered, it can be of but little consequence to him or to others by which authority it is done. And should anyone in any case be content that his oath shall go unkept on a merely unsubstantial controversy as to *how* it shall be kept?

Again: In any law upon this subject ought not all the safeguards of liberty known in civilized and humane jurisprudence to be introduced, so that a free man be not in any case surrendered as a slave? And might it not be well at the same time to provide by law for the enforcement of that clause in the Constitution which guarantees that "the citizens of each State shall be entitled to all privileges and immunities of citizens in the several States"?

I take the official oath to-day with no mental reservations and with no purpose to construe the Constitution or laws by any hypercritical rules; and while I do not choose now to specify particular acts of Congress as proper to be enforced, I do suggest that it will be much safer for all, both in official and private stations, to conform to and abide by all those acts which stand unrepealed than to violate any of them trusting to find impunity in having them held to be unconstitutional.

It is seventy-two years since the first inauguration of a President under our National Constitution. During that period fifteen different and greatly distinguished citizens have in succession administered the executive branch of the Government. They have conducted it through many perils, and generally with great success. Yet, with all this scope of precedent, I now enter upon the same task for the brief constitutional term of four years under great and peculiar difficulty. A disruption of the Federal Union, heretofore only menaced, is now formidably attempted.

I hold that in contemplation of universal law and of the Constitution the Union of these States is perpetual. Perpetuity is implied, if not expressed, in the fundamental law of all national governments. It is safe to assert that no government proper ever had a provision in its organic law for its own termination. Continue to execute all the express provisions of our National Constitution, and the Union will endure forever, it being impossible to destroy it except by some action not provided for in the instrument itself.

Again: If the United States be not a government proper, but an association of States in the nature of contract merely, can it, as a contract, be peaceably unmade by less than all the parties who made it? One party to a contract may violate it—break it, so to speak—but does it not require all to lawfully rescind it?

Descending from these general principles, we find the proposition that in legal contemplation the Union is perpetual confirmed by the history of the Union itself. The Union is much older than the Constitution. It was formed, in fact, by the Articles of Association in 1774. It was matured and continued by the Declaration of Independence in 1776. It was further matured, and the faith of all the then thirteen States expressly plighted and engaged that it should be perpetual, by the Articles of Confederation in 1778. And finally, in 1787, one of the declared objects for ordaining and establishing the Constitution was "*to form a more perfect Union.*"

But if destruction of the Union by one or by a part only of the States be lawfully possible, the Union is *less* perfect than before the Constitution, having lost the vital element of perpetuity.

It follows from these views that no State upon its own mere motion can lawfully get out of the Union; that *resolves* and *ordinances* to that effect are legally void, and that acts of violence within any State or States against the authority of the United States are insurrectionary or revolutionary, according to circumstances.

I therefore consider that in view of the Constitution and the laws the Union is unbroken, and to the extent of my ability I shall take care, as the Constitution itself expressly enjoins upon me, that the laws of the Union be faithfully executed in all the States. Doing this I deem to be only a simple duty on my part, and I shall perform it so far as practicable unless my rightful masters, the American people, shall withhold the requisite means or in some authoritative manner direct the contrary. I trust this will not be regarded as a menace, but only as the declared purpose of the Union that it *will* constitutionally defend and maintain itself.

In doing this there needs to be no bloodshed or violence, and there shall be none unless it be forced upon the national authority. The power confided to me will be used to hold, occupy, and possess the property and places belonging to the Government and to collect the duties and imposts; but beyond what may be necessary for these objects, there will be no invasion, no using of force against or among the people anywhere. Where hostility to the United States in any interior locality shall be so great and universal as to prevent competent resident citizens from holding the Federal offices, there will be no attempt to force obnoxious strangers among the people for that object. While the strict legal right may exist in the Government to enforce the exercise of these offices, the attempt to do so would be so irritating and so nearly impracticable withal that I deem it better to forego for the time the uses of such offices.

The mails, unless repelled, will continue to be furnished in all parts of the Union. So far as possible the people everywhere shall have that sense of perfect security which is most favorable to calm thought and reflection. The course here indicated will be followed unless current events and experience shall show a modification or change to be proper, and in every case and exigency my best discretion will be exercised, according to circumstances actually existing and with a view and a hope of a peaceful solution of the national troubles and the restoration of fraternal sympathies and affections.

That there are persons in one section or another who seek to destroy the Union at all events and are glad of any pretext to do it I will neither affirm nor deny; but if there be such, I need address no word to them. To those, however, who really love the Union may I not speak?

Before entering upon so grave a matter as the destruction of our national fabric, with all its benefits, its memories, and its hopes, would it not be wise to ascertain precisely why we do it? Will you hazard so desperate a step while there is any possibility that any portion of the ills you fly from have no real existence? Will you, while the certain ills you fly to are greater than all the real ones you fly from, will you risk the commission of so fearful a mistake?

All profess to be content in the Union if all constitutional rights can be maintained. Is it true, then, that any right plainly written in the Constitution has been denied? I think not. Happily, the human mind is so constituted that no party can reach to the audacity of doing this. Think, if you can, of a single instance in which a plainly written provision of the Constitution has ever been denied. If by the mere force of numbers a majority should deprive a minority of any clearly written constitutional right, it might in a moral point of view justify revolution; certainly would if such right were a vital one. But such is not our case. All the vital rights of minorities and of individuals are so plainly assured to them by affirmations and negations, guaranties and prohibitions, in the Constitution that controversies never arise concerning them. But no organic law can ever be framed with a provision specifically applicable to every question which may occur in practical administration. No foresight can anticipate nor any document of reasonable length contain express provisions for all possible questions. Shall fugitives from labor be surrendered by national or by State authority? The Constitution does not expressly say. *May* Congress prohibit slavery in the Territories? The Constitution does not expressly say. *Must* Congress protect slavery in the Territories? The Constitution does not expressly say.

From questions of this class spring all our constitutional controversies, and we divide upon them into majorities and minorities. If the minority will not acquiesce, the majority must, or the Government must cease. There is no other alternative, for continuing the Government is acquiescence on one side or the other. If a minority in such case will secede rather than acquiesce, they make a precedent which in turn will divide and ruin them, for a minority of their own will secede from them whenever a majority refuses to be controlled by such minority. For instance, why may not any portion of a new confederacy a year or two hence arbitrarily secede again, precisely as portions of the present Union now claim to secede from it? All who cherish disunion sentiments are now being educated to the exact temper of doing this.

Is there such perfect identity of interests among the States to compose a new union as to produce harmony only and prevent renewed secession?

Plainly the central idea of secession is the essence of anarchy. A majority held in restraint by constitutional checks and limitations, and always changing easily with deliberate changes of popular opinions and sentiments, is the only true sovereign of a free people. Whoever rejects it does of necessity fly to anarchy or to despotism. Unanimity is impossible. The rule of a minority, as a permanent arrangement, is wholly inadmissible; so that, rejecting the majority principle, anarchy or despotism in some form is all that is left.

I do not forget the position assumed by some that constitutional questions are to be decided by the Supreme Court, nor do I deny that such decisions must be binding in any case upon the parties to a suit as to the object of that suit, while they are also entitled to very high respect and consideration in all parallel cases by all other departments of the Government. And while it is obviously possible that such decision may be erroneous in any given case, still the evil effect following it, being limited to that particular case, with the chance that it may be overruled and never become a precedent for other cases, can better be borne than could the evils of a different practice. At the same time, the candid citizen must confess that if the policy of the Government upon vital questions affecting the whole people is to be irrevocably fixed by decisions of the Supreme Court, the instant they are made in ordinary litigation between parties in personal actions the people will have ceased to be their own rulers, having to that extent practically resigned their Government into the hands of that eminent tribunal. Nor is there in this view any assault upon the court or the judges. It is a duty from which they may not shrink to decide cases properly brought before them, and it is no fault of theirs if others seek to turn their decisions to political purposes.

Cne section of our country believes slavery is *right* and ought to be extended, while the other believes it is *wrong* and ought not to be extended. This is the only substantial dispute. The fugitive-slave clause of the Constitution and the law for the suppression of the foreign slave trade are each as well enforced, perhaps, as any law can ever be in a community where the moral sense of the people imperfectly supports the law itself. The great body of the people abide by the dry legal obligation in both cases, and a few break over in each. This, I think, can not be perfectly cured, and it would be worse in both cases *after* the separation of the sections than before. The foreign slave trade, now imperfectly suppressed, would be ultimately revived without restriction in one section, while fugitive slaves, now only partially surrendered, would not be surrendered at all by the other.

Physically speaking, we can not separate. We can not remove our respective sections from each other nor build an impassable wall between them. A husband and wife may be divorced and go out of the presence and beyond the reach of each other, but the different parts of our country can not do this. They can not but remain face to face, and intercourse, either amicable or hostile, must continue between them. Is it possible, then, to make that intercourse more advantageous or more satisfactory *after* separation than *before?* Can aliens make treaties easier than friends can make laws? Can treaties be more faithfully enforced between aliens than laws can among friends? Suppose you go to war, you can not fight always; and when, after much loss on both sides and no gain on either, you cease fighting, the identical old questions, as to terms of intercourse, are again upon you.

This country, with its institutions, belongs to the people who inhabit it. Whenever they shall grow weary of the existing Government, they can exercise their *constitutional* right of amending it or their *revolutionary* right to dismember or overthrow it. I can not be ignorant of the fact that many worthy and patriotic citizens are desirous of having the National Constitution amended. While I make no recommendation of amendments, I fully recognize the rightful authority of the people over the whole subject, to be exercised in either of the modes prescribed in the instrument itself; and I should, under existing circumstances, favor rather than oppose a fair opportunity being afforded the people to act upon it. I will venture to add that to me the convention mode seems preferable, in that it allows amendments to originate with the people themselves, instead of only permitting them to take or reject propositions originated by others, not especially chosen for the purpose, and which might not be precisely such as they would wish to either accept or refuse. I understand a proposed amendment to the Constitution—which amendment, however, I have not seen—has passed Congress, to the effect that the Federal Government shall never interfere with the domestic institutions of the States, including that of persons held to service. To avoid misconstruction of what I have said, I depart from my purpose not to speak of particular amendments so far as to say that, holding such a provision to now be implied constitutional law, I have no objection to its being made express and irrevocable.

The Chief Magistrate derives all his authority from the people, and they have conferred none upon him to fix terms for the separation of the States. The people themselves can do this also if they choose, but the Executive as such has nothing to do with it. His duty is to administer the present Government as it came to his hands and to transmit it unimpaired by him to his successor.

Why should there not be a patient confidence in the ultimate justice of the people? Is there any better or equal hope in the world? In our present differences, is either party without faith of being in the right? If the Almighty Ruler of Nations, with His eternal truth and justice, be on your side of the North, or on yours of the South, that truth and that justice will surely prevail by the judgment of this great tribunal of the American people.

By the frame of the Government under which we live this same people have wisely given their public servants but little power for mischief, and have with equal wisdom provided for the return of that little to their own hands at very short intervals. While the people retain their virtue and vigilance no Administration by any extreme of wickedness or folly can very seriously injure the Government in the short space of four years.

My countrymen, one and all, think calmly and *well* upon this whole subject. Nothing valuable can be lost by taking time. If there be an object to *hurry* any of you in hot haste to a step which you would never take *deliberately*, that object will be frustrated by taking time; but no good object can be frustrated by it. Such of you as are now dissatisfied still have the old Constitution unimpaired, and, on the sensitive point, the laws of your own framing under it; while the new Administration will have no immediate power, if it would, to change either. If it were admitted that you who are dissatisfied hold the right side in the dispute, there still is no single good reason for precipitate action. Intelligence, patriotism, Christianity, and a firm reliance on Him who has never yet forsaken this favored land are still competent to adjust in the best way all our present difficulty.

In *your* hands, my dissatisfied fellow-countrymen, and not in *mine*, is the momentous issue of civil war. The Government will not assail *you*. You can have no conflict without being yourselves the aggressors. *You* have no oath registered in heaven to destroy the Government, while *I* shall have the most solemn one to "preserve, protect, and defend it."

I am loath to close. We are not enemies, but friends. We must not be enemies.   Though passion may have strained it must not break our bonds of affection.   The mystic chords of memory, stretching from every battlefield and patriot grave to every living heart and hearthstone all over this broad land, will yet swell the chorus of the Union, when again touched, as surely they will be, by the better angels of our nature.

MARCH 4, 1861.

SPECIAL MESSAGES.

To the Senate: WASHINGTON, *March 16, 1861.*

The Senate has transmitted to me a copy of the message sent by my predecessor to that body on the 21st day of February last, proposing to take its advice on the subject of a proposition made by the British Government through its minister here to refer the matter in controversy between that Government and the Government of the United States to the arbitrament of the King of Sweden and Norway, the King of the Netherlands, or the Republic of the Swiss Confederation.

In that message my predecessor stated that he wished to submit to the Senate the precise questions following, namely:

Will the Senate approve a treaty referring to either of the sovereign powers above named the dispute now existing between the Governments of the United States and Great Britain concerning the boundary line between Vancouvers Island and the American continent?   In case the referee shall find himself unable to decide where the line is by the description of it in the treaty of 15th June, 1846, shall he be authorized to establish a line according to the treaty as nearly as possible?   Which of the three powers named by Great Britain as an arbiter shall be chosen by the United States?

I find no reason to disapprove of the course of my predecessor in this important matter, but, on the contrary, I not only shall receive the advice of the Senate therein cheerfully, but I respectfully ask the Senate for their advice on the three questions before recited.

ABRAHAM LINCOLN.

WASHINGTON, *March 26, 1861.*

To the Senate of the United States:

I have received a copy of a resolution of the Senate passed on the 25th instant, requesting me, if in my opinion not incompatible with the public interest, to communicate to the Senate the dispatches of Major Robert Anderson to the War Department during the time he has been in command of Fort Sumter.

On examining the correspondence thus called for I have, with the highest respect for the Senate, come to the conclusion that at the present moment the publication of it would be inexpedient.

ABRAHAM LINCOLN.

PROCLAMATIONS.

By the President of the United States.

A PROCLAMATION.

Whereas the laws of the United States have been for some time past and now are opposed and the execution thereof obstructed in the States of South Carolina, Georgia, Alabama, Florida, Mississippi, Louisiana, and Texas by combinations too powerful to be suppressed by the ordinary course of judicial proceedings or by the powers vested in the marshals by law:

Now, therefore, I, Abraham Lincoln, President of the United States, in virtue of the power in me vested by the Constitution and the laws, have thought fit to call forth, and hereby do call forth, the militia of the several States of the Union to the aggregate number of 75,000, in order to suppress said combinations and to cause the laws to be duly executed.

The details for this object will be immediately communicated to the State authorities through the War Department.

I appeal to all loyal citizens to favor, facilitate, and aid this effort to maintain the honor, the integrity, and the existence of our National Union and the perpetuity of popular government and to redress wrongs already long enough endured.

I deem it proper to say that the first service assigned to the forces hereby called forth will probably be to repossess the forts, places, and property which have been seized from the Union; and in every event the utmost care will be observed, consistently with the objects aforesaid, to avoid any devastation, any destruction of or interference with property, or any disturbance of peaceful citizens in any part of the country.

And I hereby command the persons composing the combinations aforesaid to disperse and retire peaceably to their respective abodes within twenty days from this date.

Deeming that the present condition of public affairs presents an extraordinary occasion, I do hereby, in virtue of the power in me vested by the Constitution, convene both Houses of Congress. Senators and Representatives are therefore summoned to assemble at their respective chambers at 12 o'clock noon on Thursday, the 4th day of July next, then and there to consider and determine such measures as, in their wisdom, the public safety and interest may seem to demand.

In witness whereof I have hereunto set my hand and caused the seal of the United States to be affixed.

[SEAL.]   Done at the city of Washington, this 15th day of April, A. D. 1861, and of the Independence of the United States the eighty-fifth.

                                                    ABRAHAM LINCOLN.
By the President:

WILLIAM H. SEWARD, *Secretary of State.*

BY THE PRESIDENT OF THE UNITED STATES OF AMERICA.

A PROCLAMATION.

Whereas an insurrection against the Government of the United States has broken out in the States of South Carolina, Georgia, Alabama, Florida, Mississippi, Louisiana, and Texas, and the laws of the United States for the collection of the revenue can not be effectually executed therein conformably to that provision of the Constitution which requires duties to be uniform throughout the United States; and

Whereas a combination of persons engaged in such insurrection have threatened to grant pretended letters of marque to authorize the bearers thereof to commit assaults on the lives, vessels, and property of good citizens of the country lawfully engaged in commerce on the high seas and in waters of the United States; and

Whereas an Executive proclamation has been already issued requiring the persons engaged in these disorderly proceedings to desist therefrom, calling out a militia force for the purpose of repressing the same, and convening Congress in extraordinary session to deliberate and determine thereon:

Now, therefore, I, Abraham Lincoln, President of the United States, with a view to the same purposes before mentioned and to the protection of the public peace and the lives and property of quiet and orderly citizens pursuing their lawful occupations, until Congress shall have assembled and deliberated on the said unlawful proceedings or until the same shall have ceased, have further deemed it advisable to set on foot a blockade of the ports within the States aforesaid, in pursuance of the laws of the United States and of the law of nations in such case provided. For this purpose a competent force will be posted so as to prevent entrance and exit of vessels from the ports aforesaid. If, therefore, with a view to violate such blockade, a vessel shall approach or shall attempt to leave either of the said ports, she will be duly warned by the commander of one of the blockading vessels, who will indorse on her register the fact and date of such warning, and if the same vessel shall again attempt to enter or leave the blockaded port she will be captured and sent to the nearest convenient port for such proceedings against her and her cargo as prize as may be deemed advisable.

And I hereby proclaim and declare that if any person, under the pretended authority of the said States or under any other pretense, shall molest a vessel of the United States or the persons or cargo on board of her, such person will be held amenable to the laws of the United States for the prevention and punishment of piracy.

In witness whereof I have hereunto set my hand and caused the seal of the United States to be affixed.

[SEAL.]   Done at the city of Washington, this 19th day of April, A. D. 1861, and of the Independence of the United States the eighty-fifth.   ABRAHAM LINCOLN.

By the President:

WILLIAM H. SEWARD, *Secretary of State.*

BY THE PRESIDENT OF THE UNITED STATES OF AMERICA.

A PROCLAMATION.

Whereas, for the reasons assigned in my proclamation of the 19th instant, a blockade of the ports of the States of South Carolina, Georgia, Florida, Alabama, Louisiana, Mississippi, and Texas was ordered to be established; and

Whereas since that date public property of the United States has been seized, the collection of the revenue obstructed, and duly commissioned officers of the United States, while engaged in executing the orders of their superiors, have been arrested and held in custody as prisoners or have been impeded in the discharge of their official duties, without due legal process, by persons claiming to act under authorities of the States of Virginia and North Carolina, an efficient blockade of the ports of those States will also be established.

In witness whereof I have hereunto set my hand and caused the seal of the United States to be affixed.

[SEAL.]   Done at the city of Washington, this 27th day of April, A. D. 1861, and of the Independence of the United States the eighty-fifth.   ABRAHAM LINCOLN.

By the President:

WILLIAM H. SEWARD, *Secretary of State.*

BY THE PRESIDENT OF THE UNITED STATES.

A PROCLAMATION.

Whereas existing exigencies demand immediate and adequate measures for the protection of the National Constitution and the preservation of the National Union by the suppression of the insurrectionary combinations now existing in several States for opposing the laws of the Union and obstructing the execution thereof, to which end a military force in addition to that called forth by my proclamation of the 15th day of April in the present year appears to be indispensably necessary :

Now, therefore, I, Abraham Lincoln, President of the United States and Commander in Chief of the Army and Navy thereof and of the militia of the several States when called into actual service, do hereby call into the service of the United States 42,034 volunteers to serve for the period of three years, unless sooner discharged, and to be mustered into service as infantry and cavalry. The proportions of each arm and the details of enrollment and organization will be made known through the Department of War.

And I also direct that the Regular Army of the United States be increased by the addition of eight regiments of infantry, one regiment of cavalry, and one regiment of artillery, making altogether a maximum aggregate increase of 22,714 officers and enlisted men, the details of which increase will also be made known through the Department of War.

And I further direct the enlistment for not less than one or more than three years of 18,000 seamen, in addition to the present force, for the naval service of the United States. The details of the enlistment and organization will be made known through the Department of the Navy.

The call for volunteers hereby made and the direction for the increase of the Regular Army and for the enlistment of seamen hereby given, together with the plan of organization adopted for the volunteer and for the regular forces hereby authorized, will be submitted to Congress as soon as assembled.

In the meantime I earnestly invoke the cooperation of all good citizens in the measures hereby adopted for the effectual suppression of unlawful violence, for the impartial enforcement of constitutional laws, and for the speediest possible restoration of peace and order, and with these of happiness and prosperity, throughout our country.

In testimony whereof I have hereunto set my hand and caused the seal of the United States to be affixed.

[SEAL.]   Done at the city of Washington, this 3d day of May, A. D. 1861, and of the Independence of the United States the eighty-fifth.

ABRAHAM LINCOLN.

By the President :

WILLIAM H. SEWARD, *Secretary of State.*

BY THE PRESIDENT OF THE UNITED STATES OF AMERICA

A PROCLAMATION.

Whereas an insurrection exists in the State of Florida by which the lives, liberty, and property of loyal citizens of the United States are endangered; and

Whereas it is deemed proper that all needful measures should be taken for the protection of such citizens and all officers of the United States in the discharge of their public duties in the State aforesaid:

Now, therefore, be it known that I, Abraham Lincoln, President of the United States, do hereby direct the commander of the forces of the United States on the Florida coast to permit no person to exercise any office or authority upon the islands of Key West, the Tortugas, and Santa Rosa which may be inconsistent with the laws and Constitution of the United States, authorizing him at the same time, if he shall find it necessary, to suspend there the writ of *habeas corpus* and to remove from the vicinity of the United States fortresses all dangerous or suspected persons.

In witness whereof I have hereunto set my hand and caused the seal of the United States to be affixed.

[SEAL.]   Done at the city of Washington, this 10th day of May, A. D. 1861, and of the Independence of the United States the eighty-fifth.

         ABRAHAM LINCOLN.

By the President:
     WILLIAM H. SEWARD,
         Secretary of State.

EXECUTIVE ORDERS.

Lieutenant-General SCOTT.   WASHINGTON, *April 25, 1861.*

MY DEAR SIR: The Maryland legislature assembles to-morrow at Annapolis, and not improbably will take action to arm the people of that State against the United States. The question has been submitted to and considered by me whether it would not be justifiable, upon the ground of necessary defense, for you, as General in Chief of the United States Army, to arrest or disperse the members of that body. I think it would not be justifiable nor efficient for the desired object.

First. They have a clearly legal right to assemble, and we can not know in advance that their action will not be lawful and peaceful, and if we wait until they shall have acted their arrest or dispersion will not lessen the effect of their action.

Secondly. We can not permanently prevent their action. If we arrest them, we can not long hold them as prisoners, and when liberated they will immediately reassemble and take their action; and precisely the same if we simply disperse them—they will immediately reassemble in some other place.

I therefore conclude that it is only left to the Commanding General to watch and await their action, which, if it shall be to arm their people against the United States, he is to adopt the most prompt and efficient means to counteract, even, if necessary, to the bombardment of their cities and, in the extremest necessity, the suspension of the writ of *habeas corpus*.

Your obedient servant,   ABRAHAM LINCOLN.

The COMMANDING GENERAL OF THE ARMY OF THE UNITED STATES:

You are engaged in suppressing an insurrection against the laws of the United States. If at any point on or in the vicinity of any military line which is now or which shall be used between the city of Philadelphia and the city of Washington you find resistance which renders it necessary to suspend the writ of *habeas corpus* for the public safety, you personally, or through the officer in command at the point where resistance occurs, are authorized to suspend that writ.

Given under my hand and the seal of the United States, at the city [SEAL.] of Washington, this 27th day of April, 1861, and of the Independence of the United States the eighty-fifth.

ABRAHAM LINCOLN.

By the President of the United States:

WILLIAM H. SEWARD,
Secretary of State.

GENERAL ORDERS, NO. 13.

WAR DEPARTMENT,
ADJUTANT-GENERAL'S OFFICE,
Washington, April 30, 1861.

The President directs that all officers of the Army, except those who have entered the service since the 1st instant, take and subscribe anew the oath of allegiance to the United States of America, as set forth in the tenth article of war.

Commanding officers will see to the prompt execution of this order, and report accordingly.

By order: L. THOMAS,
Adjutant-General.

To all who shall see these presents, greeting:

Know ye that, reposing special trust and confidence in the patriotism, valor, fidelity, and ability of Colonel Robert Anderson, United States Army, I have empowered him, and do hereby empower him, to receive into the Army of the United States as many regiments of volunteer troops from the State of Kentucky and from the western part of the State of Virginia as shall be willing to engage in the service of the United States for the term of three years upon the terms and according to the plan proposed by the proclamation of May 3, 1861, and General Orders, No. 15, from the War Department, of May 4, 1861.

The troops whom he receives shall be on the same footing in every respect as those of the like kind called for in the proclamation above cited, except that the officers shall be commissioned by the United States. He is therefore carefully and diligently to discharge the duty hereby devolved upon him by doing and performing all manner of things thereunto belonging.

Given under my hand, at the city of Washington, this 7th day of May, A. D. 1861, and in the eighty-fifth year of the Independence of the United States.

ABRAHAM LINCOLN.

By the President:
SIMON CAMERON,
Secretary of War.

STATE DEPARTMENT, *June 20, 1861.*

The LIEUTENANT-GENERAL COMMANDING THE ARMIES OF THE UNITED STATES:

You or any officer you may designate will, in your discretion, suspend the writ of *habeas corpus* so far as may relate to Major Chase, lately of the Engineer Corps of the Army of the United States, now alleged to be guilty of treasonable practices against this Government.

ABRAHAM LINCOLN.

By the President:
WILLIAM H. SEWARD.

The COMMANDING GENERAL, ARMY OF THE UNITED STATES:

You are engaged in suppressing an insurrection against the laws of the United States. If at any point on or in the vicinity of any military line which is now or which shall be used between the city of New York and the city of Washington you find resistance which renders it necessary to suspend the writ of *habeas corpus* for the public safety, you personally, or through the officer in command at the point where resistance occurs, are authorized to suspend that writ.

Given under my hand and the seal of the United States, at the city [SEAL.] of Washington, this 2d day of July, A. D. 1861, and of the Independence of the United States the eighty-fifth.

ABRAHAM LINCOLN.

By the President:
WILLIAM H. SEWARD,
Secretary of State.

SPECIAL SESSION MESSAGE.

JULY 4, 1861.

Fellow-Citizens of the Senate and House of Representatives:

Having been convened on an extraordinary occasion, as authorized by the Constitution, your attention is not called to any ordinary subject of legislation.

At the beginning of the present Presidential term, four months ago, the functions of the Federal Government were found to be generally suspended within the several States of South Carolina, Georgia, Alabama, Mississippi, Louisiana, and Florida, excepting only those of the Post-Office Department.

Within these States all the forts, arsenals, dockyards, custom-houses, and the like, including the movable and stationary property in and about them, had been seized and were held in open hostility to this Government, excepting only Forts Pickens, Taylor, and Jefferson, on and near the Florida coast, and Fort Sumter, in Charleston Harbor, South Carolina. The forts thus seized had been put in improved condition, new ones had been built, and armed forces had been organized and were organizing, all avowedly with the same hostile purpose.

The forts remaining in the possession of the Federal Government in and near these States were either besieged or menaced by warlike preparations, and especially Fort Sumter was nearly surrounded by well-protected hostile batteries, with guns equal in quality to the best of its own and outnumbering the latter as perhaps ten to one. A disproportionate share of the Federal muskets and rifles had somehow found their way into these States, and had been seized to be used against the Government. Accumulations of the public revenue lying within them had been seized for the same object. The Navy was scattered in distant seas, leaving but a very small part of it within the immediate reach of the Government. Officers of the Federal Army and Navy had resigned in great numbers, and of those resigning a large proportion had taken up arms against the Government. Simultaneously and in connection with all this the purpose to sever the Federal Union was openly avowed. In accordance with this purpose, an ordinance had been adopted in each of these States declaring the States respectively to be separated from the National Union. A formula for instituting a combined government of these States had been promulgated, and this illegal organization, in the character of Confederate States, was already invoking recognition, aid, and intervention from foreign powers.

Finding this condition of things and believing it to be an imperative duty upon the incoming Executive to prevent, if possible, the consummation of such attempt to destroy the Federal Union, a choice of means to that end became indispensable. This choice was made, and was declared in the inaugural address. The policy chosen looked to the exhaustion of all peaceful measures before a resort to any stronger ones. It sought only to hold the public places and property not already wrested from the Government and to collect the revenue, relying for the rest on time, discussion, and the ballot box. It promised a continuance of the mails at Government expense to the very people who were resisting the Government, and it gave repeated pledges against any disturbance to any of the people or any of their rights. Of all that which a President might constitutionally and justifiably do in such a case, everything was forborne without which it was believed possible to keep the Government on foot.

On the 5th of March, the present incumbent's first full day in office, a letter of Major Anderson, commanding at Fort Sumter, written on the 28th of February and received at the War Department on the 4th of March, was by that Department placed in his hands. This letter expressed the professional opinion of the writer that reenforcements could not be thrown into that fort within the time for his relief rendered necessary by the limited supply of provisions, and with a view of holding possession of the same, with a force of less than 20,000 good and well-disciplined men. This opinion was concurred in by all the officers of his command, and their memoranda on the subject were made inclosures of Major Anderson's letter. The whole was immediately laid before Lieutenant-General Scott, who at once concurred with Major Anderson in opinion. On reflection, however, he took full time, consulting with other officers, both of the Army and the Navy, and at the end of four days came reluctantly, but decidedly, to the same conclusion as before. He also stated at the same time that no such sufficient force was then at the control of the Government or could be raised and brought to the ground within the time when the provisions in the fort would be exhausted. In a purely military point of view this reduced the duty of the Administration in the case to the mere matter of getting the garrison safely out of the fort.

It was believed, however, that to so abandon that position under the circumstances would be utterly ruinous; that the *necessity* under which it was to be done would not be fully understood; that by many it would be construed as a part of a *voluntary* policy; that at home it would discourage the friends of the Union, embolden its adversaries, and go far to insure to the latter a recognition abroad; that, in fact, it would be our national destruction consummated. This could not be allowed. Starvation was not yet upon the garrison, and ere it would be reached *Fort Pickens* might be reenforced. This last would be a clear indication of *policy*, and would better enable the country to accept the evacuation of Fort Sumter as a military *necessity*. An order was at once directed to be sent for the landing of the troops from the steamship *Brooklyn* into Fort Pickens. This order could not go by land but must take the longer and slower route by sea. The first return news from the order was received just one week before the fall of Fort Sumter. The news itself was that the officer commanding the *Sabine*, to which vessel the troops had been transferred from the *Brooklyn*, acting upon some *quasi* armistice of the late Administration (and of the existence of which the present Administration, up to the time the order was dispatched, had only too vague and uncertain rumors to fix attention), had refused to land the troops. To now reenforce Fort Pickens before a crisis would be reached at Fort Sumter was impossible, rendered so by the near exhaustion of provisions in the latter-named fort. In precaution against such a conjuncture the Government had a few days before commenced preparing an expedition, as well adapted as might be, to relieve Fort Sumter, which expedition was intended to be ultimately used or not, according to circumstances. The strongest anticipated case for using it was now presented, and it was resolved to send it forward. As had been intended in this contingency, it was also resolved to notify the governor of South Carolina that he might expect an attempt would be made to provision the fort, and that if the attempt should not be resisted there would be no effort to throw in men, arms, or ammunition without further notice, or in case of an attack upon the fort. This notice was accordingly given, whereupon the fort was attacked and bombarded to its fall, without even awaiting the arrival of the provisioning expedition.

It is thus seen that the assault upon and reduction of Fort Sumter was in no sense a matter of self-defense on the part of the assailants. They well knew that the garrison in the fort could by no possibility commit aggression upon them. They knew—they were expressly notified—that the giving of bread to the few brave and hungry men of the garrison was all which would on that occasion be attempted, unless themselves, by resisting so much, should provoke more. They knew that this Government desired to keep the garrison in the fort, not to assail them, but merely to maintain visible possession, and thus to preserve the Union from actual and immediate dissolution, trusting, as hereinbefore stated, to time, discussion, and the ballot box for final adjustment; and they assailed and reduced the fort for precisely the reverse object—to drive out the visible authority of the Federal Union, and thus force it to immediate dissolution. That this was their object the Executive well understood; and having said to them in the inaugural address, "You can have no conflict without being yourselves the aggressors," he took pains not only to keep this declaration good, but also to keep the case so free from the power of ingenious sophistry as that the world should not be able to misunderstand it. By the affair at Fort Sumter, with its surrounding circumstances, that point was reached. Then and thereby the assailants of the Government began the conflict of arms, without a gun in sight or in expectancy to return their fire, save only the few in the fort, sent to that harbor years before for their own protection, and still ready to give that protection in whatever was lawful. In this act, discarding all else, they have forced upon the country the distinct issue, "Immediate dissolution or blood."

And this issue embraces more than the fate of these United States. It presents to the whole family of man the question whether a constitutional republic, or democracy—a government of the people by the same people—can or can not maintain its territorial integrity against its own domestic foes. It presents the question whether discontented individuals, too few in numbers to control administration according to organic law in any case, can always, upon the pretenses made in this case, or on any other pretenses, or arbitrarily without any pretense, break up their government, and thus practically put an end to free government upon the earth. It forces us to ask, Is there in all republics this inherent and fatal weakness? Must a government of necessity be too *strong* for the liberties of its own people, or too *weak* to maintain its own existence?

So viewing the issue, no choice was left but to call out the war power of the Government and so to resist force employed for its destruction by force for its preservation.

The call was made, and the response of the country was most gratifying, surpassing in unanimity and spirit the most sanguine expectation. Yet none of the States commonly called slave States, except Delaware, gave a regiment through regular State organization. A few regiments have been organized within some others of those States by individual enterprise and received into the Government service. Of course the seceded States, so called (and to which Texas had been joined about the time of the inauguration), gave no troops to the cause of the Union. The border States, so called, were not uniform in their action, some of them being almost *for* the Union, while in others, as Virginia, North Carolina, Tennessee, and Arkansas, the Union sentiment was nearly repressed and silenced. The course taken in Virginia was the most remarkable, perhaps the most important. A convention elected by the people of that State to consider this very question of disrupting the Federal Union was in session at the capital of Virginia when Fort Sumter fell. To this body the people had chosen a large majority of *professed* Union men. Almost immediately after the fall of Sumter many members of that majority went over to the original disunion minority, and with them adopted an ordinance for withdrawing the State from the Union. Whether this change was wrought by their great approval of the assault upon Sumter or their great resentment at the Government's resistance to that assault is not definitely known. Although they submitted the ordinance for ratification to a vote of the people, to be taken on a day then somewhat more than a month distant, the convention and the legislature (which was also in session at the same time and place), with leading men of the State not members of either, immediately commenced acting as if the State were already out of the Union. They pushed military preparations vigorously forward all over the State. They seized the United States armory at Harpers Ferry and the navy-yard at Gosport, near Norfolk. They received—perhaps invited—into their State large bodies of troops, with their warlike appointments, from the so-called seceded States. They formally entered into a treaty of temporary alliance and cooperation with the so-called "Confederate States," and sent members to their congress at Montgomery; and, finally, they permitted the insurrectionary government to be transferred to their capital at Richmond.

The people of Virginia have thus allowed this giant insurrection to make its nest within her borders, and this Government has no choice left but to deal with it *where* it finds it; and it has the less regret, as the loyal citizens have in due form claimed its protection. Those loyal citizens this Government is bound to recognize and protect, as being Virginia.

In the border States, so called—in fact, the Middle States—there are those who favor a policy which they call "armed neutrality;" that is, an arming of those States to prevent the Union forces passing one way or the disunion the other over their soil. This would be disunion completed. Figuratively speaking, it would be the building of an impassable wall along the line of separation, and yet not quite an impassable one, for, under the guise of neutrality, it would tie the hands of the Union men and freely pass supplies from among them to the insurrectionists, which it could not do as an open enemy. At a stroke it would take all the trouble off the hands of secession, except only what proceeds from the external blockade. It would do for the disunionists that which of all things they most desire—feed them well and give them disunion without a struggle of their own. It recognizes no fidelity to the Constitution, no obligation to maintain the Union; and while very many who have favored it are doubtless loyal citizens, it is, nevertheless, very injurious in effect.

Recurring to the action of the Government, it may be stated that at first a call was made for 75,000 militia, and rapidly following this a proclamation was issued for closing the ports of the insurrectionary districts by proceedings in the nature of blockade. So far all was believed to be strictly legal. At this point the insurrectionists announced their purpose to enter upon the practice of privateering.

Other calls were made for volunteers to serve three years unless sooner discharged, and also for large additions to the Regular Army and Navy. These measures, whether strictly legal or not, were ventured upon under what appeared to be a popular demand and a public necessity, trusting then, as now, that Congress would readily ratify them. It is believed that nothing has been done beyond the constitutional competency of Congress.

Soon after the first call for militia it was considered a duty to authorize the Commanding General in proper cases, according to his discretion, to suspend the privilege of the writ of *habeas corpus*, or, in other words, to arrest and detain without resort to the ordinary processes and forms of law such individuals as he might deem dangerous to the public safety. This authority has purposely been exercised but very sparingly. Nevertheless, the legality and propriety of what has been done under it are questioned, and the attention of the country has been called to the proposition that one who is sworn to "take care that the laws be faithfully executed" should not himself violate them. Of course some consideration was given to the questions of power and propriety before this matter was acted upon. The whole of the laws which were required to be faithfully executed were being resisted and failing of execution in nearly one-third of the States. Must they be allowed to finally fail of execution, even had it been perfectly clear that by the use of the means necessary to their execution some single law, made in such extreme tenderness of the citizen's liberty that practically it relieves more of the guilty than of the innocent, should to a very limited extent be violated? To state the question more directly, Are all the laws *but one* to go unexecuted, and the Government itself go to pieces lest that one be violated? Even in such a case, would not the official oath be broken if the Government should be overthrown when it was believed that disregarding the single law would tend to preserve it? But it was not believed that this question was presented. It was not believed that any law was violated. The provision of the Constitution that "the privilege of the writ of *habeas corpus* shall not be suspended unless when, in cases of rebellion or invasion, the public safety may require it" is equivalent to a provision—is a provision—that such privilege may be suspended when, in cases of rebellion or invasion, the public safety *does* require it. It was decided that we have a case of rebellion and that the public safety does require the qualified suspension of the privilege of the writ which was authorized to be made. Now it is insisted that Congress, and not the Executive, is vested with this power; but the Constitution itself is silent as to which or who is to exercise the power; and as the provision was plainly made for a dangerous emergency, it can not be believed the framers of the instrument intended that in every case the danger should run its course until Congress could be called together, the very assembling of which might be prevented, as was intended in this case, by the rebellion.

No more extended argument is now offered, as an opinion at some length will probably be presented by the Attorney-General. Whether there shall be any legislation upon the subject, and, if any, what, is submitted entirely to the better judgment of Congress.

The forbearance of this Government had been so extraordinary and so long continued as to lead some foreign nations to shape their action as if they supposed the early destruction of our National Union was probable. While this on discovery gave the Executive some concern, he is now happy to say that the sovereignty and rights of the United States are now everywhere practically respected by foreign powers, and a general sympathy with the country is manifested throughout the world.

The reports of the Secretaries of the Treasury, War, and the Navy will give the information in detail deemed necessary and convenient for your deliberation and action, while the Executive and all the Departments will stand ready to supply omissions or to communicate new facts considered important for you to know.

It is now recommended that you give the legal means for making this contest a short and a decisive one; that you place at the control of the Government for the work at least 400,000 men and $400,000,000. That number of men is about one-tenth of those of proper ages within the regions where apparently *all* are willing to engage, and the sum is less than a twenty-third part of the money value owned by the men who seem ready to devote the whole. A debt of $600,000,000 *now* is a less sum per head than was the debt of our Revolution when we came out of that struggle, and the money value in the country now bears even a greater proportion to what it was *then* than does the population. Surely each man has as strong a motive *now* to *preserve* our liberties as each had *then* to *establish* them.

A right result at this time will be worth more to the world than ten times the men and ten times the money. The evidence reaching us from the country leaves no doubt that the material for the work is abundant, and that it needs only the hand of legislation to give it legal sanction and the hand of the Executive to give it practical shape and efficiency. One of the greatest perplexities of the Government is to avoid receiving troops faster than it can provide for them. In a word, the people will save their Government if the Government itself will do its part only indifferently well.

It might seem at first thought to be of little difference whether the present movement at the South be called "secession" or "rebellion." The movers, however, well understand the difference. At the beginning they knew they could never raise their treason to any respectable magnitude by any name which implies *violation* of law. They knew their people possessed as much of moral sense, as much of devotion to law and order, and as much pride in and reverence for the history and Government of their common country as any other civilized and patriotic people. They knew they could make no advancement directly in the teeth of these strong and noble sentiments. Accordingly, they commenced by an insidious debauching of the public mind. They invented an ingenious sophism, which, if conceded, was followed by perfectly logical steps through all the incidents to the complete destruction of the Union. The sophism itself is that any State of the Union may *consistently* with the National Constitution, and therefore *lawfully* and *peacefully*, withdraw from the Union without the consent of the Union or of any other State. The little disguise that the supposed right is to be exercised only for just cause, themselves to be the sole judge of its justice, is too thin to merit any notice.

With rebellion thus sugar coated they have been drugging the public mind of their section for more than thirty years, and until at length they have brought many good men to a willingness to take up arms against the Government the day *after* some assemblage of men have enacted the farcical pretense of taking their State out of the Union who could have been brought to no such thing the day *before*.

This sophism derives much, perhaps the whole, of its currency from the assumption that there is some omnipotent and sacred supremacy pertaining to a *State*—to each State of our Federal Union. Our States have neither more nor less power than that reserved to them in the Union by the Constitution, no one of them ever having been a State *out* of the Union. The original ones passed into the Union even *before* they cast off their British colonial dependence, and the new ones each came into the Union directly from a condition of dependence, excepting Texas; and even Texas, in its temporary independence, was never designated a State. The new ones only took the designation of States on coming into the Union, while that name was first adopted for the old ones in and by the Declaration of Independence. Therein the "United Colonies" were declared to be "free and independent States;" but even then the object plainly was not to declare their independence of *one another* or of the *Union*, but directly the contrary, as their mutual pledge and their mutual action before, at the time, and afterwards abundantly show. The express plighting of faith by each and all of the original thirteen in the Articles of Confederation, two years later, that the Union shall be perpetual is most conclusive. Having never been States, either in substance or in name, *outside* of the Union, whence this magical omnipotence of "State rights," asserting a claim of power to lawfully destroy the Union itself? Much is said about the "sovereignty" of the States, but the word even is not in the National Constitution, nor, as is believed, in any of the State constitutions. What is a "sovereignty" in the political sense of the term? Would it be far wrong to define it "a political community without a political superior"? Tested by this, no one of our States, except Texas, ever was a sovereignty; and even Texas gave up the character on coming into the Union, by which act she acknowledged the Constitution of the United States and the laws and treaties of the United States made in pursuance of the Constitution to be for her the supreme law of the land. The States have their status in the Union, and they have no other legal status. If they break from this, they can only do so against law and by revolution. The Union, and not themselves separately, procured their independence and their liberty. By conquest or purchase the Union gave each of them whatever of independence and liberty it has. The Union is older than any of the States, and, in fact, it created them as States. Originally some dependent colonies made the Union, and in turn the Union threw off their old dependence for them and made them States, such as they are.   Not one of them ever had a State constitution independent of the Union.   Of course it is not forgotten that all the new States framed their constitutions before they entered the Union, nevertheless dependent upon and preparatory to coming into the Union.

Unquestionably the States have the powers and rights reserved to them in and by the National Constitution; but among these surely are not included all conceivable powers, however mischievous or destructive, but at most such only as were known in the world at the time as governmental powers; and certainly a power to destroy the Government itself had never been known as a governmental—as a merely administrative power.   This relative matter of national power and State rights, as a principle, is no other than the principle of *generality* and *locality*.   Whatever concerns the whole should be confided to the whole—to the General Government—while whatever concerns *only* the State should be left exclusively to the State.   This is all there is of original principle about it.   Whether the National Constitution in defining boundaries between the two has applied the principle with exact accuracy is not to be questioned.   We are all bound by that defining without question.

What is now combated is the position that secession is *consistent* with the Constitution—is *lawful* and *peaceful*.   It is not contended that there is any express law for it, and nothing should ever be implied as law which leads to unjust or absurd consequences.   The nation purchased with money the countries out of which several of these States were formed.   Is it just that they shall go off without leave and without refunding?   The nation paid very large sums (in the aggregate, I believe, nearly a hundred millions) to relieve Florida of the aboriginal tribes. Is it just that she shall now be off without consent or without making any return?   The nation is now in debt for money applied to the benefit of these so-called seceding States in common with the rest.   Is it just either that creditors shall go unpaid or the remaining States pay the whole?   A part of the present national debt was contracted to pay the old debts of Texas.   Is it just that she shall leave and pay no part of this herself?

Again: If one State may secede, so may another; and when all shall have seceded none is left to pay the debts.   Is this quite just to creditors?   Did we notify them of this sage view of ours when we borrowed their money?   If we now recognize this doctrine by allowing the seceders to go in peace, it is difficult to see what we can do if others choose to go or to extort terms upon which they will promise to remain.

The seceders insist that our Constitution admits of secession.   They have assumed to make a national constitution of their own, in which of necessity they have either *discarded* or *retained* the right of secession, as they insist it exists in ours.   If they have discarded it, they thereby admit that on principle it ought not to be in ours.   If they have retained

Executive Mansion
Washington, Nov 21. 1864

To Mrs Bixby, Boston, Mass,

Dear Madam.

I have been shown in the files of the War Department a statement of the Adjutant General of Massachusetts that you are the mother of five sons who have died gloriously on the field of battle. I feel how weak and fruitless must be any word of mine which should attempt to beguile you from the grief of a loss so overwhelming. But I cannot refrain from tendering you the consolation that may be found in the thanks of the republic they died to save. I pray that our Heavenly Father may assuage the anguish of your bereavement, and leave you only the cherished memory of the loved and lost, and the solemn pride that must be yours to have laid so costly a sacrifice upon the altar of freedom.

Yours very sincerely and respectfully.

A. Lincoln.

FACSIMILE—PRESIDENT LINCOLN'S LETTER TO MRS. BIXBY

THE BIXBY LETTER.

Than the famous letter of Abraham Lincoln to Mrs. Bixby, nothing reveals better Lincoln's tenderness, his sadness at the sacrifices demanded by the war, his adamantine love of the Union, and his ever-throbbing humaneness. The simple but pulsating words with which he commiserated the martyred widow who had given all her sons over to death that the Union might be undivided have made the "Bixby Letter" a classic which is fittingly placed by the side of the immortal Gettysburg address.

it, by their own construction of ours they show that to be consistent they must secede from one another whenever they shall find it the easiest way of settling their debts or effecting any other selfish or unjust object. The principle itself is one of disintegration, and upon which no government can possibly endure.

If all the States save one should assert the power to *drive* that one out of the Union, it is presumed the whole class of seceder politicians would at once deny the power and denounce the act as the greatest outrage upon State rights. But suppose that precisely the same act, instead of being called "driving the one out," should be called "the seceding of the others from that one," it would be exactly what the seceders claim to do, unless, indeed, they make the point that the one, because it is a minority, may rightfully do what the others, because they are a majority, may not rightfully do. These politicians are subtle and profound on the rights of minorities. They are not partial to that power which made the Constitution and speaks from the preamble, calling itself "we, the people."

It may well be questioned whether there is to-day a majority of the legally qualified voters of any State, except, perhaps, South Carolina, in favor of disunion. There is much reason to believe that the Union men are the majority in many, if not in every other one, of the so-called seceded States. The contrary has not been demonstrated in any one of them. It is ventured to affirm this even of Virginia and Tennessee; for the result of an election held in military camps, where the bayonets are all on one side of the question voted upon, can scarcely be considered as demonstrating popular sentiment. At such an election all that large class who are at once *for* the Union and *against* coercion would be coerced to vote against the Union.

It may be affirmed without extravagance that the free institutions we enjoy have developed the powers and improved the condition of our whole people beyond any example in the world. Of this we now have a striking and an impressive illustration. So large an army as the Government has now on foot was never before known without a soldier in it but who had taken his place there of his own free choice. But more than this, there are many single regiments whose members, one and another, possess full practical knowledge of all the arts, sciences, professions, and whatever else, whether useful or elegant, is known in the world; and there is scarcely one from which there could not be selected a President, a Cabinet, a Congress, and perhaps a court, abundantly competent to administer the Government itself. Nor do I say this is not true also in the army of our late friends, now adversaries in this contest; but if it is, so much better the reason why the Government which has conferred such benefits on both them and us should not be broken up. Whoever in any section proposes to abandon such a government would do well to consider in deference to what principle it is that he does it; what better he is likely to get in its stead; whether the substitute will give, or be intended to give, so much of good to the people. There are some foreshadowings on this subject. Our adversaries have adopted some declarations of independence in which, unlike the good old one penned by Jefferson, they omit the words ''all men are created equal.'' Why? They have adopted a temporary national constitution, in the preamble of which, unlike our good old one signed by Washington, they omit '' We, the people,'' and substitute ''We, the deputies of the sovereign and independent States.'' Why? Why this deliberate pressing out of view the rights of men and the authority of the people?

This is essentially a people's contest. On the side of the Union it is a struggle for maintaining in the world that form and substance of government whose leading object is to elevate the condition of men; to lift artificial weights from all shoulders; to clear the paths of laudable pursuit for all; to afford all an unfettered start and a fair chance in the race of life. Yielding to partial and temporary departures, from necessity, this is the leading object of the Government for whose existence we contend.

I am most happy to believe that the plain people understand and appreciate this. It is worthy of note that while in this the Government's hour of trial large numbers of those in the Army and Navy who have been favored with the offices have resigned and proved false to the hand which had pampered them, not one common soldier or common sailor is known to have deserted his flag.

Great honor is due to those officers who remained true despite the example of their treacherous associates; but the greatest honor and most important fact of all is the unanimous firmness of the common soldiers and common sailors. To the last man, so far as known, they have successfully resisted the traitorous efforts of those whose commands but an hour before they obeyed as absolute law. This is the patriotic instinct of plain people. They understand without an argument that the destroying the Government which was made by Washington means no good to them.

Our popular Government has often been called an experiment. Two points in it our people have already settled—the successful *establishing* and the successful *administering* of it. One still remains—its successful *maintenance* against a formidable internal attempt to overthrow it. It is now for them to demonstrate to the world that those who can fairly carry an election can also suppress a rebellion; that ballots are the rightful and peaceful successors of bullets, and that when ballots have fairly and constitutionally decided there can be no successful appeal back to bullets; that there can be no successful appeal except to ballots themselves at succeeding elections. Such will be a great lesson of peace, teaching men that what they can not take by an election neither can they take it by a war; teaching all the folly of being the beginners of a war.

Lest there be some uneasiness in the minds of candid men as to what is to be the course of the Government toward the Southern States *after* the rebellion shall have been suppressed, the Executive deems it proper to say it will be his purpose then, as ever, to be guided by the Constitution and the laws, and that he probably will have no different understanding of the powers and duties of the Federal Government relatively to the rights of the States and the people under the Constitution than that expressed in the inaugural address.

He desires to preserve the Government, that it may be administered for all as it was administered by the men who made it. Loyal citizens everywhere have the right to claim this of their government, and the government has no right to withhold or neglect it. It is not perceived that in giving it there is any coercion, any conquest, or any subjugation in any just sense of those terms.

The Constitution provides, and all the States have accepted the provision, that "the United States shall guarantee to every State in this Union a republican form of government." But if a State may lawfully go out of the Union, having done so it may also discard the republican form of government; so that to prevent its going out is an indispensable *means* to the *end* of maintaining the guaranty mentioned; and when an end is lawful and obligatory the indispensable means to it are also lawful and obligatory.

It was with the deepest regret that the Executive found the duty of employing the war power in defense of the Government forced upon him. He could but perform this duty or surrender the existence of the Government. No compromise by public servants could in this case be a cure; not that compromises are not often proper, but that no popular government can long survive a marked precedent that those who carry an election can only save the government from immediate destruction by giving up the main point upon which the people gave the election. The people themselves, and not their servants, can safely reverse their own deliberate decisions.

As a private citizen the Executive could not have consented that these institutions shall perish; much less could he in betrayal of so vast and so sacred a trust as these free people had confided to him. He felt that he had no moral right to shrink, nor even to count the chances of his own life, in what might follow. In full view of his great responsibility he has so far done what he has deemed his duty. You will now, according to your own judgment, perform yours. He sincerely hopes that your views and your action may so accord with his as to assure all faithful citizens who have been disturbed in their rights of a certain and speedy restoration to them under the Constitution and the laws.

And having thus chosen our course, without guile and with pure purpose, let us renew our trust in God and go forward without fear and with manly hearts.

ABRAHAM LINCOLN.

SPECIAL MESSAGES.

To the House of Representatives: WASHINGTON, *July 11, 1861.*

In answer to the resolution of the House of Representatives of the 9th instant, requesting a copy of correspondence upon the subject of the incorporation of the Dominican Republic with the Spanish Monarchy, I transmit a report from the Secretary of State, to whom the resolution was referred.
                              ABRAHAM LINCOLN.

WASHINGTON, *July, 1861.*

To the Senate and House of Representatives:

I transmit to Congress a copy of correspondence between the Secretary of State and Her Britannic Majesty's envoy extraordinary and minister plenipotentiary accredited to this Government, relative to an exhibition of the products of industry of all nations which is to take place at London in the course of next year. As citizens of the United States may justly pride themselves upon their proficiency in industrial arts, it is desirable that they should have proper facilities toward taking part in the exhibition. With this view I recommend such legislation by Congress at this session as may be necessary for that purpose.
                              ABRAHAM LINCOLN.

WASHINGTON, *July 19, 1861.*

To the Senate of the United States:

I transmit to the Senate, for its advice with a view to a formal execution of the instrument, the draft of a treaty informally agreed upon between the United States and the Delaware tribe of Indians, relative to certain lands of that tribe.
                              ABRAHAM LINCOLN.

WASHINGTON, *July 19, 1861.*

To the Senate and House of Representatives:

As the United States have, in common with Great Britain and France, a deep interest in the preservation and development of the fisheries adjacent to the northeastern coast and islands of this continent, it seems proper that we should concert with the Governments of those countries such measures as may be conducive to those important objects. With this view I transmit to Congress a copy of a correspondence between the Secretary of State and the British minister here, in which the latter proposes on behalf of his Government the appointment of a joint commission to inquire into the matter, in order that such ulterior measures may be adopted as may be advisable for the objects proposed. Such legislation is recommended as may be necessary to enable the Executive to provide for a commissioner on behalf of the United States. ABRAHAM LINCOLN.

WASHINGTON, *July 25, 1861.*

To the House of Representatives:

In answer to the resolution of the House of Representatives of the 22d instant, requesting a copy of the correspondence between this Government and foreign powers with reference to maritime rights, I transmit a report from the Secretary of State. ABRAHAM LINCOLN.

WASHINGTON, *July 25, 1861.*

To the House of Representatives:

In answer to the resolution of the House of Representatives of the 15th instant, requesting a copy of the correspondence between this Government and foreign powers on the subject of the existing insurrection in the United States, I transmit a report from the Secretary of State. ABRAHAM LINCOLN.

WASHINGTON, *July 27, 1861.*

To the Senate:

In answer to the resolution of the Senate of the 25th instant, relative to the instructions to the ministers of the United States abroad in reference to the rebellion now existing in the southern portion of the Union, I transmit a report from the Secretary of State. ABRAHAM LINCOLN.

WASHINGTON, *July 27, 1861.*

To the House of Representatives:

In answer to the resolution of the House of Representatives of the 24th instant, asking the grounds, reasons, and evidence upon which the police commissioners of Baltimore were arrested and are now detained as prisoners at Fort McHenry, I have to state that it is judged to be incompatible with the public interest at this time to furnish the information called for by the resolution. ABRAHAM LINCOLN.

EXECUTIVE OFFICE, *July 29, 1861.*

Hon. H. HAMLIN,
 President of the Senate.

SIR: I transmit herewith, to be laid before the Senate for its constitutional action thereon, articles of agreement and convention,* with accompanying papers. ABRAHAM LINCOLN.

* With confederated tribes of Arapahoe and Cheyenne Indians of the Upper Arkansas River.

To the Senate of the United States: JULY 30, 1861.

In answer to the resolution of the Senate of the 19th instant, requesting information concerning the *quasi* armistice alluded to in my message
of the 4th instant,* I transmit a report from the Secretary of the Navy.

ABRAHAM LINCOLN.

To the Senate of the United States: JULY 30, 1861.

In answer to the resolution of the Senate of the 23d instant, requesting
information concerning the imprisonment of Lieutenant John J. Worden
[John L. Worden], of the United States Navy, I transmit a report from
the Secretary of the Navy.   ABRAHAM LINCOLN.

WASHINGTON, *August 1, 1861.*
To the Senate of the United States:

I submit herewith, for consideration with a view to ratification, a postal
treaty between the United States of America and the United Mexican
States, concluded by their respective plenipotentiaries on the 31st ultimo.

ABRAHAM LINCOLN.

WASHINGTON, *August 2, 1861.*
To the House of Representatives:

In answer to the resolution of the House of Representatives of yesterday, requesting information regarding the imprisonment of loyal citizens
of the United States by the forces now in rebellion against this Government, I transmit a report from the Secretary of State and the copy of a
telegraphic dispatch by which it was accompanied.

ABRAHAM LINCOLN.

To the Senate of the United States: AUGUST 2, 1861.

The resolution of your honorable body which is herewith returned has
been submitted to the Secretary of the Navy, who has made the report
upon it which I have the honor to inclose herewith.

I have the honor to add that the same rule stated by the Secretary of
the Navy is found in section 5 of the Army Regulations published in
1861.   It certainly is competent for Congress to change this rule by law,
but it is respectfully suggested that a rule of so long standing and of so
extensive application should not be hastily changed, nor by any authority
less than the full lawmaking power.

ABRAHAM LINCOLN.

* See p. 3223.

NAVY DEPARTMENT, *August 2, 1861.*

The PRESIDENT OF THE UNITED STATES.

SIR: I have the honor to acknowledge the receipt of the resolution of the Senate of the 31st ultimo, in relation to the recent nominations of lieutenants of marines, which nominations were directed to "be returned to the President and he be informed that the Senate adhere to the opinion expressed in the resolution passed by them on the 19th of July instant, and that the Senate are of opinion that rank and position in the Army, Navy, or Marine Corps should not be decided by lot, but that, all other things being equal, preference should be given to age."

If I understand correctly the resolution of the Senate, it is an expression of opinion on the part of that body against the Army Regulations, which are made applicable to the Marine Corps—regulations that have been in existence almost from the commencement of the Government.

In the published edition of Army Regulations when Mr. Calhoun was Secretary of War, section 1, article 3, it is expressly stated that the questions respecting the rank of officers arising from the sameness of dates in commissions of the same grade shall be decided, first, by a reference to the relative rank of the parties in the regular forces (including the United States Marine Corps) at the time the present appointments or promotions were made; second, by reference to former rank therein taken away by derangement or disbandment; third, by reference to former rank therein given up by resignation; fourth, by lottery.

And in the last edition of Army Regulations, before me, published in 1857, it is specified in article 2, section 5, that "when commissions are of the same date the rank is to be decided between officers of the same regiment or corps by the order of appointment; between officers of different regiments or corps, first, by rank in actual service when appointed; second, by former rank and service in the Army or Marine Corps; third, by lottery among such as have not been in the military service of the United States."

The rule here laid down governed in the appointment of the lieutenants of marines who have been nominated the present session to the Senate. Their order of rank was determined by lottery, agreeably to the published Army Regulations, and applied by those regulations specifically to the Marine Corps.

The gentlemen thus appointed in conformity to regulations have been mustered into service and done duty under fire. One of the number has fallen in the rank and place assigned him according to those regulations, and to set them aside and make a new order in conflict with the regulations will, I apprehend, be deemed, if not *ex post facto*, almost invidious.

In this matter the Department has no feeling, but it is desirable that it should be distinctly settled whether hereafter the Army Regulations are to govern in the question of rank in the Marine Corps or whether they are to be set aside by resolution of the Senate.

I have the honor to return the papers and subscribe myself, very respectfully, your obedient servant,

GIDEON WELLES.

EXECUTIVE MANSION, *August 5, 1861.*

To the Senate of the United States:

In answer to the resolution of your honorable body of date July 31, 1861, requesting the President to inform the Senate whether the Hon. James H. Lane, a member of that body from Kansas, has been appointed a brigadier-general in the Army of the United States, and, if so, whether he has accepted such appointment, I have the honor to transmit herewith certain papers, numbered 1, 2, 3, 4, 5, 6, and 7, which taken together explain themselves, and which contain all the information I possess upon the questions propounded.

It was my intention, as shown by my letter of June 20, 1861, to appoint Hon. James H. Lane, of Kansas, a brigadier-general of United States Volunteers, in anticipation of the act of Congress since passed for raising such volunteers; and I have no further knowledge upon the subject except as derived from the papers herewith inclosed.

ABRAHAM LINCOLN.

PROCLAMATIONS.

BY THE PRESIDENT OF THE UNITED STATES OF AMERICA.

A PROCLAMATION.

Whereas a joint committee of both Houses of Congress has waited on the President of the United States and requested him to "recommend a day of public humiliation, prayer, and fasting to be observed by the people of the United States with religious solemnities and the offering of fervent supplications to Almighty God for the safety and welfare of these States, His blessings on their arms, and a speedy restoration of peace;" and

Whereas it is fit and becoming in all people at all times to acknowledge and revere the supreme government of God, to bow in humble submission to His chastisements, to confess and deplore their sins and transgressions in the full conviction that the fear of the Lord is the beginning of wisdom, and to pray with all fervency and contrition for the pardon of their past offenses and for a blessing upon their present and prospective action; and

Whereas when our own beloved country, once, by the blessing of God, united, prosperous, and happy, is now afflicted with faction and civil war, it is peculiarly fit for us to recognize the hand of God in this terrible visitation, and in sorrowful remembrance of our own faults and crimes as a nation and as individuals to humble ourselves before Him and to pray for His mercy—to pray that we may be spared further punishment, though most justly deserved; that our arms may be blessed and made effectual for the reestablishment of law, order, and peace throughout the wide extent of our country; and that the inestimable boon of civil and religious liberty, earned under His guidance and blessing by the labors and sufferings of our fathers, may be restored in all its original excellence:

Therefore I, Abraham Lincoln, President of the United States, do appoint the last Thursday in September next as a day of humiliation, prayer, and fasting for all the people of the nation. And I do earnestly recommend to all the people, and especially to all ministers and teachers of religion of all denominations and to all heads of families, to observe and keep that day according to their several creeds and modes of worship in all humility and with all religious solemnity, to the end that the united prayer of the nation may ascend to the Throne of Grace and bring down plentiful blessings upon our country.

In testimony whereof I have hereunto set my hand and caused the seal of the United States to be affixed, this 12th day of August, [SEAL.] A. D. 1861, and of the Independence of the United States of America the eighty-sixth.

ABRAHAM LINCOLN.

By the President:

WILLIAM H. SEWARD, *Secretary of State.*

BY THE PRESIDENT OF THE UNITED STATES OF AMERICA.

A PROCLAMATION.

Whereas on the 15th day of April, 1861, the President of the United States, in view of an insurrection against the laws, Constitution, and Government of the United States which had broken out within the States of South Carolina, Georgia, Alabama, Florida, Mississippi, Louisiana, and Texas, and in pursuance of the provisions of the act entitled "An act to provide for calling forth the militia to execute the laws of the Union, suppress insurrections, and repel invasions, and to repeal the act now in force for that purpose," approved February 28, 1795, did call forth the militia to suppress said insurrection and to cause the laws of the Union to be duly executed, and the insurgents have failed to disperse by the time directed by the President; and

Whereas such insurrection has since broken out, and yet exists, within the States of Virginia, North Carolina, Tennessee, and Arkansas; and

Whereas the insurgents in all the said States claim to act under the authority thereof, and such claim is not disclaimed or repudiated by the persons exercising the functions of government in such State or States or in the part or parts thereof in which such combinations exist, nor has such insurrection been suppressed by said States:

Now, therefore, I, Abraham Lincoln, President of the United States, in pursuance of an act of Congress approved July 13, 1861, do hereby declare that the inhabitants of the said States of Georgia, South Carolina, Virginia, North Carolina, Tennessee, Alabama, Louisiana, Texas, Arkansas, Mississippi, and Florida (except the inhabitants of that part of the State of Virginia lying west of the Alleghany Mountains and of such other parts of that State and the other States hereinbefore named as may maintain a loyal adhesion to the Union and the Constitution or may be from time to time occupied and controlled by forces of the United States engaged in the dispersion of said insurgents) are in a state of insurrection against the United States, and that all commercial intercourse between the same and the inhabitants thereof, with the exceptions aforesaid, and the citizens of other States and other parts of the United States is unlawful, and will remain unlawful until such insurrection shall cease or has been suppressed; that all goods and chattels, wares and merchandise, coming from any of said States, with the exceptions aforesaid, into other parts of the United States without the special license and permission of the President, through the Secretary of the Treasury, or proceeding to any of said States, with the exceptions aforesaid, by land or water, together with the vessel or vehicle conveying the same or conveying persons to or from said States, with said exceptions, will be forfeited to the United States; and that from and after fifteen days from the issuing of this proclamation all ships and vessels belonging in whole or in part to any citizen or inhabitant of any of said States, with said exceptions, found at sea or in any port of the United States will be forfeited to the United States; and I hereby enjoin upon all district attorneys, marshals, and officers of the revenue and of the military and naval forces of the United States to be vigilant in the execution of said act and in the enforcement of the penalties and forfeitures imposed or declared by it, leaving any party who may think himself aggrieved thereby to his application to the Secretary of the Treasury for the remission of any penalty or forfeiture, which the said Secretary is authorized by law to grant if in his judgment the special circumstances of any case shall require such remission.

In witness whereof I have hereunto set my hand and caused the seal of the United States to be affixed.

[SEAL.] Done at the city of Washington, this 16th day of August, A. D. 1861, and of the Independence of the United States the eighty-sixth.

ABRAHAM LINCOLN.

By the President:
WILLIAM H. SEWARD,
Secretary of State.

EXECUTIVE ORDERS.

JULY 31, 1861.

The marshal of the United States in the vicinity of forts where political prisoners are held will supply decent lodging and subsistence for such prisoners, unless they shall prefer to provide in those respects for themselves, in which cases they will be allowed to do so by the commanding officers in charge.

Approved, and the Secretary of State will transmit the order to marshals, the Lieutenant-General, and Secretary of the Interior.

ABRAHAM LINCOLN.

AUGUST 7, 1861.

By the fifty-seventh article of the act of Congress entitled "An act for establishing rules and articles for the government of the armies of the United States," approved April 10, 1806, holding correspondence with or giving intelligence to the enemy, either directly or indirectly, is made punishable by death, or such other punishment as shall be ordered by the sentence of a court-martial. Public safety requires strict enforcement of this article.

It is therefore ordered, That all correspondence and communication, verbally or by writing, printing, or telegraphing, respecting operations of the Army or military movements on land or water, or respecting the troops, camps, arsenals, intrenchments, or military affairs within the several military districts, by which intelligence shall be, directly or indirectly, given to the enemy, without the authority and sanction of the major-general in command, be, and the same are, absolutely prohibited, and from and after the date of this order persons violating the same will be proceeded against under the fifty-seventh article of war.

SIMON CAMERON.

Approved:

A. LINCOLN.

GENERAL ORDER.

EXECUTIVE OF THE UNITED STATES, *October 4, 1861.*

Flag-officers of the United States Navy authorized to wear a square flag at the mizzenmast head will take rank with major-generals of the United States Army.

ABRAHAM LINCOLN.

WASHINGTON, *October 14, 1861.*

Lieutenant-General WINFIELD SCOTT:

The military line of the United States for the suppression of the insurrection may be extended so far as Bangor, in Maine. You and any officer acting under your authority are hereby authorized to suspend the writ of *habeas corpus* in any place between that place and the city of Washington.

ABRAHAM LINCOLN.

By the President:
WILLIAM H. SEWARD,
Secretary of State.

GENERAL ORDERS, No. 94.

WAR DEPARTMENT,
ADJUTANT-GENERAL'S OFFICE,
Washington, November 1, 1861.

The following order from the President of the United States, announcing the retirement from active command of the honored veteran Lieutenant-General Winfield Scott, will be read by the Army with profound regret:

EXECUTIVE MANSION,
Washington, November 1, 1861.

On the 1st day of November, A. D. 1861, upon his own application to the President of the United States, Brevet Lieutenant-General Winfield Scott is ordered to be placed, and hereby is placed, upon the list of retired officers of the Army of the United States, without reduction in his current pay, subsistence, or allowances.

The American people will hear with sadness and deep emotion that General Scott has withdrawn from the active control of the Army, while the President and a unanimous Cabinet express their own and the nation's sympathy in his personal affliction and their profound sense of the important public services rendered by him to his country during his long and brilliant career, among which will ever be gratefully distinguished his faithful devotion to the Constitution, the Union, and the flag when assailed by parricidal rebellion.

ABRAHAM LINCOLN.

The President is pleased to direct that Major-General George B. McClellan assume the command of the Army of the United States. The headquarters of the Army will be established in the city of Washington. All communications intended for the Commanding General will hereafter be addressed direct to the Adjutant-General. The duplicate returns, orders, and other papers heretofore sent to the Assistant Adjutant-General, Headquarters of the Army, will be discontinued.

By order of the Secretary of War:

L. THOMAS,
Adjutant-General.

EXECUTIVE MANSION,
Washington, November 5, 1861.

The governor of the State of Missouri, acting under the direction of the convention of that State, proposes to the Government of the United States that he will raise a military force, to serve within the State as State militia during the war there, to cooperate with the troops in the service of the United States in repelling the invasion of the State and suppressing rebellion therein; the said State militia to be embodied and to be held in the camp and in the field, drilled, disciplined, and governed according to the Army Regulations and subject to the Articles of War; the said State militia not to be ordered out of the State except for the immediate defense of the State of Missouri, but to cooperate with the troops in the service of the United States in military operations within the State or necessary to its defense, and when officers of the State militia act with officers in the service of the United States of the same grade the officers of the United States service shall command the combined force; the State militia to be armed, equipped, clothed, subsisted, transported, and paid by the United States during such time as they shall be actually engaged as an embodied military force in service in accordance with Regulations of the United States Army or general orders as issued from time to time.

In order that the Treasury of the United States may not be burdened with the pay of unnecessary officers, the governor proposes that, although the State law requires him to appoint upon the general staff an adjutant-general, a commissary-general, an inspector-general, a quartermaster-general, a paymaster-general, and a surgeon-general, each with the rank of colonel of cavalry, yet he proposes that the Government of the United States pay only the adjutant-general, the quartermaster-general, and inspector-general, their services being necessary in the relations which would exist between the State militia and the United States. The governor further proposes that, while he is allowed by the State law to appoint aids-de-camp to the governor at his discretion, with the rank of colonel, three only shall be reported to the United States for payment. He also proposes that the State militia shall be commanded by a single major-general and by such number of brigadier-generals as shall allow one for a brigade of not less than four regiments, and that no greater number of staff officers shall be appointed for regimental, brigade, and division duties than as provided for in the act of Congress of the 22d July, 1861; and that, whatever be the rank of such officers as fixed by the law of the State, the compensation that they shall receive from the United States shall only be that which belongs to the rank given by said act of Congress to officers in the United States service performing the same duties.

The field officers of a regiment in the State militia are one colonel, one lieutenant-colonel, and one major, and the company officers are a captain, a first lieutenant, and a second lieutenant.

The governor proposes that, as the money to be disbursed is the money of the United States, such staff officers in the service of the United States as may be necessary to act as disbursing officers for the State militia shall be assigned by the War Department for that duty; or, if such can not be spared from their present duty, he will appoint such persons disbursing officers for the State militia as the President of the United States may designate. Such regulations as may be required, in the judgment of the President, to insure regularity of returns and to protect the United States from any fraudulent practices shall be observed and obeyed by all in office in the State militia.

The above propositions are accepted on the part of the United States, and the Secretary of War is directed to make the necessary orders upon the Ordnance, Quartermaster's, Commissary, Pay, and Medical departments to carry this agreement into effect. He will cause the necessary staff officers in the United States service to be detailed for duty in connection with the Missouri State militia, and will order them to make the necessary provision in their respective offices for fulfilling this agreement. All requisitions upon the different officers of the United States under this agreement to be made in substance in the same mode for the Missouri State militia as similar requisitions are made for troops in the service of the United States; and the Secretary of War will cause any additional regulations that may be necessary to insure regularity and economy in carrying this agreement into effect to be adopted and communicated to the governor of Missouri for the government of the Missouri State militia.

[Indorsement.]

NOVEMBER 6, 1861.

This plan approved, with the modification that the governor stipulates that when he commissions a major-general of militia it shall be the same person at the time in command of the United States Department of the West; and in case the United States shall change such commander of the department, he (the governor) will revoke the State commission given to the person relieved and give one to the person substituted to the United States command of said department.

A. LINCOLN.

GENERAL ORDERS, NO. 96.

WAR DEPARTMENT,
ADJUTANT-GENERAL'S OFFICE,
Washington, November 7, 1861.

Authority to raise a force of State militia, to serve during the war, is granted, by direction of the President, to the governor of Missouri. This force is to cooperate with the troops in the service of the United States in repelling the invasion of the State of Missouri and in suppressing rebellion therein. It is to be held, in camp and in the field, drilled, disciplined, and governed according to the Regulations of the United States Army and subject to the Articles of War; but it is not to be ordered out of the State of Missouri except for the immediate defense of the said State.

The State forces thus authorized will be, during such time as they shall be actually engaged as an embodied military force in active service, armed, equipped, clothed, subsisted, transported, and paid by the United States in accordance with the Regulations of the United States Army and such orders as may from time to time be issued from the War Department, and in no other manner; and they shall be considered as disbanded from the service of the United States whenever the President may so direct.

In connection with this force the governor is authorized to appoint the following officers, who will be recognized and paid by the United States, to wit: One major-general, to command the whole of the State forces brought into service, who shall be the same person appointed by the President to command the United States Military Department of the West, and shall retain his commission as major-general of the State forces only during his command of the said department; one adjutant-general, one inspector-general, and one quartermaster-general, each with the rank and pay of a colonel of cavalry; three aids-de-camp to the governor, each with the rank and pay of a colonel of infantry; brigadier-generals at the rate of one to a brigade of not less than four regiments; and division, brigade, and regimental staff officers not to exceed in numbers those provided for in the organization prescribed by the act approved July 22, 1861, "for the employment of volunteers," nor to be more highly compensated by the United States, whatever their nominal rank in the State service, than officers performing the same duties under that act.

The field officers of a regiment to be one colonel, one lieutenant-colonel, and one major, and the officers of a company to be one captain, one first and one second lieutenant.

When officers of the said State forces shall act in conjunction with officers of the United States Army of the same grade, the latter shall command the combined force.

All disbursements of money made to these troops or in consequence of their employment by the United States shall be made by disbursing officers of the United States Army, assigned by the War Department, or specially appointed by the President for that purpose, who will make their requisitions upon the different supply departments in the same manner for the Missouri State forces as similar requisitions are made for other volunteer troops in the service of the United States.

The Secretary of War will cause any additional regulations that may be necessary for the purpose of promoting economy, insuring regularity of returns, and protecting the United States from fraudulent practices to be adopted and published for the government of the said State forces, and the same will be obeyed and observed by all in office under the authority of the State of Missouri.

By order:

JULIUS P. GARESCHÉ,
Assistant Adjutant-General.

GENERAL ORDERS, No. 100.

HEADQUARTERS OF THE ARMY,
ADJUTANT-GENERAL'S OFFICE,
Washington, November 16, 1861.

Complaint has been made to the President of the United States that certain persons within the State of Virginia, in places occupied by the forces of the United States, claim to be incumbents of civil offices—State, county, and municipal—by alleged authority from the Commonwealth of Virginia, in disregard and violation of the "declaration of the people of Virginia represented in convention at the city of Wheeling, Thursday, June 13, 1861," and of the ordinances of said convention, and of the acts of the general assembly held by authority of said convention.

It is therefore ordered, by direction of the President, that if any person shall hereafter attempt within the State of Virginia, under the alleged authority of said Commonwealth, to exercise any official powers of a civil nature within the limits of any of the commands of the occupying forces of the United States, unless in pursuance of the declaration and ordinances of the convention assembled at Wheeling on the 13th day of June, 1861, and the acts of the general assembly held by authority of said convention, such attempt shall be treated as an act of hostility against the United States, and such person shall be taken into military custody.

Commanding officers are directed to enforce this order within their respective commands.

*   *   *   *   *   *   *

By command of Major-General McClellan:

L. THOMAS, *Adjutant-General.*

EXECUTIVE MANSION, *Washington, November 27, 1861.*

The municipal authorities of Washington and Georgetown, in this District, having appointed to-morrow, the 28th instant, as a day of thanksgiving, the several Departments will on that occasion be closed, in order that the officers of the Government may partake in the ceremonies.

ABRAHAM LINCOLN.

FIRST ANNUAL MESSAGE.

WASHINGTON, *December 3, 1861.*

Fellow-Citizens of the Senate and House of Representatives:

In the midst of unprecedented political troubles we have cause of great gratitude to God for unusual good health and most abundant harvests.

You will not be surprised to learn that in the peculiar exigencies of the times our intercourse with foreign nations has been attended with profound solicitude, chiefly turning upon our own domestic affairs.

THE BOMBARDMENT OF FORT SUMTER

BOMBARDMENT OF FORT SUMTER.

The story of the bombardment and fall of Fort Sumter is best told by Abraham Lincoln (page 3221). In fact, his messages form the most remarkable treatise ever written on the moral aspect of the great conflict.

"Judged by the loss of life, no battle could be more insignificant," says Rhodes. "Not a man on either side was killed. Judged by the train of events which ensued, few contests in our history have been more momentous."

"The people of the North," he continues, "to the last praying and hoping that actual hostilities might be averted, were profoundly moved. . . . With excitement and with sorrow they followed the course of the bombardment; with stern determination their minds accepted the policy which this grave event portended, and when on Monday, April 15, 1861, they read of the President's call for 75,000 militia . . . they gave with one voice their approval of the policy foreshadowed, and rose almost as one man to the support of their chief magistrate."

No commencement of hostilities could have better suited Lincoln. He had avoided striking the first blow; so had Davis; but Davis's subordinates blundered and "at the darkest moment in the history of the republic," said Emerson, "when it looked as if the Nation would be dismembered, pulverized into its original elements, the attack on Fort Sumter crystallized the North into a unit, and the hope of mankind was saved." See the article entitled "Fort Sumter (S. C.), Fired on," in the Encyclopedic Index.

During all the bombardment, the flag was not hit, and remained flying exultantly and defiantly above the smoke of battle.

A disloyal portion of the American people have during the whole year been engaged in an attempt to divide and destroy the Union. A nation which endures factious domestic division is exposed to disrespect abroad, and one party, if not both, is sure sooner or later to invoke foreign intervention.

Nations thus tempted to interfere are not always able to resist the counsels of seeming expediency and ungenerous ambition, although measures adopted under such influences seldom fail to be unfortunate and injurious to those adopting them.

The disloyal citizens of the United States who have offered the ruin of our country in return for the aid and comfort which they have invoked abroad have received less patronage and encouragement than they probably expected. If it were just to suppose, as the insurgents have seemed to assume, that foreign nations in this case, discarding all moral, social, and treaty obligations, would act solely and selfishly for the most speedy restoration of commerce, including especially the acquisition of cotton, those nations appear as yet not to have seen their way to their object more directly or clearly through the destruction than through the preservation of the Union. If we could dare to believe that foreign nations are actuated by no higher principle than this, I am quite sure a sound argument could be made to show them that they can reach their aim more readily and easily by aiding to crush this rebellion than by giving encouragement to it.

The principal lever relied on by the insurgents for exciting foreign nations to hostility against us, as already intimated, is the embarrassment of commerce. Those nations, however, not improbably saw from the first that it was the Union which made as well our foreign as our domestic commerce. They can scarcely have failed to perceive that the effort for disunion produces the existing difficulty, and that one strong nation promises more durable peace and a more extensive, valuable, and reliable commerce than can the same nation broken into hostile fragments.

It is not my purpose to review our discussions with foreign states, because, whatever might be their wishes or dispositions, the integrity of our country and the stability of our Government mainly depend not upon them, but on the loyalty, virtue, patriotism, and intelligence of the American people. The correspondence itself, with the usual reservations, is herewith submitted.

I venture to hope it will appear that we have practiced prudence and liberality toward foreign powers, averting causes of irritation and with firmness maintaining our own rights and honor.

Since, however, it is apparent that here, as in every other state, foreign dangers necessarily attend domestic difficulties, I recommend that adequate and ample measures be adopted for maintaining the public defenses on every side. While under this general recommendation provision for defending our seacoast line readily occurs to the mind, I also in the same connection ask the attention of Congress to our great lakes and rivers. It is believed that some fortifications and depots of arms and munitions, with harbor and navigation improvements, all at well-selected points upon these, would be of great importance to the national defense and preservation. I ask attention to the views of the Secretary of War, expressed in his report, upon the same general subject.

I deem it of importance that the loyal regions of east Tennessee and western North Carolina should be connected with Kentucky and other faithful parts of the Union by railroad. I therefore recommend, as a military measure, that Congress provide for the construction of such road as speedily as possible. Kentucky no doubt will cooperate, and through her legislature make the most judicious selection of a line. The northern terminus must connect with some existing railroad, and whether the route shall be from Lexington or Nicholasville to the Cumberland Gap, or from Lebanon to the Tennessee line, in the direction of Knoxville, or on some still different line, can easily be determined. Kentucky and the General Government cooperating, the work can be completed in a very short time, and when done it will be not only of vast present usefulness, but also a valuable permanent improvement, worth its cost in all the future.

Some treaties, designed chiefly for the interests of commerce, and having no grave political importance, have been negotiated, and will be submitted to the Senate for their consideration.

Although we have failed to induce some of the commercial powers to adopt a desirable melioration of the rigor of maritime war, we have removed all obstructions from the way of this humane reform except such as are merely of temporary and accidental occurrence.

I invite your attention to the correspondence between Her Britannic Majesty's minister accredited to this Government and the Secretary of State relative to the detention of the British ship *Perthshire* in June last by the United States steamer *Massachusetts* for a supposed breach of the blockade. As this detention was occasioned by an obvious misapprehension of the facts, and as justice requires that we should commit no belligerent act not founded in strict right as sanctioned by public law, I recommend that an appropriation be made to satisfy the reasonable demand of the owners of the vessel for her detention.

I repeat the recommendation of my predecessor in his annual message to Congress in December last in regard to the disposition of the surplus which will probably remain after satisfying the claims of American citizens against China, pursuant to the awards of the commissioners under the act of the 3d of March, 1859. If, however, it should not be deemed advisable to carry that recommendation into effect, I would suggest that authority be given for investing the principal, over the proceeds of the surplus referred to, in good securities, with a view to the satisfaction of such other just claims of our citizens against China as are not unlikely to arise hereafter in the course of our extensive trade with that Empire.

By the act of the 5th of August last Congress authorized the President to instruct the commanders of suitable vessels to defend themselves against and to capture pirates. This authority has been exercised in a single instance only. For the more effectual protection of our extensive and valuable commerce in the Eastern seas especially, it seems to me that it would also be advisable to authorize the commanders of sailing vessels to recapture any prizes which pirates may make of United States vessels and their cargoes, and the consular courts now established by law in Eastern countries to adjudicate the cases in the event that this should not be objected to by the local authorities.

If any good reason exists why we should persevere longer in withholding our recognition of the independence and sovereignty of Hayti and Liberia, I am unable to discern it. Unwilling, however, to inaugurate a novel policy in regard to them without the approbation of Congress, I submit for your consideration the expediency of an appropriation for maintaining a chargé d'affaires near each of those new States. It does not admit of doubt that important commercial advantages might be secured by favorable treaties with them.

The operations of the Treasury during the period which has elapsed since your adjournment have been conducted with signal success. The patriotism of the people has placed at the disposal of the Government the large means demanded by the public exigencies. Much of the national loan has been taken by citizens of the industrial classes, whose confidence in their country's faith and zeal for their country's deliverance from present peril have induced them to contribute to the support of the Government the whole of their limited acquisitions. This fact imposes peculiar obligations to economy in disbursement and energy in action.

The revenue from all sources, including loans, for the financial year ending on the 30th of June, 1861, was $86,835,900.27, and the expenditures for the same period, including payments on account of the public debt, were $84,578,834.47, leaving a balance in the Treasury on the 1st of July of $2,257,065.80. For the first quarter of the financial year ending on the 30th of September, 1861, the receipts from all sources, including the balance of the 1st of July, were $102,532,509.27, and the expenses $98,239,733.09, leaving a balance on the 1st of October, 1861, of $4,292,776.18.

Estimates for the remaining three quarters of the year and for the financial year 1863, together with his views of ways and means for meeting the demands contemplated by them, will be submitted to Congress by the Secretary of the Treasury. It is gratifying to know that the expenditures made necessary by the rebellion are not beyond the resources of the loyal people. and to believe that the same patriotism which has thus far sustained the Government will continue to sustain it till peace and union shall again bless the land.

I respectfully refer to the report of the Secretary of War for information respecting the numerical strength of the Army and for recommendations having in view an increase of its efficiency and the well-being of the various branches of the service intrusted to his care. It is gratifying to know that the patriotism of the people has proved equal to the occasion, and that the number of troops tendered greatly exceeds the force which Congress authorized me to call into the field.

I refer with pleasure to those portions of his report which make allusion to the creditable degree of discipline already attained by our troops and to the excellent sanitary condition of the entire Army.

The recommendation of the Secretary for an organization of the militia upon a uniform basis is a subject of vital importance to the future safety of the country, and is commended to the serious attention of Congress.

The large addition to the Regular Army, in connection with the defection that has so considerably diminished the number of its officers, gives peculiar importance to his recommendation for increasing the corps of cadets to the greatest capacity of the Military Academy.

By mere omission, I presume, Congress has failed to provide chaplains for hospitals occupied by volunteers. This subject was brought to my notice, and I was induced to draw up the form of a letter, one copy of which, properly addressed, has been delivered to each of the persons, and at the dates respectively named and stated in a schedule, containing also the form of the letter marked A, and herewith transmitted.

These gentlemen, I understand, entered upon the duties designated at the times respectively stated in the schedule, and have labored faithfully therein ever since. I therefore recommend that they be compensated at the same rate as chaplains in the Army. I further suggest that general provision be made for chaplains to serve at hospitals, as well as with regiments.

The report of the Secretary of the Navy presents in detail the operations of that branch of the service, the activity and energy which have characterized its administration, and the results of measures to increase its efficiency and power. Such have been the additions, by construction and purchase, that it may almost be said a navy has been created and brought into service since our difficulties commenced.

Besides blockading our extensive coast, squadrons larger than ever before assembled under our flag have been put afloat and performed deeds which have increased our naval renown.

I would invite special attention to the recommendation of the Secretary for a more perfect organization of the Navy by introducing additional grades in the service.

The present organization is defective and unsatisfactory, and the suggestions submitted by the Department will, it is believed, if adopted, obviate the difficulties alluded to, promote harmony, and increase the efficiency of the Navy.

There are three vacancies on the bench of the Supreme Court—two by the decease of Justices Daniel and McLean and one by the resignation of Justice Campbell. I have so far forborne making nominations to fill these vacancies for reasons which I will now state. Two of the outgoing judges resided within the States now overrun by revolt, so that if successors were appointed in the same localities they could not now serve upon their circuits; and many of the most competent men there probably would not take the personal hazard of accepting to serve, even here, upon the Supreme bench. I have been unwilling to throw all the appointments northward, thus disabling myself from doing justice to the South on the return of peace; although I may remark that to transfer to the North one which has heretofore been in the South would not, with reference to territory and population, be unjust.

During the long and brilliant judicial career of Judge McLean his circuit grew into an empire—altogether too large for any one judge to give the courts therein more than a nominal attendance—rising in population from 1,470,018 in 1830 to 6,151,405 in 1860.

Besides this, the country generally has outgrown our present judicial system. If uniformity was at all intended, the system requires that all the States shall be accommodated with circuit courts, attended by Supreme judges, while, in fact, Wisconsin, Minnesota, Iowa, Kansas, Florida, Texas, California, and Oregon have never had any such courts. Nor can this well be remedied without a change in the system, because the adding of judges to the Supreme Court, enough for the accommodation of all parts of the country with circuit courts, would create a court altogether too numerous for a judicial body of any sort. And the evil, if it be one, will increase as new States come into the Union. Circuit courts are useful or they are not useful. If useful, no State should be denied them; if not useful, no State should have them. Let them be provided for all or abolished as to all.

Three modifications occur to me, either of which, I think, would be an improvement upon our present system. Let the Supreme Court be of convenient number in every event; then, first, let the whole country be divided into circuits of convenient size, the Supreme judges to serve in a number of them corresponding to their own number, and independent circuit judges be provided for all the rest; or, secondly, let the Supreme judges be relieved from circuit duties and circuit judges provided for all the circuits; or, thirdly, dispense with circuit courts altogether, leaving the judicial functions wholly to the district courts and an independent Supreme Court.

I respectfully recommend to the consideration of Congress the present condition of the statute laws, with the hope that Congress will be able to find an easy remedy for many of the inconveniences and evils which constantly embarrass those engaged in the practical administration of them. Since the organization of the Government Congress has enacted some 5,000 acts and joint resolutions, which fill more than 6,000 closely printed pages and are scattered through many volumes. Many of these acts have been drawn in haste and without sufficient caution, so that their provisions are often obscure in themselves or in conflict with each other, or at least so doubtful as to render it very difficult for even the best-informed persons to ascertain precisely what the statute law really is.

It seems to me very important that the statute laws should be made as plain and intelligible as possible, and be reduced to as small a compass as may consist with the fullness and precision of the will of the Legislature and the perspicuity of its language. This well done would, I think, greatly facilitate the labors of those whose duty it is to assist in the administration of the laws, and would be a lasting benefit to the people, by placing before them in a more accessible and intelligible form the laws which so deeply concern their interests and their duties.

I am informed by some whose opinions I respect that all the acts of Congress now in force and of a permanent and general nature might be revised and rewritten so as to be embraced in one volume (or at most two volumes) of ordinary and convenient size; and I respectfully recommend to Congress to consider of the subject, and if my suggestion be approved to devise such plan as to their wisdom shall seem most proper for the attainment of the end proposed.

One of the unavoidable consequences of the present insurrection is the entire suppression in many places of all the ordinary means of administering civil justice by the officers and in the forms of existing law. This is the case, in whole or in part, in all the insurgent States; and as our armies advance upon and take possession of parts of those States the practical evil becomes more apparent. There are no courts nor officers to whom the citizens of other States may apply for the enforcement of their lawful claims against citizens of the insurgent States, and there is a vast amount of debt constituting such claims. Some have estimated it as high as $200,000,000, due in large part from insurgents in open rebellion to loyal citizens who are even now making great sacrifices in the discharge of their patriotic duty to support the Government.

Under these circumstances I have been urgently solicited to establish by military power courts to administer summary justice in such cases. I have thus far declined to do it, not because I had any doubt that the end proposed—the collection of the debts—was just and right in itself, but because I have been unwilling to go beyond the pressure of necessity in the unusual exercise of power. But the powers of Congress, I suppose, are equal to the anomalous occasion, and therefore I refer the whole matter to Congress, with the hope that a plan may be devised for the administration of justice in all such parts of the insurgent States and Territories as may be under the control of this Government, whether by a voluntary return to allegiance and order or by the power of our arms; this, however, not to be a permanent institution, but a temporary substitute, and to cease as soon as the ordinary courts can be reestablished in peace.

It is important that some more convenient means should be provided, if possible, for the adjustment of claims against the Government, especially in view of their increased number by reason of the war. It is as much the duty of Government to render prompt justice against itself in favor of citizens as it is to administer the same between private individuals. The investigation and adjudication of claims in their nature belong to the judicial department. Besides, it is apparent that the attention of Congress will be more than usually engaged for some time to come with great national questions. It was intended by the organization of the Court of Claims mainly to remove this branch of business from the halls of Congress; but while the court has proved to be an effective and valuable means of investigation, it in great degree fails to effect the object of its creation for want of power to make its judgments final.

Fully aware of the delicacy, not to say the danger, of the subject, I commend to your careful consideration whether this power of making judgments final may not properly be given to the court, reserving the right of appeal on questions of law to the Supreme Court, with such other provisions as experience may have shown to be necessary.

I ask attention to the report of the Postmaster-General, the following being a summary statement of the condition of the Department:

The revenue from all sources during the fiscal year ending June 30, 1861, including the annual permanent appropriation of $700,000 for the transportation of "free mail matter," was $9,049,296.40, being about 2 per cent less than the revenue for 1860.

The expenditures were $13,606,759.11, showing a decrease of more than 8 per cent as compared with those of the previous year and leaving an excess of expenditure over the revenue for the last fiscal year of $4,557,462.71.

The gross revenue for the year ending June 30, 1863, is estimated at an increase of 4 per cent on that of 1861, making $8,683,000, to which should be added the earnings of the Department in carrying free matter, viz, $700,000, making $9,383,000.

The total expenditures for 1863 are estimated at $12,528,000, leaving an estimated deficiency of $3,145,000 to be supplied from the Treasury in addition to the permanent appropriation.

The present insurrection shows, I think, that the extension of this District across the Potomac River at the time of establishing the capital here was eminently wise, and consequently that the relinquishment of that portion of it which lies within the State of Virginia was unwise and dangerous. I submit for your consideration the expediency of regaining that part of the District and the restoration of the original boundaries thereof through negotiations with the State of Virginia.

The report of the Secretary of the Interior, with the accompanying documents, exhibits the condition of the several branches of the public business pertaining to that Department. The depressing influences of the insurrection have been specially felt in the operations of the Patent and General Land Offices. The cash receipts from the sales of public lands during the past year have exceeded the expenses of our land system only about $200,000. The sales have been entirely suspended in the Southern States, while the interruptions to the business of the country and the diversion of large numbers of men from labor to military service have obstructed settlements in the new States and Territories of the Northwest.

The receipts of the Patent Office have declined in nine months about $100,000, rendering a large reduction of the force employed necessary to make it self-sustaining.

The demands upon the Pension Office will be largely increased by the insurrection. Numerous applications for pensions, based upon the casualties of the existing war, have already been made. There is reason to believe that many who are now upon the pension rolls and in receipt of the bounty of the Government are in the ranks of the insurgent army or giving them aid and comfort. The Secretary of the Interior has directed a suspension of the payment of the pensions of such persons upon proof of their disloyalty. I recommend that Congress authorize that officer to cause the names of such persons to be stricken from the pension rolls.

The relations of the Government with the Indian tribes have been greatly disturbed by the insurrection, especially in the southern superintendency and in that of New Mexico. The Indian country south of Kansas is in the possession of insurgents from Texas and Arkansas. The agents of the United States appointed since the 4th of March for this superintendency have been unable to reach their posts, while the most of those who were in office before that time have espoused the insurrectionary cause, and assume to exercise the powers of agents by virtue of commissions from the insurrectionists. It has been stated in the public press that a portion of those Indians have been organized as a military force and are attached to the army of the insurgents. Although the Government has no official information upon this subject, letters have been written to the Commissioner of Indian Affairs by several prominent chiefs giving assurance of their loyalty to the United States and expressing a wish for the presence of Federal troops to protect them. It is believed that upon the repossession of the country by the Federal forces the Indians will readily cease all hostile demonstrations and resume their former relations to the Government.

Agriculture, confessedly the largest interest of the nation, has not a department nor a bureau, but a clerkship only, assigned to it in the Government. While it is fortunate that this great interest is so independent in its nature as to not have demanded and extorted more from the Government, I respectfully ask Congress to consider whether something more can not be given voluntarily with general advantage.

Annual reports exhibiting the condition of our agriculture, commerce, and manufactures would present a fund of information of great practical value to the country. While I make no suggestion as to details, I venture the opinion that an agricultural and statistical bureau might profitably be organized.

The execution of the laws for the suppression of the African slave trade has been confided to the Department of the Interior. It is a subject of gratulation that the efforts which have been made for the suppression of this inhuman traffic have been recently attended with unusual success. Five vessels being fitted out for the slave trade have been seized and condemned. Two mates of vessels engaged in the trade and one person in equipping a vessel as a slaver have been convicted and subjected to the penalty of fine and imprisonment, and one captain, taken with a cargo of Africans on board his vessel, has been convicted of the highest grade of offense under our laws, the punishment of which is death.

The Territories of Colorado, Dakota, and Nevada, created by the last Congress, have been organized, and civil administration has been inaugurated therein under auspices especially gratifying when it is considered that the leaven of treason was found existing in some of these new countries when the Federal officers arrived there.

The abundant natural resources of these Territories, with the security and protection afforded by organized government, will doubtless invite to them a large immigration when peace shall restore the business of the country to its accustomed channels. I submit the resolutions of the legislature of Colorado, which evidence the patriotic spirit of the people of the Territory. So far the authority of the United States has been upheld in all the Territories, as it is hoped it will be in the future. I commend their interests and defense to the enlightened and generous care of Congress.

I recommend to the favorable consideration of Congress the interests of the District of Columbia. The insurrection has been the cause of much suffering and sacrifice to its inhabitants, and as they have no representative in Congress that body should not overlook their just claims upon the Government.

At your late session a joint resolution was adopted authorizing the President to take measures for facilitating a proper representation of the industrial interests of the United States at the exhibition of the industry of all nations to be holden at London in the year 1862. I regret to say I have been unable to give personal attention to this subject—a subject at once so interesting in itself and so extensively and intimately connected with the material prosperity of the world. Through the Secretaries of

State and of the Interior a plan or system has been devised and partly matured, and which will be laid before you.

Under and by virtue of the act of Congress entitled "An act to confiscate property used for insurrectionary purposes," approved August 6, 1861, the legal claims of certain persons to the labor and service of certain other persons have become forfeited, and numbers of the latter thus liberated are already dependent on the United States and must be provided for in some way. Besides this, it is not impossible that some of the States will pass similar enactments for their own benefit respectively, and by operation of which persons of the same class will be thrown upon them for disposal. In such case I recommend that Congress provide for accepting such persons from such States, according to some mode of valuation, in lieu, *pro tanto*, of direct taxes, or upon some other plan to be agreed on with such States respectively; that such persons, on such acceptance by the General Government, be at once deemed free, and that in any event steps be taken for colonizing both classes (or the one first mentioned if the other shall not be brought into existence) at some place or places in a climate congenial to them. It might be well to consider, too, whether the free colored people already in the United States could not, so far as individuals may desire, be included in such colonization.

To carry out the plan of colonization may involve the acquiring of territory, and also the appropriation of money beyond that to be expended in the territorial acquisition. Having practiced the acquisition of territory for nearly sixty years, the question of constitutional power to do so is no longer an open one with us. The power was questioned at first by Mr. Jefferson, who, however, in the purchase of Louisiana, yielded his scruples on the plea of great expediency. If it be said that the only legitimate object of acquiring territory is to furnish homes for white men, this measure effects that object, for the emigration of colored men leaves additional room for white men remaining or coming here. Mr. Jefferson, however, placed the importance of procuring Louisiana more on political and commercial grounds than on providing room for population.

On this whole proposition, including the appropriation of money with the acquisition of territory, does not the expediency amount to absolute necessity—that without which the Government itself can not be perpetuated?

The war continues. In considering the policy to be adopted for suppressing the insurrection I have been anxious and careful that the inevitable conflict for this purpose shall not degenerate into a violent and remorseless revolutionary struggle. I have therefore in every case thought it proper to keep the integrity of the Union prominent as the primary object of the contest on our part, leaving all questions which are not of vital military importance to the more deliberate action of the Legislature.

In the exercise of my best discretion I have adhered to the blockade of the ports held by the insurgents, instead of putting in force by proclamation the law of Congress enacted at the late session for closing those ports.

So also, obeying the dictates of prudence, as well as the obligations of law, instead of transcending I have adhered to the act of Congress to confiscate property used for insurrectionary purposes. If a new law upon the same subject shall be proposed, its propriety will be duly considered. The Union must be preserved, and hence all indispensable means must be employed. We should not be in haste to determine that radical and extreme measures, which may reach the loyal as well as the disloyal, are indispensable.

The inaugural address at the beginning of the Administration and the message to Congress at the late special session were both mainly devoted to the domestic controversy out of which the insurrection and consequent war have sprung. Nothing now occurs to add or subtract to or from the principles or general purposes stated and expressed in those documents.

The last ray of hope for preserving the Union peaceably expired at the assault upon Fort Sumter, and a general review of what has occurred since may not be unprofitable. What was painfully uncertain then is much better defined and more distinct now, and the progress of events is plainly in the right direction. The insurgents confidently claimed a strong support from north of Mason and Dixon's line, and the friends of the Union were not free from apprehension on the point. This, however, was soon settled definitely, and on the right side. South of the line noble little Delaware led off right from the first. Maryland was made to *seem* against the Union. Our soldiers were assaulted, bridges were burned, and railroads torn up within her limits, and we were many days at one time without the ability to bring a single regiment over her soil to the capital. Now her bridges and railroads are repaired and open to the Government; she already gives seven regiments to the cause of the Union, and none to the enemy; and her people, at a regular election, have sustained the Union by a larger majority and a larger aggregate vote than they ever before gave to any candidate or any question. Kentucky, too, for some time in doubt, is now decidedly and, I think, unchangeably ranged on the side of the Union. Missouri is comparatively quiet, and, I believe, can not again be overrun by the insurrectionists. These three States of Maryland, Kentucky, and Missouri, neither of which would promise a single soldier at first, have now an aggregate of not less than 40,000 in the field for the Union, while of their citizens certainly not more than a third of that number, and they of doubtful whereabouts and doubtful existence, are in arms against us. After a somewhat bloody struggle of months, winter closes on the Union people of western Virginia, leaving them masters of their own country.

An insurgent force of about 1,500, for months dominating the narrow peninsular region constituting the counties of Accomac and Northampton, and known as Eastern Shore of Virginia, together with some contiguous parts of Maryland, have laid down their arms, and the people there have renewed their allegiance to and accepted the protection of the old flag. This leaves no armed insurrectionist north of the Potomac or east of the Chesapeake.

Also we have obtained a footing at each of the isolated points on the southern coast of Hatteras, Port Royal, Tybee Island (near Savannah), and Ship Island; and we likewise have some general accounts of popular movements in behalf of the Union in North Carolina and Tennessee.

These things demonstrate that the cause of the Union is advancing steadily and certainly southward.

Since your last adjournment Lieutenant-General Scott has retired from the head of the Army. During his long life the nation has not been unmindful of his merit; yet on calling to mind how faithfully, ably, and brilliantly he has served the country, from a time far back in our history, when few of the now living had been born, and thenceforward continually, I can not but think we are still his debtors. I submit, therefore, for your consideration what further mark of recognition is due to him, and to ourselves as a grateful people.

With the retirement of General Scott came the Executive duty of appointing in his stead a General in Chief of the Army. It is a fortunate circumstance that neither in council nor country was there, so far as I know, any difference of opinion as to the proper person to be selected. The retiring chief repeatedly expressed his judgment in favor of General McClellan for the position, and in this the nation seemed to give a unanimous concurrence. The designation of General McClellan is therefore in considerable degree the selection of the country as well as of the Executive, and hence there is better reason to hope there will be given him the confidence and cordial support thus by fair implication promised, and without which he can not with so full efficiency serve the country.

It has been said that one bad general is better than two good ones, and the saying is true if taken to mean no more than that an army is better directed by a single mind, though inferior, than by two superior ones at variance and cross-purposes with each other.

And the same is true in all joint operations wherein those engaged *can* have none but a common end in view and *can* differ only as to the choice of means. In a storm at sea no one on board *can* wish the ship to sink, and yet not unfrequently all go down together because too many will direct and no single mind can be allowed to control.

It continues to develop that the insurrection is largely, if not exclusively, a war upon the first principle of popular government—the rights of the people. Conclusive evidence of this is found in the most grave and maturely considered public documents, as well as in the general tone of the insurgents. In those documents we find the abridgment of the existing right of suffrage and the denial to the people of all right to participate in the selection of public officers except the legislative boldly advocated, with labored arguments to prove that large control of the people in government is the source of all political evil. Monarchy itself is sometimes hinted at as a possible refuge from the power of the people.

In my present position I could scarcely be justified were I to omit raising a warning voice against this approach of returning despotism.

It is not needed nor fitting here that a general argument should be made in favor of popular institutions, but there is one point, with its connections, not so hackneyed as most others, to which I ask a brief attention. It is the effort to place *capital* on an equal footing with, if not above, *labor* in the structure of government. It is assumed that labor is available only in connection with capital; that nobody labors unless somebody else, owning capital, somehow by the use of it induces him to labor. This assumed, it is next considered whether it is best that capital shall *hire* laborers, and thus induce them to work by their own consent, or *buy* them and drive them to it without their consent. Having proceeded so far, it is naturally concluded that all laborers are either *hired* laborers or what we call slaves. And further, it is assumed that whoever is once a hired laborer is fixed in that condition for life.

Now there is no such relation between capital and labor as assumed, nor is there any such thing as a free man being fixed for life in the condition of a hired laborer. Both these assumptions are false, and all inferences from them are groundless.

Labor is prior to and independent of capital. Capital is only the fruit of labor, and could never have existed if labor had not first existed. Labor is the superior of capital, and deserves much the higher consideration. Capital has its rights, which are as worthy of protection as any other rights. Nor is it denied that there is, and probably always will be, a relation between labor and capital producing mutual benefits. The error is in assuming that the whole labor of community exists within that relation. A few men own capital, and that few avoid labor themselves, and with their capital hire or buy another few to labor for them. A large majority belong to neither class—neither work for others nor have others working for them. In most of the Southern States a majority of the whole people of all colors are neither slaves nor masters, while in the Northern a large majority are neither hirers nor hired. Men, with their families—wives, sons, and daughters—work for themselves on their farms, in their houses, and in their shops, taking the whole product to themselves, and asking no favors of capital on the one hand nor of hired laborers or slaves on the other. It is not forgotten that a considerable number of persons mingle their own labor with capital; that is, they labor with their own hands and also buy or hire others to labor for them; but this is only a mixed and not a distinct class. No principle stated is disturbed by the existence of this mixed class.

Again, as has already been said, there is not of necessity any such thing as the free hired laborer being fixed to that condition for life. Many independent men everywhere in these States a few years back in their lives were hired laborers. The prudent, penniless beginner in the world labors for wages awhile, saves a surplus with which to buy tools or land for himself, then labors on his own account another while, and at length hires another new beginner to help him. This is the just and generous and prosperous system which opens the way to all, gives hope to all, and consequent energy and progress and improvement of condition to all. No men living are more worthy to be trusted than those who toil up from poverty; none less inclined to take or touch aught which they have not honestly earned. Let them beware of surrendering a political power which they already possess, and which if surrendered will surely be used to close the door of advancement against such as they and to fix new disabilities and burdens upon them till all of liberty shall be lost.

From the first taking of our national census to the last are seventy years, and we find our population at the end of the period eight times as great as it was at the beginning. The increase of those other things which men deem desirable has been even greater. We thus have at one view what the popular principle, applied to Government through the machinery of the States and the Union, has produced in a given time, and also what if firmly maintained it promises for the future. There are already among us those who if the Union be preserved will live to see it contain 250,000,000. The struggle *of* to-day is not altogether *for* to-day; it is for a vast future also. With a reliance on Providence all the more firm and earnest, let us proceed in the great task which events have devolved upon us.

ABRAHAM LINCOLN.

SPECIAL MESSAGES.

WASHINGTON, December 4, 1861.

To the House of Representatives:

I transmit herewith a report from the Secretary of State, in reply to the resolution of the House of Representatives of the 31st July last, upon the subject of increasing and extending trade and commerce of the United States with foreign countries.

ABRAHAM LINCOLN.

WASHINGTON, December 4, 1861.

To the House of Representatives:

I transmit herewith a report from the Secretary of State, in reply to the resolution of the House of Representatives of the 13th July last, in relation to the correspondence between this Government and foreign nations respecting the rights of blockade, privateering, and the recognition of the so-called Confederate States.

ABRAHAM LINCOLN.

WASHINGTON, *December 5, 1861.*
To the Senate of the United States:

I transmit to the Senate, for its consideration with a view to ratification, a treaty between the United States of America and His Majesty the King of Hanover, concerning the abolition of the Stade or Brunshausen dues, signed at Berlin on the 6th November, 1861.

ABRAHAM LINCOLN.

WASHINGTON, *December 9, 1861.*
To the House of Representatives:

I transmit herewith a report from the Secretary of State, in reply to the resolution of the House of the 4th instant, relative to the intervention of certain European powers in the affairs of Mexico.

ABRAHAM LINCOLN.

EXECUTIVE MANSION,
Washington, December 14, 1861.
To the Senate of the United States:

In compliance with the resolution of your honorable body "that the President be requested to furnish to the Senate copies of the charges, testimony, and finding of the recent court of inquiry in the case of Colonel Dixon S. Miles, of the United States Army," I have the honor to transmit herewith the copies desired, which have been procured from the War Department.

ABRAHAM LINCOLN.

WASHINGTON, *December 16, 1861.*
To the Senate of the United States:

I submit to the Senate, for consideration with a view to ratification, the amendments introduced by the Constituent National Assembly of Bolivia in its decree of ratification into the treaty of peace, friendship, commerce, and navigation concluded with that Republic on the 13th of May, 1858, an official translation of which decree accompanies this message, with the original treaty. As the time within which the exchange of ratifications should be effected is limited, I recommend, in view of the delay which must necessarily occur and the difficulty of reaching the seat of Government of that Republic, that the time within which such exchange shall take place be extended in the following terms: "Within such period as may be mutually convenient to both Governments."

ABRAHAM LINCOLN.

WASHINGTON, *December 17, 1861.*

To the Senate and House of Representatives:

I transmit to the Senate and House of Representatives copies of the correspondence between the Secretary of State, Secretary of War, and the governor of the State of Maine on the subject of the fortification of the seacoast and Lakes.   ABRAHAM LINCOLN.

WASHINGTON, *December 17, 1861.*

To the Senate of the United States:

I transmit to the Senate, for its advice, a copy of a draft for a convention with the Republic of Mexico, proposed to the Government of that Republic by Mr. Corwin, the minister of the United States accredited to that Government, together with the correspondence relating to it.

As the subject is of momentous interest to the two Governments at this juncture, the early consideration of it by the Senate is very desirable.

ABRAHAM LINCOLN.

WASHINGTON, *December 20, 1861.*

To the Senate and House of Representatives:

I transmit to Congress a letter from the secretary of the executive committee of the commission appointed to represent the interests of those American citizens who may desire to become exhibitors at the industrial exhibition to be held in London in 1862, and a memorial of that commission, with a report of the executive committee thereof and copies of circulars announcing the decisions of Her Majesty's commissioners in London, giving directions to be observed in regard to articles intended for exhibition, and also of circular forms of application, demands for space, approvals, etc., according to the rules prescribed by the British commissioners.

As these papers fully set forth the requirements necessary to enable those citizens of the United States who may wish to become exhibitors to avail themselves of the privileges of the exhibition, I commend them to your early consideration, especially in view of the near approach of the time when the exhibition will begin.   ABRAHAM LINCOLN.

WASHINGTON, *December 23, 1861.*

To the House of Representatives:

In compliance with the resolution of the House of Representatives of the 13th July last, requesting information respecting the Asiatic cooly trade, I transmit a report from the Secretary of State, with the documents which accompanied it.   ABRAHAM LINCOLN.

By the President of the United States of America:

A Proclamation.

Whereas, on the twenty-second day of September, in the year of our Lord one thousand eight hundred and sixty-two, a proclamation was issued by the President of the United States, containing, among other things, the following, to wit:

"That on the first day of January, in the "year of our Lord one thousand eight hundred "and sixty-three, all persons held as slaves within "any State or designated part of a State, the people "whereof shall then be in rebellion against the "United States, shall be then, thenceforward, and "forever free; and the Executive Government of the "United States, including the military and naval "authority thereof, will recognize and maintain "the freedom of such persons, and will do no act "or acts to repress such persons, or any of them, "in any efforts they may make for their actual "freedom.
"That the Executive will, on the first day

PREAMBLE TO THE EMANCIPATION PROCLAMATION.

day first above mentioned, order and designate as the States and parts of States wherein the people thereof respectively, are this day in rebellion against the United States, the following, to wit:

Arkansas, Texas, Louisiana, (except the Parishes of St. Bernard, Plaquemines, Jefferson, St. John, St. Charles, St. James Ascension, Assumption, Terrebonne, Lafourche, St. Mary, St. Martin, and Orleans, including the City of New Orleans) Mississippi, Alabama, Florida, Georgia, South Carolina, North Carolina, and Virginia, (except the forty-eight counties designated as West Virginia, and also the counties of Berkley, Accomac, Northampton, Elizabeth City, York, Princess Ann, and Norfolk, including the cities of Norfolk and Portsmouth, and which excepted parts are, for the present, left precisely as if this proclamation were not issued.

And by virtue of the power, and for the purpose aforesaid, I do order and declare that all persons held as slaves within said designated States, and parts of States, are, and henceforward shall be free; and that the Executive

PAGE FROM LINCOLN'S EMANCIPATION PROCLAMATION.

government of the United States, including the military and naval authorities thereof, will recognize and maintain the freedom of said persons.

And I hereby enjoin upon the people so declared to be free to abstain from all violence, unless in necessary self-defence; and I recommend to them that, in all cases when allowed, they labor faithfully for reasonable wages.

And I further declare and make known, that such persons of suitable condition, will be received into the armed service of the United States to garrison forts, positions, stations, and other places, and to man vessels of all sorts in said service.

And upon this act, sincerely believed to be an act of justice, warranted by the Constitution, upon military necessity, I invoke the considerate judgment of mankind, and the gracious favor of Almighty God.

In witness whereof, I have hereunto set my hand and caused the seal of the United States to be affixed.

Done at the city of Washington, this first day of January, in the year of our Lord

PAGE FROM LINCOLN'S EMANCIPATION PROCLAMATION.

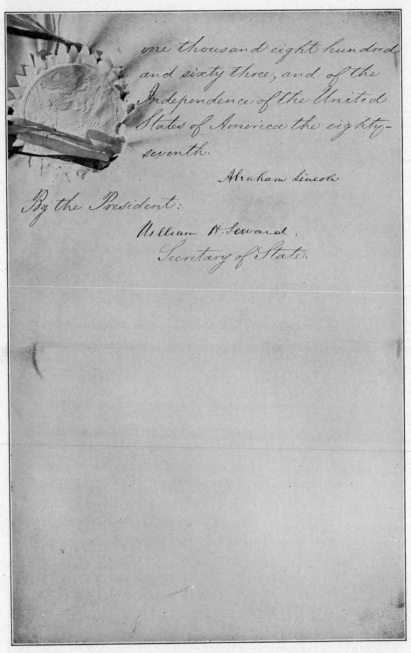

one thousand eight hundred and sixty three, and of the Independence of the United States of America the eighty-seventh.

Abraham Lincoln

By the President:

William H. Seward,
Secretary of State.

LAST PAGE OF EMANCIPATION PROCLAMATION WITH SIGNATURES OF LINCOLN AND SECRETARY SEWARD.

"SIGNING THE EMANCIPATION PROCLAMATION" hangs over the landing of the eastern grand staircase in the Capitol. This famous picture was painted by Frank B. Carpenter from studies of Lincoln made in the White House, where he resided for a considerable time for that purpose. It was presented to Congress in 1878 by Mrs. Elizabeth Thompson.

The Proclamation of Emancipation

WASHINGTON, *December 30, 1861.*

To the Senate and House of Representatives:

I transmit to Congress a correspondence which has taken place between the Secretary of State and authorities of Great Britain and France on the subject of the recent removal of certain citizens* of the United States from the British mail steamer *Trent* by order of Captain Wilkes, in command of the United States war steamer *San Jacinto.*

ABRAHAM LINCOLN.

WASHINGTON, *January 2, 1862.*

To the Senate and House of Representatives:

I transmit to Congress a copy of a letter to the Secretary of State from James R. Partridge, secretary to the executive committee to the industrial exhibition to be held in London in the course of the present year, and a copy of the correspondence to which it refers, relative to a vessel for the purpose of taking such articles as persons in this country may wish to exhibit on that occasion. As it appears that no naval vessel can be spared for the purpose, I recommend that authority be given to charter a suitable merchant vessel, in order that facilities similar to those afforded by the Government for the exhibition of 1851 may also be extended to those citizens of the United States who may desire to contribute to the exhibition of this year.

ABRAHAM LINCOLN.

WASHINGTON, D. C., *January 3, 1862.*

To the Senate of the United States:

I transmit to the Senate, for its constitutional action thereon, a treaty concluded on the 15th November, 1861, between William W. Ross, agent on the part of the United States, and the chiefs and headmen of the tribe of Pottawatomie Indians, with accompanying communications from the Secretary of the Interior and Commissioner of Indian Affairs, the latter of which proposes certain modifications of said treaty, which are also referred for the consideration of the Senate.

ABRAHAM LINCOLN.

WASHINGTON, *January 10, 1862.*

To the Senate and House of Representatives:

I transmit to Congress a translation of an instruction to the minister of His Majesty the Emperor of Austria accredited to this Government, and a copy of a note to that minister from the Secretary of State, relative to the questions involved in the taking from the British steamer

---

*James M. Mason and John Slidell, Confederate envoys to England and France, respectively, and two others.

Trent of certain citizens of the United States by order of Captain Wilkes, of the United States Navy. This correspondence may be considered as a sequel to that previously communicated to Congress relating to the same subject.

ABRAHAM LINCOLN.

WASHINGTON, *January 17, 1862.*

To the Senate and House of Representatives:

I transmit to Congress a translation of an instruction to the minister of His Majesty the King of Prussia accredited to this Government, and a copy of a note to that minister from the Secretary of State, relating to the capture and detention of certain citizens of the United States, passengers on board the British steamer *Trent*, by order of Captain Wilkes, of the United States Navy.

ABRAHAM LINCOLN.

WASHINGTON, D. C., *January 17, 1862.*

To the Senate of the United States:

I transmit herewith, for the consideration of the Senate, a petition of certain members of the Pottawatomie tribe of Indians, complaining of the treaty made by W. W. Ross on the 15th November last with that tribe, which treaty was laid before the Senate for its constitutional action in my communication to that body dated the 6th [3d] instant.

A letter of the 16th instant from the Secretary of the Interior, inclosing a report of the Commissioner of Indian Affairs dated the 15th instant, in relation to the subject, is also herewith transmitted.

ABRAHAM LINCOLN.

WASHINGTON, D. C., *January, 1862.*

To the Senate of the United States:

I transmit herewith, for the constitutional action of the Senate, articles of agreement and convention concluded at Niobrara, Nebraska Territory, on the 14th day of November, 1860, between J. Shaw Gregory, agent on the part of the United States, and the chiefs and headmen of the Poncas tribe of Indians, being supplementary to the treaty with said tribe made on the 12th day of March, 1858.

I also transmit a letter, dated the 4th instant, from the Secretary of the Interior, inclosing a copy of a report of the Commissioner of Indian Affairs of the 20th September, 1861, in relation to the subject.

ABRAHAM LINCOLN.

WASHINGTON, *January 24, 1862.*

To the Senate and House of Representatives:

I submit to Congress the accompanying copy of a correspondence between the Secretary of State, the Spanish minister, and the Secretary of the Navy, concerning the case of the bark *Providencia*, a Spanish vessel seized on her voyage from Havana to New York by a steamer of the United States Blockading Squadron and subsequently released. I recommend the appropriation of the amount of the award of the referee.

ABRAHAM LINCOLN.

WASHINGTON, *January 24, 1862.*
To the Senate of the United States:

I lay before the Senate a dispatch which has just been received from Mr. Corwin, our minister to Mexico. It communicates important information concerning the war which is waged against Mexico by the combined powers of Spain, France, and Great Britain.

Mr. Corwin asks instructions by which to regulate his proceedings so as to save our national interests in the case of an adjustment of the difficulties between the belligerents. I have heretofore submitted to the Senate a request for its advice upon the question pending by treaty for making a loan to Mexico, which Mr. Corwin thinks will in any case be expedient. It seems to be my duty now to solicit an early action of the Senate upon the subject, to the end that I may cause such instructions to be given to Mr. Corwin as will enable him to act in the manner which, while it will most carefully guard the interests of our country, will at the same time be most beneficial to Mexico.

ABRAHAM LINCOLN.

WASHINGTON, *January 28, 1862.*
To the Senate of the United States:

I submit to the Senate, for its consideration with a view to ratification, a treaty of extradition concluded by Mr. Corwin with the Mexican Government on the 11th of December last.

I also submit a postal convention concluded by that gentleman at the same time, and a copy of his dispatch of the 24th of the same month explanatory of the provisions of both these instruments, and the reasons for the nonratification by Mexico of the postal convention concluded in this city on the 31st of July last and approved by the Senate on the 6th of August.

A copy of a letter from the Postmaster-General to the Secretary of State in relation to Mr. Corwin's postal convention is also herewith communicated. The advice of the Senate as to the expediency of accepting that convention as a substitute for the one of the 31st of July last is requested.

ABRAHAM LINCOLN.

WASHINGTON, *January 31, 1862.*
To the Senate and House of Representatives:

As a sequel to the correspondence on the subject previously communicated, I transmit to Congress extracts from a dispatch of the 20th ultimo from Mr. Adams, United States minister at London, to the Secretary of State, and a copy of an instruction from Earl Russell to Lord Lyons of the 10th instant, relative to the removal of certain citizens of the United States from the British mail steamer *Trent* by order of the commander of the United States war steamer *San Jacinto.*

ABRAHAM LINCOLN.

WASHINGTON CITY, *February 4, 1862.*

To the Senate of the United States:

The third section of the "Act further to promote the efficiency of the Navy," approved December 21, 1861, provides—

That the President of the United States, by and with the advice and consent of the Senate, shall have the authority to detail from the retired list of the Navy for the command of squadrons and single ships such officers as he may believe that the good of the service requires to be thus placed in command; and such officers may, if upon the recommendation of the President of the United States they shall receive a vote of thanks of Congress for their services and gallantry in action against an enemy, be restored to the active list, and not otherwise.

In conformity with this law, Captain Samuel F. Du Pont, of the Navy, was nominated to the Senate for continuance as the flag-officer in command of the squadron which recently rendered such important service to the Union in the expedition to the coast of South Carolina.

Believing that no occasion could arise which would more fully correspond with the intention of the law or be more pregnant with happy influence as an example, I cordially recommend that Captain Samuel F. Du Pont receive a vote of thanks of Congress for his services and gallantry displayed in the capture of Forts Walker and Beauregard, commanding the entrance of Port Royal Harbor, on the 7th of November, 1861.

ABRAHAM LINCOLN.

WASHINGTON, *February 7, 1862.*

To the Senate of the United States:

In answer to the resolution of the Senate of the 5th instant, requesting a communication of any recent correspondence relating to the presentation of American citizens to the Court of France, I transmit a copy of a dispatch of the 14th ultimo from the United States minister at Paris to the Secretary of State and of an instruction of Mr. Seward to Mr. Dayton of the 3d instant.

ABRAHAM LINCOLN.

WASHINGTON, *February 12, 1862.*

To the Senate and House of Representatives:

I transmit to Congress a copy of a special treaty between the United States and His Majesty the King of Hanover for the abolition of the Stade dues, which was signed at Berlin on the 6th of November last.   In this treaty, already approved by the Senate and ratified on the part of the United States, it is stipulated that the sums specified in Articles III and IV to be paid to the Hanoverian Government shall be paid at Berlin on the day of the exchange of ratifications. I therefore recommend that seasonable provision be made to enable the Executive to carry this stipulation into effect.

ABRAHAM LINCOLN.

WASHINGTON CITY, *February 15, 1862.*
To the Senate and House of Representatives of the United States:

The third section of the "Act further to promote the efficiency of the Navy," approved December 21, 1861, provides—

That the President of the United States, by and with the advice and consent of the Senate, shall have the authority to detail from the retired list of the Navy for the command of squadrons and single ships such officers as he may believe that the good of the service requires to be thus placed in command; and such officers may, if upon the recommendation of the President of the United States they shall receive a vote of thanks of Congress for their services and gallantry in action against an enemy, be restored to the active list, and not otherwise.

In conformity with this law, Captain Louis M. Goldsborough, of the Navy, was nominated to the Senate for continuance as the flag-officer in command of the North Atlantic Blockading Squadron, which recently rendered such important service to the Union in the expedition to the coast of North Carolina.

Believing that no occasion could arise which would more fully correspond with the intention of the law or be more pregnant with happy influence as an example, I cordially recommend that Captain Louis M. Goldsborough receive a vote of thanks of Congress for his services and gallantry displayed in the combined attack of the forces commanded by him and Brigadier-General Burnside in the capture of Roanoke Island and the destruction of rebel gunboats on the 7th, 8th, and 10th of February, 1862.

ABRAHAM LINCOLN.

WASHINGTON, *February 21, 1862.*
To the Senate and House of Representatives:

The President of the United States was last evening plunged into affliction by the death of a beloved child. The heads of the Departments, in consideration of this distressing event, have thought it would be agreeable to Congress and to the American people that the official and private buildings occupied by them should not be illuminated in the evening of the 22d instant.

WILLIAM H. SEWARD.   CALEB B. SMITH.
S. P. CHASE.   M. BLAIR.
EDWIN M. STANTON.   EDWARD BATES.
GIDEON WELLES.

WASHINGTON, *February 25, 1862.*

To the Senate and House of Representatives:

I transmit to Congress a copy of an instruction from Prince Gortchakoff to Mr. De Stoeckl, the minister of His Imperial Majesty the Emperor of Russia accredited to this Government, and of a note of the Secretary of State to the latter, relative to the adjustment of the question between the United States and Great Britain growing out of the removal of certain of our citizens from the British mail steamer *Trent* by order of the commander of the United States war steamer *San Jacinto.*

ABRAHAM LINCOLN.

WASHINGTON, *February 26, 1862.*

To the Senate and House of Representatives:

In transmitting to Congress the accompanying copy of two letters, bearing date the 14th of February, 1861, from His Majesty the Major King of Siam to the President of the United States, and of the President's answer thereto, I submit for their consideration the question as to the proper place of deposit of the gifts received with the royal letters referred to.

ABRAHAM LINCOLN.

WASHINGTON, *February 27, 1862.*

To the Senate of the United States:

Lieutenant-General Scott has advised me that while he would cheerfully accept a commission as additional minister to Mexico, with a view to promote the interests of the United States and of peace, yet his infirmities are such that he could not be able to reach the capital of that country by any existing mode of travel, and he therefore deems it his duty to decline the important mission I had proposed for him. For this reason I withdraw the nomination in this respect heretofore submitted to the Senate. It is hardly necessary to add that the nomination was made without any knowledge of it on his part.

ABRAHAM LINCOLN.

WASHINGTON, *March 3, 1862.*

To the Senate and House of Representatives:

I transmit to Congress a copy of a dispatch to the Secretary of State from the minister resident of the United States at Lisbon, concerning recent measures which have been adopted by the Government of Portugal intended to encourage the growth and to enlarge the area of the culture of cotton in its African possessions.

ABRAHAM LINCOLN.

WASHINGTON, *March 3, 1862.*

To the Senate and House of Representatives:

I transmit to Congress a translation of an instruction to the minister of His Majesty the King of Italy accredited to this Government, and a copy of a note to that minister from the Secretary of State, relating to the settlement of the question arising out of the capture and detention of certain citizens of the United States, passengers on board the British steamer *Trent,* by order of Captain Wilkes, of the United States Navy.

ABRAHAM LINCOLN.

WASHINGTON, *March 3, 1862.*

To the Senate of the United States:

I transmit to the Senate a translation of a note addressed to the Secretary of State on the 1st instant by General P. A. Herran, envoy extraordinary and minister plenipotentiary of the Granadian Confederation, with a translation of the communication accompanying that note from the special commissioner of that Republic, together with a copy of a letter from the special commissioner of the United States of the 26th ultimo, under the convention of the 10th September, 1857, setting forth the impracticability of disposing of the cases submitted to the joint commission now in session under the convention within the period prescribed therein.

I recommend, therefore, that the Senate consent to the extension of time for —— days from and after the expiration of the time limited by the convention. ABRAHAM LINCOLN.

WASHINGTON, *March 3, 1862.*

To the House of Representatives of the United States:

I transmit herewith a communication* of the Secretary of War, inclosing a report of the Adjutant-General, in answer to a resolution of the House of Representatives of the 22d of January, 1862.

ABRAHAM LINCOLN.

WASHINGTON, *March 5, 1862.*

To the Senate of the United States:

I submit to the Senate, for its consideration, a copy of a message addressed to that body by my immediate predecessor on the 12th February, 1861, relating to the award made by the joint commission under the convention between the United States and Paraguay of the 4th February, 1859, together with the original ''journal of the proceedings'' of the commission and a printed copy of the ''statements and arguments—and for

---

* Relating to assignment of officers of the Army to duty.

the Republic," and request the advice of the Senate as to the final acquiescence in or rejection of the award of the commissioner by the Government of the United States. As the "journal" is an original document, pertaining to the archives of the Department of State, it is proper, when the Senate shall have arrived at a conclusion on the subject, that the volume be returned to the custody of the Secretary of State.

ABRAHAM LINCOLN.

MARCH 6, 1862.

Fellow-Citizens of the Senate and House of Representatives:

I recommend the adoption of a joint resolution by your honorable bodies, which shall be substantially as follows:

Resolved, That the United States ought to cooperate with any State which may adopt gradual abolishment of slavery, giving to such State pecuniary aid, to be used by such State, in its discretion, to compensate for the inconveniences, public and private, produced by such change of system.

If the proposition contained in the resolution does not meet the approval of Congress and the country, there is the end; but if it does command such approval, I deem it of importance that the States and people immediately interested should be at once distinctly notified of the fact, so that they may begin to consider whether to accept or reject it. The Federal Government would find its highest interest in such a measure, as one of the most efficient means of self-preservation. The leaders of the existing insurrection entertain the hope that this Government will ultimately be forced to acknowledge the independence of some part of the disaffected region, and that all the slave States north of such part will then say, "The Union for which we have struggled being already gone, we now choose to go with the Southern section." To deprive them of this hope substantially ends the rebellion, and the initiation of emancipation completely deprives them of it as to all the States initiating it. The point is not that *all* the States tolerating slavery would very soon, if at all, initiate emancipation; but that while the offer is equally made to all, the more northern shall by such initiation make it certain to the more southern that in no event will the former ever join the latter in their proposed confederacy. I say "initiation" because, in my judgment, gradual and not sudden emancipation is better for all. In the mere financial or pecuniary view any member of Congress with the census tables and Treasury reports before him can readily see for himself how very soon the current expenditures of this war would purchase, at fair valuation, all the slaves in any named State. Such a proposition on the part of the General Government sets up no claim of a right by Federal authority to interfere with slavery within State limits, referring, as it does, the absolute control of the subject in each case to the State and its people immediately interested. It is proposed as a matter of perfectly free choice with them.

In the annual message last December I thought fit to say "the Union

must be preserved, and hence all indispensable means must be employed.''
I said this not hastily, but deliberately. War has been made and continues to be an indispensable means to this end. A practical reacknowl-
edgment of the national authority would render the war unnecessary,
and it would at once cease. If, however, resistance continues, the war
must also continue; and it is impossible to foresee all the incidents which
may attend and all the ruin which may follow it. Such as may seem
indispensable or may obviously promise great efficiency toward ending
the struggle must and will come.

The proposition now made (though an offer only), I hope it may be
esteemed no offense to ask whether the pecuniary consideration tendered
would not be of more value to the States and private persons concerned
than are the institution and property in it in the present aspect of affairs.

While it is true that the adoption of the proposed resolution would be
merely initiatory, and not within itself a practical measure, it is recommended in the hope that it would soon lead to important practical results.
In full view of my great responsibility to my God and to my country, I
earnestly beg the attention of Congress and the people to the subject.

ABRAHAM LINCOLN.

WASHINGTON, D. C., *March 7, 1862.*
To the Senate of the United States:

I transmit herewith, for the constitutional action of the Senate thereon,
a treaty concluded at Paola, Kans., on the 18th day of August, between
Seth Clover, commissioner on the part of the United States, and the
delegates of the united tribes of Kaskaskia and Peoria, Piankeshaw,
and Wea Indians.

I also transmit a communication of the Secretary of the Interior of the
6th instant and accompanying papers from the Acting Commissioner of
Indian Affairs, in relation to the subject.

ABRAHAM LINCOLN.

WASHINGTON, *March 12, 1862.*
To the Senate of the United States:

In compliance with the resolution of the Senate of the 11th instant,
requesting "a copy of any correspondence on the records or files of the
Department of State in regard to railway systems in Europe," I transmit a report from the Secretary of State and the papers by which it was
accompanied.

ABRAHAM LINCOLN.

WASHINGTON, *March 14, 1862.*
To the Senate of the United States:

With reference to my recent message on the subject of claims of citizens of the United States on the Government of Paraguay, I transmit a

copy of three memorials of the claimants and of their closing arguments in the case, together with extracts from a dispatch from Mr. Bowlin, the late commissioner of the United States to that country. These extracts show that President Lopez offered and expected to pay a large sum of money as a compromise of the claims.

ABRAHAM LINCOLN.

WASHINGTON, *March 14, 1862.*

To the Senate and House of Representatives:

I submit to Congress the accompanying copy of a correspondence between the Secretary of State, the Danish chargé d'affaires, and the Secretary of the Navy, concerning the case of the bark *Jorgen Lorentzen,* a Danish vessel seized on her voyage from Rio Janeiro to Havana by the United States ship *Morning Light* and subsequently released. I recommend the appropriation of the amount of the award of the referees.

ABRAHAM LINCOLN.

WASHINGTON CITY, *March 20, 1862.*

To the Senate and House of Representatives:

The third section of the "Act further to promote the efficiency of the Navy," approved December 21, 1861, provides—

That the President of the United States, by and with the advice and consent of the Senate, shall have the authority to detail from the retired list of the Navy for the command of squadrons and single ships such officers as he may believe that the good of the service requires to be thus placed in command; and such officers may, if upon the recommendation of the President of the United States they shall receive a vote of thanks of Congress for their services and gallantry in action against an enemy, be restored to the active list, and not otherwise.

In conformity with this law, Captain Samuel F. Du Pont, of the Navy, was nominated to the Senate for continuance as the flag-officer in command of the squadron which recently rendered such important service to the Union in the expedition to the coasts of South Carolina, Georgia, and Florida.

Believing that no occasion could arise which would more fully correspond with the intention of the law or be more pregnant with happy influence as an example, I cordially recommend that Captain Samuel F. Du Pont receive a vote of thanks of Congress for his service and gallantry displayed in the capture since the 21st December, 1861, of various points on the coasts of Georgia and Florida, particularly Brunswick, Cumberland Island and Sound, Amelia Island, the towns of St. Marys, St. Augustine, and Jacksonville and Fernandina.

ABRAHAM LINCOLN.

WASHINGTON, *March 26, 1862.*

To the Senate and House of Representatives:

I transmit a copy of a communication* of the 21st of December last addressed to the Secretary of State by the governor of the Territory of Nevada, and commend to the particular attention of Congress those parts of it which show that further legislation is desirable for the public welfare in that quarter. ABRAHAM LINCOLN.

WASHINGTON, *March 31, 1862.*

To the Senate of the United States:

I transmit to the Senate, for its consideration with a view to ratification, a treaty of commerce and navigation between the United States and the Ottoman Empire, signed at Constantinople on the 25th of last month. Extracts from a dispatch of the same date, upon the subject of the treaty, from Mr. Morris, the United States minister at Constantinople, to the Secretary of State, are also herewith communicated.

It will be noticed that the exchange of ratifications is to take place within three months from the date of the instrument. This renders it desirable that the Senate should decide in regard to it as soon as this may be convenient, for if that decision be favorable the ratifications of this Government must reach Constantinople prior to the expiration of the three months adverted to. ABRAHAM LINCOLN.

WASHINGTON, *April 5, 1862.*

To the House of Representatives:

In compliance with the resolution of the House of Representatives of yesterday, requesting any information which may have been received at the Department of State showing the system of revenue and finance now existing in any foreign country, I transmit a copy of a recent dispatch from Mr. Pike, the United States minister at The Hague. This is understood to be the only information on the subject of the resolution recently received which has not been made public.

ABRAHAM LINCOLN.

WASHINGTON, *April 10, 1862.*

To the Senate of the United States:

I transmit to the Senate, for its consideration with a view to ratification, a treaty between the United States and Her Britannic Majesty for the suppression of the slave trade. A copy of the correspondence between the Secretary of State and Lord Lyons on the subject of the treaty is also herewith transmitted. ABRAHAM LINCOLN.

---

* Containing a narrative of incidents pertaining to the government of the Territory of Nevada.

WASHINGTON, *April 14, 1862.*

To the House of Representatives:

In compliance with the resolution of the House of Representatives of the 3d ultimo, requesting information in regard to the present condition of Mexico, I transmit a report from the Secretary of State and the documents by which it was accompanied.

ABRAHAM LINCOLN.

WASHINGTON, *April 15, 1862.*

To the Senate of the United States:

On the 26th of June, 1860, the Senate approved of the treaty of friendship and commerce between the United States and Nicaragua, signed on the 16th of March, 1859, with certain amendments.

On the next day, namely, June 27, 1860, the Senate adopted a resolution extending the period for the exchange of the ratifications of the treaty for six months from that date; that is, until the 27th of December, 1860.

Although the amendments of the Senate were immediately transmitted to our minister in Nicaragua for submission to the Government of that Republic, he failed, notwithstanding earnest efforts, to induce that Government to call an extra session of Congress to take into consideration the amendments of the Senate of the United States within the supplementary time named in the resolution of June 27, 1860, for the exchange of ratifications.

It was not until the 25th of March, 1861, nearly three months after the expiration of the six months extended by the Senate resolution, that the Congress of Nicaragua acted favorably upon the amendments of the Senate of the United States.

A translation of the decree of the Nicaraguan Government approving the treaty as amended, with an additional amendment, is herewith inclosed.

It will be perceived that while the ratification of Nicaragua recites literally the second amendment of the Senate and accepts it with an additional clause, it does not in explicit terms accept the first amendment of the Senate, striking out the last clause of the sixteenth article.

That amendment is of so much importance that the adoption or rejection of it by the Government of Nicaragua should not be left to construction or inference.

The final amendment of that Government properly extended the time of exchanging ratifications for an additional twelve months. That time has expired. For obvious reasons connected with our internal affairs, the subject has not sooner been submitted to the Senate, but the treaty is now laid before that body, with this brief historical sketch and the decree of the Nicaraguan Government, for such further advice as may be deemed necessary and proper in regard to the acceptance or rejection of the amendments of Nicaragua.

ABRAHAM LINCOLN.

WASHINGTON, *April 15, 1862.*

To the Senate of the United States:

In consequence of the delay attending the approval by the Senate of the extradition treaty with Mexico signed on the 11th December last, it is impossible to effect the exchange of ratifications of that and the postal convention of the same date within the period assigned by those instruments.

I recommend, therefore, the passage of a resolution at the earliest practicable moment extending the time specified in the eighth article of the extradition treaty and in the twelfth article of the postal convention for the exchange of ratifications for sixty days from and after the 11th June next, the date of the expiration of the period named for that purpose in both instruments. ABRAHAM LINCOLN.

WASHINGTON, D. C., *April 15, 1862.*

To the Senate of the United States:

I transmit herewith, for the consideration and such constitutional action as the Senate may deem proper to take, a treaty negotiated on the 6th March, 1861, between late Agent Vanderslice, on the part of the United States, and certain delegates of the Sac and Fox of the Missouri and the Iowa tribes of Indians; also certain petitions of said tribes, praying that the treaty may be ratified with an amendment as set forth in said petitions. A letter of the Secretary of the Interior, with a report of the Commissioner of Indian Affairs and letter of the present agent of the Indians, accompany the treaty and petitions.

ABRAHAM LINCOLN.

APRIL 16, 1862.

Fellow-Citizens of the Senate and House of Representatives:

The act entitled "An act for the release of certain persons held to service or labor in the District of Columbia" has this day been approved and signed.

I have never doubted the constitutional authority of Congress to abolish slavery in this District, and I have ever desired to see the national capital freed from the institution in some satisfactory way. Hence there has never been in my mind any question upon the subject except the one of expediency, arising in view of all the circumstances. If there be matters within and about this act which might have taken a course or shape more satisfactory to my judgment, I do not attempt to specify them. I am gratified that the two principles of compensation and colonization are both recognized and practically applied in the act.

In the matter of compensation, it is provided that claims may be presented within ninety days from the passage of the act, "but not thereafter;" and there is no saving for minors, femes covert, insane or absent persons. I presume this is an omission by mere oversight, and I recommend that it be supplied by an amendatory or supplemental act.

ABRAHAM LINCOLN.

WASHINGTON, *April 18, 1862.*

To the Senate and House of Representatives:

I transmit to Congress a copy of a correspondence between the Secretary of State and Benjamin E. Brewster, of Philadelphia, relative to the arrest in that city of Simon Cameron, late Secretary of War, at the suit of Pierce Butler, for trespass *vi et armis*, assault and battery, and false imprisonment.

ABRAHAM LINCOLN.

EXECUTIVE MANSION,
Washington, April 24, 1862.

To the Senate of the United States:

In obedience to your resolution of the 17th instant, I herewith communicate the testimony and judgment of the recent naval court of inquiry in the case of Lieutenant Charles E. Fleming, of the United States Navy; also the testimony and finding of the naval retiring board in the case of the said Lieutenant Fleming.

I have the honor to state that the judgment and finding aforesaid have not been approved by me.

ABRAHAM LINCOLN.

WASHINGTON, *April 26, 1862.*

To the House of Representatives:

In compliance with the resolution of the House of Representatives of the 24th of February last, requesting information in regard to insurgent privateers in foreign ports, I transmit a report from the Secretary of State and the documents by which it was accompanied.

ABRAHAM LINCOLN.

EXECUTIVE MANSION,
Washington, May 1, 1862.

To the Senate of the United States:

In answer to the resolution of the Senate in relation to Brigadier-General Stone, I have the honor to state that he was arrested and imprisoned under my general authority, and upon evidence which, whether he be guilty or innocent, required, as appears to me, such proceedings to be had against him for the public safety. I deem it incompatible with the public interest, as also, perhaps, unjust to General Stone, to make a more particular statement of the evidence.

He has not been tried because in the state of military operations at the time of his arrest and since the officers to constitute a court-martial and for witnesses could not be withdrawn from duty without serious injury to the service. He will be allowed a trial without any unnecessary delay, the charges and specifications will be furnished him in due season, and every facility for his defense will be afforded him by the War Department.

ABRAHAM LINCOLN.

EXECUTIVE MANSION,
Washington, May 1, 1862.

To the Senate of the United States:

In accordance with the suggestion of the Secretary of the Treasury contained in the accompanying letter, I have the honor to transmit the inclosed petition and report thereon of the Third Auditor for the consideration of Congress.

ABRAHAM LINCOLN.

WASHINGTON, D. C., *May 14, 1862.*

To the Senate and House of Representatives:

The third section of the "Act further to promote the efficiency of the Navy," approved 21st of December, 1861, provides—

That the President of the United States, by and with the advice and consent of the Senate, shall have the authority to detail from the retired list of the Navy for the command of squadrons and single ships such officers as he may believe that the good of the service requires to be thus placed in command; and such officers may, if upon the recommendation of the President of the United States they shall receive a vote of thanks of Congress for their services and gallantry in action against an enemy, be restored to the active list, and not otherwise.

In conformity with this law, Captain David G. Farragut was nominated to the Senate for continuance as the flag-officer in command of the squadron which recently rendered such important service to the Union by his successful operations on the Lower Mississippi and capture of New Orleans.

Believing that no occasion could arise which would more fully correspond with the intention of the law or be more pregnant with happy influence as an example, I cordially recommend that Captain D. G. Farragut receive a vote of thanks of Congress for his services and gallantry displayed in the capture since 21st December, 1861, of Forts Jackson and St. Philip, city of New Orleans, and the destruction of various rebel gunboats, rams, etc.

ABRAHAM LINCOLN.

WASHINGTON, D. C., *May 14, 1862.*

To the Senate and House of Representatives:

I submit herewith a list of naval officers who commanded vessels engaged in the recent brilliant operations of the squadron commanded by Flag-Officer Farragut, which led to the capture of Forts Jackson and St. Philip, city of New Orleans, and the destruction of rebel gunboats, rams, etc., in April, 1862. For their services and gallantry on those occasions I cordially recommend that they should by name receive a vote of thanks of Congress.

LIST.

Captain Theodorus Bailey.
Captain Henry W. Morris.
Captain Thomas T. Craven.
Commander Henry H. Bell.
Commander Samuel Phillips Lee.
Commander Samuel Swartwout.
Commander Melancton Smith.
Commander Charles Stewart Boggs.
Commander John De Camp.
Commander James Alden.
Commander David D. Porter.
Commander Richard Wainwright.
Commander William B. Renshaw.
Lieutenant Commanding Abram D. Harrell.
Lieutenant Commanding Edward Donaldson.
Lieutenant Commanding George H. Preble.
Lieutenant Commanding Edward T. Nichols.
Lieutenant Commanding Jonathan M. Wainwright.
Lieutenant Commanding John Guest.
Lieutenant Commanding Charles H. B. Caldwell.
Lieutenant Commanding Napoleon B. Harrison.
Lieutenant Commanding Albert N. Smith.
Lieutenant Commanding Pierce Crosby.
Lieutenant Commanding George M. Ransom.
Lieutenant Commanding Watson Smith.
Lieutenant Commanding John H. Russell.
Lieutenant Commanding Walter W. Queen.
Lieutenant Commanding K. Randolph Breese.
Acting Lieutenant Commanding Selim E. Woodworth.
Acting Lieutenant Commanding Charles H. Baldwin.

ABRAHAM LINCOLN.

EXECUTIVE OFFICE, *May, 1862.*

To the Senate of the United States:

I transmit herewith, for the constitutional action of the Senate, a treaty negotiated on the 13th of March, 1862, between H. W. Farnsworth, a commissioner on the part of the United States, and the authorized representatives of the Kansas tribe of Indians.

A communication from the Secretary of the Interior, together with a letter of the Commissioner of Indian Affairs, suggesting certain amendments to the treaty and inclosing papers relating thereto, are also transmitted.

ABRAHAM LINCOLN.

WASHINGTON, *May 21, 1862.*

To the Senate:

In answer to the resolution of the Senate of the 14th instant, requesting information in regard to arrests in the State of Kentucky, I transmit a report from the Secretary of War, to whom the resolution was referred.

ABRAHAM LINCOLN.

WASHINGTON, *May 22, 1862.*

To the House of Representatives:

In compliance with the resolution of the House of Representatives of the 20th instant, requesting information in regard to the indemnity obtained by the consul-general of the United States at Alexandria, Egypt, for the maltreatment of Faris-El-Hakim, an agent in the employ of the American missionaries in that country, I transmit a report from the Secretary of State and the documents by which it was accompanied.

ABRAHAM LINCOLN.

WASHINGTON, *May 23, 1862.*

To the House of Representatives:

I transmit a report from the Secretary of State, in answer to the resolution of the House of Representatives of the 22d instant, calling for further correspondence relative to Mexican affairs.

ABRAHAM LINCOLN.

[The same message was sent to the Senate, in answer to a resolution of that body.]

WASHINGTON, *May 26, 1862.*

To the Senate and House of Representatives:

The insurrection which is yet existing in the United States and aims at the overthrow of the Federal Constitution and the Union was clandestinely prepared during the winter of 1860 and 1861, and assumed an open organization in the form of a treasonable provisional government at Montgomery, in Alabama, on the 18th day of February, 1861. On the 12th day of April, 1861, the insurgents committed the flagrant act of civil war by the bombardment and capture of Fort Sumter, which cut off the hope of immediate conciliation. Immediately afterwards all the roads and avenues to this city were obstructed, and the capital was put into the condition of a siege. The mails in every direction were stopped, and the lines of telegraph cut off by the insurgents, and military and naval forces which had been called out by the Government for the defense of Washington were prevented from reaching the city by organized and combined treasonable resistance in the State of Maryland. There was no adequate and effective organization for the public defense. Congress had indefinitely adjourned. There was no time to convene them. It became necessary for me to choose whether, using only the existing means, agencies, and processes which Congress had provided, I should let the Government fall at once into ruin or whether, availing myself of the broader powers conferred by the Constitution in cases of insurrection, I would make an effort to save it, with all its blessings, for the present age and for posterity.

I thereupon summoned my constitutional advisers, the heads of all the Departments, to meet on Sunday, the 20th day of April, 1861, at the office of the Navy Department, and then and there, with their unanimous concurrence, I directed that an armed revenue cutter should proceed to sea to afford protection to the commercial marine, and especially the California treasure ships then on their way to this coast. I also directed the commandant of the navy-yard at Boston to purchase or charter and arm as quickly as possible five steamships for purposes of public defense. I directed the commandant of the navy-yard at Philadelphia to purchase or charter and arm an equal number for the same purpose. I directed the commandant at New York to purchase or charter and arm an equal number. I directed Commander Gillis to purchase or charter and arm and put to sea two other vessels. Similar directions were given to Commodore Du Pont, with a view to the opening of passages by water to and from the capital. I directed the several officers to take the advice and obtain the aid and efficient services in the matter of His Excellency Edwin D. Morgan, the governor of New York, or in his absence George D. Morgan, William M. Evarts, R. M. Blatchford, and Moses H. Grinnell, who were by my directions especially empowered by the Secretary of the Navy to act for his Department in that crisis in matters pertaining to the forwarding of troops and supplies for the public defense.

On the same occasion I directed that Governor Morgan and Alexander Cummings, of the city of New York, should be authorized by the Secretary of War, Simon Cameron, to make all necessary arrangements for the transportation of troops and munitions of war, in aid and assistance of the officers of the Army of the United States, until communication by mails and telegraph should be completely reestablished between the cities of Washington and New York. No security was required to be given by them, and either of them was authorized to act in case of inability to consult with the other.

On the same occasion I authorized and directed the Secretary of the Treasury to advance, without requiring security, $2,000,000 of public money to John A. Dix, George Opdyke, and Richard M. Blatchford, of New York, to be used by them in meeting such requisitions as should be directly consequent upon the military and naval measures necessary for the defense and support of the Government, requiring them only to act without compensation and to report their transactions when duly called upon.

The several Departments of the Government at that time contained so large a number of disloyal persons that it would have been impossible to provide safely through official agents only for the performance of the duties thus confided to citizens favorably known for their ability, loyalty, and patriotism.

The several orders issued upon these occurrences were transmitted by private messengers, who pursued a circuitous way to the seaboard cities, inland across the States of Pennsylvania and Ohio and the northern lakes. I believe that by these and other similar measures taken in that crisis, some of which were without any authority of law, the Government was saved from overthrow. I am not aware that a dollar of the public funds thus confided without authority of law to unofficial persons was either lost or wasted, although apprehensions of such misdirection occurred to me as objections to those extraordinary proceedings, and were necessarily overruled.

I recall these transactions now because my attention has been directed to a resolution which was passed by the House of Representatives on the 30th day of last month, which is in these words:

Resolved, That Simon Cameron, late Secretary of War, by investing Alexander Cummings with the control of large sums of the public money and authority to purchase military supplies without restriction, without requiring from him any guaranty for the faithful performance of his duties, when the services of competent public officers were available, and by involving the Government in a vast number of contracts with persons not legitimately engaged in the business pertaining to the subject-matter of such contracts, especially in the purchase of arms for future delivery, has adopted a policy highly injurious to the public service, and deserves the censure of the House.

Congress will see that I should be wanting equally in candor and in justice if I should leave the censure expressed in this resolution to rest exclusively or chiefly upon Mr. Cameron. The same sentiment is unanimously entertained by the heads of Departments who participated in the proceedings which the House of Representatives has censured. It is due to Mr. Cameron to say that although he fully approved the proceedings they were not moved nor suggested by himself, and that not only the President, but all the other heads of Departments, were at least equally responsible with him for whatever error, wrong, or fault was committed in the premises.

ABRAHAM LINCOLN.

WASHINGTON, *May 30, 1862.*

To the Senate of the United States:

I transmit to the Senate, for its consideration with a view to ratification, a treaty of amity, commerce, consular privileges, and extradition between the United States and the Republic of Salvador, signed in this city on the 29th instant. It is believed that though this instrument contains no stipulation which may not be found in some subsisting treaty between the United States and foreign powers, it will prove to be mutually advantageous. Several of the Republics of this hemisphere, among which is Salvador, are alarmed at a supposed sentiment tending to reactionary movements against republican institutions on this continent. It seems, therefore, to be proper that we should show to any of them who may apply for that purpose that, compatibly with our cardinal policy and with an enlightened view of our own interests, we are willing to encourage them by strengthening our ties of good will and good neighborhood with them.

ABRAHAM LINCOLN.

WASHINGTON, *June 4, 1862.*

To the Senate of the United States:

In compliance with the resolution of the Senate of the 29th ultimo, adopted in executive session, requesting information in regard to the claims of citizens of the United States on Paraguay and the correspondence relating thereto, I transmit a report from the Secretary of State and the documents by which it was accompanied.

ABRAHAM LINCOLN.

WASHINGTON, *June 4, 1862.*

To the House of Representatives:

I transmit herewith a report of the Secretary of War, in answer to the resolution of the House of Representatives of the 2d of June, in relation to the authority and action of the Hon. Edward Stanly, military governor of North Carolina.

ABRAHAM LINCOLN.

WASHINGTON, *June 10, 1862.*

To the Senate and House of Representatives:

I transmit to Congress a copy of a treaty for the suppression of the African slave trade, between the United States and Her Britannic Majesty, signed in this city on the 7th of April last, and the ratifications of which were exchanged at London on the 20th ultimo.

A copy of the correspondence which preceded the conclusion of the instrument between the Secretary of State and Lord Lyons, Her Britannic Majesty's envoy extraordinary and minister plenipotentiary, is also herewith transmitted.

It is desirable that such legislation as may be necessary to carry the treaty into effect should be enacted as soon as may comport with the convenience of Congress.

ABRAHAM LINCOLN.

EXECUTIVE MANSION,
Washington, June 12, 1862.

To the Honorable House of Representatives:

In obedience to the resolution of your honorable body of the 9th instant, requesting certain information in regard to the circuit court of the United States for the State of California, and the judge of said court, I have the honor to transmit a letter of the Attorney-General, with copies of two other letters and of an indorsement of my own upon one of them; all which, taken together, contain all the information within my power to give upon the subject.

ABRAHAM LINCOLN.

EXECUTIVE MANSION,
Washington, June 13, 1862.

Fellow-Citizens of the Senate and House of Representatives:

I herewith transmit a memorial addressed and presented to me in behalf of the State of New York in favor of enlarging the locks of the Erie and Oswego Canal. While I have not given nor have leisure to give the subject a careful examination, its great importance is obvious and unquestionable. The large amount of valuable statistical information which is collated and presented in the memorial will greatly facilitate the mature consideration of the subject, which I respectfully ask for it at your hands.

ABRAHAM LINCOLN.

EXECUTIVE MANSION,
Washington City, June 17, 1862.

The SPEAKER OF THE HOUSE OF REPRESENTATIVES:

The resolution of the House of Representatives of the 9th instant, asking whether any legislation is necessary in order to give effect to the provisions of the act of April 16, 1862, providing for the reorganization of the Medical Department of the Army, was referred to the Secretary of War, whose report thereon is herewith communicated.

ABRAHAM LINCOLN.

WASHINGTON, *June 23, 1862.*

To the Senate of the United States:

On the 7th day of December, 1861, I submitted to the Senate the project of a treaty between the United States and Mexico which had been proposed to me by Mr. Corwin, our minister to Mexico, and respectfully requested the advice of the Senate thereupon.

On the 25th day of February last a resolution was adopted by the Senate to the effect "that it is not advisable to negotiate a treaty that will require the United States to assume any portion of the principal or interest of the debt of Mexico, or that will require the concurrence of European powers.''

This resolution having been duly communicated to me, notice thereof was immediately given by the Secretary of State to Mr. Corwin, and he was informed that he was to consider his instructions upon the subject referred to modified by this resolution and would govern his course accordingly. That dispatch failed to reach Mr. Corwin, by reason of the disturbed condition of Mexico, until a very recent date, Mr. Corwin being without instructions, or thus practically left without instructions, to negotiate further with Mexico.

In view of the very important events occurring there, he has thought that the interests of the United States would be promoted by the conclusion of two treaties which should provide for a loan to that Republic. He has therefore signed such treaties, and they having been duly ratified by the Government of Mexico he has transmitted them to me for my consideration. The action of the Senate is of course conclusive against an acceptance of the treaties on my part. I have, nevertheless, thought it just to our excellent minister in Mexico and respectful to the Government of that Republic to lay the treaties before the Senate, together with the correspondence which has occurred in relation to them. In performing this duty I have only to add that the importance of the subject thus submitted to the Senate can not be overestimated, and I shall cheerfully receive and consider with the highest respect any further advice the Senate may think proper to give upon the subject.

ABRAHAM LINCOLN.

EXECUTIVE MANSION,
Washington, June 26, 1862.

To the Senate of the United States:

The accompanying treaty, made and concluded at the city of Washington on the 24th day of June, 1862, between the United States and the united bands of the Ottawa Indians of Blanchards Fork and of Roche de Boeuf, in Kansas, is transmitted for the consideration and constitutional action of the Senate, agreeably to recommendation of inclosed letter from the Secretary of the Interior of this date.

ABRAHAM LINCOLN.

WASHINGTON, *July 1, 1862.*

To the Senate and House of Representatives:

I most cordially recommend that Captain Andrew H. Foote, of the United States Navy, receive a vote of thanks of Congress for his eminent services in organizing the flotilla on the Western waters, and for his gallantry at Fort Henry, Fort Donelson, Island No. 10, and at various other places, whilst in command of the naval forces, embracing a period of nearly ten months.   ABRAHAM LINCOLN.

WASHINGTON, D. C., *July 5, 1862.*

To the Senate of the United States:

I transmit herewith, for the constitutional action of the Senate thereon, a treaty negotiated in this city on the 3d instant with the Sac and Fox Indians of the Mississippi.

Letters from the Secretary of the Interior and Commissioner of Indian Affairs accompany the treaty.   ABRAHAM LINCOLN.

WASHINGTON, *July 9, 1862.*

To the Senate of the United States:

I transmit to the Senate, for consideration with a view to ratification, a postal convention with Costa Rica, concluded at San Jose on the 9th June last.   ABRAHAM LINCOLN.

WASHINGTON, D. C., *July 11, 1862.*

To the Senate of the United States:

I transmit to the Senate, for its constitutional action thereon, a treaty negotiated at the Kickapoo Agency on the 28th of June, 1862, between Charles B. Keith, commissioner on the part of the United States, and the chiefs, headmen, and delegates of the Kickapoo Indians of Kansas.

A letter of the Commissioner of Indian Affairs of the 10th instant is also transmitted, suggesting amendments to the treaty for the consideration of the Senate.   ABRAHAM LINCOLN.

WASHINGTON, D. C., *July 11, 1862.*

To the Senate and House of Representatives:

I recommend that the thanks of Congress be given to the following officers of the United States Navy:

Captain James L. Lardner, for meritorious conduct at the battle of Port Royal and distinguished services on the coast of the United States against the enemy.

Captain Charles Henry Davis, for distinguished services in conflict with the enemy at Fort Pillow, at Memphis, and for successful operations at other points in the waters of the Mississippi River.

Commander John A. Dahlgren, for distinguished services in the line of his profession, improvements in ordnance, and zealous and efficient labors in the ordnance branch of the service.

Commander Stephen C. Rowan, for distinguished services in the waters of North Carolina, and particularly in the capture of Newbern, being in chief command of the naval forces.

Commander David D. Porter, for distinguished services in the conception and preparation of the means used for the capture of the forts below New Orleans, and for highly meritorious conduct in the management of the mortar flotilla during the bombardment of Forts Jackson and St. Philip.

Captain Silas H. Stringham, now on the retired list. for distinguished services in the capture of Forts Hatteras and Clark.

ABRAHAM LINCOLN.

WASHINGTON, *July 12, 1862.*

To the House of Representatives:

I transmit a report of the Secretary of State upon the subject of the resolution of the House of Representatives of the 9th ultimo, requesting information in regard to the relations between the United States and foreign powers.

ABRAHAM LINCOLN.

WASHINGTON, D. C., *July 14, 1862.*

Fellow-Citizens of the Senate and House of Representatives:

Herewith is a draft of a bill to compensate any State which may abolish slavery within its limits, the passage of which substantially as presented I respectfully and earnestly recommend.

ABRAHAM LINCOLN.

Be it enacted by the Senate and House of Representatives of the United States of America in Congress assembled, That whenever the President of the United States shall be satisfied that any State shall have lawfully abolished slavery within and throughout such State, either immediately or gradually, it shall be the duty of the President, assisted by the Secretary of the Treasury, to prepare and deliver to such State an amount of 6 per cent interest-bearing bonds of the United States equal to the aggregate value at $—— per head of all the slaves within such State as reported by the census of the year 1860; the whole amount for any one State to be delivered at once if the abolishment be immediate, or in equal annual installments if it be gradual, interest to begin running on each bond at the time of its delivery, and not before.

And be it further enacted, That if any State, having so received any such bonds, shall at any time afterwards by law reintroduce or tolerate slavery within its limits contrary to the act of abolishment upon which such bonds shall have been received, said bonds so received by said State shall at once be null and void, in whosesoever hands they may be, and such State shall refund to the United States all interest which may have been paid on such bonds.

EXECUTIVE MANSION,
Washington, July 15, 1862.

Hon. SOLOMON FOOT,
  President pro tempore of the Senate.

SIR: Please inform the Senate that I shall be obliged if they will postpone the adjournment at least one day beyond the time which I understand to be now fixed for it.

  Your obedient servant,
                                    ABRAHAM LINCOLN.

[The same message was addressed to Hon. Galusha A. Grow, Speaker of the House of Representatives.]

JULY 17, 1862.

Fellow-Citizens of the Senate and House of Representatives:

Considering the bill for "An act to suppress insurrection, to punish treason and rebellion, to seize and confiscate the property of rebels, and for other purposes," and the joint resolution explanatory of said act as being substantially one, I have approved and signed both.

Before I was informed of the passage of the resolution I had prepared the draft of a message stating objections to the bill becoming a law, a copy of which draft is herewith transmitted.

                                    ABRAHAM LINCOLN.

Fellow-Citizens of the House of Representatives:

I herewith return to your honorable body, in which it originated, the bill for an act entitled "An act to suppress treason and rebellion, to seize and confiscate the property of rebels, and for other purposes," together with my objections to its becoming a law.

There is much in the bill to which I perceive no objection. It is wholly prospective, and touches neither person nor property of any loyal citizen, in which particulars it is just and proper. The first and second sections provide for the conviction and punishment of persons who shall be guilty of treason and persons who shall "incite, set on foot, assist, or engage in any rebellion or insurrection against the authority of the United States or the laws thereof, or shall give aid and comfort thereto, or shall engage in or give aid and comfort to any such existing rebellion or insurrection." By fair construction persons within these sections are not to be punished without regular trials in duly constituted courts, under the forms and all the substantial provisions of law and of the Constitution applicable to their several cases. To this I perceive no objection, especially as such persons would be within the general pardoning power and also the special provision for pardon and amnesty contained in this act.

It is also provided that the slaves of persons convicted under these sections shall be free. I think there is an unfortunate form of expression rather than a substantial objection in this. It is startling to say that Congress can free a slave within a State, and yet if it were said the ownership of the slave had first been transferred to the nation and that Congress had then liberated him the difficulty would at once vanish. And this is the real case. The traitor against the General Government forfeits his slave at least as justly as he does any other property, and he forfeits both to the Government against which he offends. The Government, so far as there can be ownership, thus owns the forfeited slaves, and the question for Congress in regard to them is, "Shall they be made free or be sold to new masters?" I perceive no objection to Congress deciding in advance that they shall be free. To the high honor of Kentucky, as I am informed, she has been the owner of some slaves by escheat and has sold none, but liberated all. I hope the same is true of some other States. Indeed I do not believe it would be physically possible for the General Government to return persons so circumstanced to actual slavery. I believe there would be physical resistance to it which could neither be turned aside by argument nor driven away by force. In this view I have no objection to this feature of the bill. Another matter involved in these two sections, and running through other parts of the act, will be noticed hereafter.

I perceive no objection to the third and fourth sections.

So far as I wish to notice the fifth and sixth sections, they may be considered together. That the enforcement of these sections would do no injustice to the persons embraced within them is clear. That those who make a causeless war should be compelled to pay the cost of it is too obviously just to be called in question. To give governmental protection to the property of persons who have abandoned it and gone on a crusade to overthrow that same government is absurd if considered in the mere light of justice. The severest justice may not always be the best policy. The principle of seizing and appropriating the property of the persons embraced within these sections is certainly not very objectionable, but a justly discriminating application of it would be very difficult, and to a great extent impossible. And would it not be wise to place a power of remission somewhere, so that these persons may know they have something to lose by persisting and something to save by desisting? I am not sure whether such power of remission is or is not within section 13.

Without any special act of Congress, I think our military commanders, when, in military phrase, "they are within the enemy's country," should in an orderly manner seize and use whatever of real or personal property may be necessary or convenient for their commands, at the same time preserving in some way the evidence of what they do.

What I have said in regard to slaves while commenting on the first and second sections is applicable to the ninth, with the difference that no provision is made in the whole act for determining whether a particular individual slave does or does not fall within the classes defined in that section. He is to be free upon certain conditions, but whether those conditions do or do not pertain to him no mode of ascertaining is provided. This could be easily supplied.

To the tenth section I make no objection. The oath therein required seems to be proper, and the remainder of the section is substantially identical with a law already existing.

The eleventh section simply assumes to confer discretionary powers upon the Executive. Without the law I have no hesitation to go as far in the direction indicated as I may at any time deem expedient. And I am ready to say now, I think it is proper for our military commanders to employ as laborers as many persons of African descent as can be used to advantage.

The twelfth and thirteenth sections are somewhat better than objectionable, and the fourteenth is entirely proper if all other parts of the act shall stand.

That to which I chiefly object pervades most parts of the act, but more distinctly appears in the first, second, seventh, and eighth sections. It is the sum of those provisions which results in the divesting of title forever. For the causes of treason and the ingredients of treason not amounting to the full crime it declares forfeiture extending beyond the lives of the guilty parties, whereas the Constitution of the United States declares that "no attainder of treason shall work corruption of blood, or forfeiture except during the life of the person attainted." True, there seems to be no formal attainder in this case; still, I think the greater punishment can not be constitutionally inflicted in a different form for the same offense. With great respect I am constrained to say I think this feature of the act is unconstitutional. It would not be difficult to modify it.

I may remark that this provision of the Constitution, put in language borrowed from Great Britain, applies only in this country to real or landed estate.

Again, this act, by proceedings *in rem*, forfeits property for the ingredients of treason without a conviction of the supposed criminal or a personal hearing given him in any proceeding. That we may not touch property lying within our reach because we can not give personal notice to an owner who is absent endeavoring to destroy the Government is certainly not very satisfactory. Still, the owner may not be thus engaged; and I think a reasonable time should be provided for such parties to appear and have personal hearings. Similar provisions are not uncommon in connection with proceedings *in rem*.

For the reasons stated, I return the bill to the House, in which it originated.

JULY 17, 1862.

Fellow-Citizens of the Senate and House of Representatives:

I have inadvertently omitted so long to inform you that in March last Mr. Cornelius Vanderbilt, of New York, gratuitously presented to the United States the ocean steamer *Vanderbilt*, by many esteemed the finest merchant ship in the world. She has ever since been and still is doing valuable service to the Government. For the patriotic act in making this magnificent and valuable present to the country, I recommend that some suitable acknowledgment be made.

ABRAHAM LINCOLN.

VETO MESSAGES.

JUNE 23, 1862.

To the Senate of the United States:

The bill which has passed the House of Representatives and the Senate entitled "An act to repeal that part of an act of Congress which prohibits the circulation of bank notes of a less denomination than $5 in the District of Columbia" has received my attentive consideration, and I now return it to the Senate, in which it originated, with the following objections:

1. The bill proposes to repeal the existing legislation prohibiting the circulation of bank notes of a less denomination than $5 within the District of Columbia without permitting the issuing of such bills by banks not now legally authorized to issue them. In my judgment it will be found impracticable in the present condition of the currency to make such a discrimination. The banks have generally suspended specie payments, and a legal sanction given to the circulation of the irredeemable notes of one class of them will almost certainly be so extended in practical operation as to include those of all classes, whether authorized or unauthorized. If this view be correct, the currency of the District,

should this act become a law will certainly and greatly deteriorate, to the serious injury of honest trade and honest labor.

2. This bill seems to contemplate no end which can not be otherwise more certainly and beneficially attained. During the existing war it is peculiarly the duty of the National Government to secure to the people a sound circulating medium. This duty has been under existing circumstances satisfactorily performed, in part at least, by authorizing the issue of United States notes, receivable for all Government dues except customs, and made a legal tender for all debts, public and private, except interest on public debt. The object of the bill submitted to me, namely, that of providing a small-note currency during the present suspension, can be fully accomplished by authorizing the issue, as part of any new emission of United States notes made necessary by the circumstances of the country, of notes of a similar character but of less denomination than $5. Such an issue would answer all the beneficial purposes of the bill, would save a considerable amount to the Treasury in interest, would greatly facilitate payments to soldiers and other creditors of small sums, and would furnish to the people a currency as safe as their own Government.

Entertaining these objections to the bill, I feel myself constrained to withhold from it my approval and return it for the further consideration and action of Congress. ABRAHAM LINCOLN.

EXECUTIVE MANSION, *July 2, 1862.*
To the Senate of the United States:

I herewith return to your honorable body, in which it originated, an act entitled "An act to provide for additional medical officers of the volunteer service," without my approval.

My reason for so doing is that I have approved an act of the same title passed by Congress after the passage of the one first mentioned for the express purpose of correcting errors in and superseding the same, as I am informed. ABRAHAM LINCOLN.

PROCLAMATIONS.

BY THE PRESIDENT OF THE UNITED STATES OF AMERICA.

A PROCLAMATION.

It is recommended to the people of the United States that they assemble in their customary places of meeting for public solemnities on the 22d day of February instant and celebrate the anniversary of the birth of the Father of his Country by causing to be read to them his immortal Farewell Address.

Given under my hand and the seal of the United States, at Washington, the 19th day of February, A. D. 1862, and of the Independence of the United States of America the eighty-sixth.

[SEAL.]

ABRAHAM LINCOLN.

By the President:

WILLIAM H. SEWARD,
Secretary of State.

BY THE PRESIDENT OF THE UNITED STATES OF AMERICA.

A PROCLAMATION.

It has pleased Almighty God to vouchsafe signal victories to the land and naval forces engaged in suppressing an internal rebellion, and at the same time to avert from our country the dangers of foreign intervention and invasion.

It is therefore recommended to the people of the United States that at their next weekly assemblages in their accustomed places of public worship which shall occur after notice of this proclamation shall have been received they especially acknowledge and render thanks to our Heavenly Father for these inestimable blessings, that they then and there implore spiritual consolation in behalf of all who have been brought into affliction by the casualties and calamities of sedition and civil war, and that they reverently invoke the divine guidance for our national counsels, to the end that they may speedily result in the restoration of peace, harmony, and unity throughout our borders and hasten the establishment of fraternal relations among all the countries of the earth.

In witness whereof I have hereunto set my hand and caused the seal of the United States to be affixed.

[SEAL.] Done at the city of Washington, this 10th day of April, A. D. 1862, and of the Independence of the United States the eighty-sixth.

ABRAHAM LINCOLN.

By the President:

WILLIAM H. SEWARD,
Secretary of State.

BY THE PRESIDENT OF THE UNITED STATES OF AMERICA.

A PROCLAMATION.

Whereas by my proclamation of the 19th of April, 1861, it was declared that the ports of certain States, including those of Beaufort, in the State of North Carolina; Port Royal, in the State of South Carolina;

and New Orleans, in the State of Louisiana, were, for reasons therein set forth, intended to be placed under blockade; and

Whereas the said ports of Beaufort, Port Royal, and New Orleans have since been blockaded; but as the blockade of the same ports may now be safely relaxed with advantage to the interests of commerce:

Now, therefore, be it known that I, Abraham Lincoln, President of the United States, pursuant to the authority in me vested by the fifth section of the act of Congress approved on the 13th of July last, entitled "An act further to provide for the collection of duties on imports, and for other purposes," do hereby declare that the blockade of the said ports of Beaufort, Port Royal, and New Orleans shall so far cease and determine, from and after the 1st day of June next, that commercial intercourse with those ports, except as to persons, things, and information contraband of war, may from that time be carried on subject to the laws of the United States and to the limitations and in pursuance of the regulations which are prescribed by the Secretary of the Treasury in his order of this date, which is appended to this proclamation.

In witness whereof I have hereunto set my hand and caused the seal of the United States to be affixed.

[SEAL.]   Done at the city of Washington, this 12th day of May, A. D. 1862, and of the Independence of the United States the eighty-sixth.   ABRAHAM LINCOLN.

By the President:
    WILLIAM H. SEWARD,
        Secretary of State.

REGULATIONS RELATING TO TRADE WITH PORTS OPENED BY PROCLAMATION.

TREASURY DEPARTMENT, *May 12, 1862.*

1. To vessels clearing from foreign ports and destined to ports opened by the proclamation of the President of the United States of this date, namely, Beaufort, in North Carolina; Port Royal, in South Carolina, and New Orleans, in Louisiana, licenses will be granted by consuls of the United States upon satisfactory evidence that the vessels so licensed will convey no persons, property, or information contraband of war either to or from the said ports, which licenses shall be exhibited to the collector of the port to which said vessels may be respectively bound immediately on arrival, and, if required, to any officer in charge of the blockade; and on leaving either of said ports every vessel will be required to have a clearance from the collector of the customs, according to law, showing no violation of the conditions of the license. Any violation of said conditions will involve the forfeiture and condemnation of the vessel and cargo and the exclusion of all parties concerned from any further privilege of entering the United States during the war for any purpose whatever.

2. To vessels of the United States clearing coastwise for the ports aforesaid licenses can only be obtained from the Treasury Department.

3. In all other respects the existing blockade remains in full force and effect as hitherto established and maintained, nor is it relaxed by the proclamation except in regard to the ports to which the relaxation is by that instrument expressly applied.

S. P. CHASE, *Secretary of the Treasury.*

BY THE PRESIDENT OF THE UNITED STATES OF AMERICA.

A PROCLAMATION.

Whereas there appears in the public prints what purports to be a proclamation of Major-General Hunter, in the words and figures following, to wit:

HEADQUARTERS DEPARTMENT OF THE SOUTH,
Hilton Head, S. C., May 9, 1862.

General Orders, No. 11.—The three States of Georgia, Florida, and South Carolina, comprising the Military Department of the South, having deliberately declared themselves no longer under the protection of the United States of America, and having taken up arms against the said United States, it becomes a military necessity to declare them under martial law This was accordingly done on the 25th day of April, 1862. Slavery and martial law in a free country are altogether incompatible; the persons in these three States—Georgia, Florida, and South Carolina—heretofore held as slaves are therefore declared forever free.

DAVID HUNTER,
Major-General Commanding.

Official:

ED. W. SMITH,
Acting Assistant Adjutant-General.

And whereas the same is producing some excitement and misunderstanding:

Therefore I, Abraham Lincoln, President of the United States, proclaim and declare that the Government of the United States had no knowledge, information, or belief of an intention on the part of General Hunter to issue such a proclamation, nor has it yet any authentic information that the document is genuine; and, further, that neither General Hunter nor any other commander or person has been authorized by the Government of the United States to make proclamations declaring the slaves of any State free, and that the supposed proclamation now in question, whether genuine or false, is altogether void so far as respects such declaration.

I further make known that whether it be competent for me, as Commander in Chief of the Army and Navy, to declare the slaves of any State or States free, and whether at any time, in any case, it shall have become a necessity indispensable to the maintenance of the Government to exercise such supposed power, are questions which, under my responsibility, I reserve to myself, and which I can not feel justified in leaving to the decision of commanders in the field. These are totally different questions from those of police regulations in armies and camps.

On the 6th day of March last, by a special message, I recommended to Congress the adoption of a joint resolution to be substantially as follows:

Resolved, That the United States ought to cooperate with any State which may adopt a gradual abolishment of slavery, giving to such State pecuniary aid, to be used by such State, in its discretion, to compensate for the inconveniences, public and private, produced by such change of system

The resolution, in the language above quoted, was adopted by large majorities in both branches of Congress, and now stands an authentic, definite, and solemn proposal of the nation to the States and people most immediately interested in the subject-matter. To the people of those States I now earnestly appeal—I do not argue; I beseech you to make the arguments for yourselves; you can not, if you would, be blind to the signs of the times. I beg of you a calm and enlarged consideration of them, ranging, if it may be, far above personal and partisan politics. This proposal makes common cause for a common object, casting no reproaches upon any. It acts not the Pharisee. The change it contemplates would come gently as the dews of heaven, not rending or wrecking anything. Will you not embrace it? So much good has not been done by one effort in all past time as, in the providence of God, it is now your high privilege to do. May the vast future not have to lament that you have neglected it.

In witness whereof I have hereunto set my hand and caused the seal of the United States to be affixed.

[SEAL.]　　Done at the city of Washington, this 19th day of May, A. D. 1862, and of the Independence of the United States the eighty-sixth.

ABRAHAM LINCOLN.

By the President:

WILLIAM H. SEWARD, *Secretary of State.*

BY THE PRESIDENT OF THE UNITED STATES OF AMERICA.

A PROCLAMATION.

Whereas in and by the second section of an act of Congress passed on the 7th day of June, A. D. 1862, entitled "An act for the collection of direct taxes in insurrectionary districts within the United States, and for other purposes," it is made the duty of the President to declare, on or before the 1st day of July then next following, by his proclamation, in what States and parts of States insurrection exists:

Now, therefore, be it known that I, Abraham Lincoln, President of the United States of America, do hereby declare and proclaim that the States of South Carolina, Florida, Georgia, Alabama, Louisiana, Texas, Mississippi, Arkansas, Tennessee, North Carolina, and the State of Virginia except the following counties—Hancock, Brooke, Ohio, Marshall, Wetzel, Marion, Monongalia, Preston, Taylor, Pleasants, Tyler, Ritchie, Doddridge, Harrison, Wood, Jackson, Wirt, Roane, Calhoun, Gilmer, Barbour, Tucker, Lewis, Braxton, Upshur, Randolph, Mason, Putnam, Kanawha, Clay, Nicholas, Cabell, Wayne, Boone, Logan, Wyoming, Webster, Fayette, and Raleigh—are now in insurrection and rebellion, and by reason thereof the civil authority of the United States is obstructed so that the provisions of the "Act to provide increased revenue

THE BATTLE OF MALVERN HILL

CAVALRY CHARGE

BATTLE OF MALVERN HILL.

The Battle of Malvern Hill represents the last of the severe engagements fought in McClellan's Peninsular campaign, with the Confederate capital as its objective. Malvern Hill is a high plateau above the James River, sloping towards Richmond. The Army of the Potomac occupied it on July 1, 1862, and was strongly entrenched on its heights. Nevertheless, Lee determined to take Malvern Hill by storm, and planned a general frontal attack. Lee's plans were bungled, however, and the first attack was delivered by only one Confederate division, which was beaten off without much trouble. The second attack was delivered with the full force of Lee's army, but the deadly musketry and artillery of the Union troops, coupled with the destructive fire of the Union gunboats in the James River, fully 150 feet below the heights on which the battle was fought, proved too much for the Confederates, who retired with great loss. The entire engagement represented one of the severest battles of the Civil War, as can be seen from the fact that Union forces lost 1,734 men, with 8,062 wounded and 6,053 missing, while the Confederates lost 3,478 men, with 16,261 wounded and an unreported number missing. (See Malvern Hill (Va.). Battle of, in Encyclopedic Index.)

from imports, to pay the interest on the public debt, and for other purposes," approved August 5, 1861, can not be peaceably executed; and that the taxes legally chargeable upon real estate under the act last aforesaid lying within the States and parts of States as aforesaid, together with a penalty of 50 *per centum* of said taxes, shall be a lien upon the tracts or lots of the same, severally charged, till paid.

In witness whereof I have hereunto set my hand and caused the seal of the United States to be affixed.

[SEAL.]   Done at the city of Washington, this 1st day of July, A. D. 1862, and of the Independence of the United States of America the eighty-sixth.   ABRAHAM LINCOLN.

By the President:
    F. W. SEWARD,
       Acting Secretary of State.

BY THE PRESIDENT OF THE UNITED STATES OF AMERICA.

A PROCLAMATION.

In pursuance of the sixth section of the act of Congress entitled "An act to suppress insurrection and to punish treason and rebellion, to seize and confiscate property of rebels, and for other purposes," approved July 17, 1862, and which act and the joint resolution explanatory thereof are herewith published, I, Abraham Lincoln, President of the United States, do hereby proclaim to and warn all persons within the contemplation of said sixth section to cease participating in, aiding, countenancing, or abetting the existing rebellion or any rebellion against the Government of the United States and to return to their proper allegiance to the United States on pain of the forfeitures and seizures as within and by said sixth section provided.

In testimony whereof I have hereunto set my hand and caused the seal of the United States to be affixed.

[SEAL.]   Done at the city of Washington, this 25th day of July, A. D. 1862, and of the Independence of the United States the eighty-seventh.   ABRAHAM LINCOLN.

By the President:
    WILLIAM H. SEWARD,
       Secretary of State.

[From Statutes at Large (Little, Brown & Co.), Vol. XII, p. 589.]

AN ACT to suppress insurrection, to punish treason and rebellion, to seize and confiscate the property of rebels, and for other purposes.

Be it enacted by the Senate and House of Representatives of the United States of America in Congress assembled, That every person who shall hereafter commit the crime of treason against the United States, and shall be adjudged guilty thereof, shall suffer death, and all his slaves, if any, shall be declared and made free; or, at the discretion of the court, he shall be imprisoned for not less than five years and fined not less than $10,000, and all his slaves, if any, shall be declared and made free; said fine shall be levied and collected on any or all of the property, real and personal, excluding slaves, of which the said person so convicted was the owner at the time of committing the said crime, any sale or conveyance to the contrary notwithstanding.

SEC. 2. *And be it further enacted,* That if any person shall hereafter incite, set on foot, assist, or engage in any rebellion or insurrection against the authority of the United States or the laws thereof, or shall give aid or comfort thereto, or shall engage in or give aid and comfort to any such existing rebellion or insurrection, and be convicted thereof, such person shall be punished by imprisonment for a period not exceeding ten years, or by a fine not exceeding $10,000, and by the liberation of all his slaves, if any he have; or by both of said punishments, at the discretion of the court.

SEC. 3. *And be it further enacted*, That every person guilty of either of the offenses described in this act shall be forever incapable and disqualified to hold any office under the United States.

SEC. 4. *And be it further enacted*, That this act shall not be construed in any way to affect or alter the prosecution, conviction, or punishment of any person or persons guilty of treason against the United States before the passage of this act, unless such person is convicted under this act.

SEC. 5. *And be it further enacted*, That to insure the speedy termination of the present rebellion it shall be the duty of the President of the United States to cause the seizure of all the estate and property, money, stocks, credits, and effects of the persons hereinafter named in this section, and to apply and use the same and the proceeds thereof for the support of the Army of the United States; that is to say:

First. Of any person hereafter acting as an officer of the army or navy of the rebels in arms against the Government of the United States.

Secondly. Of any person hereafter acting as president, vice-president, member of congress, judge of any court, cabinet officer, foreign minister, commissioner, or consul of the so-called Confederate States of America.

Thirdly. Of any person acting as governor of a State, member of a convention or legislature, or judge of any court of any of the so-called Confederate States of America.

Fourthly. Of any person who, having held an office of honor, trust, or profit in the United States, shall hereafter hold an office in the so-called Confederate States of America.

Fifthly. Of any person hereafter holding any office or agency under the government of the so-called Confederate States of America, or under any of the several States of the said Confederacy, or the laws thereof, whether such office or agency be national, State, or municipal in its name or character: *Provided*, That the persons thirdly, fourthly, and fifthly above described shall have accepted their appointment or election since the date of the pretended ordinance of secession of the State, or shall have taken an oath of allegiance to or to support the constitution of the so-called Confederate States.

Sixthly. Of any person who owning property in any loyal State or Territory of the United States, or in the District of Columbia, shall hereafter assist and give aid and comfort to such rebellion; and all sales, transfers, or conveyances of any such property shall be null and void; and it shall be a sufficient bar to any suit brought by such person for the possession or the use of such property, or any of it, to allege and prove that he is one of the persons described in this section.

SEC. 6. *And be it further enacted*, That if any person within any State or Territory of the United States, other than those named as aforesaid, after the passage of this act, being engaged in armed rebellion against the Government of the United States, or aiding or abetting such rebellion, shall not, within sixty days after public warning and proclamation duly given and made by the President of the United States, cease to aid, countenance, and abet such rebellion, and return to his allegiance to the United States, all the estate and property, moneys, stocks, and credits of such person shall be liable to seizure as aforesaid, and it shall be the duty of the President to seize and use them as aforesaid, or the proceeds thereof. And all sales, transfers, or conveyances of any such property after the expiration of the said sixty days from the date of such warning and proclamation shall be null and void; and it shall be a sufficient bar to any suit brought by such person for the possession or the use of such property, or any of it, to allege and prove that he is one of the persons described in this section.

SEC. 7. *And be it further enacted*, That to secure the condemnation and sale of any of such property, after the same shall have been seized, so that it may be made available for the purpose aforesaid, proceedings *in rem* shall be instituted in the name of the United States in any district court thereof, or in any Territorial court, or in the United States district court for the District of Columbia, within which the property above described, or any part thereof, may be found, or into which the same, if movable, may first be brought, which proceedings shall conform as nearly as may be to proceedings in admiralty or revenue cases; and if said property, whether real or personal, shall be found to have belonged to a person engaged in rebellion, or who has given aid or comfort thereto, the same shall be condemned as enemies' property and become the property of the United States, and may be disposed of as the court shall decree and the proceeds thereof paid into the Treasury of the United States for the purposes aforesaid.

SEC. 8. *And be it further enacted*, That the several courts aforesaid shall have power to make such orders, establish such forms of decree and sale, and direct such deeds and conveyances to be executed and delivered by the marshals thereof where real estate shall be the subject of sale as shall fitly and efficiently effect the purposes of this act, and vest in the purchasers of such property good and valid titles thereto. And the said courts shall have power to allow such fees and charges of their officers as shall be reasonable and proper in the premises.

SEC. 9. *And be it further enacted*, That all slaves of persons who shall hereafter be engaged in rebellion against the Government of the United States, or who shall in any way give aid or comfort thereto, escaping from such persons and taking refuge within the lines of the army, and all slaves captured from such persons or deserted by them and coming under the control of the Government of the United States, and all slaves of such persons found on [or] being within any place occupied by rebel forces and afterwards occupied by the forces of the United States, shall be deemed captives of war, and shall be forever free of their servitude, and not again held as slaves.

SEC. 10. *And be it further enacted*, That no slave escaping into any State, Territory, or the District of Columbia from any other State shall be delivered up or in any way impeded or hindered of his liberty except for crime or some offense against the laws, unless the person claiming said fugitive shall first make oath that the person to whom the labor or service of such fugitive is alleged to be due is his lawful owner and has not borne arms against the United States in the present rebellion nor in any way given aid and comfort thereto; and no person engaged in the military or naval service of the United States shall, under any pretense whatever, assume to decide on the validity of the claim of any person to the service or labor of any other person, or surrender up any such person to the claimant, on pain of being dismissed from the service.

SEC. 11. *And be it further enacted*, That the President of the United States is authorized to employ as many persons of African descent as he may deem necessary and proper for the suppression of this rebellion, and for this purpose he may organize and use them in such manner as he may judge best for the public welfare.

SEC. 12. *And be it further enacted,* That the President of the United States is hereby authorized to make provision for the transportation, colonization, and settlement, in some tropical country beyond the limits of the United States, of such persons of the African race, made free by the provisions of this act, as may be willing to emigrate, having first obtained the consent of the Government of said country to their protection and settlement within the same, with all the rights and privileges of freemen.

SEC. 13. *And be it further enacted,* That the President is hereby authorized, at any time hereafter, by proclamation, to extend to persons who may have participated in the existing rebellion in any State or part thereof pardon and amnesty, with such exceptions and at such time and on such conditions as he may deem expedient for the public welfare.

SEC. 14. *And be it further enacted,* That the courts of the United States shall have full power to institute proceedings, make orders and decrees, issue process, and do all other things necessary to carry this act into effect.

Approved, July 17, 1862.

[From Statutes at Large (Little, Brown & Co.), Vol. XII, p. 627.]

JOINT RESOLUTION explanatory of "An act to suppress insurrection, to punish treason and rebellion, to seize and confiscate the property of rebels, and for other purposes."

Resolved by the Senate and House of Representatives of the United States of America in Congress assembled, That the provisions of the third clause of the fifth section of "An act to suppress insurrection, to punish treason and rebellion, to seize and confiscate the property of rebels, and for other purposes" shall be so construed as not to apply to any act or acts done prior to the passage thereof, nor to include any member of a State legislature or judge of any State court who has not in accepting or entering upon his office taken an oath to support the constitution of the so-called "Confederate States of America;" nor shall any punishment or proceedings under said act be so construed as to work a forfeiture of the real estate of the offender beyond his natural life.

Approved, July 17, 1862.

BY THE PRESIDENT OF THE UNITED STATES OF AMERICA.

A PROCLAMATION.

I, Abraham Lincoln, President of the United States of America and Commander in Chief of the Army and Navy thereof, do hereby proclaim and declare that hereafter, as heretofore, the war will be prosecuted for the object of practically restoring the constitutional relation between the United States and each of the States and the people thereof in which States that relation is or may be suspended or disturbed.

That it is my purpose, upon the next meeting of Congress, to again recommend the adoption of a practical measure tendering pecuniary aid to the free acceptance or rejection of all slave States, so called, the people whereof may not then be in rebellion against the United States, and which States may then have voluntarily adopted, or thereafter may voluntarily adopt, immediate or gradual abolishment of slavery within their respective limits; and that the effort to colonize persons of African descent with their consent upon this continent or elsewhere, with the previously obtained consent of the governments existing there, will be continued.

That on the 1st day of January, A. D. 1863, all persons held as slaves within any State or designated part of a State the people whereof shall then be in rebellion against the United States shall be then, thenceforward, and forever free; and the executive government of the United States, including the military and naval authority thereof, will recognize and maintain the freedom of such persons and will do no act or acts to repress such persons, or any of them, in any efforts they may make for their actual freedom.

That the Executive will on the 1st day of January aforesaid, by proclamation, designate the States and parts of States, if any, in which the people thereof, respectively, shall then be in rebellion against the United States; and the fact that any State or the people thereof shall on that day be in good faith represented in the Congress of the United States by members chosen thereto at elections wherein a majority of the qualified voters of such State shall have participated shall, in the absence of strong countervailing testimony, be deemed conclusive evidence that such State and the people thereof are not then in rebellion against the United States.

That attention is hereby called to an act of Congress entitled "An act to make an additional article of war," approved March 13, 1862, and which act is in the words and figure following:

Be it enacted by the Senate and House of Representatives of the United States of America in Congress assembled, That hereafter the following shall be promulgated as an additional article of war for the government of the Army of the United States, and shall be obeyed and observed as such :

ART. —. All officers or persons in the military or naval service of the United States are prohibited from employing any of the forces under their respective commands for the purpose of returning fugitives from service or labor who may have escaped from any persons to whom such service or labor is claimed to be due, and any officer who shall be found guilty by a court-martial of violating this article shall be dismissed from the service.

SEC. 2. *And be it further enacted,* That this act shall take effect from and after its passage.

Also to the ninth and tenth sections of an act entitled "An act to suppress insurrection, to punish treason and rebellion, to seize and confiscate the property of rebels, and for other purposes," approved July 17, 1862, and which sections are in the words and figures following :

SEC. 9. *And be it further enacted,* That all slaves of persons who shall hereafter be engaged in rebellion against the Government of the United States, or who shall in any way give aid or comfort thereto, escaping from such persons and taking refuge within the lines of the army, and all slaves captured from such persons or deserted by them and coming under the control of the Government of the United States, and all slaves of such persons found on [or] being within any place occupied by rebel forces and afterwards occupied by the forces of the United States, shall be deemed captives of war and shall be forever free of their servitude and not again held as slaves.

SEC. 10. *And be it further enacted,* That no slave escaping into any State, Territory, or the District of Columbia from any other State shall be delivered up or in any way impeded or hindered of his liberty except for crime or some offense against the laws, unless the person claiming said fugitive shall first make oath that the person to whom the labor or service of such fugitive is alleged to be due is his lawful owner and has not borne arms against the United States in the present rebellion nor in any way given aid and comfort thereto, and no person engaged in the military or naval service of the United States shall, under any pretense whatever, assume to decide on the validity of the claim of any person to the service or labor of any other person or surrender up any such person to the claimant on pain of being dismissed from the service.

And I do hereby enjoin upon and order all persons engaged in the military and naval service of the United States to observe, obey, and enforce within their respective spheres of service the act and sections above recited.

And the Executive will in due time recommend that all citizens of the United States who shall have remained loyal thereto throughout the rebellion shall, upon the restoration of the constitutional relation between the United States and their respective States and people, if that relation shall have been suspended or disturbed, be compensated for all losses by acts of the United States, including the loss of slaves.

In witness whereof I have hereunto set my hand and caused the seal of the United States to be affixed.

[SEAL.] Done at the city of Washington, this 22d day of September, A. D. 1862, and of the Independence of the United States the eighty-seventh.

ABRAHAM LINCOLN.

By the President:

WILLIAM H. SEWARD, *Secretary of State.*

BY THE PRESIDENT OF THE UNITED STATES OF AMERICA.

A PROCLAMATION.

Whereas it has become necessary to call into service not only volunteers, but also portions of the militia of the States by draft in order to suppress the insurrection existing in the United States, and disloyal persons are not adequately restrained by the ordinary processes of law from hindering this measure and from giving aid and comfort in various ways to the insurrection:

Now, therefore, be it ordered, first, that during the existing insurrection, and as a necessary measure for suppressing the same, all rebels and insurgents, their aiders and abettors, within the United States, and all persons discouraging volunteer enlistments, resisting militia drafts, or guilty of any disloyal practice affording aid and comfort to rebels against the authority of the United States, shall be subject to martial law and liable to trial and punishment by courts-martial or military commissions; second, that the writ of *habeas corpus* is suspended in respect to all persons arrested, or who are now or hereafter during the rebellion shall be imprisoned in any fort, camp, arsenal, military prison, or other place of confinement by any military authority or by the sentence of any court-martial or military commission.

In witness whereof I have hereunto set my hand and caused the seal of the United States to be affixed.

[SEAL.]   Done at the city of Washington, this 24th day of September, A. D. 1862, and of the Independence of the United States the eighty-seventh.   ABRAHAM LINCOLN

By the President:
    WILLIAM H. SEWARD,
            Secretary of State.

EXECUTIVE ORDERS.

Major-General H. W. HALLECK,
    Commanding in the Department of Missouri.

GENERAL: As an insurrection exists in the United States and is in arms in the State of Missouri, you are hereby authorized and empowered to suspend the writ of *habeas corpus* within the limits of the military division under your command and to exercise martial law as you find it necessary, in your discretion, to secure the public safety and the authority of the United States.

In witness whereof I have hereunto set my hand and caused the seal of the United States to be affixed, at Washington, this 2d day of December, A. D. 1861.

[SEAL.]

ABRAHAM LINCOLN.

By the President:
    WILLIAM H. SEWARD,
            Secretary of State.

GENERAL ORDERS, No. 111.

HEADQUARTERS OF THE ARMY,
    ADJUTANT-GENERAL'S OFFICE,
        Washington, December 30, 1861.

*   *   *   *   *   *   *

JOINT RESOLUTION expressive of the recognition by Congress of the gallant and patriotic services of the late Brigadier-General Nathaniel Lyon and the officers and soldiers under his command at the battle of Springfield, Mo.

Resolved by the Senate and House of Representatives of the United States of America in Congress assembled, 1. That Congress deems it just and proper to enter upon its records a recognition of the eminent and patriotic services of the late Brigadier-General Nathaniel Lyon. The country to whose service he devoted his life will guard and preserve his fame as a part of its own glory.

2. That the thanks of Congress are hereby given to the brave officers and soldiers who, under the command of the late General Lyon, sustained the honor of the flag and achieved victory against overwhelming numbers at the battle of Springfield, in Missouri; and that, in order to commemorate an event so honorable to the country and to themselves, it is ordered that each regiment engaged shall be authorized to bear upon its colors the word "Springfield," embroidered in letters of gold. And the President of the United States is hereby requested to cause these resolutions to be read at the head of every regiment in the Army of the United States.

The President of the United States directs that the foregoing joint resolution be read at the head of every regiment in the Army of the United States.

By command of Major-General McClellan:

L. THOMAS,
Adjutant-General.

WAR DEPARTMENT, *January 22, 1862.*

The President, Commander in Chief of the Army and Navy, has received information of a brilliant victory by the United States forces over a large body of armed traitors and rebels at Mill Springs, in the State of Kentucky. He returns thanks to the gallant officers and soldiers who won that victory, and when the official reports shall be received the military and personal valor displayed in battle will be acknowledged and rewarded in a fitting manner.

The courage that encountered and vanquished the greatly superior numbers of the rebel force, pursued and attacked them in their intrenchments, and paused not until the enemy was completely routed merits and receives commendation.

The purpose of this war is to attack, pursue, and destroy a rebellious enemy and to deliver the country from danger menaced by traitors. Alacrity, daring, courageous spirit, and patriotic zeal on all occasions and under every circumstance are expected from the Army of the United States. In the prompt and spirited movements and daring battle of Mill Springs the nation will realize its hopes, and the people of the United States will rejoice to honor every soldier and officer who proves his courage by charging with the bayonet and storming intrenchments or in the blaze of the enemy's fire.

By order of the President:

EDWIN M. STANTON,
Secretary of War.

PRESIDENT'S GENERAL WAR ORDER NO. 1.

EXECUTIVE MANSION,
Washington, January 27, 1862.

Ordered, That the 22d day of February, 1862, be the day for a general movement of the land and naval forces of the United States against the insurgent forces; that especially the army at and about Fortress Monroe, the Army of the Potomac, the Army of Western Virginia, the army near Munfordville, Ky., the army and flotilla at Cairo, and a naval force in the Gulf of Mexico be ready to move on that day.

That all other forces, both land and naval, with their respective commanders, obey existing orders for the time and be ready to obey additional orders when duly given.

That the heads of Departments, and especially the Secretaries of War and of the Navy, with all their subordinates, and the General in Chief, with all other commanders and subordinates of land and naval forces, will severally be held to their strict and full responsibilities for prompt execution of this order.

ABRAHAM LINCOLN.

PRESIDENT'S SPECIAL WAR ORDER NO. 1.

EXECUTIVE MANSION,
Washington, January 31, 1862.

Ordered, That all the disposable force of the Army of the Potomac, after providing safely for the defense of Washington, be formed into an expedition for the immediate object of seizing and occupying a point upon the railroad southwestward of what is known as Manassas Junction; all details to be in the discretion of the General in Chief, and the expedition to move before or on the 22d day of February next.

A. LINCOLN.

WAR DEPARTMENT,
Washington City, February 11, 1862.

Ordered, That D. C. McCallum be, and he is hereby, appointed military director and superintendent of railroads in the United States, with authority to enter upon, take possession of, hold, and use all railroads, engines, cars, locomotives, equipments, appendages, and appurtenances that may be required for the transport of troops, arms, ammunition, and military supplies of the United States, and to do and perform all acts and things that may be necessary or proper to be done for the safe and speedy transport aforesaid.

By order of the President, Commander in Chief of the Army and Navy of the United States:

EDWIN M. STANTON,
Secretary of War.

WAR DEPARTMENT, *February 13, 1862.*

Ordered, 1. That all applications to go south across the military lines of the United States be made to Major-General John A. Dix, commanding at Baltimore, who will grant or refuse the same at his discretion.

2. That all prisoners of war and other persons imprisoned by authority of any department of the Government who shall be released on parole or exchange shall report themselves immediately on their arrival at Baltimore to Major-General Dix and be subject to his direction while remaining in that city. Any failure to observe this order will be taken as a forfeiture of the parole or exchange.

The regulation heretofore existing which required passes across the military lines of the United States to be signed by the Secretary of State and countersigned by the General Commanding is rescinded.

By order of the President:　　　　EDWIN M. STANTON,
　　　　　　　　　　　　　　　　　　Secretary of War.

EXECUTIVE ORDER NO. 1, RELATING TO POLITICAL PRISONERS.

WAR DEPARTMENT,
Washington, February 14, 1862.

The breaking out of a formidable insurrection based on a conflict of political ideas, being an event without precedent in the United States, was necessarily attended by great confusion and perplexity of the public mind. Disloyalty before unsuspected suddenly became bold, and treason astonished the world by bringing at once into the field military forces superior in number to the standing Army of the United States.

Every department of the Government was paralyzed by treason. Defection appeared in the Senate, in the House of Representatives, in the Cabinet, in the Federal courts; ministers and consuls returned from foreign countries to enter the insurrectionary councils or land or naval forces; commanding and other officers of the Army and in the Navy betrayed our councils or deserted their posts for commands in the insurgent forces. Treason was flagrant in the revenue and in the post-office service, as well as in the Territorial governments and in the Indian reserves.

Not only governors, judges, legislators, and ministerial officers in the States, but even whole States rushed one after another with apparent unanimity into rebellion. The capital was besieged and its connection with all the States cut off.

Even in the portions of the country which were most loyal political combinations and secret societies were formed furthering the work of disunion, while, from motives of disloyalty or cupidity or from excited passions or perverted sympathies, individuals were found furnishing men, money, and materials of war and supplies to the insurgents' military and naval forces. Armies, ships, fortifications, navy-yards, arsenals, military posts, and garrisons one after another were betrayed or abandoned to the insurgents.

Congress had not anticipated, and so had not provided for, the emergency. The municipal authorities were powerless and inactive. The judicial machinery seemed as if it had been designed, not to sustain the Government, but to embarrass and betray it.

Foreign intervention, openly invited and industriously instigated by the abettors of the insurrection, became imminent, and has only been prevented by the practice of strict and impartial justice, with the most perfect moderation, in our intercourse with nations.

The public mind was alarmed and apprehensive, though fortunately not distracted or disheartened. It seemed to be doubtful whether the Federal Government, which one year before had been thought a model worthy of universal acceptance, had indeed the ability to defend and maintain itself.

Some reverses, which, perhaps, were unavoidable, suffered by newly levied and inefficient forces, discouraged the loyal and gave new hopes to the insurgents. Voluntary enlistments seemed about to cease and desertions commenced. Parties speculated upon the question whether conscription had not become necessary to fill up the armies of the United States.

In this emergency the President felt it his duty to employ with energy the extraordinary powers which the Constitution confides to him in cases of insurrection. He called into the field such military and naval forces, unauthorized by the existing laws, as seemed necessary. He directed measures to prevent the use of the post-office for treasonable correspondence. He subjected passengers to and from foreign countries to new passport regulations, and he instituted a blockade, suspended the writ of *habeas corpus* in various places, and caused persons who were represented to him as being or about to engage in disloyal and treasonable practices to be arrested by special civil as well as military agencies and detained in military custody when necessary to prevent them and deter others from such practices. Examinations of such cases were instituted, and some of the persons so arrested have been discharged from time to time under circumstances or upon conditions compatible, as was thought, with the public safety.

Meantime a favorable change of public opinion has occurred. The line between loyalty and disloyalty is plainly defined. The whole structure of the Government is firm and stable. Apprehension of public danger and facilities for treasonable practices have diminished with the passions which prompted heedless persons to adopt them. The insurrection is believed to have culminated and to be declining.

The President, in view of these facts, and anxious to favor a return to the normal course of the Administration as far as regard for the public welfare will allow, directs that all political prisoners or state prisoners now held in military custody be released on their subscribing to a parole engaging them to render no aid or comfort to the enemies in hostility to the United States.

The Secretary of War will, however, in his discretion, except from the effect of this order any persons detained as spies in the service of the insurgents, or others whose release at the present moment may be deemed incompatible with the public safety.

To all persons who shall be so released and who shall keep their parole the President grants an amnesty for any past offenses of treason or disloyalty which they may have committed.

Extraordinary arrests will hereafter be made under the direction of the military authorities alone.

By order of the President:

EDWIN M. STANTON,
Secretary of War.

THE PRESIDENT'S THANKS TO THE FORCES THAT CAPTURED FORT HENRY AND ROANOKE ISLAND.

WASHINGTON CITY, D. C., *February 15, 1862.*

The President, Commander in Chief of the Army and Navy, returns thanks to Brigadier-General Burnside and Flag-Officer Goldsborough, and to Brigadier-General Grant and Flag-Officer Foote, and the land and naval forces under their respective commands, for their gallant achievements in the capture of Fort Henry and at Roanoke Island. While it will be no ordinary pleasure for him to acknowledge and reward in a becoming manner the valor of the living, he also recognizes his duty to pay fitting honor to the memory of the gallant dead. The charge at Roanoke Island, like the bayonet charge at Mill Springs, proves that the close grapple and sharp steel of loyal and patriotic soldiers must always put rebels and traitors to flight.

The late achievements of the Navy show that the flag of the Union, once borne in proud glory around the world by naval heroes, will soon again float over every rebel city and stronghold, and that it shall forever be honored and respected as the emblem of liberty and union in every land and upon every sea.

By order of the President:

EDWIN M. STANTON,
Secretary of War.

GIDEON WELLES,
Secretary of the Navy.

WAR DEPARTMENT,
Washington City, D. C., February 17, 1862.

Brigadier-General F. W. LANDER:

The President directs me to say that he has observed with pleasure the activity and enterprise manifested by yourself and the officers and soldiers of your command. You have shown how much may be done in the worst weather and worst roads by a spirited officer at the head of a small force of brave men, unwilling to waste life in camp when the enemies of their country are within reach. Your brilliant success is a happy presage of what may be expected when the Army of the Potomac shall be led to the field by their gallant general.

EDWIN M. STANTON,
Secretary of War.

GENERAL ORDERS, No. 16.

HEADQUARTERS OF THE ARMY,
ADJUTANT-GENERAL'S OFFICE,
Washington, February 18, 1862.

I. The following concurrent resolutions of the two Houses of the Congress of the United States are published for the information of the Army:

Resolved, That the two Houses will assemble in the Chamber of the House of Representatives on Saturday, the 22d day of February instant, at 12 o'clock meridian, and that in the presence of the two Houses of Congress thus assembled the Farewell Address of George Washington to the people of the United States shall be read; and that the President of the Senate and the Speaker of the House of Representatives be requested to invite the President of the United States, the heads of the several Departments, the judges of the Supreme Court, the representatives from all foreign governments near this Government, and such officers of the Army and Navy and distinguished citizens as may then be at the seat of Government to be present on that occasion.

Resolved, That the President of the United States, Commander in Chief of the Army and Navy, be requested to direct that orders be issued for the reading to the Army and Navy of the United States of the Farewell Address of George Washington, or such parts thereof as he may select, on the 22d day of February instant.

II. In compliance with the foregoing resolutions, the President of the United States, Commander in Chief of the Army and Navy, orders that the following extracts from the Farewell Address of George Washington be read to the troops at every military post and at the head of the several regiments and corps of the Army:

Interwoven as is the love of liberty with every ligament of your hearts, no recommendation of mine is necessary to fortify or confirm the attachment.

The unity of government which constitutes you one people is also now dear to you. It is justly so, for it is a main pillar in the edifice of your real independence, the support of your tranquillity at home, your peace abroad, of your safety, of your prosperity, of that very liberty which you so highly prize. But as it is easy to foresee that from different causes and from different quarters much pains will be taken, many artifices employed, to weaken in your minds the conviction of this truth, as this is the point in your political fortress against which the batteries of internal and external enemies will be most constantly and actively (though often covertly and insidiously) directed, it is of infinite moment that you should properly estimate the immense value of your national union to your collective and individual happiness; that you should cherish a cordial, habitual, and immovable attachment to it; accustoming yourselves to think and speak of it as of the palladium of your political safety and prosperity; watching for its preservation with jealous anxiety; discountenancing whatever may suggest even a suspicion that it can in any event be abandoned, and indignantly frowning upon the first dawning of every attempt to alienate any portion of our country from the rest or to enfeeble the sacred ties which now link together the various parts.

For this you have every inducement of sympathy and interest. Citizens by birth or choice of a common country, that country has a right to concentrate your affections. The name of American, which belongs to you in your national capacity, must always exalt the just pride of patriotism more than any appellation derived from local discriminations. With slight shades of difference, you have the same religion, manners, habits, and political principles. You have in a common cause fought and triumphed together. The independence and liberty you possess are the work of joint councils and joint efforts, of common dangers, sufferings, and successes.

*   *   *   *   *   *   *

While, then, every part of our country thus feels an immediate and particular interest in union, all the parts combined can not fail to find in the united mass of means and efforts greater strength, greater resource, proportionably greater security from external danger, a less frequent interruption of their peace by foreign nations, and, what is of inestimable value, they must derive from union an exemption from those broils and wars between themselves which so frequently afflict neighboring countries not tied together by the same governments, which their own rivalships alone would be sufficient to produce, but which opposite foreign alliances, attachments, and intrigues would stimulate and imbitter. Hence, likewise, they will avoid the necessity of those overgrown military establishments which, under any form of government, are inauspicious to liberty, and which are to be regarded as particularly hostile to republican liberty. In this sense it is that your union ought to be considered as a main prop of your liberty, and that the love of the one ought to endear to you the preservation of the other.

*   *   *   *   *   *   *

To the efficacy and permanency of your union a government for the whole is indispensable. No alliances, however strict, between the parts can be an adequate substitute. They must inevitably experience the infractions and interruptions which all alliances in all times have experienced. Sensible of this momentous truth, you have improved upon your first essay by the adoption of a Constitution of Government better calculated than your former for an intimate union and for the efficacious management of your common concerns. This Government, the offspring of our own choice, uninfluenced and unawed, adopted upon full investigation and mature deliberation, completely free in its principles, in the distribution of its powers, uniting security with energy, and containing within itself a provision for its own amendment, has a just claim to your confidence and your support. Respect for its authority, compliance with its laws, acquiescence in its measures, are duties enjoined by the fundamental maxims of true liberty. The basis of our political systems is the right of the people to make and to alter their constitutions of government. But the constitution which at any time exists till changed by an explicit and authentic act of the whole people is sacredly obligatory upon all. The very idea of the power and the right of the people to establish government presupposes the duty of every individual to obey the established government.

All obstructions to the execution of the laws, all combinations and associations, under whatever plausible character, with the real design to direct, control, counteract, or awe the regular deliberation and action of the constituted authorities, are destructive of this fundamental principle and of fatal tendency. They serve to organize faction; to give it an artificial and extraordinary force; to put in the place of the delegated will of the nation the will of a party, often a small but artful and enterprising minority of the community, and, according to the alternate triumphs of different parties. to make the public administration the mirror of the ill-concerted and incongruous projects of faction rather than the organ of consistent and wholesome plans, digested by common counsels and modified by mutual interests.

*   *   *   *   *   *   *

Of all the dispositions and habits which lead to political prosperity, religion and morality are indispensable supports. In vain would that man claim the tribute of patriotism who should labor to subvert these great pillars of human happiness—these firmest props of the duties of men and citizens. The mere politician, equally with the pious man, ought to respect and to cherish them. A volume could not trace all their connections with private and public felicity. Let it simply be asked, Where is the security for property, for reputation, for life, if the sense of religious obligation *desert* the oaths which are the instruments of investigation in courts of justice? And let us with caution indulge the supposition that morality can be maintained without religion. Whatever may be conceded to the influence of refined education on minds of peculiar structure, reason and experience both forbid us to expect that national morality can prevail in exclusion of religious principle.

It is substantially true that virtue or morality is a necessary spring of popular government. The rule indeed extends with more or less force to every species of free government. Who that is a sincere friend to it can look with indifference upon attempts to shake the foundation of the fabric? Promote, then, as an object of primary importance, institutions for the general diffusion of knowledge. In proportion as the structure of a government gives force to public opinion, it is essential that public opinion should be enlightened.

   *   *   *   *   *   *   *

Observe good faith and justice toward all nations. Cultivate peace and harmony with all. Religion and morality enjoin this conduct. And can it be that good policy does not equally enjoin it? It will be worthy of a free, enlightened, and at no distant period a great nation to give to mankind the magnanimous and too novel example of a people always guided by an exalted justice and benevolence? Who can doubt that in the course of time and things the fruits of such a plan would richly repay any temporary advantages which might be lost by a steady adherence to it? Can it be that Providence has not connected the permanent felicity of a nation with its virtue? The experiment, at least, is recommended by every sentiment which ennobles human nature. Alas! is it rendered impossible by its vices?

   *   *   *   *   *   *   *

Harmony, liberal intercourse with all nations, are recommended by policy, humanity, and interest. But even our commercial policy should hold an equal and impartial hand, neither seeking nor granting exclusive favors or preferences; consulting the natural course of things; diffusing and diversifying by gentle means the streams of commerce, but forcing nothing; establishing with powers so disposed, in order to give trade a stable course, to define the rights of our merchants, and to enable the Government to support them, conventional rules of intercourse, the best that present circumstances and mutual opinion will permit, but temporary and liable to be from time to time abandoned or varied as experience and circumstances shall dictate; constantly keeping in view that it is folly in one nation to look for disinterested favors from another; that it must pay with a portion of its independence for whatever it may accept under that character; that by such acceptance it may place itself in the condition of having given equivalents for nominal favors, and yet of being reproached with ingratitude for not giving more. There can be no greater error than to expect or calculate upon real favors from nation to nation. It is an illusion which experience must cure, which a just pride ought to discard.

In offering to you, my countrymen, these counsels of an old and affectionate friend I dare not hope they will make the strong and lasting impression I could wish—that they will control the usual current of the passions or prevent our nation from running the course which has hitherto marked the destiny of nations. But if I may even flatter myself that they may be productive of some partial benefit, some occasional good—that they may now and then recur to moderate the fury of party spirit, to warn against the mischiefs of foreign intrigue, to guard against the impostures of pretended patriotism—this hope will be a full recompense for the solicitude for your welfare by which they have been dictated.

*　　*　　*　　*　　*　　*　　*

Though in reviewing the incidents of my Administration I am unconscious of intentional error, I am nevertheless too sensible of my defects not to think it probable that I may have committed many errors. Whatever they may be, I fervently beseech the Almighty to avert or mitigate the evils to which they may tend. I shall also carry with me the hope that my country will never cease to view them with indulgence, and that, after forty-five years of my life dedicated to its service with an upright zeal, the faults of incompetent abilities will be consigned to oblivion, as myself must soon be to the mansions of rest.

Relying on its kindness in this as in other things, and actuated by that fervent love toward it which is so natural to a man who views in it the native soil of himself and his progenitors for several generations, I anticipate with pleasing expectation that retreat in which I promise myself to realize without alloy the sweet enjoyment of partaking in the midst of my fellow-citizens the benign influence of good laws under a free government—the ever-favorite object of my heart, and the happy reward, as I trust, of our mutual cares, labors, and dangers.

By command of Major-General McClellan:

L. THOMAS,
Adjutant-General.

WAR DEPARTMENT,
Washington City, D. C., February 18, 1862.

Ordered by the President, Commander in Chief of the Army and Navy of the United States, That on the 22d day of February, in the Hall of the House of Representatives, immediately after the Farewell Address of George Washington shall have been read, the rebel flags lately captured by the United States forces shall be presented to Congress by the Adjutant-General, to be disposed of as Congress may direct.

By order of the President:

EDWIN M. STANTON,
Secretary of War.

WAR DEPARTMENT,
Washington City, February 25, 1862.

Ordered, first. On and after the 26th day of February instant the President, by virtue of the act of Congress, takes military possession of all the telegraph lines in the United States.

Second. All telegraphic communications in regard to military operations not expressly authorized by the War Department, the General Commanding, or the generals commanding armies in the field, in the several departments, are absolutely forbidden.

Third. All newspapers publishing military news, however obtained and by whatever medium received, not authorized by the official authority mentioned in the preceding paragraph will be excluded thereafter from receiving information by telegraph or from transmitting their papers by railroad.

Fourth. Edward S. Sanford is made military supervisor of telegraphic messages throughout the United States. Anson Stager is made military superintendent of all telegraph lines and offices in the United States.

Fifth. This possession and control of the telegraph lines is not intended to interfere in any respect with the ordinary affairs of the companies or with private business.

By order of the President:

EDWIN M. STANTON,
Secretary of War.

WAR DEPARTMENT,
Washington, February 27, 1862.

It is ordered, first. That a special commission of two persons, one of military rank and the other in civil life, be appointed to examine the cases of the state prisoners remaining in the military custody of the United States, and to determine whether, in view of the public safety and the existing rebellion, they should be discharged or remain in military custody or be remitted to the civil tribunals for trial.

Second. That Major-General John A. Dix, commanding in Baltimore, and the Hon. Edwards Pierrepont, of New York, be, and they are hereby, appointed commissioners for the purposes above mentioned, and they are authorized to examine, hear, and determine the cases aforesaid, *ex parte* and in a summary manner, at such times and places as in their discretion they may appoint, and make full report to the War Department.

By order of the President:

EDWIN M. STANTON,
Secretary of War.

BY THE PRESIDENT OF THE UNITED STATES.

WASHINGTON, *February 28, 1862.*

Considering that the existing circumstances of the country allow a partial restoration of commercial intercourse between the inhabitants of those parts of the United States heretofore declared to be in insurrection and the citizens of the loyal States of the Union, and exercising the authority and discretion confided to me by the act of Congress approved July 13, 1861, entitled "An act further to provide for the collection of duties on imports, and for other purposes," I hereby license and permit such commercial intercourse in all cases within the rules and regulations which have been or may be prescribed by the Secretary of the Treasury for the conducting and carrying on of the same on the inland waters and ways of the United States.

ABRAHAM LINCOLN.

PRESIDENT'S GENERAL WAR ORDER NO. 2.

EXECUTIVE MANSION,
Washington, March 8, 1862.

Ordered, 1. That the major-general commanding the Army of the Potomac proceed forthwith to organize that part of the said army destined to enter upon active operations (including the reserve, but excluding the troops to be left in the fortifications about Washington) into four army corps, to be commanded according to seniority of rank, as follows:

First Corps to consist of four divisions, and to be commanded by Major-General I. McDowell.

Second Corps to consist of three divisions, and to be commanded by Brigadier-General E. V. Sumner.

Third Corps to consist of three divisions, and to be commanded by Brigadier-General S. P. Heintzelman.

Fourth Corps to consist of three divisions, and to be commanded by Brigadier-General E. D. Keyes.

2. That the divisions now commanded by the officers above assigned to the commands of army corps shall be embraced in and form part of their respective corps.

3. The forces left for the defense of Washington will be placed in command of Brigadier-General James S. Wadsworth, who shall also be military governor of the District of Columbia.

4. That this order be executed with such promptness and dispatch as not to delay the commencement of the operations already directed to be undertaken by the Army of the Potomac.

5. A fifth army corps, to be commanded by Major-General N. P. Banks, will be formed from his own and General Shields's (late General Lander's) divisions.

ABRAHAM LINCOLN.

PRESIDENT'S GENERAL WAR ORDER NO. 3.

EXECUTIVE MANSION,
Washington, March 8, 1862.

Ordered, That no change of the base of operations of the Army of the Potomac shall be made without leaving in and about Washington such a force as in the opinion of the General in Chief and the commanders of all the army corps shall leave said city entirely secure.

That no more than two army corps (about 50,000 troops) of said Army of the Potomac shall be moved *en route* for a new base of operations until the navigation of the Potomac from Washington to the Chesapeake Bay shall be freed from enemy's batteries and other obstructions, or until the President shall hereafter give express permission.

That any movements as aforesaid *en route* for a new base of operations which may be ordered by the General in Chief, and which may be intended to move upon the Chesapeake Bay, shall begin to move upon the bay as early as the 18th day of March instant, and the General in Chief shall be responsible that it so move as early as that day.

Ordered, That the Army and Navy cooperate in an immediate effort to capture the enemy's batteries upon the Potomac between Washington and the Chesapeake Bay.

A. LINCOLN.

PRESIDENT'S SPECIAL WAR ORDER No. 3.

EXECUTIVE MANSION,
Washington, March 11, 1862.

Major-General McClellan having personally taken the field at the head of the Army of the Potomac, until otherwise ordered he is relieved from the command of the other military departments, he retaining command of the Department of the Potomac.

Ordered further, That the departments now under the respective commands of Generals Halleck and Hunter, together with so much of that under General Buell as lies west of a north and south line indefinitely drawn through Knoxville, Tenn., be consolidated and designated the Department of the Mississippi, and that until otherwise ordered Major-General Halleck have command of said department.

Ordered also, That the country west of the Department of the Potomac and east of the Department of the Mississippi be a military department, to be called the Mountain Department, and that the same be commanded by Major-General Frémont.

That all the commanders of departments, after the receipt of this order by them, respectively report severally and directly to the Secretary of War, and that prompt, full, and frequent reports will be expected of all and each of them.

ABRAHAM LINCOLN

WAR DEPARTMENT, *March 13, 1862.*
Major-General GEORGE B. McCLELLAN:

The President, having considered the plan of operations agreed upon by yourself and the commanders of army corps, makes no objection to the same, but gives the following directions as to its execution:

1. Leave such force at Manassas Junction as shall make it entirely certain that the enemy shall not repossess himself of that position and line of communication.

2. Leave Washington entirely secure.

3. Move the remainder of the force down the Potomac, choosing a new base at Fortress Monroe, or anywhere between here and there, or, at all events, move such remainder of the army at once in pursuit of the enemy by some route.

EDWIN M. STANTON, *Secretary of War.*

[From the Daily National Intelligencer, March 28, 1862.]

NAVY DEPARTMENT, *March 15, 1862.*

Lieutenant JOHN L. WORDEN, United States Navy,
Commanding United States Steamer Monitor, Washington.

SIR: The naval action which took place on the 10th instant between the *Monitor* and *Merrimac* at Hampton Roads, when your vessel, with two guns, engaged a powerful armored steamer of at least eight guns, and after a few hours' conflict repelled her formidable antagonist, has excited general admiration and received the applause of the whole country.

The President directs me, while earnestly and deeply sympathizing with you in the injuries which you have sustained, but which it is believed are but temporary, to thank you and your command for the heroism you have displayed and the great service you have rendered.

The action of the 10th and the performance, power, and capabilities of the *Monitor* must effect a radical change in naval warfare.

Flag-Officer Goldsborough, in your absence, will be furnished by the Department with a copy of this letter of thanks and instructed to cause it to be read to the officers and crew of the *Monitor.*

I am, very respectfully, your obedient servant,

GIDEON WELLES.

WAR DEPARTMENT,
Washington, D. C., April 5, 1862.

Major-General JOHN A. DIX:

Ordered, That Major-General John A. Dix, commanding at Baltimore, be, and he is, authorized and empowered at his discretion—

First. To assume and exercise control over the police of the city of Baltimore; to supersede and remove the civil police or any part thereof and establish a military police in said city.

Second. To arrest and imprison disloyal persons, declare martial law, and suspend the writ of *habeas corpus* in the city of Baltimore or any part of his command, and to exercise and perform all military power, function, and authority that he may deem proper for the safety of his command or to secure obedience and respect to the authority and Government of the United States.

By order of the President:

EDWIN M. STANTON,
Secretary of War.

[From the Daily National Intelligencer, May 17, 1862.]

The skillful and gallant movements of Major-General John E. Wool and the forces under his command, which resulted in the surrender of Norfolk and the evacuation of strong batteries erected by the rebels on Sewells

Point and Craney Island and the destruction of the rebel ironclad steamer *Merrimac*, are regarded by the President as among the most important successes of the present war. He therefore orders that his thanks as Commander in Chief of the Army and Navy be communicated by the War Department to Major-General John E. Wool and the officers and soldiers of his command for their gallantry and good conduct in the brilliant operations mentioned.

By order of the President, made at the city of Norfolk on the 11th day of May, 1862:

EDWIN M. STANTON,
Secretary of War.

WAR DEPARTMENT, *May 25, 1862.*

Ordered: By virtue of the authority vested by act of Congress, the President takes military possession of all the railroads in the United States from and after this date until further order, and directs that the respective railroad companies, their officers and servants, shall hold themselves in readiness for the transportation of such troops and munitions of war as may be ordered by the military authorities, to the exclusion of all other business.

By order of the Secretary of War:

M. C. MEIGS,
Quartermaster-General.

WAR DEPARTMENT,
Washington, D. C., May 28, 1862.

Colonel HAUPT.

SIR: You are hereby appointed chief of construction and transportation in the Department of the Rappahannock, with the rank of colonel, and attached to the staff of Major-General McDowell.

You are authorized to do whatever you may deem expedient to open for use in the shortest possible time all military railroads now or hereafter required in said department; to use the same for transportation under such rules and regulations as you may prescribe; to appoint such assistants and employees as you may deem necessary, define their duties and fix their compensation; to make requisitions upon any of the military authorities, with the approval of the Commanding General, for such temporary or permanent details of men as may be required for the construction or protection of lines of communication; to use such Government steamers and transports as you may deem necessary; to pass free of charge in such steamers and transports and on other military roads all persons whose services may be required in construction or transportation; to purchase all such machinery, rolling stock, and supplies as the proper use and operation of the said railroads may require, and certify the same to the Quartermaster-General, who shall make payment therefor. You are also authorized to form a permanent corps of artificers, organized, officered, and equipped in such manner as you may prescribe; to supply said corps with rations, transportation, tools, and implements by requisitions upon the proper departments; to employ civilians as foremen and assistants, under such rules and rates of compensation as you may deem expedient; to make such additions to ordinary rations when actually at work as you may deem necessary.

You are also authorized to take possession of and use all railroads, engines, cars, buildings, machinery, and appurtenances within the geographical limits of the Department of the Rappahannock, and all authority heretofore given to other parties which may in any way conflict with the instructions herein contained are and will be without force and effect in the said Department of the Rappahannock from and after this date.

By order of the President, Commander in Chief of the Army and Navy of the United States:

EDWIN M. STANTON,
Secretary of War.

WAR DEPARTMENT,
Washington City, D. C., May 30, 1862.

All regiments of militia or of three-months' volunteers who have offered their services under the recent call of the War Department, and who have so far perfected their organization as to be able to report for orders at St. Louis, at Columbus, or at Washington City by the 10th of June, will be mustered into the service of the United States for three months from that date, the pay of each volunteer or militiaman commencing from the date of his enlistment.

Under the call for three-years' volunteers 50,000 men will be accepted as raised and reported by the respective State governors.

By order of the President:

EDWIN M. STANTON,
Secretary of War.

NEW YORK, *June 30, 1862.*

To the Governors of the several States:

The capture of New Orleans, Norfolk, and Corinth by the national forces has enabled the insurgents to concentrate a large force at and about Richmond, which place we must take with the least possible delay; in fact, there will soon be no formidable insurgent force except at Richmond. With so large an army there, the enemy can threaten us on the Potomac and elsewhere. Until we have reestablished the national authority, all these places must be held, and we must keep a respectable force in front of Washington. But this, from the diminished strength of our Army by sickness and casualties, renders an addition to it necessary in order to close the struggle which has been prosecuted for the last three months with energy and success. Rather than hazard the misapprehension of our military condition and of groundless alarm by a call for troops by proclamation, I have deemed it best to address you in this form. To accomplish the object stated we require without delay 150,000 men, including those recently called for by the Secretary of War. Thus reenforced our gallant Army will be enabled to realize the hopes and expectations of the Government and the people.

ABRAHAM LINCOLN.

The PRESIDENT: JUNE 28, 1862.

The undersigned, governors of States of the Union, impressed with the belief that the citizens of the States which they respectively represent are of one accord in the hearty desire that the recent successes of the Federal arms may be followed up by measures which must insure the speedy restoration of the Union, and believing that, in view of the present state of the important military movements now in progress and the reduced condition of our effective forces in the field, resulting from the usual and unavoidable casualties in the service, the time has arrived for prompt and vigorous measures to be adopted by the people in support of the great interests committed to your charge, respectfully request, if it meets with your entire approval, that you at once call upon the several States for such number of men as may be required to fill up all military organizations now in the field, and add to the armies heretofore organized such additional number of men as may, in your judgment, be necessary to garrison and hold all the numerous cities and military positions that have been captured by our armies, and to speedily crush the rebellion that still exists in several of the Southern States, thus practically restoring to the civilized world our great and good Government. All believe that the decisive moment is near at hand, and to that end the people of the United States are desirous to aid promptly in furnishing all reenforcements that you may deem needful to sustain our Government.

ISRAEL WASHBURN, Jr., Governor of Maine; H. S. BERRY, Governor of New Hampshire; FREDERICK HOLBROOK, Governor of Vermont; WILLIAM A. BUCKINGHAM, Governor of Connecticut; E. D. MORGAN, Governor of New York; CHARLES S. OLDEN, Governor of New Jersey; A. G. CURTIN, Governor of Pennsylvania; A. W. BRADFORD, Governor of Maryland; F. H. PEIRPOINT, Governor of Virginia; AUSTIN BLAIR, Governor of Michigan; J. B. TEMPLE, President Military Board of Kentucky; ANDREW JOHNSON, Governor of Tennessee; H. R. GAMBLE, Governor of Missouri; O. P. MORTON, Governor of Indiana; DAVID TODD, Governor of Ohio; ALEXANDER RAMSEY, Governor of Minnesota; RICHARD YATES, Governor of Illinois; EDWARD SALOMON, Governor of Wisconsin.

EXECUTIVE MANSION,
Washington, July 1, 1862.

GENTLEMEN: Fully concurring in the wisdom of the views expressed to me in so patriotic a manner by you in the communication of the 28th day of June, I have decided to call into the service an additional force of 300,000 men. I suggest and recommend that the troops should be chiefly of infantry. The quota of your State would be ———. I trust that they may be enrolled without delay, so as to bring this unnecessary and injurious civil war to a speedy and satisfactory conclusion. An order fixing the quotas of the respective States will be issued by the War Department to-morrow.

ABRAHAM LINCOLN.

EXECUTIVE MANSION,
Washington, July 11, 1862.

Ordered, That Major-General Henry W. Halleck be assigned to command the whole land forces of the United States as General in Chief, and that he repair to this capital as soon as he can with safety to the positions and operations within the department under his charge.

A. LINCOLN.

Whereas, in the judgment of the President, the public safety does require that the railroad line called and known as the Southwest Branch of the Pacific Railroad in the State of Missouri be repaired, extended, and completed from Rolla to Lebanon, in the direction to Springfield, in the said State, the same being necessary to the successful and economical conduct of the war and to the maintenance of the authority of the Government in the Southwest:

Therefore, under and in virtue of the act of Congress entitled "An act to authorize the President of the United States in certain cases to take possession of railroad and telegraph lines, and for other purposes," approved January 31, 1862, it is—

Ordered, That the portion of the said railroad line which reaches from Rolla to Lebanon be repaired, extended, and completed, so as to be made available for the military uses of the Government, as speedily as may be. And inasmuch as, upon the part of the said line from Rolla to the stream called Little Piney a considerable portion of the necessary work has already been done by the railroad company, and the road to this extent may be completed at comparatively small cost, it is ordered that the said line from Rolla to and across Little Piney be first completed, and as soon as possible.

The Secretary of War is charged with the execution of this order. And to facilitate the speedy execution of the work, he is directed, at his discretion, to take possession and control of the whole or such part of the said railroad line, and the whole or such part of the rolling stock, offices, shops, buildings, and all their appendages and appurtenances, as he may judge necessary or convenient for the early completion of the road from Rolla to Lebanon.

Done at the city of Washington, July 11, 1862.

ABRAHAM LINCOLN

GENERAL ORDERS, NO. 82.

WAR DEPARTMENT,
ADJUTANT-GENERAL'S OFFICE,
Washington, July 21, 1862.

The following order has been received from the President of the United States:

Representations have been made to the President by the ministers of various foreign powers in amity with the United States that subjects of such powers have during the present insurrection been obliged or required by military authorities to take an oath of general or qualified allegiance to this Government. It is the duty of all aliens residing in the United States to submit to and obey the laws and respect the authority of the Government. For any proceeding or conduct inconsistent with this obligation and subversive of that authority they may rightfully be subjected to military restraints when this may be necessary. But they can not be required to take an oath of allegiance to this Government, because it conflicts with the duty they owe to their own sovereigns. All such obligations heretofore taken are therefore remitted and annulled. Military commanders will abstain from imposing similar obligations in future, and will in lieu thereof adopt such other restraints of the character indicated as they shall find necessary, convenient, and effectual for the public safety. It is further directed that whenever any order shall be made affecting the personal liberty of an alien reports of the same and of the causes thereof shall be made to the War Department for the consideration of the Department of State.

By order of the Secretary of War:

L. THOMAS,
Adjutant-General.

WAR DEPARTMENT, *July 22, 1862.*

1. *Ordered,* That military commanders within the States of Virginia, South Carolina, Georgia, Florida, Alabama, Mississippi, Louisiana, Texas, and Arkansas in an orderly manner seize and use any property, real or personal, which may be necessary or convenient for their several commands as supplies or for other military purposes; and that while property may be destroyed for proper military objects, none shall be destroyed in wantonness or malice.

2. That military and naval commanders shall employ as laborers within and from said States so many persons of African descent as can be advantageously used for military or naval purposes, giving them reasonable wages for their labor.

3. That as to both property and persons of African descent accounts shall be kept sufficiently accurate and in detail to show quantities and amounts and from whom both property and such persons shall have

come, as a basis upon which compensation can be made in proper cases; and the several Departments of this Government shall attend to and perform their appropriate parts toward the execution of these orders.

By order of the President:
EDWIN M. STANTON,
Secretary of War.

GENERAL ORDERS, No. 89.

WAR DEPARTMENT,
ADJUTANT-GENERAL'S OFFICE,
Washington, July 25, 1862.

I. The following order of the President of the United States communicates information of the death of ex-President Martin Van Buren:

WASHINGTON, *July 25, 1862.*

The President with deep regret announces to the people of the United States the decease, at Kinderhook, N. Y., on the 24th instant, of his honored predecessor Martin Van Buren.

This event will occasion mourning in the nation for the loss of a citizen and a public servant whose memory will be gratefully cherished. Although it has occurred at a time when his country is afflicted with division and civil war, the grief of his patriotic friends will measurably be assuaged by the consciousness that while suffering with disease and seeing his end approaching his prayers were for the restoration of the authority of the Government of which he had been the head and for peace and good will among his fellow-citizens.

As a mark of respect for his memory, it is ordered that the Executive Mansion and the several Executive Departments, except those of War and the Navy, be immediately placed in mourning and all business be suspended during to-morrow.

It is further ordered that the War and Navy Departments cause suitable military and naval honors to be paid on this occasion to the memory of the illustrious dead.

ABRAHAM LINCOLN.

II. On the day after the receipt of this order the troops will be paraded at 10 o'clock a. m. and the order read to them. The national flag will be displayed at half-staff. At dawn of day thirteen guns will be fired, and afterwards at intervals of thirty minutes between rising and setting sun a single gun, and at the close of the day a national salute of thirty-four guns. The officers of the Army will wear crape on the left arm and on their swords and the colors of the several regiments will be put in mourning for the period of six months.

By order of the Secretary of War:
L. THOMAS,
Adjutant-General.

GENERAL ORDER.

NAVY DEPARTMENT, *July 25, 1862.*

The death of ex-President Martin Van Buren is announced in the following order of the President of the United States:

[For order see preceding page.]

In pursuance of the foregoing order, it is hereby directed that thirty minute guns, commencing at noon, be fired on the day after the receipt of this general order at the navy-yards, naval stations, and on board the vessels of the Navy in commission; that their flags be displayed at half-mast for one week, and that crape be worn on the left arm by all officers of the Navy for a period of six months.

GIDEON WELLES, *Secretary of the Navy.*

WAR DEPARTMENT,
Washington City, D. C., July 31, 1862.

The absence of officers and privates from their duty under various pretexts while receiving pay, at great expense and burden to the Government, makes it necessary that efficient measures be taken to enforce their return to duty or that their places be supplied by those who will not take pay while rendering no service. This evil, moreover, tends greatly to discourage the patriotic impulses of those who would contribute to support the families of faithful soldiers.

It is therefore ordered by the President—

I. That on Monday, the 11th day of August, all leaves of absence and furloughs, by whomsoever given, unless by the War Department, are revoked and absolutely annulled, and all officers capable of service are required forthwith to join their respective commands and all privates capable of service to join their regiments, under penalty of a dismissal from the service, or such penalty as a court-martial may award, unless the absence be occasioned by lawful cause.

II. The only excuses allowed for the absence of officers or privates after the 11th day of August are:

First. The order or leave of the War Department.

Second. Disability from wounds received in service.

Third. Disability from disease that renders the party unfit for military duty. But any officer or private whose health permits him to visit watering places or places of amusement, or to make social visits or walk about the town, city, or neighborhood in which he may be, will be considered fit for military duty and as evading duty by absence from his command or ranks.

III. On Monday, the 18th day of August, at 10 o'clock a. m., each regiment and corps shall be mustered. The absentees will be marked, three lists of the same made out, and within forty-eight hours after the muster one copy shall be sent to the Adjutant-General of the Army, one to the commander of the corps, the third to be retained; and all officers and privates fit for duty absent at that time will be regarded as absent without cause, their pay will be stopped, and they dismissed from the service or treated as deserters unless restored; and no officer shall be restored to his rank unless by the judgment of a court of inquiry, to be approved by the President, he shall establish that his absence was with good cause.

IV. Commanders of corps, divisions, brigades, regiments, and detached posts are strictly enjoined to enforce the muster and return aforesaid. Any officer failing in his duty herein will be deemed guilty of gross neglect of duty and be dismissed from the service.

V. A commissioner shall be appointed by the Secretary of War to superintend the execution of this order in the respective States.

The United States marshals in the respective districts, the mayor and chief of police of any town or city, the sheriff of the respective counties in each State, all postmasters and justices of the peace, are authorized to act as special provost-marshals to arrest any officer or private soldier fit for duty who may be found absent from his command without just cause and convey him to the nearest military post or depot. The transportation, reasonable expenses of this duty, and $5 will be paid for each officer or private so arrested and delivered.

By order of the President:

            E. M. STANTON, *Secretary of War.*

                WAR DEPARTMENT,
        Washington City, D. C., August 4, 1862.

Ordered, I. That a draft of 300,000 militia be immediately called into the service of the United States, to serve for nine months unless sooner discharged. The Secretary of War will assign the quotas to the States and establish regulations for the draft.

II. That if any State shall not by the 15th of August furnish its quota of the additional 300,000 volunteers authorized by law the deficiency of volunteers in that State will also be made up by special draft from the militia. The Secretary of War will establish regulations for this purpose.

III. Regulations will be prepared by the War Department and presented to the President with the object of securing the promotion of officers of the Army and Volunteers for meritorious and distinguished services and of preventing the nomination or appointment in the military service of incompetent or unworthy officers. The regulations will also provide for ridding the service of such incompetent persons as now hold commissions in it.

By order of the President:

            EDWIN M. STANTON, *Secretary of War.*

WAR DEPARTMENT,
Washington, D. C., August 8, 1862.

By direction of the President of the United States, it is hereby ordered that until further order no citizen liable to be drafted into the militia shall be allowed to go to a foreign country. And all marshals, deputy marshals, and military officers of the United States are directed, and all police authorities, especially at the ports of the United States on the seaboard and on the frontier, are requested, to see that this order is faithfully carried into effect. And they are hereby authorized and directed to arrest and detain any person or persons about to depart from the United States in violation of this order, and report to Major L. C. Turner, judge-advocate at Washington City, for further instructions respecting the person or persons so arrested or detained.

II. Any person liable to draft who shall absent himself from his county or State before such draft is made will be arrested by any provost-marshal or other United States or State officer, wherever he may be found within the jurisdiction of the United States, and be conveyed to the nearest military post or depot and placed on military duty for the term of the draft; and the expenses of his own arrest and conveyance to such post or depot, and also the sum of $5, as a reward to the officer who shall make such arrest, shall be deducted from his pay.

III. The writ of *habeas corpus* is hereby suspended in respect to all persons so arrested and detained, and in respect to all persons arrested for disloyal practices.

EDWIN M. STANTON,
Secretary of War.

WAR DEPARTMENT,
Washington City, D. C., August 14, 1862.

ORDER RESPECTING VOLUNTEERS AND MILITIA.

Ordered, first. That after the 15th of this month bounty and advanced pay shall not be paid to volunteers for any new regiments, but only to volunteers for regiments now in the field and volunteers to fill up new regiments now organizing, but not yet full.

Second. Volunteers to fill up new regiments now organizing will be received and paid the bounty and advanced pay until the 22d day of this month, and if not completed by that time the incomplete regiments will be consolidated and superfluous officers mustered out.

Third. Volunteers to fill up the old regiments will be received and paid the bounty and advanced pay until the 1st day of September.

Fourth. The draft for 300,000 militia called for by the President will be made on Wednesday, the 3d day of September, between the hours of 9 a. m. and 5 p. m., and continue from day to day between the same hours until completed.

Fifth. If the old regiments should not be filled up by volunteers before the 1st day of September, a special draft will be ordered for the deficiency.

Sixth. The exigencies of the service require that officers now in the field should remain with their commands, and no officer now in the field in the regular or volunteer service will under any circumstances be detailed to accept a new command.

By order of the President:

EDWIN M. STANTON,
Secretary of War.

SPECIAL ORDERS, No. 218.

HEADQUARTERS OF THE ARMY,
ADJUTANT-GENERAL'S OFFICE,
Washington, September 2, 1862.

* * * * * * *

By direction of the President, all the clerks and employees of the civil Departments and all the employees on the public buildings in Washington will be immediately organized into companies, under the direction of Brigadier-General Wadsworth, and will be armed and supplied with ammunition, for the defense of the capital.

By command of Major-General Halleck:

E. D. TOWNSEND,
Assistant Adjutant-General.

EXECUTIVE ORDER ESTABLISHING A PROVISIONAL COURT IN LOUISIANA.

EXECUTIVE MANSION,
Washington City, October 20, 1862.

The insurrection which has for some time prevailed in several of the States of this Union, including Louisiana, having temporarily subverted and swept away the civil institutions of that State, including the judiciary and the judicial authorities of the Union, so that it has become necessary to hold the State in military occupation, and it being indispensably necessary that there shall be some judicial tribunal existing there capable of administering justice, I have therefore thought it proper to appoint, and I do hereby constitute, a provisional court, which shall be a court of record, for the State of Louisiana; and I do hereby appoint Charles A. Peabody, of New York, to be a provisional judge to hold said court, with authority to hear, try, and determine all causes, civil and criminal, including causes in law, equity, revenue, and admiralty, and particularly all such powers and jurisdiction as belong to the district and circuit courts of the United States, conforming his proceedings so far as possible to the course of proceedings and practice which has been customary in the courts of the United States and Louisiana, his judgment to be final and conclusive. And I do hereby authorize and empower the said judge to make and establish such rules and regulations as may be necessary for the exercise of his jurisdiction, and empower the said judge to appoint a prosecuting attorney, marshal, and clerk of the said court, who shall perform the functions of attorney, marshal, and clerk according to such proceedings and practice as before mentioned and such rules and regulations as may be made and established by said judge. These appointments are to continue during the pleasure of the President, not extending beyond the military occupation of the city of New Orleans or the restoration of the civil authority in that city and in the State of Louisiana. These officers shall be paid, out of the contingent fund of the War Department, compensation as follows: The judge at the rate of $3,500 per annum; the prosecuting attorney, including the fees, at the rate of $3,000 per annum; the marshal, including the fees, at the rate of $3,000 per annum; and the clerk, including the fees, at the rate of $2,500 per annum; such compensations to be certified by the Secretary of War. A copy of this order, certified by the Secretary of War and delivered to such judge, shall be deemed and held to be a sufficient commission.

ABRAHAM LINCOLN,
President of the United States.

EXECUTIVE MANSION,
Washington, October 29, 1862.

Two associate justices of the Supreme Court of the United States having been appointed since the last adjournment of said court, and consequently no allotment of the members of said court to the several circuits having been made by them, according to the fifth section of the act of Congress entitled "An act to amend the judicial system of the United States," approved April 29, 1802, I, Abraham Lincoln, President of the United States, in virtue of said section, do make an allotment of the justices of said court to the circuits now existing by law, as follows:

For the first circuit: Nathan Clifford, associate justice.
For the second circuit: Samuel Nelson, associate justice.
For the third circuit: Robert C. Grier, associate justice.
For the fourth circuit: Roger B. Taney, Chief Justice.
For the fifth circuit: James M. Wayne, associate justice.
For the sixth circuit: John Catron, associate justice.
For the seventh circuit: Noah H. Swayne, associate justice.
For the eighth circuit: David Davis, associate justice.
For the ninth circuit: Samuel F. Miller, associate justice.

ABRAHAM LINCOLN.

EXECUTIVE MANSION,
Washington, November 5, 1862.

By direction of the President, it is ordered that Major-General Mc-
Clellan be relieved from the command of the Army of the Potomac, and
that Major-General Burnside take the command of that army; also that
Major-General Hunter take command of the corps in said army which
is now commanded by General Burnside; that Major-General Fitz John
Porter be relieved from the command of the corps he now commands in
said army, and that Major-General Hooker take command of said corps.

The General in Chief is authorized, in [his] discretion, to issue an order
substantially as the above forthwith, or so soon as he may deem proper.

A. LINCOLN.

EXECUTIVE MANSION, *November 7, 1862.*

Ordered, That Brigadier-General Ellet report to Rear-Admiral Porter
for instructions, and act under his direction until otherwise ordered by
the War Department.

ABRAHAM LINCOLN.

EXECUTIVE MANSION,
Washington, November 12, 1862.

Ordered, first. That clearances issued by the Treasury Department for
vessels or merchandise bound for the port of Norfolk for the military
necessities of the department, certified by the military commandant at
Fort Monroe, shall be allowed to enter said port.

Second. That vessels and domestic produce from Norfolk, permitted
by the military commandant at Fort Monroe for the military purposes of
his command, shall on his permit be allowed to pass from said port to
their destination in any port not blockaded by the United States.

A. LINCOLN.

[From the Daily National Intelligencer, November 25, 1862.]

EXECUTIVE MANSION, *November 13, 1862.*

Ordered by the President of the United States, That the Attorney-General be charged with the superintendence and direction of all proceedings
to be had under the act of Congress of the 17th of July, 1862, entitled
"An act to suppress insurrection, to punish treason and rebellion, to
seize and confiscate the property of rebels, and for other purposes," in
so far as may concern the seizure, prosecution, and condemnation of the
estate, property, and effects of rebels and traitors, as mentioned and provided for in the fifth, sixth, and seventh sections of the said act of Congress. And the Attorney-General is authorized and required to give to
the attorneys and marshals of the United States such instructions and

THE IRON-CLAD MERRIMAC DESTROYING THE CUMBERLAND

THE MONITOR AND THE MERRIMAC

THE *MERRIMAC* AND THE *MONITOR*.

The Confederates, who had their share of able naval officers, raised the United States frigate *Merrimac,* which had been burned and sunk by the Federals when they evacuated Norfolk in April, 1861, and proceeded to convert her into an ironclad, after European plans. She was the first truly armorclad vessel. The Federal authorities, learning of her existence, built the *Monitor* from plans by Ericcson. Each knowing of the other's preparations, it was a race to get finished first.

The command of the James River and the adjacent waters was particularly vital to the Union forces in their campaign against Richmond, but the *Merrimac* reached the scene of action first. On March 8, 1862, the blockading squadron in Hampton Roads sighted a sort of half-submerged crocodile, accompanied by several tenders. Three frigates made for the enemy, but got into low water and grounded. The "crocodile" continued until at Newport News the *Cumberland* and *Congress* frigates assailed her. Their shot and balls from shore batteries bounded off her sides like rubber. Without firing a shot she got within easy range, poured a broadside into the *Congress,* then, vomiting iron all the way, dashed for the *Cumberland,* and rammed a great hole in her side. Sinking fast, the *Cumberland* continued to fight, discharging her cannon until the water covered them, and went down with colors flying. The *Merrimac* then set the *Congress* on fire with hot shot.

The next morning, when the *Merrimac* returned to complete her work, she was received by the *Monitor,* that "cheesebox on a raft." For four hours they fought, when the *Merrimac* retreated, its power and terror forever gone. See the article "Merrimac" in the index.

directions as he may find needful and convenient touching all such seizures, prosecutions, and condemnations, and, moreover, to authorize all such attorneys and marshals, whenever there may be reasonable ground to fear any forcible resistance to them in the discharge of their respective duties in this behalf, to call upon any military officer in command of the forces of the United States to give to them such aid, protection, and support as may be necessary to enable them safely and efficiently to discharge their respective duties; and all such commanding officers are required promptly to obey such call, and to render the necessary service as far as may be in their power consistently with their other duties.

ABRAHAM LINCOLN.

By the President:
 EDWARD BATES,
  Attorney-General.

GENERAL ORDER RESPECTING THE OBSERVANCE OF THE SABBATH DAY IN THE ARMY AND NAVY.

EXECUTIVE MANSION,
Washington, November 15, 1862.

The President, Commander in Chief of the Army and Navy, desires and enjoins the orderly observance of the Sabbath by the officers and men in the military and naval service. The importance for man and beast of the prescribed weekly rest, the sacred rights of Christian soldiers and sailors, a becoming deference to the best sentiment of a Christian people, and a due regard for the divine will demand that Sunday labor in the Army and Navy be reduced to the measure of strict necessity.

The discipline and character of the national forces should not suffer nor the cause they defend be imperiled by the profanation of the day or name of the Most High. "At this time of public distress," adopting the words of Washington in 1776, "men may find enough to do in the service of God and their country without abandoning themselves to vice and immorality." The first general order issued by the Father of his Country after the Declaration of Independence indicates the spirit in which our institutions were founded and should ever be defended:

The General hopes and trusts that every officer and man will endeavor to live and act as becomes a Christian soldier defending the dearest rights and liberties of his country.

ABRAHAM LINCOLN.

EXECUTIVE MANSION,
Washington City, November 21, 1862.

Ordered, That no arms, ammunition, or munitions of war be cleared or allowed to be exported from the United States until further order; that any clearances for arms, ammunition, or munitions of war issued heretofore by the Treasury Department be vacated if the articles have not passed without the United States, and the articles stopped; that the Secretary of War hold possession of the arms, etc., recently seized by his order at Rouses Point, bound for Canada.

ABRAHAM LINCOLN.

SECOND ANNUAL MESSAGE.

DECEMBER 1, 1862.

Fellow-Citizens of the Senate and House of Representatives:

Since your last annual assembling another year of health and bountiful harvests has passed, and while it has not pleased the Almighty to bless us with a return of peace, we can but press on, guided by the best light He gives us, trusting that in His own good time and wise way all will yet be well.

The correspondence touching foreign affairs which has taken place during the last year is herewith submitted, in virtual compliance with a request to that effect made by the House of Representatives near the close of the last session of Congress.

If the condition of our relations with other nations is less gratifying than it has usually been at former periods, it is certainly more satisfactory than a nation so unhappily distracted as we are might reasonably have apprehended. In the month of June last there were some grounds to expect that the maritime powers which at the beginning of our domestic difficulties so unwisely and unnecessarily, as we think, recognized the insurgents as a belligerent would soon recede from that position, which has proved only less injurious to themselves than to our own country. But the temporary reverses which afterwards befell the national arms, and which were exaggerated by our own disloyal citizens abroad, have hitherto delayed that act of simple justice.

The civil war, which has so radically changed for the moment the occupations and habits of the American people, has necessarily disturbed the social condition and affected very deeply the prosperity of the nations with which we have carried on a commerce that has been steadily increasing throughout a period of half a century. It has at the same time excited political ambitions and apprehensions which have produced a profound agitation throughout the civilized world. In this unusual agitation we have forborne from taking part in any controversy between foreign states and between parties or factions in such states. We have attempted no propagandism and acknowledged no revolution. But we have left to every nation the exclusive conduct and management of its own affairs. Our struggle has been, of course, contemplated by foreign nations with reference less to its own merits than to its supposed and often exaggerated effects and consequences resulting to those nations themselves. Nevertheless, complaint on the part of this Government, even if it were just, would certainly be unwise.

The treaty with Great Britain for the suppression of the slave trade has been put into operation with a good prospect of complete success. It is an occasion of special pleasure to acknowledge that the execution of it on the part of Her Majesty's Government has been marked with a jealous respect for the authority of the United States and the rights of their moral and loyal citizens.

The convention with Hanover for the abolition of the Stade dues has been carried into full effect under the act of Congress for that purpose.

A blockade of 3,000 miles of seacoast could not be established and vigorously enforced in a season of great commercial activity like the present without committing occasional mistakes and inflicting unintentional injuries upon foreign nations and their subjects.

A civil war occurring in a country where foreigners reside and carry on trade under treaty stipulations is necessarily fruitful of complaints of the violation of neutral rights. All such collisions tend to excite misapprehensions, and possibly to produce mutual reclamations between nations which have a common interest in preserving peace and friendship. In clear cases of these kinds I have so far as possible heard and redressed complaints which have been presented by friendly powers. There is still, however, a large and an augmenting number of doubtful cases upon which the Government is unable to agree with the governments whose protection is demanded by the claimants. There are, moreover, many cases in which the United States or their citizens suffer wrongs from the naval or military authorities of foreign nations which the governments of those states are not at once prepared to redress. I have proposed to some of the foreign states thus interested mutual conventions to examine and adjust such complaints. This proposition has been made especially to Great Britain, to France, to Spain, and to Prussia. In each case it has been kindly received, but has not yet been formally adopted.

I deem it my duty to recommend an appropriation in behalf of the owners of the Norwegian bark *Admiral P. Tordenskiold*, which vessel was in May, 1861, prevented by the commander of the blockading force off Charleston from leaving that port with cargo, notwithstanding a similar privilege had shortly before been granted to an English vessel. I have directed the Secretary of State to cause the papers in the case to be communicated to the proper committees.

Applications have been made to me by many free Americans of African descent to favor their emigration, with a view to such colonization as was contemplated in recent acts of Congress. Other parties, at home and abroad—some from interested motives, others upon patriotic considerations, and still others influenced by philanthropic sentiments—have suggested similar measures, while, on the other hand, several of the Spanish American Republics have protested against the sending of such colonies to their respective territories.   Under these circumstances I have declined to move any such colony to any state without first obtaining the consent of its government, with an agreement on its part to receive and protect such emigrants in all the rights of freemen; and I have at the same time offered to the several States situated within the Tropics, or having colonies there, to negotiate with them, subject to the advice and consent of the Senate, to favor the voluntary emigration of persons of that class to their respective territories, upon conditions which shall be equal, just, and humane.   Liberia and Hayti are as yet the only countries to which colonists of African descent from here could go with certainty of being received and adopted as citizens; and I regret to say such persons contemplating colonization do not seem so willing to migrate to those countries as to some others, nor so willing as I think their interest demands.   I believe, however, opinion among them in this respect is improving, and that ere long there will be an augmented and considerable migration to both these countries from the United States.

The new commercial treaty between the United States and the Sultan of Turkey has been carried into execution.

A commercial and consular treaty has been negotiated, subject to the Senate's consent, with Liberia, and a similar negotiation is now pending with the Republic of Hayti. A considerable improvement of the national commerce is expected to result from these measures.

Our relations with Great Britain, France, Spain, Portugal, Russia, Prussia, Denmark, Sweden, Austria, the Netherlands, Italy, Rome, and the other European States remain undisturbed.   Very favorable relations also continue to be maintained with Turkey, Morocco, China, and Japan.

During the last year there has not only been no change of our previous relations with the independent States of our own continent, but more friendly sentiments than have heretofore existed are believed to be entertained by these neighbors, whose safety and progress are so intimately connected with our own.   This statement especially applies to Mexico, Nicaragua, Costa Rica, Honduras, Peru, and Chile.

The commission under the convention with the Republic of New Granada closed its session without having audited and passed upon all the claims which were submitted to it.   A proposition is pending to revive the convention, that it may be able to do more complete justice. The joint commission between the United States and the Republic of Costa Rica has completed its labors and submitted its report.

I have favored the project for connecting the United States with Europe by an Atlantic telegraph, and a similar project to extend the telegraph from San Francisco to connect by a Pacific telegraph with the line which is being extended across the Russian Empire.

The Territories of the United States, with unimportant exceptions, have remained undisturbed by the civil war; and they are exhibiting such evidence of prosperity as justifies an expectation that some of them will soon be in a condition to be organized as States and be constitutionally admitted into the Federal Union.

The immense mineral resources of some of those Territories ought to be developed as rapidly as possible. Every step in that direction would have a tendency to improve the revenues of the Government and diminish the burdens of the people. It is worthy of your serious consideration whether some extraordinary measures to promote that end can not be adopted. The means which suggests itself as most likely to be effective is a scientific exploration of the mineral regions in those Territories with a view to the publication of its results at home and in foreign countries—results which can not fail to be auspicious.

The condition of the finances will claim your most diligent consideration. The vast expenditures incident to the military and naval operations required for the suppression of the rebellion have hitherto been met with a promptitude and certainty unusual in similar circumstances, and the public credit has been fully maintained. The continuance of the war, however, and the increased disbursements made necessary by the augmented forces now in the field demand your best reflections as to the best modes of providing the necessary revenue without injury to business and with the least possible burdens upon labor.

The suspension of specie payments by the banks soon after the commencement of your last session made large issues of United States notes unavoidable. In no other way could the payment of the troops and the satisfaction of other just demands be so economically or so well provided for. The judicious legislation of Congress, securing the receivability of these notes for loans and internal duties and making them a legal tender for other debts, has made them an universal currency, and has satisfied, partially at least, and for the time, the long-felt want of an uniform circulating medium, saving thereby to the people immense sums in discounts and exchanges.

A return to specie payments, however, at the earliest period compatible with due regard to all interests concerned should ever be kept in view. Fluctuations in the value of currency are always injurious, and to reduce these fluctuations to the lowest possible point will always be a leading purpose in wise legislation. Convertibility, prompt and certain convertibility, into coin is generally acknowledged to be the best and surest safeguard against them; and it is extremely doubtful whether a circulation of United States notes payable in coin and sufficiently large for the wants of the people can be permanently, usefully, and safely maintained.

Is there, then, any other mode in which the necessary provision for the public wants can be made and the great advantages of a safe and uniform currency secured?

I know of none which promises so certain results and is at the same time so unobjectionable as the organization of banking associations, under a general act of Congress, well guarded in its provisions. To such associations the Government might furnish circulating notes, on the security of United States bonds deposited in the Treasury. These notes, prepared under the supervision of proper officers, being uniform in appearance and security and convertible always into coin, would at once protect labor against the evils of a vicious currency and facilitate commerce by cheap and safe exchanges.

A moderate reservation from the interest on the bonds would compensate the United States for the preparation and distribution of the notes and a general supervision of the system, and would lighten the burden of that part of the public debt employed as securities. The public credit, moreover, would be greatly improved and the negotiation of new loans greatly facilitated by the steady market demand for Government bonds which the adoption of the proposed system would create.

It is an additional recommendation of the measure, of considerable weight, in my judgment, that it would reconcile as far as possible all existing interests by the opportunity offered to existing institutions to reorganize under the act, substituting only the secured uniform national circulation for the local and various circulation, secured and unsecured, now issued by them.

The receipts into the Treasury from all sources, including loans and balance from the preceding year, for the fiscal year ending on the 30th June, 1862, were $583,885,247.06, of which sum $49,056,397.62 were derived from customs; $1,795,331.73 from the direct tax; from public lands, $152,203.77; from miscellaneous sources, $931,787.64; from loans in all forms, $529,692,460.50. The remainder, $2,257,065.80, was the balance from last year.

The disbursements during the same period were: For Congressional, executive, and judicial purposes, $5,939,009.29; for foreign intercourse, $1,339,710.35; for miscellaneous expenses, including the mints, loans, Post-Office deficiencies, collection of revenue, and other like charges, $14,129,771.50; for expenses under the Interior Department, $3,102,-985.52; under the War Department, $394,368,407.36; under the Navy Department, $42,674,569.69; for interest on public debt, $13,190,324.45; and for payment of public debt, including reimbursement of temporary loan and redemptions, $96,096,922.09; making an aggregate of $570,-841,700.25, and leaving a balance in the Treasury on the 1st day of July, 1862, of $13,043,546.81.

It should be observed that the sum of $96,096,922.09, expended for reimbursements and redemption of public debt, being included also in the loans made, may be properly deducted both from receipts and expenditures, leaving the actual receipts for the year $487,788,324.97, and the expenditures $474,744,778.16.

Other information on the subject of the finances will be found in the report of the Secretary of the Treasury, to whose statements and views I invite your most candid and considerate attention.

The reports of the Secretaries of War and of the Navy are herewith transmitted. These reports, though lengthy, are scarcely more than brief abstracts of the very numerous and extensive transactions and operations conducted through those Departments. Nor could I give a summary of them here upon any principle which would admit of its being much shorter than the reports themselves. I therefore content myself with laying the reports before you and asking your attention to them.

It gives me pleasure to report a decided improvement in the financial condition of the Post-Office Department as compared with several preceding years. The receipts for the fiscal year 1861 amounted to $8,349,296.40, which embraced the revenue from all the States of the Union for three quarters of that year. Notwithstanding the cessation of revenue from the so-called seceded States during the last fiscal year, the increase of the correspondence of the loyal States has been sufficient to produce a revenue during the same year of $8,299,820.90, being only $50,000 less than was derived from all the States of the Union during the previous year. The expenditures show a still more favorable result. The amount expended in 1861 was $13,606,759.11. For the last year the amount has been reduced to $11,125,364.13, showing a decrease of about $2,481,000 in the expenditures as compared with the preceding year, and about $3,750,000 as compared with the fiscal year 1860. The deficiency in the Department for the previous year was $4,551,966.98. For the last fiscal year it was reduced to $2,112,814.57. These favorable results are in part owing to the cessation of mail service in the insurrectionary States and in part to a careful review of all expenditures in that Department in the interest of economy. The efficiency of the postal service, it is believed, has also been much improved. The Postmaster-General has also opened a correspondence through the Department of State with foreign governments proposing a convention of postal representatives for the purpose of simplifying the rates of foreign postage and to expedite the foreign mails. This proposition, equally important to our adopted citizens and to the commercial interests of this country, has been favorably entertained and agreed to by all the governments from whom replies have been received.

I ask the attention of Congress to the suggestions of the Postmaster-General in his report respecting the further legislation required, in his opinion, for the benefit of the postal service.

The Secretary of the Interior reports as follows in regard to the public lands:

The public lands have ceased to be a source of revenue. From the 1st July, 1861, to the 30th September, 1862, the entire cash receipts from the sale of lands were $137,476.26—a sum much less than the expenses of our land system during the same period. The homestead law, which will take effect on the 1st of January next, offers such inducements to settlers that sales for cash can not be expected to an extent sufficient to meet the expenses of the General Land Office and the cost of surveying and bringing the land into market.

The discrepancy between the sum here stated as arising from the sales of the public lands and the sum derived from the same source as reported from the Treasury Department arises, as I understand, from the fact that the periods of time, though apparently, were not really coincident at the beginning point, the Treasury report including a considerable sum now which had previously been reported from the Interior, sufficiently large to greatly overreach the sum derived from the three months now reported upon by the Interior and not by the Treasury.

The Indian tribes upon our frontiers have during the past year manifested a spirit of insubordination, and at several points have engaged in open hostilities against the white settlements in their vicinity. The tribes occupying the Indian country south of Kansas renounced their allegiance to the United States and entered into treaties with the insurgents. Those who remained loyal to the United States were driven from the country. The chief of the Cherokees has visited this city for the purpose of restoring the former relations of the tribe with the United States. He alleges that they were constrained by superior force to enter into treaties with the insurgents, and that the United States neglected to furnish the protection which their treaty stipulations required.

In the month of August last the Sioux Indians in Minnesota attacked the settlements in their vicinity with extreme ferocity, killing indiscriminately men, women, and children. This attack was wholly unexpected, and therefore no means of defense had been provided. It is estimated that not less than 800 persons were killed by the Indians, and a large amount of property was destroyed. How this outbreak was induced is not definitely known, and suspicions, which may be unjust, need not to be stated. Information was received by the Indian Bureau from different sources about the time hostilities were commenced that a simultaneous attack was to be made upon the white settlements by all the tribes between the Mississippi River and the Rocky Mountains. The State of Minnesota has suffered great injury from this Indian war. A large portion of her territory has been depopulated, and a severe loss has been sustained by the destruction of property. The people of that State manifest much anxiety for the removal of the tribes beyond the limits of the State as a guaranty against future hostilities. The Commissioner of Indian Affairs will furnish full details. I submit for your especial consideration whether our Indian system shall not be remodeled. Many wise and good men have impressed me with the belief that this can be profitably done.

I submit a statement of the proceedings of commissioners, which shows the progress that has been made in the enterprise of constructing the

Pacific Railroad. And this suggests the earliest completion of this road, and also the favorable action of Congress upon the projects now pending before them for enlarging the capacities of the great canals in New York and Illinois, as being of vital and rapidly increasing importance to the whole nation, and especially to the vast interior region hereinafter to be noticed at some greater length. I purpose having prepared and laid before you at an early day some interesting and valuable statistical information upon this subject. The military and commercial importance of enlarging the Illinois and Michigan Canal and improving the Illinois River is presented in the report of Colonel Webster to the Secretary of War, and now transmitted to Congress. I respectfully ask attention to it.

To carry out the provisions of the act of Congress of the 15th of May last, I have caused the Department of Agriculture of the United States to be organized.

The Commissioner informs me that within the period of a few months this Department has established an extensive system of correspondence and exchanges, both at home and abroad, which promises to effect highly beneficial results in the development of a correct knowledge of recent improvements in agriculture, in the introduction of new products, and in the collection of the agricultural statistics of the different States.

Also, that it will soon be prepared to distribute largely seeds, cereals, plants, and cuttings, and has already published and liberally diffused much valuable information in anticipation of a more elaborate report, which will in due time be furnished, embracing some valuable tests in chemical science now in progress in the laboratory.

The creation of this Department was for the more immediate benefit of a large class of our most valuable citizens, and I trust that the liberal basis upon which it has been organized will not only meet your approbation, but that it will realize at no distant day all the fondest anticipations of its most sanguine friends and become the fruitful source of advantage to all our people.

On the 22d day of September last a proclamation was issued by the Executive, a copy of which is herewith submitted.

In accordance with the purpose expressed in the second paragraph of that paper, I now respectfully recall your attention to what may be called "compensated emancipation."

A nation may be said to consist of its territory, its people, and its laws. The territory is the only part which is of certain durability. "One generation passeth away and another generation cometh, but the earth abideth forever." It is of the first importance to duly consider and estimate this ever-enduring part. That portion of the earth's surface which is owned and inhabited by the people of the United States is well adapted to be the home of one national family, and it is not well adapted for two or more. Its vast extent and its variety of climate and productions are of advantage in this age for one people, whatever they might have been in former ages. Steam, telegraphs, and intelligence have brought these to be an advantageous combination for one united people.

In the inaugural address I briefly pointed out the total inadequacy of disunion as a remedy for the differences between the people of the two sections. I did so in language which I can not improve, and which, therefore, I beg to repeat:

One section of our country believes slavery is *right* and ought to be extended, while the other believes it is *wrong* and ought not to be extended. This is the only substantial dispute. The fugitive-slave clause of the Constitution and the law for the suppression of the foreign slave trade are each as well enforced, perhaps, as any law can ever be in a community where the moral sense of the people imperfectly supports the law itself. The great body of the people abide by the dry legal obligation in both cases, and a few break over in each. This, I think, can not be perfectly cured, and it would be worse in both cases *after* the separation of the sections than before. The foreign slave trade, now imperfectly suppressed, would be ultimately revived without restriction in one section, while fugitive slaves, now only partially surrendered, would not be surrendered at all by the other.

Physically speaking, we can not separate. We can not remove our respective sections from each other nor build an impassable wall between them. A husband and wife may be divorced and go out of the presence and beyond the reach of each other, but the different parts of our country can not do this. They can not but remain face to face, and intercourse, either amicable or hostile, must continue between them. Is it possible, then, to make that intercourse more advantageous or more satisfactory *after* separation than *before?* Can aliens make treaties easier than friends can make laws? Can treaties be more faithfully enforced between aliens than laws can among friends? Suppose you go to war, you can not fight always; and when, after much loss on both sides and no gain on either, you cease fighting, the identical old questions, as to terms of intercourse, are again upon you.

There is no line, straight or crooked, suitable for a national boundary upon which to divide. Trace through, from east to west, upon the line between the free and slave country, and we shall find a little more than one-third of its length are rivers, easy to be crossed, and populated, or soon to be populated, thickly upon both sides; while nearly all its remaining length are merely surveyors' lines, over which people may walk back and forth without any consciousness of their presence. No part of this line can be made any more difficult to pass by writing it down on paper or parchment as a national boundary. The fact of separation, if it comes, gives up on the part of the seceding section the fugitive-slave clause, along with all other constitutional obligations upon the section seceded from, while I should expect no treaty stipulation would ever be made to take its place.

But there is another difficulty. The great interior region bounded east by the Alleghanies, north by the British dominions, west by the Rocky Mountains, and south by the line along which the culture of corn and cotton meets, and which includes part of Virginia, part of Tennessee, all of Kentucky, Ohio, Indiana, Michigan, Wisconsin, Illinois, Missouri, Kansas, Iowa, Minnesota, and the Territories of Dakota, Nebraska, and part of Colorado, already has above 10,000,000 people, and will have

50,000,000 within fifty years if not prevented by any political folly or mistake. It contains more than one-third of the country owned by the United States—certainly more than 1,000,000 square miles. Once half as populous as Massachusetts already is, it would have more than 75,000,000 people. A glance at the map shows that, territorially speaking, it is the great body of the Republic. The other parts are but marginal borders to it, the magnificent region sloping west from the Rocky Mountains to the Pacific being the deepest and also the richest in undeveloped resources. In the production of provisions, grains, grasses, and all which proceed from them this great interior region is naturally one of the most important in the world. Ascertain from the statistics the small proportion of the region which has as yet been brought into cultivation, and also the large and rapidly increasing amount of its products, and we shall be overwhelmed with the magnitude of the prospect presented. And yet this region has no seacoast—touches no ocean anywhere. As part of one nation, its people now find, and may forever find, their way to Europe by New York, to South America and Africa by New Orleans, and to Asia by San Francisco; but separate our common country into two nations, as designed by the present rebellion, and every man of this great interior region is thereby cut off from some one or more of these outlets, not perhaps by a physical barrier, but by embarrassing and onerous trade regulations.

And this is true, *wherever* a dividing or boundary line may be fixed. Place it between the now free and slave country, or place it south of Kentucky or north of Ohio, and still the truth remains that none south of it can trade to any port or place north of it, and none north of it can trade to any port or place south of it, except upon terms dictated by a government foreign to them. These outlets, east, west, and south, are indispensable to the well-being of the people inhabiting and to inhabit this vast interior region. *Which* of the three may be the best is no proper question. All are better than either, and all of right belong to that people and to their successors forever. True to themselves, they will not ask *where* a line of separation shall be, but will vow rather that there shall be no such line. Nor are the marginal regions less interested in these communications to and through them to the great outside world. They, too, and each of them, must have access to this Egypt of the West without paying toll at the crossing of any national boundary.

Our national strife springs not from our permanent part; not from the land we inhabit; not from our national homestead. There is no possible severing of this but would multiply and not mitigate evils among us. In all its adaptations and aptitudes it demands union and abhors separation. In fact, it would ere long force reunion, however much of blood and treasure the separation might have cost.

Our strife pertains to ourselves—to the passing generations of men—and it can without convulsion be hushed forever with the passing of one generation.

In this view I recommend the adoption of the following resolution and articles amendatory to the Constitution of the United States:

Resolved by the Senate and House of Representatives of the United States of America in Congress assembled (*two-thirds of both Houses concurring*), That the following articles be proposed to the legislatures (or conventions) of the several States as amendments to the Constitution of the United States, all or any of which articles, when ratified by three-fourths of the said legislatures (or conventions), to be valid as part or parts of the said Constitution, viz:

ART. —. Every State wherein slavery now exists which shall abolish the same therein at any time or times before the 1st day of January, A. D. 1900, shall receive compensation from the United States as follows, to wit:

The President of the United States shall deliver to every such State bonds of the United States bearing interest at the rate of —— per cent per annum to an amount equal to the aggregate sum of —— for each slave shown to have been therein by the Eighth Census of the United States, said bonds to be delivered to such State by installments or in one parcel at the completion of the abolishment, accordingly as the same shall have been gradual or at one time within such State; and interest shall begin to run upon any such bond only from the proper time of its delivery as aforesaid. Any State having received bonds as aforesaid and afterwards reintroducing or tolerating slavery therein shall refund to the United States the bonds so received, or the value thereof, and all interest paid thereon.

ART. —. All slaves who shall have enjoyed actual freedom by the chances of the war at any time before the end of the rebellion shall be forever free; but all owners of such who shall not have been disloyal shall be compensated for them at the same rates as is provided for States adopting abolishment of slavery, but in such way that no slave shall be twice accounted for.

ART. —. Congress may appropriate money and otherwise provide for colonizing free colored persons with their own consent at any place or places without the United States.

I beg indulgence to discuss these proposed articles at some length. Without slavery the rebellion could never have existed; without slavery it could not continue.

Among the friends of the Union there is great diversity of sentiment and of policy in regard to slavery and the African race amongst us. Some would perpetuate slavery; some would abolish it suddenly and without compensation; some would abolish it gradually and with compensation; some would remove the freed people from us, and some would retain them with us; and there are yet other minor diversities. Because of these diversities we waste much strength in struggles among ourselves. By mutual concession we should harmonize and act together. This would be compromise, but it would be compromise among the friends and not with the enemies of the Union. These articles are intended to embody a plan of such mutual concessions. If the plan shall be adopted, it is assumed that emancipation will follow, at least in several of the States.

As to the first article, the main points are, first, the emancipation; secondly, the length of time for consummating it (thirty-seven years); and, thirdly, the compensation.

The emancipation will be unsatisfactory to the advocates of perpetual slavery, but the length of time should greatly mitigate their dissatisfaction. The time spares both races from the evils of sudden derangement—in fact, from the necessity of any derangement—while most of those whose habitual course of thought will be disturbed by the measure will have passed away before its consummation. They will never see it. Another class will hail the prospect of emancipation, but will deprecate the length of time. They will feel that it gives too little to the now living slaves. But it really gives them much. It saves them from the vagrant destitution which must largely attend immediate emancipation in localities where their numbers are very great, and it gives the inspiring assurance that their posterity shall be free forever. The plan leaves to each State choosing to act under it to abolish slavery now or at the end of the century, or at any intermediate time, or by degrees extending over the whole or any part of the period, and it obliges no two States to proceed alike. It also provides for compensation, and generally the mode of making it. This, it would seem, must further mitigate the dissatisfaction of those who favor perpetual slavery, and especially of those who are to receive the compensation. Doubtless some of those who are to pay and not to receive will object. Yet the measure is both just and economical. In a certain sense the liberation of slaves is the destruction of property—property acquired by descent or by purchase, the same as any other property. It is no less true for having been often said that the people of the South are not more responsible for the original introduction of this property than are the people of the North; and when it is remembered how unhesitatingly we all use cotton and sugar and share the profits of dealing in them, it may not be quite safe to say that the South has been more responsible than the North for its continuance. If, then, for a common object this property is to be sacrificed, is it not just that it be done at a common charge?

And if with less money, or money more easily paid, we can preserve the benefits of the Union by this means than we can by the war alone, is it not also economical to do it? Let us consider it, then. Let us ascertain the sum we have expended in the war since compensated emancipation was proposed last March, and consider whether if that measure had been promptly accepted by even some of the slave States the same sum would not have done more to close the war than has been otherwise done. If so, the measure would save money, and in that view would be a prudent and economical measure. Certainly it is not so easy to pay *something* as it is to pay *nothing*, but it is easier to pay a *large* sum than it is to pay a *larger* one. And it is easier to pay any sum *when* we are able than it is to pay it *before* we are able. The war requires large sums, and requires them at once. The aggregate sum necessary for compensated emancipation of course would be large. But it would require no ready cash, nor the bonds even any faster than the emancipation progresses. This might not, and probably would not, close before the end of the thirty-seven years. At that time we shall probably have a hundred millions of people to share the burden, instead of thirty-one millions as now. And not only so, but the increase of our population may be expected to continue for a long time after that period as rapidly as before, because our territory will not have become full. I do not state this inconsiderately. At the same ratio of increase which we have maintained, on an average, from our first national census, in 1790, until that of 1860, we should in 1900 have a population of 103,208,415. And why may we not continue that ratio far beyond that period? Our abundant room, our broad national homestead, is our ample resource. Were our territory as limited as are the British Isles, very certainly our population could not expand as stated. Instead of receiving the foreign born as now, we should be compelled to send part of the native born away. But such is not our condition. We have 2,963,000 square miles. Europe has 3,800,000, with a population averaging 73⅓ persons to the square mile. Why may not our country at some time average as many? Is it less fertile? Has it more waste surface by mountains, rivers, lakes, deserts, or other causes? Is it inferior to Europe in any natural advantage? If, then, we are at some time to be as populous as Europe, how soon? As to when this *may* be, we can judge by the past and the present; as to when it *will* be, if ever, depends much on whether we maintain the Union. Several of our States are already above the average of Europe—73⅓ to the square mile. Massachusetts has 157; Rhode Island, 133; Connecticut, 99; New York and New Jersey, each 80. Also two other great States, Pennsylvania and Ohio, are not far below, the former having 63 and the latter 59. The States already above the European average, except New York, have increased in as rapid a ratio since passing that point as ever before, while no one of them is equal to some other parts of our country in natural capacity for sustaining a dense population.

Taking the nation in the aggregate, and we find its population and ratio of increase for the several decennial periods to be as follows:

Year.	Population.	Ratio of increase.
		Per cent.
1790.	3,929,827	....
1800.	5,305,937	35.02
1810.	7,239,814	36.45
1820.	9,638,131	33.13
1830.	12,866,020	33.49
1840.	17,069,453	32.67
1850.	23,191,876	35.87
1860.	31,443,790	35.58

This shows an average decennial increase of 34.60 per cent in population through the seventy years from our first to our last census yet taken. It is seen that the ratio of increase at no one of these seven periods is either 2 per cent below or 2 per cent above the average, thus showing how inflexible, and consequently how reliable, the law of increase in our case is. Assuming that it will continue, it gives the following results:

Year.	Population.
1870	42,323,341
1880	56,967,216
1890	76,677,872
1900	103,208,415
1910	138,918,526
1920	186,984,335
1930	251,680,914

These figures show that our country *may* be as populous as Europe now is at some point between 1920 and 1930—say about 1925—our territory, at 73⅓ persons to the square mile, being of capacity to contain 217,186,000.

And we *will* reach this, too, if we do not ourselves relinquish the chance by the folly and evils of disunion or by long and exhausting war springing from the only great element of national discord among us. While it can not be foreseen exactly how much one huge example of secession, breeding lesser ones indefinitely, would retard population, civilization, and prosperity, no one can doubt that the extent of it would be very great and injurious.

The proposed emancipation would shorten the war, perpetuate peace, insure this increase of population, and proportionately the wealth of the country. With these we should pay all the emancipation would cost, together with our other debt, easier than we should pay our other debt without it. If we had allowed our old national debt to run at 6 per cent per annum, simple interest, from the end of our revolutionary struggle until to-day, without paying anything on either principal or interest, each man of us would owe less upon that debt now than each man owed upon it then; and this because our increase of men through the whole period has been greater than 6 per cent—has run faster than the interest upon the debt. Thus time alone relieves a debtor nation, so long as its population increases faster than unpaid interest accumulates on its debt.

This fact would be no excuse for delaying payment of what is justly due, but it shows the great importance of time in this connection—the great advantage of a policy by which we shall not have to pay until we number 100,000,000 what by a different policy we would have to pay now, when we number but 31,000,000. In a word, it shows that a dollar will be much harder to pay for the war than will be a dollar for emancipation on the proposed plan. And then the latter will cost no blood, no precious life. It will be a saving of both.

As to the second article, I think it would be impracticable to return to bondage the class of persons therein contemplated. Some of them, doubtless, in the property sense belong to loyal owners, and hence provision is made in this article for compensating such.

The third **article relates** to the future of the freed people. It does not oblige, but merely authorizes Congress to aid in colonizing such as may consent. This ought not to be regarded as objectionable on the one hand or on the other, insomuch as it comes to nothing unless by the mutual consent of the people to be deported and the American voters, through their representatives in Congress.

I can not make it better known than it already is that I strongly favor colonization; and yet I wish to say there is an objection urged against free colored persons remaining in the country which is largely imaginary, if not sometimes malicious.

It is insisted that their presence would injure and displace white labor and white laborers. If there ever could be a proper time for mere catch arguments, that time surely is not now. In times like the present men should utter nothing for which they would not willingly be responsible through time and in eternity. Is it true, then, that colored people can displace any more white labor by being free than by remaining slaves? If they stay in their old places, they jostle no white laborers; if they leave their old places, they leave them open to white laborers. Logically, there is neither more nor less of it. Emancipation, even without deportation, would probably enhance the wages of white labor, and very surely would not reduce them. Thus the customary amount of labor would still have to be performed—the freed people would surely not do more than their old proportion of it, and very probably for a time would do less, leaving an increased part to white laborers, bringing their labor into greater demand, and consequently enhancing the wages of it. With deportation, even to a limited extent, enhanced wages to white labor is mathematically certain. Labor is like any other commodity in the market—increase the demand for it and you increase the price of it. Reduce the supply of black labor by colonizing the black laborer out of the country, and by precisely so much you increase the demand for and wages of white labor.

But it is dreaded that the freed people will swarm forth and cover the whole land. Are they not already in the land? Will liberation make them any more numerous? Equally distributed among the whites of the whole country, and there would be but one colored to seven whites. Could the one in any way greatly disturb the seven? There are many communities now having more than one free colored person to seven whites and this without any apparent consciousness of evil from it. The District of Columbia and the States of Maryland and Delaware are all in this condition. The District has more than one free colored to six whites, and yet in its frequent petitions to Congress I believe it has never presented the presence of free colored persons as one of its grievances. But why should emancipation South send the free people North? People of any color

BATTLES OF ANTIETAM AND FAIR OAKS

BATTLE OF ANTIETAM.

This engagement was fought on September 17, 1862, by the Confederate forces under General Lee, who commanded 51,844 men, and the Union forces under General McClellan, who commanded 75,316 men. Two days previously Lee had abandoned Harper's Ferry, and massed his forces, which had hitherto been divided, in the Antietam valley, near Sharpsburg, Md., where he was joined by Jackson. At dawn on the 17th, Hooker attacked Jackson's division, but was met with stubborn resistance. Hooker himself was seriously wounded, but his forces were winning, when Lee weakened his centre by dispatching fresh troops to Jackson's assistance, and the Federal forces were once more checked. On the other fronts, however, the Confederates had decidedly the worse of the encounter. The ever cautious McClellan did not push the conflict on the 18th, and on the 19th Lee removed across the Potomac. It is estimated that the Union loss was 2,108 men killed and 9,549 wounded, whereas the Confederate loss was 2,700 men killed and 9,024 wounded. (See Antietam, Battle of, in Encyclopedic Index.)

BATTLE OF FAIR OAKS.

The Battle of Fair Oaks, sometimes called the Battle of Seven Pines, was fought near Richmond on May 31, 1862. McClellan's forces were divided by the Chickahominy River, and General Johnston took advantage of the Union predicament to launch an attack. The Union forces under General Casey had to fall back before the Confederate attack, thus forcing the forces back of them into the bogs and swamps of the river. The situation looked black for the Federals, but McClellan, on the other side of the river, sent a division under General Sumner to the relief of Casey's men, who were thus enabled to extricate themselves. On the next day, the Confederates were driven back, and much of the lost ground was regained. General Johnston was severely wounded in the battle, and the command of the Confederate Army was turned over to Robert Lee on June 2. (See Seven Pines and Fair Oaks (Va.), Battle of, in Encyclopedic Index.)

With a view to ascertain this, the subject was referred to a commission of the United States and French naval officers at New York, with a naval officer of Italy as an arbiter. The conclusion arrived at was that the collision was occasioned by the failure of the *San Jacinto* seasonably to reverse her engine. It then became necessary to ascertain the amount of indemnification due to the injured party. The United States consul-general at Havana was consequently instructed to confer with the consul of France on this point, and they have determined that the sum of $9,500 is an equitable allowance under the circumstances.

I recommend an appropriation of this sum for the benefit of the owners of the *Jules et Marie.*

A copy of the letter of Mr. Shufeldt, the consul-general of the United States at Havana, to the Secretary of State on the subject is herewith transmitted.

ABRAHAM LINCOLN.

WASHINGTON, D. C., *December 8, 1862.*

To the Senate and House of Representatives:

In conformity to the law of July 16, 1862, I most cordially recommend that Commander John L. Worden, United States Navy, receive a vote of thanks of Congress for the eminent skill and gallantry exhibited by him in the late remarkable battle between the United States ironclad steamer *Monitor,* under his command, and the rebel ironclad steamer *Merrimac,* in March last.

The thanks of Congress for his services on the occasion referred to were tendered by a resolution approved July 11, 1862, but the recommendation is now specially made in order to comply with the requirements of the ninth section of the act of July 16, 1862, which is in the following words, viz:

That any line officer of the Navy or Marine Corps may be advanced one grade if upon recommendation of the President by name he receives the thanks of Congress for highly distinguished conduct in conflict with the enemy or for extraordinary heroism in the line of his profession.

ABRAHAM LINCOLN.

WASHINGTON, D. C., *December 9, 1862.*

To the Senate of the United States:

In compliance with the resolution of the Senate of the United States of the 13th of March last, requesting a copy of the correspondence relative to the attempted seizure of Mr. Fauchet by the commander of the *Africa* within the waters of the United States, I transmit a report from the Secretary of State and the documents by which it was accompanied.

ABRAHAM LINCOLN.

WASHINGTON, D. C., *December 10, 1862.*
To the Senate and House of Representatives:

In conformity to the law of July 16, 1862, I most cordially recommend that Lieutenant-Commander George U. Morris, United States Navy, receive a vote of thanks of Congress for the determined valor and heroism displayed in his defense of the United States ship of war *Cumberland*, temporarily under his command, in the naval engagement at Hampton Roads on the 8th March, 1862, with the rebel ironclad steam frigate *Merrimac.*

ABRAHAM LINCOLN.

WASHINGTON, *December 10, 1862.*
To the House of Representatives:

In answer to the resolution of the House of Representatives of the 17th of July last, requesting the communication of correspondence relating to the arrest of a part of the crew of the brig *Sumter* at Tangier, Morocco, I herewith transmit a report from the Secretary of State.

ABRAHAM LINCOLN.

To the Senate of the United States:

In compliance with your resolution of December 5, 1862, requesting the President "to furnish the Senate with all information in his possession touching the late Indian barbarities in the State of Minnesota, and also the evidence in his possession upon which some of the principal actors and headmen were tried and condemned to death," I have the honor to state that on receipt of said resolution I transmitted the same to the Secretary of the Interior, accompanied by a note a copy of which is herewith inclosed, marked A, and in response to which I received through that Department a letter of the Commissioner of Indian Affairs, a copy of which is herewith inclosed, marked B.

I further state that on the 8th day of November last I received a long telegraphic dispatch from Major-General Pope, at St. Paul, Minn., simply announcing the names of the persons sentenced to be hanged. I immediately telegraphed to have transcripts of the records in all the cases forwarded to me, which transcripts, however, did not reach me until two or three days before the present meeting of Congress. Meantime I received, through telegraphic dispatches and otherwise, appeals in behalf of the condemned, appeals for their execution, and expressions of opinion as to proper policy in regard to them and to the Indians generally in that vicinity, none of which, as I understand, falls within the scope of your inquiry. After the arrival of the transcripts of records, but before I had sufficient opportunity to examine them, I received a joint letter from one of the Senators and two of the Representatives from Minnesota, which contains some statements of fact not found in the records of the trials, and for which reason I herewith transmit a copy, marked C. I also, for the same reason, inclose a printed memorial of the citizens of St. Paul addressed to me and forwarded with the letter aforesaid.

Anxious to not act with so much clemency as to encourage another outbreak on the one hand, nor with so much severity as to be real cruelty on the other, I caused a careful examination of the records of trials to be made, in view of first ordering the execution of such as had been proved guilty of violating females. Contrary to my expectations, only two of this class were found. I then directed a further examination, and a classification of all who were proven to have participated in *massacres*, as distinguished from participation in *battles*. This class numbered forty, and included the two convicted of female violation. One of the number is strongly recommended by the commission which tried them for commutation to ten years' imprisonment. I have ordered the other thirty-nine to be executed on Friday, the 19th instant. The order was dispatched from here on Monday, the 8th instant, by a messenger to General Sibley, and a copy of which order is herewith transmitted, marked D.

An abstract of the evidence as to the forty is herewith inclosed, marked E.

To avoid the immense amount of copying, I lay before the Senate the original transcripts of the records of trials as received by me.

This is as full and complete a response to the resolution as it is in my power to make.

ABRAHAM LINCOLN.

DECEMBER 11, 1862.

WASHINGTON, *December 11, 1862.*

To the Senate of the United States:

I transmit to the Senate, for its consideration with a view to ratification, a treaty between the United States and the Republic of Liberia, signed at London by the plenipotentiaries of the parties on the 21st of October last.

ABRAHAM LINCOLN.

DECEMBER 12, 1862.

Fellow-Citizens of the Senate and House of Representatives:

I have in my possession three valuable swords, formerly the property of General David E. Twiggs, which I now place at the disposal of Congress. They are forwarded to me from New Orleans by Major-General Benjamin F. Butler. If they or any of them shall be by Congress disposed of in reward or compliment of military service, I think General Butler is entitled to the first consideration. A copy of the General's letter to me accompanying the swords is herewith transmitted.

ABRAHAM LINCOLN.

WASHINGTON, D. C., *December 13, 1862.*

To the Senate of the United States:

In the list of nominations transmitted to the Senate under date of the 1st instant Captain William M. Glendy, United States Navy, was included therein for promotion to the grade of commodore.

Since submitting this nomination it appears that this officer was ineligible for the advancement to which he had been nominated in consequence of his age, being 62 on the 23d of May, 1862, and under the law of 21st December, 1861, should, had this fact been known to the Navy Department, have been transferred to the retired list on the day when he completed sixty-two years.

The nomination of Captain Glendy is accordingly withdrawn.

It is due to this officer to state that at the period of the passage of the law of December, 1861, he was and still is absent on duty on a foreign station, and the certificate of his age required by the Navy Department was only received a few days since.

ABRAHAM LINCOLN.

WASHINGTON, *December 18, 1862.*

To the Senate and House of Representatives:

I transmit a copy of a dispatch to the Secretary of State from Mr. Adams, United States minister at London, and of the correspondence to which it refers between that gentleman and Mr. Panizzi, the principal librarian of the British Museum, relative to certain valuable publications presented to the Library of Congress.

ABRAHAM LINCOLN.

WASHINGTON, *December 22, 1862.*

To the Senate of the United States:

In compliance with the resolution of the Senate of the 15th instant, requesting a copy of the report of the Hon. Reverdy Johnson,* I transmit a communication from the Secretary of State and the documents by which it was accompanied.

ABRAHAM LINCOLN.

WASHINGTON, *December 24, 1862.*

To the Senate and House of Representatives:

I transmit, for the consideration of Congress, a report from the Secretary of State on the subject of consular pupils.

ABRAHAM LINCOLN.

* United States commissioner at New Orleans.

WASHINGTON, *January 2, 1863.*

To the Senate and House of Representatives:

I submit to Congress the expediency of extending to other Departments of the Government the authority conferred on the President by the eighth section of the act of the 8th of May, 1792, to appoint a person to temporarily discharge the duties of Secretary of State, Secretary of the Treasury, and Secretary of War in case of the death, absence from the seat of Government, or sickness of either of those officers.

ABRAHAM LINCOLN.

WASHINGTON, *January 3, 1863.*

To the Senate of the United States:

I transmit to the Senate, for consideration with a view to ratification, a convention for the mutual adjustment of claims between the United States and Ecuador, signed by the respective plenipotentiaries of the two Governments in Guayaquil on the 25th November ultimo.

ABRAHAM LINCOLN.

WASHINGTON, *January 5, 1863.*

To the House of Representatives:

In compliance with the resolution of the House of Representatives of the 22d ultimo, in relation to the alleged interference of our minister to Mexico in favor of the French, I transmit a report from the Secretary of State and the papers with which it is accompanied.

ABRAHAM LINCOLN.

WASHINGTON, *January 9, 1863.*

To the Senate and House of Representatives:

I transmit for the consideration of Congress, and with a view to the adoption of such measures in relation to the subject of it as may be deemed expedient, a copy of a note of the 8th instant addressed to the Secretary of State by the minister resident of the Hanseatic Republics accredited to this Government, concerning an international agricultural exhibition to be held next summer in the city of Hamburg.

ABRAHAM LINCOLN.

WASHINGTON, *January 14, 1863.*

To the House of Representatives:

The Secretary of State has submitted to me a resolution of the House of Representatives of the 5th instant, which has been delivered to him, and which is in the following words:

Resolved, That the Secretary of State be requested to communicate to this House, if not in his judgment incompatible with the public interest, why our minister in

New Granada has not presented his credentials to the actual Government of that country; also the reasons for which Señor Murillo is not recognized by the United States as the diplomatic representative of the Mosquera Government of that country; also what negotiations have been had, if any, with General Herran, as the representative of Ospina's Government in New Granada, since it went into existence.

On the 12th day of December, 1846, a treaty of amity. peace, and concord was concluded between the United States of America and the Republic of New Granada, which is still in force. On the 7th day of December, 1847, General Pedro Alcántara Herran, who had been duly accredited, was received here as the envoy extraordinary and minister plenipotentiary of that Republic. On the 30th day of August, 1849, Señor Don Rafael Rivas was received by this Government as chargé d'affaires of the same Republic. On the 5th day of December, 1851, a consular convention was concluded between that Republic and the United States, which treaty was signed on behalf of the Republic of Granada by the same Señor Rivas. This treaty is still in force. On the 27th of April, 1852, Señor Don Victoriano de Diego Paredes was received as chargé d'affaires of the Republic of New Granada. On the 20th of June, 1855, General Pedro Alcántara Herran was again received as envoy extraordinary and minister plenipotentiary, duly accredited by the Republic of New Granada, and he has ever since remained, under the same credentials, as the representative of that Republic near the Government of the United States. On the 10th of September, 1857, a claims convention was concluded between the United States and the Republic of Granada. This convention is still in force, and has in part been executed. In May, 1858, the constitution of the Republic was remodeled, and the nation assumed the political title of "The Granadian Confederacy." This fact was formally announced to this Government, but without any change in their representative here. Previously to the 4th day of March, 1861, a revolutionary war against the Republic of New Granada, which had thus been recognized and treated with by the United States, broke out in New Granada, assuming to set up a new government under the name of "The United States of Colombia." This war has had various vicissitudes, sometimes favorable, sometimes adverse, to the revolutionary movements. The revolutionary organization has hitherto been simply a military provisionary power, and no definitive constitution of government has yet been established in New Granada in place of that organized by the constitution of 1858. The minister of the United States to the Granadian Confederacy, who was appointed on the 29th day of May, 1861, was directed, in view of the occupation of the capital by the revolutionary party and of the uncertainty of the civil war, not to present his credentials to either the Government of the Granadian Confederacy or to the provisional military Government, but to conduct his affairs informally, as is customary in such cases, and to report the progress of events and await the instructions of this Government. The advices which have been received from him have not hitherto been sufficiently conclusive to determine me to recognize the revolutionary Government. General Herran being here, with full authority from the Government of New Granada, which had been so long recognized by the United States, I have not received any representative from the revolutionary Government, which has not yet been recognized, because such a proceeding would, in itself be an act of recognition.

Official communications have been had on various incidental and occasional questions with General Herran as the minister plenipotentiary and envoy extraordinary of the Granadian Confederacy, but in no other character. No definitive measure or proceeding has resulted from these communications, and a communication of them at present would not, in my judgment, be compatible with the public interest.

ABRAHAM LINCOLN.

To the Senate and House of Representatives: JANUARY 17, 1863.

I have signed the joint resolution to provide for the immediate payment of the Army and Navy of the United States, passed by the House of Representatives on the 14th and by the Senate on the 15th instant.

The joint resolution is a simple authority, amounting, however, under existing circumstances, to a direction, to the Secretary of the Treasury to make an additional issue of $100,000,000 in United States notes, if so much money is needed, for the payment of the Army and Navy.

My approval is given in order that every possible facility may be afforded for the prompt discharge of all arrears of pay due to our soldiers and our sailors.

While giving this approval, however, I think it my duty to express my sincere regret that it has been found necessary to authorize so large an additional issue of United States notes, when this circulation and that of the suspended banks together have become already so redundant as to increase prices beyond real values, thereby augmenting the cost of living to the injury of labor, and the cost of supplies to the injury of the whole country.

It seems very plain that continued issues of United States notes without any check to the issues of suspended banks and without adequate provision for the raising of money by loans and for funding the issues so as to keep them within due limits must soon produce disastrous consequences; and this matter appears to me so important that I feel bound to avail myself of this occasion to ask the special attention of Congress to it.

That Congress has power to regulate the currency of the country can hardly admit of doubt, and that a judicious measure to prevent the deterioration of this currency, by a seasonable taxation of bank circulation or otherwise, is needed seems equally clear. Independently of this general consideration, it would be unjust to the people at large to exempt banks enjoying the special privilege of circulation from their just proportion of the public burdens.

In order to raise money by way of loans most easily and cheaply, it is clearly necessary to give every possible support to the public credit. To that end a uniform currency, in which taxes, subscriptions to loans, and all other ordinary public dues, as well as all private dues, may be paid, is almost, if not quite, indispensable. Such a currency can be furnished by banking associations, organized under a general act of Congress, as suggested in my message at the beginning of the present session. The securing of this circulation by the pledge of United States bonds, as therein suggested, would still further facilitate loans by increasing the present and causing a future demand for such bonds.

In view of the actual financial embarrassments of the Government and of the greater embarrassments sure to come if the necessary means of relief be not afforded, I feel that I should not perform my duty by a simple announcement of my approval of the joint resolution, which proposes relief only by increasing circulation, without expressing my earnest desire that measures such in substance as those I have just referred to may receive the early sanction of Congress.

By such measures, in my opinion, will payment be most certainly secured, not only to the Army and Navy, but to all honest creditors of the Government, and satisfactory provision made for future demands on the Treasury.

ABRAHAM LINCOLN.

WASHINGTON, *January 20, 1863.*

To the Senate of the United States:

I transmit herewith a report from the Secretary of State, in answer to the resolution of the Senate relative to the correspondence between this Government and the Mexican minister in relation to the exportation of articles contraband of war for the use of the French army in Mexico.

ABRAHAM LINCOLN.

EXECUTIVE MANSION,
Washington, January 21, 1863.

Gentlemen of the Senate and House of Representatives:

I submit herewith, for your consideration, the joint resolutions of the corporate authorities of the city of Washington adopted September 27, 1862, and a memorial of the same under date of October 28, 1862, both relating to and urging the construction of certain railroads concentrating upon the city of Washington.

In presenting this memorial and the joint resolutions to you I am not prepared to say more than that the subject is one of great practical importance and that I hope it will receive the attention of Congress.

ABRAHAM LINCOLN.

WASHINGTON, *January 23, 1863.*

To the Senate and House of Representatives:

I transmit, for the consideration of Congress, a report from the Secretary of State, transmitting the regulations, decrees, and orders for the government of the United States consular courts in Turkey.

ABRAHAM LINCOLN.

WASHINGTON, *January 26, 1863.*

To the Senate of the United States:

In compliance with the resolution of the Senate of the 13th instant, requesting a copy of certain correspondence respecting the capture of British vessels sailing from one British port to another having on board contraband of war intended for the use of the insurgents, I have the honor to transmit a report from the Secretary of State and the documents by which it was accompanied.

ABRAHAM LINCOLN.

WASHINGTON CITY, *January 28, 1863.*

To the Senate and House of Representatives:

In conformity to the law of July 16, 1862, I most cordially recommend that Commander David D. Porter, United States Navy, acting rear-admiral, commanding the Mississippi Squadron, receive a vote of thanks of Congress for the bravery and skill displayed in the attack on the post of Arkansas, which surrendered to the combined military and naval forces on the 10th instant.

ABRAHAM LINCOLN.

WASHINGTON, *February 4, 1863.*

To the House of Representatives:

In compliance with the resolution of the House of Representatives of the 5th December last, requesting information upon the present condition of Mexico, I transmit a report from the Secretary of State and the papers by which it was accompanied.

ABRAHAM LINCOLN.

WASHINGTON, D. C., *February 4, 1863.*

To the Senate of the United States:

In pursuance of the joint resolution of Congress approved 3d February, 1863, tendering its thanks to Commander John L. Worden, United States Navy, I nominate that officer to be a captain in the Navy on the active list from the 3d February, 1863.

It may be proper to state that the number of captains authorized by the second section of the act of 16th July, 1862, is now full, but presuming that the meaning of the ninth section of the same act is that the officer receiving the vote of thanks shall immediately be advanced one grade I have made the nomination.

ABRAHAM LINCOLN.

WASHINGTON, *February 5, 1863.*
Tc the Senate of the United States:

I submit to the Senate, for consideration with a view to ratification, a "convention between the United States of America and the Republic of Peru for the settlement of the pending claims of the citizens of either country against the other," signed at Lima on the 12th January ultimo, with the following amendment:

Article 1, strike out the words "the claims of the American citizens Dr. Charles Easton, Edmund Sartori, and the owners of the whale ship *William Lee* against the Government of Peru, and the Peruvian citizen Stephen Montano against the Government of the United States," and insert: *all claims of citizens of the United States against the Government of Peru and of citizens of Peru against the Government of the United States which have not been embraced in conventional or diplomatic agreement between the two Governments or their plenipotentiaries, and statements of which soliciting the interposition of either Government may previously to the exchange of the ratifications of this convention have been filed in the Department of State at Washington or the department for foreign affairs at Lima, etc.*

This amendment is considered desirable, as there are believed to be other claims proper for the consideration of the commission which are not among those specified in the original article, and because it is at least questionable whether either Government would be justified in incurring the expense of a commission for the sole purpose of disposing of the claims mentioned in that article.

ABRAHAM LINCOLN.

WASHINGTON, *February 5, 1863.*
To the Senate of the United States:

I submit to the Senate, for consideration with a view to ratification, a "convention between the United States of America and the Republic of Peru, providing for the reference to the King of Belgium of the claims arising out of the capture and confiscation of the ships *Lizzie Thompson* and *Georgiana*," signed at Lima on the 20th December, 1862.

ABRAHAM LINCOLN.

WASHINGTON, *February 6, 1863.*
To the Senate of the United States:

In compliance with the resolution of the Senate of the United States of yesterday, requesting information in regard to the death of General Ward, a citizen of the United States in the military service of the Chinese Government, I transmit a copy of a dispatch of the 27th of October last, and of its accompaniment, from the minister of the United States in China.

ABRAHAM LINCOLN.

WASHINGTON, *February 6, 1863.*
To the Senate of the United States:

I transmit herewith a report* from the Secretary of State, with accompanying documents, in answer to the resolution of the Senate of the 30th ultimo.

ABRAHAM LINCOLN.

WASHINGTON, *February 10, 1863.*
To the Senate of the United States:

In answer to the resolution of the Senate of yesterday, requesting information touching the visit of Mr. Mercier to Richmond in April last, I transmit a report from the Secretary of State, to whom the resolution was referred.

ABRAHAM LINCOLN.

WASHINGTON, D. C., *February 12, 1863.*
To the Senate of the United States:

On the 4th of September, 1862, Commander George Henry Preble, United States Navy, then senior officer in command of the naval force off the harbor of Mobile, was guilty of inexcusable neglect in permitting the armed steamer *Oreto* in open daylight to run the blockade. For his omission to perform his whole duty on that occasion and the injury thereby inflicted on the service and the country, his name was stricken from the list of naval officers and he was dismissed the service.

Since his dismissal earnest application has been made for his restoration to his former position by Senators and naval officers, on the ground that his fault was an error of judgment, and that the example in his case has already had its effect in preventing a repetition of similar neglect.

I therefore, on this application and representation, and in consideration of his previous fair record, do hereby nominate George Henry Preble to be a commander in the Navy from the 16th July, 1862, to take rank on the active list next after Commander Edward Donaldson, and to fill a vacancy occasioned by the death of Commander J. M. Wainwright.

ABRAHAM LINCOLN.

WASHINGTON, D. C., *February 12, 1863.*
To the Senate of the United States:

On the 24th August, 1861, Commander Roger Perry, United States Navy, was dismissed from the service under a misapprehension in regard to his loyalty to the Government, from the circumstance that several oaths were transmitted to him and the Navy Department failed to receive any recognition of them. After his dismissal, and upon his assurance that the oath failed to reach him and his readiness to execute it, he was

---

* Relating to the building of ships of war for the Japanese Government.

recommissioned to his original position on the 4th September following. On the same day, 4th September, he was ordered to command the sloop of war *Vandalia;* on the 22d this order was revoked and he was ordered to duty in the Mississippi Squadron, and on the 23d January, 1862, was detached sick, and has since remained unemployed. The advisory board under the act of 16th July, 1862, did not recommend him for further promotion.

This last commission, having been issued during the recess of the Senate, expired at the end of the succeeding session, 17th July, 1862, from which date, not having been nominated to the Senate, he ceased to be a commander in the Navy.

To correct the omission to nominate this officer to the Senate at its last session, I now nominate Commander Roger Perry to be a commander in the Navy from the 14th September, 1855, to take his relative position on the list of commanders not recommended for further promotion.

ABRAHAM LINCOLN.

WASHINGTON, *February 12, 1863.*
To the Senate of the United States:

In answer to the resolution of the Senate of the 10th instant, requesting information on the subjects of mediation, arbitration, or other measures looking to the termination of the existing civil war, I transmit a report from the Secretary of State and the documents by which it was accompanied.

ABRAHAM LINCOLN.

WASHINGTON, *February 13, 1863.*
To the Senate of the United States:

I transmit to the Senate, in answer to their resolution of the 12th instant, the accompanying report* from the Secretary of State.

ABRAHAM LINCOLN.

WASHINGTON, *February 13, 1863.*
Hon. GALUSHA A. GROW,
    Speaker of the House of Representatives.

SIR: I herewith communicate to the House of Representatives, in answer to their resolution of the 18th of December last, a report from the Secretary of the Interior, containing all the information in the possession of the Department respecting the causes of the recent outbreaks of the Indian tribes in the Northwest which has not heretofore been transmitted to Congress.

ABRAHAM LINCOLN.

* Relating to the use of negroes by the French army in Mexico.

EXECUTIVE OFFICE, *February 17, 1863.*

To the Senate of the United States:

I transmit herewith, for the constitutional action of the Senate thereon, a treaty made and concluded on the 3d day of February, 1863, between W. W. Ross, commissioner on the part of the United States, and the chiefs and headmen of the Pottawatomie Nation of Indians of Kansas, which, it appears from the accompanying letter from the Secretary of the Interior of the 17th instant, is intended to be amendatory of the treaty concluded with said Indians on the 15th November, 1862.

ABRAHAM LINCOLN.

WASHINGTON, *February 18, 1863.*

To the Senate of the United States:

I transmit to the Senate, for consideration with a view to its ratification, an additional article to the treaty between the United States and Great Britain of the 7th of April, 1862, for the suppression of the African slave trade, which was concluded and signed at Washington on the 17th instant by the Secretary of State and Her Britannic Majesty's minister accredited to this Government.

ABRAHAM LINCOLN.

WASHINGTON, D. C., *February 19, 1863.*

To the Senate of the United States:

Congress on my recommendation passed a resolution, approved 7th February, 1863, tendering its thanks to Commodore Charles Henry Davis for "distinguished service in conflict with the enemy at Fort Pillow, at Memphis, and for successful operations at other points in the waters of the Mississippi River."

I therefore, in conformity with the seventh section of the act approved 16th July, 1862, nominate Commodore Charles Henry Davis to be a rear-admiral in the Navy on the active list from the 7th February, 1863.

Captain John A. Dahlgren having in said resolution of the 7th February in like manner received the thanks of Congress "for distinguished service in the line of his profession, improvements in ordnance, and zealous and efficient labors in the ordnance branch of the service," I therefore, in conformity with the seventh section of the act of 16th July, 1862, nominate Captain John A. Dahlgren to be a rear-admiral in the Navy on the active list from the 7th February, 1863.

The ninth section of the act of July, 1862, authorizes "any line officer of the Navy or Marine Corps to be advanced one grade if upon recommendation of the President by name he receives the thanks of Congress for highly distinguished conduct in conflict with the enemy or for extraordinary heroism in the line of his profession," and Captain Stephen C. Rowan and Commander David D. Porter having each on my recommendation received the thanks of Congress for distinguished service, by resolution of the 7th February, 1863, I do therefore nominate Captain Stephen C. Rowan to be a commodore in the Navy on the active list from the 7th February, 1863. Commander David D. Porter to be a captain in the Navy on the active list from the 7th February, 1863.

If this nomination should be confirmed, there will be vacancies in the several grades to which these officers are nominated for promotion.

ABRAHAM LINCOLN.

WAR DEPARTMENT,
Washington City, February 25, 1863.

The PRESIDENT OF THE UNITED STATES SENATE.

SIR: In answer to the Senate resolution of the 21st instant, I have the honor to inclose herewith a letter of the 24th instant from the Secretary of War, by which it appears that there are 438 assistant quartermasters, 387 commissaries of subsistence, and 343 additional paymasters now in the volunteer service, including those before the Senate for confirmation.

I am, sir, very respectfully, your obedient servant,

ABRAHAM LINCOLN.

WASHINGTON, D. C., *February 25, 1863.*
To the Senate of the United States:

I nominate Passed Midshipmen Samuel Pearce and Nathaniel T. West, now on the retired list, to be ensigns in the Navy on the retired list.

These nominations are made in conformity with the fourth section of the act to amend an act entitled "An act to promote the efficiency of the Navy," approved 16th January, 1857, and are induced by the following considerations:

The pay of a passed midshipman on the retired list as fixed by the "Act for the better organization of the military establishment," approved 3d August, 1861, amounted, including rations, to $788 per annum. By the "Act to establish and equalize the grade of line officers of the United States Navy," approved 16th July, 1862, the grade or rank of passed midshipman, which was the next below that of master, was discontinued and that of ensign was established, being now the next grade below that of master and the only grade in the line list between those of master and midshipman. The same act fixes the pay of officers on the retired list, omitting the grade of passed midshipman, and prohibits the allowance of rations to retired officers. The effect of this was to reduce the pay of a passed midshipman on the retired list from $788 to $350 per annum, or less than half of previous rate.

This was no doubt an unintended result of the law, operating exclusively on the two passed midshipmen then on the retired list, and their

By the President of the United States of America.

A Proclamation.

Whereas, by the Act of Congress approved the 31st day of December, last, the State of West Virginia was declared to be one of the United States of America, and was admitted into the Union on an equal footing with the original States in all respects whatever; upon the condition that certain changes should be duly made in the proposed Constitution for that State;

And, whereas, proof of a compliance with that condition as required by the Second Section of the Act aforesaid, has been submitted to me;

Now, therefore, be it known, that I Abraham Lincoln, President of the United States, do, hereby, in pursuance of the Act of Congress aforesaid, declare and proclaim that the said act shall take effect and be in force; from and after sixty days from the date hereof.

In witness whereof, I have hereunto set my hand

PROCLAMATION ADMITTING WEST VIRGINIA TO THE
UNION OF STATES.

and caused the Seal of the United States to be affixed.

Done at the city of Washington, this twentieth day of April, in the year of our Lord one thousand eight hundred and sixty-three; and of the Independence of the United States the eighty-seventh.

Abraham Lincoln

By the President.

William H. Seward,
Secretary of State.

LAST PAGE AND SIGNATURES TO PROCLAMATION ADMITTING
WEST VIRGINIA.

promotion or transfer to the equivalent grade of ensign would not completely indemnify them, the pay of an ensign on the retired list being only $500 per annum. It is the only relief, however, which is deemed within the intention of the existing laws, and it is the more willingly recommended in this case, as there is nothing in the character of the officers to be relieved which would make it objectionable. These are the only cases of the kind.

ABRAHAM LINCOLN.

WASHINGTON, *February 28, 1863.*
To the Senate of the United States:

In compliance with the resolution of the Senate of the 26th instant, requesting a copy of any correspondence which may have taken place between me and workingmen in England, I transmit the papers mentioned in the subjoined list.

ABRAHAM LINCOLN.

WASHINGTON, *February 28, 1863.*
To the Senate and House of Representatives:

I transmit, for the consideration of Congress, a dispatch to the Secretary of State from the United States consul at Liverpool, and the address to which it refers, of the distressed operatives of Blackburn, in England, to the New York relief committee and to the inhabitants of the United States generally.

ABRAHAM LINCOLN.

WASHINGTON, *March 2, 1863.*
To the Senate and House of Representatives:

I transmit to Congress a copy of a preamble and joint resolution of the legislative assembly of the Territory of New Mexico, accepting the benefits of the act of Congress approved the 2d of July last, entitled "An act donating public lands to the several States and Territories which may provide colleges for the benefit of agriculture and the mechanic arts."

ABRAHAM LINCOLN.

PROCLAMATION.

BY THE PRESIDENT OF THE UNITED STATES OF AMERICA.

A PROCLAMATION.

Whereas on the 22d day of September, A. D. 1862, a proclamation was issued by the President of the United States, containing, among other things, the following, to wit:

That on the 1st day of January, A. D. 1863, all persons held as slaves within any State or designated part of a State the people whereof shall then be in rebellion against the United States shall be then, thenceforward, and forever free; and the executive government of the United States, including the military and naval authority thereof, will recognize and maintain the freedom of such persons and will do no act or acts to repress such persons, or any of them, in any efforts they may make for their actual freedom.

That the Executive will on the 1st day of January aforesaid, by proclamation, designate the States and parts of States, if any, in which the people thereof, respectively, shall then be in rebellion against the United States; and the fact that any State or the people thereof shall on that day be in good faith represented in the Congress of the United States by members chosen thereto at elections wherein a majority of the qualified voters of such States shall have participated shall, in the absence of strong countervailing testimony, be deemed conclusive evidence that such State and the people thereof are not then in rebellion against the United States.

Now, therefore, I, Abraham Lincoln, President of the United States, by virtue of the power in me vested as Commander in Chief of the Army and Navy of the United States in time of actual armed rebellion against the authority and Government of the United States, and as a fit and necessary war measure for suppressing said rebellion, do, on this 1st day of January, A. D. 1863, and in accordance with my purpose so to do, publicly proclaimed for the full period of one hundred days from the day first above mentioned, order and designate as the States and parts of States wherein the people thereof, respectively, are this day in rebellion against the United States the following, to wit:

Arkansas, Texas, Louisiana (except the parishes of St. Bernard, Plaquemines, Jefferson, St. John, St. Charles, St. James, Ascension, Assumption, Terrebonne, Lafourche, St. Mary, St. Martin, and Orleans, including the city of New Orleans), Mississippi, Alabama, Florida, Georgia, South Carolina, North Carolina, and Virginia (except the forty-eight counties designated as West Virginia, and also the counties of Berkeley, Accomac, Northampton, Elizabeth City, York, Princess Anne, and Norfolk, including the cities of Norfolk and Portsmouth), and which excepted parts are for the present left precisely as if this proclamation were not issued.

And by virtue of the power and for the purpose aforesaid, I do order and declare that all persons held as slaves within said designated States and parts of States are and henceforward shall be free, and that the executive government of the United States, including the military and naval authorities thereof, will recognize and maintain the freedom of said persons.

And I hereby enjoin upon the people so declared to be free to abstain from all violence, unless in necessary self-defense; and I recommend to them that in all cases when allowed they labor faithfully for reasonable wages.

And I further declare and make known that such persons of suitable condition will be received into the armed service of the United States to garrison forts, positions, stations, and other places and to man vessels of all sorts in said service.

And upon this act, sincerely believed to be an act of justice, warranted by the Constitution upon military necessity, I invoke the considerate judgment of mankind and the gracious favor of Almighty God.

In witness whereof I have hereunto set my hand and caused the seal of the United States to be affixed.

[SEAL.]   Done at the city of Washington, this 1st day of January, A. D. 1863, and of the Independence of the United States of America the eighty-seventh.

ABRAHAM LINCOLN.

By the President:

WILLIAM H. SEWARD, *Secretary of State.*

EXECUTIVE ORDERS.

EXECUTIVE MANSION,
Washington, December 22, 1862.

To the Army of the Potomac:

I have just read your commanding general's preliminary report of the battle of Fredericksburg. Although you were not successful, the attempt was not an error nor the failure other than an accident. The courage with which you in an open field maintained the contest against an intrenched foe and the consummate skill and success with which you crossed and recrossed the river in face of the enemy show that you possess all the qualities of a great army, which will yet give victory to the cause of the country and of popular government. Condoling with the mourners for the dead and sympathizing with the severely wounded, I congratulate you that the number of both is comparatively so small.

I tender to you, officers and soldiers, the thanks of the nation.

ABRAHAM LINCOLN.

EXECUTIVE MANSION,
Washington, January 4, 1863.

Hon. GIDEON WELLES,
    Secretary of the Navy.

DEAR SIR: As many persons who come well recommended for loyalty and service to the Union cause, and who are refugees from rebel oppression in the State of Virginia, make application to me for authority and permission to remove their families and property to protection within the Union lines by means of our armed gunboats on the Potomac River and Chesapeake Bay, you are hereby requested to hear and consider all such applications and to grant such assistance to this class of persons as in your judgment their merits may render proper and as may in each case be consistent with the perfect and complete efficiency of the naval service and with military expediency.

ABRAHAM LINCOLN.

EXECUTIVE MANSION, *January 8, 1863.*
Ordered by the President:

Whereas on the 13th day of November, 1862, it was ordered that the Attorney-General be charged with the superintendence and direction of all proceedings to be had under the act of Congress of the 17th of July, entitled "An act to suppress insurrection, to punish treason and rebellion, and to seize and confiscate the property of rebels, and for other purposes," in so far as may concern the seizure, prosecution, and condemnation of the estate, property, and effects of rebels and traitors, as mentioned and provided for in the fifth, sixth, and seventh sections of the said act of Congress; and

Whereas since that time it has been ascertained that divers prosecutions have been instituted in the courts of the United States for the condemnation of property of rebels and traitors under the act of Congress of August 6, 1861, entitled "An act to confiscate property used for insurrectionary purposes," which equally require the superintending care of the Government: Therefore

It is now further ordered by the President, That the Attorney-General be charged with superintendence and direction of all proceedings to be had under the said last-mentioned act (the act of 1861) as fully in all respects as under the first-mentioned act (the act of 1862).

                                                ABRAHAM LINCOLN.
By the President:
    EDW. BATES,
        Attorney-General.

Whereas by the twelfth section of an act of Congress entitled "An act to aid in the construction of a railroad and telegraph line from the Missouri River to the Pacific Ocean, and to secure to the Government the use of the same for postal, military, and other purposes," approved July 1, 1862, it is made the duty of the President of the United States to determine the uniform width of the track of the entire line of the said railroad and the branches of the same; and

Whereas application has been made to me by the Leavenworth, Pawnee and Western Railroad Company, a company authorized by the act of Congress above mentioned to construct a branch of said railroad, to fix the gauge thereof:

Now, therefore, I, Abraham Lincoln, President of the United States of America, do determine that the uniform width of the track of said railroad and all its branches which are provided for in the aforesaid act of Congress shall be 5 feet, and that this order be filed in the office of the Secretary of the Interior for the information and guidance of all concerned.

Done at the city of Washington, this 21st day of January, A. D. 1863.

                                                ABRAHAM LINCOLN.

' PROCLAMATION.

BY THE PRESIDENT OF THE UNITED STATES OF AMERICA.

A PROCLAMATION.

Whereas objects of interest to the United States require that the Senate should be convened at 12 o'clock on the 4th of March next to receive and act upon such communications as may be made to it on the part of the Executive:

Now, therefore, I, Abraham Lincoln, President of the United States, have considered it to be my duty to issue this my proclamation, declaring that an extraordinary occasion requires the Senate of the United States to convene for the transaction of business at the Capitol, in the city of Washington, on the 4th day of March next, at 12 o'clock at noon on that day, of which all who shall at that time be entitled to act as members of that body are hereby required to take notice.

Given under my hand and the seal of the United States, at Washington, the 28th day of February, A. D. 1863, and of the Independence of the United States of America the eighty-seventh.

[SEAL.]

ABRAHAM LINCOLN.

By the President:

WILLIAM H. SEWARD,
Secretary of State.

SPECIAL MESSAGES.

WASHINGTON, *March 5, 1863.*

To the Senate of the United States:

For the reasons stated by the Secretary of War, I present the nomination of the persons named in the accompanying communication for confirmation of the rank which they held at the time they fell in the service of their country.

ABRAHAM LINCOLN.

WAR DEPARTMENT,
Washington, March 5, 1863.

The PRESIDENT OF THE UNITED STATES.

SIR: The following-named persons having fallen in battle after having received appointments to the grades for which they are herein nominated, I have the honor to propose that their names be submitted to the Senate for confirmation of their rank, as a token of this Government's approbation of their distinguished merit. This has been the practice of the Department in similar cases, brevet nominations and confirmations having been made after the decease of gallant officers.

To be major-generals.

Brigadier-General Philip Kearney, of the United States Volunteers, July 14, 1862. (Killed in the battle of Chantilly.)

Brigadier-General Israel B. Richardson, of the United States Volunteers, July 4, 1862. (Died of wounds received at the battle of Antietam.)

Brigadier-General Jesse L. Reno, of the United States Volunteers, July 18, 1862. (Killed in the battle of South Mountain.)

To be brigadier-general.

Captain William R. Terrill, of the Fifth United States Artillery, September 9, 1862. (Killed in the battle of Perryville.)

I am, sir, with great respect, your obedient servant,

EDWIN M. STANTON,
Secretary of War.

WASHINGTON, *March 5, 1863.*
To the Senate of the United States:

For the reasons stated by the Secretary of War, I present the nomination of the persons named in the accompanying communication for confirmation of the rank of major-general, in which capacity they were acting at the time they fell in battle.

ABRAHAM LINCOLN.

WAR DEPARTMENT,
Washington, March 5, 1863.
The PRESIDENT OF THE UNITED STATES.

SIR: The following-named persons having fallen in battle while performing the duty and exercising command as major-generals, a rank which they had earned in the service of their country, I have the honor to propose that their names be submitted to the Senate for confirmation, as a token of the Government's appreciation of their distinguished merit. This is in accordance with the practice in similar cases, brevet nominations and confirmations having been made after the decease of gallant officers.

To be major-generals of volunteers.

Brigadier-General Joseph K. F. Mansfield, of the United States Army, July 19, 1862. (Died of wounds received in the battle of Antietam, Md.)

Brigadier-General Isaac I. Stevens, of the United States Volunteers, July 18, 1862. [Killed in the battle of Chantilly, Va.)

I am, sir, with great respect, your obedient servant,

EDWIN M. STANTON,
Secretary of War.

EXECUTIVE MANSION, *March 12, 1863.*
To the Senate of the United States:

I herewith transmit to the Senate, for its consideration and ratification, a treaty with the chiefs and headmen of the Chippewas of the Mississippi and the Pillagers and Lake Winnibigoshish bands of Chippewa Indians.

ABRAHAM LINCOLN.

PROCLAMATIONS.

[From Final Report of the Provost-Marshal-General (March 17, 1866), p. 218.]

BY THE PRESIDENT OF THE UNITED STATES.

A PROCLAMATION.

EXECUTIVE MANSION, *March 10, 1863.*

In pursuance of the twenty-sixth section of the act of Congress entitled "An act for enrolling and calling out the national forces, and for other purposes," approved on the 3d day of March, 1863, I, Abraham Lincoln, President and Commander in Chief of the Army and Navy of the United States, do hereby order and command that all soldiers enlisted or drafted in the service of the United States now absent from their regiments without leave shall forthwith return to their respective regiments.

And I do hereby declare and proclaim that all soldiers now absent from their respective regiments without leave who shall, on or before the 1st day of April, 1863, report themselves at any rendezvous designated by the general orders of the War Department No. 58, hereto annexed, may be restored to their respective regiments without punishment, except the forfeiture of pay and allowances during their absence; and all who do not return within the time above specified shall be arrested as deserters and punished as the law provides; and

Whereas evil-disposed and disloyal persons at sundry places have enticed and procured soldiers to desert and absent themselves from their regiments, thereby weakening the strength of the armies and prolonging the war, giving aid and comfort to the enemy, and cruelly exposing the gallant and faithful soldiers remaining in the ranks to increased hardships and danger:

I do therefore call upon all patriotic and faithful citizens to oppose and resist the aforementioned dangerous and treasonable crimes, and to aid in restoring to their regiments all soldiers absent without leave, and to assist in the execution of the act of Congress "for enrolling and calling out the national forces, and for other purposes," and to support the proper authorities in the prosecution and punishment of offenders against said act and in suppressing the insurrection and rebellion.

In testimony whereof I have hereunto set my hand.

Done at the city of Washington, this 10th day of March, A. D. 1863, and of the Independence of the United States the eighty-seventh.

ABRAHAM LINCOLN.

By the President:
EDWIN M. STANTON,
Secretary of War.

GENERAL ORDERS, NO. 58.

WAR DEPARTMENT,
ADJUTANT-GENERAL'S OFFICE,
Washington, March 10, 1863.

I. The following is the twenty-sixth section of the act "for enrolling and calling out the national forces, and for other purposes," approved March 3, 1863:

"SEC. 26. *And be it further enacted*, That immediately after the passage of this act the President shall issue his proclamation declaring that all soldiers now absent from their regiments without leave may return, within a time specified, to such place or places as he may indicate in his proclamation, and be restored to their respective regiments without punishment, except the forfeiture of their pay and allowances during their absence; and all deserters who shall not return within the time so specified by the President shall, upon being arrested, be punished as the law provides."

I II. The following places* are designated as rendezvous to which soldiers absent without leave may report themselves to the officers named on or before the 1st day of April next under the proclamation of the President of this date.

III. Commanding officers at the above-named places of rendezvous, or, in the absence of commanding officers, superintendents of recruiting service, recruiting officers, and mustering and disbursing officers, will take charge of all soldiers presenting themselves as above directed and cause their names to be enrolled, and copy of said roll will, on or before the 10th day of April, be sent to the Adjutant-General of the Army.

The soldiers so reporting themselves will be sent without delay to their several regiments, a list of those sent being furnished to the commanding officer of the regiment and a duplicate to the Adjutant-General of the Army. The commanding officer of the regiment will immediately report to the Adjutant-General of the Army the receipt of any soldiers so sent to him.

By order of the Secretary of War:

L. THOMAS,
Adjutant-General.

BY THE PRESIDENT OF THE UNITED STATES OF AMERICA.

A PROCLAMATION.

Whereas the Senate of the United States, devoutly recognizing the supreme authority and just government of Almighty God in all the affairs of men and of nations, has by a resolution requested the President to designate and set apart a day for national prayer and humiliation; and

Whereas it is the duty of nations as well as of men to own their dependence upon the overruling power of God, to confess their sins and transgressions in humble sorrow, yet with assured hope that genuine repentance will lead to mercy and pardon, and to recognize the sublime truth, announced in the Holy Scriptures and proven by all history, that those nations only are blessed whose God is the Lord;

And, insomuch as we know that by His divine law nations, like individuals, are subjected to punishments and chastisements in this world, may we not justly fear that the awful calamity of civil war which now desolates the land may be but a punishment inflicted upon us for our

* Omitted.

presumptuous sins, to the needful end of our national reformation as a whole people? We have been the recipients of the choicest bounties of Heaven; we have been preserved these many years in peace and prosperity; we have grown in numbers, wealth, and power as no other nation has ever grown. But we have forgotten God. We have forgotten the gracious hand which preserved us in peace and multiplied and enriched and strengthened us, and we have vainly imagined, in the deceitfulness of our hearts, that all these blessings were produced by some superior wisdom and virtue of our own. Intoxicated with unbroken success, we have become too self-sufficient to feel the necessity of redeeming and preserving grace, too proud to pray to the God that made us.

It behooves us, then, to humble ourselves before the offended Power, to confess our national sins, and to pray for clemency and forgiveness.

Now, therefore, in compliance with the request, and fully concurring in the views of the Senate, I do by this my proclamation designate and set apart Thursday, the 30th day of April, 1863, as a day of national humiliation, fasting, and prayer. And I do hereby request all the people to abstain on that day from their ordinary secular pursuits, and to unite at their several places of public worship and their respective homes in keeping the day holy to the Lord and devoted to the humble discharge of the religious duties proper to that solemn occasion.

All this being done in sincerity and truth, let us then rest humbly in the hope authorized by the divine teachings that the united cry of the nation will be heard on high and answered with blessings no less than the pardon of our national sins and the restoration of our now divided and suffering country to its former happy condition of unity and peace.

In witness whereof I have hereunto set my hand and caused the seal of the United States to be affixed.

[SEAL.] Done at the city of Washington, this 30th day of March, A. D. 1863, and of the Independence of the United States the eighty-seventh.

ABRAHAM LINCOLN.

By the President:

WILLIAM H. SEWARD, *Secretary of State.*

BY THE PRESIDENT OF THE UNITED STATES OF AMERICA.

A PROCLAMATION.

Whereas, in pursuance of the act of Congress approved July 13, 1861, I did, by proclamation dated August 16, 1861, declare that the inhabitants of the States of Georgia, South Carolina, Virginia, North Carolina, Tennessee, Alabama, Louisiana, Texas, Arkansas, Mississippi, and Florida (except the inhabitants of that part of Virginia lying west of the Alleghany Mountains and of such other parts of that State and the other States hereinbefore named as might maintain a legal adhesion to the

Union and the Constitution or might be from time to time occupied and controlled by forces of the United States engaged in the dispersion of said insurgents) were in a state of insurrection against the United States, and that all commercial intercourse between the same and the inhabitants thereof, with the exceptions aforesaid, and the citizens of other States and other parts of the United States was unlawful and would remain unlawful until such insurrection should cease or be suppressed, and that all goods and chattels, wares and merchandise, coming from any of said States, with the exceptions aforesaid, into other parts of the United States without the license and permission of the President, through the Secretary of the Treasury, or proceeding to any of said States, with the exceptions aforesaid, by land or water, together with the vessel or vehicle conveying the same to or from said States, with the exceptions aforesaid, would be forfeited to the United States; and

Whereas experience has shown that the exceptions made in and by said proclamation embarrass the due enforcement of said act of July 13, 1861, and the proper regulation of the commercial intercourse authorized by said act with the loyal citizens of said States:

Now, therefore, I, Abraham Lincoln, President of the United States, do hereby revoke the said exceptions, and declare that the inhabitants of the States of Georgia, South Carolina, North Carolina, Tennessee, Alabama, Louisiana, Texas, Arkansas, Mississippi, Florida, and Virginia (except the forty-eight counties of Virginia designated as West Virginia, and except also the ports of New Orleans, Key West, Port Royal, and Beaufort, in North Carolina) are in a state of insurrection against the United States, and that all commercial intercourse not licensed and conducted as provided in said act between the said States and the inhabitants thereof, with the exceptions aforesaid, and the citizens of other States and other parts of the United States is unlawful and will remain unlawful until such insurrection shall cease or has been suppressed and notice thereof has been duly given by proclamation; and all cotton, tobacco, and other products, and all other goods and chattels, wares and merchandise, coming from any of said States, with the exceptions aforesaid, into other parts of the United States, or proceeding to any of said States, with the exceptions aforesaid, without the license and permission of the President, through the Secretary of the Treasury, will, together with the vessel or vehicle conveying the same, be forfeited to the United States.

In witness whereof I have hereunto set my hand and caused the seal of the United States to be affixed.

[SEAL.] Done at the city of Washington, this 2d day of April, A. D. 1863, and of the Independence of the United States of America the eighty-seventh.

ABRAHAM LINCOLN.

By the President:

WILLIAM H. SEWARD, *Secretary of State.*

ABRAHAM LINCOLN, PRESIDENT OF THE UNITED STATES OF AMERICA.

To all to whom these presents shall come, greeting:

Know ye that, whereas a paper bearing date the 31st day of December last, purporting to be an agreement between the United States and one Bernard Kock for immigration of persons of African extraction to a dependency of the Republic of Hayti, was signed by me on behalf of the party of the first part; but whereas the said instrument was and has since remained incomplete in consequence of the seal of the United States not having been thereunto affixed; and whereas I have been moved by considerations by me deemed sufficient to withhold my authority for affixing the said seal:

Now, therefore, be it known that I, Abraham Lincoln, President of the United States, do hereby authorize the Secretary of State to cancel my signature to the instrument aforesaid.

Done at Washington, this 16th day of April, A. D. 1863.

[SEAL.]   ABRAHAM LINCOLN.

By the President:

WILLIAM H. SEWARD,
Secretary of State.

BY THE PRESIDENT OF THE UNITED STATES OF AMERICA.

A PROCLAMATION.

Whereas by the act of Congress approved the 31st day of December last the State of West Virginia was declared to be one of the United States of America, and was admitted into the Union on an equal footing with the original States in all respects whatever, upon the condition that certain changes should be duly made in the proposed constitution for that State; and

Whereas proof of a compliance with that condition, as required by the second section of the act aforesaid has been submitted to me:

Now, therefore, be it known that I, Abraham Lincoln, President of the United States, do hereby, in pursuance of the act of Congress aforesaid, declare and proclaim that the said act shall take effect and be in force from and after sixty days from the date hereof.

In witness whereof I have hereunto set my hand and caused the seal of the United States to be affixed.

[SEAL.]   Done at the city of Washington, this 20th day of April, A. D. 1863, and of the Independence of the United States the eighty-seventh.   ABRAHAM LINCOLN.

By the President:

WILLIAM H. SEWARD,
Secretary of State.

BY THE PRESIDENT OF THE UNITED STATES OF AMERICA.

A PROCLAMATION.

Whereas the Congress of the United States at its last session enacted a law entitled "An act for enrolling and calling out the national forces and for other purposes," which was approved on the 3d day of March last; and

Whereas it is recited in the said act that there now exists in the United States an insurrection and rebellion against the authority thereof, and it is, under the Constitution of the United States, the duty of the Government to suppress insurrection and rebellion, to guarantee to each State a republican form of government, and to preserve the public tranquillity; and

Whereas for these high purposes a military force is indispensable, to raise and support which all persons ought willingly to contribute; and

Whereas no service can be more praiseworthy and honorable than that which is rendered for the maintenance of the Constitution and Union and the consequent preservation of free government; and

Whereas, for the reasons thus recited, it was enacted by the said statute that all able-bodied male citizens of the United States and persons of foreign birth who shall have declared on oath their intention to become citizens under and in pursuance of the laws thereof, between the ages of 20 and 45 years (with certain exceptions not necessary to be here mentioned), are declared to constitute the national forces, and shall be liable to perform military duty in the service of the United States when called out by the President for that purpose; and

Whereas it is claimed by and in behalf of persons of foreign birth within the ages specified in said act who have heretofore declared on oath their intentions to become citizens under and in pursuance of the laws of the United States, and who have not exercised the right of suffrage or any other political franchise under the laws of the United States or of any of the States thereof, that they are not absolutely concluded by their aforesaid declaration of intention from renouncing their purpose to become citizens, and that, on the contrary, such persons, under treaties or the law of nations, retain a right to renounce that purpose and to forego the privileges of citizenship and residence within the United States under the obligations imposed by the aforesaid act of Congress:

Now, therefore, to avoid all misapprehensions concerning the liability of persons concerned to perform the service required by such enactment, and to give it full effect, I do hereby order and proclaim that no plea of alienage will be received or allowed to exempt from the obligations imposed by the aforesaid act of Congress any person of foreign birth who shall have declared on oath his intention to become a citizen of the United States under the laws thereof, and who shall be found within the United States at any time during the continuance of the present insurrection and rebellion or after the expiration of the period of sixty-five days from the date of this proclamation, nor shall any such plea of alienage be allowed in favor of any such person who has so as aforesaid declared his intention to become a citizen of the United States and shall have exercised at any time the right of suffrage or any other political franchise within the United States under the laws thereof or under the laws of any of the several States.

In witness whereof I have hereunto set my hand and caused the seal of the United States to be affixed.

[SEAL.] Done at the city of Washington, this 8th day of May, A. D. 1863, and of the Independence of the United States the eighty-seventh.

ABRAHAM LINCOLN.

By the President:
WILLIAM H. SEWARD, *Secretary of State.*

BY THE PRESIDENT OF THE UNITED STATES OF AMERICA.

A PROCLAMATION.

Whereas the armed insurrectionary combinations now existing in several of the States are threatening to make inroads into the States of Maryland, West Virginia, Pennsylvania, and Ohio, requiring immediately an additional military force for the service of the United States:

Now, therefore, I, Abraham Lincoln, President of the United States and Commander in Chief of the Army and Navy thereof and of the militia of the several States when called into actual service, do hereby call into the service of the United States 100,000 militia from the States following, namely: From the State of Maryland, 10,000; from the State of Pennsylvania, 50,000; from the State of Ohio, 30,000; from the State of West Virginia, 10,000—to be mustered into the service of the United States forthwith and to serve for the period of six months from the date of such muster into said service, unless sooner discharged; to be mustered in as infantry, artillery, and cavalry, in proportions which will be made known through the War Department, which Department will also designate the several places of rendezvous. These militia to be organized according to the rules and regulations of the volunteer service and such orders as may hereafter be issued. The States aforesaid will be respectively credited under the enrollment act for the militia services rendered under this proclamation.

In testimony whereof I have hereunto set my hand and caused the seal of the United States to be affixed.

[SEAL.] Done at the city of Washington, this 15th day of June, A. D. 1863, and of the Independence of the United States the eighty seventh.

ABRAHAM LINCOLN.

By the President:
WILLIAM H. SEWARD, *Secretary of State.*

By the President of the United States of America.

A PROCLAMATION.

It has pleased Almighty God to hearken to the supplications and prayers of an afflicted people and to vouchsafe to the Army and the Navy of the United States victories on land and on the sea so signal and so effective as to furnish reasonable grounds for augmented confidence that the Union of these States will be maintained, their Constitution preserved, and their peace and prosperity permanently restored. But these victories have been accorded not without sacrifices of life, limb, health, and liberty, incurred by brave, loyal, and patriotic citizens. Domestic affliction in every part of the country follows in the train of these fearful bereavements. It is meet and right to recognize and confess the presence of the Almighty Father and the power of His hand equally in these triumphs and in these sorrows:

Now, therefore, be it known that I do set apart Thursday, the 6th day of August next, to be observed as a day for national thanksgiving, praise, and prayer, and I invite the people of the United States to assemble on that occasion in their customary places of worship and in the forms approved by their own consciences render the homage due to the Divine Majesty for the wonderful things He has done in the nation's behalf and invoke the influence of His Holy Spirit to subdue the anger which has produced and so long sustained a needless and cruel rebellion, to change the hearts of the insurgents, to guide the counsels of the Government with wisdom adequate to so great a national emergency, and to visit with tender care and consolation throughout the length and breadth of our land all those who, through the vicissitudes of marches, voyages, battles, and sieges, have been brought to suffer in mind, body, or estate, and finally to lead the whole nation through the paths of repentance and submission to the divine will back to the perfect enjoyment of union and fraternal peace.

In witness whereof I have hereunto set my hand and caused the seal of the United States to be affixed.

[SEAL.] Done at the city of Washington, this 15th day of July, A. D. 1863, and of the Independence of the United States of America the eighty-eighth. ABRAHAM LINCOLN.

By the President:

WILLIAM H. SEWARD, *Secretary of State.*

By the President of the United States of America.

A PROCLAMATION.

Whereas the Constitution of the United States has ordained that the privilege of the writ of *habeas corpus* shall not be suspended unless when, in cases of rebellion or invasion, the public safety may require it; and

Whereas a rebellion was existing on the 3d day of March, 1863, which rebellion is still existing; and

Whereas by a statute which was approved on that day it was enacted by the Senate and House of Representatives of the United States in Congress assembled that during the present insurrection the President of the United States, whenever in his judgment the public safety may require, is authorized to suspend the privilege of the writ of *habeas corpus* in any case throughout the United States or any part thereof; and

Whereas, in the judgment of the President, the public safety does require that the privilege of the said writ shall now be suspended throughout the United States in the cases where, by the authority of the President of the United States, military, naval, and civil officers of the United States, or any of them, hold persons under their command or in their custody, either as prisoners of war, spies, or aiders or abettors of the enemy, or officers, soldiers, or seamen enrolled or drafted or mustered or enlisted in or belonging to the land or naval forces of the United States, or as deserters therefrom, or otherwise amenable to military law or the rules and articles of war or the rules or regulations prescribed for the military or naval services by authority of the President of the United States, or for resisting a draft, or for any other offense against the military or naval service:

Now, therefore, I, Abraham Lincoln, President of the United States, do hereby proclaim and make known to all whom it may concern that the privilege of the writ of *habeas corpus* is suspended throughout the United States in the several cases before mentioned, and that this suspension will continue throughout the duration of the said rebellion or until this proclamation shall, by a subsequent one to be issued by the President of the United States, be modified or revoked. And I do hereby require all magistrates, attorneys, and other civil officers within the United States and all officers and others in the military and naval services of the United States to take distinct notice of this suspension and to give it full effect, and all citizens of the United States to conduct and govern themselves accordingly and in conformity with the Constitution of the United States and the laws of Congress in such case made and provided.

In testimony whereof I have hereunto set my hand and caused the seal of the United States to be affixed this 15th day of September,
[SEAL.]   A. D. 1863, and of the Independence of the United States of America the eighty-eighth.

By the President: ABRAHAM LINCOLN.

WILLIAM H. SEWARD, *Secretary of State.*

BY THE PRESIDENT OF THE UNITED STATES OF AMERICA.

A PROCLAMATION.

Whereas in my proclamation of the 27th of April, 1861, the ports of the States of Virginia and North Carolina were, for reasons therein set forth, placed under blockade; and

Whereas the port of Alexandria, Va., has since been blockaded, but as the blockade of said port may now be safely relaxed with advantage to the interests of commerce:

Now, therefore, be it known that I, Abraham Lincoln, President of the United States, pursuant to the authority in me vested by the fifth section of the act of Congress approved on the 13th of July, 1861, entitled "An act further to provide for the collection of duties on imports and for other purposes," do hereby declare that the blockade of the said port of Alexandria shall so far cease and determine from and after this date that commercial intercourse with said port, except as to persons, things, and information contraband of war, may from this date be carried on, subject to the laws of the United States and to the limitations and in pursuance of the regulations which are prescribed by the Secretary of the Treasury in his order which is appended to my proclamation of the 12th of May, 1862.

In witness whereof I have hereunto set my hand and caused the seal of the United States to be affixed.

[SEAL.]   Done at the city of Washington, this 24th day of September, A. D. 1863, and of the Independence of the United States the eighty-eighth.

ABRAHAM LINCOLN.

By the President:

WILLIAM H. SEWARD, *Secretary of State.*

BY THE PRESIDENT OF THE UNITED STATES OF AMERICA.

A PROCLAMATION.

The year that is drawing toward its close has been filled with the blessings of fruitful fields and healthful skies. To these bounties, which are so constantly enjoyed that we are prone to forget the source from which they come, others have been added which are of so extraordinary a nature that they can not fail to penetrate and soften even the heart which is habitually insensible to the ever-watchful providence of Almighty God.

In the midst of a civil war of unequaled magnitude and severity, which has sometimes seemed to foreign states to invite and to provoke their aggression, peace has been preserved with all nations, order has been maintained, the laws have been respected and obeyed, and harmony has prevailed everywhere, except in the theater of military conflict, while that theater has been greatly contracted by the advancing armies and navies of the Union.

Needful diversions of wealth and of strength from the fields of peaceful industry to the national defense have not arrested the plow, the shuttle, or the ship; the ax has enlarged the borders of our settlements, and the mines, as well of iron and coal as of the precious metals, have yielded even more abundantly than heretofore. Population has steadily increased notwithstanding the waste that has been made in the camp, the siege, and the battlefield, and the country, rejoicing in the conscious-

BATTLE OF GETTYSBURG

An Incident of the Confederate Retreat

THE BATTLE OF GETTYSBURG

The three-days Battle of Gettysburg is described in the Encyclopedic Index, under the heading " Gettysburg, Battle of."

On the morning of the 4th of July, the press of the North contained this notice: " The President announces to the country that news from the Army of the Potomac, up to 10 p.m. of the 3rd, is such as to cover that army with the highest honor, to promise a great success to the cause of the Union, and to claim the condolence of all for the many gallant fallen, and that for this he especially desires that on this day. He whose will, not ours, should ever be done, be everywhere remembered and reverenced with profoundest gratitude."

Had the war been one between two nations, it would have terminated then and there in a treaty of peace dictated by the victor at Gettysburg.

ness of augmented strength and vigor, is permitted to expect continuance of years with large increase of freedom.

No human counsel hath devised nor hath any mortal hand worked out these great things. They are the gracious gifts of the Most High God, who, while dealing with us in anger for our sins, hath nevertheless remembered mercy.

It has seemed to me fit and proper that they should be solemnly, reverently, and gratefully acknowledged, as with one heart and one voice, by the whole American people. I do therefore invite my fellow-citizens in every part of the United States, and also those who are at sea and those who are sojourning in foreign lands, to set apart and observe the last Thursday of November next as a day of thanksgiving and praise to our beneficent Father who dwelleth in the heavens. And I recommend to them that while offering up the ascriptions justly due to Him for such singular deliverances and blessings they do also, with humble penitence for our national perverseness and disobedience, commend to His tender care all those who have become widows, orphans, mourners, or sufferers in the lamentable civil strife in which we are unavoidably engaged, and fervently implore the interposition of the Almighty hand to heal the wounds of the nation and to restore it, as soon as may be consistent with the divine purposes, to the full enjoyment of peace, harmony, tranquillity, and union.

In testimony whereof I have hereunto set my hand and caused the seal of the United States to be affixed.

[SEAL.]   Done at the city of Washington, this 3d day of October, A. D. 1863, and of the Independence of the United States the eighty-eighth.

ABRAHAM LINCOLN.

By the President:

WILLIAM H. SEWARD, *Secretary of State.*

BY THE PRESIDENT OF THE UNITED STATES OF AMERICA.

A PROCLAMATION.

Whereas the term of service of a part of the volunteer forces of the United States will expire during the coming year; and

Whereas, in addition to the men raised by the present draft, it is deemed expedient to call out 300,000 volunteers to serve for three years or the war, not, however, exceeding three years:

Now, therefore, I, Abraham Lincoln, President of the United States and Commander in Chief of the Army and Navy thereof and of the militia of the several States when called into actual service, do issue this my proclamation, calling upon the governors of the different States to raise and have enlisted into the United States service for the various companies and regiments in the field from their respective States their quotas of 300,000 men.

I further proclaim that all volunteers thus called out and duly enlisted shall receive advance pay, premium, and bounty, as heretofore communicated to the governors of States by the War Department through the Provost-Marshal-General's Office by special letters.

I further proclaim that all volunteers received under this call, as well as all others not heretofore credited, shall be duly credited on and deducted from the quotas established for the next draft.

I further proclaim that if any State shall fail to raise the quota assigned to it by the War Department under this call, then a draft for the deficiency in said quota shall be made on said State, or on the districts of said State, for their due proportion of said quota; and the said draft shall commence on the 5th day of January, 1864.

And I further proclaim that nothing in this proclamation shall interfere with existing orders, or those which may be issued, for the present draft in the States where it is now in progress or where it has not yet commenced.

The quotas of the States and districts will be assigned by the War Department, through the Provost-Marshal-General's Office, due regard being had for the men heretofore furnished, whether by volunteering or drafting, and the recruiting will be conducted in accordance with such instructions as have been or may be issued by that Department.

In issuing this proclamation I address myself not only to the governors of the several States, but also to the good and loyal people thereof, invoking them to lend their willing, cheerful, and effective aid to the measures thus adopted, with a view to reenforce our victorious armies now in the field and bring our needful military operations to a prosperous end, thus closing forever the fountains of sedition and civil war.

In witness whereof I have hereunto set my hand and caused the seal of the United States to be affixed.

[SEAL.] Done at the city of Washington, this 17th day of October, A. D. 1863, and of the Independence of the United States the eighty-eighth. ABRAHAM LINCOLN.

By the President:

WILLIAM H. SEWARD, *Secretary of State.*

EXECUTIVE ORDERS.

EXECUTIVE MANSION,
Washington, March 31, 1863.

Whereas by the act of Congress approved July 13, 1861, entitled "An act to provide for the collection of duties on imports, and for other purposes," all commercial intercourse between the inhabitants of such States as should by proclamation be declared in insurrection against the United

States and the citizens of the rest of the United States was prohibited so long as such condition of hostility should continue, except as the same shall be licensed and permitted by the President to be conducted and carried on only in pursuance of rules and regulations prescribed by the Secretary of the Treasury; and

Whereas it appears that a partial restoration of such intercourse between the inhabitants of sundry places and sections heretofore declared in insurrection in pursuance of said act and the citizens of the rest of the United States will favorably affect the public interests:

Now, therefore, I, Abraham Lincoln, President of the United States, exercising the authority and discretion confided to me by the said act of Congress, do hereby license and permit such commercial intercourse between the citizens of loyal States and the inhabitants of such insurrectionary States in the cases and under the restrictions described and expressed in the regulations prescribed by the Secretary of the Treasury bearing even date with these presents, or in such other regulations as he may hereafter, with my approval, prescribe.

ABRAHAM LINCOLN.

EXECUTIVE MANSION,
Washington, June 22, 1863.

Whereas the act of Congress approved the 3d day of March, A. D. 1863, entitled "An act to provide circuit courts for the districts of California and Oregon, and for other purposes," authorized the appointment of one additional associate justice of the Supreme Court of the United States, and provided that the districts of California and Oregon should constitute the tenth circuit and that the other circuits should remain as then constituted by law; and

Whereas Stephen J. Field was appointed the said additional associate justice of the Supreme Court since the last adjournment of said court, and consequently he was not allotted to the said circuit according to the fifth section of the act of Congress entitled "An act to amend the judicial system of the United States," approved the 29th day of April, 1802:

Now I, Abraham Lincoln, President of the United States, under the authority of said section, do allot the said associate justice, Stephen J. Field, to the said tenth circuit.

ABRAHAM LINCOLN.

Attest:

TITIAN J. COFFEY,
Attorney-General ad interim.

WAR DEPARTMENT,
Washington, July 4, 1863—10 a. m.

The President announces to the country that news from the Army of the Potomac up to 10 o'clock p. m. of the 3d is such as to cover that army with the highest honor, to promise a great success to the cause of the Union, and to claim the condolence of all for the many gallant fallen; and that for this he especially desires that on this day He whose will, not ours, should ever be done be everywhere remembered and ever reverenced with profoundest gratitude.

ABRAHAM LINCOLN.

GENERAL ORDERS, No. 211.

WAR DEPARTMENT,
ADJUTANT-GENERAL'S OFFICE,
Washington, July 9, 1863.

ORDER ABOLISHING MILITARY GOVERNORSHIP OF ARKANSAS.

Ordered, That the appointment of John S. Phelps as military governor of the State of Arkansas and of Amos F. Eno as secretary be revoked, and the office of military governor in said State is abolished, and that all authority, appointments, and power heretofore granted to and exercised by them, or either of them, as military governor or secretary, or by any person or persons appointed by or acting under them, is hereby revoked and annulled.

By order of the President:

E. D. TOWNSEND,
Assistant Adjutant-General.

EXECUTIVE MANSION,
Washington, July 25, 1863.

Hon. SECRETARY OF THE NAVY.

SIR: Certain matters have come to my notice, and considered by me, which induce me to believe that it will conduce to the public interest for you to add to the general instructions given to our naval commanders in relation to contraband trade propositions substantially as follows, to wit:

First. You will avoid the reality, and as far as possible the appearance, of using any neutral port to watch neutral vessels, and then to dart out and seize them on their departure.

NOTE.—Complaint is made that this has been practiced at the port of St. Thomas, which practice, if it exists, is disapproved and must cease.

Second. You will not in any case detain the crew of a captured neutral vessel or any other subject of a neutral power on board such vessel, as prisoners of war or otherwise, except the small number necessary as witnesses in the prize court.

NOTE.—The practice here forbidden is also charged to exist, which, if true, is disapproved and must cease.

My dear sir, it is not intended to be insinuated that you have been remiss in the performance of the arduous and responsible duties of your Department, which, I take pleasure in affirming, has in your hands been conducted with admirable success. Yet, while your subordinates are almost of necessity brought into angry collision with the subjects of foreign states, the representatives of those states and yourself do not come into immediate contact for the purpose of keeping the peace, in spite of such collisions. At that point there is an ultimate and heavy responsibility upon me.

What I propose is in strict accordance with international law, and is therefore unobjectionable; whilst, if it does no other good, it will contribute to sustain a considerable portion of the present British ministry in their places, who, if displaced, are sure to be replaced by others more unfavorable to us.

Your obedient servant, ABRAHAM LINCOLN.

EXECUTIVE MANSION,
Washington, July 30, 1863.

It is the duty of every government to give protection to its citizens, of whatever class, color, or condition, and especially to those who are duly organized as soldiers in the public service. The law of nations and the usages and customs of war, as carried on by civilized powers, permit no distinction as to color in the treatment of prisoners of war as public enemies. To sell or enslave any captured person on account of his color, and for no offense against the laws of war, is a relapse into barbarism and a crime against the civilization of the age.

The Government of the United States will give the same protection to all its soldiers, and if the enemy shall sell or enslave anyone because of his color the offense shall be punished by retaliation upon the enemy's prisoners in our possession.

It is therefore ordered, That for every soldier of the United States killed in violation of the laws of war a rebel soldier shall be executed, and for every one enslaved by the enemy or sold into slavery a rebel soldier shall be placed at hard labor on the public works and continued at such labor until the other shall be released and receive the treatment due to a prisoner of war.

ABRAHAM LINCOLN.

EXECUTIVE MANSION,
Washington City, August 25, 1863.

Ordered, first. That clearances issued by the Treasury Department for vessels or merchandise bound for the port of New Orleans for the military necessities of the department, certified by Brigadier-General Shepley, the military governor of Louisiana, shall be allowed to enter said port.

Second. That vessels and domestic produce from New Orleans permitted by the military governor of Louisiana at New Orleans for the military purpose of his department shall on his permit be allowed to pass from said port to its destination to any port not blockaded by the United States.

A. LINCOLN.

WAR DEPARTMENT,
Washington City, August 31, 1863.

Ordered, That the Executive order of November 21, 1862, prohibiting the exportation of arms, ammunition, or munitions of war from the United States, be, and the same hereby is, modified so far as to permit the exportation of imported arms, ammunition, and munitions of war to the ports whence they were shipped for the United States.

By order of the President: [EDWIN M. STANTON.]

EXECUTIVE MANSION,
Washington, September 4, 1863.

Ordered, That the Executive order dated November 21, 1862, prohibiting the exportation from the United States of arms, ammunition, or munitions of war, under which the commandants of departments were, by order of the Secretary of War dated May 13, 1863, directed to prohibit the purchase and sale for exportation from the United States of all horses and mules within their respective commands, and to take and appropriate to the use of the United States any horses, mules, and live stock designed for exportation, be so far modified that any arms heretofore imported into the United States may be reexported to the place of original shipment, and that any live stock raised in any State or Territory bounded by the Pacific Ocean may be exported from any port of such State or Territory.

ABRAHAM LINCOLN.

WAR DEPARTMENT,
Washington City, September 24, 1863.

Ordered by the President of the United States, That Major-General Hooker be, and he is hereby, authorized to take military possession of all railroads, with their cars, locomotives, plants, and equipments, that may be necessary for the execution of the military operation committed to his charge; and all officers, agents, and employees of said roads are directed to render their aid and assistance therein and to respect and obey his commands, pursuant to the act of Congress in such case made and provided.

EDWIN M. STANTON, *Secretary of War.*

EXECUTIVE MANSION,
Washington, November 10, 1863.

In consideration of the peculiar circumstances and pursuant to the comity deemed to be due to friendly powers, any tobacco in the United

States belonging to the government either of France, Austria, or any other state with which this country is at peace, and which tobacco was purchased and paid for by such government prior to the 4th day of March, 1861, may be exported from any port of the United States under the supervision and upon the responsibility of naval officers of such governments and in conformity to such regulations as may be presented by the Secretary of State of the United States, and not otherwise.

ABRAHAM LINCOLN.

THIRD ANNUAL MESSAGE.

DECEMBER 8, 1863.

Fellow-Citizens of the Senate and House of Representatives:

Another year of health and of sufficiently abundant harvests has passed. For these, and especially for the improved condition of our national affairs, our renewed and profoundest gratitude to God is due.

We remain in peace and friendship with foreign powers.

The efforts of disloyal citizens of the United States to involve us in foreign wars to aid an inexcusable insurrection have been unavailing. Her Britannic Majesty's Government, as was justly expected, have exercised their authority to prevent the departure of new hostile expeditions from British ports. The Emperor of France has by a like proceeding promptly vindicated the neutrality which he proclaimed at the beginning of the contest. Questions of great intricacy and importance have arisen out of the blockade and other belligerent operations between the Government and several of the maritime powers, but they have been discussed and, as far as was possible, accommodated in a spirit of frankness, justice, and mutual good will. It is especially gratifying that our prize courts, by the impartiality of their adjudications, have commanded the respect and confidence of maritime powers.

The supplemental treaty between the United States and Great Britain for the suppression of the African slave trade, made on the 17th day of February last, has been duly ratified and carried into execution. It is believed that so far as American ports and American citizens are concerned that inhuman and odious traffic has been brought to an end.

I shall submit for the consideration of the Senate a convention for the adjustment of possessory claims in Washington Territory arising out of the treaty of the 15th June, 1846, between the United States and Great Britain, and which have been the source of some disquiet among the citizens of that now rapidly improving part of the country.

A novel and important question, involving the extent of the maritime jurisdiction of Spain in the waters which surround the island of Cuba, has been debated without reaching an agreement, and it is proposed in an amicable spirit to refer it to the arbitrament of a friendly power. A convention for that purpose will be submitted to the Senate.

I have thought it proper, subject to the approval of the Senate, to concur with the interested commercial powers in an arrangement for the liquidation of the Scheldt dues, upon the principles which have been heretofore adopted in regard to the imposts upon navigation in the waters of Denmark.

The long-pending controversy between this Government and that of Chile touching the seizure at Sitana, in Peru, by Chilean officers, of a large amount in treasure belonging to citizens of the United States has been brought to a close by the award of His Majesty the King of the Belgians, to whose arbitration the question was referred by the parties. The subject was thoroughly and patiently examined by that justly respected magistrate, and although the sum awarded to the claimants may not have been as large as they expected there is no reason to distrust the wisdom of His Majesty's decision. That decision was promptly complied with by Chile when intelligence in regard to it reached that country.

The joint commission under the act of the last session for carrying into effect the convention with Peru on the subject of claims has been organized at Lima, and is engaged in the business intrusted to it.

Difficulties concerning interoceanic transit through Nicaragua are in course of amicable adjustment.

In conformity with principles set forth in my last annual message, I have received a representative from the United States of Colombia, and have accredited a minister to that Republic.

Incidents occurring in the progress of our civil war have forced upon my attention the uncertain state of international questions touching the rights of foreigners in this country and of United States citizens abroad. In regard to some governments these rights are at least partially defined by treaties. In no instance, however, is it expressly stipulated that in the event of civil war a foreigner residing in this country within the lines of the insurgents is to be exempted from the rule which classes him as a belligerent, in whose behalf the Government of his country can not expect any privileges or immunities distinct from that character. I regret to say, however, that such claims have been put forward, and in some instances in behalf of foreigners who have lived in the United States the greater part of their lives.

There is reason to believe that many persons born in foreign countries who have declared their intention to become citizens, or who have been fully naturalized, have evaded the military duty required of them by denying the fact and thereby throwing upon the Government the burden of proof. It has been found difficult or impracticable to obtain this proof, from the want of guides to the proper sources of information. These might be supplied by requiring clerks of courts where declarations of intention may be made or naturalizations effected to send periodically lists of the names of the persons naturalized or declaring their intention to become citizens to the Secretary of the Interior, in whose Department those names might be arranged and printed for general information.

There is also reason to believe that foreigners frequently become citizens of the United States for the sole purpose of evading duties imposed by the laws of their native countries, to which on becoming naturalized here they at once repair, and though never returning to the United States they still claim the interposition of this Government as citizens. Many altercations and great prejudices have heretofore arisen out of this abuse. It is therefore submitted to your serious consideration. It might be advisable to fix a limit beyond which no citizen of the United States residing abroad may claim the interposition of his Government.

The right of suffrage has often been assumed and exercised by aliens under pretenses of naturalization, which they have disavowed when drafted into the military service. I submit the expediency of such an amendment of the law as will make the fact of voting an estoppel against any plea of exemption from military service or other civil obligation on the ground of alienage.

In common with other Western powers, our relations with Japan have been brought into serious jeopardy through the perverse opposition of the hereditary aristocracy of the Empire to the enlightened and liberal policy of the Tycoon, designed to bring the country into the society of nations. It is hoped, although not with entire confidence, that these difficulties may be peacefully overcome. I ask your attention to the claim of the minister residing there for the damages he sustained in the destruction by fire of the residence of the legation at Yedo.

Satisfactory arrangements have been made with the Emperor of Russia, which, it is believed, will result in effecting a continuous line of telegraph through that Empire from our Pacific coast.

I recommend to your favorable consideration the subject of an international telegraph across the Atlantic Ocean, and also of a telegraph between this capital and the national forts along the Atlantic seaboard and the Gulf of Mexico. Such communications, established with any reasonable outlay, would be economical as well as effective aids to the diplomatic, military, and naval service.

The consular system of the United States, under the enactments of the last Congress, begins to be self-sustaining, and there is reason to hope that it may become entirely so with the increase of trade which will ensue whenever peace is restored. Our ministers abroad have been faithful in defending American rights. In protecting commercial interests our consuls have necessarily had to encounter increased labors and responsibilities growing out of the war. These they have for the most part met and discharged with zeal and efficiency. This acknowledgment justly includes those consuls who, residing in Morocco, Egypt, Turkey,

Japan, China, and other Oriental countries, are charged with complex functions and extraordinary powers.

The condition of the several organized Territories is generally satisfactory, although Indian disturbances in New Mexico have not been entirely suppressed. The mineral resources of Colorado, Nevada, Idaho, New Mexico, and Arizona are proving far richer than has been heretofore understood. I lay before you a communication on this subject from the governor of New Mexico. I again submit to your consideration the expediency of establishing a system for the encouragement of immigration. Although this source of national wealth and strength is again flowing with greater freedom than for several years before the insurrection occurred, there is still a great deficiency of laborers in every field of industry, especially in agriculture and in our mines, as well of iron and coal as of the precious metals. While the demand for labor is much increased here, tens of thousands of persons, destitute of remunerative occupation, are thronging our foreign consulates and offering to emigrate to the United States if essential, but very cheap, assistance can be afforded them. It is easy to see that under the sharp discipline of civil war the nation is beginning a new life. This noble effort demands the aid and ought to receive the attention and support of the Government.

Injuries unforeseen by the Government and unintended may in some cases have been inflicted on the subjects or citizens of foreign countries, both at sea and on land, by persons in the service of the United States. As this Government expects redress from other powers when similar injuries are inflicted by persons in their service upon citizens of the United States, we must be prepared to do justice to foreigners. If the existing judicial tribunals are inadequate to this purpose, a special court may be authorized, with power to hear and decide such claims of the character referred to as may have arisen under treaties and the public law. Conventions for adjusting the claims by joint commission have been proposed to some governments, but no definitive answer to the proposition has yet been received from any.

In the course of the session I shall probably have occasion to request you to provide indemnification to claimants where decrees of restitution have been rendered and damages awarded by admiralty courts, and in other cases where this Government may be acknowledged to be liable in principle and where the amount of that liability has been ascertained by an informal arbitration.

The proper officers of the Treasury have deemed themselves required by the law of the United States upon the subject to demand a tax upon the incomes of foreign consuls in this country. While such a demand may not in strictness be in derogation of public law, or perhaps of any existing treaty between the United States and a foreign country, the expediency of so far modifying the act as to exempt from tax the income of such consuls as are not citizens of the United States, derived from the emoluments of their office or from property not situated in the United States, is submitted to your serious consideration. I make this suggestion upon the ground that a comity which ought to be reciprocated exempts our consuls in all other countries from taxation to the extent thus indicated. The United States, I think, ought not to be exceptionally illiberal to international trade and commerce.

The operations of the Treasury during the last year have been successfully conducted. The enactment by Congress of a national banking law has proved a valuable support of the public credit, and the general legislation in relation to loans has fully answered the expectations of its favorers. Some amendments may be required to perfect existing laws, but no change in their principles or general scope is believed to be needed.

Since these measures have been in operation all demands on the Treasury, including the pay of the Army and Navy, have been promptly met and fully satisfied. No considerable body of troops, it is believed, were ever more amply provided and more liberally and punctually paid, and it may be added that by no people were the burdens incident to a great war ever more cheerfully borne.

The receipts during the year from all sources, including loans and balance in the Treasury at its commencement, were $901,125,674.86, and the aggregate disbursements $895,796,630.65, leaving a balance on the 1st of July, 1863, of $5,329,044.21. Of the receipts there were derived from customs $69,059,642.40, from internal revenue $37,640,787.95, from direct tax $1,485,103.61, from lands $167,617.17, from miscellaneous sources $3,046,615.35, and from loans $776,682,361.57, making the aggregate $901,125,674.86. Of the disbursements there were for the civil service $23,253,922.08, for pensions and Indians $4,216,520.79, for interest on public debt $24,729,846.51, for the War Department $599,298,600.83, for the Navy Department $63,211,105.27, for payment of funded and temporary debt $181,086,635.07, making the aggregate $895,796,630.65 and leaving the balance of $5,329,044.21. But the payment of funded and temporary debt, having been made from moneys borrowed during the year, must be regarded as merely nominal payments and the moneys borrowed to make them as merely nominal receipts, and their amount, $181,086,635.07, should therefore be deducted both from receipts and disbursements. This being done there remains as actual receipts $720,039,039.79 and the actual disbursements $714,709,995.58, leaving the balance as already stated.

The actual receipts and disbursements for the first quarter and the estimated receipts and disbursements for the remaining three quarters of the current fiscal year (1864) will be shown in detail by the report of the Secretary of the Treasury, to which I invite your attention. It is sufficient to say here that it is not believed that actual results will exhibit a state of the finances less favorable to the country than the estimates of that officer heretofore submitted, while it is confidently expected that at the close of the year both disbursements and debt will be found very considerably less than has been anticipated.

The report of the Secretary of War is a document of great interest. It consists of—

1. The military operations of the year, detailed in the report of the General in Chief.

2. The organization of colored persons into the war service.

3. The exchange of prisoners, fully set forth in the letter of General Hitchcock.

4. The operations under the act for enrolling and calling out the national forces, detailed in the report of the Provost-Marshal-General.

5. The organization of the invalid corps, and

6. The operation of the several departments of the Quartermaster-General, Commissary-General, Paymaster-General, Chief of Engineers, Chief of Ordnance, and Surgeon-General.

It has appeared impossible to make a valuable summary of this report, except such as would be too extended for this place, and hence I content myself by asking your careful attention to the report itself.

The duties devolving on the naval branch of the service during the year and throughout the whole of this unhappy contest have been discharged with fidelity and eminent success. The extensive blockade has been constantly increasing in efficiency as the Navy has expanded, yet on so long a line it has so far been impossible to entirely suppress illicit trade. From returns received at the Navy Department it appears that more than 1,000 vessels have been captured since the blockade was instituted, and that the value of prizes already sent in for adjudication amounts to over $13,000,000.

The naval force of the United States consists at this time of 588 vessels completed and in the course of completion, and of these 75 are ironclad or armored steamers. The events of the war give an increased interest and importance to the Navy which will probably extend beyond the war itself.

The armored vessels in our Navy completed and in service, or which are under contract and approaching completion, are believed to exceed in number those of any other power; but while these may be relied upon for harbor defense and coast service, others of greater strength and capacity will be necessary for cruising purposes and to maintain our rightful position on the ocean.

The change that has taken place in naval vessels and naval warfare since the introduction of steam as a motive power for ships of war demands either a corresponding change in some of our existing navy-yards or the establishment of new ones for the construction and necessary repair of modern naval vessels. No inconsiderable embarrassment, delay, and public injury have been experienced from the want of such governmental establishments. The necessity of such a navy-yard, so furnished, at some suitable place upon the Atlantic seaboard has on repeated occasions been brought to the attention of Congress by the Navy Department, and is again presented in the report of the Secretary which accompanies this communication. I think it my duty to invite your special attention to this subject, and also to that of establishing a yard and depot for naval purposes upon one of the Western rivers. A naval force has been created on those interior waters, and under many disadvantages, within little more than two years, exceeding in numbers the whole naval force of the country at the commencement of the present Administration. Satisfactory and important as have been the performances of the heroic men of the Navy at this interesting period, they are scarcely more wonderful than the success of our mechanics and artisans in the production of war vessels, which has created a new form of naval power.

Our country has advantages superior to any other nation in our resources of iron and timber, with inexhaustible quantities of fuel in the immediate vicinity of both, and all available and in close proximity to navigable waters. Without the advantage of public works, the resources of the nation have been developed and its power displayed in the construction of a Navy of such magnitude, which has at the very period of its creation rendered signal service to the Union.

The increase of the number of seamen in the public service from 7,500 men in the spring of 1861 to about 34,000 at the present time has been accomplished without special legislation or extraordinary bounties to promote that increase. It has been found, however, that the operation of the draft, with the high bounties paid for army recruits, is beginning to affect injuriously the naval service, and will, if not corrected, be likely to impair its efficiency by detaching seamen from their proper vocation and inducing them to enter the Army. I therefore respectfully suggest that Congress might aid both the army and naval services by a definite provision on this subject which would at the same time be equitable to the communities more especially interested.

I commend to your consideration the suggestions of the Secretary of the Navy in regard to the policy of fostering and training seamen and also the education of officers and engineers for the naval service. The Naval Academy is rendering signal service in preparing midshipmen for the highly responsible duties which in after life they will be required to perform. In order that the country should not be deprived of the proper quota of educated officers, for which legal provision has been made at the naval school, the vacancies caused by the neglect or omission to make nominations from the States in insurrection have been filled by the Secretary of the Navy. The school is now more full and complete than at any former period, and in every respect entitled to the favorable consideration of Congress.

During the past fiscal year the financial condition of the Post-Office Department has been one of increasing prosperity, and I am gratified in being able to state that the actual postal revenue has nearly equaled the entire expenditures, the latter amounting to $11,314,206.84 and the former to $11,163,789.59, leaving a deficiency of but $150,417.25. In 1860, the year immediately preceding the rebellion, the deficiency amounted to $5,656,705.49, the postal receipts of that year being $2,645,722.19 less than those of 1863. The decrease since 1860 in the annual amount of transportation has been only about 25 per cent, but the annual expenditure on account of the same has been reduced 35 per cent. It is manifest, therefore, that the Post-Office Department may become self-sustaining in a few years, even with the restoration of the whole service.

The international conference of postal delegates from the principal countries of Europe and America, which was called at the suggestion of the Postmaster-General, met at Paris on the 11th of May last and concluded its deliberations on the 8th of June. The principles established by the conference as best adapted to facilitate postal intercourse between nations and as the basis of future postal conventions inaugurate a general system of uniform international charges at reduced rates of postage, and can not fail to produce beneficial results.

I refer you to the report of the Secretary of the Interior, which is herewith laid before you, for useful and varied information in relation to the public lands, Indian affairs, patents, pensions, and other matters of public concern pertaining to his Department.

The quantity of land disposed of during the last and the first quarter of the present fiscal years was 3,841,549 acres, of which 161,911 acres were sold for cash, 1,456,514 acres were taken up under the homestead law, and the residue disposed of under laws granting lands for military bounties, for railroad and other purposes. It also appears that the sale of the public lands is largely on the increase.

It has long been a cherished opinion of some of our wisest statesmen that the people of the United States had a higher and more enduring interest in the early settlement and substantial cultivation of the public lands than in the amount of direct revenue to be derived from the sale of them. This opinion has had a controlling influence in shaping legislation upon the subject of our national domain. I may cite as evidence of this the liberal measures adopted in reference to actual settlers; the grant to the States of the overflowed lands within their limits, in order to their being reclaimed and rendered fit for cultivation; the grants to railway companies of alternate sections of land upon the contemplated lines of their roads, which when completed will so largely multiply the facilities for reaching our distant possessions. This policy has received its most signal and beneficent illustration in the recent enactment granting homesteads to actual settlers. Since the 1st day of January last the before-mentioned quantity of 1,456,514 acres of land have been taken up under its provisions. This fact and the amount of sales furnish gratifying evidence of increasing settlement upon the public lands, notwithstanding the great struggle in which the energies of the nation have been engaged, and which has required so large a withdrawal of our citizens from their accustomed pursuits. I cordially concur in the recommendation of the Secretary of the Interior suggesting a modification of the act in favor of those engaged in the military and naval service of the United States. I doubt not that Congress will cheerfully adopt such measures as will, without essentially changing the general features of the system, secure to the greatest practicable extent its benefits to those who have left their homes in the defense of the country in this arduous crisis.

I invite your attention to the views of the Secretary as to the propriety of raising by appropriate legislation a revenue from the mineral lands of the United States.

The measures provided at your last session for the removal of certain Indian tribes have been carried into effect. Sundry treaties have been negotiated, which will in due time be submitted for the constitutional action of the Senate. They contain stipulations for extinguishing the possessory rights of the Indians to large and valuable tracts of lands. It is hoped that the effect of these treaties will result in the establishment of permanent friendly relations with such of these tribes as have been brought into frequent and bloody collision with our outlying settlements and emigrants. Sound policy and our imperative duty to these wards of the Government demand our anxious and constant attention to their material well-being, to their progress in the arts of civilization, and, above all, to that moral training which under the blessing of Divine Providence will confer upon them the elevated and sanctifying influences, the hopes and consolations, of the Christian faith.

I suggested in my last annual message the propriety of remodeling our Indian system. Subsequent events have satisfied me of its necessity. The details set forth in the report of the Secretary evince the urgent need for immediate legislative action.

I commend the benevolent institutions established or patronized by the Government in this District to your generous and fostering care.

The attention of Congress during the last session was engaged to some extent with a proposition for enlarging the water communication between the Mississippi River and the northeastern seaboard, which proposition, however, failed for the time. Since then, upon a call of the greatest respectability, a convention has been held at Chicago upon the same subject, a summary of whose views is contained in a memorial addressed to the President and Congress, and which I now have the honor to lay before you. That this interest is one which ere long will force its own way I do not entertain a doubt, while it is submitted entirely to your wisdom as to what can be done now. Augmented interest is given to this subject by the actual commencement of work upon the Pacific Railroad, under auspices so favorable to rapid progress and completion. The enlarged navigation becomes a palpable need to the great road.

I transmit the second annual report of the Commissioner of the Department of Agriculture, asking your attention to the developments in that vital interest of the nation.

When Congress assembled a year ago, the war had already lasted nearly twenty months, and there had been many conflicts on both land and sea, with varying results; the rebellion had been pressed back into reduced limits; yet the tone of public feeling and opinion, at home and abroad, was not satisfactory. With other signs, the popular elections then just past indicated uneasiness among ourselves, while, amid much that was cold and menacing, the kindest words coming from Europe were uttered in accents of pity that we were too blind to surrender a hopeless cause. Our commerce was suffering greatly by a few armed vessels built upon and furnished from foreign shores, and we were threatened with such additions from the same quarter as would sweep our trade from the sea and raise our blockade. We had failed to elicit from European Governments anything hopeful upon this subject. The preliminary emancipation proclamation, issued in September, was running its assigned period to the beginning of the new year. A month later the final proclamation came, including the announcement that colored men of suitable condition would be received into the war service. The policy of emancipation and of employing black soldiers gave to the future a new aspect, about which hope and fear and doubt contended in uncertain conflict. According to our political system, as a matter of civil administration, the General Government had no lawful power to effect emancipation in any State, and for a long time it had been hoped that the rebellion could be suppressed without resorting to it as a military measure. It was all the while deemed possible that the necessity for it might come, and that if it should the crisis of the contest would then be presented. It came, and, as was anticipated, it was followed by dark and doubtful days. Eleven months having now passed, we are permitted to take another review. The rebel borders are pressed still farther back, and by the complete opening of the Mississippi the country dominated by the rebellion is divided into distinct parts, with no practical communication between them. Tennessee and Arkansas have been substantially cleared of insurgent control, and influential citizens in each, owners of slaves and advocates of slavery at the beginning of the rebellion, now declare openly for emancipation in their respective States. Of those States not included in the emancipation proclamation, Maryland and Missouri, neither of which three years ago would tolerate any restraint upon the extension of slavery into new Territories, only dispute now as to the best mode of removing it within their own limits.

Of those who were slaves at the beginning of the rebellion full 100,000 are now in the United States military service, about one-half of which number actually bear arms in the ranks, thus giving the double advantage of taking so much labor from the insurgent cause and supplying the places

GUN AND MORTAR BOATS ON THE MISSISSIPPI

LEE'S RETREAT AFTER THE BATTLE OF GETTYSBURG

RIVER OPERATIONS OF THE CIVIL WAR

In these days of railroad transportation the importance of the Mississippi River before and during the Civil War can hardly be realized. So essential was it that the Confederates considered that their control of its navigation would ultimately force the Western States to join them. Lincoln, a Westerner, was impregnated with this sentiment. From a military point of view Federal success on the Mississippi was a vital wound to the Confederacy. Across its broad bosom Texas sent her grain and beef for the army, and Louisiana her sugar. It was an avenue for munitions of war, sent from abroad to Mexico.

In 1862 the Confederate line ran from Columbus on the Mississippi, to Fort Henry on the Tennessee, to Fort Donelson on the Cumberland, and thence to Bowling Green. On February 6, 1862, Foote's gunboats, of the types shown in the illustration, reduced Fort Henry. On February 14th the troops under Grant combined with the gunboats to reduce Fort Donelson. During the remainder of the year the river was opened down to Vicksburg. When on July 3, 1863, Grant received the surrender of Vicksburg, the final outcome of the war was settled.

Various river battles are described in the Encyclopedic Index, as for instance, "New Madrid (Mo.), Battle of," "Island No. 10 (Tenn.), Battle of," "Vicksburg (Miss.), Battle of," and "Arkansas Post, Battle of."

which otherwise must be filled with so many white men. So far as tested, it is difficult to say they are not as good soldiers as any. No servile insurrection or tendency to violence or cruelty has marked the measures of emancipation and arming the blacks. These measures have been much discussed in foreign countries, and, contemporary with such discussion, the tone of public sentiment there is much improved. At home the same measures have been fully discussed, supported, criticised, and denounced, and the annual elections following are highly encouraging to those whose official duty it is to bear the country through this great trial. Thus we have the new reckoning. The crisis which threatened to divide the friends of the Union is past.

Looking now to the present and future, and with reference to a resumption of the national authority within the States wherein that authority has been suspended, I have thought fit to issue a proclamation, a copy of which is herewith transmitted.* On examination of this proclamation it will appear, as is believed, that nothing will be attempted beyond what is amply justified by the Constitution. True, the form of an oath is given, but no man is coerced to take it. The man is only promised a pardon in case he voluntarily takes the oath. The Constitution authorizes the Executive to grant or withhold the pardon at his own absolute discretion, and this includes the power to grant on terms, as is fully established by judicial and other authorities.

It is also proffered that if in any of the States named a State government shall be in the mode prescribed set up, such government shall be recognized and guaranteed by the United States, and that under it the State shall, on the constitutional conditions, be protected against invasion and domestic violence. The constitutional obligation of the United States to guarantee to every State in the Union a republican form of government and to protect the State in the cases stated is explicit and full. But why tender the benefits of this provision only to a State government set up in this particular way? This section of the Constitution contemplates a case wherein the element within a State favorable to republican government in the Union may be too feeble for an opposite and hostile element external to or even within the State, and such are precisely the cases with which we are now dealing.

An attempt to guarantee and protect a revived State government, constructed in whole or in preponderating part from the very element against whose hostility and violence it is to be protected, is simply absurd. There must be a test by which to separate the opposing elements, so as to build only from the sound; and that test is a sufficiently liberal one which accepts as sound whoever will make a sworn recantation of his former unsoundness.

But if it be proper to require as a test of admission to the political body an oath of allegiance to the Constitution of the United States and to the

*See proclamation dated December 8, 1863, pp. 3414-3416.

Union under it, why also to the laws and proclamations in regard to slavery? Those laws and proclamations were enacted and put forth for the purpose of aiding in the suppression of the rebellion. To give them their fullest effect there had to be a pledge for their maintenance. In my judgment, they have aided and will further aid the cause for which they were intended. To now abandon them would be not only to relinquish a lever of power, but would also be a cruel and an astounding breach of faith. I may add at this point that while I remain in my present position I shall not attempt to retract or modify the emancipation proclamation, nor shall I return to slavery any person who is free by the terms of that proclamation or by any of the acts of Congress. For these and other reasons it is thought best that support of these measures shall be included in the oath, and it is believed the Executive may lawfully claim it in return for pardon and restoration of forfeited rights, which he has clear constitutional power to withhold altogether or grant upon the terms which he shall deem wisest for the public interest. It should be observed also that this part of the oath is subject to the modifying and abrogating power of legislation and supreme judicial decision.

The proposed acquiescence of the National Executive in any reasonable temporary State arrangement for the freed people is made with the view of possibly modifying the confusion and destitution which must at best attend all classes by a total revolution of labor throughout whole States. It is hoped that the already deeply afflicted people in those States may be somewhat more ready to give up the cause of their affliction if to this extent this vital matter be left to themselves, while no power of the National Executive to prevent an abuse is abridged by the proposition.

The suggestion in the proclamation as to maintaining the political framework of the States on what is called reconstruction is made in the hope that it may do good without danger of harm. It will save labor and avoid great confusion.

But why any proclamation now upon this subject? This question is beset with the conflicting views that the step might be delayed too long or be taken too soon. In some States the elements for resumption seem ready for action, but remain inactive apparently for want of a rallying point—a plan of action. Why shall A adopt the plan of B rather than B that of A? And if A and B should agree, how can they know but that the General Government here will reject their plan? By the proclamation a plan is presented which may be accepted by them as a rallying point, and which they are assured in advance will not be rejected here. This may bring them to act sooner than they otherwise would.

The objections to a premature presentation of a plan by the National Executive consist in the danger of committals on points which could be more safely left to further developments. Care has been taken to so shape the document as to avoid embarrassments from this source. Saying that on certain terms certain classes will be pardoned with rights restored, it is not said that other classes or other terms will never be included. Saying that reconstruction will be accepted if presented in a specified way, it is not said it will never be accepted in any other way.

The movements by State action for emancipation in several of the States not included in the emancipation proclamation are matters of profound gratulation. And while I do not repeat in detail what I have heretofore so earnestly urged upon this subject, my general views and feelings remain unchanged; and I trust that Congress will omit no fair opportunity of aiding these important steps to a great consummation.

In the midst of other cares, however important, we must not lose sight of the fact that the war power is still our main reliance. To that power alone can we look yet for a time to give confidence to the people in the contested regions that the insurgent power will not again overrun them. Until that confidence shall be established little can be done anywhere for what is called reconstruction. Hence our chiefest care must still be directed to the Army and Navy, who have thus far borne their harder part so nobly and well; and it may be esteemed fortunate that in giving the greatest efficiency to these indispensable arms we do also honorably recognize the gallant men, from commander to sentinel, who compose them, and to whom more than to others the world must stand indebted for the home of freedom disenthralled, regenerated, enlarged, and perpetuated.   ABRAHAM LINCOLN.

SPECIAL MESSAGES.

WASHINGTON, D. C., *December 8, 1863.*

To the Senate and House of Representatives:

In conformity to the law of July 16, 1862, I most cordially recommend that Captain John Rodgers, United States Navy, receive a vote of thanks from Congress for the eminent skill and gallantry exhibited by him in the engagement with the rebel armed ironclad steamer *Fingal*, alias *Atlanta*, whilst in command of the United States ironclad steamer *Weehawken*, which led to her capture on the 17th June, 1863, and also for the zeal, bravery, and general good conduct shown by this officer on many occasions.

This recommendation is specially made in order to comply with the requirements of the ninth section of the aforesaid act, which is in the following words, viz:

That any line officer of the Navy or Marine Corps may be advanced one grade if upon recommendation of the President by name he receives the thanks of Congress for highly distinguished conduct in conflict with the enemy or for extraordinary heroism in the line of his profession.   ABRAHAM LINCOLN.

WASHINGTON, D. C., *December 8, 1863.*

To the Senate of the United States:

Congress, on my recommendation, passed a resolution, approved 7th February, 1863, tendering its thanks to Commander D. D. Porter "for the bravery and skill displayed in the attack on the post of Arkansas on the 10th January, 1863," and in consideration of those services, together with his efficient labors and vigilance subsequently displayed in thwarting the efforts of the rebels to obstruct the Mississippi and its tributaries and the important part rendered by the squadron under his command, which led to the surrender of Vicksburg.

I do therefore, in conformity to the seventh section of the act approved 16th July, 1862, nominate Commander D. D. Porter to be a rear-admiral in the Navy on the active list from the 4th July, 1863, to fill an existing vacancy.

ABRAHAM LINCOLN.

WASHINGTON, *December 10, 1863.*

To the Senate and House of Representatives:

I transmit herewith a report, dated the 9th instant, with the accompanying papers, received from the Secretary of State in compliance with the requirements of the sixteenth and eighteenth sections of the act entitled "An act to regulate the diplomatic and consular systems of the United States," approved August 18, 1856.

ABRAHAM LINCOLN.

EXECUTIVE MANSION,
Washington, December, 1863.

To the Senate of the United States:

I lay before the Senate, for its constitutional action thereon, a treaty concluded at Le Roy, Kans., on the 29th day of August, 1863, between William P. Dole, Commissioner of Indian Affairs, and William G. Coffin, superintendent of Indian affairs of the southern superintendency, commissioners on the part of the United States, and the chiefs and headmen of the Great and Little Osage tribe of Indians of the State of Kansas.

A communication from the Secretary of the Interior, dated the 12th instant, accompanies the treaty.

ABRAHAM LINCOLN.

EXECUTIVE MANSION,
Washington, December, 1863.

To the Senate of the United States:

I lay before the Senate, for its constitutional action thereon, a treaty concluded on the 7th day of October, 1863, at Conejos, Colorado Territory, between John Evans, governor and *ex officio* superintendent of Indian affairs of said Territory; Michael Steck, superintendent of Indian affairs for the Territory of New Mexico; Simeon Whitely and Lafayette Head,

Indian agents, commissioners on the part of the United States, and the chiefs and warriors of the Tabeguache band of Utah Indians.

I also transmit a report of the Secretary of the Interior of the 12th instant, submitting the treaty; an extract from the last annual report of Governor Evans, of Colorado Territory, relating to its negotiation, and a map upon which is delineated the boundaries of the country ceded by the Indians and that retained for their own use.

ABRAHAM LINCOLN.

EXECUTIVE MANSION,
Washington, December, 1863.

To the Senate of the United States:

I lay before the Senate, for its constitutional action thereon, a treaty concluded at the city of Washington on the 6th day of April, 1863, between John P. Usher, commissioner on the part of the United States, and the chiefs and headmen of the Comanche, Kiowa, and Apache tribes of Indians, duly authorized thereto.

A letter of the Secretary of the Interior of the 12th instant accompanies the treaty.

ABRAHAM LINCOLN.

EXECUTIVE MANSION,
Washington, December, 1863.

To the Senate of the United States:

I lay before the Senate, for its constitutional action thereon, a treaty concluded at the Sac and Fox Agency, in Kansas, on the 2d day of September, 1863, between William P. Dole, Commissioner of Indian Affairs, commissioner on the part of the United States, and the New York Indians, represented by duly authorized members of the bands of said tribe.

A letter of the Secretary of the Interior of the 12th instant accompanies the treaty.

ABRAHAM LINCOLN.

EXECUTIVE MANSION,
Washington, December, 1863.

To the Senate of the United States:

I lay before the Senate, for its constitutional action thereon, a treaty concluded at the Sac and Fox Agency, in Kansas, on the 3d day of September, 1863, between William P. Dole, Commissioner of Indian Affairs, and William G. Coffin, superintendent of Indian affairs for the southern superintendency, on the part of the United States, and the Creek Nation of Indians, represented by its chiefs.

A letter from the Secretary of the Interior, dated the 12th instant, accompanies the treaty.

ABRAHAM LINCOLN.

EXECUTIVE MANSION,
Washington, December, 1863.

To the Senate of the United States:

I lay before the Senate, for its constitutional action thereon, a treaty concluded at the Sac and Fox Agency, in Kansas, on the 4th day of September, 1863, between William P. Dole, Commissioner of Indian Affairs, and Henry W. Martin, agent for the Sacs and Foxes, commissioners on the part of the United States, and the united tribes of Sac and Fox Indians of the Mississippi.

A letter from the Secretary of the Interior, dated the 12th instant, accompanies the treaty.   ABRAHAM LINCOLN.

WASHINGTON, *December 15, 1863.*

To the Senate of the United States:

In answer to the resolution of the Senate of the 11th of March last, requesting certain information touching persons in the service of this Government, I transmit a report from the Secretary of State, to whom the resolution was referred.   ABRAHAM LINCOLN.

WASHINGTON, *December 17, 1863.*

To the Senate of the United States:

I transmit to the Senate, for consideration with a view to its ratification, a convention between the United States and Her Britannic Majesty for the final adjustment of the claims of the Hudsons Bay and Pugets Sound Agricultural Companies, signed in this city on the 1st day of July last (1863).   ABRAHAM LINCOLN.

DECEMBER 17, 1863.

To the Senate and House of Representatives of the United States:

Herewith I lay before you a letter addressed to myself by a committee of gentlemen representing the freedmen's aid societies in Boston, New York, Philadelphia, and Cincinnati. The subject of the letter, as indicated above, is one of great magnitude and importance, and one which these gentlemen, of known ability and high character, seem to have considered with great attention and care. Not having the time to form a mature judgment of my own as to whether the plan they suggest is the best, I submit the whole subject to Congress, deeming that their attention thereto is almost imperatively demanded.

ABRAHAM LINCOLN.

WASHINGTON, *December 22, 1863.*

To the Senate of the United States:

I transmit to the Senate, for its consideration with a view to ratification, two conventions between the United States and His Belgian Majesty, signed at Brussels on the 20th May and the 20th of July last, respectively, and both relating to the extinguishment of the Scheldt dues, etc. A copy of so much of the correspondence between the Secretary of State and Mr. Sanford, the minister resident of the United States at Brussels, on the subject of the conventions as is necessary to a full understanding of it is also herewith transmitted.

ABRAHAM LINCOLN.

WASHINGTON, *December 23, 1863.*
To the Senate and House of Representatives:

I transmit to Congress a copy of the report to the Secretary of State of the commissioners on the part of the United States under the convention with Peru of the 12th of January last, on the subject of claims. It will be noticed that two claims of Peruvian citizens on this Government have been allowed. An appropriation for the discharge of the obligations of the United States in these cases is requested.

ABRAHAM LINCOLN.

JANUARY 5, 1864.
Gentlemen of the Senate and House of Representatives:

By a joint resolution of your honorable bodies approved December 23, 1863, the paying of bounties to veteran volunteers, as now practiced by the War Department, is, to the extent of $300 in each case, prohibited after this 5th day of the present month. I transmit for your consideration a communication from the Secretary of War, accompanied by one from the Provost-Marshal-General to him, both relating to the subject above mentioned. I earnestly recommend that the law be so modified as to allow bounties to be paid as they now are, at least until the ensuing 1st day of February.

I am not without anxiety lest I appear to be importunate in thus recalling your attention to a subject upon which you have so recently acted, and nothing but a deep conviction that the public interest demands it could induce me to incur the hazard of being misunderstood on this point. The Executive approval was given by me to the resolution mentioned, and it is now by a closer attention and a fuller knowledge of facts that I feel constrained to recommend a reconsideration of the subject.

ABRAHAM LINCOLN.

WASHINGTON, *January 7, 1864.*
To the Senate and House of Representatives:

I transmit to Congress a copy of the decree of the court of the United States for the southern district of New York, awarding the sum of $17,150.66 for the illegal capture of the British schooner *Glen*, and request that an appropriation of that amount may be made as an indemnification to the parties interested.

ABRAHAM LINCOLN.

EXECUTIVE MANSION,
Washington, January, 1864.

To the Senate of the United States:

I herewith lay before the Senate, for its constitutional action thereon, the following-described treaties, viz:

A treaty made at Fort Bridger, Utah Territory, on the 2d day of July, 1863, between the United States and the chiefs, principal men, and warriors of the eastern bands of the Shoshonee Nation of Indians.

A treaty made at Box Elder, Utah Territory, on the 30th day of July, 1863, between the United States and the chiefs and warriors of the northwestern bands of the Shoshonee Nation of Indians.

A treaty made at Ruby Valley, Nevada Territory, on the 1st day of October, 1863, between the United States and the chiefs, principal men, and warriors of the Shoshonee Nation of Indians.

A treaty made at Tuilla Valley, Utah Territory, on the 12th day of October, 1863, between the United States and the chiefs, principal men, and warriors of the Goship bands of Shoshonee Indians.

A treaty made at Soda Springs, in Idaho Territory, on the 14th day of October, 1863, between the United States and the chiefs of the mixed bands of Bannacks and Shoshonees, occupying the valley of the Shoshonee River.

A letter of the Secretary of the Interior of the 5th instant, a copy of a report of the 30th ultimo, from the Commissioner of Indian Affairs, a copy of a communication from Governor Doty, superintendent of Indian Affairs, Utah Territory, dated November 10, 1863, relating to the Indians parties to the several treaties herein named, and a map, furnished by that gentleman, are herewith transmitted.

ABRAHAM LINCOLN,

EXECUTIVE MANSION,
Washington, January, 1864.

To the Senate of the United States:

I herewith lay before the Senate, for its constitutional action thereon, a treaty made at the Old Crossing of Red Lake River, in the State of Minnesota, on the 2d day of October, 1863, between Alexander Ramsey and Ashley C. Morrill, commissioners on the part of the United States, and the chiefs, headmen, and warriors of the Red Lake and Pembina bands of Chippewa Indians.

A letter of the Secretary of the Interior of the 8th instant, together with a communication from the Commissioner of Indian Affairs of the 5th instant and copies of Mr. Ramsey's report and journal, relating to the treaty, and a map showing the territory ceded, are herewith transmitted.

ABRAHAM LINCOLN.

EXECUTIVE MANSION, *January 12, 1864.*

To the Senate of the United States:

In accordance with the request of the Senate conveyed in their resolution of the 16th of December, 1863, desiring any information in my possession relative to the alleged exceptional treatment of Kansas troops when captured by those in rebellion, I have the honor to transmit a communication from the Secretary of War, accompanied by reports from the General in Chief of the Army and the Commissary-General of Prisoners relative to the subject-matter of the resolution.

ABRAHAM LINCOLN.

JANUARY 20, 1864.

Gentlemen of the Senate and House of Representatives:

In accordance with a letter addressed by the Secretary of State, with my approval, to the Hon. Joseph A. Wright, of Indiana, that patriotic and distinguished gentleman repaired to Europe and attended the International Agricultural Exhibition, held at Hamburg last year, and has since his return made a report to me, which, it is believed, can not fail to be of general interest, and especially so to the agricultural community. I transmit for your consideration copies of the letters and report. While it appears by the letter that no reimbursement of expenses or compensation was promised him, I submit whether reasonable allowance should not be made him for them.

ABRAHAM LINCOLN.

WASHINGTON, *January 21, 1864.*

To the Senate of the United States:

In compliance with the resolution of the Senate of yesterday, respecting the recent destruction by fire of the Church of the Compañía at Santiago, Chile, and the efforts of citizens of the United States to rescue the victims of the conflagration, I transmit a report from the Secretary of State, with the papers accompanying it.

ABRAHAM LINCOLN.

WASHINGTON, *January 23, 1864.*

To the Senate of the United States:

I transmit to the Senate a copy of a dispatch of the 12th of April last, addressed by Anson Burlingame, esq., the minister of the United States to China, to the Secretary of State, relative to a modification of the twenty-first article of a treaty between the United States and China of the 18th of June, 1858, a printed copy of which is also herewith transmitted.

These papers are submitted to the consideration of the Senate with a view to their advice and consent being given to the modification of the said twenty-first article, as explained in the said dispatch and its accompaniments.

ABRAHAM LINCOLN.

WASHINGTON, *January 29, 1864.*

To the Senate of the United States:

I transmit herewith a report from the Secretary of State, in answer to the resolution of the Senate respecting the correspondence with the authorities of Great Britain in' relation to the proposed pursuit of hostile bands of the Sioux Indians into the Hudson Bay territories.

ABRAHAM LINCOLN.

WASHINGTON, *February 4, 1864.*

To the Senate:

In compliance with the resolution of the Senate of the 26th ultimo, requesting ''a copy of all the correspondence between the authorities of the United States and the rebel authorities on the exchange of prisoners, and the different propositions connected with that subject,'' I transmit herewith a report from the Secretary of War and the papers with which it is accompanied.

ABRAHAM LINCOLN.

WASHINGTON, *February 5, 1864.*

To the Senate of the United States:

In answer to the resolution of the Senate of yesterday on the subject of a reciprocity treaty with the Sandwich Islands, I transmit a report from the Secretary of State, to whom the resolution was referred.

ABRAHAM LINCOLN.

WASHINGTON, *February 16, 1864.*

To the Senate and House of Representatives:

I transmit to Congress a report from the Secretary of State, with the accompanying papers, relative to the claim on this Government of the owners of the French ship *La Manche*, and recommend an appropriation for the satisfaction of the claim, pursuant to the award of the arbitrators.

ABRAHAM LINCOLN.

WASHINGTON, *February 16, 1864.*

To the House of Representatives of the United States:

In answer to the resolution of the House of Representatives of the 8th instant, requesting information touching the arrest of the United States consul-general to the British North American Provinces, and certain official communications respecting Canadian commerce, I transmit a report from the Secretary of State and the documents by which it was accompanied.

ABRAHAM LINCOLN.

WASHINGTON, *February 22, 1864.*

To the Senate and House of Representatives:

I transmit to Congress the copy of a correspondence which has recently taken place between Her Britannic Majesty's minister accredited to this Government and the Secretary of State, in order that the expediency of sanctioning the acceptance by the master of the American schooner *Highlander* of a present of a watch which the lords of the committee of Her Majesty's privy council for trade propose to present to him in recognition of services rendered by him to the crew of the British vessel *Pearl* may be taken into consideration.

ABRAHAM LINCOLN.

EXECUTIVE MANSION, *February, 1864.*

To the Senate of the United States:

I communicate to the Senate herewith, for its constitutional action thereon, the articles of agreement and convention made and concluded at the city of Washington on the 25th day of the present month by and between William P. Dole, as commissioner on the part of the United States, and the duly authorized delegates of the Swan Creek and Black River Chippewas and the Munsees or Christian Indians in Kansas.

ABRAHAM LINCOLN.

WASHINGTON, *February 29, 1864.*

To the House of Representatives:

In answer to the resolution of the House of Representatives of the 26th instant, I transmit herewith a report from the Secretary of War, relative to the reenlistment of veteran volunteers.

ABRAHAM LINCOLN.

EXECUTIVE MANSION,
Washington, February 29, 1864.

To the Senate of the United States:

I nominate Ulysses S. Grant, now a major-general in the military service, to be lieutenant-general in the Army of the United States.

ABRAHAM LINCOLN.

EXECUTIVE MANSION, *March, 1864.*

To the Senate of the United States:

I transmit herewith a report * of the Secretary of the Interior of the 11th instant, containing the information requested in Senate resolution of the 29th ultimo.

ABRAHAM LINCOLN.

* Relating to the amount of money received for the sale of the Wea trust lands in Kansas, etc.

EXECUTIVE MANSION, *March 9, 1864.*

To the Senate of the United States:

In compliance with a resolution of the Senate of the 1st instant, respecting the points of commencement of the Union Pacific Railroad, on the one hundredth degree of west longitude, and of the branch road, from the western boundary of Iowa to the said one hundredth degree of longitude, I transmit the accompanying report from the Secretary of the Interior, containing the information called for.

I deem it proper to add that on the 17th day of November last an Executive order was made upon this subject and delivered to the vice-president of the Union Pacific Railroad Company, which fixed the point on the western boundary of the State of Iowa from which the company should construct their branch road to the one hundredth degree of west longitude, and declared it to be within the limits of the township in Iowa opposite the town of Omaha, in Nebraska.   Since then the company has represented to me that upon actual surveys made it has determined upon the precise point of departure of their said branch road from the Missouri River, and located the same as described in the accompanying report of the Secretary of the Interior, which point is within the limits designated in the order of November last; and inasmuch as that order is not of record in any of the Executive Departments, and the company having desired a more definite one, I have made the order of which a copy is herewith, and caused the same to be filed in the Department of the Interior.   ABRAHAM LINCOLN.

EXECUTIVE OFFICE, *March 12, 1864.*

To the Senate of the United States:

In obedience to the resolution of the Senate of the 28th of January last, I communicate herewith a report, with accompanying papers, from the Secretary of the Interior, showing what portion of the appropriations for the colonization of persons of African descent has been expended and the several steps which have been taken for the execution of the acts of Congress on that subject.   ABRAHAM LINCOLN.

WASHINGTON, *March 14, 1864.*

To the Senate and House of Representatives:

I transmit to Congress a copy of a treaty between the United States and Great Britain for the final settlement of the claims of the Hudsons Bay and Pugets Sound Agricultural Companies, concluded on the 1st of July last, the ratifications of which were exchanged in this city on the 5th instant, and recommend an appropriation to carry into effect the first, second, and third articles thereof.   ABRAHAM LINCOLN.

WASHINGTON, *March 14, 1864.*

To the Senate and House of Representatives:

On the 25th day of November, 1862, a convention for the mutual adjustment of claims pending between the United States and Ecuador was signed at Quito by the plenipotentiaries of the contracting parties. A copy is herewith inclosed.

This convention, already ratified by this Government, has been sent to Quito for the customary exchange of ratifications, which it is not doubted will be promptly effected. As the stipulations of the instrument require that the commissioners who are to be appointed pursuant to its provisions shall meet at Guayaquil within ninety days after such exchange, it is desirable that the legislation necessary to give effect to the convention on the part of the United States should anticipate the usual course of proceeding.

I therefore invite the early attention of Congress to the subject.

ABRAHAM LINCOLN.

EXECUTIVE OFFICE,
Washington, March 22, 1864.

To the Senate of the United States:

I herewith lay before the Senate, for its constitutional action thereon, a treaty made and concluded in Washington City on the 18th instant by and between William P. Dole, Commissioner of Indian Affairs, and the Shawnee Indians, represented by their duly authorized delegates.

A report of the Secretary of the Interior and a communication of the Commissioner of Indian Affairs accompany the treaty.

ABRAHAM LINCOLN.

WASHINGTON, *March 24, 1864.*

To the Senate of the United States:

In reply to the resolution of the Senate of the 15th instant, in relation to the establishment of monarchical governments in Central and South America, I transmit a report from the Secretary of State, to whom the subject was referred.

ABRAHAM LINCOLN.

MARCH 29, 1864.

To the Senate and House of Representatives:

Mr. Charles B. Stuart, consulting engineer, appointed such by me upon invitation of the governor of New York, according to a law of that State, has made a report upon the proposed improvements to pass gunboats from tide water to the northern and northwestern lakes, which report is herewith respectfully submitted for your consideration.

ABRAHAM LINCOLN.

EXECUTIVE OFFICE,
Washington, April 4, 1864.

To the Senate of the United States:

I herewith lay before the Senate, for its constitutional action thereon, a treaty concluded June 9, 1863, between C. H. Hale, superintendent of Indian affairs, Charles Hutchins and S. D. Howe, Indian agents, on the part of the United States, and the chiefs, headmen, and delegates of the Nez Percé tribe of Indians in Washington Territory.

A report of the Secretary of the Interior of the 1st instant, with a letter from the Commissioner of Indian Affairs of the 2d ultimo, proposing amendments to the treaty, together with a report of Superintendent Hale on the subject and a synopsis of the proceedings of the council held with the Nez Percé Indians, are herewith transmitted for the consideration of the Senate.

ABRAHAM LINCOLN.

WASHINGTON, *April 7, 1864.*

To the House of Representatives:

I transmit herewith a report from the Secretary of War, in answer to the resolution of the House of Representatives of the 4th instant, in relation to Major N. H. McLean.

ABRAHAM LINCOLN.

WASHINGTON CITY, *April 15, 1864.*

To the Senate of the United States:

I herewith lay before the Senate, for its constitutional action thereon, a supplemental treaty negotiated on the 12th of April, 1864, with the Red Lake and Pembina bands of Chippewa Indians.

A report of the Secretary of the Interior of this date and a communication from the Acting Commissioner of Indian Affairs accompany the treaty.

ABRAHAM LINCOLN.

WASHINGTON, *April 23, 1864.*

To the Senate of the United States:

I transmit herewith a report from the Secretary of War, in answer to the resolutions passed by the Senate in executive session on the 14th and 18th of April, 1864.

ABRAHAM LINCOLN.

WAR DEPARTMENT,
Washington City, April 22, 1864.

The PRESIDENT OF THE UNITED STATES.

SIR: In answer to the Senate resolutions of April 14 and April 18, I have the honor to state that the nominations of Colonel Hiram Burnham, Colonel Edward M.

McCook, Colonel Lewis A. Grant, and Colonel Edward Hatch are not either of them made to fill any vacancy in the proper sense of that term. They are not made to fill a command vacated by any other general, but are independent nominations, and if confirmed the officers will be assigned to such command as the General Commanding may deem proper. But in consequence of the resignations of Generals Miller, Boyle, and Beatty and the death of General Champlin, their confirmations will be within the number of brigadiers allowed by law.

Your obedient servant,

EDWIN M. STANTON,
Secretary of War.

WASHINGTON, *April 23, 1864.*

To the Senate and House of Representatives:

I transmit to Congress a copy of a note of the 19th instant from Lord Lyons to the Secretary of State, on the subject of two British naval officers who recently received medical treatment at the naval hospital at Norfolk. The expediency of authorizing Surgeon Solomon Sharp to accept the piece of plate to which the note refers, as an acknowledgment of his services, is submitted to your consideration.

ABRAHAM LINCOLN.

To the House of Representatives: APRIL 28, 1864.

In obedience to the resolution of your honorable body a copy of which is herewith returned, I have the honor to make the following brief statement, which is believed to contain the information sought.

Prior to and at the meeting of the present Congress Robert C. Schenck, of Ohio, and Frank P. Blair, jr., of Missouri, members elect thereto, by and with the consent of the Senate held commissions from the Executive as major-generals in the Volunteer Army. General Schenck tendered the resignation of his said commission and took his seat in the House of Representatives at the assembling thereof upon the distinct verbal understanding with the Secretary of War and the Executive that he might at any time during the session, at his own pleasure, withdraw said resignation and return to the field. General Blair was, by temporary assignment of General Sherman, in command of a corps through the battles in front of Chattanooga and in the march to the relief of Knoxville, which occurred in the latter days of November and early days of December last, and of course was not present at the assembling of Congress. When he subsequently arrived here, he sought and was allowed by the Secretary of War and the Executive the same conditions and promise as allowed and made to General Schenck. General Schenck has not applied to withdraw his resignation, but when General Grant was made lieutenant-general, producing some change of commanders, General Blair sought to be assigned to the command of a corps. This was made known to Generals Grant and Sherman and assented to by them, and the particular corps for him designated. This was all arranged and understood, as now remembered, so much as a month ago, but the formal withdrawal of General Blair's resignation and making the order assigning him to the command of a corps were not consummated at the War Department until last week, perhaps on the 23d of April instant. As a summary of the whole, it may be stated that General Blair holds no military commission or appointment other than as herein stated, and that it is believed he is now acting as a major-general upon the assumed validity of the commission herein stated, in connection with the facts herein stated, and not otherwise. There are some letters, notes, telegrams, orders, entries, and perhaps other documents in connection with this subject, which it is believed would throw no additional light upon it, but which will be cheerfully furnished if desired.

ABRAHAM LINCOLN.

APRIL 28, 1864.

To the Honorable the Senate and House of Representatives:

I have the honor to transmit herewith an address to the President of the United States, and through him to both Houses of Congress, on the condition and wants of the people of east Tennessee, and asking their attention to the necessity of some action on the part of the Government for their relief, and which address is presented by a committee of an organization called "The East Tennessee Relief Association."

Deeply commiserating the condition of these most loyal and suffering people, I am unprepared to make any specific recommendation for their relief. The military is doing and will continue to do the best for them within its power. Their address represents that the construction of direct railroad communication between Knoxville and Cincinnati by way of central Kentucky would be of great consequence in the present emergency. It may be remembered that in the annual message of December, 1861, such railroad construction was recommended. I now add that, with the hearty concurrence of Congress, I would yet be pleased to construct a road, both for the relief of these people and for its continuing military importance.

ABRAHAM LINCOLN.

WASHINGTON, *April 29, 1864.*

To the Senate of the United States:

In compliance with the resolution of the Senate of the 27th instant, requesting information in regard to the condition of affairs in the Territory of Nevada, I transmit a copy of a letter of the 25th of last month addressed to the Secretary of State by James W. Nye, the governor of that Territory.

ABRAHAM LINCOLN.

Executive Mansion,

Washington,   , 186 .

Four score and seven years ago our fathers brought forth, upon this continent, a new nation, conceived in Liberty, and dedicated to the proposition that "all men are created equal"

Now we are engaged in a great civil war, testing whether that nation, or any nation so conceived, and so dedicated, can long endure. We are met on a great battle field of that war. We have come to dedicate a portion of it, as a final resting place for those who here gave their lives, that the nation might live. This we may, in all propriety do. But, in a larger sense, we can not dedicate— we can not consecrate— we can not hallow, this ground— The brave men, living and dead, who struggled here, have hallowed it, far above our poor power to add or detract. The world will little note, nor long remember what we say here; while it can never forget what they did here.

It is rather for us, the living, to stand here, we here be dedicated to us to the great task remaining before us—

that, from these honored dead we take in=

creased devotion to that cause for which

they here gave the last full measure of de=

votion— that we here highly resolve then

these dead shall not have died in vain; that

the nation, shall have a new birth of free

dom; and that government of the people by

the people for the people, shall not per=

ish from the earth.

THE GETTYSBURG ADDRESS.

Immediately after the battle of Gettysburg, Congress set aside the battlefield as a national burial-ground for soldiers; and it was at the dedication of the new national cemetery on November 19, 1863, that Lincoln delivered the address which has forever afterwards been called by the name of the little town in Pennsylvania. There is some dispute as to the manner in which the address was prepared, one legend running that Lincoln wrote it in a few minutes on the back of an official government envelope while on the special train which was conveying him to the dedication ceremonies. The consensus of valid opinion, however, indicates that the address was prepared with great care in Washington some days before it was delivered, although Lincoln may have slightly revised it on the evening before or the day of the dedication itself. Lincoln held a written copy of his remarks in his hand when he rose to speak after the two hours' address of Edward Everett, whose sonorous and polished phrases had mightily moved the audience before him. The fewness and the simplicity of Lincoln's immortal words, after Everett's lengthy peroration, could not but engrave them indelibly on the minds of those who were privileged to hear them.

MAY 2, 1864.

To the Honorable the House of Representatives:

In compliance with the request contained in your resolution of the 29th ultimo, a copy of which resolution is herewith returned, I have the honor to transmit the following:

EXECUTIVE MANSION,
Washington, November 2, 1863.

Hon. MONTGOMERY BLAIR.

MY DEAR SIR: Some days ago I understood you to say that your brother, General Frank Blair, desired to be guided by my wishes as to whether he will occupy his seat in Congress or remain in the field. My wish, then, is compounded of what I believe will be best for the country and best for him, and it is that he will come here, put his military commission in my hands, take his seat, go into caucus with our friends, abide the nominations, help elect the nominees, and thus aid to organize a House of Representatives which will really support the Government in the war. If the result shall be the election of himself as Speaker, let him serve in that position; if not, let him retake his commission and return to the Army. For the country, this will heal a dangerous schism. For him, it will relieve from a dangerous position. By a misunderstanding, as I think, he is in danger of being permanently separated from those with whom only he can ever have a real sympathy—the sincere opponents of slavery. It will be a mistake if he shall allow the provocations offered him by insincere timeservers to drive him from the house of his own building. He is young yet. He has abundant talents, quite enough to occupy all his time without devoting any to temper. He is rising in military skill and usefulness. His recent appointment to the command of a corps by one so competent to judge as General Sherman proves this. In that line he can serve both the country and himself more profitably than he could as a Member of Congress upon the floor. The foregoing is what I would say if Frank Blair were my brother instead of yours.

Yours, truly,

A. LINCOLN.

HEADQUARTERS MIDDLE DEPARTMENT, EIGHTH ARMY CORPS,
Baltimore, Md., November 13, 1863.

Hon. E. M. STANTON,
Secretary of War.

SIR: Inclosed I forward to the President my resignation, to take effect on the 5th of December.

I respectfully request, however, that I may be relieved from my command at an earlier day, say by the 20th instant, or as soon thereafter as some officer can be ordered to succeed me. While I desire to derange the plans or hurry the action of the Department as little as possible, it will be a great convenience to me to secure some little time before the session of Congress for a necessary journey and for some preparations for myself and family in view of my approaching change of residence and occupation. I could also spend two or three days very profitably, I think, to the service of my successor after his arrival here.

I have the honor to be, very respectfully, your obedient servant,

ROBT. C. SCHENCK, *Major-General.*

HEADQUARTERS MIDDLE DEPARTMENT, EIGHTH ARMY CORPS,
Baltimore, Md., November 13, 1863.

The PRESIDENT OF THE UNITED STATES.

SIR: Having concluded to accept the place of Member of Congress in the House of Representatives, to which I was elected in October, 1862, I hereby tender the resignation of my commission as a major-general of United States Volunteers, to take effect on the 5th day of December next.

I shall leave the military service with much reluctance and a sacrifice of personal feelings and desires, and only consent to do so in the hope that in another capacity I may be able to do some effective service in the cause of my country and Government in this time of peculiar trial.

I have the honor to be, very respectfully, your obedient servant,

ROBT. C. SCHENCK,
Major-General.

[Indorsement on the foregoing letter.]

The resignation of General Schenck is accepted, and he is authorized to turn over his command to Brigadier-General Lockwood at any time.

EDWIN M. STANTON,
Secretary of War.

ADJUTANT-GENERAL'S OFFICE,
Washington, November 21, 1863.

Major-General ROBERT C. SCHENCK,
United States Volunteers, Commanding Middle Department, Baltimore, Md.

SIR: Your resignation has been accepted by the President of the United States, to take effect the 5th day of December, 1863.

I am, sir, very respectfully, your obedient servant,

E. D. TOWNSEND,
Assistant Adjutant-General.

WASHINGTON, *January 1, 1864.*

The PRESIDENT OF THE UNITED STATES,
Washington City, D. C.:

I hereby tender my resignation as a major-general of the United States Volunteers.
Respectfully,

FRANK P. BLAIR,
Major-General, United States Volunteers.

JANUARY 12, 1864.

Accepted, by order of the President.

EDWIN M. STANTON,
Secretary of War.

ADJUTANT-GENERAL'S OFFICE,
Washington, January 12, 1864.

Major-General FRANCIS P. BLAIR,
U. S. Volunteers.

(Care of Hon. M. Blair, Washington, D. C.)

SIR: Your resignation has been accepted by the President of the United States, to take effect this day.

I am, sir, very respectfully, your obedient servant,

JAS. A. HARDIE,
Assistant Adjutant-General.

[Telegram.]

EXECUTIVE MANSION,
Washington, D. C., March 15, 1864.

Lieutenant-General GRANT,
Nashville, Tenn.:

General McPherson having been assigned to the command of a department, could not General Frank Blair, without difficulty or detriment to the service, be assigned to command the corps he commanded a while last autumn?

A. LINCOLN.

[Telegram.]

NASHVILLE, TENN., *March 16. 1864—10 a. m.*

His Excellency the PRESIDENT:

General Logan commands the corps referred to in your dispatch. I will see General Sherman in a few days and consult him about the transfer, and answer.

U. S. GRANT,
Lieutenant-General.

[Telegram.]

NASHVILLE, TENN., *March 17, 1864.*

His Excellency A. LINCOLN,
President of the United States:

General Sherman is here. He consents to the transfer of General Logan to the Seventeenth Corps and the appointment of General F. P. Blair to the Fifteenth Corps.

U. S. GRANT,
Lieutenant-General.

[Telegram.]

HUNTSVILLE, ALA., *March 26, 1864.*

His Excellency A. LINCOLN,
President of the United States:

I understand by the papers that it is contemplated to make a change of commanders of the Fifteenth and Seventeenth Army Corps, so as to transfer me to the Seventeenth. I hope this will not be done. I fully understand the organization of the Fifteenth Corps now, of which I have labored to complete the organization this winter. Earnestly hope that the change may not be made.

JOHN A. LOGAN,
Major-General.

[Telegram.]

OFFICE UNITED STATES MILITARY TELEGRAPH,
War Department.

The following telegram received at Washington 9 a. m. March 31, 1864, from Culpeper Court-House, 11.30 p. m., dated March 30, 1864:

"Major-General W. T. SHERMAN,
"*Nashville:*

"General F. P. Blair will be assigned to the Seventeenth (17th) Corps, and not the Fifteenth (15th). Assign General Joseph Hooker, subject to the approval of the President, to any other corps command you may have, and break up the anomaly of one general commanding two (2) corps.
"U. S. GRANT,
"*Lieutenant-General, Commanding.*"

From a long dispatch of April 2, 1864, from General Sherman to General Grant, presenting his plan for disposing the forces under his command, the following extracts, being the only parts pertinent to the subject now under consideration, are taken:

After a full consultation with all my army commanders, I have settled down to the following conclusions, to which I would like to have the President's consent before I make the orders:

* * * * * * *

Third. General McPherson. * * * His [three] corps to be commanded by Major-Generals Logan, Blair, and Dodge. * * *

OFFICE UNITED STATES MILITARY TELEGRAPH,
War Department.

The following telegram received at Washington 3 p. m. April 10, 1864, from Cul
peper Court-House, Va., 10 p. m., dated April 9, 1864:

"Major-General H. W. HALLECK,
"Chief of Staff:

"Will you please ascertain if General F. P. Blair is to be sent to General Sherman.
If not, an army-corps commander will have to be named for the Fifteenth Corps.

"U. S. GRANT, *Lieutenant-General.*"

WASHINGTON, *April 20, 1864.*
The PRESIDENT:

You will do me a great favor by giving the order assigning me to the command of
the Seventeenth Army Corps immediately, as I desire to leave Washington the next
Saturday to join the command. I also request the assignment of Captain Andrew J.
Alexander, of Third Regiment United States Cavalry, as adjutant-general of the Seventeenth Corps, with the rank of lieutenant-colonel. The present adjutant, or rather the
former adjutant, Colonel Clark, has, I understand, been retained by General McPherson
as adjutant-general of the department, and the place of adjutant-general of the corps
is necessarily vacant.

I also request the appointment of George A. Maguire, formerly captain Thirty-first
Missouri Volunteer Infantry, as major and aid-de-camp, and Lieutenant Logan Tompkins, Twenty-first Missouri Volunteer Infantry, as captain and aid-de-camp on my
staff.

Respectfully, FRANK P. BLAIR.

[Indorsements.]

Honorable SECRETARY OF WAR: APRIL 21, 1864.

Please have General Halleck make the proper order in this case.

A. LINCOLN.

Referred to General Halleck, chief of staff.

EDWIN M. STANTON, *Secretary of War.*

EXECUTIVE MANSION,
Washington, April 23, 1864.
Honorable SECRETARY OF WAR.

MY DEAR SIR: According to our understanding with Major-General Frank P. Blair
at the time he took his seat in Congress last winter, he now asks to withdraw his
resignation as major-general, then tendered, and be sent to the field. Let this be
done. Let the order sending him be such as shown me to-day by the Adjutant-General, only dropping from it the names of Maguire and Tompkins.

Yours, truly, A. LINCOLN.

[Indorsement.]

APRIL 23, 1864.
Referred to the Adjutant-General.

EDWIN M. STANTON, *Secretary of War.*

WASHINGTON CITY, D. C., *April 23, 1864.*
Hon. E. M. STANTON,
Secretary of War:

I respectfully request to withdraw my resignation as major-general of the United
States Volunteers, tendered on the 12th day of January, 1864.

Respectfully,

FRANK P. BLAIR.

GENERAL ORDERS, No. 178.

WAR DEPARTMENT,
ADJUTANT-GENERAL'S OFFICE,
Washington, April 23, 1864.

I. Major-General F. P. Blair, jr., is assigned to the command of the Seventeenth Army Corps.

II. Captain Andrew J. Alexander, Third Regiment United States Cavalry, is assigned as assistant adjutant-general of the Seventeenth Army Corps, with the rank of lieutenant-colonel, under the tenth section of the act approved July 17, 1862.

By order of the President of the United States:

E. D. TOWNSEND,
Assistant Adjutant-General.

The foregoing constitutes all sought by the resolution so far as is remembered or has been found upon diligent search.

ABRAHAM LINCOLN.

MAY 7, 1864.

To the Senate of the United States:

In compliance with the request contained in a resolution of the Senate dated April 30, 1864, I herewith transmit to your honorable body a copy of the opinion by the Attorney-General on the rights of colored persons in the Army or volunteer service of the United States, together with the accompanying papers.

ABRAHAM LINCOLN.

WASHINGTON, *May 12, 1864.*

To the Senate of the United States:

In answer to the resolution of the Senate of the 9th instant, requesting a copy of correspondence relative to a controversy between the Republics of Chile and Bolivia, I transmit a report from the Secretary of State, to whom the resolution was referred.

ABRAHAM LINCOLN.

EXECUTIVE MANSION,
Washington, May 14, 1864.

To the Senate of the United States:

I transmit herewith a report of the Secretary of the Interior of the 14th instant, and accompanying papers, in answer to a resolution of the Senate of the 14th ultimo, in the following words, viz:

Resolved, That the President of the United States be requested to communicate to the Senate the reasons, if any exist, why the refugee Indians in the State of Kansas are not returned to their homes.

ABRAHAM LINCOLN.

EXECUTIVE MANSION,
Washington, May 17, 1864.

To the Senate of the United States:

I herewith lay before the Senate, for its constitutional action thereon, a treaty concluded on the 7th instant in this city between William P. Dole, Commissioner of Indian Affairs, and Clark W. Thompson, superintendent of Indian affairs, northern superintendency, on the part of the United States, and the chief Hole-in-the-day and Mis-qua-dace for and on behalf of the Chippewas of the Mississippi, and the Pillager and Lake Winnibigoshish bands of Chippewa Indians in Minnesota.

A communication from the Secretary of the Interior of the 17th instant, with a statement and copies of reports of the Commissioner of Indian Affairs of the 12th and 17th instant, accompany the treaty.

ABRAHAM LINCOLN.

WASHINGTON, D. C., *May 24, 1864.*

To the Senate of the United States:

I recommend Lieutenant-Commander Francis A. Roe for advancement in his grade five numbers, to take rank next after Lieutenant-Commander John H. Upshur, for distinguished conduct in battle in command of the United States steamer *Sassacus* in her attack on and attempt to run down the rebel ironclad ram *Albemarle* on the 5th of May, 1864.

I also recommend that First Assistant Engineer James M. Hobby be advanced thirty numbers in his grade for distinguished conduct in battle and extraordinary heroism, as mentioned in the report of Lieutenant-Commander Francis A. Roe, commanding the United States steamer *Sassacus* in her action with the rebel ram *Albemarle* on the 5th May, 1864.

ABRAHAM LINCOLN.

WASHINGTON, *May 24, 1864.*

To the House of Representatives:

In answer to the resolution of the House of Representatives of yesterday on the subject of the joint resolution of the 4th of last month relative to Mexico, I transmit a report from the Secretary of State, to whom the resolution was referred.

ABRAHAM LINCOLN.

WASHINGTON, *May 28, 1864.*

To the Senate of the United States:

In reply to a resolution of the Senate of the 25th instant, relating to Mexican affairs, I transmit a partial report from the Secretary of State of this date, with the papers therein mentioned.

ABRAHAM LINCOLN.

WASHINGTON, *May 31, 1864.*

To the Senate of the United States:

I transmit to the Senate, in answer to their resolution of the 28th instant, a report* from the Secretary of State, with accompanying documents.

ABRAHAM LINCOLN.

WASHINGTON, D. C., *June 8, 1864.*

To the Senate and House of Representatives:

I have the honor to submit, for the consideration of Congress, a letter and inclosure † from the Secretary of War, with my concurrence in the recommendation therein made.

ABRAHAM LINCOLN.

WASHINGTON, *June 13, 1864.*

To the Senate of the United States:

In compliance with the resolution of the Senate of the 4th of March, 1864, I transmit herewith a report from the Secretary of War in the case of William Yokum, with accompanying papers.

ABRAHAM LINCOLN.

WASHINGTON, *June 13, 1864.*

To the Senate of the United States:

I transmit herewith, for consideration with a view to ratification, a convention between the United States of America and the United Colombian States, signed by the plenipotentiaries of the contracting powers on the 10th February last, providing for a revival of the joint commission on claims under the convention of 10th September, 1857, with New Granada.

ABRAHAM LINCOLN.

WASHINGTON, *June 18, 1864.*

To the Senate of the United States:

In further answer to the Senate's resolution of the 28th ultimo, requesting to be informed whether the President "has, and when, authorized a person alleged to have committed a crime against Spain or any of its dependencies to be delivered up to officers of that Government, and whether such delivery was had, and, if so, under what authority of law or of treaty it was done," I transmit a copy of a dispatch of the 10th instant to the Secretary of State from the acting consul of the United States at Havana.

ABRAHAM LINCOLN.

---

* Relating to the delivery of a person charged with crime against Spain to the officers of that Government.

† Report from the Provost-Marshal-General, showing the result of the draft to fill a deficiency in the quotas of certain States, and recommending a repeal of the clause in the enrollment act commonly known as the three-hundred-dollar clause.

EXECUTIVE MANSION, *June 21, 1864.*

To the Senate of the United States:

I herewith communicate to the Senate, for its constitutional action thereon, the articles of agreement and convention made and concluded at the city of Washington on the 15th instant between the United States and the Delaware Indians of Kansas, referred to in the accompanying communication of the present date from the Secretary of the Interior.

ABRAHAM LINCOLN.

EXECUTIVE MANSION, *Washington, June 24, 1864.*

To the Senate of the United States:

I herewith lay before the Senate, for its constitutional action thereon, a treaty made and concluded at the city of Washington on the 11th day of June, 1864, by and between William P. Dole, Commissioner of Indian Affairs, and Hiram W. Farnsworth, United States Indian agent, commissioners on the part of the United States, and the chiefs and headmen of the Kansas tribe of Indians.

A communication of the Secretary of the Interior of the 18th instant, with a copy of report of Commissioner of Indian Affairs of the 13th instant, accompany the treaty.   ABRAHAM LINCOLN.

WASHINGTON, *June 28, 1864.*

To the Senate of the United States:

In answer to the resolution of the Senate of the 24th instant, requesting information in regard to the alleged enlistment in foreign countries of recruits for the military and naval service of the United States, I transmit reports from the Secretaries of State, of War, and of the Navy, respectively.   ABRAHAM LINCOLN.

WASHINGTON, *June 28, 1864.*

To the Senate of the United States:

In compliance with the resolution of the Senate of the 16th of last month, requesting information in regard to the maltreatment of passengers and seamen on board ships plying between New York and Aspinwall, I transmit a report from the Secretary of State, to whom the resolution was referred.   ABRAHAM LINCOLN.

WASHINGTON, *July 2, 1864.*

To the Senate of the United States:

In answer to the resolution of the Senate of the 6th ultimo, requesting information upon the subject of the African slave trade, I transmit a report from the Secretary of State and the papers by which it was accompanied.

ABRAHAM LINCOLN.

PROCLAMATIONS.

A PROCLAMATION.

Whereas in and by the Constitution of the United States it is provided that the President "shall have power to grant reprieves and pardons for offenses against the United States, except in cases of impeachment;" and

Whereas a rebellion now exists whereby the loyal State governments of several States have for a long time been subverted, and many persons have committed and are now guilty of treason against the United States; and

Whereas, with reference to said rebellion and treason, laws have been enacted by Congress declaring forfeitures and confiscation of property and liberation of slaves, all upon terms and conditions therein stated, and also declaring that the President was thereby authorized at any time thereafter, by proclamation, to extend to persons who may have participated in the existing rebellion in any State or part thereof pardon and amnesty, with such exceptions and at such times and on such conditions as he may deem expedient for the public welfare; and

Whereas the Congressional declaration for limited and conditional pardon accords with well-established judicial exposition of the pardoning power; and

Whereas, with reference to said rebellion, the President of the United States has issued several proclamations with provisions in regard to the liberation of slaves; and

Whereas it is now desired by some persons heretofore engaged in said rebellion to resume their allegiance to the United States and to reinaugurate loyal State governments within and for their respective States:

Therefore, I, Abraham Lincoln, President of the United States, do proclaim, declare, and make known to all persons who have, directly or by implication, participated in the existing rebellion, except as hereinafter excepted, that a full pardon is hereby granted to them and each of them, with restoration of all rights of property, except as to slaves and in property cases where rights of third parties shall have intervened, and upon the condition that every such person shall take and subscribe an oath and thenceforward keep and maintain said oath inviolate, and which oath shall be registered for permanent preservation and shall be of the tenor and effect following, to wit:

I, ——— ———, do solemnly swear, in presence of Almighty God, that I will henceforth faithfully support, protect, and defend the Constitution of the United States and the Union of the States thereunder; and that I will in like manner abide by and faithfully support all acts of Congress passed during the existing rebellion with reference to slaves, so long and so far as not repealed, modified, or held void by Congress or by decision of the Supreme Court; and that I will in like manner abide by and faithfully support all proclamations of the President made during the existing rebellion having reference to slaves, so long and so far as not modified or declared void by decision of the Supreme Court.   So help me God.

The persons excepted from the benefits of the foregoing provisions are all who are or shall have been civil or diplomatic officers or agents of the so-called Confederate Government; all who have left judicial stations under the United States to aid the rebellion; all who are or shall have been military or naval officers of said so-called Confederate Government above the rank of colonel in the army or of lieutenant in the navy; all who left seats in the United States Congress to aid the rebellion; all who resigned commissions in the Army or Navy of the United States and afterwards aided the rebellion; and all who have engaged in any way in treating colored persons, or white persons in charge of such, otherwise than lawfully as prisoners of war, and which persons may have been found in the United States service as soldiers, seamen, or in any other capacity.

And I do further proclaim, declare, and make known that whenever, in any of the States of Arkansas, Texas, Louisiana, Mississippi, Tennessee, Alabama, Georgia, Florida, South Carolina, and North Carolina, a number of persons, not less than one-tenth in number of the votes cast in such State at the Presidential election of the year A. D. 1860, each having taken the oath aforesaid, and not having since violated it, and being a qualified voter by the election law of the State existing immediately before the so-called act of secession, and excluding all others, shall reestablish a State government which shall be republican and in nowise contravening said oath, such shall be recognized as the true government of the State, and the State shall receive thereunder the benefits of the constitutional provision which declares that "the United States shall guarantee to every State in this Union a republican form of government and shall protect each of them against invasion, and, on application of the legislature, or the executive (when the legislature can not be convened), against domestic violence."

And I do further proclaim, declare, and make known that any provision which may be adopted by such State government in relation to the freed people of such State which shall recognize and declare their permanent freedom, provide for their education, and which may yet be consistent as a temporary arrangement with their present condition as a laboring, landless, and homeless class, will not be objected to by the National Executive.

And it is suggested as not improper that in constructing a loyal State government in any State the name of the State, the boundary, the subdivisions, the constitution, and the general code of laws as before the rebellion be maintained, subject only to the modifications made necessary by the conditions hereinbefore stated, and such others, if any, not contravening said conditions and which may be deemed expedient by those framing the new State government.

To avoid misunderstanding, it may be proper to say that this proclamation, so far as it relates to State governments, has no reference to States wherein loyal State governments have all the while been maintained. And for the same reason it may be proper to further say that whether members sent to Congress from any State shall be admitted to seats constitutionally rests exclusively with the respective Houses, and not to any extent with the Executive. And, still further, that this proclamation is intended to present the people of the States wherein the national authority has been suspended and loyal State governments have been subverted a mode in and by which the national authority and loyal State governments may be reestablished within said States or in any of them; and while the mode presented is the best the Executive can suggest, with his present impressions, it must not be understood that no other possible mode would be acceptable.

Given under my hand at the city of Washington, the 8th day of December, A. D. 1863, and of the Independence of the United States of America the eighty-eighth.

[SEAL.]

ABRAHAM LINCOLN.

By the President:

WILLIAM H. SEWARD, *Secretary of State.*

BY THE PRESIDENT OF THE UNITED STATES OF AMERICA.

A PROCLAMATION.

Whereas by an act of the Congress of the United States of the 24th of May, 1828, entitled "An act in addition to an act entitled 'An act concerning discriminating duties of tonnage and impost' and to equalize the duties on Prussian vessels and their cargoes," it is provided that upon satisfactory evidence being given to the President of the United States by the government of any foreign nation that no discriminating duties of tonnage or impost are imposed or levied in the ports of the said nation upon vessels wholly belonging to citizens of the United States or upon the produce, manufactures, or merchandise imported in the same from the United States or from any foreign country, the President is thereby authorized to issue his proclamation declaring that the foreign discriminating duties of tonnage and impost within the United States are and shall be suspended and discontinued so far as respects the vessels of the said foreign nation and the produce, manufactures, or merchandise imported into the United States in the same from the said foreign nation or from any other foreign country, the said suspension to take effect from the time of such notification being given to the President of the United States and to continue so long as the reciprocal exemption of vessels belonging to citizens of the United States and their cargoes, as aforesaid, shall be continued, and no longer; and

Whereas satisfactory evidence has lately been received by me through an official communication of Señor Don Luis Molina, envoy extraordinary and minister plenipotentiary of the Republic of Nicaragua, under date of the 28th of November, 1863, that no other or higher duties of tonnage and impost have been imposed or levied since the 2d day of August, 1838, in the ports of Nicaragua upon vessels wholly belonging to citizens of the United States and upon the produce, manufactures, or merchandise imported in the same from the United States and from any foreign country whatever than are levied on Nicaraguan ships and their cargoes in the same ports under like circumstances:

Now, therefore, I, Abraham Lincoln, President of the United States of America, do hereby declare and proclaim that so much of the several acts imposing discriminating duties of tonnage and impost within the United States are and shall be suspended and discontinued so far as respects the vessels of Nicaragua and the produce, manufactures, and merchandise imported into the United States in the same from the dominions of Nicaragua and from any other foreign country whatever, the said suspension to take effect from the day above mentioned and to continue thenceforward so long as the reciprocal exemption of the vessels of the United States and the produce, manufactures, and merchandise imported into the dominions of Nicaragua in the same, as aforesaid, shall be continued on the part of the Government of Nicaragua.

Given under my hand at the city of Washington, the 16th day of December, A. D. 1863, and the eighty-eighth of the Independence of the United States.

[SEAL.]

ABRAHAM LINCOLN.

By the President:

WILLIAM H. SEWARD,
Secretary of State.

BY THE PRESIDENT OF THE UNITED STATES OF AMERICA.

A PROCLAMATION.

Whereas by my proclamation of the 19th of April, 1861, the ports of the States of South Carolina, Georgia, Alabama, Florida, Mississippi, Louisiana, and Texas were, for reasons therein set forth, placed under blockade; and

Whereas the port of Brownsville, in the district of Brazos Santiago, in the State of Texas, has since been blockaded, but as the blockade of said port may now be safely relaxed with advantage to the interests of commerce:

Now, therefore, be it known that I, Abraham Lincoln, President of the United States, pursuant to the authority in me vested by the fifth section of the act of Congress approved on the 13th of July, 1861, entitled "An act further to provide for the collection of duties on imports and for other purposes," do hereby declare that the blockade of the said port of Brownsville shall so far cease and determine from and after this date that commercial intercourse with said port, except as to persons, things, and information hereinafter specified, may from this date be carried on subject to the laws of the United States, to the regulations prescribed by the Secretary of the Treasury, and, until the rebellion shall have been suppressed, to such orders as may be promulgated by the general commanding the department or by an officer duly authorized by him and commanding at said port. This proclamation does not authorize or allow the shipment or conveyance of persons in or intending to enter the service of the insurgents, or of things or information intended for their use or for their aid or comfort, nor, except upon the permission of the Secretary of War or of some officer duly authorized by him, of the following prohibited articles, namely: Cannon, mortars, firearms, pistols, bombs, grenades, powder, saltpeter, sulphur, balls, bullets, pikes, swords, boarding caps (always excepting the quantity of the said articles which may be necessary for the defense of the ship and those who compose the crew), saddles, bridles, cartridge-bag material, percussion and other caps, clothing adapted for uniforms, sailcloth of all kinds, hemp and cordage, intoxicating drinks other than beer and light native wines.

To vessels clearing from foreign ports and destined to the port of Brownsville, opened by this proclamation, licenses will be granted by consuls of the United States upon satisfactory evidence that the vessel so licensed will convey no persons, property, or information excepted or prohibited above either to or from the said port, which licenses shall be exhibited to the collector of said port immediately on arrival, and, if required, to any officer in charge of the blockade; and on leaving said port every vessel will be required to have a clearance from the collector of the customs, according to law, showing no violation of the conditions of the license. Any violations of said conditions will involve the forfeiture and condemnation of the vessel and cargo and the exclusion of all parties concerned from any further privilege of entering the United States during the war for any purpose whatever.

In all respects except as herein specified the existing blockade remains in full force and effect as hitherto established and maintained, nor is it relaxed by this proclamation except in regard to the port to which relaxation is or has been expressly applied.

In witness whereof I have hereunto set my hand and caused the seal of the United States to be affixed.

[SEAL.] Done at the city of Washington, this 18th day of February, A. D. 1864, and of the Independence of the United States the eighty-eighth.

ABRAHAM LINCOLN.

By the President:

WILLIAM H. SEWARD, *Secretary of State.*

BY THE PRESIDENT OF THE UNITED STATES OF AMERICA.

A PROCLAMATION.

Whereas it has become necessary to define the cases in which insurgent enemies are entitled to the benefits of the proclamation of the President of the United States which was made on the 8th day of December, 1863, and the manner in which they shall proceed to avail themselves of those benefits; and

Whereas the objects of that proclamation were to suppress the insurrection and to restore the authority of the United States; and

Whereas the amnesty therein proposed by the President was offered with reference to these objects alone:

Now, therefore, I, Abraham Lincoln, President of the United States, do hereby proclaim and declare that the said proclamation does not apply to the cases of persons who at the time when they seek to obtain the benefits thereof by taking the oath thereby prescribed are in military, naval, or civil confinement or custody, or under bonds, or on parole of the civil, military, or naval authorities or agents of the United States as prisoners of war, or persons detained for offenses of any kind, either before or after conviction, and that, on the contrary, it does apply only to those persons who, being yet at large and free from any arrest, confinement, or duress, shall voluntarily come forward and take the said oath with the purpose of restoring peace and establishing the national authority. Prisoners excluded from the amnesty offered in the said proclamation may apply to the President for clemency, like all other offenders, and their applications will receive due consideration.

I do further declare and proclaim that the oath prescribed in the aforesaid proclamation of the 8th of December, 1863, may be taken and subscribed before any commissioned officer, civil, military, or naval, in the service of the United States or any civil or military officer of a State or Territory not in insurrection who by the laws thereof may be qualified for administering oaths. All officers who receive such oaths are hereby authorized to give certificates thereon to the persons respectively by whom they are made, and such officers are hereby required to transmit the original records of such oaths at as early a day as may be convenient to the Department of State, where they will be deposited and remain in the archives of the Government. The Secretary of State will keep a register thereof, and will on application, in proper cases, issue certificates of such records in the customary form of official certificates.

In testimony whereof I have hereunto set my hand and caused the seal of the United States to be affixed.

[SEAL.]   Done at the city of Washington, the 26th day of March, A. D. 1864, and of the Independence of the United States the eighty-eighth.

ABRAHAM LINCOLN.

By the President:

WILLIAM H. SEWARD, *Secretary of State.*

ABRAHAM LINCOLN, PRESIDENT OF THE UNITED STATES OF AMERICA.

To all whom it may concern:

An exequatur bearing date the 3d day of May, 1850, having been issued to Charles Hunt, a citizen of the United States, recognizing him as consul of Belgium for St. Louis, Mo., and declaring him free to exercise and enjoy such functions, powers, and privileges as are allowed to the consuls of the most favored nations in the United States, and the said Hunt having sought to screen himself from his military duty to his country in consequence of thus being invested with the consular functions of a foreign power in the United States, it is deemed advisable that the said Charles Hunt should no longer be permitted to continue in the exercise of said functions, powers, and privileges:

These are, therefore, to declare that I no longer recognize the said Charles Hunt as consul of Belgium for St. Louis, Mo., and will not permit him to exercise or enjoy any of the functions, powers, or privileges allowed to consuls of that nation, and that I do hereby wholly revoke and annul the said exequatur heretofore given and do declare the same to be absolutely null and void from this day forward.

In testimony whereof I have caused these letters to be made patent and the seal of the United States of America to be hereunto affixed.

[SEAL.] Given under my hand, at Washington, this 19th day of May, A. D. 1864, and of the Independence of the United States of America the eighty-eighth.

ABRAHAM LINCOLN.

By the President:

WILLIAM H. SEWARD,
Secretary of State.

BY THE PRESIDENT OF THE UNITED STATES OF AMERICA.

A PROCLAMATION.

Whereas by a proclamation which was issued on the 15th day of April, 1861, the President of the United States announced and declared that the laws of the United States had been for some time past, and then were, opposed and the execution thereof obstructed in certain States therein mentioned by combinations too powerful to be suppressed by the ordinary course of judicial proceedings or by the powers vested in the marshals by law; and

Whereas immediately after the issuing of the said proclamation the land and naval forces of the United States were put into activity to suppress the said insurrection and rebellion; and

Whereas the Congress of the United States by an act approved on the 3d day of March, 1863, did enact that during the said rebellion the

President of the United States, whenever in his judgment the public safety may require it, is authorized to suspend the privilege of the writ of *habeas corpus* in any case throughout the United States or in any part thereof; and

Whereas the said insurrection and rebellion still continue, endangering the existence of the Constitution and Government of the United States; and

Whereas the military forces of the United States are now actively engaged in suppressing the said insurrection and rebellion in various parts of the States where the said rebellion has been successful in obstructing the laws and public authorities, especially in the States of Virginia and Georgia; and

Whereas on the 15th day of September last the President of the United States duly issued his proclamation, wherein he declared that the privilege of the writ of *habeas corpus* should be suspended throughout the United States in the cases where, by the authority of the President of the United States, military, naval, and civil officers of the United States, or any of them, hold persons under their command or in their custody, either as prisoners of war, spies, or aiders or abettors of the enemy, or officers, soldiers, or seamen enrolled or drafted or mustered or enlisted in or belonging to the land or naval forces of the United States, or as deserters therefrom, or otherwise amenable to military law or the rules and articles of war or the rules or regulations prescribed for the military or naval services by authority of the President of the United States, or for resisting a draft, or for any other offense against the military or naval service; and

Whereas many citizens of the State of Kentucky have joined the forces of the insurgents, and such insurgents have on several occasions entered the said State of Kentucky in large force, and, not without aid and comfort furnished by disaffected and disloyal citizens of the United State residing therein, have not only greatly disturbed the public peace, but have overborne the civil authorities and made flagrant civil war, destroying property and life in various parts of that State; and

Whereas it has been made known to the President of the United States by the officers commanding the national armies that combinations have been formed in the said State of Kentucky with a purpose of inciting rebel forces to renew the said operations of civil war within the said State and thereby to embarrass the United States armies now operating in the said States of Virginia and Georgia and even to endanger their safety:

Now, therefore, I, Abraham Lincoln, President of the United States, by virtue of the authority vested in me by the Constitution and laws, do hereby declare that in my judgment the public safety especially requires that the suspension of the privilege of the writ of *habeas corpus*, so proclaimed in the said proclamation of the 15th of September, 1863, be made

THE BATTLE OF THE WILDERNESS

MARCHING TO THE BATTLEFIELD—BALL'S BLUFF

FIGHTING A WAY THROUGH THE WILDERNESS

From May 3d, when Grant led the Army of the Potomac across the Rapidan into the Wilderness to crush Lee, until June 12th, when he led it across the James, they fought incessantly. His losses (54,929 men) were almost equal to the number of Lee's army when the fighting began.

This illustration truthfully portrays the character of the fighting. Artillery could not be used effectually, and it was hand-to-hand for the most part. Yet, in spite of the horrors of constant battle, in spite of the brush-fires that consumed the wounded, in spite of privation, when Grant rode along the lines he was cheered tumultuously. The army reached a fork in the road; to turn one way meant retreat, to turn the other meant an advance on Richmond; and when the column set its face toward the rebel capital the men shouted with joy.

For accounts of the terrific fighting, see the articles in the Encyclopedic Index, entitled "Wilderness (Va.), Battle of," "Spottsylvania Court House (Va.), Battle of," and "Cold Harbor (Va.), Battle of."

effectual and be duly enforced in and throughout the said State of Kentucky, and that martial law be for the present established therein. I do therefore hereby require of the military officers in the said State that the privileges of the writ of *habeas corpus* be effectually suspended within the said State, according to the aforesaid proclamation, and that martial law be established therein, to take effect from the date of this proclamation, the said suspension and establishment of martial law to continue until this proclamation shall be revoked or modified, but not beyond the period when the said rebellion shall have been suppressed or come to an end. And I do hereby require and command as well all military officers as all civil officers and authorities existing or found within the said State of Kentucky to take notice of this proclamation and to give full effect to the same.

The martial law herein proclaimed and the things in that respect herein ordered will not be deemed or taken to interfere with the holding of lawful elections, or with the proceedings of the constitutional legislature of Kentucky, or with the administration of justice in the courts of law existing therein between citizens of the United States in suits or proceedings which do not affect the military operations or the constituted authorities of the Government of the United States.

In testimony whereof I have hereunto set my hand and caused the seal of the United States to be affixed

[SEAL.] Done at the city of Washington, this 5th day of July, A. D. 1864, and of the Independence of the United States the eighty-ninth.

ABRAHAM LINCOLN.

By the President:

WILLIAM H. SEWARD,
Secretary of State.

BY THE PRESIDENT OF THE UNITED STATES.

A PROCLAMATION.

Whereas the Senate and House of Representatives at their last session adopted a concurrent resolution, which was approved on the 2d day of July instant and which was in the words following, namely:

That the President of the United States be requested to appoint a day for humiliation and prayer by the people of the United States; that he request his constitutional advisers at the head of the Executive Departments to unite with him as Chief Magistrate of the nation, at the city of Washington, and the members of Congress, and all magistrates, all civil, military, and naval officers, all soldiers, sailors, and marines, with all loyal and law-abiding people, to convene at their usual places of worship, or wherever they may be, to confess and to repent of their manifold sins; to implore the compassion and forgiveness of the Almighty, that, if consistent with His will, the existing rebellion may be speedily suppressed and the supremacy of the Constitution and laws of the United States may be established throughout all the States; to implore

Him, as the Supreme Ruler of the World, not to destroy us as a people, nor suffer us to be destroyed by the hostility or connivance of other nations or by obstinate adhesion to our own counsels, which may be in conflict with His eternal purposes, and to implore Him to enlighten the mind of the nation to know and do His will, humbly believing that it is in accordance with His will that our place should be maintained as a united people among the family of nations; to implore Him to grant to our armed defenders and the masses of the people that courage, power of resistance, and endurance necessary to secure that result; to implore Him in His infinite goodness to soften the hearts, enlighten the minds, and quicken the consciences of those in rebellion, that they may lay down their arms and speedily return to their allegiance to the United States, that they may not be utterly destroyed, that the effusion of blood may be stayed, and that unity and fraternity may be restored and peace established throughout all our borders:

Now, therefore, I, Abraham Lincoln, President of the United States, cordially concurring with the Congress of the United States in the penitential and pious sentiments expressed in the aforesaid resolution and heartily approving of the devotional design and purpose thereof, do hereby appoint the first Thursday of August next to be observed by the people of the United States as a day of national humiliation and prayer.

I do hereby further invite and request the heads of the Executive Departments of this Government, together with all legislators, all judges and magistrates, and all other persons exercising authority in the land, whether civil, military, or naval, and all soldiers, seamen, and marines in the national service, and all the other loyal and law-abiding people of the United States, to assemble in their preferred places of public worship on that day, and there and then to render to the almighty and merciful Ruler of the Universe such homages and such confessions and to offer to Him such supplications as the Congress of the United States have in their aforesaid resolution so solemnly, so earnestly, and so reverently recommended.

In testimony whereof I have hereunto set my hand and caused the seal of the United States to be affixed.

[SEAL.] Done at the city of Washington, this 7th day of July, A. D. 1864, and of the Independence of the United States the eighty-ninth.

ABRAHAM LINCOLN.

By the President:

WILLIAM H. SEWARD,
Secretary of State.

BY THE PRESIDENT OF THE UNITED STATES.

A PROCLAMATION.

Whereas at the late session Congress passed a bill "to guarantee to certain States whose governments have been usurped or overthrown a republican form of government," a copy of which is hereunto annexed; and

Whereas the said bill was presented to the President of the United

States for his approval less than one hour before the *sine die* adjournment of said session, and was not signed by him; and

Whereas the said bill contains, among other things, a plan for restoring the States in rebellion to their proper practical relation in the Union, which plan expresses the sense of Congress upon that subject, and which plan it is now thought fit to lay before the people for their consideration:

Now, therefore, I, Abraham Lincoln, President of the United States, do proclaim, declare, and make known that while I am (as I was in December last, when, by proclamation, I propounded a plan for restoration) unprepared by a formal approval of this bill to be inflexibly committed to any single plan of restoration, and while I am also unprepared to declare that the free State constitutions and governments already adopted and installed in Arkansas and Louisiana shall be set aside and held for naught, thereby repelling and discouraging the loyal citizens who have set up the same as to further effort, or to declare a constitutional competency in Congress to abolish slavery in States, but am at the same time sincerely hoping and expecting that a constitutional amendment abolishing slavery throughout the nation may be adopted, nevertheless I am fully satisfied with the system for restoration contained in the bill as one very proper plan for the loyal people of any State choosing to adopt it, and that I am and at all times shall be prepared to give the Executive aid and assistance to any such people so soon as the military resistance to the United States shall have been suppressed in any such State and the people thereof shall have sufficiently returned to their obedience to the Constitution and the laws of the United States, in which cases military governors will be appointed with directions to proceed according to the bill.

In testimony whereof I have hereunto set my hand and caused the seal of the United States to be affixed.

[SEAL.] Done at the city of Washington, this 8th day of July, A. D. 1864, and of the Independence of the United States the eighty-ninth.

ABRAHAM LINCOLN.

By the President:
WILLIAM H. SEWARD,
Secretary of State.

[H. R. 244, Thirty-eighth Congress, first session.]

AN ACT to guarantee to certain States whose governments have been usurped or overthrown a republican form of government.

Be it enacted by the Senate and House of Representatives of the United States of America in Congress assembled, That in the States declared in rebellion against the United States the President shall, by and with the advice and consent of the Senate, appoint for each a provisional governor, whose pay and emoluments shall not exceed that of a brigadier-general of volunteers, who shall be charged with the civil administration of such State until a State government therein shall be recognized as hereinafter provided.

SEC. 2. *And be it further enacted*, That so soon as the military resistance to the United States shall have been suppressed in any such State and the people thereof shall have sufficiently returned to their obedience to the Constitution and the laws of the United States the provisional governor shall direct the marshal of the United States, as speedily as may be, to name a sufficient number of deputies, and to enroll all white male citizens of the United States resident in the State in their respective counties, and to request each one to take the oath to support the Constitution of the United States, and in his enrollment to designate those who take and those who refuse to take that oath, which rolls shall be forthwith returned to the provisional governor; and if the persons taking that oath shall amount to a majority of the persons enrolled in the State, he shall, by proclamation, invite the loyal people of the State to elect delegates to a convention charged to declare the will of the people of the State relative to the reestablishment of a State government, subject to and in conformity with the Constitution of the United States.

SEC. 3. *And be it further enacted*, That the convention shall consist of as many members as both houses of the last constitutional State legislature, apportioned by the provisional governor among the counties, parishes, or districts of the State, in proportion to the white population returned as electors by the marshal in compliance with the provisions of this act. The provisional governor shall, by proclamation, declare the number of delegates to be elected by each county, parish, or election district; name a day of election not less than thirty days thereafter; designate the places of voting in each county, parish, or district, conforming as nearly as may be convenient to the places used in the State elections next preceding the rebellion; appoint one or more commissioners to hold the election at each place of voting, and provide an adequate force to keep the peace during the election.

SEC. 4. *And be it further enacted*, That the delegates shall be elected by the loyal white male citizens of the United States of the age of 21 years, and resident at the time in the county, parish, or district in which they shall offer to vote, and enrolled as aforesaid, or absent in the military service of the United States, and who shall take and subscribe the oath of allegiance to the United States in the form contained in the act of Congress of July 2, 1862; and all such citizens of the United States who are in the military service of the United States shall vote at the headquarters of their respective commands, under such regulations as may be prescribed by the provisional governor for the taking and return of their votes; but no person who has held or exercised any office, civil or military, State or Confederate, under the rebel usurpation, or who has voluntarily borne arms against the United States, shall vote or be eligible to be elected as delegate at such election.

SEC. 5. *And be it further enacted*, That the said commissioners, or either of them, shall hold the election in conformity with this act, and, so far as may be consistent therewith, shall proceed in the manner used in the State prior to the rebellion. The oath of allegiance shall be taken and subscribed on the poll book by every voter in the form above prescribed, but every person known by or proved to the commissioners to have held or exercised any office, civil or military, State or Confederate, under the rebel usurpation, or to have voluntarily borne arms against the United States, shall be excluded though he offer to take the oath; and in case any person who shall have borne arms against the United States shall offer to vote, he shall be deemed to have borne arms voluntarily unless he shall prove the contrary by the testimony of a qualified voter. The poll book, showing the name and oath of each voter, shall be returned to the provisional governor by the commissioners of election, or the one acting, and the provisional governor shall canvass such returns and declare the person having the highest number of votes elected.

SEC. 6. *And be it further enacted*, That the provisional governor shall, by proclamation, convene the delegates elected as aforesaid at the capital of the State on a day not more than three months after the election, giving at least thirty days' notice of such day. In case the said capital shall in his judgment be unfit, he shall in his proclamation appoint another place. He shall preside over the deliberations of the convention and administer to each delegate, before taking his seat in the convention, the oath of allegiance to the United States in the form above prescribed.

SEC. 7. *And be it further enacted*, That the convention shall declare on behalf of the people of the State their submission to the Constitution and laws of the United States, and shall adopt the following provisions, hereby prescribed by the United States in the execution of the constitutional duty to guarantee a republican form of government to every State, and incorporate them in the constitution of the State; that is to say:

First. No person who has held or exercised any office, civil or military (except offices merely ministerial and military offices below the grade of colonel), State or Confederate, under the usurping power, shall vote for or be a member of the legislature or governor.

Second. Involuntary servitude is forever prohibited, and the freedom of all persons is guaranteed in said State.

Third. No debt, State or Confederate, created by or under the sanction of the usurping power shall be recognized or paid by the State.

SEC. 8. *And be it further enacted*, That when the convention shall have adopted those provisions it shall proceed to reestablish a republican form of government and ordain a constitution containing those provisions, which, when adopted, the convention shall by ordinance provide for submitting to the people of the State entitled to vote under this law, at an election to be held in the manner prescribed by the act for the election of delegates, but at a time and place named by the convention, at which election the said electors, and none others, shall vote directly for or against such constitution and form of State government. And the returns of said election shall be made to the provisional governor, who shall canvass the same in the presence of the electors, and if a majority of the votes cast shall be for the constitution and form of government, he shall certify the same, with a copy thereof, to the President of the United States, who, after obtaining the assent of Congress, shall, by proclamation, recognize the government so established, and none other, as the constitutional government of the State; and from the date of such recognition, and not before, Senators and Representatives and electors for President and Vice-President may be elected in such State, according to the laws of the State and of the United States.

SEC. 9. *And be it further enacted*, That if the convention shall refuse to reestablish the State government on the conditions aforesaid the provisional governor shall declare it dissolved; but it shall be the duty of the President, whenever he shall have reason to believe that a sufficient number of the people of the State entitled to vote under this act, in number not less than a majority of those enrolled as aforesaid, are willing to reestablish a State government on the conditions aforesaid, to direct the provisional governor to order another election of delegates to a convention for the purpose and in the manner prescribed in this act, and to proceed in all respects as hereinbefore provided, either to dissolve the convention or to certify the State government reestablished by it to the President.

SEC. 10. *And be it further enacted*, That until the United States shall have recognized a republican form of State government the provisional governor in each of said States shall see that this act and the laws of the United States and the laws of the State in force when the State government was overthrown by the rebellion are faithfully executed within the State; but no law or usage whereby any person was heretofore held in involuntary servitude shall be recognized or enforced by any court or officer in such State; and the laws for the trial and punishment of white persons shall extend to all persons, and jurors shall have the qualifications of voters under this law for delegates to the convention. The President shall appoint such officer provided for by the laws of the State when its government was overthrown as he may find necessary to the civil administration of the State, all which officers shall be entitled to receive the fees and emoluments provided by the State laws for such officers.

SEC. 11. *And be it further enacted*, That until the recognition of a State government as aforesaid the provisional governor shall, under such regulations as he may prescribe, cause to be assessed, levied, and collected, for the year 1864 and every year thereafter, the taxes provided by the laws of such State to be levied during the fiscal year preceding the overthrow of the State government thereof, in the manner prescribed by the laws of the State, as nearly as may be; and the officers appointed as aforesaid are vested with all powers of levying and collecting such taxes, by distress or sale, as were vested in any officers or tribunal of the State government aforesaid for those purposes. The proceeds of such taxes shall be accounted for to the provisional governor and be by him applied to the expenses of the administration of the laws in such State, subject to the direction of the President, and the surplus shall be deposited in the Treasury of the United States to the credit of such State, to be paid to the State upon an appropriation therefor to be made when a republican form of government shall be recognized therein by the United States.

SEC. 12. *And be it further enacted*, That all persons held to involuntary servitude or labor in the States aforesaid are hereby emancipated and discharged therefrom, and they and their posterity shall be forever free. And if any such persons or their posterity shall be restrained of liberty under pretense of any claim to such service or labor, the courts of the United States shall, on *habeas corpus*, discharge them.

SEC. 13. *And be it further enacted*, That if any person declared free by this act, or any law of the United States or any proclamation of the President, be restrained of liberty with intent to be held in or reduced to involuntary servitude or labor, the person convicted before a court of competent jurisdiction of such act shall be punished by fine of not less than $1,500 and be imprisoned not less than five nor more than twenty years.

SEC. 14. *And be it further enacted*, That every person who shall hereafter hold or exercise any office, civil or military (except offices merely ministerial and military offices below the grade of colonel), in the rebel service, State or Confederate, is hereby declared not to be a citizen of the United States.

BY THE PRESIDENT OF THE UNITED STATES OF AMERICA.

A PROCLAMATION.

Whereas by the act approved July 4, 1864, entitled "An act further to regulate and provide for the enrolling and calling out the national forces and for other purposes," it is provided that the President of the United States may, "at his discretion, at any time hereafter, call for any number of men, as volunteers for the respective terms of one, two, and three years for military service," and "that in case the quota or any part thereof of any town, township, ward of a city, precinct, or election district, or of a county not so subdivided, shall not be filled within the space of fifty days after such call, then the President shall immediately order a draft for one year to fill such quota or any part thereof which may be unfilled;" and

Whereas the new enrollment heretofore ordered is so far completed as that the aforementioned act of Congress may now be put in operation for recruiting and keeping up the strength of the armies in the field, for garrisons, and such military operations as may be required for the purpose of suppressing the rebellion and restoring the authority of the United States Government in the insurgent States:

Now, therefore, I, Abraham Lincoln, President of the United States, do issue this my call for 500,000 volunteers for the military service: *Provided, nevertheless,* That this call shall be reduced by all credits which may be established under section 8 of the aforesaid act on account of persons who have entered the naval service during the present rebellion and by credits for men furnished to the military service in excess of calls heretofore made. Volunteers will be accepted under this call for one, two, or three years, as they may elect, and will be entitled to the bounty provided by the law for the period of service for which they enlist.

And I hereby proclaim, order, and direct that immediately after the 5th day of September, 1864, being fifty days from the date of this call, a draft for troops to serve for one year shall be had in every town, township, ward of a city, precinct, or election district, or county not so subdivided, to fill the quota which shall be assigned to it under this call or any part thereof which may be unfilled by volunteers on the said 5th day of September, 1864.

In testimony whereof I have hereunto set my hand and caused the seal of the United States to be affixed.

[SEAL.]   Done at the city of Washington, this 18th day of July, A. D. 1864, and of the Independence of the United States the eighty-ninth.

ABRAHAM LINCOLN.

By the President:

WILLIAM H. SEWARD,
    Secretary of State.

BY THE PRESIDENT OF THE UNITED STATES OF AMERICA.

A PROCLAMATION.

Whereas the act of Congress of the 28th of September, 1850, entitled "An act to create additional collection districts in the State of California, and to change the existing districts therein, and to modify the existing collection districts in the United States," extends to merchandise warehoused under bond the privilege of being exported to the British North American Provinces adjoining the United States in the manner prescribed in the act of Congress of the 3d of March, 1845, which designates certain frontier ports through which merchandise may be exported, and further provides "that such other ports, situated on the frontiers of the United States adjoining the British North American Provinces, as may hereafter be found expedient may have extended to them the like privileges on the recommendation of the Secretary of the Treasury and proclamation duly made by the President of the United States specially designating the ports to which the aforesaid privileges are to be extended:"

Now, therefore, I, Abraham Lincoln, President of the United States of America, in accordance with the recommendation of the Secretary of the Treasury, do hereby declare and proclaim that the port of Newport, in the State of Vermont, is and shall be entitled to all the privileges in regard to the exportation of merchandise in bond to the British North American Provinces adjoining the United States which are extended to the ports enumerated in the seventh section of the act of Congress of the 3d of March, 1845, aforesaid, from and after the date of this proclamation

In witness whereof I have hereunto set my hand and caused the seal of the United States to be affixed.

[SEAL.]   Done at the city of Washington, this 18th day of August, A. D. 1864, and of the Independence of the United States of America the eighty-ninth.

ABRAHAM LINCOLN.

By the President:

WILLIAM H. SEWARD,
Secretary of State.

BY THE PRESIDENT OF THE UNITED STATES OF AMERICA.

A PROCLAMATION.

It has pleased Almighty God to prolong our national life another year, defending us with His guardian care against unfriendly designs from abroad and vouchsafing to us in His mercy many and signal victories over the enemy, who is of our own household. It has also pleased our Heavenly Father to favor as well our citizens in their homes as our soldiers in their camps and our sailors on the rivers and seas with unusual health. He has largely augmented our free population by emancipation and by immigration, while He has opened to us new sources of wealth and has crowned the labor of our workingmen in every department of industry with abundant rewards. Moreover, He has been pleased to animate and inspire our minds and hearts with fortitude, courage, and resolution sufficient for the great trial of civil war into which we have been brought by our adherence as a nation to the cause of freedom and humanity, and to afford to us reasonable hopes of an ultimate and happy deliverance from all our dangers and afflictions:

Now, therefore, I, Abraham Lincoln, President of the United States, do hereby appoint and set apart the last Thursday in November next as a day which I desire to be observed by all my fellow-citizens, wherever they may then be, as a day of thanksgiving and praise to Almighty God, the beneficent Creator and Ruler of the Universe. And I do further recommend to my fellow-citizens aforesaid that on that occasion they do reverently humble themselves in the dust and from thence offer up penitent and fervent prayers and supplications to the Great Disposer of Events for a return of the inestimable blessings of peace, union, and harmony throughout the land which it has pleased Him to assign as a dwelling place for ourselves and for our posterity throughout all generations.

In testimony whereof I have hereunto set my hand and caused the seal of the United States to be affixed.

[SEAL.]   Done at the city of Washington, this 20th day of October, A. D. 1864, and of the Independence of the United States the eighty-ninth.

ABRAHAM LINCOLN.

By the President:

WILLIAM H. SEWARD,
    Secretary of State.

BY THE PRESIDENT OF THE UNITED STATES OF AMERICA.

A PROCLAMATION.

Whereas the Congress of the United States passed an act, which was approved on the 21st day of March last, entitled "An act to enable the people of Nevada to form a constitution and State government and for the admission of such State into the Union on an equal footing with the original States;" and

Whereas the said constitution and State government have been formed, pursuant to the conditions prescribed by the fifth section of the act of Congress aforesaid, and the certificate required by the said act and also a copy of the constitution and ordinances have been submitted to the President of the United States:

Now, therefore, be it known that I, Abraham Lincoln, President of the United States, in accordance with the duty imposed upon me by the act of Congress aforesaid, do hereby declare and proclaim that the said State of Nevada is admitted into the Union on an equal footing with the original States.

In witness whereof I have hereunto set my hand and caused the seal of the United States to be affixed.

[SEAL.]   Done at the city of Washington, this 31st day of October, A. D. 1864, and of the Independence of the United States the eighty-ninth.

ABRAHAM LINCOLN.

By the President:

WILLIAM H. SEWARD,
    Secretary of State.

BY THE PRESIDENT OF THE UNITED STATES OF AMERICA.

A PROCLAMATION.

Whereas by my proclamation of the 19th of April, 1861, it was declared that the ports of certain States, including those of Norfolk, in the State of Virginia, Fernandina and Pensacola, in the State of Florida, were, for reasons therein set forth, intended to be placed under blockade; and

Whereas the said ports were subsequently blockaded accordingly, but having for some time past been in the military possession of the United States, it is deemed advisable that they should be opened to domestic and foreign commerce:

Now, therefore, be it known that I, Abraham Lincoln, President of the United States, pursuant to the authority in me vested by the fifth section of the act of Congress approved on the 13th of July, 1861, entitled "An act further to provide for the collection of duties on imports, and for other purposes," do hereby declare that the blockade of the said ports of Norfolk, Fernandina, and Pensacola shall so far cease and determine, from and after the 1st day of December next, that commercial intercourse with those ports, except as to persons, things, and information contraband of war, may from that time be carried on, subject to the laws of the United States, to the limitations and in pursuance of the regulations which may be prescribed by the Secretary of the Treasury, and to such military and naval regulations as are now in force or may hereafter be found necessary.

In witness whereof I have hereunto set my hand and caused the seal of the United States to be affixed.

[SEAL.]   Done at the city of Washington, this 19th day of November, A. D. 1864, and of the Independence of the United States the eighty-ninth.

ABRAHAM LINCOLN.

By the President:

WILLIAM H. SEWARD,
Secretary of State.

EXECUTIVE ORDERS.

EXECUTIVE MANSION,
Washington, D. C., December 7, 1863.

Reliable information being received that the insurgent force is retreating from east Tennessee under circumstances rendering it probable that the Union forces can not hereafter be dislodged from that important position, and esteeming this to be of high national consequence, I recommend that all loyal people do, on receipt of this information, assemble at their places of worship and render special homage and gratitude to Almighty God for this great advancement of the national cause.

A. LINCOLN.

GENERAL ORDERS, NO. 398.

WAR DEPARTMENT,
ADJUTANT-GENERAL'S OFFICE,
Washington, December 21, 1863.

The following joint resolution by the Senate and House of Representatives of the United States is published to the Army:

JOINT RESOLUTION of thanks to Major-General Ulysses S. Grant and the officers and soldiers who have fought under his command during this rebellion, and providing that the President of the United States shall cause a medal to be struck, to be presented to Major-General Grant in the name of the people of the United States of America.

Be it resolved by the Senate and House of Representatives of the United States of America in Congress assembled, That the thanks of Congress be, and they hereby are, presented to Major-General Ulysses S. Grant, and through him to the officers and soldiers who have fought under his command during this rebellion, for their gallantry and good conduct in the battles in which they have been engaged; and that the President of the United States be requested to cause a gold medal to be struck, with suitable emblems, devices, and inscriptions, to be presented to Major-General Grant.

SEC. 2. *And be it further resolved,* That when the said medal shall have been struck the President shall cause a copy of this joint resolution to be engrossed on parchment, and shall transmit the same, together with the said medal, to Major-General Grant, to be presented to him in the name of the people of the United States of America.

SEC. 3. *And be it further resolved,* That a sufficient sum of money to carry this resolution into effect is hereby appropriated out of any money in the Treasury not otherwise appropriated.

SCHUYLER COLFAX,
Speaker of the House of Representatives.
H. HAMLIN,
Vice-President of the United States and President of the Senate.

Approved, December 17, 1863.

ABRAHAM LINCOLN.

By order of the Secretary of War:

E. D. TOWNSEND,
Assistant Adjutant-General.

EXECUTIVE MANSION, *January 9, 1864.*

Information having been received that Caleb B. Smith, late Secretary of the Interior, has departed this life at his residence in Indiana, it is ordered that the executive buildings at the seat of the Government be draped in mourning for the period of fourteen days in honor of his memory as a prudent and loyal counselor and a faithful and effective coadjutor of the Administration in a time of public difficulty and peril.

The Secretary of State will communicate a copy of this order to the family of the deceased, together with proper expressions of the profound sympathy of the President and the heads of Departments in their irreparable bereavement.

ABRAHAM LINCOLN.

WAR DEPARTMENT,
Washington City, January 12, 1864.

It is hereby ordered, That all orders and records relating to the Missouri troops, designated, respectively, as Missouri State Militia (M. S. M.) and as Enrolled Missouri Militia (E. M. M.), and which are or have been on file in the offices of the adjutant-generals or their assistants at the different headquarters located in the State of Missouri, shall be open to the inspection of the general assembly of Missouri or of persons commissioned by it, and that copies of such records be furnished them when called for.

By order of the President:

EDWIN M. STANTON,
Secretary of War.

EXECUTIVE MANSION, *February 1, 1864.*

Ordered, That a draft for 500,000 men, to serve for three years or during the war, be made on the 10th day of March next for the military service of the United States, crediting and deducting therefrom so many as may have been enlisted or drafted into the service prior to the 1st day of March and not heretofore credited.

ABRAHAM LINCOLN.

EXECUTIVE MANSION, *February 1, 1864.*

Hon. EDWIN M. STANTON,
Secretary of War.

SIR: You are directed to have a transport (either a steam or sailing vessel, as may be deemed proper by the Quartermaster-General) sent to the colored colony established by the United States at the island of Vache, on the coast of San Domingo, to bring back to this country such of the colonists there as desire to return. You will have the transport furnished with suitable supplies for that purpose, and detail an officer of the Quartermaster's Department, who, under special instructions to be given, shall have charge of the business. The colonists will be brought to Washington, unless otherwise hereafter directed, and be employed and provided for at the camps for colored persons around that city. Those only will be brought from the island who desire to return, and their effects will be brought with them.

ABRAHAM LINCOLN.

GENERAL ORDERS, No. 76.

WAR DEPARTMENT,
ADJUTANT-GENERAL'S OFFICE,
Washington, February 26, 1864.

SENTENCE OF DESERTERS.

The President directs that the sentences of all deserters who have been condemned by court-martial to death, and that have not been otherwise acted upon by him, be mitigated to imprisonment during the war at the Dry Tortugas, Florida, where they will be sent under suitable guards by orders from army commanders.

The commanding generals, who have power to act on proceedings of courts-martial in such cases, are authorized in special cases to restore to duty deserters under sentence, when in their judgment the service will be thereby benefited.

Copies of all orders issued under the foregoing instructions will be immediately forwarded to the Adjutant-General and to the Judge-Advocate-General.

By order of the Secretary of War:

E. D. TOWNSEND,
Assistant Adjutant-General.

EXECUTIVE MANSION,
Washington, March 7, 1864.

Whereas by an Executive order of the 10th of November last permission was given to export certain tobacco belonging to the French Government from insurgent territory, which tobacco was supposed to have been purchased and paid for prior to the 4th day of March, 1861; but whereas it was subsequently ascertained that a part at least of the said tobacco had been purchased subsequently to that date, which fact made it necessary to suspend the carrying into effect of the said order; but whereas, pursuant to mutual explanations, a satisfactory understanding upon the subject has now been reached, it is directed that the order aforesaid may be carried into effect, it being understood that the quantity of French tobacco so to be exported shall not exceed 7,000 hogsheads, and that it is the same tobacco respecting the exportation of which application was originally made by the French Government.

ABRAHAM LINCOLN.

In pursuance of the provisions of section 14 of the act of Congress entitled "An act to aid in the construction of a railroad and telegraph line from the Missouri River to the Pacific Ocean, and to secure to the Government the use of the same for postal, military, and other purposes," approved July 1, 1862, authorizing and directing the President of the United States to fix the point on the western boundary of the State of Iowa from which the Union Pacific Railroad Company is by said section authorized and required to construct a single line of railroad and telegraph upon the most direct and practicable route, subject to the approval of the President of the United States, so as to form a connection with the lines of said company at some point on the one hundredth meridian of longitude in said section named, I, Abraham Lincoln, President of the United States, do, upon the application of the said company, designate and establish such first above-named point on the western boundary of the State of Iowa east of and opposite to the east line of section 10, in township 15 north, of range 13 east, of the sixth principal meridian, in the Territory of Nebraska.

Done at the city of Washington, this 7th day of March, A. D. 1864.

ABRAHAM LINCOLN.

EXECUTIVE MANSION,
Washington, D. C., March 10, 1864.

Under the authority of an act of Congress to revive the grade of lieutenant-general in the United States Army, approved February 29, 1864, Lieutenant-General Ulysses S. Grant, United States Army, is assigned to the command of the armies of the United States.

ABRAHAM LINCOLN.

GENERAL ORDERS, No. 98.

WAR DEPARTMENT,
ADJUTANT-GENERAL'S OFFICE,
Washington, March 12, 1864.

The President of the United States orders as follows:

I. Major-General H. W. Halleck is, at his own request, relieved from duty as General in Chief of the Army, and Lieutenant-General U. S. Grant is assigned to the command of the armies of the United States. The headquarters of the Army will be in Washington and also with Lieutenant-General Grant in the field.

II. Major-General H. W. Halleck is assigned to duty in Washington as chief of staff of the Army, under the direction of the Secretary of War and the Lieutenant-General Commanding. His orders will be obeyed and respected accordingly.

III. Major-General W. T. Sherman is assigned to the command of the Military Division of the Mississippi, composed of the departments of the Ohio, the Cumberland, the Tennessee and the Arkansas.

IV. Major-General J. B. McPherson is assigned to the command of the Department and Army of the Tennessee.

V. In relieving Major-General Halleck from duty as General in Chief, the President desires to express his approbation and thanks for the able and zealous manner in which the arduous and responsible duties of that position have been performed.

By order of the Secretary of War:

E. D. TOWNSEND,
Assistant Adjutant-General.

EXECUTIVE MANSION,
Washington, March 14, 1864.

In order to supply the force required to be drafted for the Navy and to provide an adequate reserve force for all contingencies, in addition to the 500,000 men called for February 1, 1864, a call is hereby made and a draft ordered for 200,000 men for the military service (Army, Navy, and Marine Corps) of the United States.

The proportional quotas for the different wards, towns, townships, precincts, or election districts, or counties, will be made known through the Provost-Marshal-General's Bureau, and account will be taken of the credits and deficiencies on former quotas.

The 15th day of April, 1864, is designated as the time up to which the numbers required from each ward of a city, town, etc., may be raised by voluntary enlistment, and drafts will be made in each ward of a city, town, etc., which shall not have filled the quota assigned to it within the time designated for the number required to fill said quotas. The drafts will be commenced as soon after the 15th of April as practicable.

The Government bounties as now paid continue until April 1, 1864, at which time the additional bounties cease. On and after that date $100 bounty only will be paid, as provided by the act approved July 22, 1861.

ABRAHAM LINCOLN.

EXECUTIVE MANSION, *April 2, 1864.*

Ordered, That the Executive order of September 4, 1863, in relation to the exportation of live stock from the United States, be so extended as to prohibit the exportation of all classes of salted provisions from any part of the United States to any foreign port, except that meats cured, salted, or packed in any State or Territory bordering on the Pacific Ocean may be exported from any port of such State or Territory.

ABRAHAM LINCOLN.

The PRESIDENT OF THE UNITED STATES:

I. The governors of Ohio, Indiana, Illinois, Iowa, and Wisconsin offer to the President infantry troops for the approaching campaign as follows:

Ohio 30,000
Indiana 20,000
Illinois 20,000
Iowa 10,000
Wisconsin 5,000

II. The term of service to be one hundred days, reckoning from the date of muster into the service of the United States, unless sooner discharged.

III. The troops to be mustered into the service of the United States by regiments, when the regiments are filled up, according to regulations, to the minimum strength, the regiments to be organized according to the regulations of the War Department. The whole number to be furnished within twenty days from date of notice of the acceptance of this proposition.

IV. The troops to be clothed, armed, equipped, subsisted, transported, and paid as other United States infantry volunteers, and to serve in fortifications, or wherever their services may be required, within or without their respective States.

V. No bounty to be paid the troops, nor the service charged or credited on any draft.

VI. The draft for three years' service to go on in any State or district where the quota is not filled up; but if any officer or soldier in this special service should be drafted he shall be credited for the service rendered

JOHN BROUGH,
Governor of Ohio

O. P. MORTON,
Governor of Indiana

RICHARD YATES,
Governor of Illinois.

WM. M. STONE,
Governor of Iowa.

JAMES T. LEWIS,
Governor of Wisconsin.

APRIL 23, 1864.

The foregoing proposition of the governors is accepted, and the Secretary of War is directed to carry it into execution.

A. LINCOLN.

EXECUTIVE MANSION,
Washington, May 9, 1864.

To the Friends of the Union and Liberty:

Enough is known of the army operations within the last five days to claim our especial gratitude to God, while what remains undone demands our most sincere prayers to and reliance upon Him, without whom all human efforts are in vain. I recommend that all patriots, at their homes, in their places of public worship, and wherever they may be, unite in common thanksgiving and prayer to Almighty God.

ABRAHAM LINCOLN.

EXECUTIVE MANSION,
Washington, May 18, 1864.

Major-General JOHN A. DIX,
Commanding at New York:

Whereas there has been wickedly and traitorously printed and published this morning in the New York World and New York Journal of Commerce, newspapers printed and published in the city of New York, a false and spurious proclamation purporting to be signed by the President and to be countersigned by the Secretary of State, which publication is of a treasonable nature, designed to give aid and comfort to the enemies of the United States and to the rebels now at war against the Government and their aiders and abettors, you are therefore hereby commanded forthwith to arrest and imprison in any fort or military prison in your command the editors, proprietors, and publishers of the aforesaid newspapers, and all such persons as, after public notice has been given of the falsehood of said publication, print and publish the same with intent to give aid and comfort to the enemy; and you will hold the persons so arrested in close custody until they can be brought to trial before a military commission for their offense. You will also take possession by military force of the printing establishments of the New York World and Journal of Commerce, and hold the same until further orders, and prohibit any further publication therefrom.

A. LINCOLN.

EXECUTIVE MANSION, *Washington, D. C.*

The President of the United States directs that the four persons whose names follow, to wit, Hon. Clement C. Clay, Hon. Jacob Thompson, Professor James P. Holcombe, George N. Sanders, shall have safe conduct to the city of Washington in company with the Hon. Horace Greeley, and shall be exempt from arrest or annoyance of any kind from any officer of the United States during their journey to the said city of Washington.

By order of the President:

JOHN HAY,
Major and Assistant Adjutant-General.

EXECUTIVE MANSION,
Washington, July 18, 1864.

To whom it may concern:

Any proposition which embraces the restoration of peace, the integrity of the whole Union, and the abandonment of slavery, and which comes by and with an authority that can control the armies now at war against the United States, will be received and considered by the executive government of the United States, and will be met by liberal terms on other substantial and collateral points; and the bearer or bearers thereof shall have safe conduct both ways.

ABRAHAM LINCOLN.

EXECUTIVE MANSION, *Washington, August 31, 1864.*

Any person or persons engaged in bringing out cotton, in strict conformity with authority given by W. P. Fessenden, Secretary of the United States Treasury, must not be hindered by the War, Navy, or any other Department of the Government or any person engaged under any of said Departments.

ABRAHAM LINCOLN.

EXECUTIVE MANSION, *September 3, 1864.*

The national thanks are tendered by the President to Major-General William T. Sherman and the gallant officers and soldiers of his command before Atlanta for the distinguished ability, courage, and perseverance displayed in the campaign in Georgia, which, under divine favor, has resulted in the capture of the city of Atlanta. The marches, battles, sieges, and other military operations that have signalized this campaign must render it famous in the annals of war, and have entitled those who have participated therein to the applause and thanks of the nation.

ABRAHAM LINCOLN.

EXECUTIVE MANSION,
Washington City, September 3, 1864.

Ordered, first. That on Monday, the 5th day of September, commencing at the hour of 12 o'clock noon, there shall be given a salute of 100 guns at the arsenal and navy-yard at Washington, and on Tuesday, the 6th of September, or on the day after the receipt of this order, at each arsenal and navy-yard in the United States, for the recent brilliant achievements of the fleet and land forces of the United States in the harbor of Mobile and in the reduction of Fort Powell, Fort Gaines, and Fort Morgan. The Secretary of War and Secretary of the Navy will issue the necessary directions in their respective Departments for the execution of this order.

Second. That on Wednesday, the 7th day of September, commencing at the hour of 12 o'clock noon, there shall be fired a salute of 100 guns at the arsenal at Washington, and at New York, Boston, Philadelphia, Baltimore, Pittsburg, Newport, Ky., and St. Louis, and at New Orleans, Mobile, Pensacola, Hilton Head, and New Berne the day after the receipt of this order, for the brilliant achievements of the army under command of Major-General Sherman in the State of Georgia and the capture of Atlanta. The Secretary of War will issue directions for the execution of this order.

ABRAHAM LINCOLN.

EXECUTIVE MANSION, *Washington, September 3, 1864.*

The signal success that Divine Providence has recently vouchsafed to the operations of the United States fleet and army in the harbor of

Mobile, and the reduction of Fort Powell, Fort Gaines, and Fort Morgan, and the glorious achievements of the army under Major-General Sherman in the State of Georgia, resulting in the capture of the city of Atlanta, call for devout acknowledgment to the Supreme Being, in whose hands are the destinies of nations. It is therefore requested that on next Sunday, in all places of public worship in the United States, thanksgiving be offered to Him for His mercy in preserving our national existence against the insurgent rebels who so long have been waging a cruel war against the Government of the United States for its overthrow; and also that prayer be made for the divine protection to our brave soldiers and their leaders in the field, who have so often and so gallantly periled their lives in battling with the enemy, and for blessing and comfort from the Father of Mercies to the sick, wounded, and prisoners, and to the orphans and widows of those who have fallen in the service of their country; and that He will continue to uphold the Government of the United States against all the efforts of public enemies and secret foes.

ABRAHAM LINCOLN.

EXECUTIVE MANSION, *September 3, 1864.*

The national thanks are tendered by the President to Admiral Farragut and Major-General Canby for the skill and harmony with which the recent operations in Mobile Harbor and against Fort Powell, Fort Gaines, and Fort Morgan were planned and carried into execution; also to Admiral Farragut and Major-General Granger, under whose immediate command they were conducted, and to the gallant commanders on sea and land, and to the sailors and soldiers engaged in the operations, for their energy and courage, which, under the blessing of Providence, have been crowned with brilliant success and have won for them the applause and thanks of the nation.

ABRAHAM LINCOLN.

EXECUTIVE MANSION,
Washington City, September 10, 1864.

The term of one hundred days for which the National Guard of Ohio volunteered having expired, the President directs an official acknowledgment to be made of their patriotic and valuable services during the recent campaigns. The term of service of their enlistment was short, but distinguished by memorable events. In the Valley of the Shenandoah, on the Peninsula, in the operations on the James River, around Petersburg and Richmond, in the battle of Monocacy, and in the intrenchments of Washington, and in other important service, the National Guard of Ohio performed with alacrity the duty of patriotic volunteers, for which they are entitled to and are hereby tendered, through the governor of their State, the national thanks.

The Secretary of War is directed to transmit a copy of this order to the governor of Ohio and to cause a certificate of their honorable service to be delivered to the officers and soldiers of the Ohio National Guard who recently served in the military force of the United States as volunteers for one hundred days.

ABRAHAM LINCOLN.

EXECUTIVE MANSION, *September 24, 1864.*

I. Congress having authorized the purchase for the United States of the product of States declared in insurrection, and the Secretary of the Treasury having designated New Orleans, Memphis, Nashville, Pensacola, Port Royal, Beaufort, N. C., and Norfolk as places of purchase, and with my approval appointed agents and made regulations under which said products may be purchased: Therefore,

II. All persons, except such as may be in the civil, military, or naval service of the Government, having in their possession any products of States declared in insurrection which said agents are authorized to purchase, and all persons owning or controlling such products therein, are authorized to convey such products to either of the places which have been hereby or may hereafter be designated as places of purchase, and such products so destined shall not be liable to detention, seizure, or forfeiture while *in transitu* or in store awaiting transportation.

III. Any person having the certificate of a purchasing agent, as prescribed by Treasury Regulations, VIII, is authorized to pass, with the necessary means of transportation, to the points named in said certificate, and to return therefrom with the products required for the fulfillment of the stipulations set forth in said certificate.

IV. Any person having sold and delivered to a purchasing agent any products of an insurrectionary State in accordance with the regulations in relation thereto, and having in his possession a certificate setting forth the fact of such purchase and sale, the character and quantity of products, and the aggregate amount paid therefor, as prescribed by Regulation IX, shall be permitted by the military authority commanding at the place of sale to purchase from any authorized dealer at such place, or any other place in a loyal State, merchandise and other articles not contraband of war nor prohibited by the order of the War Department, nor coin, bullion, or foreign exchange, to an amount not exceeding in value one-third of the aggregate value of the products sold by him, as certified by the agent purchasing; and the merchandise and other articles so purchased may be transported by the same route and to the same place from and by which the products sold and delivered reached the purchasing agent, as set forth in the certificate; and such merchandise and other articles shall have safe conduct, and shall not be subject to detention, seizure, or forfeiture while being transported to the places and by the route set forth in the said certificate.

V. Generals commanding military districts and commandants of military posts and detachments, and officers commanding fleets, flotillas, and gunboats, will give safe conduct to persons and products, merchandise, and other articles duly authorized as aforesaid, and not contraband of war or prohibited by order of the War Department, or the orders of such generals commanding, or other duly authorized military or naval officer, made in pursuance thereof; and all persons hindering or preventing such safe conduct of persons or property will be deemed guilty of a military offense and punished accordingly.

VI. Any person transporting or attempting to transport any merchandise or other articles, except in pursuance of regulations of the Secretary of the Treasury dated July 29, 1864, or in pursuance of this order, or transporting or attempting to transport any merchandise or other articles contraband of war or forbidden by any order of the War Department, will be deemed guilty of a military offense and punished accordingly; and all products of insurrectionary States found *in transitu* to any other person or place than a purchasing agent and a designated place of purchase shall be seized and forfeited to the United States, except such as may be moving to a loyal State under duly authorized permits of a proper officer of the Treasury Department, as prescribed by Regulation XXXVIII, concerning ''commercial intercourse,'' dated July 29, 1864, or such as may have been found abandoned or have been captured and are moving in pursuance of the act of March 12, 1863.

VII. No military or naval officer of the United States, or person in the military or naval service, nor any civil officer, except such as are appointed for that purpose, shall engage in trade or traffic in the products of insurrectionary States, or furnish transportation therefor, under pain of being deemed guilty of unlawful trading with the enemy and punished accordingly.

VIII. The Secretary of War will make such general orders or regulations as will insure the proper observance and execution of this order, and the Secretary of the Navy will give instructions to officers commanding fleets, flotillas, and gunboats in conformity therewith.

ABRAHAM LINCOLN.

EXECUTIVE MANSION,
Washington, October 1, 1864.

SPECIAL EXECUTIVE ORDER RETURNING THANKS TO THE VOLUN-
TEERS FOR ONE HUNDRED DAYS FROM THE STATES OF INDIANA,
ILLINOIS, IOWA, AND WISCONSIN.

The term of one hundred days for which volunteers from the States of Indiana, Illinois, Iowa, and Wisconsin volunteered, under the call of their respective governors, in the months of May and June, to aid in the campaign of General Sherman, having expired, the President directs an official acknowledgment to be made of their patriotic service. It was their good fortune to render efficient service in the brilliant operations in the Southwest and to contribute to the victories of the national arms over the rebel forces in Georgia under command of Johnston and Hood. On all occasions and in every service to which they were assigned their duty as patriotic volunteers was performed with alacrity and courage, for which they are entitled to and are hereby tendered the national thanks through the governors of their respective States.

The Secretary of War is directed to transmit a copy of this order to the governors of Indiana, Illinois, Iowa, and Wisconsin and to cause a certificate of their honorable service to be delivered to the officers and soldiers of the States above named who recently served in the military force of the United States as volunteers for one hundred days.

A. LINCOLN.

EXECUTIVE MANSION,
Washington, October 12, 1864.

The Japanese Government having caused the construction at New York of a vessel of war called the *Fusigama*, and application having been made for the clearance of the same, in order that it may proceed to Japan, it is ordered, in view of the state of affairs in that country and of its relation with the United States, that a compliance with the application be for the present suspended.

ABRAHAM LINCOLN.

GENERAL ORDERS, NO. 282.

WAR DEPARTMENT,
ADJUTANT-GENERAL'S OFFICE,
Washington, November 14, 1864.

Ordered by the President, I. That the resignation of George B. Mc-Clellan as major-general in the United States Army, dated November 8 and received by the Adjutant-General on the 10th instant, be accepted as of the 8th of November.

II. That for the personal gallantry, military skill, and just confidence in the courage and patriotism of his troops displayed by Philip H. Sheridan on the 19th day of October at Cedar Run, whereby, under the blessing of Providence, his routed army was reorganized, a great national disaster averted, and a brilliant victory achieved over the rebels for the third time in pitched battle within thirty days, Philip H. Sheridan is appointed major-general in the United States Army, to rank as such from the 8th day of November, 1864.

By order of the President of the United States:

E. D. TOWNSEND, *Assistant Adjutant-General.*

EXECUTIVE MANSION,
Washington, December 3, 1864.

A war steamer, called the *Funayma Solace*, having been built in this country for the Japanese Government and at the instance of that Government, it is deemed to comport with the public interest, in view of the unsettled condition of the relations of the United States with that Empire, that the steamer should not be allowed to proceed to Japan. If, however, the Secretary of the Navy should ascertain that the steamer is adapted to our service, he is authorized to purchase her, but the purchase money will be held in trust toward satisfying any valid claims which may be presented by the Japanese on account of the construction of the steamer and the failure to deliver the same, as above set forth.

ABRAHAM LINCOLN.

FOURTH ANNUAL MESSAGE.

DECEMBER 6, 1864

Fellow-Citizens of the Senate and House of Representatives:

Again the blessings of health and abundant harvests claim our profoundest gratitude to Almighty God.

The condition of our foreign affairs is reasonably satisfactory.

Mexico continues to be a theater of civil war. While our political relations with that country have undergone no change, we have at the same time strictly maintained neutrality between the belligerents.

At the request of the States of Costa Rica and Nicaragua, a competent engineer has been authorized to make a survey of the river San Juan and the port of San Juan. It is a source of much satisfaction that the difficulties which for a moment excited some political apprehensions and caused a closing of the interoceanic transit route have been amicably adjusted, and that there is a good prospect that the route will soon be reopened with an increase of capacity and adaptation. We could not exaggerate either the commercial or the political importance of that great improvement.

It would be doing injustice to an important South American State not to acknowledge the directness, frankness, and cordiality with which the United States of Colombia have entered into intimate relations with this Government. A claims convention has been constituted to complete the unfinished work of the one which closed its session in 1861.

The new liberal constitution of Venezuela having gone into effect with the universal acquiescence of the people, the Government under it has been recognized and diplomatic intercourse with it has opened in a cordial and friendly spirit. The long-deferred Aves Island claim has been satis-factorily paid and discharged.

Mutual payments have been made of the claims awarded by the late joint commission for the settlement of claims between the United States and Peru. An earnest and cordial friendship continues to exist between the two countries, and such efforts as were in my power have been used to remove misunderstanding and avert a threatened war between Peru and Spain.

Our relations are of the most friendly nature with Chile, the Argentine Republic, Bolivia, Costa Rica, Paraguay, San Salvador, and Hayti.

During the past year no differences of any kind have arisen with any of those Republics, and, on the other hand, their sympathies with the United States are constantly expressed with cordiality and earnestness.

The claim arising from the seizure of the cargo of the brig *Macedonian* in 1821 has been paid in full by the Government of Chile.

Civil war continues in the Spanish part of San Domingo, apparently without prospect of an early close.

Official correspondence has been freely opened with Liberia, and it gives us a pleasing view of social and political progress in that Republic. It may be expected to derive new vigor from American influence, improved by the rapid disappearance of slavery in the United States.

I solicit your authority to furnish to the Republic a gunboat at moderate cost, to be reimbursed to the United States by installments. Such a vessel is needed for the safety of that State against the native African races, and in Liberian hands it would be more effective in arresting the African slave trade than a squadron in our own hands. The possession of the least organized naval force would stimulate a generous ambition in the Republic, and the confidence which we should manifest by furnishing it would win forbearance and favor toward the colony from all civilized nations.

The proposed overland telegraph between America and Europe, by the way of Behrings Straits and Asiatic Russia, which was sanctioned by Congress at the last session, has been undertaken, under very favorable circumstances, by an association of American citizens, with the cordial good will and support as well of this Government as of those of Great Britain and Russia. Assurances have been received from most of the South American States of their high appreciation of the enterprise and their readiness to cooperate in constructing lines tributary to that world-encircling communication. I learn with much satisfaction that the noble design of a telegraphic communication between the eastern coast of America and Great Britain has been renewed, with full expectation of its early accomplishment.

Thus it is hoped that with the return of domestic peace the country will be able to resume with energy and advantage its former high career of commerce and civilization.

Our very popular and estimable representative in Egypt died in April last. An unpleasant altercation which arose between the temporary incumbent of the office and the Government of the Pasha resulted in a suspension of intercourse. The evil was promptly corrected on the arrival of the successor in the consulate, and our relations with Egypt, as well as our relations with the Barbary Powers, are entirely satisfactory.

The rebellion which has so long been flagrant in China has at last been suppressed, with the cooperating good offices of this Government and of the other Western commercial States. The judicial consular establishment there has become very difficult and onerous, and it will need legislative revision to adapt it to the extension of our commerce and to the more intimate intercourse which has been instituted with the Government and people of that vast Empire. China seems to be accepting with hearty good will the conventional laws which regulate commercial and social intercourse among the Western nations.

Owing to the peculiar situation of Japan and the anomalous form of its Government, the action of that Empire in performing treaty stipulations is inconstant and capricious. Nevertheless, good progress has been effected by the Western powers, moving with enlightened concert. Our own pecuniary claims have been allowed or put in course of settlement, and the inland sea has been reopened to commerce. There is reason also to believe that these proceedings have increased rather than diminished the friendship of Japan toward the United States.

The ports of Norfolk, Fernandina, and Pensacola have been opened by proclamation. It is hoped that foreign merchants will now consider whether it is not safer and more profitable to themselves, as well as just to the United States, to resort to these and other open ports than it is to pursue, through many hazards and at vast cost, a contraband trade with other ports which are closed, if not by actual military occupation, at least by a lawful and effective blockade.

For myself, I have no doubt of the power and duty of the Executive, under the law of nations, to exclude enemies of the human race from an asylum in the United States. If Congress should think that proceedings in such cases lack the authority of law, or ought to be further regulated by it, I recommend that provision be made for effectually preventing foreign slave traders from acquiring domicile and facilities for their criminal occupation in our country.

It is possible that if it were a new and open question the maritime powers, with the lights they now enjoy, would not concede the privileges of a naval belligerent to the insurgents of the United States, destitute, as they are, and always have been, equally of ships of war and of ports and harbors. Disloyal emissaries have been neither less assiduous nor more successful during the last year than they were before that time in their efforts, under favor of that privilege, to embroil our country in foreign wars. The desire and determination of the governments of the maritime states to defeat that design are believed to be as sincere as and can not be more earnest than our own. Nevertheless, unforeseen political difficulties have arisen, especially in Brazilian and British ports and on the northern boundary of the United States, which have required, and are likely to continue to require, the practice of constant vigilance and a just and conciliatory spirit on the part of the United States, as well as of the nations concerned and their governments.

Commissioners have been appointed under the treaty with Great Britain on the adjustment of the claims of the Hudsons Bay and Pugets Sound Agricultural Companies, in Oregon, and are now proceeding to the execution of the trust assigned to them.

In view of the insecurity of life and property in the region adjacent to the Canadian border, by reason of recent assaults and depredations committed by inimical and desperate persons who are harbored there, it has been thought proper to give notice that after the expiration of six months, the period conditionally stipulated in the existing arrangement with Great Britain, the United States must hold themselves at liberty to increase their naval armament upon the Lakes if they shall find that proceeding necessary. The condition of the border will necessarily come into consideration in connection with the question of continuing or modifying the rights of transit from Canada through the United States, as well as the regulation of imposts, which were temporarily established by the reciprocity treaty of the 5th June, 1854.

I desire, however, to be understood while making this statement that the colonial authorities of Canada are not deemed to be intentionally unjust or unfriendly toward the United States, but, on the contrary, there is every reason to expect that, with the approval of the Imperial Government, they will take the necessary measures to prevent new incursions across the border.

The act passed at the last session for the encouragement of immigration has so far as was possible been put into operation. It seems to need amendment which will enable the officers of the Government to prevent the practice of frauds against the immigrants while on their way and on their arrival in the ports, so as to secure them here a free choice of avocations and places of settlement. A liberal disposition toward this great national policy is manifested by most of the European States, and ought to be reciprocated on our part by giving the immigrants effective national protection. I regard our immigrants as one of the principal replenishing streams which are appointed by Providence to repair the ravages of internal war and its wastes of national strength and health. All that is necessary is to secure the flow of that stream in its present fullness, and to that end the Government must in every way make it manifest that it neither needs nor designs to impose involuntary military service upon those who come from other lands to cast their lot in our country.

The financial affairs of the Government have been successfully administered during the last year. The legislation of the last session of Congress has beneficially affected the revenues, although sufficient time has not yet elapsed to experience the full effect of several of the provisions of the acts of Congress imposing increased taxation.

The receipts during the year from all sources, upon the basis of warrants signed by the Secretary of the Treasury, including loans and the balance in the Treasury on the 1st day of July, 1863, were $1,394,796,007.62, and the aggregate disbursements, upon the same basis, were $1,298,056,-101.89, leaving a balance in the Treasury, as shown by warrants, of $96,739,905.73.

Deduct from these amounts the amount of the principal of the public debt redeemed and the amount of issues in substitution therefor, and the actual cash operations of the Treasury were: Receipts, $884,076,646.57; disbursements, $865,234,087.86; which leaves a cash balance in the Treasury of $18,842,558.71.

Of the receipts there were derived from customs $102,316,152.99, from lands $588,333.29, from direct taxes $475,648.96, from internal revenue $109,741,134.10, from miscellaneous sources $47,511,448.10, and from loans applied to actual expenditures, including former balance, $623,-443,929.13.

There were disbursed for the civil service $27,505,599.46, for pensions and Indians $7,517,930.97, for the War Department $690,791,842.97, for the Navy Department $85,733,292.77, for interest on the public debt $53,685,421.69, making an aggregate of $865,234,087.86 and leaving a balance in the Treasury of $18,842,558.71, as before stated.

For the actual receipts and disbursements for the first quarter and the estimated receipts and disbursements for the three remaining quarters of the current fiscal year, and the general operations of the Treasury in detail, I refer you to the report of the Secretary of the Treasury. I concur with him in the opinion that the proportion of moneys required to meet the expenses consequent upon the war derived from taxation should be still further increased; and I earnestly invite your attention to this subject, to the end that there may be such additional legislation as shall be required to meet the just expectations of the Secretary.

The public debt on the 1st day of July last, as appears by the books of the Treasury, amounted to $1,740,690,489.49. Probably, should the war continue for another year, that amount may be increased by not far from five hundred millions. Held, as it is, for the most part by our own people, it has become a substantial branch of national, though private, property. For obvious reasons the more nearly this property can be distributed among all the people the better. To favor such general distribution, greater inducements to become owners might, perhaps, with good effect and without injury be presented to persons of limited means. With this view I suggest whether it might not be both competent and expedient for Congress to provide that a limited amount of some future issue of public securities might be held by any *bona fide* purchaser exempt from taxation and from seizure for debt, under such restrictions and limitations as might be necessary to guard against abuse of so important a privilege. This would enable every prudent person to set aside a small annuity against a possible day of want.

Privileges like these would render the possession of such securities to the amount limited most desirable to every person of small means who might be able to save enough for the purpose. The great advantage of citizens being creditors as well as debtors with relation to the public debt is obvious. Men readily perceive that they can not be much oppressed by a debt which they owe to themselves.

The public debt on the 1st day of July last, although somewhat exceeding the estimate of the Secretary of the Treasury made to Congress at the commencement of the last session, falls short of the estimate of that officer made in the preceding December as to its probable amount at the beginning of this year by the sum of $3,995,097.31. This fact exhibits a satisfactory condition and conduct of the operations of the Treasury.

The national banking system is proving to be acceptable to capitalists and to the people. On the 25th day of November 584 national banks had been organized, a considerable number of which were conversions from State banks. Changes from State systems to the national system are rapidly taking place, and it is hoped that very soon there will be in the United States no banks of issue not authorized by Congress and no bank-note circulation not secured by the Government. That the Government and the people will derive great benefit from this change in the banking systems of the country can hardly be questioned. The national system will create a reliable and permanent influence in support of the national credit and protect the people against losses in the use of paper money. Whether or not any further legislation is advisable for the suppression of State-bank issues it will be for Congress to determine. It seems quite clear that the Treasury can not be satisfactorily conducted unless the Government can exercise a restraining power over the bank-note circulation of the country.

The report of the Secretary of War and the accompanying documents will detail the campaigns of the armies in the field since the date of the last annual message, and also the operations of the several administrative bureaus of the War Department during the last year. It will also specify the measures deemed essential for the national defense and to keep up and supply the requisite military force.

The report of the Secretary of the Navy presents a comprehensive and satisfactory exhibit of the affairs of that Department and of the naval service. It is a subject of congratulation and laudable pride to our countrymen that a Navy of such vast proportions has been organized in so brief a period and conducted with so much efficiency and success.

The general exhibit of the Navy, including vessels under construction on the 1st of December, 1864, shows a total of 671 vessels, carrying 4,610 guns, and of 510,396 tons, being an actual increase during the year, over and above all losses by shipwreck or in battle, of 83 vessels, 167 guns, and 42,427 tons.

The total number of men at this time in the naval service, including officers, is about 51,000.

There have been captured by the Navy during the year 324 vessels, and the whole number of naval captures since hostilities commenced is 1,379, of which 267 are steamers.

The gross proceeds arising from the sale of condemned prize property thus far reported amount to $14,396,250.51. A large amount of such proceeds is still under adjudication and yet to be reported.

The total expenditure of the Navy Department of every description, including the cost of the immense squadrons that have been called into existence from the 4th of March, 1861, to the 1st of November, 1864, is $238,647,262.35.

Your favorable consideration is invited to the various recommendations of the Secretary of the Navy, especially in regard to a navy-yard and suitable establishment for the construction and repair of iron vessels and the machinery and armature for our ships, to which reference was made in my last annual message.

Your attention is also invited to the views expressed in the report in relation to the legislation of Congress at its last session in respect to prize on our inland waters.

I cordially concur in the recommendation of the Secretary as to the propriety of creating the new rank of vice-admiral in our naval service.

Your attention is invited to the report of the Postmaster-General for a detailed account of the operations and financial condition of the Post-Office Department.

The postal revenues for the year ending June 30, 1864, amounted to $12,438,253.78 and the expenditures to $12,644,786.20, the excess of expenditures over receipts being $206,652.42.

The views presented by the Postmaster-General on the subject of special grants by the Government in aid of the establishment of new lines of ocean mail steamships and the policy he recommends for the development of increased commercial intercourse with adjacent and neighboring countries should receive the careful consideration of Congress.

It is of noteworthy interest that the steady expansion of population, improvement, and governmental institutions over the new and unoccupied portions of our country have scarcely been checked, much less impeded or destroyed, by our great civil war, which at first glance would seem to have absorbed almost the entire energies of the nation.

The organization and admission of the State of Nevada has been completed in conformity with law, and thus our excellent system is firmly established in the mountains, which once seemed a barren and uninhabitable waste between the Atlantic States and those which have grown up on the coast of the Pacific Ocean.

The Territories of the Union are generally in a condition of prosperity and rapid growth. Idaho and Montana, by reason of their great distance and the interruption of communication with them by Indian hostilities, have been only partially organized; but it is understood that these difficulties are about to disappear, which will permit their governments, like those of the others, to go into speedy and full operation.

As intimately connected with and promotive of this material growth of the nation, I ask the attention of Congress to the valuable information and important recommendations relating to the public lands, Indian affairs, the Pacific Railroad, and mineral discoveries contained in the report of the Secretary of the Interior which is herewith transmitted, and which report also embraces the subjects of patents, pensions, and other topics of public interest pertaining to his Department.

The quantity of public land disposed of during the five quarters ending on the 30th of September last was 4,221,342 acres, of which 1,538,614 acres were entered under the homestead law. The remainder was located with military land warrants, agricultural scrip certified to States for railroads, and sold for cash. The cash received from sales and location fees was $1,019,446.

The income from sales during the fiscal year ending June 30, 1864, was $678,007.21, against $136,077.95 received during the preceding year. The aggregate number of acres surveyed during the year has been equal to the quantity disposed of, and there is open to settlement about 133,000,000 acres of surveyed land.

The great enterprise of connecting the Atlantic with the Pacific States by railways and telegraph lines has been entered upon with a vigor that gives assurance of success, notwithstanding the embarrassments arising from the prevailing high prices of materials and labor. The route of the main line of the road has been definitely located for 100 miles westward from the initial point at Omaha City, Nebr., and a preliminary location of the Pacific Railroad of California has been made from Sacramento eastward to the great bend of the Truckee River in Nevada.

Numerous discoveries of gold, silver, and cinnabar mines have been added to the many heretofore known, and the country occupied by the Sierra Nevada and Rocky mountains and the subordinate ranges now teems with enterprising labor, which is richly remunerative. It is believed that the product of the mines of precious metals in that region has during the year reached, if not exceeded, one hundred millions in value.

It was recommended in my last annual message that our Indian system be remodeled. Congress at its last session, acting upon the recommendation, did provide for reorganizing the system in California, and it is believed that under the present organization the management of the Indians there will be attended with reasonable success. Much yet remains to be done to provide for the proper government of the Indians in other parts of the country, to render it secure for the advancing settler, and to provide for the welfare of the Indian. The Secretary reiterates his recommendations, and to them the attention of Congress is invited.

The liberal provisions made by Congress for paying pensions to invalid soldiers and sailors of the Republic and to the widows, orphans, and dependent mothers of those who have fallen in battle or died of disease contracted or of wounds received in the service of their country have been diligently administered. There have been added to the pension rolls during the year ending the 30th day of June last the names of 16,770 invalid soldiers and of 271 disabled seamen, making the present number of army invalid pensioners 22,767 and of navy invalid pensioners 712.

Of widows, orphans, and mothers 22,198 have been placed on the army pension rolls and 248 on the navy rolls. The present number of army pensioners of this class is 25,433 and of navy pensioners 793. At the beginning of the year the number of Revolutionary pensioners was 1,430. Only 12 of them were soldiers, of whom 7 have since died. The remainder are those who under the law receive pensions because of relationship to Revolutionary soldiers. During the year ending the 30th of June, 1864, $4,504,616.92 have been paid to pensioners of all classes.

I cheerfully commend to your continued patronage the benevolent institutions of the District of Columbia which have hitherto been established or fostered by Congress, and respectfully refer for information concerning them and in relation to the Washington Aqueduct, the Capitol, and other matters of local interest to the report of the Secretary.

The Agricultural Department, under the supervision of its present energetic and faithful head, is rapidly commending itself to the great and vital interest it was created to advance It is peculiarly the people's Department, in which they feel more directly concerned than in any other. I commend it to the continued attention and fostering care of Congress.

The war continues. Since the last annual message all the important lines and positions then occupied by our forces have been maintained and our arms have steadily advanced, thus liberating the regions left in rear, so that Missouri, Kentucky, Tennessee, and parts of other States have again produced reasonably fair crops.

The most remarkable feature in the military operations of the year is General Sherman's attempted march of 300 miles directly through the insurgent region. It tends to show a great increase of our relative strength that our General in Chief should feel able to confront and hold in check every active force of the enemy, and yet to detach a well-appointed large army to move on such an expedition. The result not yet being known, conjecture in regard to it is not here indulged.

Important movements have also occurred during the year to the effect of molding society for durability in the Union. Although short of complete success, it is much in the right direction that 12,000 citizens in each of the States of Arkansas and Louisiana have organized loyal State governments, with free constitutions, and are earnestly struggling to maintain and administer them. The movements in the same direction, more extensive though less definite, in Missouri, Kentucky, and Tennessee should not be overlooked. But Maryland presents the example of complete success. Maryland is secure to liberty and union for all the future. The genius of rebellion will no more claim Maryland. Like another foul spirit being driven out, it may seek to tear her, but it will woo her no more.

At the last session of Congress a proposed amendment of the Constitution abolishing slavery throughout the United States passed the Senate, but failed for lack of the requisite two-thirds vote in the House of Representatives. Although the present is the same Congress and nearly the same members, and without questioning the wisdom or patriotism of those who stood in opposition, I venture to recommend the reconsideration and passage of the measure at the present session. Of course the abstract question is not changed; but an intervening election shows almost certainly that the next Congress will pass the measure if this does not. Hence there is only a question of *time* as to when the proposed amendment will go to the States for their action. And as it is to so go at all events, may we not agree that the sooner the better? It is not claimed that the election has imposed a duty on members to change their views or their votes any further than, as an additional element to be considered, their judgment may be affected by it. It is the voice of the people now for the first time heard upon the question. In a great national crisis like ours unanimity of action among those seeking a common end is very desirable—almost indispensable. And yet no approach to such unanimity is attainable unless some deference shall be paid to the will of the majority simply because it is the will of the majority. In this case the common end is the maintenance of the Union, and among the means to secure that end such will, through the election, is most clearly declared in favor of such constitutional amendment.

The most reliable indication of public purpose in this country is derived through our popular elections. Judging by the recent canvass and its result, the purpose of the people within the loyal States to maintain the integrity of the Union was never more firm nor more nearly unanimous than now. The extraordinary calmness and good order with which the millions of voters met and mingled at the polls give strong assurance of this. Not only all those who supported the Union ticket, so called, but a great majority of the opposing party also may be fairly claimed to entertain and to be actuated by the same purpose. It is an unanswerable argument to this effect that no candidate for any office whatever, high or low, has ventured to seek votes on the avowal that

SHERMAN'S MARCH FROM ATLANTA TO THE SEA

LANDING REINFORCEMENTS AT FORT PICKENS, FLORIDA

SHERMAN'S MARCH FROM ATLANTA TO THE SEA

The State of Georgia had never felt the scourge of war. Its rich planters
were strong for a continuance of the struggle. The fertile soil supported not
only her own people but also the Confederate army of Georgia and Lee's Army
of Virginia. Sherman suggested to Grant that he be permitted to leave
Thomas with an army to oppose the Confederate General Hood, and with
the remainder of his troops march through Georgia from Atlanta to the seaboard. Grant and Lincoln reluctantly granted the desired permission, and
for thirty-two days, from November 12 to December 14, 1864, the authorities at Washington heard no word from him. He made the march, cutting
a sixty-mile-wide swath of ruin and devastation, so that, according to Jefferson
Davis, the whole Confederacy was terrified. Two hundred and sixty-five
miles of railroad were irreparably destroyed. Plantations were denuded of
stock and produce. Sherman reported having done $100,000,000 worth of
damage.

See the articles "Atlanta, Battle of," "Nashville, Battle of," "Franklin,
Battle of," and "Fort McAllister, Battle of," in the Encyclopedic Index.

he was for giving up the Union. There have been much impugning of motives and much heated controversy as to the proper means and best mode of advancing the Union cause, but on the distinct issue of Union or no Union the politicians have shown their instinctive knowledge that there is no diversity among the people. In affording the people the fair opportunity of showing one to another and to the world this firmness and unanimity of purpose, the election has been of vast value to the national cause.

The election has exhibited another fact not less valuable to be known— the fact that we do not approach exhaustion in the most important branch of national resources, that of living men. While it is melan choly to reflect that the war has filled so many graves and carried mourning to so many hearts, it is some relief to know that, compared with the surviving, the fallen have been so few. While corps and divisions and brigades and regiments have formed and fought and dwindled and gone out of existence, a great majority of the men who composed them are still living. The same is true of the naval service. The election returns prove this. So many voters could not else be found. The States regularly holding elections, both now and four years ago, to wit, California, Connecticut, Delaware, Illinois, Indiana, Iowa, Kentucky, Maine, Maryland, Massachusetts, Michigan, Minnesota, Missouri, New Hampshire, New Jersey, New York, Ohio, Oregon, Pennsylvania, Rhode Island, Vermont, West Virginia, and Wisconsin, cast 3,982,011 votes now, against 3,870,222 cast then, showing an aggregate now of 3,982,011. To this is to be added 33,762 cast now in the new States of Kansas and Nevada, which States did not vote in 1860, thus swelling the aggregate to 4,015,773 and the net increase during the three years and a half of war to 145,551. A table is appended showing particulars. To this again should be added the number of all soldiers in the field from Massachusetts, Rhode Island, New Jersey, Delaware, Indiana, Illinois, and California, who by the laws of those States could not vote away from their homes, and which number can not be less than 90,000. Nor yet is this all. The number in organized Territories is triple now what it was four years ago, while thousands, white and black, join us as the national arms press back the insurgent lines. So much is shown, affirmatively and negatively, by the election. It is not material to inquire *how* the increase has been produced or to show that it would have been *greater* but for the war, which is probably true. The important fact remains demonstrated that we have *more* men *now* than we had when the war *began;* that we are not exhausted nor in process of exhaustion; that we are *gaining* strength and may if need be maintain the contest indefinitely. This as to men. Material resources are now more complete and abundant than ever.

The national resources, then, are unexhausted, and, as we believe, inexhaustible. The public purpose to reestablish and maintain the national authority is unchanged, and, as we believe, unchangeable. The manner

III

of continuing the effort remains to choose. On careful consideration of all the evidence accessible it seems to me that no attempt at negotiation with the insurgent leader could result in any good. He would accept nothing short of severance of the Union, precisely what we will not and can not give. His declarations to this effect are explicit and oft repeated. He does not attempt to deceive us. He affords us no excuse to deceive ourselves. He can not voluntarily reaccept the Union; we can not voluntarily yield it. Between him and us the issue is distinct, simple, and inflexible. It is an issue which can only be tried by war and decided by victory. If we yield, we are beaten; if the Southern people fail him, he is beaten. Either way it would be the victory and defeat following war. What is true, however, of him who heads the insurgent cause is not necessarily true of those who follow. Although he can not reaccept the Union, they can. Some of them, we know, already desire peace and reunion. The number of such may increase. They can at any moment have peace simply by laying down their arms and submitting to the national authority under the Constitution. After so much the Government could not, if it would, maintain war against them. The loyal people would not sustain or allow it. If questions should remain, we would adjust them by the peaceful means of legislation, conference, courts, and votes, operating only in constitutional and lawful channels. Some certain, and other possible, questions are and would be beyond the Executive power to adjust; as, for instance, the admission of members into Congress and whatever might require the appropriation of money. The Executive power itself would be greatly diminished by the cessation of actual war. Pardons and remissions of forfeitures, however, would still be within Executive control. In what spirit and temper this control would be exercised can be fairly judged of by the past.

A year ago general pardon and amnesty, upon specified terms, were offered to all except certain designated classes, and it was at the same time made known that the excepted classes were still within contemplation of special clemency. During the year many availed themselves of the general provision, and many more would, only that the signs of bad faith in some led to such precautionary measures as rendered the practical process less easy and certain. During the same time also special pardons have been granted to individuals of the excepted classes, and no voluntary application has been denied. Thus practically the door has been for a full year open to all except such as were not in condition to make free choice; that is, such as were in custody or under constraint. It is still so open to all. But the time may come, probably will come, when public duty shall demand that it be closed and that in lieu more rigorous measures than heretofore shall be adopted.

In presenting the abandonment of armed resistance to the national authority on the part of the insurgents as the only indispensable condition to ending the war on the part of the Government, I retract nothing heretofore said as to slavery. I repeat the declaration made a year ago, that "while I remain in my present position I shall not attempt to retract or modify the emancipation proclamation, nor shall I return to slavery any person who is free by the terms of that proclamation or by any of the acts of Congress." If the people should, by whatever mode or means, make it an Executive duty to reenslave such persons, another, and not I, must be their instrument to perform it.

In stating a single condition of peace I mean simply to say that the war will cease on the part of the Government whenever it shall have ceased on the part of those who began it.

ABRAHAM LINCOLN.

Table showing the aggregate votes in the States named at the Presidential elections respectively, in 1860 and 1864.

State.	1860.	1864.
California	118,840	*110,000
Connecticut	77,246	86,616
Delaware	16,039	16,924
Illinois	339,693	348,235
Indiana	272,143	280,645
Iowa	128,331	143,331
Kentucky	146,216	*91,300
Maine	97,918	115,141
Maryland	92,502	72,703
Massachusetts	169,533	175,487
Michigan	154,747	162,413
Minnesota	34,799	42,534
Missouri	165,538	*90,000
New Hampshire	65,953	69,111
New Jersey	121,125	128,680
New York	675,156	730,664
Ohio	442,441	470,745
Oregon	14,410	†14,410
Pennsylvania	476,442	572,697
Rhode Island	19,931	22,187
Vermont	42,844	55,811
West Virginia	46,195	33,874
Wisconsin	152,180	148,513
	3,870,222	3,982,011
Kansas		17,234
Nevada		16,528
		33,762
		3,982,011
Total		4,015,773
		3,870,222
Net increase		145,551

* Nearly.   † Estimated.

SPECIAL MESSAGES.

WASHINGTON CITY, *December 5, 1864.*

To the Senate and House of Representatives:

In conformity to the law of July 16, 1862, I most cordially recommend that Captain John A. Winslow, United States Navy, receive a vote of thanks from Congress for the skill and gallantry exhibited by him in the brilliant action, while in command of the United States steamer *Kearsarge*, which led to the total destruction of the piratical craft *Alabama* on the 19th of June, 1864—a vessel superior in tonnage, superior in number of guns, and superior in number of crew.

This recommendation is specially made in order to comply with the requirements of the ninth section of the aforesaid act, which is in the following words, namely:

That any line officer of the Navy or Marine Corps may be advanced one grade if upon recommendation of the President by name he receives the thanks of Congress for highly distinguished conduct in conflict with the enemy or for extraordinary heroism in the line of his profession.

ABRAHAM LINCOLN.

WASHINGTON CITY, *December 5, 1864.*

To the Senate and House of Representatives:

In conformity to the law of July 16, 1862, I most cordially recommend that Lieutenant William B. Cushing, United States Navy, receive a vote of thanks from Congress for his important, gallant, and perilous achievement in destroying the rebel ironclad steamer *Albemarle* on the night of the 27th of October, 1864, at Plymouth, N. C.

The destruction of so formidable a vessel, which had resisted the continued attacks of a number of our vessels on former occasions, is an important event touching our future naval and military operations, and would reflect honor on any officer, and redounds to the credit of this young officer and the few brave comrades who assisted in this successful and daring undertaking.

This recommendation is specially made in order to comply with the requirements of the ninth section of the aforesaid act, which is in the following words, namely:

That any line officer of the Navy or Marine Corps may be advanced one grade if upon recommendation of the President by name he receives the thanks of Congress for highly distinguished conduct in conflict with the enemy or for extraordinary heroism in the line of his profession.

ABRAHAM LINCOLN.

WASHINGTON CITY, *December 5, 1864.*

To the Senate of the United States:

By virtue of the authority contained in the sixth section of the act of 21st April, 1864, which enacts "that any officer in the naval service, by and with the advice and consent of the Senate, may be advanced not exceeding thirty numbers in his own grade for distinguished conduct in battle or extraordinary heroism," I recommend Commander William H. Macomb, United States Navy, for advancement in his grade ten numbers, to take rank next after Commander William Ronckendorff, for distinguished conduct in the capture of the town of Plymouth, N. C., with its batteries, ordnance stores, etc., on the 31st October, 1864, by a portion of the naval division under his command. The affair was executed in a most creditable manner.

ABRAHAM LINCOLN.

WASHINGTON CITY, *December 5, 1864.*

To the Senate of the United States:

By virtue of the authority contained in the sixth section of the act of 21st April, 1864, which enacts "that any officer in the naval service, by and with the advice and consent of the Senate, may be advanced not exceeding thirty numbers in his own grade for distinguished conduct in battle or extraordinary heroism," I recommend Lieutenant-Commander James S. Thornton, United States Navy, the executive officer of the United States steamer *Kearsarge*, for advancement in his grade ten numbers, to take rank next after Lieutenant-Commander William D. Whiting, for his good conduct and faithful discharge of his duties in the brilliant action with the rebel steamer *Alabama*, which led to the destruction of that vessel on the 19th June, 1864.

ABRAHAM LINCOLN.

WASHINGTON, *December 7, 1864.*

To the Senate of the United States:

In answer to the Senate's resolution of yesterday, requesting information in regard to aid furnished to the rebellion by British subjects, I transmit a report from the Secretary of State and the documents by which it was accompanied.

ABRAHAM LINCOLN.

WASHINGTON, *December 13, 1864.*

To the Senate of the United States:

I transmit to the Senate, for consideration with a view to ratification, "a treaty of friendship, commerce, and navigation between the United States of America and the Republic of Honduras," signed by their respective plenipotentiaries at Comayagua on the 4th of July (1864) last.

ABRAHAM LINCOLN.

WASHINGTON, *December 13, 1864.*

To the Senate of the United States:

I transmit to the Senate, for consideration with a view to ratification, "a treaty of amity, commerce, and navigation, and for the extradition of fugitive criminals, between the United States of America and the Republic of Hayti, signed by their respective plenipotentiaries at Port au Prince on the 3d of November " last.

ABRAHAM LINCOLN.

WASHINGTON, *January 7, 1865.*

To the Senate and House of Representatives:

I transmit to Congress a copy of two treaties between the United States and Belgium, for the extinguishment of the Scheldt dues, etc., concluded on the 20th of May, 1863, and 20th of July, 1863, respectively, the ratifications of which were exchanged at Brussels on the 24th of June last; and I recommend an appropriation to carry into effect the provisions thereof relative to the payment of the proportion of the United States toward the capitalization of the said dues.

ABRAHAM LINCOLN.

EXECUTIVE MANSION,
Washington, January 9, 1865.

Hon. SCHUYLER COLFAX,
    Speaker House of Representatives.

SIR: I transmit herewith the letter of the Secretary of War, with accompanying report of the Adjutant-General, in reply to the resolution of the House of Representatives dated December 7, 1864, requesting me "to communicate to the House the report made by Colonel Thomas M. Key of an interview between himself and General Howell Cobb on the 14th day of June, 1862, on the bank of the Chickahominy, on the subject of the exchange of prisoners of war."

I am, sir, very respectfully, your obedient servant,

ABRAHAM LINCOLN.

WASHINGTON, *January 9, 1865.*

To the Senate of the United States:

In compliance with the resolution of the Senate of the 15th ultimo, requesting information concerning an arrangement limiting the naval armament on the Lakes, I transmit a report of this date from the Secretary of State, to whom the resolution was referred.

ABRAHAM LINCOLN.

EXECUTIVE MANSION,
Washington, January 17, 1865.

To the Senate of the United States:

I herewith lay before the Senate, for its constitutional action thereon, a treaty concluded at the Isabella Indian Reservation, in the State of Michigan, on the 18th day of October, 1864, between H. J. Alvord, special commissioner, and D. C. Leach, United States Indian agent, acting as commissioner on the part of the United States, and the chiefs and headmen of the Chippewas of Saginaw, Swan Creek, and Black River, in the State of Michigan, parties to the treaty of August 2, 1855, with amendments.

A letter of the Secretary of the Interior of the 12th instant and a copy of a communication of the Commissioner of Indian Affairs of the 22d ultimo, with inclosure, accompany the treaty.

ABRAHAM LINCOLN.

WASHINGTON, D. C., *January 31, 1865.*

Hon. H. HAMLIN,
    President of the Senate:

I transmit herewith a communication from the Secretary of War, covering papers bearing on the arrest and imprisonment of Colonel Richard T. Jacobs, lieutenant-governor of the State of Kentucky, and Colonel Frank Wolford, one of the Presidential electors of that State, requested by resolution of the Senate dated December 20, 1864.

ABRAHAM LINCOLN.

WASHINGTON, *February 4, 1865.*

To the Senate of the United States:

In compliance with the resolution of the Senate of the 13th ultimo, requesting information upon the present condition of Mexico and the case of the French war transport steamer *Rhine*, I transmit a report from the Secretary of State and the papers by which it was accompanied.

ABRAHAM LINCOLN.

WASHINGTON, *February 8, 1865.*

To the Senate and House of Representatives:

I transmit to Congress a copy of a note of the 4th instant addressed by J. Hume Burnley, esq., Her Britannic Majesty's chargé d'affaires, to the Secretary of State, relative to a sword which it is proposed to present to Captain Henry S. Stellwagen, commanding the United States frigate *Constitution*, as a mark of gratitude for his services to the British brigantine *Mersey*. The expediency of sanctioning the acceptance of the gift is submitted to your consideration. ABRAHAM LINCOLN.

EXECUTIVE MANSION, *February 8, 1865.*

To the Honorable the Senate and House of Representatives:

The joint resolution entitled "Joint resolution declaring certain States not entitled to representation in the electoral college" has been signed by the Executive in deference to the view of Congress implied in its passage and presentation to him. In his own view, however, the two Houses of Congress, convened under the twelfth article of the Constitution, have complete power to exclude from counting all electoral votes deemed by them to be illegal, and it is not competent for the Executive to defeat or obstruct that power by a veto, as would be the case if his action were at all essential in the matter. He disclaims all right of the Executive to interfere in any way in the matter of canvassing or counting electoral votes, and he also disclaims that by signing said resolution he has expressed any opinion on the recitals of the preamble or any judgment of his own upon the subject of the resolution.

ABRAHAM LINCOLN.

WASHINGTON, *February 10, 1865.*

To the Senate of the United States:

In answer to the resolution of the Senate of the 8th instant, requesting information concerning recent conversations or communications with insurgents under Executive sanction, I transmit a report from the Secretary of State, to whom the resolution was referred.

ABRAHAM LINCOLN.

EXECUTIVE MANSION, *February 10, 1865.*

To the Honorable the House of Representatives:

In response to your resolution of the 8th instant, requesting information in relation to a conference recently held in Hampton Roads, I have the honor to state that on the day of the date I gave Francis P. Blair, sr., a card, written on as follows, to wit:

DECEMBER 28, 1864.

Allow the bearer, F. P. Blair, sr., to pass our lines, go South, and return.

A. LINCOLN.

That at the time I was informed that Mr. Blair sought the card as a means of getting to Richmond, Va., but he was given no authority to speak or act for the Government, nor was I informed of anything he would say or do on his own account or otherwise. Afterwards Mr. Blair told me that he had been to Richmond and had seen Mr. Jefferson Davis; and he (Mr. B.) at the same time left with me a manuscript letter, as follows, to wit:

RICHMOND, VA., *January 12, 1865.*

F. P. BLAIR, Esq.

SIR: I have deemed it proper, and probably desirable to you, to give you in this form the substance of remarks made bv me, to be repeated by you to President Lincoln, etc., etc.

I have no disposition to find obstacles in forms, and am willing, now as heretofore, to enter into negotiations for the restoration of peace, and am ready to send a commission whenever I have reason to suppose it will be received, or to receive a commission if the United States Government shall choose to send one. That notwithstanding the rejection of our former offers, I would, if you could promise that a commissioner, minister, or other agent would be received, appoint one immediately, and renew the effort to enter into conference with a view to secure peace to the two countries.

Yours, etc.,

JEFFERSON DAVIS.

Afterwards, and with the view that it should be shown to Mr. Davis, I wrote and delivered to Mr. Blair a letter, as follows, to wit:

WASHINGTON, *January 18, 1865.*

F. P. BLAIR, Esq.

SIR: Your having shown me Mr. Davis's letter to you of the 12th instant, you may say to him that I have constantly been, am now, and shall continue ready to receive any agent whom he or any other influential person now resisting the national authority may informally send to me with the view of securing peace to the people of our one common country.

Yours, etc.,

A. LINCOLN.

Afterwards Mr. Blair dictated for and authorized me to make an entry on the back of my retained copy of the letter last above recited, which entry is as follows:

JANUARY 28, 1865.

To-day Mr. Blair tells me that on the 21st instant he delivered to Mr. Davis the original of which the within is a copy, and left it with him; that at the time of delivering it Mr. Davis read it over twice in Mr. Blair's presence, at the close of which he (Mr. Blair) remarked that the part about "our one common country" related to the part of Mr. Davis's letter about "the two countries," to which Mr. Davis replied that he so understood it.

A. LINCOLN.

Afterwards the Secretary of War placed in my hands the following telegram, indorsed by him, as appears:

OFFICE UNITED STATES MILITARY TELEGRAPH,
War Department.

The following telegram received at Washington January 29, 1865, from headquarters Army of James, 6.30 p. m., January 29, 1865:

"Hon. EDWIN M. STANTON,
"*Secretary of War:*

"The following dispatch just received from Major-General Parke, who refers it to me for my action. I refer it to you in Lieutenant-General Grant's absence.

"E. O. C. ORD, *Major-General, Commanding.*"

'HEADQUARTERS ARMY OF POTOMAC,
'*January 29, 1865—4 p. m.*

Major-General E. O. C. ORD,
'*Headquarters Army of James:*

'The following dispatch is forwarded to you for your action. Since I have no knowledge of General Grant's having had any understanding of this kind, I refer the matter to you as the ranking officer present in the two armies.

'JNO. G. PARKE, *Major-General, Commanding.*'

'FROM HEADQUARTERS NINTH ARMY CORPS, *29th.*
'Major-General JNO. G. PARKE,
      '*Headquarters Army of Potomac:*

'Alexander H. Stephens, R. M. T. Hunter, and J. A. Campbell desire to cross my lines, in accordance with an understanding claimed to exist with Lieutenant-General Grant, on their way to Washington as peace commissioners. Shall they be admitted? They desire an early answer, to come through immediately. Would like to reach City Point to-night if they can. If they can not do this, they would like to come through at 10 a. m. to-morrow morning.

      'O. B. WILCOX,
      '*Major-General, Commanding Ninth Corps.*'

      "JANUARY 29—8.30 p. m.

"Respectfully referred to the President for such instructions as he may be pleased to give.

      "EDWIN M. STANTON,
      "*Secretary of War.*"

It appears that about the time of placing the foregoing telegram in my hands the Secretary of War dispatched General Ord as follows, to wit:

      WAR DEPARTMENT,
      Washington City, January 29, 1865—10 p. m.
      (Sent at 2 a. m. 30th.)

Major-General ORD.

SIR: This Department has no knowledge of any understanding by General Grant to allow any person to come within his lines as commissioner of any sort. You will therefore allow no one to come into your lines under such character or profession until you receive the President's instructions, to whom your telegram will be submitted for his directions.

      EDWIN M. STANTON,
      Secretary of War.

Afterwards, by my direction, the Secretary of War telegraphed General Ord as follows, to wit:

      WAR DEPARTMENT,
      Washington, D. C., January 30, 1865—10.30 a. m.

Major-General E. O. C. ORD,
      Headquarters Army of the James.

SIR: By direction of the President, you are instructed to inform the three gentlemen, Messrs. Stephens, Hunter, and Campbell, that a messenger will be dispatched to them at or near where they now are without unnecessary delay.

      EDWIN M. STANTON,
      Secretary of War.

Afterwards I prepared and put into the hands of Major Thomas T. Eckert the following instructions and message:

      EXECUTIVE MANSION,
      Washington, January 30, 1865.

Major T. T. ECKERT.

SIR: You will proceed with the documents placed in your hands, and on reaching General Ord will deliver him the letter addressed to him by the Secretary of War; then, by General Ord's assistance, procure an interview with Messrs. Stephens, Hunter, and Campbell, or any of them. Deliver to him or them the paper on which your own letter is written. Note on the copy which you retain the time of delivery and to whom delivered. Receive their answer in writing, waiting a reasonable time for it, and which, if it contain their decision to come through without further condition, will be your warrant to ask General Ord to pass them through, as directed in the letter of the Secretary of War to him. If by their answer they decline to come, or propose other terms, do not have them pass through. And this being your whole duty, return and report to me.

A. LINCOLN.

CITY POINT, VA., *February 1, 1865.*

Messrs. ALEXANDER H. STEPHENS, J. A. CAMPBELL, and R. M. T. HUNTER.

GENTLEMEN: I am instructed by the President of the United States to place this paper in your hands, with the information that if you pass through the United States military lines it will be understood that you do so for the purpose of an informal conference on the basis of the letter a copy of which is on the reverse side of this sheet, and that if you choose to pass on such understanding, and so notify me in writing, I will procure the commanding general to pass you through the lines and to Fortress Monroe under such military precautions as he may deem prudent, and at which place you will be met in due time by some person or persons for the purpose of such informal conference; and, further, that you shall have protection, safe conduct, and safe return in all events.

THOMAS T. ECKERT,
Major and Aid-de-Camp.

WASHINGTON, *January 18, 1865.*

F. P. BLAIR, Esq.

SIR: Your having shown me Mr. Davis's letter to you of the 12th instant, you may say to him that I have constantly been, am now, and shall continue ready to receive any agent whom he or any other influential person now resisting the national authority may informally send to me with the view of securing peace to the people of our one common country.

Yours, etc.,

A. LINCOLN.

Afterwards, but before Major Eckert had departed, the following dispatch was received from General Grant:

OFFICE UNITED STATES MILITARY TELEGRAPH,
War Department.

The following telegram received at Washington January 31, 1865, from City Point, Va., 10.30 a. m., January 30, 1865:

"His Excellency ABRAHAM LINCOLN,
"*President of the United States:*

"The following communication was received here last evening:

'PETERSBURG, VA., *January 30, 1865.*

'Lieutenant-General U. S. GRANT,
'*Commanding Armies United States.*

'SIR: We desire to pass your lines under safe conduct, and to proceed to Washington to hold a conference with President Lincoln upon the subject of the existing war, and with a view of ascertaining upon what terms it may be terminated, in pursuance of the course indicated by him in his letter to Mr. Blair of January 18, 1865, of which we presume you have a copy; and if not, we wish to see you in person, if convenient, and to confer with you upon the subject.

'Very respectfully, yours,

'ALEXANDER H. STEPHENS.
'J. A. CAMPBELL.
'R. M. T. HUNTER.'

"I have sent directions to receive these gentlemen, and expect to have them at my quarters this evening, awaiting your instructions.

"U. S. GRANT,
"*Lieutenant-General, Commanding Armies United States*"

This, it will be perceived, transferred General Ord's agency in the matter to General Grant. I resolved, however, to send Major Eckert forward with his message, and accordingly telegraphed General Grant as follows, to wit:

EXECUTIVE MANSION,
Washington, January 31, 1865.
(Sent at 1.30 p. m.)

Lieutenant-General GRANT,
City Point, Va.:

A messenger is coming to you on the business contained in your dispatch. Detain the gentlemen in comfortable quarters until he arrives, and then act upon the message he brings as far as applicable, it having been made up to pass through General Ord's hands, and when the gentlemen were supposed to be beyond our lines

A. LINCOLN.

When Major Eckert departed, he bore with him a letter of the Secretary of War to General Grant, as follows, to wit:

WAR DEPARTMENT,
Washington, D. C., January 30, 1865.

Lieutenant-General GRANT,
Commanding, etc.

GENERAL: The President desires that you will please procure for the bearer, Major Thomas T. Eckert, an interview with Messrs. Stephens, Hunter, and Campbell, and if on his return to you he requests it pass them through our lines to Fortress Monroe by such route and under such military precautions as you may deem prudent, giving them protection and comfortable quarters while there, and that you let none of this have any effect upon your movements or plans.

By order of the President:

EDWIN M. STANTON,
Secretary of War.

Supposing the proper point to be then reached, I dispatched the Secretary of State with the following instructions, Major Eckert, however, going ahead of him:

EXECUTIVE MANSION,
Washington, January 31, 1865.

Hon. WILLIAM H. SEWARD,
Secretary of State:

You will proceed to Fortress Monroe, Va., there to meet and informally confer with Messrs. Stephens, Hunter, and Campbell on the basis of my letter to F. P. Blair, esq., of January 18, 1865, a copy of which you have.

You will make known to them that three things are indispensable, to wit:

1. The restoration of the national authority throughout all the States.

2. No receding by the Executive of the United States on the slavery question from the position assumed thereon in the ate annual message to Congress and in preceding documents.

3. No cessation of hostilities short of an end of the war and the disbanding of all forces hostile to the Government.

You will inform them that all propositions of theirs not inconsistent with the above will be considered and passed upon in a spirit of sincere liberality. You will hear all they may choose to say and report it to me.

You will not assume to definitely consummate anything.

Yours, etc.,

ABRAHAM LINCOLN.

On the day of its date the following telegram was sent to General Grant:

WAR DEPARTMENT,
Washington, D. C., February 1, 1865.
(Sent at 9.30 a. m.)

Lieutenant-General GRANT,
City Point, Va.:

Let nothing which is transpiring change, hinder, or delay your military movements or plans.

A. LINCOLN.

Afterwards the following dispatch was received from General Grant:

OFFICE UNITED STATES MILITARY TELEGRAPH,
War Department.

The following telegram received at Washington 2.30 p. m. February 1, 1865, from City Point, Va., February 1, 12.30 p. m., 1865:

"His Excellency A. LINCOLN,
"*President United States:*

"Your dispatch received. There will be no armistice in consequence of the presence of Mr. Stephens and others within our lines. The troops are kept in readiness to move at the shortest notice if occasion should justify it.

"U. S. GRANT, *Lieutenant-General.*"

To notify Major Eckert that the Secretary of State would be at Fortress Monroe, and to put them in communication, the following dispatch was sent:

WAR DEPARTMENT,
Washington, D. C., February 1, 1865.

Major T. T. ECKERT,
Care of General Grant, City Point, Va.:

Call at Fortress Monroe and put yourself under direction of Mr. S., whom you will find there.

A. LINCOLN.

On the morning of the 2d instant the following telegrams were received by me respectively from the Secretary of State and Major Eckert:

FORT MONROE, VA., *February 1, 1865—11.30 p. m.*

The PRESIDENT OF THE UNITED STATES:

Arrived at 10 this evening. Richmond party not here. I remain here.

WILLIAM H. SEWARD.

CITY POINT, VA., *February 1, 1865—10 p. m.*

His Excellency A. LINCOLN,
President of the United States:

I have the honor to report the delivery of your communication and my letter at 4.15 this afternoon, to which I received a reply at 6 p. m., but not satisfactory.

At 8 p. m. the following note, addressed to General Grant, was received:

'Lieutenant-General GRANT.   "CITY POINT, VA., *February 1, 1865.*

"SIR: We desire to go to Washington City to confer informally with the President personally in reference to the matters mentioned in his letter to Mr. Blair of the 18th January ultimo, without any personal compromise on any question in the letter. We have the permission to do so from the authorities in Richmond.

"Very respectfully, yours,
                                        "ALEX. H. STEPHENS.
                                        "R. M. T. HUNTER.
                                        "J. A. CAMPBELL."

At 9.30 p. m. I notified them that they could not proceed further unless they complied with the terms expressed in my letter. The point of meeting designated in the above note would not, in my opinion, be insisted upon. Think Fort Monroe would be acceptable. Having complied with my instructions, I will return to Washington to-morrow unless otherwise ordered.
                                        THOS. T. ECKERT, *Major, etc.*

On reading this dispatch of Major Eckert I was about to recall him and the Secretary of State, when the following telegram of General Grant to the Secretary of War was shown me:

                    OFFICE UNITED STATES MILITARY TELEGRAPH,
                                        War Department.

The following telegram received at Washington 4.35 a. m. February 2, 1865, from City Point, Va., February 1, 10.30 p. m., 1865:

"Hon. EDWIN M. STANTON,
        "*Secretary of War:*

"Now that the interview between Major Eckert, under his written instructions, and Mr. Stephens and party has ended, I will state confidentially, but not officially to become a matter of record, that I am convinced upon conversation with Messrs. Stephens and Hunter that their intentions are good and their desire sincere to restore peace and union. I have not felt myself at liberty to express even views of my own or to account for my reticency. This has placed me in an awkward position, which I could have avoided by not seeing them in the first instance. I fear now their going back without any expression from anyone in authority will have a bad influence. At the same time, I recognize the difficulties in the way of receiving these informal commissioners at this time, and do not know what to recommend. I am sorry, however, that Mr. Lincoln can not have an interview with the two named in this dispatch, if not all three now within our lines. Their letter to me was all that the President's instructions contemplated to secure their safe conduct if they had used the same language to Major Eckert.
                                        "U. S. GRANT, *Lieutenant-General.*"

This dispatch of General Grant changed my purpose, and accordingly I telegraphed him and the Secretary of State, respectively, as follows:

                                        WAR DEPARTMENT,
                            Washington, D. C., February 2, 1865.
                                        (Sent at 9 a. m.)

Lieutenant-General GRANT,
        City Point, Va.:

Say to the gentlemen I will meet them personally at Fortress Monroe as soon as I can get there.
                                        A. LINCOLN.

WAR DEPARTMENT,
Washington, D. C., February 2, 1865.

(Sent at 9 a. m.)

Hon. WILLIAM H. SEWARD,
Fortress Monroe, Va.:

Induced by a dispatch from General Grant, I join you at Fort Monroe as soon as I can come.

A. LINCOLN.

Before starting, the following dispatch was shown me. I proceeded, nevertheless.

OFFICE UNITED STATES MILITARY TELEGRAPH,
War Department.

The following telegram received at Washington February 2, 1865, from City Point, Va., 9 a. m., February 2, 1865:

"Hon. WILLIAM H. SEWARD,
"*Secretary of State, Fort Monroe:*

"The gentlemen here have accepted the proposed terms, and will leave for Fort Monroe at 9.30 a. m.

"U. S. GRANT,
"*Lieutenant-General.*"

(Copy to Hon. Edwin M. Stanton, Secretary of War, Washington.)

On the night of the 2d I reached Hampton Roads, found the Secretary of State and Major Eckert on a steamer anchored offshore, and learned of them that the Richmond gentlemen were on another steamer also anchored offshore, in the Roads, and that the Secretary of State had not yet seen or communicated with them. I ascertained that Major Eckert had literally complied with his instructions, and I saw for the first time the answer of the Richmond gentlemen to him, which in his dispatch to me of the 1st he characterizes as "not satisfactory." That answer is as follows, to wit:

CITY POINT, VA., *February 1, 1865.*

THOMAS T. ECKERT,
Major and Aid-de-Camp.

MAJOR: Your note, delivered by yourself this day, has been considered. In reply we have to say that we were furnished with a copy of the letter of President Lincoln to Francis P. Blair, esq., of the 18th of January ultimo, another copy of which is appended to your note.

Our instructions are contained in a letter of which the following is a copy:

"RICHMOND, *January 28, 1865.*

"In conformity with the letter of Mr. Lincoln, of which the foregoing is a copy, you are to proceed to Washington City for informal conference with him upon the issues involved in the existing war, and for the purpose of securing peace to the two countries.

'With great respect, your obedient servant,

"JEFFERSON DAVIS."

The substantial object to be obtained by the informal conference is to ascertain upon what terms the existing war can be terminated honorably.

Our instructions contemplate a personal interview between President Lincoln and ourselves at Washington City, but with this explanation we are ready to meet any person or persons that President Lincoln may appoint at such place as he may designate.

Our earnest desire is that a just and honorable peace may be agreed upon, and we are prepared to receive or to submit propositions which may possibly lead to the attainment of that end.

Very respectfully, yours,

ALEXANDER H. STEPHENS.
R. M. T. HUNTER.
JOHN A. CAMPBELL.

A note of these gentlemen, subsequently addressed to General Grant, has already been given in Major Eckert's dispatch of the 1st instant.

I also here saw, for the first time, the following note addressed by the Richmond gentlemen to Major Eckert:

THOMAS T. ECKERT,
    Major and Aid-de-Camp.

CITY POINT, VA., *February 2, 1865.*

MAJOR: In reply to your verbal statement that your instructions did not allow you to alter the conditions upon which a passport could be given to us, we say that we are willing to proceed to Fortress Monroe and there to have an informal conference with any person or persons that President Lincoln may appoint on the basis of his letter to Francis P. Blair of the 18th of January ultimo, or upon any other terms or conditions that he may hereafter propose not inconsistent with the essential principles of self-government and popular rights, upon which our institutions are founded.

It is our earnest wish to ascertain, after a free interchange of ideas and information, upon what principles and terms, if any, a just and honorable peace can be established without the further effusion of blood, and to contribute our utmost efforts to accomplish such a result.

We think it better to add that in accepting your passport we are not to be understood as committing ourselves to anything but to carry to this informal conference the views and feelings above expressed.

Very respectfully, yours, etc.,

ALEXANDER H. STEPHENS.
J. A. CAMPBELL.
R. M. T. HUNTER.

NOTE.—The above communication was delivered to me at Fort Monroe at 4.30 p. m. February 2 by Lieutenant-Colonel Babcock, of General Grant's staff.

THOMAS T. ECKERT,
Major and Aid-de-Camp.

On the morning of the 3d the three gentlemen, Messrs. Stephens, Hunter, and Campbell, came aboard of our steamer and had an interview with the Secretary of State and myself of several hours' duration. No question of preliminaries to the meeting was then and there made or mentioned; no other person was present; no papers were exchanged or produced; and it was in advance agreed that the conversation was to be informal and verbal merely. On our part the whole substance of the instructions to the Secretary of State hereinbefore recited was stated and insisted upon, and nothing was said inconsistent therewith; while by the other party it was not said that in any event or on any condition they *ever* would consent to reunion, and yet they equally omitted to declare that they *never* would so

JEFFERSON DAVIS—CONFEDERATE CAPITOL—LEE IN WAR TIME

THE FORMATION OF THE SOUTHERN CONFEDERACY

The reasons put forward by Southerners for their secession are considered by Lincoln in his first inaugural address and the following, messages. Jefferson Davis was a representative of the Southern aristocracy as Lincoln was of the Northern working classes. Many writers quote Milton's description of the fallen angel, Lucifer, in describing Jefferson Davis's mental powers. His face in the photograph seems eloquent of pride, decision and commanding intellect. Robert E. Lee's character has been the subject of so much eulogy that no comment is necessary.

The Encyclopedic Index articles, " Civil War " and " Confederate States," give a brief narrative of events.

Lincoln's messages form the greatest Exposition of the Northern Cause ever written; for profundity of thought, for accuracy of analysis, and for clearness and beauty of language they have remained, and will always remain, unrivalled.

consent. They seemed to desire a postponement of that question and the adoption of some other course first, which, as some of them seemed to argue, might or might not lead to reunion, but which course we thought would amount to an indefinite postponement. The conference ended without result.

The foregoing, containing, as is believed, all the information sought, is respectfully submitted.   ABRAHAM LINCOLN.

WASHINGTON, *February 13, 1865.*

To the Senate and House of Representatives:

I transmit to Congress a copy of a dispatch of the 12th ultimo, addressed to the Secretary of State by the minister resident of the United States at Stockholm, relating to an international exhibition to be held at Bergen, in Norway, during the coming summer. The expediency of any legislation upon the subject is submitted for your consideration.

ABRAHAM LINCOLN.

WASHINGTON, *February 13, 1865.*

To the Senate and House of Representatives:

I transmit to Congress a copy of a note of the 2d instant, addressed to the Secretary of State by the Commander J. C. de Figaniere a Moraô, envoy extraordinary and minister plenipotentiary of His Most Faithful Majesty the King of Portugal, calling attention to a proposed international exhibition at the city of Oporto, to be opened in August next, and inviting contributions thereto of the products of American manufactures and industry. The expediency of any legislation on the subject is submitted for your consideration.   ABRAHAM LINCOLN.

WASHINGTON, *February 25, 1865.*

To the Senate of the United States:

In compliance with the resolution of the Senate of the 23d instant, I transmit herewith a report from the Secretary of War, with the accompanying General Orders, No. 23,* issued by Major-General Banks at New Orleans, February 3, 1864.   ABRAHAM LINCOLN.

EXECUTIVE MANSION,
Washington, February 27, 1865.

To the Senate of the United States:

I herewith lay before the Senate, for its constitutional action thereon, a treaty made and concluded with the Klamath and Modoc tribes of Indians of Oregon, at Fort Klamath, on the 5th day of October, 1864.

A letter of the Secretary of the Interior of this date, a copy of the

* On the subject of compensated plantation labor, public or private.

report of the Commissioner of Indian Affairs of the 24th instant, and a communication of the superintendent of Indian affairs in Oregon accompany the treaty.

ABRAHAM LINCOLN.

EXECUTIVE MANSION,
Washington, D. C., February 28, 1865.

Hon. H. HAMLIN,
    President United States Senate.

SIR: In reply to the resolution of the Senate dated February 14, 1865, I transmit herewith a communication from the Secretary of War, forwarding a copy of the report of the court of inquiry "in respect to the explosion of the mine in front of Petersburg."

I am, sir, very respectfully, your obedient servant,

ABRAHAM LINCOLN.

WASHINGTON, D. C., *March 2, 1865.*

Hon. SCHUYLER COLFAX,
    Speaker of the House of Representatives:

I transmit herewith the report of the Secretary of War, which, with my permission, has been delayed until the present time to enable the Lieutenant-General to furnish his report.

A. LINCOLN.

[The same message was addressed to the President of the Senate.]

WASHINGTON, *March 3, 1865.*

To the Senate and House of Representatives:

I herewith transmit to Congress a report, dated 1st instant, with the accompanying papers, received from the Secretary of State in compliance with the requirements of the eighteenth section of the act entitled "An act to regulate the diplomatic and consular systems of the United States," approved August 18, 1856.

ABRAHAM LINCOLN.

VETO MESSAGE.*

EXECUTIVE MANSION, *January 5, 1865.*

To the House of Representatives of the United States:

I herewith return to your honorable body, in which it originated, a "Joint resolution to correct certain clerical errors in the internal-revenue act," without my approval.

My reason for so doing is that I am informed that this joint resolution

* Pocket veto.

was prepared during the last moments of the last session of Congress for the purpose of correcting certain errors of reference in the internal-revenue act which were discovered on an examination of an official copy procured from the State Department a few hours only before the adjournment. It passed the House and went to the Senate, where a vote was taken upon it, but by some accident it was not presented to the President of the Senate for his signature.

Since the adjournment of the last session of Congress other errors of a kind similar to those which this resolution was designed to correct have been discovered in the law, and it is now thought most expedient to include all the necessary corrections in one act or resolution.

The attention of the proper committee of the House has, I am informed, been already directed to the preparation of a bill for this purpose.

ABRAHAM LINCOLN.

PROCLAMATIONS.

BY THE PRESIDENT OF THE UNITED STATES.

A PROCLAMATION.

Whereas by the act approved July 4, 1864, entitled "An act further to regulate and provide for the enrolling and calling out the national forces, and for other purposes," it is provided that the President of the United States may, "at his discretion, at any time hereafter, call for any number of men, as volunteers for the respective terms of one, two, and three years for military service," and "that in case the quota or any part thereof of any town, township, ward of a city, precinct, or election district, or of any county not so subdivided, shall not be filled within the space of fifty days after such call, then the President shall immediately order a draft for one year to fill such quota or any part thereof which may be unfilled;" and

Whereas by the credits allowed in accordance with the act of Congress on the call for 500,000 men, made July 18, 1864, the number of men to be obtained under that call was reduced to 280,000; and

Whereas the operations of the enemy in certain States have rendered it impracticable to procure from them their full quotas of troops under said call; and

Whereas from the foregoing causes but 240,000 men have been put into the Army, Navy, and Marine Corps under the said call of July 18, 1864, leaving a deficiency on that call of two hundred and sixty thousand (260,000):

Now, therefore, I, Abraham Lincoln, President of the United States of

America, in order to supply the aforesaid deficiency and to provide for casualties in the military and naval service of the United States, do issue this my call for three hundred thousand (300,000) volunteers to serve for one, two, or three years. The quotas of the States, districts, and subdistricts under this call will be assigned by the War Department through the bureau of the Provost-Marshal-General of the United States, and "in case the quota or any part thereof of any town, township, ward of a city, precinct, or election district, or of any county not so subdivided, shall not be filled" before the 15th day of February, 1865, then a draft shall be made to fill such quota or any part thereof under this call which may be unfilled on said 15th day of February, 1865.

In testimony whereof I have hereunto set my hand and caused the seal of the United States to be affixed.

[SEAL.]   Done at the city of Washington, this 19th day of December, A. D. 1864, and of the Independence of the United States the eighty-ninth.

ABRAHAM LINCOLN.

By the President:
    WILLIAM H. SEWARD,
        Secretary of State.

BY THE PRESIDENT OF THE UNITED STATES OF AMERICA.

A PROCLAMATION.

Whereas the act of Congress of the 28th of September, 1850, entitled "An act to create additional collection districts in the State of California, and to change the existing districts therein, and to modify the existing collection districts in the United States," extends to merchandise warehoused under bond the privilege of being exported to the British North American Provinces adjoining the United States in the manner prescribed in the act of Congress of the 3d of March, 1845, which designates certain frontier ports through which merchandise may be exported, and further provides "that such other ports situated on the frontiers of the United States adjoining the British North American Provinces as may hereafter be found expedient may have extended to them the like privileges on the recommendation of the Secretary of the Treasury and proclamation duly made by the President of the United States specially designating the ports to which the aforesaid privileges are to be extended:"

Now, therefore, I, Abraham Lincoln, President of the United States of America, in accordance with the recommendation of the Secretary of the Treasury, do hereby declare and proclaim that the port of St. Albans, in the State of Vermont, is and shall be entitled to all the privileges in regard to the exportation of merchandise in bond to the British North American Provinces adjoining the United States which are extended to the ports enumerated in the seventh section of the act of Congress of the 3d of March, 1845, aforesaid, from and after the date of this proclamation.

In witness whereof I have hereunto set my hand and caused the seal of the United States to be affixed.

[SEAL.]   Done at the city of Washington, this 10th day of January, A. D. 1865, and of the Independence of the United States of America the eighty-ninth.

                                                    ABRAHAM LINCOLN.

By the President:
    WILLIAM H. SEWARD,
                Secretary of State.

BY THE PRESIDENT OF THE UNITED STATES OF AMERICA.

A PROCLAMATION.

Whereas objects of interest to the United States require that the Senate should be convened at 12 o'clock on the 4th of March next to receive and act upon such communications as may be made to it on the part of the Executive:

Now, therefore, I, Abraham Lincoln, President of the United States, have considered it to be my duty to issue this my proclamation, declaring that an extraordinary occasion requires the Senate of the United States to convene for the transaction of business at the Capitol, in the city of Washington, on the 4th day of March next, at 12 o'clock at noon on that day, of which all who shall at that time be entitled to act as members of that body are hereby required to take notice.

Given under my hand and the seal of the United States at Washington, the 17th day of February, A. D. 1865, and of the Independence of the United States of America the eighty-ninth.

[SEAL.]

                                                    ABRAHAM LINCOLN.

By the President:
    WILLIAM H. SEWARD,
                Secretary of State.

EXECUTIVE ORDERS.

EXECUTIVE MANSION, *December 10, 1864.*

Ordered, first. That Major-General William F. Smith and the Hon. Henry Stanbery be, and they are hereby, appointed special commissioners to investigate and report, for the information of the President, upon the civil and military administration in the military division bordering upon and west of the Mississippi, under such instructions as shall be issued by authority of the President and the War Department.

Second. Said commissioners shall have power to examine witnesses upon oath, and to take such proofs, orally or in writing, upon the subject-matters of investigation as they may deem expedient, and return the same together with their report.

Third. All officers and persons in the military, naval, and revenue services, or in any branch of the public service under the authority of the United States Government, are required, upon subpœna issued by direction of the said commissioners, to appear before them at such time and place as may be designated in said subpœna and to give testimony on oath touching such matters as may be inquired of by the commissioners, and to produce such books, papers, writings, and documents as they may be notified or required to produce by the commissioners, and as may be in their possession.

Fourth. Said special commissioners shall also investigate and report upon any other matters that may hereafter be directed by the Secretary of War, and shall with all convenient dispatch make report to him in writing of their investigation, and shall also from time to time make special reports to the Secretary of War upon such matters as they may deem of importance to the public interests.

Fifth. The Secretary of War shall assign to the said commissioners such aid and assistance as may be required for the performance of their duties, and make such just and reasonable allowances and compensation for the said commissioners and for the persons employed by them as he may deem proper.

ABRAHAM LINCOLN.

DEPARTMENT OF STATE,
Washington, December 17, 1864.

The President directs that, except immigrant passengers directly entering an American port by sea, henceforth no traveler shall be allowed to enter the United States from a foreign country without a passport. If a citizen, the passport must be from this Department or from some United States minister or consul abroad; and if an alien, from the competent authority of his own country, the passport to be countersigned by a diplomatic agent or consul of the United States. This regulation is intended to apply especially to persons proposing to come to the United States from the neighboring British Provinces. Its observance will be strictly enforced by all officers, civil, military, and naval, in the service of the United States, and the State and municipal authorities are requested to aid in its execution. It is expected, however, that no immigrant passenger coming in manner aforesaid will be obstructed, or any other persons who may set out on their way hither before intelligence of this regulation could reasonably be expected to reach the country from which they may have started.

WILLIAM H. SEWARD.

WASHINGTON, D. C., *December 31, 1864.*

By the authority conferred upon the President of the United States by the second section of the act of Congress approved July 2, 1864, entitled " An act to amend an act to aid in the construction of a railroad and telegraph line from the Missouri River to the Pacific Ocean," etc., I, Abraham Lincoln, President of the United States, do hereby designate the Merchants' National Bank, Boston ; the Chicago and Rock Island Railroad Company's office, Chicago ; the First National Bank at Philadelphia; the First National Bank at Baltimore ; the First National Bank at Cincinnati, and the Third National Bank at St. Louis, in addition to the general office of the Union Pacific Railroad Company in the city of New York, as the places at which the said Union Pacific Railroad Company shall cause books to be kept open to receive subscriptions to the capital stock of said company. ABRAHAM LINCOLN.

EXECUTIVE MANSION, *Washington City, January 20, 1865.*

Ordered, That no clearances for the exportation of hay from the United States be granted until further orders, unless the same shall have been placed on shipboard before the publication hereof.

ABRAHAM LINCOLN.

EXECUTIVE MANSION, *Washington City, February 6, 1865.*

Whereas complaints are made in some localities respecting the assignments of quotas and credits allowed for the pending call of troops to fill up the armies:

Now, in order to determine all controversies in respect thereto and to avoid any delay in filling up the armies, it is ordered that the Attorney-General, Brigadier-General Richard Delafield, and Colonel C. W. Foster be, and they are hereby, constituted a board to examine into the proper quotas and credits of the respective States and districts under the call of December 19, 1864, with directions, if any errors be found therein, to make such corrections as the law and facts may require and report their determination to the Provost-Marshal-General. The determination of said board to be final and conclusive, and the draft to be made in conformity therewith.

2. The Provost-Marshal-General is ordered to make the draft in the respective districts as speedily as the same can be done after the 15th of this month. ABRAHAM LINCOLN.

WASHINGTON, *February 13, 1865.*

To the Military Officers Commanding in West Tennessee:

While I can not order as within requested, allow me to say that it is my wish for you to relieve the people from all burdens, harassments and oppressions so far as is possible consistently with your military necessities;

that the object of the war being to restore and maintain the blessings of peace and good government, I desire you to help, and not hinder, every advance in that direction.

Of your military necessities you must judge and execute, but please do so in the spirit and with the purpose above indicated.

ABRAHAM LINCOLN.

[From the Daily National Intelligencer, February 22, 1865.]

DEPARTMENT OF STATE,
Washington, February 21, 1865.

The Department buildings will be illuminated on the night of Washington's birthday, in honor of the recent triumphs of the Union.

By order of the President:

WILLIAM H. SEWARD.

SECOND INAUGURAL ADDRESS.

FELLOW-COUNTRYMEN: At this second appearing to take the oath of the Presidential office there is less occasion for an extended address than there was at the first. Then a statement somewhat in detail of a course to be pursued seemed fitting and proper. Now, at the expiration of four years, during which public declarations have been constantly called forth on every point and phase of the great contest which still absorbs the attention and engrosses the energies of the nation, little that is new could be presented. The progress of our arms, upon which all else chiefly depends, is as well known to the public as to myself, and it is, I trust, reasonably satisfactory and encouraging to all. With high hope for the future, no prediction in regard to it is ventured.

On the occasion corresponding to this four years ago all thoughts were anxiously directed to an impending civil war. All dreaded it, all sought to avert it. While the inaugural address was being delivered from this place, devoted altogether to *saving* the Union without war, insurgent agents were in the city seeking to *destroy* it without war—seeking to dissolve the Union and divide effects by negotiation. Both parties deprecated war, but one of them would *make* war rather than let the nation survive, and the other would *accept* war rather than let it perish, and the war came.

One-eighth of the whole population were colored slaves, not distributed generally over the Union, but localized in the southern part of it. These slaves constituted a peculiar and powerful interest. All knew that this interest was somehow the cause of the war. To strengthen, perpetuate, and extend this interest was the object for which the insurgents would rend the Union even by war, while the Government claimed no right to do more than to restrict the territorial enlargement of it. Neither party expected for the war the magnitude or the duration which it has already attained. Neither anticipated that the *cause* of the conflict might cease with or even before the conflict itself should cease. Each looked for an easier triumph, and a result less fundamental and astounding. Both read the same Bible and pray to the same God, and each invokes His aid against the other. It may seem strange that any men should dare to ask a just God's assistance in wringing their bread from the sweat of other men's faces, but let us judge not, that we be not judged. The prayers of both could not be answered. That of neither has been answered fully. The Almighty has His own purposes. "Woe unto the world because of offenses; for it must needs be that offenses come, but woe to that man by whom the offense cometh." If we shall suppose that American slavery is one of those offenses which, in the providence of God, must needs come, but which, having continued through His appointed time, He now wills to remove, and that He gives to both North and South this terrible war as the woe due to those by whom the offense came, shall we discern therein any departure from those divine attributes which the believers in a living God always ascribe to Him? Fondly do we hope, fervently do we pray, that this mighty scourge of war may speedily pass away. Yet, if God wills that it continue until all the wealth piled by the bondsman's two hundred and fifty years of unrequited toil shall be sunk, and until every drop of blood drawn with the lash shall be paid by another drawn with the sword, as was said three thousand years ago, so still it must be said "the judgments of the Lord are true and righteous altogether."

With malice toward none, with charity for all, with firmness in the right as God gives us to see the right, let us strive on to finish the work we are in, to bind up the nation's wounds, to care for him who shall have borne the battle and for his widow and his orphan, to do all which may achieve and cherish a just and lasting peace among ourselves and with all nations.

MARCH 4, 1865.

SPECIAL MESSAGES.

WASHINGTON, D. C., *March 8, 1865.*

To the Senate of the United States:

The fourth section of the law of 16th January, 1857, provides that reserved officers may be promoted on the reserved list, by and with the advice and consent of the Senate, and under this authority various officers of the Navy have been promoted one grade from time to time.

I therefore nominate Commander John J. Young, now on the reserved list, to be a captain in the Navy on the reserved list from the 12th August, 1854, the date when he was entitled to his regular promotion had he not been overslaughed. It is due to this officer to state that he was passed over in consequence of physical disability, this disability having occurred in the discharge of his duties; and prior to his misfortune he bore the reputation of an efficient and correct officer, and subsequently has evinced a willingness to perform whatever duties were assigned him.

ABRAHAM LINCOLN.

WASHINGTON, *March 8, 1865.*

To the Senate of the United States:

In answer to the Senate's resolution of the 6th instant, requesting the return of a certain joint resolution,* I transmit a report from the Secretary of State.

ABRAHAM LINCOLN.

PROCLAMATIONS.

BY THE PRESIDENT OF THE UNITED STATES OF AMERICA.

A PROCLAMATION.

Whereas the twenty-first section of the act of Congress approved on the 3d instant, entitled "An act to amend the several acts heretofore passed to provide for the enrolling and calling out the national forces and for other purposes," requires "that, in addition to the other lawful penalties of the crime of desertion from the military or naval service, all persons who have deserted the military or naval service of the United States who shall not return to said service or report themselves to a provost-marshal within sixty days after the proclamation hereinafter mentioned shall be deemed and taken to have voluntarily relinquished and forfeited their rights of citizenship and their rights to become citizens, and such deserters shall be forever incapable of holding any office of trust or profit under the United States or of exercising any rights of citizens thereof; and all persons who shall hereafter desert the military or naval service, and all persons who, being duly enrolled, shall depart the jurisdiction of the district in which he is enrolled or go beyond the limits of the United States with intent to avoid any draft into the military or naval service duly ordered, shall be liable to the penalties of this section. And the President is hereby authorized and required, forthwith on the passage of this act, to issue his proclamation setting forth the provisions of this section, in which proclamation the President is requested to notify all

---

* Entitled "Joint resolution in relation to certain railroads."

deserters returning within sixty days as aforesaid that they shall be pardoned on condition of returning to their regiments and companies or to such other organizations as they may be assigned to until they shall have served for a period of time equal to their original term of enlistment:"

Now, therefore, be it known that I, Abraham Lincoln, President of the United States, do issue this my proclamation, as required by said act, ordering and requiring all deserters to return to their proper posts; and I do hereby notify them that all deserters who shall, within sixty days from the date of this proclamation, viz, on or before the 10th day of May, 1865, return to service or report themselves to a provost-marshal shall be pardoned, on condition that they return to their regiments and companies or to such other organizations as they may be assigned to and serve the remainder of their original terms of enlistment and in addition thereto a period equal to the time lost by desertion.

In testimony whereof I have hereunto set my hand and caused the seal of the United States to be affixed.

[SEAL.]   Done at the city of Washington, this 11th day of March, A. D. 1865, and of the Independence of the United States the eighty-ninth.

ABRAHAM LINCOLN.

By the President:

WILLIAM H. SEWARD,
Secretary of State.

BY THE PRESIDENT OF THE UNITED STATES OF AMERICA.

A PROCLAMATION.

Whereas reliable information has been received that hostile Indians within the limits of the United States have been furnished with arms and munitions of war by persons dwelling in conterminous foreign territory, and are thereby enabled to prosecute their savage warfare upon the exposed and sparse settlements of the frontier:

Now, therefore, be it known that I, Abraham Lincoln, President of the United States of America, do hereby proclaim and direct that all persons detected in that nefarious traffic shall be arrested and tried by court-martial at the nearest military post, and if convicted shall receive the punishment due to their deserts.

In witness whereof I have hereunto set my hand and caused the seal of the United States to be affixed.

[SEAL.]   Done at the city of Washington, this 17th day of March, A. D. 1865, and of the Independence of the United States the eighty-ninth.

ABRAHAM LINCOLN.

By the President :

WILLIAM H. SEWARD,
Secretary of State.

BY THE PRESIDENT OF THE UNITED STATES OF AMERICA.

A PROCLAMATION.

Whereas by my proclamations of the 19th and 27th days of April, A. D. 1861, the ports of the United States in the States of Virginia, North Carolina, South Carolina, Georgia, Florida, Alabama, Mississippi, Louisiana, and Texas were declared to be subject to blockade; but

Whereas the said blockade has, in consequence of actual military occupation by this Government, since been conditionally set aside or relaxed in respect to the ports of Norfolk and Alexandria, in the State of Virginia; Beaufort, in the State of North Carolina; Port Royal, in the State of South Carolina; Pensacola and Fernandina, in the State of Florida; and New Orleans, in the State of Louisiana; and

Whereas by the fourth section of the act of Congre   pproved on the 13th of July, 1861, entitled "An act further to provide or the collection of duties on imports, and for other purposes," the President, for the reasons therein set forth, is authorized to close certain ports of entry:

Now, therefore, be it known that I, Abraham Lincoln, President of the United States, do hereby proclaim that the ports of Richmond, Tappahannock, Cherrystone, Yorktown, and Petersburg, in Virginia; of Camden (Elizabeth City), Edenton, Plymouth, Washington, Newbern, Ocracoke, and Wilmington, in North Carolina; of Charleston, Georgetown, and Beaufort, in South Carolina; of Savannah, St. Marys, and Brunswick (Darien), in Georgia; of Mobile, in Alabama; of Pearl River (Shieldsboro), Natchez, and Vicksburg, in Mississippi; of St. Augustine, Key West, St. Marks (Port Leon), St. Johns (Jacksonville), and Apalachicola, in Florida; of Teche (Franklin), in Louisiana; of Galveston, La Salle, Brazos de Santiago (Point Isabel), and Brownsville, in Texas, are hereby closed, and all right of importation, warehousing, and other privileges shall, in respect to the ports aforesaid, cease until they shall have again been opened by order of the President; and if while said ports are so closed any ship or vessel from beyond the United States or having on board any articles subject to duties shall attempt to enter any such port, the same, together with its tackle, apparel, furniture, and cargo, shall be forfeited to the United States.

In witness whereof I have hereunto set my hand and caused the seal of the United States to be affixed.

[SEAL.]   Done at the city of Washington, this 11th day of April, A. D. 1865, and of the Independence of the United States of America the eighty-ninth.

ABRAHAM LINCOLN.

By the President:

WILLIAM H. SEWARD,
Secretary of State.

BY THE PRESIDENT OF THE UNITED STATES OF AMERICA.

A PROCLAMATION.

Whereas by my proclamation of this date the port of Key West, in the State of Florida, was inadvertently included among those which are not open to commerce:

Now, therefore, be it known that I, Abraham Lincoln, President of the United States, do hereby declare and make known that the said port of Key West is and shall remain open to foreign and domestic commerce upon the same conditions by which that commerce has there hitherto been governed.

In testimony whereof I have hereunto set my hand and caused the seal of the United States to be affixed.

[SEAL.]   Done at the city of Washington, this 11th day of April, A. D. 1865, and of the Independence of the United States of America the eighty-ninth.

ABRAHAM LINCOLN.

By the President:

WILLIAM H. SEWARD, *Secretary of State.*

BY THE PRESIDENT OF THE UNITED STATES OF AMERICA.

A PROCLAMATION.

Whereas for some time past vessels of war of the United States have been refused in certain foreign ports privileges and immunities to which they were entitled by treaty, public law, or the comity of nations, at the same time that vessels of war of the country wherein the said privileges and immunities have been withheld have enjoyed them fully and uninterruptedly in ports of the United States, which condition of things has not always been forcibly resisted by the United States, although, on the other hand, they have not at any time failed to protest against and declare their dissatisfaction with the same. In the view of the United States, no condition any longer exists which can be claimed to justify the denial to them by any one of such nations of customary naval rights as has heretofore been so unnecessarily persisted in.

Now, therefore, I, Abraham Lincoln, President of the United States, do hereby make known that if after a reasonable time shall have elapsed for intelligence of this proclamation to have reached any foreign country in whose ports the said privileges and immunities shall have been refused as aforesaid they shall continue to be so refused, then and thenceforth the same privileges and immunities shall be refused to the vessels of war of that country in the ports of the United States; and this refusal shall continue until war vessels of the United States shall have been placed upon an entire equality in the foreign ports aforesaid with similar vessels of other countries. The United States, whatever claim or pretense may have existed heretofore, are now, at least, entitled to claim and concede an entire and friendly equality of rights and hospitalities with all maritime nations.

In witness whereof I have hereunto set my hand and caused the seal of the United States to be affixed.

[SEAL.]   Done at the city of Washington, this 11th day of April, A. D. 1865, and of the Independence of the United States of America the eighty-ninth.

                                                ABRAHAM LINCOLN.

By the President:

WILLIAM H. SEWARD,
        Secretary of State.

EXECUTIVE ORDERS.

DEPARTMENT OF STATE,
Washington, March 8, 1865.

Whereas, pursuant to the order of the President of the United States, directions were issued from this Department, under date of the 17th of December, 1864, requiring passports from all travelers entering the United States, except immigrant passengers directly entering an American port from a foreign country; but whereas information has recently been received which affords reasonable grounds to expect that Her Britannic Majesty's Government and the executive and legislative branches of the government of Canada have taken and will continue to take such steps as may be looked for from a friendly neighbor and will be effectual toward preventing hostile incursions from Canadian territory into the United States, the President directs that from and after this date the order above referred to requiring passports shall be modified, and so much thereof as relates to persons entering this country from Canada shall be rescinded, saving and reserving the order in all other respects in full force.

                                                WILLIAM H. SEWARD.

DEPARTMENT OF STATE,
Washington, March 14, 1865.

The President directs that all persons who now are or hereafter shall be found within the United States who have been engaged in holding intercourse or trade with the insurgents by sea, if they are citizens of the United States or domiciled aliens, shall be arrested and held as prisoners of war until the war shall close, subject, nevertheless, to prosecution, trial, and conviction for any offense committed by them as spies or otherwise against the laws of war. The President further directs that all nonresident foreigners who now are or hereafter shall be found in the

United States, and who have been or shall have been engaged in violating the blockade of the insurgent ports, shall leave the United States within twelve days from the publication of this order, or from their subsequent arrival in the United States, if on the Atlantic side, and forty days if on the Pacific side, of the country; and such persons shall not return to the United States during the continuance of the war. Provost-marshals and marshals of the United States will arrest and commit to military custody all such offenders as shall disregard this order, whether they have passports or not, and they will be detained in such custody until the end of the war, or until discharged by subsequent orders of the President.

W. H. SEWARD,
Secretary of State.

GENERAL ORDERS, NO. 50.

WAR DEPARTMENT,
ADJUTANT-GENERAL'S OFFICE,
Washington, March 27, 1865.

Ordered, first. That at the hour of noon on the 14th day of April, 1865, Brevet Major-General Anderson will raise and plant upon the ruins of Fort Sumter, in Charleston Harbor, the same United States flag which floated over the battlements of that fort during the rebel assault, and which was lowered and saluted by him and the small force of his command when the works were evacuated on the 14th day of April, 1861.

Second. That the flag, when raised, be saluted by one hundred guns from Fort Sumter and by a national salute from every fort and rebel battery that fired upon Fort Sumter.

Third. That suitable ceremonies be had upon the occasion, under the direction of Major-General William T. Sherman, whose military operations compelled the rebels to evacuate Charleston, or, in his absence, under the charge of Major-General Q. A. Gillmore, commanding the department. Among the ceremonies will be the delivery of a public address by the Rev. Henry Ward Beecher.

Fourth. That the naval forces at Charleston and their commander on that station be invited to participate in the ceremonies of the occasion.

By order of the President of the United States:

EDWIN M. STANTON,
Secretary of War.

To all whom these presents may concern:

Whereas for some time past evil-disposed persons have crossed the borders of the United States or entered their ports by sea from countries where they are tolerated, and have committed capital felonies against the property and life of American citizens, as well in the cities as in the rural districts of the country:

Now, therefore, in the name and by the authority of the President of the United States, I do hereby make known that a reward of $1,000 will be paid at this Department for the capture of each of such offenders, upon his conviction by a civil or military tribunal, to whomsoever shall arrest and deliver such offenders into the custody of the civil or military authorities of the United States. And the like reward will be paid upon the same terms for the capture of any such persons so entering the United States whose offenses shall be committed subsequently to the publication of this notice.

A reward of $500 will be paid upon conviction for the arrest of any person who shall have aided and abetted offenders of the class before named within the territory of the United States.

Given under my hand and the seal of the Department of State, at Washington, this 4th day of April, A. D. 1865.

[SEAL.]   WILLIAM H. SEWARD,
                                                Secretary of State.

DEATH OF PRESIDENT LINCOLN.

ANNOUNCEMENT TO THE VICE-PRESIDENT.

[From the original, Department of State.]

WASHINGTON CITY, D. C.,
April 15, 1865.

ANDREW JOHNSON,
    Vice-President of the United States.

SIR: Abraham Lincoln, President of the United States, was shot by an assassin last evening at Ford's Theater, in this city, and died at the hour of twenty-two minutes after 7 o'clock.

About the same time at which the President was shot an assassin entered the sick chamber of the Hon. William H. Seward, Secretary of State, and stabbed him in several places—in the throat, neck, and face— severely if not mortally wounding him. Other members of the Secretary's family were dangerously wounded by the assassin while making his escape. By the death of President Lincoln the office of President has devolved, under the Constitution, upon you. The emergency of the Government demands that you should immediately qualify, according to the requirements of the Constitution, and enter upon the duties of President

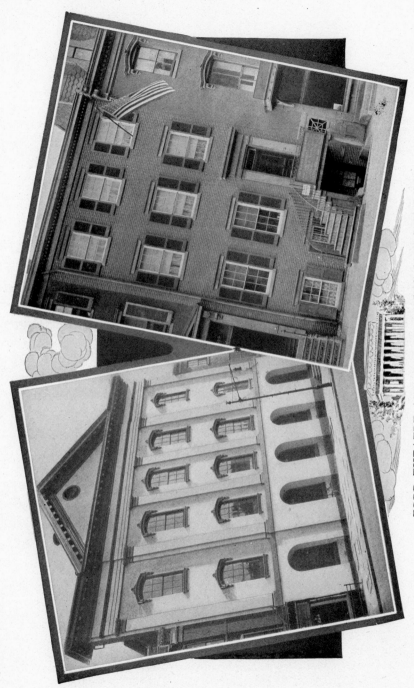

FORD THEATRE AND HOUSE WHERE LINCOLN DIED

BARBARA FRIETCHIE'S DEFIANCE

BARBARA FRIETCHIE.

Although phlegmatic historians have demonstrated conclusively that there is no basis of fact in the old legend that 95-year-old Barbara Frietchie defiantly waved the Union flag before Stonewall Jackson as he marched through the streets of Frederick, Md., every American will rejoice that the story moved Whittier to compose his stirring lines on the old woman's heroism.

of the United States. If you will please make known your pleasure, such arrangements as you deem proper will be made.

Your obedient servants,

HUGH McCULLOCH,	W. DENNISON,
Secretary of the Treasury.	*Postmaster-General.*
EDWIN M. STANTON,	J. P. USHER,
Secretary of War.	*Secretary of the Interior.*
GIDEON WELLES,	JAMES SPEED,
Secretary of Navy.	*Attorney-General.*

[From the Daily National Intelligencer, April 17, 1865.]

The Vice-President responded that it would be agreeable to him to qualify himself for the high office to which he had been so unexpectedly called, under such melancholy circumstances, at his rooms at the Kirkwood Hotel; and at 11 o'clock a.m. [15th] the oath of office was administered to him by Chief Justice Chase, of the Supreme Court of the United States, in the presence of nearly all the Cabinet officers; the Hon. Solomon Foot, United States Senator from Vermont; the Hon. Alexander Ramsey, United States Senator from Minnesota; the Hon. Richard Yates, United States Senator from Illinois; the Hon. John P. Hale, late Senator from New Hampshire; General Farnsworth, of the House of Representatives, from Illinois; F. P. Blair, sr.; Hon. Montgomery Blair, late Postmaster-General, and some others.

[For Inaugural Address of President Johnson, see pp. 305–306.]

ANNOUNCEMENT TO REPRESENTATIVES OF THE UNITED STATES ABROAD.

[From official records, Department of State.]

CIRCULAR.

DEPARTMENT OF STATE,
Washington, April 17, 1865.

SIR: The melancholy duty devolves upon me officially to apprise you of the assassination of the President at Ford's Theater, in this city, in the evening of the 14th instant. He died the next morning from the effects of the wound.

About the same time an attempt was made to assassinate the Secretary of State in his own house, where he was in bed suffering from the effects of the late accident. The attempt failed, but Mr. Seward was severely cut, on the face especially, it is supposed with a bowie knife. Mr. F W. Seward was felled by a blow or blows on the head, and for some time afterwards was apparently unconscious. Both the Secretary and Assistant Secretary are better, especially the former.

Andrew Johnson has formally entered upon the duties of President. I have been authorized temporarily to act as Secretary of State.

I am, sir, your obedient servant,

W. HUNTER, *Acting Secretary*.

ANNOUNCEMENT TO REPRESENTATIVES OF FOREIGN GOVERNMENTS IN THE UNITED STATES.

[From official records, Department of State.]

DEPARTMENT OF STATE,
Washington, April 15, 1865.

SIR: It is my great misfortune to be obliged to inform you of events not less afflicting to the people of the United States than distressing to my own feelings and the feelings of all those connected with the Government.

The President of the United States was shot with a pistol last night, while attending a theater in this city, and expired this morning from the effects of the wound. At about the same time an attempt was made to assassinate the Secretary of State, which, though it fortunately failed, left him severely, but it is hoped not dangerously, wounded with a knife or dagger. Mr. F. W. Seward was also struck on the head with a heavy weapon, and is in a critical condition from the effect of the blows.

Pursuant to the provision of the Constitution of the United States, Andrew Johnson, the Vice-President, has formally assumed the functions of President. I have by him been authorized to perform the duties of Secretary of State until otherwise ordered.

I avail myself of the occasion to offer to you the assurance of my distinguished consideration.

W. HUNTER, *Acting Secretary*.

ANNOUNCEMENT TO THE ARMY.

[From official records, War Department.]

GENERAL ORDERS, No. 66.

WAR DEPARTMENT,
ADJUTANT-GENERAL'S OFFICE,
Washington, April 16, 1865.

The following order of the Secretary of War announces to the armies of the United States the untimely and lamentable death of the illustrious Abraham Lincoln, late President of the United States:

WAR DEPARTMENT, *Washington City, April 16, 1865.*

The distressing duty has devolved upon the Secretary of War to announce to the armies of the United States that at twenty-two minutes after 7 o'clock on the morning of Saturday, the 15th day of April, 1865, Abraham Lincoln, President of the United States, died of a mortal wound inflicted upon him by an assassin.

The armies of the United States will share with their fellow-citizens the feelings of grief and horror inspired by this most atrocious murder of their great and beloved President and Commander in Chief, and with profound sorrow will mourn his death as a national calamity.

The headquarters of every department, post, station, fort, and arsenal will be draped in mourning for thirty days, and appropriate funeral honors will be paid by every army, and in every department, and at every military post, and at the Military Academy at West Point, to the memory of the late illustrious Chief Magistrate of the nation and Commander in Chief of its armies.

Lieutenant-General Grant will give the necessary instructions for carrying this order into effect.

EDWIN M. STANTON,
Secretary of War.

On the day after the receipt of this order at the headquarters of each military division, department, army, post, station, fort, and arsenal and at the Military Academy at West Point the troops and cadets will be paraded at 10 o'clock a. m. and the order read to them, after which all labors and operations for the day will cease and be suspended as far as practicable in a state of war.

The national flag will be displayed at half-staff.

At dawn of day thirteen guns will be fired, and afterwards at intervals of thirty minutes between the rising and setting sun a single gun, and at the close of the day a national salute of thirty-six guns.

The officers of the armies of the United States will wear the badge of mourning on the left arm and on their swords and the colors of their commands and regiments will be put in mourning for the period of six months.

By command of Lieutenant-General Grant:

W. A. NICHOLS, *Assistant Adjutant-General.*

ANNOUNCEMENT TO THE NAVY.

[From General Orders and Circulars, Navy Department, 1863 to 1887.]

GENERAL ORDER NO. 51.

NAVY DEPARTMENT, *Washington, April 15, 1865.*

The Department announces with profound sorrow to the officers and men of the Navy and Marine Corps the death of Abraham Lincoln, late President of the United States. Stricken down by the hand of an assassin on the evening of the 14th instant, when surrounded by his family and friends, he lingered a few hours after receiving the fatal wound, and died at 7 o'clock 22 minutes this morning.

A grateful people had given their willing confidence to the patriot and statesman under whose wise and successful administration the nation was just emerging from the civil strife which for four years has afflicted the land when this terrible calamity fell upon the country. To him our gratitude was justly due, for to him, under God, more than to any other person, are we indebted for the successful vindication of the integrity of the Union and the maintenance of the power of the Republic.

The officers of the Navy and of the Marine Corps will, as a manifestation of their respect for the exalted character, eminent position, and inestimable public services of the late President, and as an indication of their sense of the calamity which the country has sustained, wear the usual badge of mourning for six months.

The Department further directs that upon the day following the receipt of this order the commandants of squadrons, navy-yards, and stations will cause the ensign of every vessel in their several commands to be hoisted at half-mast, and a gun to be fired every half hour, beginning at sunrise and ending at sunset. The flags of the several navy-yards and marine barracks will also be hoisted at half-mast.

GIDEON WELLES,
Secretary of the Navy.

ANNOUNCEMENT TO THE REVENUE MARINE.

[From the Daily National Intelligencer, April 18, 1865.]

GENERAL ORDER.

TREASURY DEPARTMENT, *April 17, 1865.*

The Secretary of the Treasury with profound sorrow announces to the Revenue Marine the death of Abraham Lincoln, late President of the United States. He died in this city on the morning of the 15th instant, at twenty-two minutes past 7 o'clock.

The officers of the Revenue Marine will, as a manifestation of their respect for the exalted character and eminent public services of the illustrious dead and of their sense of the calamity the country has sustained by this afflicting dispensation of Providence, wear crape on the left arm and upon the hilt of the sword for six months.

It is further directed that funeral honors be paid on board all revenue vessels in commission by firing thirty-six minute guns, commencing at meridian, on the day after the receipt of this order, and by wearing their flags at half-mast.

HUGH McCULLOCH,
Secretary of the Treasury.

ACTION OF SENATORS AND REPRESENTATIVES IN WASHINGTON.

[From Appendix to Memorial Address on the Life and Character of Abraham Lincoln.]

The members of the Thirty-ninth Congress then in Washington met in the Senate reception room, at the Capitol, on the 17th of April, 1865, at noon. Hon. Lafayette S. Foster, of Connecticut, President *pro tempore* of the Senate, was called to the chair, and the Hon. Schuyler Colfax, of Indiana, Speaker of the House in the Thirty-eighth Congress, was chosen secretary.

Senator Foot, of Vermont, who was visibly affected, stated that the object of the meeting was to make arrangements relative to the funeral of the deceased President of the United States.

On motion of Senator Sumner, of Massachusetts, a committee of five members from each House was ordered to report at 4 p. m. what action would be fitting for the meeting to take.

The chairman appointed Senators Sumner, of Massachusetts; Harris, of New York; Johnson, of Maryland; Ramsey, of Minnesota, and Conness, of California, and Representatives Washburne, of Illinois; Smith, of Kentucky; Schenck, of Ohio; Pike, of Maine, and Coffroth, of Pennsylvania; and on motion of Mr. Schenck the chairman and secretary of the meeting were added to the committee, and then the meeting adjourned until 4 p. m.

The meeting reassembled at 4 p. m., pursuant to adjournment.

Mr. Sumner, from the committee heretofore appointed, reported that they had selected as pallbearers on the part of the Senate Mr. Foster, of Connecticut; Mr. Morgan, of New York; Mr. Johnson, of Maryland; Mr. Yates, of Illinois; Mr. Wade, of Ohio, and Mr. Conness, of California; on the part of the House, Mr. Dawes, of Massachusetts; Mr. Coffroth, of Pennsylvania; Mr. Smith, of Kentucky; Mr. Colfax, of Indiana; Mr. Worthington, of Nevada, and Mr. Washburne, of Illinois.

They also recommended the appointment of one member of Congress from each State and Territory to act as a Congressional committee to accompany the remains of the late President to Illinois, and presented the following names as such committee, the chairman of the meeting to have the authority of appointing hereafter for the States and Territories not represented to-day from which members may be present at the Capitol by the day of the funeral.

Maine, Mr. Pike; New Hampshire, Mr. E. H. Rollins; Vermont, Mr. Foot; Massachusetts, Mr. Sumner; Rhode Island, Mr. Anthony; Connecticut, Mr. Dixon; New York, Mr. Harris; Pennsylvania, Mr. Cowan; Ohio, Mr. Schenck; Kentucky, Mr. Smith; Indiana, Mr. Julian; Illinois, the delegation; Michigan, Mr. Chandler; Iowa, Mr. Harlan; California, Mr. Shannon; Minnesota, Mr. Ramsey; Oregon, Mr. Williams; Kansas, Mr. S. Clarke; West Virginia, Mr. Whaley; Nevada, Mr. Nye; Nebraska, Mr. Hitchcock; Colorado, Mr. Bradford; Dakota, Mr. Todd; Idaho, Mr. Wallace.

The committee also recommended the adoption of the following resolution:

Resolved, That the Sergeants-at-Arms of the Senate and House, with their necessary assistants, be requested to attend the committee accompanying the remains of the late President, and to make all the necessary arrangements.

All of which was concurred in unanimously.

Mr. Sumner, from the same committee, also reported the following, which was unanimously agreed to:

The members of the Senate and House of Representatives now assembled in Washington, humbly confessing their dependence upon Almighty God, who rules all that is done for human good, make haste at this informal meeting to express the emotions with which they have been filled by the appalling tragedy which has deprived the nation of its head and covered the land with mourning; and in further declaration of their sentiments unanimously resolve:

1. That in testimony of their veneration and affection for the illustrious dead, who has been permitted, under Providence, to do so much for his country and for liberty, they will unite in the funeral services and by an appropriate committee will accompany his remains to their place of burial in the State from which he was taken for the national service.

2. That in the life of Abraham Lincoln, who by the benignant favor of republican institutions rose from humble beginnings to the heights of power and fame, they recognize an example of purity, simplicity, and virtue which should be a lesson to mankind, while in his death they recognize a martyr whose memory will become more precious as men learn to prize those principles of constitutional order and those rights—civil, political, and human—for which he was made a sacrifice.

3. That they invite the President of the United States, by solemn proclamation, to recommend to the people of the United States to assemble on a day to be appointed by him, publicly to testify their grief and to dwell on the good which has been done on earth by him whom we now mourn.

4. That a copy of these resolutions be communicated to the President of the United States, and also that a copy be communicated to the afflicted widow of the late President as an expression of sympathy in her great bereavement.

The meeting then adjourned.

ORDERS OF THE HEADS OF THE EXECUTIVE DEPARTMENTS.

[From official records, Department of State.]

DEPARTMENT OF STATE,
Washington, April 17, 1865.

It is hereby ordered that, in honor to the memory of our late illustrious Chief Magistrate, all officers and others subject to the orders of the Secretary of State wear crape upon the left arm for the period of six months.

W. HUNTER,
Acting Secretary.

[From official records, Treasury Department.]

TREASURY DEPARTMENT,
Washington, April 17, 1865.

It is hereby ordered that, in honor to the memory of our late illustrious Chief Magistrate, all officers and others subject to the orders of the Secretary of the Treasury wear crape upon the left arm for the period of six months.

H. McCULLOCH,
Secretary of the Treasury.

[From official records, War Department.]

GENERAL ORDERS, NO. 69.

WAR DEPARTMENT,
ADJUTANT-GENERAL'S OFFICE,
Washington, April 17, 1865.

By direction of the President of the United States the War Department will be closed on Wednesday next, the day of the funeral of the late President of the United States.

Labor on that day will be suspended at all military posts and on all public works under the direction of the War Department. The flags at all military posts, stations, forts, and buildings will be kept at half-staff during the day, and at 12 o'clock m. twenty-one minute guns will be fired from all forts and at all military posts and at the Military Academy.

By order of the Secretary of War:

W. A. NICHOLS.
Assistant Adjutant-General.

[From General Orders and Circulars, Navy Department, 1863 to 1887.]

SPECIAL ORDER.

APRIL 17, 1865.

By order of the President of the United States the Navy Department will be closed on Wednesday next, the day of the funeral solemnities of the late President of the United States. Labor will also be suspended on that day at each of the navy-yards and naval stations and upon all the vessels of the United States. The flags of all vessels and at all the navy yards and stations and marine barracks will be kept at half-mast during the day, and at 12 o'clock m. twenty-one minute guns will be fired by the senior officer of each squadron and the commandants of the navy yards and stations.

GIDEON WELLES,
Secretary of the Navy.

[From the Daily National Intelligencer, April 18, 1865.]

POST-OFFICE DEPARTMENT,
Washington, April 17, 1865.

To Deputy Postmasters:

Business in all the post-offices of the United States will be suspended and the offices closed from 11 a. m. to 3 p. m. on Wednesday, the 19th instant, during the funeral solemnities of Abraham Lincoln, late President of the United States.

W. DENNISON,
Postmaster-General.

[From official records, Post-Office Department.]

SPECIAL ORDER.

POST-OFFICE DEPARTMENT,
Washington, April 18, 1865.

It is hereby ordered that, in honor of the memory of Abraham Lincoln, our lamented Chief Magistrate, the officers and employees of this Department wear crape upon the left arm for the period of six months.

W. DENNISON,
Postmaster-General.

[From official records, Department of the Interior.]

DEPARTMENT OF THE INTERIOR,
Washington, April 18, 1865.

It is hereby ordered that, in honor of the memory of the late Chief Magistrate of the nation, the officers and employees of this Department wear crape upon the left arm for the period of six months.

J. P. USHER,
Secretary.

FUNERAL ANNOUNCEMENT TO THE PUBLIC.

[From the Daily National Intelligencer, April 17, 1865.]

DEPARTMENT OF STATE,
Washington, April 17, 1865.

To the People of the United States:

The undersigned is directed to announce that the funeral ceremonies of the late lamented Chief Magistrate will take place at the Executive Mansion, in this city, at 12 o'clock m. on Wednesday, the 19th instant.

The various religious denominations throughout the country are invited to meet in their respective places of worship at that hour for the purpose of solemnizing the occasion with appropriate ceremonies.

W. HUNTER,
Acting Secretary of State.

OFFICIAL ARRANGEMENTS FOR THE FUNERAL.

[From official records, War Department.]

WAR DEPARTMENT,
ADJUTANT-GENERAL'S OFFICE,
Washington, April 17, 1865.

The following order of arrangement is directed:

ORDER OF THE PROCESSION.

FUNERAL ESCORT.
(In column of march.)

One regiment of cavalry.
Two batteries of artillery.
Battalion of marines.
Two regiments of infantry.
Commander of escort and staff.
Dismounted officers of Marine Corps, Navy, and Army, in the order named.
Mounted officers of Marine Corps, Navy, and Army, in the order named.
(All military officers to be in uniform, with side arms.)

CIVIC PROCESSION.

Marshal.
Clergy in attendance.
The Surgeon-General of the United States Army and physicians to the deceased.
Hearse.

Pallbearers.

On the part of the Senate: Mr. Foster, of Connecticut; Mr. Morgan, of New York; Mr. Johnson, of Maryland; Mr. Yates, of Illinois; Mr. Wade, of Ohio; Mr. Conness, of California.

On the part of the House: Mr. Dawes, of Massachusetts; Mr. Coffroth, of Pennsylvania; Mr. Smith, of Kentucky; Mr. Colfax, of Indiana; Mr. Worthington, of Nevada; Mr. Washburne, of Illinois.

Army: Lieutenant-General U. S. Grant; Major-General H. W. Halleck; Brevet Brigadier-General W. A. Nichols.

Navy: Vice-Admiral D. G. Farragut; Rear-Admiral W. B. Shubrick; Colonel Jacob Zelin, Marine Corps.

Civilians: O. H. Browning, George Ashman, Thomas Corwin, Simon Cameron.

Family.
Relatives.
The delegations of the States of Illinois and Kentucky, as mourners.
The President.
The Cabinet ministers.
The diplomatic corps.

Ex-Presidents.
The Chief Justice and Associate Justices of the Supreme Court.
The Senate of the United States.
Preceded by their officers.
Members of the House of Representatives of the United States.
Governors of the several States and Territories.
Legislatures of the several States and Territories.
The Federal judiciary and the judiciary of the several States and Territories.
The Assistant Secretaries of State, Treasury, War, Navy, Interior, and the Assistant
Postmasters-General, and the Assistant Attorney-General.
Officers of the Smithsonian Institution.
The members and officers of the Sanitary and Christian Commissions.
Corporate authorities of Washington, Georgetown, and other cities.
Delegations of the several States.
The reverend the clergy of the various denominations.
The clerks and employees of the several Departments and bureaus, preceded by the
heads of such bureaus and their respective chief clerks.
Such societies as may wish to join the procession.
Citizens and strangers.

The troops designated to form the escort will assemble in the Avenue, north of the President's house, and form line precisely at 11 o'clock a. m. on Wednesday, the 19th instant, with the left resting on Fifteenth street. The procession will move precisely at 2 o'clock p. m., on the conclusion of the religious services at the Executive Mansion (appointed to commence at 12 o'clock m.), when minute guns will be fired by detachments of artillery stationed near St. John's Church, the City Hall, and at the Capitol. At the same hour the bells of the several churches in Washington, Georgetown, and Alexandria will be tolled.

At sunrise on Wednesday, the 19th instant, a Federal salute will be fired from the military stations in the vicinity of Washington, minute guns between the hours of 12 and 3 o'clock, and a national salute at the setting of the sun.

The usual badge of mourning will be worn on the left arm and on the hilt of the sword.

By order of the Secretary of War:

W. A. NICHOLS,
Assistant Adjutant-General.

The funeral ceremonies took place in the East Room of the Executive Mansion at noon on the 19th of April, and the remains were then escorted to the Capitol, where they lay in state in the Rotunda.

On the morning of April 21 the remains were taken from the Capitol and placed in a funeral car, in which they were taken to Springfield, Ill. Halting at the principal cities along the route, that appropriate honors might be paid to the deceased, the funeral cortege arrived on the 3d of May at Springfield, Ill., and the next day the remains were deposited in Oak Ridge Cemetery, near that city.

GUARD OF HONOR.

[From official records, War Department.]

GENERAL ORDERS, No. 72.

WAR DEPARTMENT,
ADJUTANT-GENERAL'S OFFICE,
Washington, April 20, 1865.

The following general officers and guard of honor will accompany the remains of the late President from the city of Washington to Springfield, the capital of the State of Illinois, and continue with them until they are consigned to their final resting place:

Brevet Brigadier-General E. D. Townsend, Assistant Adjutant-General, to represent the Secretary of War.

Brevet Brigadier-General Charles Thomas, Assistant Quartermaster-General.*

Brigadier-General A. B. Eaton, Commissary-General of Subsistence.

Brevet Major-General J. G. Barnard, Lieutenant-Colonel of Engineers.

Brigadier-General G. D. Ramsay, Ordnance Department.

Brigadier-General A. P. Howe, Chief of Artillery.

Brevet Brigadier-General D. C. McCallum, Superintendent Military Railroads.

Major-General D. Hunter, United States Volunteers.

Brigadier-General J. C. Caldwell, United States Volunteers.

Twenty-five picked men, under a captain.

By order of the Secretary of War:

E. D. TOWNSEND,
Assistant Adjutant-General.

[From official records, Navy Department.]

SPECIAL ORDER.

APRIL 20, 1865.

The following officers of the Navy and Marine Corps will accompany the remains of the late President from the city of Washington to Springfield, the capital of the State of Illinois, and continue with them until they are consigned to their final resting place:

Rear-Admiral Charles Henry Davis, Chief Bureau Navigation.

Captain William Rogers Taylor, United States Navy.

Major Thomas Y. Field, United States Marine Corps.

GIDEON WELLES,
Secretary of the Navy.

*Brevet Brigadier-General James A. Ekin, Quartermaster's Department, United States Army, substituted.

ACTION OF CONGRESS.

[From Appendix to Memorial Address on the Life and Character of Abraham Lincoln.]

President Johnson, in his annual message to Congress at the commencement of the session of 1865–66, thus announced the death of his predecessor:

To express gratitude to God in the name of the people for the preservation of the United States is my first duty in addressing you. Our thoughts next revert to the death of the late President by an act of parricidal treason. The grief of the nation is still fresh. It finds some solace in the consideration that he lived to enjoy the highest proof of its confidence by entering on the renewed term of the Chief Magistracy to which he had been elected; that he brought the civil war substantially to a close; that his loss was deplored in all parts of the Union, and that foreign nations have rendered justice to his memory.

Hon. E. B. Washburne, of Illinois, immediately after the President's message had been read in the House of Representatives, offered the following joint resolution, which was unanimously adopted:

Resolved, That a committee of one member from each State represented in this House be appointed on the part of this House, to join such committee as may be appointed on the part of the Senate, to consider and report by what token of respect and affection it may be proper for the Congress of the United States to express the deep sensibility of the nation to the event of the decease of their late President, Abraham Lincoln, and that so much of the message of the President as refers to that melancholy event be referred to said committee.

On motion of Hon. Solomon Foot, the Senate unanimously concurred in the passage of the resolution, and the following joint committee was appointed, thirteen on the part of the Senate and one for every State represented (twenty-four) on the part of the House of Representatives:

Senate: Hon. Solomon Foot, Vermont; Hon. Richard Yates, Illinois; Hon. Benjamin F. Wade, Ohio; Hon. William Pitt Fessenden, Maine; Hon. Henry Wilson, Massachusetts; Hon. James R. Doolittle, Wisconsin; Hon. James H. Lane, Kansas; Hon. Ira Harris, New York; Hon. James W. Nesmith, Oregon; Hon. Henry S. Lane, Indiana; Hon. Waitman T. Willey, West Virginia; Hon. Charles R. Buckalew, Pennsylvania; Hon. John B. Henderson, Missouri.

House of Representatives: Hon. Elihu B. Washburne, Illinois; Hon. James G. Blaine, Maine; Hon. James W. Patterson, New Hampshire; Hon. Justin S. Morrill, Vermont; Hon. Nathaniel P. Banks, Massachusetts; Hon. Thomas A. Jenckes, Rhode Island; Hon. Henry C. Deming, Connecticut; Hon. John A. Griswold, New York; Hon. Edwin R. V. Wright, New Jersey; Hon. Thaddeus Stevens, Pennsylvania; Hon. John A. Nicholson, Delaware; Hon. Francis Thomas, Maryland; Hon. Robert C. Schenck, Ohio; Hon. George S. Shanklin, Kentucky; Hon. Godlove S. Orth, Indiana; Hon. Joseph W. McClurg, Missouri; Hon. Fernando C. Beaman, Michigan; Hon. John A. Kasson, Iowa; Hon. Ithamar C. Sloan, Wisconsin; Hon. William Higby, California; Hon. William Windom.

Minnesota; Hon. J. H. D. Henderson, Oregon; Hon. Sidney Clarke, Kansas; Hon. Kellian V. Whaley, West Virginia.

The joint committee made the following report, which was concurred in by both Houses *nem. con.:*

Whereas the melancholy event of the violent and tragic death of Abraham Lincoln, late President of the United States, having occurred during the recess of Congress, and the two Houses sharing in the general grief and desiring to manifest their sensibility upon the occasion of the public bereavement: Therefore,

Be it resolved by the Senate (the House of Representatives concurring), That the two Houses of Congress will assemble in the Hall of the House of Representatives on Monday, the 12th day of February next, that being his anniversary birthday, at the hour of 12 m., and that, in the presence of the two Houses there assembled, an address upon the life and character of Abraham Lincoln, late President of the United States, be pronounced by Hon. Edwin M. Stanton,* and that the President of the Senate *pro tempore* and the Speaker of the House of Representatives be requested to invite the President of the United States, the heads of the several Departments, the judges of the Supreme Court, the representatives of the foreign governments near this Government, and such officers of the Army and Navy as have received the thanks of Congress who may then be at the seat of Government to be present on the occasion.

And be it further resolved, That the President of the United States be requested to transmit a copy of these resolutions to Mrs. Lincoln, and to assure her of the profound sympathy of the two Houses of Congress for her deep personal affliction and of their sincere condolence for the late national bereavement.

[For proclamations of President Johnson recommending, in consequence of the assassination of Abraham Lincoln, late President of the United States, a day for special humiliation and prayer, see pp. 3504-3505, and for Executive order in connection therewith, see p. 3537. For Executive order closing the Executive Office and the Departments on the day of the funeral of the late President, at Springfield, Ill., see p. 3533. For Executive order closing the public offices April 14, 1866, in commemoration of the assassination of the late President, see p. 3638.

* Mr. Stanton having declined, Hon. George Bancroft, of New York, in response to an invitation from the joint committee, consented to deliver the address.

QUESTIONS.

1. When did the Federal Government take military possession of the telegraph lines and establish a censorship of the press? Pages 3309, 3310.

2. What is the fifty-seventh article of war? Page 3240.

3. Cite the nature of the obligations as well as of the frauds under naturalization laws. Pages 3381 and 3382.

4. When was a day of humiliation and mourning appointed because of the death of Lincoln? Page 3504.

5. What was the occasion for the setting apart by Lincoln of a day of fasting and prayer? Pages 3237, 3365, 3422.

6. Why was the writ of *habeas corpus* suspended by Lincoln? Pages 3299, 3371, 3420.

7. On what ground did Lincoln pardon deserters from the army? Pages 3364, 3479.

8. Were aliens required to perform military duty during the Civil War? Pages 3369 and 3381.

9. What treatment was given to American vessels in foreign ports? Page 3482.

10. What was Lincoln's proclamation as to persons supplying Indians with munitions of war? Page 3480.

SUGGESTIONS.

Lincoln's attitude on slavery changed by reason of the exigencies of the war. At the beginning of his administration, he was willing to save the Union without destroying slavery, if possible. Pages 3206, 3269, 3335. (See also Slavery, Encyclopedic Index.)

But he was unalterably opposed to secession. Pages 3206, 3221, 3227. (See Secession, Encyclopedic Index.)

When it became apparent that the destruction of the slave traffic was necessary to the preservation of the Union, Lincoln did not hesitate to strike down slavery. See the Emancipation Proclamation. Pages 3297, 3358. (See Emancipation, Encyclopedic Index. See also Comments on Amendments, page 3337, and the Thirteenth Amendment, page 31.)

Lincoln's messages are a splendid contemporary history of the Civil War, q. v., Encyclopedic Index, with references, particularly page 3206 and following.

Read Lincoln's Foreign Policy. Pages 3248, 3255, 3327, 3444.

NOTE.

For further suggestions on Lincoln's administration, see Lincoln, Abraham, Encyclopedic Index.

By reading the Foreign Policy of each President, and by scanning the messages as to the state of the nation, a thorough knowledge of the history of the United States will be acquired from the most authentic sources; because, as has been said, "Each President reviews the past, depicts the present and forecasts the future of the nation."

Andrew Johnson

April 15, 1865, to March 4, 1869

Andrew Johnson

JOHNSON

The three facts which will forever keep Andrew Johnson's name alive are that he rose from a tailor's bench to be Chief Magistrate of the Republic; that he was the only Senator of the United States from any seceding State that remained faithful to the Union, and that he was the only President of the United States who was ever impeached, although bills of impeachment were prepared against John Tyler, a fact not generally known. Not only is there great prejudice against Andrew Johnson in the public mind, but his talents are also greatly underrated. In integrity of purpose, in personal and moral courage, in intensity of patriotism he has had no superior among our Presidents. That his impeachment marks one of the most dangerous epochs of American history there can now be no question among people whose opinion is at all worthy of respect. Even intelligent Republicans now take this view of the matter.

Not long since in a lecture delivered before a college in this city, Mr. Justice John M. Harlan, of the Supreme Court of the United States, stated that as his opinion. He is certainly a competent witness.

The people of the North have never realized, and, perhaps, never will realize, the courage that was required for a man to stand for the Union in 1861 in Tennessee, Kentucky, West Virginia, or Maryland. It was as easy as falling off a log, a slippery log at that, for a man to be for the Union in Massachusetts. It was unprofitable to be anything else. It was easy to be a Confederate in South Carolina. It was dangerous to be otherwise. But in what are known as the "border States," including Tennessee, it was extremely hazardous to be one or the other. The truth is, that there really was no Civil war anywhere to any considerable extent outside of these "border States." So far as the extreme Northern States or the extreme Southern States were concerned what we term Civil war was to all intents and purposes a war between two countries foreign to each other. But in the "border States" it was not only neighborhood against neighborhood, but family against family, father against son, husband against wife, slave against master. That Johnson or any other man had the moral and physical courage to stand up against an overwhelming sentiment in his own State in that critical era is one of the marvels of history.

At the time of the firing on Fort Sumter he was not only one of the ablest men in the Senate from the South, but was also one of the most popular. At that time it appeared that by going with the South there was no station beyond his reach, and that by going with the North he had absolutely nothing to hope for in the way of political preferment.

But man proposes and God disposes, and by adhering to the Union he became President of the United States.

It is a fact known of all men who have turned their minds to a contemplation of the subject that for a man to sever his political relations or to run counter on any great question to the sentiments of the community or State in which he lived was, is, and must always be a most painful performance. That Johnson felt this there can be no question; but his love of the Union outweighed all other considerations, and he gave it a courageous, consistent and powerful support. His position probably fixed the position of thousands of Tennesseeans, for that State furnished nearly 40,000 white soldiers for the Union armies, most of them recruited from that portion of the State in which Johnson resided, and in which he had always had his greatest political influence. His love of the Union was supreme. He always said in his stump speeches that when he died he wanted to be buried with the Stars and Stripes for a winding sheet, and his wishes in this regard were gratified.

My own opinion about the matter is that he was impeached for undertaking to carry out the policy of reconciliation which Abraham Lincoln would have successfully carried out if he had lived. Lincoln would not have been impeached for doing what Johnson tried to do, because he was too strong in the hearts of what he affectionately called "the plain people of America," but that he would have suffered in popularity for so doing, there can be no question. But Johnson, being a Southerner, was under suspicion of radical Republicans from the start.

If a true history of the United States is ever written, while Andrew Johnson will not stand in the front rank of American statesmen, he will unquestionably stand in the front rank of American patriots. He did more, and risked more, to preserve the Union than was done by all the men combined who voted for his conviction. I love to remember that General John B. Henderson, of Missouri, a Republican Senator, saved the Republic from that stupendous calamity and burning shame.

Champ Clark

ELIZA McCARDLE JOHNSON

ELIZA MCCARDLE, of Tennessee, married in 1826 Andrew Johnson, a tailor, eighteen years old, whose early education she superintended perseveringly until his learning exceeded her own. Her character was simple, true and unostentatious, the duties of wife and mother being always conscientiously fulfilled. Her health being undermined by suffering during the Rebellion, she was a confirmed invalid when called to the White House, therefore Mrs. Patterson, her eldest daughter, became hostess. She presided with simple elegance, ease, grace and remarkable tact during her father's stormy administration. Their home life was delightful, and when they left Washington the whole family was much missed socially, as its popularity was widespread. Mrs. Johnson's influence over her husband was always very marked, and throughout his life she was his greatest helper and adviser. She survived him only six months.

Andrew Johnson

ANDREW JOHNSON was born in Raleigh, N. C., December 29, 1808. His parents were very poor. When he was 4 years old his father died of injuries received in rescuing a person from drowning. At the age of 10 years Andrew was apprenticed to a tailor. His early education was almost entirely neglected, and, notwithstanding his natural craving to learn, he never spent a day in school. Was taught the alphabet by a fellow-workman, borrowed a book, and learned to read. In 1824 removed to Laurens Court-House, S. C., where he worked as a journeyman tailor. In May, 1826, returned to Raleigh, and in September, with his mother and stepfather, set out for Greeneville, Tenn., in a two-wheeled cart drawn by a blind pony. Here he married Eliza McCardle, a woman of refinement, who taught him to write, and read to him while he was at work during the day. It was not until he had been in Congress that he learned to write with ease. From Greeneville went to the West, but returned after the lapse of a year. In 1828 was elected alderman; was reelected in 1829 and 1830, and in 1830 was advanced to the mayoralty, which office he held for three years. In 1831 was appointed by the county court a trustee of Rhea Academy, and about this time participated in the debates of a society at Greeneville College. In 1834 advocated the adoption of a new State constitution, by which the influence of the large landholders was abridged. In 1835 represented Greene and Washington counties in the legislature. Was defeated for the legislature in 1837, but in 1839 was reelected. In 1836 supported Hugh L. White for the Presidency, and in the political altercations between John Bell and James K. Polk, which distracted Tennessee at the time, supported the former. Mr. Johnson was the only ardent follower of Bell that failed to go over to the Whig party. Was an elector for the State at large on the Van Buren ticket in 1840, and made a State reputation by the force of his oratory. In 1841 was elected to the State senate from Greene and Hawkins counties, and while in that body was one of the " immortal thirteen " Democrats who, having it in their power to prevent the election of a Whig Senator, did so by refusing to meet the house in joint convention; also proposed that the basis of representation should rest upon white votes, without regard to the ownership of slaves. Was elected to Congress in 1843 over John A. Asken, a United States Bank Democrat, who was supported by the Whigs. His first speech was in support of the resolution to restore to General Jackson the fine imposed upon him at New Orleans; also supported the annexation of Texas. In 1845 was reelected, and supported Polk's Administration. Was regularly reelected to Congress until 1853. During this period opposed all expenditures for internal improvements that were not general; resisted and defeated the proposed contingent tax of 10 per cent on tea and coffee; made his celebrated defense of the veto power; urged the adoption of the homestead law, which was obnoxious to the extreme Southern element of his party; supported the compromise measures of 1850 as a matter of expediency, but opposed compromises in general as a sacrifice of principle. Was elected governor of Tennessee in 1853 over Gustavus A. Henry, the "Eagle Orator" of the State. In his message to the legislature he dwelt upon the homestead law and other measures for the benefit of the working classes, and earned the title of the "Mechanic Governor." Opposed the Know-nothing movement with characteristic vehemence. Was reelected governor in 1855, defeating Meredith P. Gentry, the Whig-American candidate, after a most remarkable canvass. The Kansas-Nebraska bill received his earnest support. In 1857 was elected to the United States Senate, where he urged the passage of the homestead bill, and on May 20, 1858, made his greatest speech on this subject. Opposed the grant of aid for the construction of a Pacific railroad. Was prominent in debate, and frequently clashed with Southern supporters of the Administration. His pronounced Unionism estranged him from the extremists on the Southern side, while his acceptance of slavery as an institution guaranteed by the Constitution caused him to hold aloof from the Republicans on the other. At the Democratic convention at Charleston, S. C., in 1860 was a candidate for the Presidential nomination, but received only the vote of Tennessee, and when the convention reassembled in Baltimore withdrew his name. In the canvass that followed supported John C. Breckinridge. At the session of Congress beginning in December, 1860, took decided and unequivocal grounds in opposition to secession, and on December 13 introduced a joint resolution proposing to amend the Constitution so as to elect the President and Vice-President by district votes, Senators by a direct popular vote, and to limit the terms of Federal judges to twelve years, the judges to be equally divided between slaveholding and non-slaveholding States. In his speech on this resolution, December 18 and 19, declared his unyielding opposition to secession and announced his intention to stand by and act under the Constitution. Retained his seat in the Senate until appointed by President Lincoln military governor of Tennessee, March 4, 1862. March 12 reached Nashville, and organized

a provisional government for the State; March 18 issued a proclamation in which he appealed to the people to return to their allegiance,
to uphold the law, and to accept "a full and complete amnesty for all past
acts and declarations;" April 5 removed the mayor and other officials of
Nashville for refusing to take the oath of allegiance to the United States,
and appointed others; urged the holding of Union meetings throughout
the State, and frequently attended them in person; completed the railroad
from Nashville to the Tennessee River; raised twenty-five regiments for
service in the State; December 8, 1862, issued a proclamation ordering
Congressional elections, and on the 15th levied an assessment upon the
richer Southern sympathizers "in behalf of the many helpless widows,
wives, and children in the city of Nashville who have been reduced to
poverty and wretchedness in consequence of their husbands, sons, and
fathers having been forced into the armies of this unholy and nefarious
rebellion." Was nominated for Vice-President of the United States at
the national Republican convention at Baltimore June 8, 1864, and was
elected on November 8. In his letter of acceptance of the nomination
Mr. Johnson virtually disclaimed any departure from his principles as
a Democrat, but placed his acceptance upon the ground of "the higher
duty of first preserving the Government." On the night of the 14th of
April, 1865, President Lincoln was shot by an assassin and died the next
morning. At 11 o'clock a. m. April 15 Mr. Johnson was sworn in as
President, at his rooms in the Kirkwood House, Washington, by Chief Justice Chase, in the presence of nearly all the Cabinet officers and others.
April 29, 1865, issued a proclamation for the removal of trade restrictions in most of the insurrectionary States, which, being in contraven-
tion of an act of Congress, was subsequently modified. May 9 issued an
Executive order restoring Virginia to the Union. May 22 proclaimed
all ports, except four in Texas, opened to foreign commerce on July 1,
1865. May 29 issued a general amnesty proclamation, after which the
fundamental and irreconcilable differences between President Johnson
and the party that had elevated him to power became more apparent.
He exercised the veto power to a very great extent, but it was generally nullified by the two-thirds votes of both Houses. From May 29 to
July 13, 1865, proclaimed provisional governors for North Carolina, Mississippi, Georgia, Texas, Alabama, South Carolina, and Florida, whose
duties were to reorganize the State governments. The State governments were reorganized, but the Republicans claimed that the laws
passed were so stringent in reference to the negroes that it was a worse
form of slavery than the old. The thirteenth amendment to the Constitution became a law December 18, 1865, with Mr. Johnson's concurrence.
The first breach between the President and the party in power was the
veto of the Freedmen's Bureau bill, in February, 1866, which was designed to protect, the negroes. March 27 vetoed the civil-rights bill, but
it was passed over his veto. In a message of June 22, 1866, opposed the

joint resolution proposing the fourteenth amendment to the Constitution. In June, 1866, the Republicans in Congress brought forward their plan of reconstruction, called the "Congressional plan," in contradistinction to that of the President. The chief features of the Congressional plan were to give the negroes the right to vote, to protect them in this right, and to prevent Confederate leaders from voting. January 5, 1867, vetoed the act giving negroes the right of suffrage in the District of Columbia, but it was passed over his veto. An attempt was made to impeach the President, but it failed. In January, 1867, a bill was passed to deprive the President of the power to proclaim general amnesty, which he disregarded. Measures were adopted looking to the meeting of the Fortieth and all subsequent Congresses immediately after the adjournment of the preceding. The President was deprived of the command of the Army by a rider to the army appropriation bill, which provided that his orders should only be given through the General, who was not to be removed without the previous consent of the Senate. The bill admitting Nebraska, providing that no law should ever be passed in that State denying the right of suffrage to any person because of his color or race, was vetoed by the President, but passed over his veto. March 2, 1867, vetoed the act to provide for the more efficient government of the rebel States, but it was passed over his veto. It embodied the Congressional plan of reconstruction, and divided the Southern States into five military districts, each under an officer of the Army not under the rank of brigadier-general, who was to exercise all the functions of government until the citizens had "formed a constitution of government in conformity with the Constitution of the United States in all respects." On the same day vetoed the tenure-of-office act, which was also passed over his veto. It provided that civil officers should remain in office until the confirmation of their successors; that the members of the Cabinet should be removed only with the consent of the Senate, and that when Congress was not in session the President could suspend but not remove any official, and in case the Senate at the next session should not ratify the suspension the suspended official should be reinducted into his office. August 5, 1867, requested Edwin M. Stanton to resign his office as Secretary of War. Mr. Stanton refused, was suspended, and General Grant was appointed Secretary of War *ad interim*. When Congress met, the Senate refused to ratify the suspension. General Grant then resigned, and Mr. Stanton resumed the duties of his office. The President removed him and appointed Lorenzo Thomas, Adjutant-General of the Army, Secretary of War *ad interim*. The Senate declared this act illegal, and Mr. Stanton refused to comply, and notified the Speaker of the House. On February 24, 1868, the House of Representatives resolved to impeach the President, and on March 2 and 3 articles of impeachment were agreed upon by the House of Representatives, and on the 4th were presented to the Senate. The trial began on March 30. May 16 the test vote was had;

thirty-five Senators voted for conviction and nineteen for acquittal. A change of one vote would have carried conviction. A verdict of acquittal was entered, and the Senate sitting as a court of impeachment adjourned *sine die*. After the expiration of his term the ex-President returned to Tennessee. Was a candidate for the United States Senate, but was defeated. In 1872 was an unsuccessful candidate for Congressman from the State at large. In January, 1875, was elected to the United States Senate, and took his seat at the extra session of that year. Shortly after the session began made a speech which was a skillful but bitter attack upon President Grant. While visiting his daughter near Elizabethton, in Carter County, Tenn., was stricken with paralysis July 30, 1875, and died the following day. He was buried at Greeneville, Tenn.

INAUGURAL ADDRESS.

[From the Sunday Morning Chronicle, Washington, April 16, 1865, and The Sun, Baltimore, April 17, 1865.]

GENTLEMEN: I must be permitted to say that I have been almost overwhelmed by the announcement of the sad event which has so recently occurred. I feel incompetent to perform duties so important and responsible as those which have been so unexpectedly thrown upon me. As to an indication of any policy which may be pursued by me in the administration of the Government, I have to say that that must be left for development as the Administration progresses. The message or declaration must be made by the acts as they transpire. The only assurance that I can now give of the future is reference to the past. The course which I have taken in the past in connection with this rebellion must be regarded as a guaranty of the future. My past public life, which has been long and laborious, has been founded, as I in good conscience believe, upon a great principle of right, which lies at the basis of all things. The best energies of my life have been spent in endeavoring to establish and perpetuate the principles of free government, and I believe that the Government in passing through its present perils will settle down upon principles consonant with popular rights more permanent and enduring than heretofore. I must be permitted to say, if I understand the feelings of my own heart, that I have long labored to ameliorate and elevate the condition of the great mass of the American people. Toil and an honest advocacy of the great principles of free government have been my lot. Duties have been mine; consequences are God's. This has been the foundation of my political creed, and I feel that in the end the Government will triumph and that these great principles will be permanently established.

3504 Messages and Papers of the Presidents

In conclusion, gentlemen, let me say that I want your encouragement and countenance. I shall ask and rely upon you and others in carrying the Government through its present perils. I feel in making this request that it will be heartily responded to by you and all other patriots and lovers of the rights and interests of a free people.

APRIL 15, 1865.

PROCLAMATIONS.

BY THE PRESIDENT OF THE UNITED STATES OF AMERICA.

A PROCLAMATION.

Whereas, by my direction, the Acting Secretary of State, in a notice to the public of the 17th, requested the various religious denominations to assemble on the 19th instant, on the occasion of the obsequies of Abraham Lincoln, late President of the United States, and to observe the same with appropriate ceremonies; but

Whereas our country has become one great house of mourning, where the head of the family has been taken away, and believing that a special period should be assigned for again humbling ourselves before Almighty God, in order that the bereavement may be sanctified to the nation:

Now, therefore, in order to mitigate that grief on earth which can only be assuaged by communion with the Father in heaven, and in compliance with the wishes of Senators and Representatives in Congress, communicated to me by resolutions adopted at the National Capitol, I, Andrew Johnson, President of the United States, do hereby appoint Thursday, the 25th day of May next, to be observed, wherever in the United States the flag of the country may be respected, as a day of humiliation and mourning, and I recommend my fellow-citizens then to assemble in their respective places of worship, there to unite in solemn service to Almighty God in memory of the good man who has been removed, so that all shall be occupied at the same time in contemplation of his virtues and in sorrow for his sudden and violent end.

In witness whereof I have hereunto set my hand and caused the seal of the United States to be affixed.

[SEAL.] Done at the city of Washington, the 25th day of April, A. D. 1865, and of the Independence of the United States of America the eighty-ninth.

ANDREW JOHNSON.

By the President :

W. HUNTER,
Acting Secretary of State.

By the President of the United States of America.

A PROCLAMATION.

Whereas by my proclamation of the 25th instant Thursday, the 25th day of next month, was recommended as a day for special humiliation and prayer in consequence of the assassination of Abraham Lincoln, late President of the United States; but

Whereas my attention has since been called to the fact that the day aforesaid is sacred to large numbers of Christians as one of rejoicing for the ascension of the Savior:

Now, therefore, be it known that I, Andrew Johnson, President of the United States, do hereby suggest that the religious services recommended as aforesaid should be postponed until Thursday, the 1st day of June next.

In testimony whereof I have hereunto set my hand and caused the seal of the United States to be affixed.

[SEAL.]   Done at the city of Washington, this 29th day of April, A. D. 1865, and of the Independence of the United States of America the eighty-ninth.

ANDREW JOHNSON.

By the President:
    W. Hunter,
       Acting Secretary of State.

By the President of the United States of America.

A PROCLAMATION.

Whereas it appears from evidence in the Bureau of Military Justice that the atrocious murder of the late President, Abraham Lincoln, and the attempted assassination of the Hon. William H. Seward, Secretary of State, were incited, concerted, and procured by and between Jefferson Davis, late of Richmond, Va., and Jacob Thompson, Clement C. Clay, Beverley Tucker, George N. Sanders, William C. Cleary, and other rebels and traitors against the Government of the United States harbored in Canada:

Now, therefore, to the end that justice may be done, I, Andrew Johnson, President of the United States, do offer and promise for the arrest of said persons, or either of them, within the limits of the United States, so that they can be brought to trial, the following rewards:

One hundred thousand dollars for the arrest of Jefferson Davis.

Twenty-five thousand dollars for the arrest of Clement C. Clay.

Twenty-five thousand dollars for the arrest of Jacob Thompson, late of Mississippi.

Twenty-five thousand dollars for the arrest of George N. Sanders.

Twenty-five thousand dollars for the arrest of Beverley Tucker.

Ten thousand dollars for the arrest of William C. Cleary, late clerk of Clement C. Clay.

The Provost-Marshal-General of the United States is directed to cause a description of said persons, with notice of the above rewards, to be published.

In testimony whereof I have hereunto set my hand and caused the seal of the United States to be affixed.

[SEAL.]   Done at the city of Washington, this 2d day of May, A. D. 1865, and of the Independence of the United States of America the eighty-ninth.

ANDREW JOHNSON.

By the President:

     W. HUNTER,
         Acting Secretary of State.

BY THE PRESIDENT OF THE UNITED STATES OF AMERICA.

A PROCLAMATION.

Whereas the President of the United States, by his proclamation of the 19th day of April, 1861, did declare certain States therein mentioned in insurrection against the Government of the United States; and

Whereas armed resistance to the authority of this Government in the said insurrectionary States may be regarded as virtually at an end, and the persons by whom that resistance, as well as the operations of insurgent cruisers, was directed are fugitives or captives; and

Whereas it is understood that some of those cruisers are still infesting the high seas and others are preparing to capture, burn, and destroy vessels of the United States:

Now, therefore, be it known that I, Andrew Johnson, President of the United States, hereby enjoin all naval, military, and civil officers of the United States diligently to endeavor, by all lawful means, to arrest the said cruisers and to bring them into a port of the United States, in order that they may be prevented from committing further depredations on commerce and that the persons on board of them may no longer enjoy impunity for their crimes.

And I do further proclaim and declare that if, after a reasonable time shall have elapsed for this proclamation to become known in the ports of nations claiming to have been neutrals, the said insurgent cruisers and the persons on board of them shall continue to receive hospitality in the said ports, this Government will deem itself justified in refusing hospitality to the public vessels of such nations in ports of the United States and in adopting such other measures as may be deemed advisable toward vindicating the national sovereignty.

In witness whereof I have hereunto set my hand and caused the seal of the United States to be affixed.

[SEAL.]   Done at the city of Washington, this 10th day of May, A. D. 1865, and of the Independence of the United States of America the eighty-ninth.

ANDREW JOHNSON.

By the President:
   W. HUNTER,
      Acting Secretary of State.

BY THE PRESIDENT OF THE UNITED STATES OF AMERICA.

A PROCLAMATION.

Whereas by the proclamation of the President of the 11th day of April last certain ports of the United States therein specified, which had previously been subject to blockade, were, for objects of public safety, declared, in conformity with previous special legislation of Congress, to be closed against foreign commerce during the national will, to be thereafter expressed and made known by the President; and

Whereas events and circumstances have since occurred which, in my judgment, render it expedient to remove that restriction, except as to the ports of Galveston, La Salle, Brazos de Santiago (Point Isabel), and Brownsville, in the State of Texas:

Now, therefore, be it known that I, Andrew Johnson, President of the United States, do hereby declare that the ports aforesaid, not excepted as above, shall be open to foreign commerce from and after the 1st day of July next; that commercial intercourse with the said ports may from that time be carried on, subject to the laws of the United States and in pursuance of such regulations as may be prescribed by the Secretary of the Treasury. If, however, any vessel from a foreign port shall enter any of the before-named excepted ports in the State of Texas, she will continue to be held liable to the penalties prescribed by the act of Congress approved on the 13th day of July, 1861, and the persons on board of her to such penalties as may be incurred, pursuant to the laws of war, for trading or attempting to trade with an enemy.

And I, Andrew Johnson, President of the United States, do hereby declare and make known that the United States of America do henceforth disallow to all persons trading or attempting to trade in any ports of the United States in violation of the laws thereof all pretense of belligerent rights and privileges; and I give notice that from the date of this proclamation all such offenders will be held and dealt with as pirates.

It is also ordered that all restrictions upon trade heretofore imposed in the territory of the United States east of the Mississippi River, save those relating to contraband of war, to the reservation of the rights of the United States to property purchased in the territory of an enemy, and to the 25 per cent upon purchases of cotton be removed. All provisions of the internal-revenue law will be carried into effect under the proper officers.

In witness whereof I have hereunto set my hand and caused the seal of the United States to be affixed.

[SEAL]. Done at the city of Washington, this 22d day of May, A. D. 1865, and of the Independence of the United States of America the eighty-ninth.

ANDREW JOHNSON.

By the President:

W. HUNTER,
Acting Secretary of State.

BY THE PRESIDENT OF THE UNITED STATES OF AMERICA.

A PROCLAMATION.

Whereas the President of the United States, on the 8th day of December, A. D. 1863, and on the 26th day of March, A. D. 1864, did, with the object to suppress the existing rebellion, to induce all persons to return to their loyalty, and to restore the authority of the United States, issue proclamations offering amnesty and pardon to certain persons who had, directly or by implication, participated in the said rebellion; and

Whereas many persons who had so engaged in said rebellion have, since the issuance of said proclamations, failed or neglected to take the benefits offered thereby; and

Whereas many persons who have been justly deprived of all claim to amnesty and pardon thereunder by reason of their participation, directly or by implication, in said rebellion and continued hostility to the Government of the United States since the date of said proclamations now desire to apply for and obtain amnesty and pardon.

To the end, therefore, that the authority of the Government of the United States may be restored and that peace, order, and freedom may be established, I, Andrew Johnson, President of the United States, do proclaim and declare that I hereby grant to all persons who have, directly or indirectly, participated in the existing rebellion, except as hereinafter excepted, amnesty and pardon, with restoration of all rights of property, except as to slaves and except in cases where legal proceedings under the laws of the United States providing for the confiscation of property of persons engaged in rebellion have been instituted; but upon the condition, nevertheless, that every such person shall take and subscribe the following oath (or affirmation) and thenceforward keep and maintain said oath inviolate, and which oath shall be registered for permanent preservation and shall be of the tenor and effect following, to wit:

I, ———— ————, do solemnly swear (or affirm), in presence of Almighty God, that I will henceforth faithfully support, protect, and defend the Constitution of the United

States and the Union of the States thereunder, and that I will in like manner abide by and faithfully support all laws and proclamations which have been made during the existing rebellion with reference to the emancipation of slaves. So help me God.

The following classes of persons are excepted from the benefits of this proclamation:

First. All who are or shall have been pretended civil or diplomatic officers or otherwise domestic or foreign agents of the pretended Confederate government.

Second. All who left judicial stations under the United States to aid the rebellion.

Third. All who shall have been military or naval officers of said pretended Confederate government above the rank of colonel in the army or lieutenant in the navy.

Fourth. All who left seats in the Congress of the United States to aid the rebellion.

Fifth. All who resigned or tendered resignations of their commissions in the Army or Navy of the United States to evade duty in resisting the rebellion.

Sixth. All who have engaged in any way in treating otherwise than lawfully as prisoners of war persons found in the United States service as officers, soldiers, seamen, or in other capacities.

Seventh. All persons who have been or are absentees from the United States for the purpose of aiding the rebellion.

Eighth. All military and naval officers in the rebel service who were educated by the Government in the Military Academy at West Point or the United States Naval Academy.

Ninth. All persons who held the pretended offices of governors of States in insurrection against the United States.

Tenth. All persons who left their homes within the jurisdiction and protection of the United States and passed beyond the Federal military lines into the pretended Confederate States for the purpose of aiding the rebellion.

Eleventh. All persons who have been engaged in the destruction of the commerce of the United States upon the high seas and all persons who have made raids into the United States from Canada or been engaged in destroying the commerce of the United States upon the lakes and rivers that separate the British Provinces from the United States.

Twelfth. All persons who, at the time when they seek to obtain the benefits hereof by taking the oath herein prescribed, are in military, naval, or civil confinement or custody, or under bonds of the civil, military, or naval authorities or agents of the United States as prisoners of war, or persons detained for offenses of any kind, either before or after conviction.

Thirteenth. All persons who have voluntarily participated in said rebellion and the estimated value of whose taxable property is over $20,000.

Fourteenth. All persons who have taken the oath of amnesty as prescribed in the President's proclamation of December 8, A. D. 1863, or an oath of allegiance to the Government of the United States since the date of said proclamation and who have not thenceforward kept and maintained the same inviolate.

Provided, That special application may be made to the President for pardon by any person belonging to the excepted classes, and such clemency will be liberally extended as may be consistent with the facts of the case and the peace and dignity of the United States.

The Secretary of State will establish rules and regulations for administering and recording the said amnesty oath, so as to insure its benefit to the people and guard the Government against fraud.

In testimony whereof I have hereunto set my hand and caused the seal of the United States to be affixed.

[SEAL.]   Done at the city of Washington, the 29th day of May, A. D. 1865, and of the Independence of the United States the eighty-ninth.

ANDREW JOHNSON.

By the President:

WILLIAM H. SEWARD,
Secretary of State.

BY THE PRESIDENT OF THE UNITED STATES OF AMERICA.

A PROCLAMATION.

Whereas the fourth section of the fourth article of the Constitution of the United States declares that the United States shall guarantee to every State in the Union a republican form of government and shall protect each of them against invasion and domestic violence; and

Whereas the President of the United States is by the Constitution made Commander in Chief of the Army and Navy, as well as chief civil executive officer of the United States, and is bound by solemn oath faithfully to execute the office of President of the United States and to take care that the laws be faithfully executed; and

Whereas the rebellion which has been waged by a portion of the people of the United States against the properly constituted authorities of the Government thereof in the most violent and revolting form, but whose organized and armed forces have now been almost entirely overcome, has in its revolutionary progress deprived the people of the State of North Carolina of all civil government; and

Whereas it becomes necessary and proper to carry out and enforce the obligations of the United States to the people of North Carolina in securing them in the enjoyment of a republican form of government:

Now, therefore, in obedience to the high and solemn duties imposed upon me by the Constitution of the United States and for the purpose of enabling the loyal people of said State to organize a State government whereby justice may be established, domestic tranquillity insured, and loyal citizens protected in all their rights of life, liberty, and property, I, Andrew Johnson, President of the United States and Commander in Chief of the Army and Navy of the United States, do hereby appoint William W. Holden provisional governor of the State of North Carolina, whose duty it shall be, at the earliest practicable period, to prescribe such rules and regulations as may be necessary and proper for convening a convention composed of delegates to be chosen by that portion of the people of said State who are loyal to the United States, and no others, for the purpose of altering or amending the constitution thereof, and with authority to exercise within the limits of said State all the powers necessary and proper to enable such loyal people of the State of North Carolina to restore said State to its constitutional relations to the Federal Government and to present such a republican form of State government as will entitle the State to the guaranty of the United States therefor and its people to protection by the United States against invasion, insurrection, and domestic violence: *Provided*, That in any election that may be hereafter held for choosing delegates to any State convention as aforesaid no person shall be qualified as an elector or shall be eligible as a member of such convention unless he shall have previously taken and subscribed the oath of amnesty as set forth in the President's proclamation of May 29, A. D. 1865, and is a voter qualified as prescribed by the constitution and laws of the State of North Carolina in force immediately before the 20th day of May, A. D. 1861, the date of the so-called ordinance of secession; and the said convention, when convened, or the legislature that may be thereafter assembled, will prescribe the qualification of electors and the eligibility of persons to hold office under the constitution and laws of the State—a power the people of the several States composing the Federal Union have rightfully exercised from the origin of the Government to the present time.

And I do hereby direct—

First. That the military commander of the department and all officers and persons in the military and naval service aid and assist the said provisional governor in carrying into effect this proclamation; and they are enjoined to abstain from in any way hindering, impeding, or discouraging the loyal people from the organization of a State government as herein authorized.

Second. That the Secretary of State proceed to put in force all laws of the United States the administration whereof belongs to the State Department applicable to the geographical limits aforesaid.

Third. That the Secretary of the Treasury proceed to nominate for appointment assessors of taxes and collectors of customs and internal revenue and such other officers of the Treasury Department as are authorized by law and put in execution the revenue laws of the United

States within the geographical limits aforesaid. In making appointments the preference shall be given to qualified loyal persons residing within the districts where their respective duties are to be performed; but if suitable residents of the districts shall not be found, then persons residing in other States or districts shall be appointed.

Fourth. That the Postmaster-General proceed to establish post-offices and post routes and put into execution the postal laws of the United States within the said State, giving to loyal residents the preference of appointment; but if suitable residents are not found, then to appoint agents, etc., from other States.

Fifth. That the district judge for the judicial district in which North Carolina is included proceed to hold courts within said State in accordance with the provisions of the act of Congress. The Attorney-General will instruct the proper officers to libel and bring to judgment, confiscation, and sale property subject to confiscation and enforce the administration of justice within said State in all matters within the cognizance and jurisdiction of the Federal courts.

Sixth. That the Secretary of the Navy take possession of all public property belonging to the Navy Department within said geographical limits and put in operation all acts of Congress in relation to naval affairs having application to the said State.

Seventh. That the Secretary of the Interior put in force the laws relating to the Interior Department applicable to the geographical limits aforesaid.

In testimony whereof I have hereunto set my hand and caused the seal of the United States to be affixed.

[SEAL.]   Done at the city of Washington, this 29th day of May, A. D. 1865, and of the Independence of the United States the eighty-ninth.

ANDREW JOHNSON.

By the President:
    WILLIAM H. SEWARD,
        Secretary of State.

BY THE PRESIDENT OF THE UNITED STATES OF AMERICA.

A PROCLAMATION.

Whereas the fourth section of the fourth article of the Constitution of the United States declares that the United States shall guarantee to every State in the Union a republican form of government and shall protect each of them against invasion and domestic violence; and

Whereas the President of the United States is by the Constitution made Commander in Chief of the Army and Navy, as well as chief civil